Paige Ba

Daniels College of Business, University of Denver

Amy Phillips

Daniels College of Business, University of Denver

Business Driven Information Systems

 McGraw-Hill Irwin

Boston   Burr Ridge, IL   Dubuque, IA   Madison, WI   New York   San Francisco   St. Louis
Bangkok   Bogotá   Caracas   Kuala Lumpur   Lisbon   London   Madrid   Mexico City
Milan   Montreal   New Delhi   Santiago   Seoul   Singapore   Sydney   Taipei   Toronto

The McGraw·Hill Companies

McGraw-Hill
Irwin

BUSINESS DRIVEN INFORMATION SYSTEMS

Published by McGraw-Hill/Irwin, a business unit of The McGraw-Hill Companies, Inc., 1221 Avenue of the Americas, New York, NY, 10020.
Copyright © 2008 by The McGraw-Hill Companies, Inc. All rights reserved. No part of this publication may be reproduced or distributed in any form or by any means, or stored in a database or retrieval system, without the prior written consent of The McGraw-Hill Companies, Inc., including, but not limited to, in any network or other electronic storage or transmission, or broadcast for distance learning.

Some ancillaries, including electronic and print components, may not be available to customers outside the United States.

This book is printed on acid-free paper.

3 4 5 6 7 8 9 0 CCI/CCI 0 9 8 7

ISBN 978-0-07-319558-2
MHID 0-07-319558-8

Editorial director: *Brent Gordon*
Executive editor: *Paul Ducham*
Developmental editor II: *Trina Hauger*
Marketing manager: *Sankha Basu*
Media producer: *Greg Bates*
Lead project manager: *Mary Conzachi*
Manager, New book production: *Heather D. Burbridge*
Senior designer: *Kami Carter*
Senior photo research coordinator: *Jeremy Cheshareck*
Photo researcher: *Teri Stratford*
Lead media project manager: *Brian Nacik*
Cover design: *Jillian Linder*
Interior design: *Kami Carter*
Typeface: *10/12 Utopia*
Compositor: *Laserwords Private Limited, Chennai, India*
Printer: *Courier Kendallville*

Library of Congress Cataloging-in-Publication Data

Baltzan, Paige.
    Business driven information systems/Paige Baltzan, Amy Phillips.
      p. cm.
    Includes bibliographical references and index.
    ISBN-13: 978-0-07-319558-2 (alk. paper)
    ISBN-10: 0-07-319558-8 (alk. paper)
    1. Industrial management—Data processing. 2. Information technology—Management.
  I. Phillips, Amy. II. Title.
  HD30.2.B357 2008
  658.4'038011—dc22

                              2006030375

www.mhhe.com

To Tony, Hannah, Sophie, and Gus
What do you always remember?
That I Love You!
That I'm Proud of You!

Paige

To my colleagues, Jill, David, Hans, Don, Dick,
Paul, KED, Dan, Paige, and Deborah with respect.
You are an exceptional group of professionals
and friends. Thank you very much for making
Daniels a wonderful place to park my bike.

Amy

BRIEF CONTENTS

Chapter 1   Information Systems in Business

Chapter 2   Strategic Decision Making

Chapter 3   E-Business

Chapter 4   Ethics and Information Security

Chapter 5   IT Architectures

Chapter 6   Databases and Data Warehouses

Chapter 7   Networks, Telecommunications, and Wireless Computing

Chapter 8   Supply Chain Management

Chapter 9   Customer Relationship Management

Chapter 10   Enterprise Resource Planning and Collaboration Systems

Chapter 11   Systems Development

Chapter 12   Project Management and Outsourcing

Technology Plug-In Overview

Apply Your Knowledge

Notes

Glossary

Photo Credits

Index

CONTENTS

CHAPTER 1
Information Systems in Business   1

Opening Case: Apple—Merging Technology, Business, and Entertainment   2

INTRODUCTION   5
Section 1.1 Information Systems in Business   5
INFORMATION TECHNOLOGY'S ROLE IN BUSINESS   5
  Information Technology's Impact on Business Operations   5
INFORMATION TECHNOLOGY BASICS   8
  Information versus Data   9
  IT Resources   9
  IT Cultures   9
ROLES AND RESPONSIBILITIES IN INFORMATION TECHNOLOGY   10
  The Gap Between Business Personnel and IT Personnel   12
MEASURING INFORMATION TECHNOLOGY'S SUCCESS   13
  Efficiency and Effectiveness Metrics   13
  Benchmarking—Baseline Metrics   14
  The Interrelationship Between Efficiency and Effectiveness IT Metrics   14
Section 1.2 Business Strategy   17
BUSINESS STRATEGY   17
THE FIVE FORCES MODEL—EVALUATING BUSINESS SEGMENTS   17
  Buyer Power   18
  Supplier Power   18
  Threat of Substitute Products or Services   19
  Threat of New Entrants   19
  Rivalry Among Existing Competitors   20
THE THREE GENERIC STRATEGIES—CREATING A BUSINESS FOCUS   20
VALUE CHAIN ANALYSIS—TARGETING BUSINESS PROCESSES   21
  Value Creation   21
Key Terms   24
Case Study One: Say "Charge It" with Your Cell Phone   25
Case Study Two: Innovative Business Managers   26

Case Study Three: The World Is Flat—Thomas Friedman   28
Making Business Decisions   29

CHAPTER 2
Strategic Decision Making   31

Opening Case: Revving Up Sales at Harley-Davidson   32

INTRODUCTION   35
Section 2.1 Decision-Making Systems   35
DECISION MAKING   36
TRANSACTION PROCESSING SYSTEMS   36
DECISION SUPPORT SYSTEMS   38
EXECUTIVE INFORMATION SYSTEMS   39
  Digital Dashboards   40
  Artificial Intelligence   43
  Data Mining   45
Section 2.2 Enterprise Systems   46
ENTERPRISE SYSTEMS   46
SUPPLY CHAIN MANAGEMENT   46
CUSTOMER RELATIONSHIP MANAGEMENT   47
  CRM Strategy   48
BUSINESS PROCESS REENGINEERING   49
  Finding Opportunity Using BPR   50
  Pitfalls of BPR   52
ENTERPRISE RESOURCE PLANNING   52
  ERP Software   52
  Finding the Right ERP Solution   53
Key Terms   54
Closing Case One: Consolidating Touchpoints for Saab   50
Closing Case Two: Made-to-Order Businesses   56
Closing Case Three: Delta Air Lines Plays Catch-Up   58
Making Business Decisions   60

CHAPTER 3
E-Business   62

Opening Case: Amazon.com—Not Your Average Bookstore   65

INTRODUCTION   65
Section 3.1 Business and the Internet   65

DISRUPTIVE TECHNOLOGY 65
Disruptive versus Sustaining Technology 66
The Internet—Business Disruption 67
EVOLUTION OF THE INTERNET 67
Evolution of the World Wide Web 69
ACCESSING INTERNET INFORMATION 70
Intranet 71
Extranet 71
Portal 71
Kiosk 72
PROVIDING INTERNET INFORMATION 72
Internet Service Provider 72
Online Service Provider 74
Application Service Provider 74
Section 3.2 E-Business 75
E-BUSINESS BASICS 75
E-BUSINESS MODELS 76
Business-to-Business (B2B) 76
Business-to-Consumer (B2C) 78
Consumer-to-Business (C2B) 79
Consumer-to-Consumer (C2C) 79
ORGANIZATIONAL STRATEGIES FOR E-BUSINESS 79
Marketing/Sales 80
Financial Services 80
Purchasing 82
Customer Service 83
Intermediaries 85
MEASURING E-BUSINESS SUCCESS 85
Web Site Metrics 86
E-BUSINESS BENEFITS AND CHALLENGES 87
NEW TRENDS IN E-BUSINESS, E-GOVERNMENT, AND M-COMMERCE 91
M-Commerce 91
Key Terms 93
Case Study One: eBay—The Ultimate E-Business 94
Case Study Two: Direct Groceries 97
Case Study Three: How Do You Value Friendster? 98
Making Business Decisions 99

CHAPTER 4
Ethics and Information Security 101

Opening Case: Sarbanes-Oxley: Where Information Technology, Finance, and Ethics Meet 102

INTRODUCTION 104
Section 4.1 Ethics 104
ETHICS 104
INFORMATION ETHICS 105
Information Has No Ethics 106
DEVELOPING INFORMATION MANAGEMENT POLICIES 108
Ethical Computer Use Policy 108
Information Privacy Policy 109
Acceptable Use Policy 109

E-Mail Privacy Policy 109
Internet Use Policy 111
Anti-Spam Policy 112
ETHICS IN THE WORKPLACE 113
Monitoring Technologies 113
Employee Monitoring Policies 114
Section 4.2 Information Security 115
PROTECTING INTELLECTUAL ASSETS 116
THE FIRST LINE OF DEFENSE—PEOPLE 117
THE SECOND LINE OF DEFENSE—TECHNOLOGY 121
Authentication and Authorization 121
Prevention and Resistance 122
Content Filtering 123
Encryption 124
Firewalls 124
Detection and Response 125
Key Terms 128
Closing Case One: Banks Banking on Security 129
Closing Case Two: Hacker Hunters 131
Closing Case Three: Thinking Like the Enemy 133
Making Business Decisions 134

CHAPTER 5
IT Architectures 136

Opening Case: Electronic Breaking Points 137

INTRODUCTION 140
Section 5.1 Hardware and Software Basics 140
HARDWARE BASICS 140
Central Processing Unit 140
Primary Storage 143
Secondary Storage 144
Input Devices 145
Output Devices 147
Communication Devices 148
COMPUTER CATEGORIES 148
SOFTWARE BASICS 149
System Software 149
Application Software 151
Section 5.2 Managing Enterprise Architectures 152
ENTERPRISE ARCHITECTURES 152
INFORMATION ARCHITECTURE 154
Backup and Recovery 155
Disaster Recovery 155
Information Security 157
INFRASTRUCTURE ARCHITECTURE 158
Flexibility 158
Scalability 159
Reliability 159
Availability 159
Performance 160
APPLICATION ARCHITECTURE 160
Web Services 160
Open Systems 162

Key Terms 163
Closing Case One: *Chicago Tribune's* Server Consolidation a Success 164
Closing Case Two: UPS in the Computer Repair Business 166
Closing Case Three: Fear the Penguin 167
Making Business Decisions 169

CHAPTER 6
Databases and Data Warehouses 171

Opening Case: Searching for Revenue—Google 172

INTRODUCTION 176
Section 6.1 Database Fundamentals 176
UNDERSTANDING INFORMATION 176
  Information Quality 177
DATABASE FUNDAMENTALS 180
DATABASE ADVANTAGES 180
  Increased Flexibility 181
  Increased Scalability and Performance 181
  Reduced Redundancy 181
  Increased Integrity (Quality) 181
  Increased Security 182
RELATIONAL DATABASE FUNDAMENTALS 182
  Entities, Entity Classes, and Attributes 183
  Keys and Relationships 183
DATABASE MANAGEMENT SYSTEMS 183
  Data Definition Component 185
  Data Manipulation Component 186
  Application Generation and Data Administration Components 188
INTEGRATING DATA AMONG MULTIPLE DATABASES 189
Section 6.2 Data Warehouse Fundamentals 191
ACCESSING ORGANIZATIONAL INFORMATION 191
HISTORY OF DATA WAREHOUSING 191
DATA WAREHOUSE FUNDAMENTALS 192
  Multidimensional Analysis 193
  Information Cleansing or Scrubbing 194
BUSINESS INTELLIGENCE 196
  Enabling Business Intelligence 197
DATA MINING 197
  Cluster Analysis 198
  Association Detection 199
  Statistical Analysis 199
Key Terms 202
Closing Case One: Fishing for Quality 203
Closing Case Two: Mining the Data Warehouse 205
Closing Case Three: Harrah's—Gambling Big on Technology 207
Making Business Decisions 209

CHAPTER 7
Networks, Telecommunications, and Wireless Computing 212

Opening Case: The Digital Hospital 213

INTRODUCTION 215
Section 7.1 Networks and Telecommunications 215
NETWORK BASICS 215
ARCHITECTURE 215
  Peer-to-Peer Networks 215
  Client/Server Networks 217
TOPOLOGY 218
PROTOCOLS 220
  Ethernet 220
  Transmission Control Protocol/Internet Protocol 221
MEDIA 223
  Wire Media 223
  Wireless Media 224
E-BUSINESS NETWORKS 225
Section 7.2 Wireless Computing 226
WIRELESS FIDELITY 227
  The Value of Timely Information 227
BUSINESS DRIVERS FOR WIRELESS TECHNOLOGIES 228
ADVANTAGES OF ENTERPRISE MOBILITY 229
  Bluetooth 230
  Radio Frequency Identification (RFID) 231
  Satellite 232
  Global Positioning System (GPS) 233
THE FUTURE OF WIRELESS 234
Key Terms 236
Closing Case One: Tracking Students 237
Closing Case Two: UPS versus FedEx: Head-to-Head on Wireless 238
Closing Case Three: Watching Where You Step—Prada 240
Making Business Decisions 241

CHAPTER 8
Supply Chain Management 243

Opening Case: Dell's Famous Supply Chain 244

INTRODUCTION 246
Section 8.1 Supply Chain Fundamentals 246
BASICS OF SUPPLY CHAIN 246
INFORMATION TECHNOLOGY'S ROLE IN THE SUPPLY CHAIN 247
  Visibility 250
  Consumer Behavior 250
  Competition 250
  Speed 251

SUPPLY CHAIN MANAGEMENT SUCCESS FACTORS **251**
Make the Sale to Suppliers 253
Wean Employees Off Traditional Business Practices 253
Ensure the SCM System Supports the Organizational Goals 253
Deploy in Incremental Phases and Measure and Communicate Success 253
Be Future Oriented 253
SCM SUCCESS STORIES **253**
Section 8.2 Applying a Supply Chain Design **255**
USING INFORMATION TECHNOLOGY TO DRIVE THE SUPPLY CHAIN **255**
FACILITIES DRIVER **255**
Location 256
Capacity 256
Operational Design 257
INVENTORY DRIVER **257**
Cycle Inventory 258
Safety Inventory 258
TRANSPORTATION DRIVER **259**
Method of Transportation 259
Transportation Route 259
INFORMATION DRIVER **259**
Information Sharing 260
Push versus Pull Information Strategy 260
APPLYING A SUPPLY CHAIN DESIGN **261**
FUTURE SUPPLY CHAIN TRENDS **261**
Key Terms **264**
Closing Case One: BudNet 265
Closing Case Two: Listerine's Journey 267
Closing Case Three: How Levi's Got Its Jeans into Wal-Mart 269
Making Business Decisions **271**

CHAPTER 9
Customer Relationship Management **273**

Opening Case: Customer First Awards **274**

INTRODUCTION **277**
Section 9.1 Customer Relationship Management **277**
BUSINESS BENEFITS OF CRM **277**
CRM BASICS **278**
The Evolution of CRM 278
Operational and Analytical CRM 280
USING INFORMATION TECHNOLOGY TO DRIVE OPERATIONAL CRM **280**
Marketing and Operational CRM 281
Sales and Operational CRM 281
Customer Service and Operational CRM 284

USING INFORMATION TECHNOLOGY TO DRIVE ANALYTICAL CRM **286**
Section 9.2 Customer Relationship Management Strategies **288**
CUSTOMER RELATIONSHIP MANAGEMENT'S EXPLOSIVE GROWTH **289**
CUSTOMER RELATIONSHIP MANAGEMENT SUCCESS FACTORS **290**
CURRENT TRENDS: SRM, PRM, AND ERM **291**
Supplier Relationship Management 291
Partner Relationship Management 292
Employee Relationship Management 292
FUTURE CRM TRENDS **293**
Key Terms **294**
Closing Case One: Fighting Cancer with Information 295
Closing Case Two: Calling All Canadians 297
Closing Case Three: The Ritz-Carlton—Specializing in Customers 298
Making Business Decisions **299**

CHAPTER 10
Enterprise Resource Planning and Collaboration Systems **301**

Opening Case: Campus ERP **302**

INTRODUCTION **304**
Section 10.1 Enterprise Resource Planning **304**
ENTERPRISE RESOURCE PLANNING **304**
CORE AND EXTENDED ERP COMPONENTS **305**
CORE ERP COMPONENTS **305**
Accounting and Finance ERP Components 305
Production and Materials Management ERP Components 306
Human Resources ERP Components 307
EXTENDED ERP COMPONENTS **307**
Business Intelligence Components 308
Customer Relationship Management Components 308
Supply Chain Management Components 308
E-Business Components 308
ERP VENDOR OVERVIEW **309**
ERP Software 311
Finding the Right ERP Solution 311
ERP BENEFITS AND RISKS (COST) **312**
THE CONNECTED CORPORATION—INTEGRATING SCM, CRM, AND ERP **312**
THE FUTURE OF ERP **316**
Internet 317
Interface 318
Wireless Technology 318
Section 10.2 Collaboration Systems **318**

TEAMS, PARTNERSHIPS, AND ALLIANCES 318
COLLABORATION SYSTEMS 320
KNOWLEDGE MANAGEMENT 322
    KM in Business 322
KNOWLEDGE MANAGEMENT SYSTEMS 322
    Explicit and Tacit Knowledge 323
    KM Technologies 324
    KM and Social Networking 325
CONTENT MANAGEMENT SYSTEMS 325
WORKFLOW MANAGEMENT SYSTEMS 326
GROUPWARE SYSTEMS 328
COLLABORATION TRENDS 329
Key Terms 331
Closing Case One: DreamWorks Animation Collaboration 332
Closing Case Two: Improving Highway Safety Through Collaboration 334
Closing Case Three: Saving Costs at Costco 336
Making Business Decisions 337

CHAPTER 11
Systems Development 339

Opening Case: HP's Software Problems 340

INTRODUCTION 342
Section 11.1 Developing Enterprise Applications 342
DEVELOPING SOFTWARE 342
THE SYSTEMS DEVELOPMENT LIFE CYCLE (SDLC) 343
SOFTWARE DEVELOPMENT METHODOLOGIES 344
    Waterfall Methodology 344
    Rapid Application Development Methodology (RAD) 345
    Extreme Programming Methodology 346
    Agile Methodology 347
DEVELOPING SUCCESSFUL SOFTWARE 348
    Slash the Budget 348
    If It Doesn't Work, Kill It 348
    Keep Requirements to a Minimum 348
    Test and Deliver Frequently 348
    Assign Non-IT Executives to Software Projects 348
    Section 11.2 The Systems Development Life Cycle (SDLC) 349
SYSTEMS DEVELOPMENT LIFE CYCLE 349
PHASE 1: PLANNING 349
    Identify and Select the System for Development 350
    Assess Project Feasibility 351
    Develop the Project Plan 351
PHASE 2: ANALYSIS 352
    Gather Business Requirements 352
    Create Process Diagrams 352
    Perform a Buy versus Build Analysis 353

PHASE 3: DESIGN 354
    Design the IT Infrastructure 354
    Design System Models 354
PHASE 4: DEVELOPMENT 355
    Develop the IT Infrastructure 355
    Develop the Database and Programs 356
PHASE 5: TESTING 357
    Write the Test Conditions 357
    Perform the System Testing 358
PHASE 6: IMPLEMENTATION 358
    Write Detailed User Documentation 358
    Determine Implementation Method 358
    Provide Training for the System Users 359
PHASE 7: MAINTENANCE 359
    Build a Help Desk to Support the System Users 359
    Perform System Maintenance 359
    Provide an Environment to Support System Changes 360
SOFTWARE PROBLEMS ARE BUSINESS PROBLEMS 360
    Unclear or Missing Business Requirements 360
    Skipping SDLC Phases 360
    Failure to Manage Project Scope 361
    Failure to Manage Project Plan 361
    Changing Technology 361
Key Terms 363
Closing Case One: Disaster at Denver International Airport 364
Closing Case Two: Reducing Ambiguity in Business Requirements 365
Closing Case Three: Gearing Up at REI 367
Making Business Decisions 369

CHAPTER 12
Project Management and Outsourcing 371

Opening Case: Change at Toyota 372

INTRODUCTION 375
Section 12.1 Project Management 375
PROJECT MANAGEMENT 375
PROJECT MANAGEMENT FUNDAMENTALS 377
    Choosing Strategic Projects 378
    Setting the Project Scope 379
    Managing Resources and Maintaining the Project Plan 380
CHANGE MANAGEMENT FUNDAMENTALS 381
    Preparing for Change 383
RISK MANAGEMENT FUNDAMENTALS 383
    Mitigating Risk 384
    Successful Project Management Strategies 385

Section 12.2 Outsourcing 386
OUTSOURCING 386
THE OUTSOURCING PHENOMENON 388
    Outsourcing Benefits 389
OUTSOURCING OPTIONS 390
OFFSHORE OUTSOURCING 390
    The Leaders 391
    The Up-and-Comers 393
    The Rookies 395
THE CHALLENGES OF OUTSOURCING 396
FUTURE OUTSOURCING TRENDS 398

Key Terms 399
Closing Case One: Staying on Track—Toronto Transit 400
Closing Case Two: Changing Circuits and Circuit City 401
Closing Case Three: Outsourcing Brew 403
Making Business Decisions 404
Technology Plug-In Overview 406
Apply Your Knowledge 410
Notes 450
Glossary 457
Photo Credits 471
Index 473

Business Driven Information Systems discusses various business initiatives first and how technology supports those initiatives second. The premise for this unique approach is that business initiatives should drive technology choices. Every discussion first addresses the business needs and then addresses the technology that supports those needs. This text provides the foundation that will enable students to achieve excellence in business, whether they major in operations management, manufacturing, sales, marketing, finance, human resources, accounting, or virtually any other business discipline. Business Driven Information Systems is designed to give students the ability to understand how information technology can be a point of strength for an organization.

Common business goals associated with information technology projects include reducing costs, improving productivity, improving customer satisfaction and loyalty, creating competitive advantages, streamlining supply chains, global expansion, and so on. Achieving these results is not easy. Implementing a new accounting system or marketing plan is not likely to generate long-term growth or reduce costs across an entire organization. Businesses must undertake enterprisewide initiatives to achieve broad general business goals such as reducing costs. Information technology plays a critical role in deploying such initiatives by facilitating communication and increasing business intelligence. Any individual anticipating a successful career in business whether it is in accounting, finance, human resources, or operation management must understand the basics of information technology which can be found in this text.

FORMAT, FEATURES, AND HIGHLIGHTS

Business Driven Information Systems is state-of-the-art in its discussions, presents concepts in an easy-to-understand format, and allows students to be active participants in learning. The dynamic nature of information technology requires all students, more specifically business students, to be aware of both current and emerging technologies. Students are facing complex subjects and need a clear, concise explanation to be able to understand and use the concepts throughout their careers. By engaging students with numerous case studies, exercises, projects, and questions that enforce concepts, *Business Driven Information Systems* creates a unique learning experience for both faculty and students.

- **Audience.** *Business Driven Information Systems* is designed for use in undergraduate or introductory MBA courses in Management Information Systems, which are required in many Business Administration or Management programs as part of the common body of knowledge for all business majors.

- **Logical Layout.** Students and faculty will find the text well organized with the topics flowing logically from one chapter to the next. The definition of each term is provided before it is covered in the chapter and an extensive glossary is included at the back of the text. Each chapter offers a comprehensive opening case study, introduction, learning outcomes, closing case studies, key terms, and making business decision questions. The plug-ins follow the same pedagogical elements with the exception of the exclusion of opening case and closing case studies.

- **Thorough Explanations.** Complete coverage is provided for each topic that is introduced. Explanations are written so that students can understand the ideas presented and relate them to other concepts.

- **Solid Theoretical Base.** The text relies on current theory and practice of information systems as they relate to the business environment. Current academic and professional journals cited throughout the text are found in the

Notes at the end of the book—a roadmap for additional, pertinent readings that can be the basis for learning beyond the scope of the chapters or plug-ins.

■ **Material to Encourage Discussion.** All chapters contain a diverse selection of case studies and individual and group problem-solving activities as they relate to the use of information technology in business. Three comprehensive cases at the end of each chapter reinforce content. These cases encourage students to consider what concepts have been presented and then apply those concepts to a situation they might find in an organization. Different people in an organization can view the same facts from different points of view and the cases will force students to consider some of those views.

■ **Flexibility in Teaching and Learning.** While most textbooks that are "text only" leave faculty on their own when it comes to choosing cases, *Business Driven Information Systems* goes much further. Several options are provided to faculty with case selections from a variety of sources including *CIO, Harvard Business Journal, Wired, Forbes, Business 2.0,* and *Time,* to name just a few. Therefore, faculty can use the text alone, the text and a complete selection of cases, or anything in between.

■ **Integrative Themes.** Several integrative themes recur throughout the text which adds integration to the material. Among these themes are value added techniques and methodologies, ethics and social responsibility, globalization, and gaining a competitive advantage. Such topics are essential to gaining a full understanding of the strategies that a business must recognize, formulate, and in turn implement. In addition to addressing these in the chapter material, many illustrations are provided for their relevance to business practice.

WALKTHROUGH

Learning Outcomes and Introduction

> **Introduction.** Located after the Opening Case, the introduction familiarizes students with the overall tone of the chapters. Thematic concepts are also broadly defined.

INTRODUCTION

Managers need to determine what types of hardware and software will satisfy their current and future business needs, the right time to buy the equipment, and how to protect their IT investments. This does not imply that managers need to be experts in all areas of technology; however, building a basic understanding of hardware and software can help them make the right IT investment choices.

Information technology (IT) is any computer-based tool that people use to work with information and support the information and information-processing needs of an organization. Information technology can be composed of the Internet, a personal computer, a cell phone that can access the Web, a personal digital assistant, or presentation software. All of these technologies help to perform specific information processing tasks. There are two basic categories of information technology: hardware and software. *Hardware* consists of the physical devices associated with a computer system. *Software* is the set of instructions that the hardware executes to carry out specific tasks. Software, such as Microsoft Excel, and various hardware devices, such as a keyboard and a monitor, interact to create a spreadsheet or a

> **Learning Outcomes.** These outcomes focus on what students should learn and be able to answer upon completion of the chapter or plug-in.

section 3.1 BUSINESS AND THE INTERNET

LEARNING OUTCOMES

3.1. Compare disruptive and sustaining technologies.

3.2. Explain how the Internet caused disruption among businesses.

3.3. Define the relationship between the Internet and the World Wide Web.

3.4. Describe the different methods an organization can use to access information.

3.5. Compare the three different types of service providers.

Chapter Opening Case and Opening Case Study Questions

Chapter Opening Case. To enhance student interest, each chapter begins with an opening case study that highlights an organization that has been time-tested and value proven in the business world. This feature serves to fortify concepts with relevant examples of outstanding companies. Discussion of the case is threaded throughout the chapters.

opening case study

Campus ERP

When Stefanie Fillers returned to college she needed to log in to the school's new online registration system to make certain that the courses she was taking would allow her to graduate. She also wanted to waive her participation in her college's health insurance plan. When the system crashed the day before classes began, Fillers, a senior, was annoyed. But at least she knew where her classes were—unlike most first-year students.

Opening Case Study Questions. Located at the end of each section, poignant questions connect the Chapter Opening Case Study with important chapter concepts.

OPENING CASE QUESTIONS
Campus ERP

1. How could core ERP components help improve business operations at your college?
2. How could extended ERP components help improve business operations at your college?
3. How can integrating SCM, CRM, and ERP help improve business operations at your college?
4. Review the different components in Figure 10.14. Which component would you recommend your college implement if it decided to purchase an ERP component?

Projects and Case Studies

Case Studies. This text is packed with 48 case studies illustrating how a variety of prominent organizations and business have successfully implemented many of this text's concepts. All cases are timely and promote critical thinking. Company profiles are especially appealing and relevant to your students, helping to stir classroom discussion and interest. For a full list of cases explored in *Business Driven Information Systems,* turn to the inside back cover.

Apply Your Knowledge. At the end of this text, there is a set of 50 projects aimed at reinforcing the business initiatives explored in this text. These projects help to develop the application and problem-solving skills of your students through challenging and creative business-driven scenarios.

Project 6:

Setting Boundaries

Even the most ethical people sometimes face difficult choices. Acting ethically means behaving in a principled fashion and treating other people with respect and dignity. It is simple to say, but not so simple to do since some situations are complex or ambiguous. The important role of ethics in our lives has long been recognized. As far back as 44 B.C., Cicero said that ethics are indispensable to anyone who wants to have a good career. Having said that, Cicero, along with some of the greatest minds over the centuries, struggled with what the rules of ethics should be.

Our ethics are rooted in our history, culture, and religion, and our sense of ethics may shift over time. The electronic age brings with it a new dimension in the ethics debate—the amount of personal information that we can collect and store, and the speed with which we can access and process that information.

Project Focus

In a team, discuss how you would react to the following situations:

Making Business Decisions. Small scenario-driven projects that help students focus individually on decision making as they relate to the topical elements in the chapters.

MAKING BUSINESS DECISIONS

1. **Leveraging the competitive value of the Internet**
   Physical inventories have always been a major cost component of business. Linking to suppliers in real time dramatically enhances the classic goal of inventory "turn." The Internet provides a multitude of opportunities for radically reducing the costs of designing, manufacturing, and selling goods and services. E-mango.com, a fruit e-marketplace, must take advantage of these opportunities or find itself at a significant competitive disadvantage. Identify the disadvantages that confront E-mango.com if it does not leverage the competitive value of the Internet.

End-of-Chapter Elements

Each chapter contains complete pedagogical support in the form of:

Key Terms. With page numbers referencing where they are discussed in the text.

KEY TERMS

Acceptable use policy
  (AUP) 109
Adware 114
Anti-spam policy 112
Authentication 121
Authorization 121
Backdoor program 126

Ethical computer use policy 108
Ethics 104
Fair use doctrine 104
Firewall 124
Hacker 126
Hactivist 126
Hardware key logger 114

Nonrepudiation 109
Packet tampering 127
Phishing 121
Pirated software 104
Polymorphic virus
  and worm 126
Privacy 105

Three Closing Case Studies. Reinforcing importance concepts with prominent examples from businesses and organizations. Discussion Questions follow each case study.

CLOSING CASE ONE

Consolidating Touchpoints for Saab

Saab Cars USA imports more than 37,000 Saab sedans, convertibles, and wagons annually and distributes the cars to 220 U.S. dealerships. Saab competes in the premium automotive market,

CLOSING CASE TWO

Made-to-Order Businesses

In the past, customers had two choices for purchasing products: (1) purchase a mass-produced product like a pair of jeans or a candy bar or (2) commission a custom-made item

CLOSING CASE THREE

Delta Air Lines Plays Catch-Up

The airline industry has a well-deserved reputation for creative use of IT. American Airlines is known as a leader in using IT to drive its business, and United Airlines is known as a fast follower. Delta Air Lines, while highly regarded as a well-run airline, has been a slow follower in IT. Recently, however, this has changed. In the past few years, Delta has invested more than $1.5 billion in technology, automating everything from gate and boarding tasks to baggage-handling, inventory control, and revenue accounting.

The airline reservation systems introduced by American Airlines and United Airlines, respectively, Sabre and Apollo, were the earliest examples of significant forays into business driven IT in the airline industry. The programs are inventory control systems that sell and manage available seats on upcoming flights. Travel agents received a special computer terminal

About the Plug-Ins

Located on the student CD that accompanies this text, the overall goal of the plug-ins is to provide an alternative for faculty who find themselves in the situation of having to purchase an extra book to support Microsoft Office. The plug-ins presented here offer integration with the core chapters and provides critical knowledge using essential business applications, such as Microsoft Excel, Microsoft Access, and Microsoft FrontPage. Each plug-in uses hands-on tutorials for comprehension and mastery.

PLUG-IN

T1
Personal Productivity Using IT

LEARNING OUTCOMES

1. Describe the four steps you can use to create a strong password.
2. Identify three tips you can use to manage your files.
3. Explain why you would use Microsoft's backup and recovery utility.
4. Describe the six common e-mail mistakes.
5. Explain spam and phishing and identify three ways that you can prevent each.
6. Explain the primary uses of spyware and adware.
7. Identify three things you can do to maintain your computer and keep it running smoothly.

End-of-Plug-In Elements

Each plug-in contains complete pedagogical support in the form of:

Plug-In Summary. Revisits the plug-in highlights in summary format.

Making Business Decisions. Small scenario-driven projects that help students focus individually on decision making as they relate to the topical elements in the chapters.

★ PLUG-IN SUMMARY

Microsoft Excel is a general-purpose electronic spreadsheet used to organize, calculate, and analyze data. The tasks you can perform with Excel range from preparing a simple invoice to managing an accounting ledger for a business.

Six areas in Excel were covered in this plug-in:

1. Workbooks and worksheets.
2. Working with cells and cell data.
3. Printing worksheets.
4. Formatting worksheets.
5. Formulas.
6. Working with charts and graphics.

★ MAKING BUSINESS DECISIONS

1. Stock Watcher

   Mark Martin has created a basic stock watcher worksheet that he uses to report on gains or losses from when he purchased the stock and the last recorded date and price. Mark has given you a snapshot of his spreadsheet (see Figure T2.29) that you can use to recreate this spreadsheet for yourself. Here are some basic steps to follow:

   1. Create a new workbook.
   2. Enter all the information provided in Figure T2.29.
   3. Apply the currency format to the respective columns.

Support and Supplemental Material

Business Driven Information Systems is taking supplements to a whole new level. This text focuses on engaging students, helping instructors, and achieving educational success. All supplement material is created by Paige Baltzan on the author team.

EZ TEST CD-ROM. This computerized package allows instructors to custom design, save, and generate tests. The test program permits instructors to edit, add, or delete questions from the test banks; analyze test results; and organize a database of tests and students results. In addition to the traditional test bank material BDIS offers Excel and Access questions for testing purposes. Each file comes with a Captivate solution file that walks students step-by-step through the solution, which saves instructors valuable time.

ONLINE LEARNING CENTER (www.mhhe.com/baltzan) The McGraw-Hill Higher Education Web site for *Business Driven Information Systems* includes support for students and faculty. All supplements, save the Test Bank, will be available exclusively on the OLC. This will allow the authors to continually update and add to the instructor support materials. The following materials will be available on the OLC:

Instructor's Manual (IM). The IM includes suggestions for designing the course and presenting the material. Each chapter is supported by answers to end-of-chapter questions and problems, and suggestions concerning the discussion topics and cases.

PowerPoint Presentations. A set of PowerPoint slides accompanies each chapter that features bulleted items that provide a lecture outline, plus key figures and tables from the text, and detailed teaching notes on each slide.

This text offers two sets of PowerPoint slides – one for instructors and one for students. The instructor edition comes complete with detailed teaching notes on each slide that offer discussion topics, classroom questions, and lecture points.

Additional Material PowerPoints. *Business Driven Information Systems* also offers PowerPoint slides on additional lecture material. If you want to walk your students through NetFlix' supply chain or Eddie Bauer's customer relationship management there are 10 additional sets of slides focusing on extra material not found in the text.

Sample Syllabi. Several syllabi have been developed according to different course lengths—quarters and semesters, as well as different course concentrations such as a business emphasis or a technology focus.

Classroom Exercises. Choose from over 50 engaging classroom exercises that challenge students to apply the material they are learning. For example, if you are teaching systems development start off the class with the "Skyscraper Activity" where the students build a prototype that takes them through each phase of the systems development life cycle. If you are working on tying information technology to business begin your class with the "Magazine Exercise" where students place Post-It Notes on technology articles in popular business magazines clearly demonstrating that technology is everywhere in business.

Image Library. Text figures and tables, as permission allows, are provided in a format by which they can be imported into PowerPoint for class lectures.

Multiple Data and Solution Files. For appropriate problems, there are multiple data and solution files allowing instructors to assign the same base problem with different data files.

Captivate Files. A complete set of narrated solution files for all Excel, Access, and Web development projects provide narrated step-by-step detail for each project. These are a great aid to help instructors quickly understand questions and can be posted for students to review, saving instructor time with case reviews.

Cohesion Case. The Broadway Cafe is a running case instructors can use to reinforce core material such as customer relationship management, supply chain management, business intelligence, and decision making. The case has 15 sections that challenge students to develop and expand their grandfather's coffee shop. Students receive hands-on experience in business and learn technology's true value of enabling business.

Project Files. The authors have provided files for all projects that need further support, such as data files.

Internet Links. Throughout the text are Web site addresses where related material can be obtained from the World Wide Web. These Web locations provide valuable information that, when used with the text material, provides a complete, up-to-date coverage of information technology and business.

Apply Your Knowledge

Business Driven Information Systems contains 50 projects that focus on student application of core concepts and tools. All productivity tool projects come with Captivate solution file that walks students step-by-step through the solution, which saves instructors valuable time.

Project Number	Project Name	Project Type	Focus Area	Skill Set	Page Number
1	Capitalizing on Your Career	Business	IT/MIS	Careers in IT	412
2	Achieving Alignment	Business	General Business	Business-IT Alignment	413
3	Market Dissection	Business	General Business	Porter's Five Forces	413
4	Grading Security	Business	Security	Information Security Plan/Policies	414
5	Eyes Everywhere	Business	Security	Biometrics	415
6	Setting Boundaries	Business	Ethics	Ethical Dilemmas	416
7	Contemplating Sharing	Business	Ethics	Peer-to-Peer	416
8	Dashboard Design	Business	EIS	Digital Dashboard	417
9	Great Stories	Business	CRM	Disgruntled Customers	417
10	Classic Car Problems	Business	CRM	Business Efficiency	418
11	Building Visibility	Business	SCM	Business Effectiveness	418
12	Bean Integration	Business	ERP	Information Integration	419
13	Working Together	Business	Collaboration	Workflow	420
14	Different Dimensions	Business	Business Intelligence	Data Warehouse	421
15	Connecting Components	Business	Enterprise Architecture	Developing Systems	422
16	Internet Groceries	Business	E-Business	Business Analysis	422
17	Getting Personal	Business	E-Business	Mass Customization	423
18	Express Yourself	Business	E-Business	Web Site Development	423
19	Creating a Presence	Business	E-Business	Web Site Development	424
20	GoGo Gadgets	Business	Wireless	Competitive Advantage	424
21	Back on Your Feet	Business	Enterprise Architecture	Backup and Disaster Recovery	425
22	GEM Athletic Center	Business	SDLC	Business Requirements	425
23	Confusing Coffee	Business	SDLC	Business Requirements	426
24	Picking Projects	Business	Project Management	Prioritizing Projects	426
25	Keeping Time	Business	Project Management	Project Plan	426

(*Continued*)

Project Number	Project Name	Project Type	Focus Area	Skill Set	Page Number
26	Controlling Your Spending	Excel	Personal Budget	Introductory Development: Formulas	427
27	Gearing for Cash	Excel	Cash Flow	Introductory Development: Formulas	428
28	Book Boxes	Excel	Strategic Analysis	Intermediate Development: Formulas	428
29	SplashEm	Excel	Strategic Analysis	Intermediate Development: Formulas	429
30	Tally's Purchases	Excel	Hardware and Software	Introductory Development: Formulas	430
31	Tracking Donations	Excel	Employee Relationships	Introductory Development: Formulas	430
32	All Aboard	Excel	Global Commerce	Introductory Development: Formulas	430
33	In with the Out	Excel	Outsourcing	Advanced Development: Formulas	430
34	Woods You	Excel	SCM	Advanced Development: Formulas	432
35	Bill's Boots	Excel	Profit Maximization	Intermediate Development: Formulas	432
36	Adequate Acquisitions	Excel	Break-Even Analysis	Intermediate Development: Formulas	433
37	Formatting Grades	Excel	Streamlining Data	Advanced Development: If, LookUp	433
38	Moving Espressos	Excel	SCM	Advanced Development: Absolute vs. Relative Values	434
39	Reducing Transports	Excel	SCM	Advanced Development: Pivot Table	434
40	Better Business	Excel	CRM	Intermediate Development: Pivot Table	435
41	Too Much Information	Excel	CRM	Advanced Development: Pivot Table	435
42	Gizmo Turnover	Excel	Data Mining	Advanced Development: Pivot Table	436
43	Managing Martin	Excel	Data Mining	Advanced Development: Pivot Table	436
44	Mountain Cycle	Excel	Break Even Analysis	Advanced Development: Goal Seek	437
45	Lutz Motors	Excel	Sales Analysis	Advanced Development: Scenario Manager	437
46	Animal Relations	Access	Business Analysis	Introductory Development	438
47	On-The-Level	Access	Business Intelligence	Introductory Development	439
48	iToys Inventory	Access	SCM	Intermediate Development	440
49	Call Around	Access	CRM	Intermediate Development	441
50	MoveIt	Access	Business Intelligence	Advanced Development	443

Empowered Instruction

Classroom Performance System
Engage students and assess real-time lecture retention with this simple yet powerful wireless application. You can even deliver tests that instantly grade themselves.

MIS Case Videos
Choose from our library of original video cases to illustrate important concepts or generate class discussion.

Introduction

SDLC

7: Maintenance   1: Planning

6: Implementation   2: Analysis

5: Testing   3: Design

4: Development

PowerPoint Presentations
Robust, detailed, and designed to keep students engaged. Detailed teaching notes are also included on every slide.

Introduction

Business value

Reporting Customer identification

Analyzing Customer segmentation

Predicting Customer prediction

Time

OFFSHORE OUTSOURCING

Key
- Leaders
- Up-and-Comers
- Rookies

■ Walk the students through the systems development life cycle:
- ■ *Planning phase*—involves establishing a high-level plan of the intended project and determining project goals
- ■ *Analysis phase*—involves analyzing end-user business requirements and refining project goals into defined functions and operations of the intended system
- ■ *Design phase*—involves describing the desired features and operations of the system including screen layouts, business rules, process diagrams, pseudo code, and other documentation
- ■ *Development phase*—involves taking all of the detailed design documents from the design phase and transforming them into the actual system
- ■ *Testing phase*—involves bringing all the project pieces together into a special testing environment to test for errors, bugs, and interoperability, in order to verify that the system meets all the business requirements defined in the analysis phase
- ■ *Implementation phase*—involves placing the system into production so users can begin to perform actual business operations with the system
- ■ *Maintenance phase*—involves performing changes, corrections, additions, and upgrades to ensure the system continues to meet the business goals

MIS OURCE

Software Skills & Computer Concepts
MISource provides animated tutorials and simulated practice of the core skills in Microsoft Excel, Access, and PowerPoint. MISource also animates 47 important computer concepts.

Spend less time reviewing software skills and computer literacy.

ACKNOWLEDGMENTS

Compiling the first edition of *Business Driven Information Systems* has been a tremendous undertaking and there are numerous people whom we want to heartily thank for their hard work, enthusiasm, and dedication.

This text draws from the efforts of a number of people at McGraw-Hill/Irwin. Paul Ducham, our Executive Sponsoring Editor, thank you for your insight, your intellect, and your continuous support and belief in our abilities—we simply could not have succeeded without you! Trina Hauger, our Development Editor, thank you for making all of those lists that keep us on track and focused. Mary Conzachi, our Lead Project Manager, thank you for making the difficult production process smooth and effortless.

In addition we would like to thank Brent Gordon (Editorial Director), Sankha Basu (Marketing Manager), Kami Carter (Designer), Gregory Bates (Media Producer), Brian Nacik (Media Project Manager), Heather Burbridge (Production Supervisor), and Jeremy Cheshareck (Photo Coordinator), for your support and dedication to the success of this text.

Last, but certainly not least, we offer our sincerest gratitude and deepest appreciation to our valuable reviewers whose feedback was instrumental in successfully compiling the first edition of this text.

Kamal Nayan Agarwal
Howard University

Marvin Albin
University of Southern Indiana

Sunny Baker
California State University – San Bernardino

Cynthia Barnes
Lamar University

Ozden Bayazit
Central Washington University

Jack Becker
University of North Texas

Queen Booker
Minnesota State University – Mankato

Ralph Caputo
Manhattan College

Judith Carlisle
Dowling College

Jerry Carvalho
University of Utah – Salt Lake City

Casey Cegielski
Auburn University

Robert Chi
California State University – Long Beach

Tony Coulson
California State University – San Bernardino

David Dulany
Aurora University

Lauren Eder
Rider University

Frederic Fisher
Florida State University – Tallahassee

Linda Fried
University of Colorado – Denver

James Frost
Idaho State University

John Gerdes
University of California – Riverside

Rajni Goel
Howard University

Robert Gordon
Hofstra University

Lorraine Greenwald
SUNY – Farmingdale

John Gudenas
Aurora University

Roslin Hauck
Illinois State University

Bashorat Ibragimova
University of North Texas

Rex Karsten
University of Northern Iowa

Chung Kim
Southwest Missouri State

Donald Kalmey
Indiana University Southeast

Virginia Kleist
West Virginia University

Chang Koh
University of North Texas

Al Lederer
University of Kentucky

Mark Lewis
Regis College

Stephen Loy
Eastern Kentucky University

Joan Lumpkin
Wright State University

Jane Mackay
Texas Christian University

Don McCubbrey
University of Denver

Nina McGarry
George Washington University

Bernard Merkle
California Lutheran University

Phillip Musa
University of Alabama –
Birmingham

Bijayananda Naik
University of South Dakota

Michael Pangburn
University of Oregon

Barry Pasternack
California State University
– Fullerton

Alan Graham Peace
West Virginia University

Richard Peterson
Montclair State University

John Powell
University of South Dakota

Leonard Presby
William Patterson University

Mahesh Raisinghani
Texas Women's University

Kirsten Rosacker
University of South Dakota

Marcos Schniederjans
University of Nebraska – Lincoln

Ken Sears
University of Texas – Arlington

Ganesan Shankaranarayanan
Boston University

Stephen Shao
Tennessee State University

K. David Smith
Cameron University

Ray Tsai
St. Cloud State University

Richard Turley
University of Northern Colorado

Karen Williams
University of Texas – San Antonio

James Yao
Montclair State University

Randall Young
University of North Texas

Yue Zhang
California State University
– Northridge

Paige Baltzan

Paige Baltzan teaches in the Department of Information Technology and Electronic Commerce at the Daniels College of Business at the University of Denver. She holds a B.S.B.A. specializing in MIS/Accounting from Bowling Green State University and an M.B.A. specializing in MIS from the University of Denver. She is a coauthor on several books including *Business Driven Technology*, I-Series, and a contributor to *Management Information Systems for the Information Age*.

Prior to joining the Daniels College faculty in 1999, Paige spent several years working for a large telecommunications company and an international consulting firm where she participated in client engagements in the United States as well as South America and Europe. Paige lives in Lakewood, Colorado, with her husband, Tony, and daughters, Hannah and Sophie.

Amy Phillips

Amy Phillips is a professor in the Department of Information Technology and Electronic Commerce in the Daniels College of Business at the University of Denver. Amy's main teaching and research areas involve Internet and mobile technologies. With her MCT certification, Amy works with developing training material for Microsoft's Web Services platform, .NET. With more than 22 years teaching experience, Amy has coauthored several textbooks, including *Management Information Systems for the Information Age*, 6/e, *Business Driven Technology, Business Driven Information Systems, Internet Explorer 6.0* and *PowerPoint 2003*.

Business Driven Information Systems

Information Systems in Business

1

CHAPTER

SECTION 1.1
Information Systems in Business

SECTION 1.2
Business Strategy

- Information Technology's Role in Business
- Information Technology Basics
- Roles and Responsibilities in Information Technology
- Measuring Information Technology's Success

- Identifying Competitive Advantages
- The Five Forces Model – Evaluating Business Segments
- The Three Generic Strategies – Creating a Business Focus
- Value Chain Analysis – Targeting Business Process

CHAPTER OUTLINE

Apple—Merging Technology, Business, and Entertainment

Apple Computer Inc., back from near oblivion, is setting the pace in the digital world with innovation and creativity that had been missing from the company for the past 20 years. Introduction of the iPod, a brilliant merger of technology, business, and entertainment, catapulted Apple back into the mainstream.

Capitalizing on New Trends

In 2000, Steve Jobs was fixated on developing video editing software for the Macintosh. But then he realized millions of people were using computers and CD burners to make audio CDs and to download digital songs called MP3s from illegal online services like Napster. Jobs was worried that he was looking in the wrong direction and had missed the MP3 bandwagon.

Jobs moved fast. He began by purchasing SoundStep from Jeff Robbin, a 28-year-old software engineer and former Apple employee. SoundStep was developing software that simplified the importing and compression of MP3 songs. Robbin and a couple of other programmers began writing code from scratch and created the first version of iTunes for the Mac in less than four months. This powerful and ingenious database could quickly sort tens of thousands of songs in a multitude of ways and find particular tracks in nanoseconds.

Jobs next challenged the team to make iTunes portable. He envisioned a Walkman-like player that could hold thousands of songs and be taken anywhere. The idea was to modify iTunes and build a tiny new system for what was basically a miniature computer, along with a user interface that could sort and navigate music files with the same sophistication as iTunes on the Mac. The iPod was born nine months later.

Jobs noticed that one last key element was missing, an online store for buying downloadable songs. Such a store would need an e-business infrastructure that could automatically deliver songs and track billing and payments for conceivably millions of purchases. In the spring of 2003, 18 months after the launch of the iPod, Apple's iTunes Music Store opened for business. The company's goal was to sell 1 million songs in the first six months. It hit this goal in six days.

Capitalizing on the iPod

Consumers purchased more than 14 million iPod devices during the 2005 holiday season, allowing Apple to exceed $1 billion in sales through its retail stores. Apple has now sold more than 40 million iPods. The groundbreaking product has transformed Apple from a niche computer maker into the leading purveyor of digital media.

With millions of iPods in the hands of consumers, other companies are noticing the trend and finding ways to capitalize on the product. John Lin created a prototype of a remote control for the iPod. Lin took his prototype to Macworld, where he found success. A few months later, Lin's company had Apple's blessing and a commitment for shelf space in its retail stores. "This is how Apple supports the iPod economy," Lin said.

In the iPod-dominated market, hundreds of companies have been inspired to develop more than 500 accessories—everything from rechargers for the car to $1,500 Fendi bags. Eric Tong, vice president at Belkin, a cable and peripheral manufacturer, believes that 75 percent of all iPod owners purchase at least one accessory—meaning that 30 million accessories have been sold. With most of the products priced between $10 and $200 that puts the iPod economy well over $300 million and perhaps as high as $6 billion. Popular iPod accessories include:

- Altec Lansing Technologies—iPod speakers and recharger dock ($150).
- Belkin—TuneCast mobile FM transmitter ($40).
- Etymotic Research—high-end earphones ($150).
- Griffin Technology—iTrip FM transmitter ($35).
- Kate Spade—Geneva faux-croc mini iPod holder ($55).
- Apple—socks set in six colors, green, purple, blue, orange, pink, and gray ($29).
- Apple—digital camera connector ($29).

Capitalizing on the Future

The latest iPod packs music, audiobooks, podcasts, photos, video, contacts, calendars, games, clocks, and locks in a design up to 45 percent slimmer than the original iPod. It also boasts stamina (up to 20 hours of battery life), generous capacity (30 GB or 60 GB of storage), a great personality (intuitive, customizable menus), and a touch of genius (the Apple Click Wheel). The latest features include:

- **Videos**—Choose from over 2,000 music videos at the iTunes Music Store or purchase ad-free episodes of a favorite ABC or Disney television show and watch them on the go.
- **Podcasts**—The iTunes Podcast Directory features thousands of free podcasts, or radio-style shows, including favorites from such big names as ABC News, Adam Curry, ESPN, KCRW, and WGBH.

- **Audiobooks**—The digital shelves of the iTunes Music Store are stocked with more than 11,000 audiobooks, including such exclusives as the entire Harry Potter series.
- **Photos**—With storage for up to 25,000 photos, iPod users can view photo slide shows—complete with music—on an iPod or on a TV via the optional video cable.

iPod's Impact on the Music Business

In the digital era, the unbundling of CDs through the purchase of individual tracks lets consumers pay far less to get a few of their favorite songs rather than buying an entire album. Many analysts predicted that the iPod's success coupled with the consumer's ability to choose individual song downloads would lead to increased revenues for music businesses. However, the industry is seeing individual downloads cannibalizing album profits and failing to attract new music sales. "I've still never bought a download," said Eneka Iriondo-Coysh, a 21-year-old graphic-design student in London who has owned a 10,000 song-capacity iPod for more than two years. "I do it all from my CDs," mostly hip-hop and soul.

The global music industry has been under siege for years amid declining sales. Record companies suffer from piracy, including billions of dollars in lost revenue due to bootlegged CDs. At the same time, music faces new competition for consumer time and money from video games, DVDs, and mobile phones. At traditional record stores, DVDs and games are taking an increasing amount of shelf space, squeezing out CDs. The music download numbers suggest that the iPod's iconic success is not translating into new music sales the way the evolution from vinyl albums to cassettes and then CDs did. For many users, the portable devices are just another way of stocking and listening to music, not an incentive to buy new music.

Global CD sales fell 6.7 percent to $12.4 billion in the first half of 2005, according to the London-based International Federation of the Phonographic Industry. The evidence indicates that digital downloads are not good for the music business.[1]

INTRODUCTION

nformation is everywhere. Most organizations value information as a strategic asset. Consider Apple and its iPod, iPod accessories, and iTunes Music Store. Apple's success depends heavily on information about its customers, suppliers, markets, and operations for each of these product lines. For example, Apple must be able to predict the number of people who will purchase an iPod to help estimate iPod accessory and iTunes sales within the next year. Estimating too many buyers will lead Apple to produce an excess of inventory; estimating too few buyers will potentially mean lost sales due to lack of product (resulting in even more lost revenues from iTunes downloads).

Understanding the direct impact information has on an organization's bottom line is crucial to running a successful business. This text focuses on information, business, technology, and the integrated set of activities used to run most organizations. Many of these activities are the hallmarks of business today—supply chain management, customer relationship management, enterprise resource planning, outsourcing, integration, e-business, and others.

section 1.1 INFORMATION SYSTEMS IN BUSINESS

1.1. Describe the functional areas of a business and why they must work together for the business to be successful.

1.2. Explain information technology's role in business and how you measure success.

1.3. Compare management information systems (MIS) and information technology (IT), and define the relationships among people, information technology, and information.

1.4. Compare the responsibilities of a chief information officer (CIO), chief technology officer (CTO), chief security officer (CSO), chief privacy officer (CPO), and chief knowledge officer (CKO).

1.5. Explain the gap between IT and the business, along with the primary reason this gap exists.

INFORMATION TECHNOLOGY'S ROLE IN BUSINESS

Students frequently ask, "Why do we need to study information technology?" The answer is simple: Information technology is everywhere in business. Understanding information technology provides great insight to anyone learning about business.

It is easy to demonstrate information technology's role in business by reviewing a copy of popular business magazines such as *BusinessWeek, Fortune, Business 2.0,* or *Fast Company*. Placing a marker (such as a Post-it Note) on each page that contains a technology-related article or advertisement indicates that information technology is everywhere in business (see Figure 1.1). These are *business* magazines, not *technology* magazines, yet they are filled with technology. Students who understand technology have an advantage in business.

These magazine articles typically discuss such topics as databases, customer relationship management, Web services, supply chain management, security, ethics, business intelligence, and so on. They also focus on companies such as Siebel, Oracle, Microsoft, and IBM. This text explores these topics in detail, along with reviewing the associated business opportunities and challenges.

Information Technology's Impact on Business Operations

Figure 1.2 highlights the business functions receiving the greatest benefit from information technology, along with the common business goals associated with information technology projects, according to *CIO* magazine.

Achieving the results outlined in Figure 1.2, such as reducing costs, improving productivity, and generating growth, is not easy. Implementing a new accounting

FIGURE 1.1

Technology in *Business Week*
and Fortune

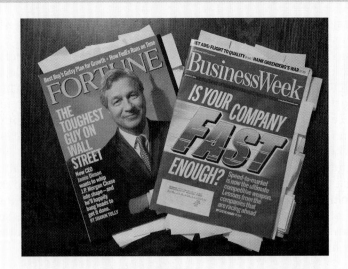

FIGURE 1.2

Business Benefits and Information Technology Project
Goals

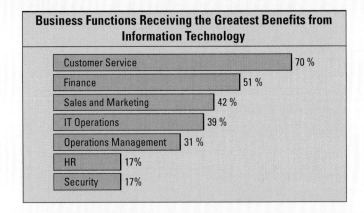

Business Functions Receiving the Greatest Benefits from Information Technology

Function	Benefit
Customer Service	70 %
Finance	51 %
Sales and Marketing	42 %
IT Operations	39 %
Operations Management	31 %
HR	17%
Security	17%

Information Technology Project Goals

Goal	Percent
Reduce Costs/Improve Productivity	81 %
Improve Customer Satisfaction/Loyalty	71 %
Create Competitive Advantage	66 %
Generate Growth	54 %
Streamline Supply Chain	37 %
Global Expansion	16%

system or marketing plan is not likely to generate long-term growth or reduce costs across an entire organization. Businesses must undertake enterprisewide initiatives to achieve broad general business goals such as reducing costs. Information technology plays a critical role in deploying such initiatives by facilitating communication and increasing business intelligence. For example, e-mail and cell phones allow people across an organization to communicate in new and innovative ways.

Understanding information technology begins with gaining an understanding of how businesses function and IT's role in creating efficiencies and effectiveness across the organization. Typical businesses operate by functional areas (often called functional silos). Each area undertakes a specific core business function (see Figure 1.3).

FIGURE 1.3

Departmental Structure of a
Typical Organization

COMMON DEPARTMENTS IN AN ORGANIZATION

ACCOUNTING		MARKETING		OPERATIONS MANAGEMENT
	HUMAN RESOURCES		PRODUCTION MANAGEMENT	
FINANCE		SALES		MANAGEMENT INFORMATION SYSTEMS

- **Accounting** provides quantitative information about the finances of the business including recording, measuring, and describing financial information.

- **Finance** deals with the strategic financial issues associated with increasing the value of the business, while observing applicable laws and social responsibilities.

- **Human resources (HR)** includes the policies, plans, and procedures for the effective management of employees (human resources).

- **Sales** is the function of selling a good or service and focuses on increasing customer sales, which increases company revenues.

- **Marketing** is the process associated with promoting the sale of goods or services. The marketing department supports the sales department by creating promotions that help sell the company's products.

- **Operations management** (also called **production management**) includes the methods, tasks, and techniques organizations use to produce goods and services. Transportation (also called logistics) is part of operations management.

- **Management information systems (MIS)** is the function that plans for, develops, implements, and maintains IT hardware, software, and the portfolio of applications that people use to support the goals of an organization.

Functional areas are anything but independent in a business. In fact, functional areas are *interdependent* (see Figure 1.4). Sales must rely on information from operations to understand inventory, place orders, calculate transportation costs, and gain insight into product availability based on production schedules. For an organization to succeed, every department or functional area must work together sharing common information and not be a "silo." Information technology can enable departments to more efficiently and effectively perform their business operations.

FIGURE 1.4

Marketing Working with
Other Organizational
Departments

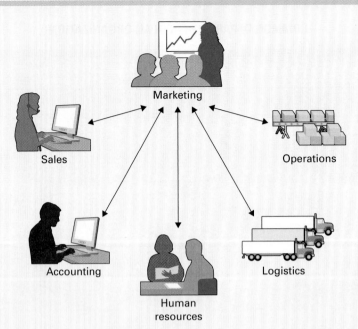

Functional organization—Each functional area has its own systems
and communicates with every other functional area (diagram
displays Marketing communicating with all other functional areas
in the organization).

Individuals anticipating a successful career in business, whether it is in accounting, finance, human resources, or operation management, must understand information technology including:

- Information technology basics.
- Roles and responsibilities in information technology.
- Measuring information technology's success.

INFORMATION TECHNOLOGY BASICS

Information technology (IT) is any computer-based tool that people use to work with information and support the information and information-processing needs of an organization. Information technology can be an important enabler of business success and innovation. This is not to say that IT *equals* business success and innovation or that IT *represents* business success and innovation. Information technology is most useful when it leverages the talents of people. Information technology in and of itself is not useful unless the right people know how to use and manage it effectively.

Management information systems is a business function just as marketing, finance, operations, and human resources management are business functions. Formally defined, *management information systems (MIS)* is the function that plans for, develops, implements, and maintains IT hardware, software, and applications that people use to support the goals of an organization. To perform the MIS function effectively, almost all organizations today, particularly large and medium-sized ones, have an internal IT department, often called Information Technology (IT), Information Systems (IS), or Management Information Systems (MIS). When beginning to learn about information technology it is important to understand:

- Information
- IT resources
- IT cultures

Information

It is important to distinguish between data and information. **Data** are raw facts that describe the characteristics of an event. Characteristics for a sales event could include the date, item number, item description, quantity ordered, customer name, and shipping details. **Information** is data converted into a meaningful and useful context. Information from sales events could include best-selling item, worst-selling item, best customer, and worst customer.

IT Resources

The plans and goals of the IT department must align with the plans and goals of the organization. Information technology can enable an organization to increase efficiency in manufacturing, retain key customers, seek out new sources of supply, and introduce effective financial management.

It is not always easy for managers to make the right choices when using IT to support (and often drive) business initiatives. Most managers understand their business initiatives well, but are often at a loss when it comes to knowing how to use and manage IT effectively in support of those initiatives. Managers who understand what IT is, and what IT can and cannot do, are in the best position for success. In essence,

- *People* use
- *information technology* to work with
- *information* (see Figure 1.5).

Those three key resources—people, information, and information technology (in that order of priority)—are inextricably linked. If one fails, they all fail. Most important, if one fails, then chances are the business will fail.

IT Cultures

An organization's culture plays a large role in determining how successfully it will share information. Culture will influence the way people use information (their information behavior) and will reflect the importance that company leaders attribute to the use of information in achieving success or avoiding failure. Four common information-sharing cultures exist in organizations today: information-functional, information-sharing, information-inquiring, and information-discovery (see Figure 1.6).[2]

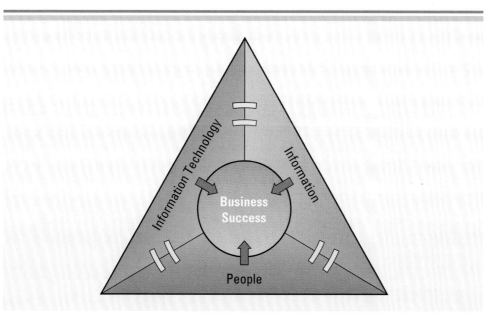

FIGURE 1.5

The Relationship among People, Information, and Information Technology

FIGURE 1.6

Different Information Cultures
Found in Organizations

Organizational Information Cultures	
Information-Functional Culture	Employees use information as a means of exercising influence or power over others. For example, a manager in sales refuses to share information with marketing. This causes marketing to need the sales manager's input each time a new sales strategy is developed.
Information-Sharing Culture	Employees across departments trust each other to use information (especially about problems and failures) to improve performance.
Information-Inquiring Culture	Employees across departments search for information to better understand the future and align themselves with current trends and new directions.
Information-Discovery Culture	Employees across departments are open to new insights about crisis and radical changes and seek ways to create competitive advantages.

An organization's IT culture can directly affect its ability to compete in the global market. If an organization operates with an information-functional culture, it will have a great degree of difficulty operating. Getting products to market quickly and creating a view of its end-to-end (or entire) business from sales to billing will be a challenge. If an organization operates with an information-discovery culture it will be able to get products to market quickly and easily see a 360-degree view of its entire organization. Employees will be able to use this view to better understand the market and create new products that offer a competitive advantage.

ROLES AND RESPONSIBILITIES IN INFORMATION TECHNOLOGY

Information technology is a relatively new functional area, having been around formally in most organizations only for about 40 years. Job titles, roles, and responsibilities often differ from organization to organization. Nonetheless, clear trends are developing toward elevating some IT positions within an organization to the strategic level.

Most organizations maintain positions such as chief executive officer (CEO), chief financial officer (CFO), and chief operations officer (COO) at the strategic level. Recently there are more IT-related strategic positions such as chief information officer (CIO), chief technology officer (CTO), chief security officer (CSO), chief privacy officer (CPO), and chief knowledge officer (CKO).

J. Greg Hanson is proud to be the first CIO of the U.S. Senate. Contrary to some perceptions, the technology found in the Senate is quite good, according to Hanson. Hanson's responsibilities include creating the Senate's technology vision, leading the IT department, and deploying the IT infrastructure. Hanson must work with everyone from the 137 network administrators to the senators themselves to ensure that everything is operating smoothly.[3]

The **chief information officer (CIO)** is responsible for (1) overseeing all uses of information technology and (2) ensuring the strategic alignment of IT with business goals and objectives. The CIO often reports directly to the CEO (see Figure 1.7 for average CIO compensation). CIOs must possess a solid understanding of every aspect of an organization coupled with tremendous insight into the capability of IT. Broad roles of a CIO include:

- *Manager*—ensure the delivery of all IT projects, on time and within budget.
- *Leader*—ensure the strategic vision of IT is in line with the strategic vision of the organization.
- *Communicator*—advocate and communicate the IT strategy by building and maintaining strong executive relationships.

FIGURE 1.7

Average CIO Compensation
by Industry

Industry	Average CIO Compensation
Wholesale/Retail/Distribution	$243,304
Finance	$210,547
Insurance	$197,697
Manufacturing	$190,250
Medical/Dental/Health Care	$171,032
Government	$118,359
Education	$93,750

FIGURE 1.8

What Concerns CIOs the
Most?

CIO's Concerns	Percentage
Enchancing customer satisfaction	94%
Security	92
Technology evaluation	89
Budgeting	87
Staffing	83
ROI analysis	66
Building new applications	64
Outsourcing hosting	45

Although CIO is considered a position within IT, CIOs must be concerned with more than just IT. According to a recent survey (see Figure 1.8), most CIOs ranked "enhancing customer satisfaction" ahead of their concerns for any specific aspect of IT. We should applaud CIOs who possess the broad business view that customer satisfaction is more crucial and critical than specific aspects of IT.

The *chief technology officer (CTO)* is responsible for ensuring the throughput, speed, accuracy, availability, and reliability of an organization's information technology. CTOs have direct responsibility for ensuring the efficiency of IT systems throughout the organization. Most CTOs possess well-rounded knowledge of all aspects of IT, including hardware, software, and telecommunications. CTO's typically report to the CIO. The role of CTO is similar to CIO, except that CIO must take on the additional responsibility of ensuring that IT aligns with the organization's strategic initiatives.

The *chief security officer (CSO)* is responsible for ensuring the security of IT systems and developing strategies and IT safeguards against attacks from hackers and viruses. The role of a CSO has been elevated in recent years because of the number of attacks from hackers and viruses. Most CSOs possess detailed knowledge of networks and telecommunications because hackers and viruses usually find their way into IT systems through networked computers.

The *chief privacy officer (CPO)* is responsible for ensuring the ethical and legal use of information within an organization. CPOs are the newest senior executive position in IT. Recently, 150 of the Fortune 500 companies added the CPO position to their list of senior executives. Many CPOs are lawyers by training, enabling them to understand the often complex legal issues surrounding the use of information.

The *chief knowledge officer (CKO)* is responsible for collecting, maintaining, and distributing the organization's knowledge. The CKO designs programs and systems that make it easy for people to reuse knowledge. These systems create repositories of organizational documents, methodologies, tools, and practices, and they establish methods for filtering the information. The CKO must continuously encourage employee contributions to keep the systems up-to-date. The CKO can contribute directly to the organization's bottom line by reducing the learning curve for new employees or employees taking on new roles.

In 1998, Danny Shaw became the first CKO at Children's Hospital in Boston. His initial task was to unite information from disparate systems to enable analysis of both the efficiency and effectiveness of the hospital's care. Shaw started by building a series of small, integrated information systems that quickly demonstrated value. He then gradually built on those successes, creating a knowledge-enabled organization one layer at a time. Shaw's information systems have enabled administrative and clinical operational analyses.[4]

All the above IT positions and responsibilities are critical to an organization's success. While many organizations may not have a different individual for each of these positions, they must have leaders taking responsibility for all these areas of concern. The individuals responsible for enterprisewide IT and IT-related issues must provide guidance and support to the organization's employees. Figure 1.9 displays the personal skills pivotal for success in an executive IT role.

The Gap Between Business Personnel and IT Personnel

One of the greatest challenges today is effective communication between business personnel and IT personnel. Figure 1.9 clearly demonstrates the importance of communication for IT executives. Business personnel possess expertise in functional areas such as marketing, accounting, sales, and so forth. IT personnel have the technological expertise. Unfortunately, a communications gap often exists between the two. Business personnel have their own vocabularies based on their experience and expertise. IT personnel have their own vocabularies consisting of acronyms and technical terms. Effective communication between business and IT personnel should be a two-way street with each side making the effort to understand each other (including written and oral communication).

Improving Communication   Business personnel must seek to increase their understanding of IT. Although they do not need to know every technical detail, it is beneficial to understand what IT can and cannot accomplish. Business managers and leaders should read business-oriented IT magazines, such as *InformationWeek* and *CIO*, to increase their IT knowledge.

At the same time, an organization must develop strategies for integrating its IT personnel into the various business functions. Too often, IT personnel are left out of strategy meetings because of the belief they do not understand the business so they

FIGURE 1.9

Skills Pivotal for Success in Executive IT Roles

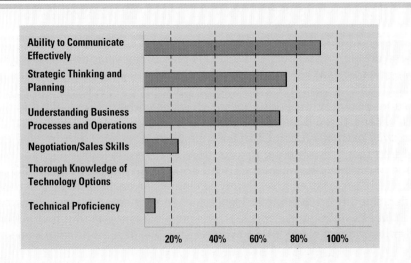

will not add any value. That is a dangerous position to take. IT personnel must understand the business if the organization is going to determine which technologies can benefit (or hurt) the business. With a little effort to communicate, IT personnel might provide information on the functionality available in an information system, which could add tremendous value to a meeting about how to improve customer service. Working together, business and IT personnel have the potential to create competitive advantages, reduce costs, and streamline business processes.

It is the CIO's responsibility to ensure effective communications between business and IT personnel. While the CIO assumes the responsibility on an enterprise-wide level, it is each employee's responsibility to communicate effectively on a personal level.

MEASURING INFORMATION TECHNOLOGY'S SUCCESS

To offer detailed information to all layers of management, General Electric Co. (GE) invested $1.5 billion in employee time, hardware, software, and other technologies to implement a real-time operations monitoring system. GE's executives use the new system to monitor sales, inventory, and savings across the company's 13 global business operations every 15 minutes. This allows GE to respond to changes, reduce cycle times, and improve risk management on an hourly basis instead of waiting for monthly or quarterly reports. GE estimates the $1.5 billion investment will provide a 33 percent return over five years.[5]

IT professionals know how to install and maintain information systems. Business professionals know how to run a successful business. But how does a company decide if an information system helps make a business successful?

The answer lies in the metrics. Designing metrics requires an expertise that neither IT nor business professionals usually possess. Metrics are about neither technology nor business strategy. The questions that arise in metrics design are almost philosophical: How do you define success? How do you apply quantifiable measures to business processes, especially qualitative ones such as customer service? What kind of information best reflects progress, or the lack of it?

Key performance indicators (KPIs) are the measures that are tied to business drivers. Metrics are the detailed measures that feed those KPIs. Performance metrics fall into a nebulous area of business intelligence that is neither technology- nor business-centered, but this area requires input from both IT and business professionals to find success. Cisco Systems implemented a cross-departmental council to create metrics for improving business process operations. The council developed metrics to evaluate the efficiency of Cisco's online order processing and discovered that due to errors, more than 70 percent of online orders required manual input and were unable to be automatically routed to manufacturing. By changing the process and adding new information systems, within six months the company doubled the percentage of orders that went directly to manufacturing.[6]

Efficiency and Effectiveness Metrics

Organizations spend enormous sums of money on IT to compete in today's fast-paced business environment. Some organizations spend up to 50 percent of their total capital expenditures on IT. To justify these expenditures, an organization must measure the payoff of these investments, their impact on business performance, and the overall business value gained.

Efficiency and effectiveness metrics are two primary types of IT metrics. *Efficiency IT metrics* measure the performance of the IT system itself such as throughput, speed, and availability. *Effectiveness IT metrics* measure the impact IT has on business processes and activities including customer satisfaction, conversion rates, and sell-through increases. Peter Drucker offers a helpful distinction between efficiency and effectiveness. Drucker states that managers "Do things right" and/or "Do the right things." Doing things right addresses efficiency—getting the most from each resource. Doing the right things addresses effectiveness—setting the right goals and objectives and ensuring they are accomplished.[7]

Efficiency focuses on the extent to which an organization is using its resources in an optimal way, while effectiveness focuses on how well an organization is achieving its goals and objectives. The two—efficiency and effectiveness—are definitely interrelated. However, success in one area does not necessarily imply success in the other.

Benchmarking—Baseline Metrics

Regardless of what is measured, how it is measured, and whether it is for the sake of efficiency or effectiveness, there must be **benchmarks**, or baseline values the system seeks to attain. **Benchmarking** is a process of continuously measuring system results, comparing those results to optimal system performance (benchmark values), and identifying steps and procedures to improve system performance.

Consider online government services (e-government) as an illustration of benchmarking efficiency IT metrics and effectiveness IT metrics (see survey results in Figure 1.10). From an effectiveness point of view, Canada ranks number one in terms of e-government satisfaction of its citizens. (The United States ranks third.) The survey, sponsored by Accenture, also included such attributes as customer-service vision, initiatives for identifying services for individual citizen segments, and approaches to offering e-government services through multiple-service delivery channels. These are all benchmarks at which Canada's government excels.[8]

In contrast, the *United Nations Division for Public Economics and Public Administration* ranks Canada sixth in terms of efficiency IT metrics. (The United States ranked first.) This particular ranking, based purely on efficiency IT metrics, includes benchmarks such as the number of computers per 100 citizens, the number of Internet hosts per 10,000 citizens, and the percentage of the citizen online population. Therefore, while Canada lags behind in IT efficiency, it is the premier e-government provider in terms of effectiveness.[9]

Governments hoping to increase their e-government presence would benchmark themselves against these sorts of efficiency and effectiveness metrics. There is a high degree of correlation between e-government efficiency and effectiveness, although it is not absolute.

The Interrelationship Between Efficiency and Effectiveness IT Metrics

Efficiency IT metrics focus on the technology itself. Figure 1.11 highlights the most common types of efficiency IT metrics.

FIGURE 1.10

E-Government Ranking for Efficiency and Effectiveness

Efficiency	Effectiveness
1. United States (3.11)	1. Canada
2. Australia (2.60)	2. Singapore
3. New Zealand (2.59)	3. United States
4. Singapore (2.58)	4. Denmark
5. Norway (2.55)	5. Australia
6. Canada (2.52)	6. Finland
7. United Kingdom (2.52)	7. Hong Kong
8. Netherlands (2.51)	8. United Kingdom
9. Denmark (2.47)	9. Germany
10. Germany (2.46)	10. Ireland

FIGURE 1.11

Common Types of Efficiency
IT Metrics

Efficiency IT Metrics	
Throughput	The amount of information that can travel through a system at any point in time.
Transaction speed	The amount of time a system takes to perform a transaction.
System availability	The number of hours a system is available for users.
Information accuracy	The extent to which a system generates the correct results when executing the same transaction numerous times.
Web traffic	Includes a host of benchmarks such as the number of page views, the number of unique visitors, and the average time spent viewing a Web page.
Response time	The time it takes to respond to user interactions such as a mouse click.

While these efficiency metrics are important to monitor, they do not always guarantee effectiveness. Effectiveness IT metrics are determined according to an organization's goals, strategies, and objectives. Here, it becomes important to consider the strategy an organization is using, such as a broad cost leadership strategy (Wal-Mart, for example), as well as specific goals and objectives such as increasing new customers by 10 percent or reducing new-product development cycle times to six months. Figure 1.12 displays the broad, general effectiveness IT metrics.

In the private sector, eBay constantly benchmarks its information technology efficiency and effectiveness. In 2005, eBay posted impressive year-end results with revenues increasing 72 percent while earnings grew 125 percent. Maintaining constant Web site availability and optimal throughput performance is critical to eBay's success.[10]

Jupiter Media Metrix ranked eBay as the Web site with the highest visitor volume (efficiency) in 2005 for the fourth year in a row, with an 80 percent growth from the previous year. The auction Web site averaged 8 million unique visitors during each week of the holiday season that year with daily peaks exceeding 12 million visitors. To ensure constant availability and reliability of its systems, eBay implemented ProactiveNet, a performance measurement and management-tracking tool. The tool

FIGURE 1.12

Common Types of Effectiveness IT Metrics

Effectiveness IT Metrics	
Usability	The ease with which people perform transactions and/or find information. A popular usability metric on the Internet is degrees of freedom, which measures the number of clicks required to find desired information.
Customer satisfaction	Measured by such benchmarks as satisfaction surveys, percentage of existing customers retained, and increases in revenue dollars per customer.
Conversion rates	The number of customers an organization "touches" for the first time and persuades to purchase its products or services. This is a popular metric for evaluating the effectiveness of banner, pop-up, and pop-under ads on the Internet.
Financial	Such as return on investment (the earning power of an organization's assets), cost-benefit analysis (the comparison of projected revenues and costs including development, maintenance, fixed, and variable), and break-even analysis (the point at which constant revenues equal ongoing costs).

FIGURE 1.13

The Interrelationships Between Efficiency and Effectiveness

allows eBay to monitor its environment against baseline benchmarks, which helps the eBay team keep tight control of its systems. The new system has resulted in improved system availability with a 150 percent increase in productivity as measured by system uptime.[11]

Be sure to consider the issue of security while determining efficiency and effectiveness IT metrics. When an organization offers its customers the ability to purchase products over the Internet, it must implement the appropriate security. It is actually inefficient for an organization to implement security measures for Internet-based transactions as compared to processing nonsecure transactions. However, an organization will probably have a difficult time attracting new customers and increasing Web-based revenue if it does not implement the necessary security measures. Purely from an efficiency IT metric point of view, security generates some inefficiency. From an organization's business strategy point of view, however, security should lead to increases in effectiveness metrics.

Figure 1.13 depicts the interrelationships between efficiency and effectiveness. Ideally, an organization should operate in the upper right-hand corner of the graph, realizing both significant increases in efficiency and effectiveness. However, operating in the upper left-hand corner (minimal effectiveness with increased efficiency) or the lower right-hand corner (significant effectiveness with minimal efficiency) may be in line with an organization's particular strategies. In general, operating in the lower left-hand corner (minimal efficiency and minimal effectiveness) is not ideal for the operation of any organization.

OPENING CASE QUESTIONS

Apple—Merging Technology, Business, and Entertainment

1. What might have happened to Apple if its top executives had not supported investment in iPods?

2. Formulate a strategy for how Apple can use efficiency IT metrics to improve its business.

3. Formulate a strategy for how Apple can use effectiveness IT metrics to improve its business.

4. Why would it be unethical for Apple to sell its iTunes customer information to other businesses?

5. Evaluate the effects on Apple's business if it failed to secure its customer information and all of it was accidentally posted to an anonymous Web site.

1.6. Explain why competitive advantages are typically temporary.

1.7. List and describe each of the five forces in Porter's Five Forces Model.

1.8. Compare Porter's three generic strategies.

1.9. Describe the relationship between business processes and value chain analysis.

IDENTIFYING COMPETITIVE ADVANTAGES

To survive and thrive, an organization must create a competitive advantage. A ***competitive advantage*** is a product or service that an organization's customers place a greater value on than similar offerings from a competitor. Unfortunately, competitive advantages are typically temporary because competitors often seek ways to duplicate the competitive advantage. In turn, organizations must develop a strategy based on a new competitive advantage.

When an organization is the first to market with a competitive advantage, it gains a first-mover advantage. The ***first-mover advantage*** occurs when an organization can significantly impact its market share by being first to market with a competitive advantage. FedEx created a first-mover advantage by creating its customer self-service software, which allows people and organizations to request parcel pick-ups, print mailing slips, and track parcels online. Other parcel delivery companies quickly began creating their own online services. Today, customer self-service on the Internet is a standard for doing business in the parcel delivery business.

As organizations develop their competitive advantages, they must pay close attention to their competition through environmental scanning. ***Environmental*** — IT field ***scanning*** is the acquisition and analysis of events and trends in the environment external to an organization. Information technology has the opportunity to play an important role in environmental scanning.

Frito-Lay, a premier provider of snack foods such as Cracker Jacks and Cheetos, does not just send its representatives into grocery stores to stock shelves; they carry handheld computers and record the product offerings, inventory, and even product locations of competitors. Frito-Lay uses this information to gain business intelligence on everything from how well competing products are selling to the strategic placement of its own products.

Organizations use three common tools to analyze and develop competitive advantages: (1) Five Forces Model, (2) three generic strategies, and (3) value chain analysis.

THE FIVE FORCES MODEL—EVALUATING BUSINESS SEGMENTS

Michael Porter's Five Forces Model is a useful tool to aid organizations facing the challenging decision of entering a new industry or industry segment. The ***Five Forces Model*** helps determine the relative attractiveness of an industry and includes:

5 forces
relative attractiveness
—industry
—segment

1. Buyer power.
2. Supplier power.
3. Threat of substitute products or services.

4. Threat of new entrants.

5. Rivalry among existing competitors (see Figure 1.14).

Buyer Power

Buyer power in the Five Forces Model is high when buyers have many choices of whom to buy from and low when their choices are few. To reduce buyer power (and create a competitive advantage), an organization must make it more attractive for customers to buy from it instead of its competition. One of the best IT-based examples is the loyalty programs that many organizations offer.

Loyalty programs reward customers based on the amount of business they do with a particular organization. The travel industry is famous for its loyalty programs such as frequent-flyer programs for airlines and frequent-guest programs for hotels. Keeping track of the activities and accounts of many thousands or millions of customers covered by loyalty programs is not practical without large-scale IT systems. Loyalty programs are a good example of using IT to reduce buyer power; because of the rewards (e.g., free airline tickets, upgrades, or hotel stays) travelers receive, they are more likely to be loyal to or give most of their business to a single organization.

Supplier Power

Supplier power in the Five Forces Model is high when buyers have few choices of whom to buy from and low when their choices are many. Supplier power is the converse of buyer power: A supplier organization in a market will want buyer power to be low. A ***supply chain*** consists of all parties involved, directly or indirectly, in the procurement of a product or raw material. In a typical supply chain, an organization will probably be both a supplier (to customers) and a customer (of other supplier organizations) (see Figure 1.15).

As a buyer, the organization can create a competitive advantage by locating alternative supply sources. IT-enabled business-to-business (B2B) marketplaces can help. A ***business-to-business (B2B) marketplace*** is an Internet-based service that brings together many buyers and sellers (discussed in detail in Chapter 3). One important variation of the B2B marketplace is a private exchange. A ***private exchange***

FIGURE 1.14

Porter's Five Forces Model

FIGURE 1.15

An Organization within the Supply Chain

is a B2B marketplace in which a single buyer posts its needs and then opens the bidding to any supplier who would care to bid. Bidding is typically carried out through a reverse auction. A ***reverse auction*** is an auction format in which increasingly lower bids are solicited from organizations willing to supply the desired product or service at an increasingly lower price. As the bids get lower and lower, more and more suppliers drop out of the auction. Ultimately, the organization with the lowest bid wins. Internet-based reverse auctions are an excellent example of the way that information technology can reduce supplier power for an organization and create a competitive advantage.

Threat of Substitute Products or Services

The ***threat of substitute products or services*** in the Five Forces Model is high when there are many alternatives to a product or service and low when there are few alternatives from which to choose. Ideally, an organization would like to be in a market in which there are few substitutes for the products or services it offers. Of course, that is seldom possible today, but an organization can still create a competitive advantage by using switching costs.

3. TSPS ↑ = many product substitutes

Switching costs are costs that can make customers reluctant to switch to another product or service. A switching cost need not have an associated *monetary* cost. Amazon.com offers an example. As customers purchase products at Amazon.com over time, Amazon develops a profile of their shopping and purchasing habits, enabling Amazon to offer products tailored to a particular customer based on the customer's profile. If the customer decides to shop elsewhere, there is an associated switching cost because the new site will not have the profile of the customer's past purchases. In this way, Amazon.com has reduced the threat of substitute products or services by creating a "cost" to the consumer to switch to another online retailer.

switching cost ↑ = reluctancy to switch ↑

The cell phone industry offers another good example of switching costs. Cell phone providers want to keep their customers as long as possible. Many cell phone providers offer their customers free phones or unlimited minutes if they will sign a one- or two-year contract. This creates a switching cost for the customers if they decide to change providers because they will be required to pay a penalty for breaking their contract. Another switching cost for the cell phone customer was losing the actual cell phone number; however, this switching cost has been removed with the implementation of *local number portability (LNP)* or the ability to "port" cell phone numbers to new providers. Within the context of Porter's Five Forces Model, eliminating this switching cost creates a greater threat of substitute products or services for the supplier. That is, customers can now expect to see more new cell phone providers cropping up over the next several years. They will compete on price, quality, and services with the big-name cell phone providers such as AT&T and Verizon because cell phone numbers can be moved from one provider to another. When businesses reduce or eliminate switching costs, the consumer gains more power.

LNP = take your call # w/ you

Threat of New Entrants

The ***threat of new entrants*** in the Five Forces Model is high when it is easy for new competitors to enter a market and low when there are significant entry barriers to

4. TNE ↑ = easy market entry

entering a market. An entry barrier is a product or service feature that customers have come to expect from organizations in a particular industry and must be offered by an entering organization to compete and survive. For example, a new bank must offer its customers an array of IT-enabled services, including ATM use, online bill paying, and account monitoring. These are significant barriers to entering the banking market. At one time, the first bank to offer such services gained a valuable first-mover advantage, but only temporarily, as other banking competitors developed their own IT systems.

Rivalry Among Existing Competitors

Rivalry among existing competitors in the Five Forces Model is high when competition is fierce in a market and low when competition is more complacent. Although competition is always more intense in some industries than in others, the overall trend is toward increased competition in almost every industry.

The retail grocery industry is intensively competitive. While Kroger, Safeway, and Albertsons in the United States compete in many different ways, essentially they try to beat or match the competition on price. Most of them have loyalty programs that give shoppers special discounts. Customers get lower prices while the store gathers valuable information on buying habits to create pricing strategies. In the future, expect to see grocery stores using wireless technologies to track customer movement throughout the store and match it to products purchased to determine product placement and pricing strategies. Such a system will be IT-based and a huge competitive advantage to the first store to implement it.

Since margins are low in the retail grocery market, grocers build efficiencies into their supply chains, connecting with their suppliers in IT-enabled information partnerships such as the one between Wal-Mart and its suppliers. Communicating with suppliers over telecommunications networks rather than using paper-based systems makes the procurement process faster, cheaper, and more accurate. That equates to lower prices for customers and increased rivalry among existing competitors.

THE THREE GENERIC STRATEGIES—CREATING A BUSINESS FOCUS

Once the relative attractiveness of an industry is determined and an organization decides to enter that market, it must formulate a strategy for entering the new market. An organization can follow Porter's three generic strategies when entering a new market: (1) broad cost leadership, (2) broad differentiation, or (3) focused strategy. Broad strategies reach a large market segment, while focused strategies target a niche market. A focused strategy concentrates on either cost leadership or differentiation. Trying to be all things to all people, however, is a recipe for disaster, since it is difficult to project a consistent image to the entire marketplace. Porter suggests that an organization is wise to adopt only one of the three generic strategies.

To illustrate the use of the three generic strategies, consider Figure 1.16. The matrix shown demonstrates the relationships among strategies (cost leadership versus differentiation) and market segmentation (broad versus focused).

- **Hyundai** is following a broad cost leadership strategy. Hyundai offers low-cost vehicles, in each particular model stratification, that appeal to a large audience.

- **Audi** is pursuing a broad differentiation strategy with its Quattro models available at several price points. Audi's differentiation is safety, and it prices its various Quattro models (higher than Hyundai) to reach a large, stratified audience.

- **Kia** has a more focused cost leadership strategy. Kia mainly offers low-cost vehicles in the lower levels of model stratification.

- **Hummer** offers the most focused differentiation strategy of any in the industry (including Mercedes-Benz).

FIGURE 1.16

Porter's Three Generic Strategies in the Auto Industry

VALUE CHAIN ANALYSIS—TARGETING BUSINESS PROCESSES

Once an organization enters a new market using one of Porter's three generic strategies, it must understand, accept, and successfully execute its business strategy. Every aspect of the organization contributes to the success (or failure) of the chosen strategy. The business processes of the organization and the value chain they create play an integral role in strategy execution.

Value Creation

A *business process* is a standardized set of activities that accomplish a specific task, such as processing a customer's order. To evaluate the effectiveness of its business processes, an organization can use Michael Porter's value chain approach. An organization creates value by performing a series of activities that Porter identified as the value chain. The *value chain* approach views an organization as a series of processes, each of which adds value to the product or service for each customer. To create a competitive advantage, the value chain must enable the organization to provide unique value to its customers. In addition to the firm's own value-creating activities, the firm operates in a value system of vertical activities including those of upstream suppliers and downstream channel members. To achieve a competitive advantage, the firm must perform one or more value-creating activities in a way that creates more overall value than do competitors. Added value is created through lower costs or superior benefits to the consumer (differentiation).

Organizations can add value by offering lower prices or by competing in a distinctive way. Examining the organization as a value chain (actually numerous distinct but inseparable value chains) leads to identifying the important activities that add value for customers and then finding IT systems that support those activities. Figure 1.17 depicts a value chain. Primary value activities, shown at the bottom of the graph, acquire raw materials and manufacture, deliver, market, sell, and provide after-sales services. Support value activities, along the top of the graph, such as firm

FIGURE 1.17

The Value Chain

each area of the value chain needs to implement IT to support the value chain & lower cost, better products & ↑ efficiencies

infrastructure, human resource management, technology development, and procurement, support the primary value activities.

The goal is to survey the customers and ask them the extent to which they believe each activity adds value to the product or service. This generates a quantifiable metric, displayed in percentages in Figure 1.17, for how each activity adds value (or reduces value). The competitive advantage decision then is to (1) target high value-adding activities to further enhance their value, (2) target low value-adding activities to increase their value, or (3) perform some combination of the two.

Organizations should attempt to use information technology to add value to both primary and support value activities. One example of a primary value activity facilitated by IT is the development of a marketing campaign management system that could target marketing campaigns more efficiently, thereby reducing marketing costs. The system would also help the organization better pinpoint target market needs, thereby increasing sales. One example of a support value activity facilitated by IT is the development of a human resources system that could more efficiently reward employees based on performance. The system could also identify employees who are at risk of leaving their jobs, allowing the organization to find additional challenges or opportunities that would help retain these employees and thus reduce turnover costs.

Value chain analysis is a highly useful tool in that it provides hard and fast numbers for evaluating the activities that add value to products and services. An organization can find additional value by analyzing and constructing its value chain in terms of Porter's Five Forces (see Figure 1.18). For example, if an organization wants to decrease its buyer's or customer's power, it can construct its value chain activity of "service after the sale" by offering high levels of quality customer service. This will increase the switching costs for its customers, thereby decreasing their power. Analyzing and constructing its support value activities can help an organization decrease the threat of new entrants. Analyzing and constructing its primary value activities can help an organization decrease the threat of substitute products or services.

A company can implement its selected strategy by means of programs, budgets, and procedures. Implementation involves organization of the firm's resources and

FIGURE 1.18

The Value Chain and Porter's Five Forces

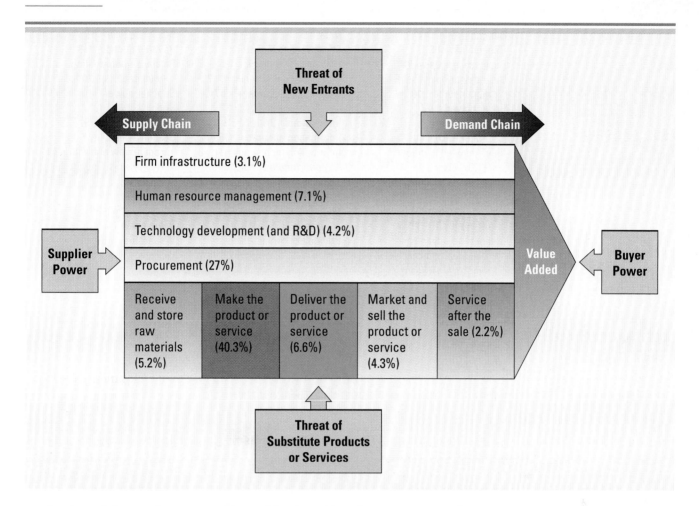

motivation of the employees to achieve objectives. How the company implements its chosen strategy can have a significant impact on its success. In a large company, the personnel implementing the strategy are usually different from those formulating the strategy. For this reason, proper communication of the strategy is critical. Failure can result if the strategy is misunderstood or if lower-level managers resist its implementation because they do not understand the process for selecting the particular strategy.

An organization must continually adapt to its competitive environment, which can cause its business strategy to change. To remain successful, an organization should use Porter's Five Forces, the three generic strategies, and value chain analysis to adopt new business strategies.

OPENING CASE QUESTIONS

Apple—Merging Technology, Business, and Entertainment

6. Did Apple gain a competitive advantage from its decision to invest in an online music business?

7. How can Apple use environmental scanning to gain business intelligence?

8. Using Porter's Five Forces Model, analyze Apple's buyer power and supplier power.

9. Which of the three generic strategies is Apple following?

10. Which of Porter's Five Forces did Apple address through its introduction of the iPod?

Benchmarking   14
Benchmark   14
Business process   21
Business-to-business (B2B)
   marketplace   18
Buyer power   18
Chief information
   officer (CIO)   10
Chief knowledge officer
   (CKO)   11
Chief privacy officer (CPO)   11
Chief security officer (CSO)   11
Chief technology
   officer (CTO)   11
Competitive advantage   17

Data   9
Effectiveness IT metrics   13
Efficiency IT metrics   13
Environmental scanning   17
First-mover advantage   17
Five Forces Model   17
Information   9
Information accuracy   15
Information technology (IT)   8
Key performance indicators
   (KPIs)   13
Loyalty program   18
Management information
   systems (MIS)   8
Private exchange   18

Response time   15
Reverse auction   19
Rivalry among existing
   competitors   20
Supplier power   18
Supply chain   18
Switching cost   19
System availability   15
Threat of new entrants   19
Threat of substitute products
   or services   19
Throughput   15
Transaction speed   15
Value chain   21
Web traffic   15

Say "Charge It" with Your Cell Phone

Wireless operators, credit card companies, and retailers are working on a technology that allows customers to purchase items by using their cell phones. For example, a customer could purchase a can of soda by dialing a telephone number on the dispensing machine and have the charge for the soda show up on the customer's cell phone bill. Working prototypes are currently in use in South Korea, Japan, and Europe.

The ability to charge items to a cell phone has significant business potential because credit cards are not nearly as popular in other countries as they are in the United States. In Japan and China, for example, people are much more likely to have a cell phone than a credit card. Japanese consumers use credit cards for only 5.6 percent of their personal spending compared with 33 percent of U.S. consumer spending.

The payoff for credit card companies and cell phone operators from this technology could be enormous. By associating a credit card with a cell phone, banks and credit card companies hope to persuade consumers to buy products, such as soda, with their cell phones instead of pocket change. Of course, they will reap transaction fees for each transaction. Mobile phone operators see the technology as a way to increase traffic on their networks as well as to position cell phones as an even more useful and, thus, essential device for consumers. Retailers envision easier transactions also leading to more sales.

MasterCard International and Nokia are currently testing a cell phone credit card for the U.S. market. The phones have a special chip programmed with the user's credit card information and a radio frequency transmitting circuit. Consumers can simply tap their phone on a special device at a checkout counter equipped with a receiving device that costs the retailer about $80. Betsy Foran-Owens, vice president for Product Services at MasterCard International, commented that with this technology, "You don't even have to get off your phone to pay. You can just tap this thing down at the register." She also noted, "If you're not going to carry cash around, what are you going to carry? Your mobile phone."

The only players who might not look favorably on the technology are the traditional telephone companies, who must certainly view the technology as just one more threat to their traditional telephone business.[12]

Questions

1. Do you view this technology as a potential threat to traditional telephone companies? If so, what counterstrategies could traditional telephone companies adopt to prepare for this technology?
2. Using Porter's Five Forces describe the barriers to entry and switching costs for this new technology.
3. Which of Porter's three generic strategies is this new technology following?
4. Describe the value chain of using cell phones as a payment method.
5. What types of regulatory issues might occur due to this type of technology?

Innovative Business Managers

BusinessWeek magazine recognized several innovative managers who have demonstrated talent, vision, and the ability to identify excellent opportunities (see Figure 1.19).

Jeffrey Immelt, General Electric (GE)

When Jeffrey Immelt took over as CEO of General Electric, he had big shoes to fill. The former CEO, Jack Welch, had left an unprecedented record as one of the top CEOs of all time. Immelt proved his ability to run the company by creating a customer-driven global culture that spawns innovation and embraces technology. The company was forecasting earnings to increase 17 percent in 2005.

Steven Reinemund, PepsiCo

Steven Reinemund has turned PepsiCo into a $27 billion food and beverage giant. "To be a leader in consumer products, it's critical to have leaders who represent the population we serve," said Reinemund, who created a diverse leadership group that defines the strategic vision for the company. Reinemund also takes a major role in mentoring and teaching his employees and demands that all senior executives do the same. The payoff: consistent double-digit earnings and solid sales at a time when many of the company's staple products—potato chips and soft drinks—are under attack for fears about childhood obesity and health concerns.

FIGURE 1.19

Innovative Business Managers

Innovative Managers	
Jeffrey Immelt, General Electric (GE)	■ Repositioned GE's portfolio with major acquisitions in health care, entertainment, and commercial finance ■ Created a more diverse, global, and customer-driven culture
Steven Reinemund, PepsiCo	■ Developed strong and diverse leadership that helped PepsiCo tap new markets ■ Attained consistent double-digit growth through product innovation and smart marketing
Steven Spielberg, Jeffrey Katzenberg, and David Geffen, DreamWorks SKG	■ Computer-animated Shrek 2 set a record with a gross of $437 million ■ IPO pulled in $812 million
Robert Nardelli, Home Depot	■ Turned a $46 billion company focused on big stores into a $70 billion chain with urban, suburban, and international outlets ■ Drive for efficiency, such as centralizing purchasing and investing in technology, pushed margins above 30 percent
John Henry, Boston Red Sox	■ Broke the most fabled curse in sports, when the Boston Red Sox won the team's first World Championship since 1918 ■ Sold out all 81 home games for the first time in team history
Phil Knight, Nike	■ Transformed a volatile, fad-driven marketing and design icon into a more shareholder-friendly company

Steven Spielberg, Jeffrey Katzenberg, and David Geffen, DreamWorks

DreamWorks, founded 10 years ago by Steven Spielberg, Jeffrey Katzenberg, and David Geffen, suffered through its share of early bombs. Finally, the studio discovered a green ogre named Shrek and quickly became the hottest studio this side of Pixar Animation. DreamWorks Animation turned a $187 million loss in 2003 into a $196 million profit in 2004, with revenues of $1.1 billion. DreamWorks plans to release two animation films per year, each taking almost four years to produce.

Robert Nardelli, Home Depot

Robert Nardelli took several risks when he became CEO of Home Depot. First, he allocated $14 billion into upgrading merchandise, renovating outdated stores, and investing in new technology such as self-checkout lanes and cordless scan guns. Second, Nardelli expanded into Mexico, China, and other regions, tapping the growing homeowner market. Finally, Nardelli bet big on carrying products for aging baby boomers who wanted to spruce up their empty nests. The moves are paying off. The company sits on $3.4 billion in cash. With 2005 revenues headed to $80 billion, Home Depot is the number two U.S. retailer after Wal-Mart.

John Henry, Boston Red Sox

John Henry earned his fortune in the global futures market by developing a proprietary futures-trading system that consistently produced double-digit returns. Henry's new system, Sabermetrics, helped him reverse the most fabled curse in sports history by leading the Boston Red Sox to the team's first World Championship since 1918. Sabermetrics mines baseball statistics to find undervalued players while avoiding long contracts for aging stars whose performance is likely to decline. With the help of Sabermetrics, Henry built one of the most effective teams in baseball.

Philip Knight, Nike

Philip Knight, who got his start by selling Japanese sneakers from the trunk of his car, built the $12 billion sports behemoth Nike. Knight and his team transformed high-performance sports equipment into high-fashion gear and forever changed the rules of sports marketing with huge endorsement contracts and in-your-face advertising. Then, just as suddenly, Nike lost focus. In early 2000, kids stopped craving the latest sneaker, the company's image took a huge hit from its labor practices, sales slumped, and costs soared.

Thus began Knight's second act. He revamped management and brought in key outsiders to oversee finances and apparel lines. Knight devoted more energy to developing new information systems. Today, Nike's earnings are less volatile and less fad-driven. In 2004, Nike's earnings increased $1 billion.[13]

Questions

1. Choose one of the companies listed above and explain how it could use a chief information officer (CIO), chief technology officer (CTO), and chief privacy officer (CPO) to improve business.
2. Why is it important for all of DreamWork's functional business areas to work together? Provide an example of what might happen if the DreamWorks marketing department failed to work with its sales department.
3. Why is information technology important to an organization like the Boston Red Sox?
4. Which of Porter's Five Forces is most important to Home Depot's business?
5. Which of the three generic strategies is PepsiCo following?
6. Explain the value chain and how a company like GE can use it to improve operations.

The World Is Flat—Thomas Friedman

In his book, *The World is Flat,* Thomas Friedman describes the unplanned cascade of technological and social shifts that effectively leveled the economic world, and "accidentally made Beijing, Bangalore, and Bethesda next-door neighbors." Chances are good that Bhavya in Bangalore will read your next X-ray, or as Friedman learned first-hand, "Grandma Betty in her bathrobe" will make your JetBlue plane reservation from her Salt Lake City home.

Friedman believes this is Globalization 3.0. "In Globalization 1.0, which began around 1492, the world went from size large to size medium. In Globalization 2.0, the era that introduced us to multinational companies, it went from size medium to size small. And then around 2000 came Globalization 3.0, in which the world went from being small to tiny. There is a difference between being able to make long-distance phone calls cheaper on the Internet and walking around Riyadh with a PDA where you can have all of Google in your pocket. It is a difference in degree that's so enormous it becomes a difference in kind," Friedman stated. Figure 1.20 displays Friedman's list of "flatteners."

Friedman writes these flatteners converged around the year 2000 and "created a flat world: a global, Web-enabled platform for multiple forms of sharing knowledge and work, irrespective of time, distance, geography, and increasingly, language." At the very moment this platform emerged, three huge economies materialized—those of India, China, and the former Soviet Union—"and 3 billion people who were out of the game, walked onto the playing field." A final

FIGURE 1.20

Thomas Friedman's 10 Forces That Flattened the World

Friedman's 10 Forces That Flattened the World	
1. **Fall of the Berlin Wall**	The events of November 9, 1989, tilted the worldwide balance of power toward democracies and free markets.
2. **Netscape IPO**	The August 9, 1995, offering sparked massive investment in fiber-optic cables.
3. **Work flow software**	The rise of applications from PayPal to VPNs enabled faster, closer coordination among far-flung employees.
4. **Open sourcing**	Self-organizing communities, such as Linux, launched a collaborative revolution.
5. **Outsourcing**	Migrating business functions to India saved money *and* a Third World economy.
6. **Offshoring**	Contract manufacturing elevated China to economic prominence.
7. **Supply chaining**	Robust networks of suppliers, retailers, and customers increased business efficiency.
8. **In-sourcing**	Logistics giants took control of customer supply chains, helping mom-and-pop shops go global.
9. **Informing**	Power searching allowed everyone to use the Internet as a "personal supply chain of knowledge."
10. **Wireless**	Wireless technologies pumped up collaboration, making it mobile and personal.

convergence may determine the fate of the United States in this chapter of globalization. A "political perfect storm," as Friedman describes it—the dot-com bust, the attacks of 9/11, and the Enron scandal—"distract us completely as a country." Just when we need to face the fact of globalization and the need to compete in a new world, "we're looking totally elsewhere."

Friedman believes that the next great breakthrough in bioscience could come from a 5-year-old who downloads the human genome in Egypt. Bill Gates's view is similar: "20 years ago, would you rather have been a B-student in Poughkeepsie or a genius in Shanghai? Twenty years ago you'd rather be a B-student in Poughkeepsie. Today, it is not even close. You'd much prefer to be the genius in Shanghai because you can now export your talents anywhere in the world."[14]

Questions

1. Do you agree or disagree with Friedman's assessment that the world is flat? Be sure to justify your answer.
2. What are the potential impacts of a flat world for a student performing a job search?
3. What can students do to prepare themselves for competing in a flat world?
4. Identify a current flattener not mentioned on Friedman's list.

MAKING BUSINESS DECISIONS

1. Competitive analysis

Cheryl O'Connell is the owner of a small, high-end retailer of women's clothing called Excelus. Excelus's business has been successful for many years, largely because of Cheryl's ability to anticipate the needs and wants of her loyal customer base and provide them with personalized service. Cheryl does not see any value in IT and does not want to invest any capital in something that will not directly affect her bottom line. Develop a proposal describing the potential IT-enabled competitive opportunities or threats Cheryl might be missing by not embracing IT. Be sure to include a Porter's Five Forces analysis and discuss which one of the three generic strategies Cheryl should pursue.

2. Applying the three generic strategies

This chapter discussed several examples of companies that pursue differentiated strategies so that they are not forced into positions where they must compete solely based on price. In a team, choose an industry and find and compare two companies, one that is competing based on price and another that is pursuing a differentiated strategy enabled by the creative use of IT. Some industries you may want to consider are clothing retailers, grocery stores, airlines, and personal computers. Prepare a presentation for the class on the ways that the company is using IT to help it differentiate and compete against the low-cost provider. Before you begin, spend some class time to make sure each team selects a different industry.

3. Using efficiency and effectiveness metrics

You are the CEO of a 500-bed acute care general hospital. Your internal IT department is responsible for running applications that support both administrative functions (e.g., patient accounting) as well as medical applications (e.g., medical records). You need assurance that your IT department is a high-quality operation in comparison to similar hospitals. What metrics should you ask your CIO to provide to give the assurance you seek? Provide the reasoning behind each suggested metric. Also, determine how the interrelationship between efficiency metrics and effectiveness metrics can drive your business's success.

4. Building Business Relationships

Synergistics Inc. is a start-up company that specializes in helping businesses build successful internal relationships. You have recently been promoted to senior manager of the Business and IT Relationship area. Sales for your new department have dwindled over the last two years for a variety of reasons including the burst of the technological stock bubble, recent economic conditions, and a poorly communicated business strategy. Your first task on the job is to prepare a report detailing the following:

- Fundamental reasons for the gap between IT and the business.
- Strategies you can take to convince the business this is an area that is critical to success.
- Strategies the business can follow to ensure synergies exist between the two sides.

5. Determining IT Organizational Structures

You are the chief executive officer for a start-up telecommunications company. The company currently has 50 employees and plans to ramp up to 3,000 by the end of the year. Your first task is to determine how you are going to model your organization. You decide to address the IT department's organizational structure first. You need to consider if you want to have a CIO, CPO, CSO, CTO, and CKO and if so, what the reporting structure will look like and why. You also need to determine the responsibilities for each executive position. Once you have compiled this information, put together a presentation describing your IT department's organizational structure.

Strategic Decision Making

2

SECTION 2.1
Decision-Making Systems

SECTION 2.2
Enterprise Systems

- Decision Making
- Transaction Processing Systems
- Decision Support Systems
- Executive Information Systems

- Enterprise Systems
- Supply Chain Management
- Customer Relationship Management
- Business Process Reengineering
- Enterprise Resource Planning

Revving Up Sales at Harley-Davidson

There is a mystique associated with a Harley-Davidson motorcycle. No other motorcycle in the world has the look, feel, and sound of a Harley-Davidson. Demand for Harley-Davidson motorcycles outweighs supply even though the company produces 300,000 motorcycles per year, which generates over $4 billion in revenues. Some models have a two-year waiting list.

The company recently won a number of awards including:

- Rated second in *ComputerWorld's* Top 100 Best Places to Work in IT.
- Rated 51st in *Fortune's* 100 Best Companies to Work For.
- Rated first in *Fortune's* 5 Most Admired Companies in the motor vehicles industry.
- Rated first in the Top 10 Sincerest Corporations by the *Harris Interactive Report.*
- Rated second in the Top 10 Overall Corporations by the *Harris Interactive Report.*

Harley-Davidson's Focus on Technology

Harley-Davidson's technology budget of $50 million is more than 2 percent of its revenue, which is far above the manufacturing industry average. More than 50 percent of this budget is devoted to developing new technologies such as sharing information, gaining business intelligence, and enhancing decision making. Harley-Davidson's commitment to technology is paying off, and by using strategic information systems, the company has reduced operating costs by $40 million.

Talon, Harley-Davidson's proprietary dealer management system, is one of its most successful information systems. Talon handles inventory, vehicle registration, warranties, and point-of-sale transactions for all Harley-Davidson dealerships. The system checks dealer inventory, generates parts orders, and analyzes global organization information. Talon gives Harley-Davidson managers a 360-degree view into enterprise-wide information that supports strategic goal setting and decision making throughout all levels of the organization.

Building Supplier Relationships

Harley-Davidson understands and values the importance of building strong relationships with its suppliers, and it invests time, energy, and resources into improving company-to-company information systems. To develop these important relationships, the company deployed Manugistics, a supply chain management (SCM) system that allows it to do business with suppliers in a collaborative, Web-based environment. The company uses the SCM software to manage material flows and improve collaboration with key suppliers.

Building Customer Relationships

Each time a customer reaches out to a company, the company has an opportunity to build a trusting relationship with that particular customer. Harley-Davidson realizes that it takes more than just building and selling motorcycles to fulfill the dreams of its customers. For this reason, the company strives to deliver unforgettable experiences along with high-quality products.

Harley-Davidson sells more than $500 million worth of parts and accessories to its loyal followers. Ken Ostermann, Harley-Davidson's manager of electronic commerce and communications, decided the company could increase parts and accessories sales if it could offer the products online. The dilemma facing Ostermann's online strategy was that selling jackets, saddlebags, and T-shirts directly to consumers would bypass Harley-Davidson's 650 dealers, who depend on the high-margin accessories to fuel profits. Ostermann's solution was to build an online store, Harley-Davidson.com, which prompts customers to select a participating Harley-Davidson dealership before placing any online orders. The selected dealership is then responsible for fulfilling the order. The strategy ensures dealers that they will remain the focal point of customers' buying experiences. The company currently receives over 1 million visitors a month to its online store. To guarantee that every customer has a highly satisfying online buying experience, the company asks the dealers to agree to a number of standards including:

- Checking online orders twice daily.
- Shipping online orders within 24 hours.
- Responding to customer inquiries within 24 hours.

Another of Harley-Davidson's customer-centric strategies is its Harley's Owners Group (HOG), which offers an array of events, rides, and benefits to its members. HOG is the largest factory-sponsored motorcycle club in the world with more than 600,000 members and is one of the key drivers helping to build a strong sense of community among Harley-Davidson owners. Harley-Davidson has built a customer following that is extremely loyal, a difficult task to accomplish in any industry.

Harley-Davidson's Corporate Culture

Harley-Davidson employees are the engine behind its outstanding performance and the foundation of the company's overall success. Harley-Davidson believes in a strong sense of corporate ethics and values, and the company's top five core values serve as a framework for the entire corporation:

- Tell the truth.
- Be fair.
- Keep your promises.
- Respect the individual.
- Encourage intellectual curiosity.

The company credits its core values as the primary reason it won the two prestigious awards from the *Harris Interactive Report*, one of the most respected consumer reviews for corporate sincerity, ethics, and standards. Sticking to strong ethics and values is and will continue to be a top priority for the company and its employees.

To enhance its enterprise further, Harley-Davidson plans to keep taking advantage of new technologies and strategies, including a Web-based approach to accessing information and an enterprisewide system to consolidate procurement at its eight U.S. facilities.[1]

INTRODUCTION

Decision-making and problem-solving abilities are now the most sought-after traits in up-and-coming executives, according to a recent survey of 1,000 executives by Caliper Associates, as reported in *The Wall Street Journal*. To put it mildly, decision makers and problem solvers have limitless career potential.[2]

Decision making and problem solving in today's electronic world encompass large-scale, opportunity-oriented, strategically focused solutions. The traditional "cookbook" approach to decision making simply will not work. This chapter focuses on technology to help make decisions, solve problems, and find new innovative opportunities. The chapter also highlights how to bring people together with the best IT processes and tools in complete, flexible solutions that can seize business opportunities and combat business challenges (see Figure 2.1).

section 2.1 DECISION-MAKING SYSTEMS

LEARNING OUTCOMES

2.1. Explain the difference between transactional information and analytical information. Be sure to provide an example of each.

2.2. Define TPS, DSS, and EIS and explain how an organization can use these systems to make decisions and gain competitive advantages.

2.3. Describe the three quantitative models typically used by decision support systems.

2.4. Describe the relationship between digital dashboards and executive information systems.

2.5. Identify the four types of artificial intelligence systems.

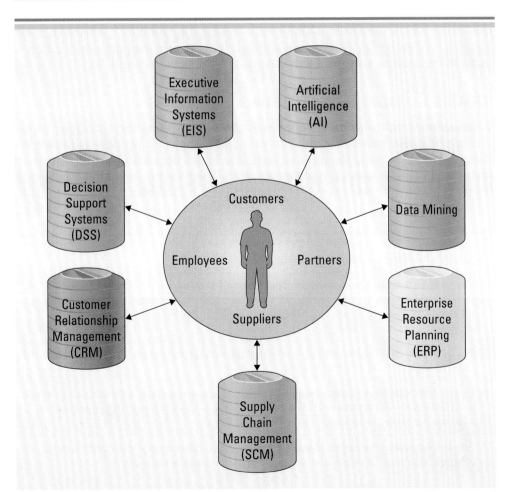

FIGURE 2.1

Examples of Decision Making, Problem Solving, and Opportunity Seizing Information Systems

DECISION MAKING

What is the value of information? The answer to this important question varies. Karsten Solheim would say the value of information is its ability to lower a company's handicap. Solheim, an avid golfer, invented a putter, one with a "ping," that led to a successful golf equipment company and the PING golf clubs. PING Inc., a privately held corporation, was the first to offer customizable golf clubs. The company prides itself on being a just-in-time manufacturer that depends on flexible information systems to make informed production decisions. PING's production systems scan large amounts of information and pull orders that meet certain criteria such as order date (this week), order priority (high), and customer type (Gold). PING then manufactures the appropriate products, allowing it to carry less than 5 percent of inventory in its warehouse. PING depends on its flexible information systems for production decision support and thanks information technology for the explosion of its business over the past decade. [3]

Business is accelerating at a breakneck pace. The more information a business acquires, the more difficult it becomes to make decisions. The amount of information people must understand to make good decisions is growing exponentially. In the past, people could rely on manual processes to make decisions because they had limited amounts of information to process. Today, with massive volumes of available information it is almost impossible for people to make decisions without the aid of information systems. Highly complex decisions—involving far more information than the human brain can comprehend—must be made in increasingly shorter time frames. Figure 2.2 highlights the primary reasons dependence on information systems to make decisions is growing and will continue to grow.

 A *model* is a simplified representation or abstraction of reality. Models can calculate risks, understand uncertainty, change variables, and manipulate time. Decision-making information systems work by building models out of organizational information to lend insight into important business issues and opportunities. Figure 2.3 displays three common types of decision-making information systems used in organizations today—transaction processing systems, decision support systems, and executive information systems. Each system uses different models to assist in decision making, problem solving, and opportunity capturing.

TRANSACTION PROCESSING SYSTEMS

Transactional information encompasses all of the information contained within a single business process or unit of work, and its primary purpose is to support the performing of daily operational tasks. Examples of transactional information include purchasing stocks, making an airline reservation, or withdrawing cash from an ATM. Organizations use transactional information when performing

---

FIGURE 2.2

Primary Reasons for Growth of Decision-Making Information Systems

Reasons for Growth of Decision-Making Information Systems
1. **People need to analyze large amounts of information**—Improvements in technology itself, innovations in communication, and globalization have resulted in a dramatic increase in the alternatives and dimensions people need to consider when making a decision or appraising an opportunity.
2. **People must make decisions quickly**—Time is of the essence and people simply do not have time to sift through all the information manually.
3. **People must apply sophisticated analysis techniques, such as modeling and forecasting, to make good decisions**—Information systems substantially reduce the time required to perform these sophisticated analysis techniques.
4. **People must protect the corporate asset of organizational information**—Information systems offer the security required to ensure organizational information remains safe.

FIGURE 2.3

IT Systems in an Enterprise

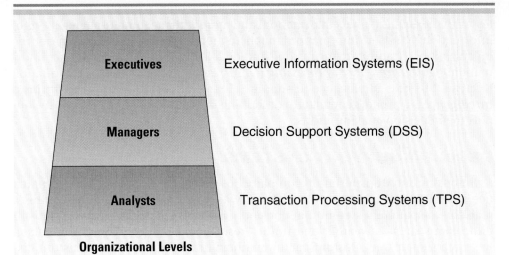

Organizational Levels

(handwritten note: Know each system & what it is for.)

operational tasks and repetitive decisions such as analyzing daily sales reports to determine how much inventory to carry.

Analytical information encompasses all organizational information, and its primary purpose is to support the performing of managerial analysis tasks. Analytical information includes transactional information along with other information such as market and industry information. Examples of analytical information include trends, sales, product statistics, and future growth projections. Managers use analytical information when making important ad hoc decisions such as whether the organization should build a new manufacturing plant or hire additional sales personnel.

(handwritten note: organize info support managerial)

The structure of a typical organization is similar to a pyramid. Organizational activities occur at different levels of the pyramid. People in the organization have unique information needs and thus require various sets of IT tools (see Figure 2.4). At the lower levels of the pyramid, people perform daily tasks such as processing transactions. ***Online transaction processing (OLTP)*** is the capturing of transaction and event information using technology to (1) process the information according to defined business rules, (2) store the information, and (3) update existing information to reflect the new information. During OLTP, the organization must capture every detail of transactions and events. A ***transaction processing system (TPS)*** is the basic business system that serves the operational level (analysts) in an organization. The most common example of a TPS is an operational accounting system such as a payroll system or an order-entry system.

FIGURE 2.4

Enterprise View of Information and Information Technology

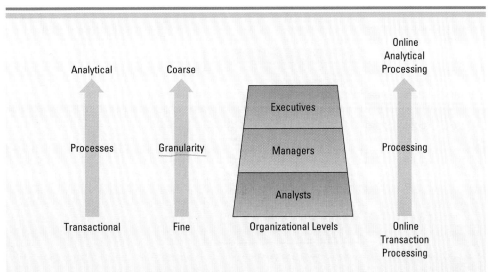

Moving up through the organizational pyramid, people (typically managers) deal less with the details ("finer" information) and more with meaningful aggregations of information ("coarser" information) that help them make broader decisions for the organization. (Granularity means fine and detailed or "coarse" and abstract information.) ***Online analytical processing (OLAP)*** is the manipulation of information to create business intelligence in support of strategic decision making. ***Business intelligence*** is a broad, general term describing information that people use to support their decision-making efforts.

DECISION SUPPORT SYSTEMS

At limousine and transportation company BostonCoach, managers must dispatch fleets of hundreds of vehicles as efficiently as possible. BostonCoach requires a real-time dispatching system that considers inventory, customer needs, and soft dimensions such as weather and traffic. Researchers at IBM's Thomas J. Watson Research Center built BostonCoach a mathematical algorithm for a custom dispatch system that combines information about weather, traffic conditions, driver locations, and customer pickup requests and determines which cars to assign to which customers. The system is so efficient that, after launching it in Atlanta, BostonCoach experienced a 20 percent increase in revenues.[4]

 A ***decision support system (DSS)***, such as BostonCoach's, models information to support managers and business professionals during the decision-making process. Three quantitative models often used by DSS include:

1. ***Sensitivity analysis*** is the study of the impact that changes in one (or more) parts of the model have on other parts of the model. Users change the value of one variable repeatedly and observe the resulting changes in other variables.

2. ***What-if analysis*** checks the impact of a change in an assumption on the proposed solution. For example, "What will happen to the supply chain if a hurricane in South Carolina reduces holding inventory from 30 percent to 10 percent?" Users repeat this analysis until they understand all the effects of various situations. Figure 2.5

FIGURE 2.5

Example of What-If Analysis in Microsoft Excel

FIGURE 2.6

Example of Goal-Seeking
Analysis in Microsoft Excel

displays an example of what-if analysis using Microsoft Excel. The tool is calculating the net effect of a 20 percent increase in sales on the company's bottom line.

3. **Goal-seeking analysis** finds the inputs necessary to achieve a goal such as a desired level of output. Instead of observing how changes in a variable affect other variables as in what-if analysis, goal-seeking analysis sets a target value (a goal) for a variable and then repeatedly changes other variables until the target value is achieved. For example, "How many customers are required to purchase a new product to increase gross profits to $5 million?" Figure 2.6 displays a goal-seeking scenario using Microsoft Excel. The model is seeking the monthly mortgage payment needed to pay off the remaining balance in 130 months.

One national insurance company uses DSSs to analyze the amount of risk the company is undertaking when it insures drivers who have a history of driving under the influence of alcohol. The DSS discovered that only 3 percent of married male homeowners in their forties received more than one DUI. The company decided to lower rates for customers falling into this category, which increased its revenue while mitigating its risk.[5]

Figure 2.7 displays how a TPS is used within a DSS. The TPS supplies transaction-based data to the DSS. The DSS summarizes and aggregates the information from the many different TPS systems, which assists managers in making informed decisions. Burlington Northern and Santa Fe Railroad (BNSF) regularly tests its railroad tracks. Each year hundreds of train derailments result from defective tracks. Using a DSS to schedule train track replacements helped BNSF decrease its rail-caused derailments by 33 percent.[6]

EXECUTIVE INFORMATION SYSTEMS

An **executive information system (EIS)** is a specialized DSS that supports senior-level executives within the organization. An EIS differs from a DSS because an EIS

FIGURE 2.7

Interaction Between TPSs and DSSs

typically contains data from external sources as well as data from internal sources (see Figure 2.8).

Consolidation, drill-down, and slice-and-dice are a few of the capabilities offered in most EISs.

- ■ **Consolidation** involves the aggregation of information and features simple roll-ups to complex groupings of interrelated information. Many organizations track financial information at a regional level and then consolidate the information at a single global level.

- ■ **Drill-down** enables users to view details, and details of details, of information. Viewing monthly, weekly, daily, or even hourly information represents drill-down capability.

- ■ **Slice-and-dice** is the ability to look at information from different perspectives. One slice of information could display all product sales during a given promotion. Another slice could display a single product's sales for all promotions.

Digital Dashboards

A common feature of an EIS is a digital dashboard. **Digital dashboards** integrate information from multiple components and tailor the information to individual preferences. Digital dashboards commonly use indicators to help executives quickly identify the status of key information or critical success factors. Following is a list of features included in a dashboard designed for a senior executive of an oil refinery:

- ■ A hot list of key performance indicators, refreshed every 15 minutes.

- ■ A running line graph of planned versus actual production for the past 24 hours.

- ■ A table showing actual versus forecasted product prices and inventories.

FIGURE 2.8

Interaction Between TPSs and EISs

- A list of outstanding alerts and their resolution status.
- A graph of crude-oil stock market prices.
- A scroll of headline news from Petroleum Company news, an industry news service.

Digital dashboards, whether basic or comprehensive, deliver results quickly. As digital dashboards become easier to use, more executives can perform their own analysis without inundating IT personnel with questions and requests for reports. According to an independent study by Nucleus Research, there is a direct correlation between use of digital dashboards and companies' return on investment (ROI). Figure 2.9 and Figure 2.10 display two different digital dashboards from Visual Mining.

EIS systems, such as digital dashboards, allow executives to move beyond reporting to using information to directly impact business performance. Digital dashboards help executives react to information as it becomes available and make decisions, solve problems, and change strategies daily instead of monthly.

Verizon Communications CIO Shaygan Kheradpir tracks 100-plus major IT systems on a single screen called "The Wall of Shaygan." Every 15 seconds, a new set of charts communicating Verizon's performance flashes onto a giant LCD screen in Kheradpir's office. The 44 screen shots cycle continuously, all day long, every day. The dashboard includes more than 300 measures of business performance that fall into one of three categories:

1. **Market pulse**—examples include daily sales numbers, market share, and subscriber turnover.
2. **Customer service**—examples include problems resolved on the first call, call center wait times, and on-time repair calls.

3. **Cost driver**—examples include number of repair trucks in the field, repair jobs completed per day, and call center productivity.

Kheradpir has memorized the screens and can tell at a glance when the lines on the charts are not trending as expected. The system informs him of events such as

FIGURE 2.9

Visual Mining NetCharts Corporate Financial Dashboard

FIGURE 2.10

Visual Mining NetCharts Marketing Communications Dashboard

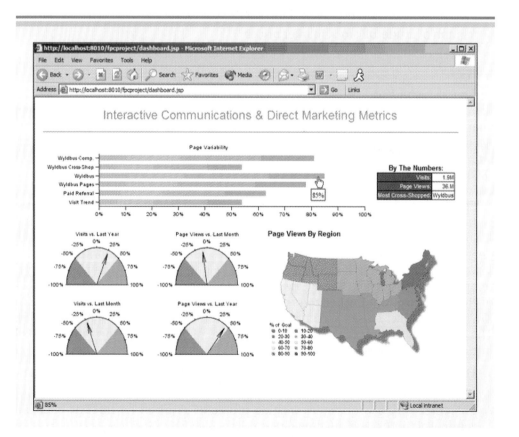

the percentage of customer calls resolved by voice systems, number of repair trucks in the field, and amount of time to resolve an IT system issue. The dashboard works the same way for 400 managers at every level of Verizon.[7]

Artificial Intelligence

Executive information systems are starting to take advantage of artificial intelligence to help executives make strategic decisions. RivalWatch, based in Santa Clara, California, offers a strategic business information service using artificial intelligence that enables organizations to track the product offerings, pricing policies, and promotions of online competitors. Clients can determine the competitors they want to watch and the specific information they wish to gather, ranging from products added, removed, or out of stock to price changes, coupons offered, and special shipping terms. Clients can check each competitor, category, and product either daily, weekly, monthly, or quarterly.

"Competing in the Internet arena is a whole different ballgame than doing business in the traditional brick-and-mortar world because you're competing with the whole world rather than the store down the block or a few miles away," said Phil Lumish, vice president of sales and marketing at RivalWatch.com. "With new products and campaigns being introduced at a breakneck pace, e-businesses need new tools to monitor the competitive environment, and our service is designed specifically to meet that need."[8]

Intelligent systems are various commercial applications of artificial intelligence. ***Artificial intelligence (AI)*** simulates human intelligence such as the ability to reason and learn. AI systems can learn or understand from experience, make sense of ambiguous or contradictory information, and even use reasoning to solve problems and make decisions effectively. AI systems can perform such tasks as boosting productivity in factories by monitoring equipment and signaling when preventive maintenance is required. The ultimate goal of AI is the ability to build a system that can mimic human intelligence. AI systems are beginning to show up everywhere:

- At Manchester Airport in England, the Hefner AI Robot Cleaner alerts passengers to security and nonsmoking rules while it scrubs up to 65,600 square feet of floor per day. Laser scanners and ultrasonic detectors keep it from colliding with passengers.
- Shell Oil's SmartPump keeps drivers in their cars on cold, wet winter days. It can service any automobile built after 1987 that has been fitted with a special gas cap and a windshield-mounted transponder that tells the robot where to insert the pump.
- Matsushita's courier robot navigates hospital hallways, delivering patient files, X-ray films, and medical supplies.
- The FireFighter AI Robot can extinguish flames at chemical plants and nuclear reactors with water, foam, powder, or inert gas. The robot puts distance between the human operator and the fire.[9]

Examples of AI Systems

AI systems dramatically increase the speed and consistency of decision making, solve problems with incomplete information, and resolve complicated issues that cannot be solved by conventional computing. There are many categories of AI systems; four of the most familiar are: (1) expert systems, (2) neural networks, (3) genetic algorithms, and (4) intelligent agents.

Expert Systems   *Expert systems* are computerized advisory programs that imitate the reasoning processes of experts in solving difficult problems. Human expertise is transferred to the expert system, and users can access the expert system for specific advice. Most expert systems reflect expertise from many humans and can therefore perform better analysis than any single expert. Typically, the system includes a knowledge base containing various accumulated experience and a set of rules for applying the knowledge base to each particular situation. The best-known expert systems play chess and assist in medical diagnosis. Expert systems are the most commonly used form of AI in the business arena because they fill the gap when human experts are difficult to find, retain, or too expensive.

Neural Networks   A *neural network*, also called an *artificial neural network*, is a category of AI that attempts to emulate the way the human brain works. The types of decisions for which neural networks are most useful are those that involve pattern or image recognition because a neural network can learn from the information it processes. Neural networks analyze large quantities of information to establish patterns and characteristics in situations where the logic or rules are unknown.

The finance industry is a veteran in neural network technology and has been relying on various forms of it for over two decades. The industry uses neural networks to review loan applications and create patterns or profiles of applications that fall into two categories: approved or denied. One neural network has become the standard for detecting credit card fraud. Since 1992, this technology has slashed fraud by 70 percent for U.S. Bancorp. Now, even small credit unions are required to use the software in order to qualify for debit-card insurance from Credit Union National Association.[10]

Fuzzy logic is a mathematical method of handling imprecise or subjective information. The basic approach is to assign values between 0 and 1 to vague or ambiguous information. The higher the value, the closer it is to 1. The value zero is used to represent nonmembership, and the value one is used to represent membership. For example, fuzzy logic is used in washing machines that determine by themselves how much water to use or how long to wash (they continue washing until the water is clean). In accounting and finance, fuzzy logic allows people to analyze information with subjective financial values (intangibles such as goodwill) that are very important considerations in economic analysis. Fuzzy logic and neural networks are often combined to express complicated and subjective concepts in a form that makes it possible to simplify the problem and apply rules that are executed with a level of certainty.

Genetic Algorithms   A *genetic algorithm* is an artificial intelligence system that mimics the evolutionary, survival-of-the-fittest process to generate increasingly better solutions to a problem. A genetic algorithm is essentially an optimizing system: It finds the combination of inputs that gives the best outputs.

Genetic algorithms are best suited to decision-making environments in which thousands, or perhaps millions, of solutions are possible. Genetic algorithms can find and evaluate solutions with many more possibilities, faster and more thoroughly than a human. Organizations face decision-making environments for all types of problems that require optimization techniques such as the following:

■ Business executives use genetic algorithms to help them decide which combination of projects a firm should invest in, taking complicated tax considerations into account.

- Investment companies use genetic algorithms to help in trading decisions.
- Telecommunication companies use genetic algorithms to determine the optimal configuration of fiber-optic cable in a network that may include as many as 100,000 connection points. The genetic algorithm evaluates millions of cable configurations and selects the one that uses the least amount of cable.[11]

Intelligent Agents   An *intelligent agent* is a special-purpose knowledge-based information system that accomplishes specific tasks on behalf of its users. Intelligent agents use their knowledge base to make decisions and accomplish tasks in a way that fulfills the intentions of a user. Intelligent agents usually have a graphical representation such as "Sherlock Holmes" for an information search agent.

One of the simplest examples of an intelligent agent is a shopping bot. A ***shopping bot*** is software that will search several retailer Web sites and provide a comparison of each retailer's offerings including price and availability. Increasingly, intelligent agents handle the majority of a company's Internet buying and selling and handle such processes as finding products, bargaining over prices, and executing transactions. Intelligent agents also have the capability to handle all supply chain buying and selling.

Another application for intelligent agents is in environmental scanning and competitive intelligence. For instance, an intelligent agent can learn the types of competitor information users want to track, continuously scan the Web for it, and alert users when a significant event occurs.

By 2010, some 4 million AI robots are expected to populate homes and businesses, performing everything from pumping gas to delivering mail. According to a new report by the United Nations and the International Federation of Robotics, more than half the AI robots will be toys and the other half will perform services. Bots will deactivate bombs, clean skyscraper windows, and vacuum homes.[12]

Data Mining

Wal-Mart consolidates point-of-sale details from its 3,000 stores and uses AI to transform the information into business intelligence. Data-mining systems sift instantly through the information to uncover patterns and relationships that would elude an army of human researchers. The results enable Wal-Mart to predict sales of every product at each store with uncanny accuracy, translating into huge savings in inventories and maximum payoff from promotional spending.

Data-mining software typically includes many forms of AI such as neural networks and expert systems. Data-mining tools apply algorithms to information sets to uncover inherent trends and patterns in the information, which analysts use to develop new business strategies. Analysts use the output from data-mining tools to build models that, when exposed to new information sets, perform a variety of data analysis functions. The analysts provide business solutions by putting together the analytical techniques and the business problem at hand, which often reveals important new correlations, patterns, and trends in information. A few of the more common forms of data-mining analysis capabilities include cluster analysis, association detection, and statistical analysis. Data mining is covered in detail in Chapter 6.

OPENING CASE QUESTIONS

Revving Up Sales at Harley-Davidson

1. How does Talon help Harley-Davidson employees improve their decision-making capabilities?
2. Identify a few key metrics a Harley-Davidson marketing executive might want to monitor on a digital dashboard.
3. How can Harley-Davidson benefit from using decision support systems in its business?

LEARNING OUTCOMES

2.6. Describe the four basic components of supply chain management.

2.7. Explain customer relationship management and the benefits it can provide an organization.

2.8. Define enterprise resource planning and explain its importance to an organization.

2.9. Identify how an organization can use business process reengineering to improve its business.

ENTERPRISE SYSTEMS

Trek, a leader in bicycle products and accessories, gained a 30 percent increase in market share by streamlining its information systems. The largest improvement realized from the new systems was the ability to obtain key management information to drive business decisions in line with the company's strategic goals. The system also included a highly successful Web site developed for the 1,400 Trek dealers where they could enter orders, check stock availability, view accounts receivable, and verify credit. Tonja Green, Trek channel manager for North America, stated, "We wanted to give our dealers an easier and quicker way to enter their orders and get information. Every week the number of Web orders increases by 25 to 30 percent due to the new system."[13]

Section 2.2 introduces supply chain management, customer relationship management, business process reengineering, and enterprise resource planning— enterprise systems organizations can use to make decisions and gain competitive advantages.

SUPPLY CHAIN MANAGEMENT

To understand a supply chain, consider a customer purchasing a Trek bike from a dealer. The supply chain begins when a customer places an order for a Trek bike with the dealer. The dealer purchases the bike from the manufacturer, Trek. Trek purchases the raw materials required to make the bike such as metal, packaging, and accessories from different suppliers. The supply chain for Trek encompasses every activity and party involved in the process of fulfilling the order from the customer for the new bike.

Supply chain management (SCM) involves the management of information flows between and among stages in a supply chain to maximize total supply chain effectiveness and profitability. The four basic components of supply chain management include:

1. **Supply chain strategy**—the strategy for managing all the resources required to meet customer demand for all products and services.
2. **Supply chain partners**—the partners chosen to deliver finished products, raw materials, and services including pricing, delivery, and payment processes along with partner relationship monitoring metrics.
3. **Supply chain operation**—the schedule for production activities including testing, packaging, and preparation for delivery. Measurements for this component include productivity and quality.
4. **Supply chain logistics**—the product delivery processes and elements including orders, warehouses, carriers, defective product returns, and invoicing.

Dozens of steps are required to achieve and carry out each of the above components. SCM software can enable an organization to generate efficiencies within these steps by automating and improving the information flows throughout and among the different supply chain components.

FIGURE 2.11

Supply Chain for a Product Purchased from Wal-Mart

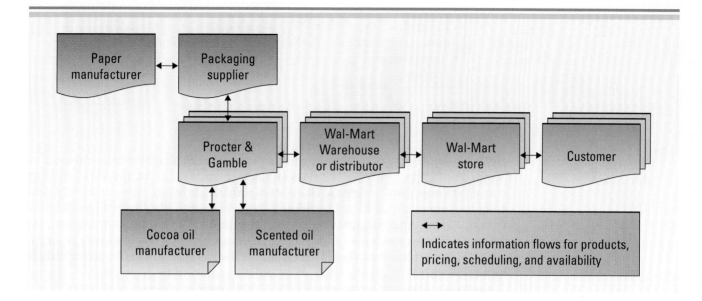

Wal-Mart and Procter & Gamble (P&G) implemented a successful SCM system, which linked Wal-Mart's distribution centers directly to P&G's manufacturing centers. Every time a Wal-Mart customer purchases a P&G product, the system sends a message directly to the factory alerting P&G to restock the product. The system also sends an automatic alert to P&G whenever a product is running low at one of Wal-Mart's distribution centers. This real-time information allows P&G to produce and deliver products to Wal-Mart without having to maintain large inventories in its warehouses. The SCM system saves time, reduces inventory, and decreases order-processing costs for P&G, which P&G passes on to Wal-Mart in the form of discounted prices.[14]

Figure 2.11 diagrams the stages of the SCM system for a customer purchasing a product from Wal-Mart. The diagram demonstrates how the supply chain is dynamic and involves the constant flow of information between the different parties. For example, a customer purchases a product from Wal-Mart and generates order information. Wal-Mart supplies the order information to its warehouse or distributor. The warehouse or distributor transfers the order information to the manufacturer, who provides pricing and availability information to the store and replenishes the product. Partners transfer all payments electronically.

Effective and efficient supply chain management systems can enable an organization to:

- Decrease the power of its buyers.
- Increase its own supplier power.
- Increase switching costs to reduce the threat of substitute products or services.
- Create entry barriers thereby reducing the threat of new entrants.
- Increase efficiencies while seeking a competitive advantage through cost leadership (see Figure 2.12).

CUSTOMER RELATIONSHIP MANAGEMENT

Today, most competitors are simply a mouse-click away. The intense competition in today's marketplace forces organizations to switch from sales-focused strategies to customer-focused strategies.

Charles Schwab recouped the cost of a multimillion-dollar customer relationship management system in less than two years. The system, developed by Siebel,

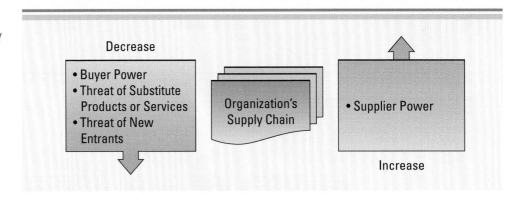

allows the brokerage firm to trace each interaction with a customer or prospective customer and then provide services (retirement planning, for instance) to each customer's needs and interests. The system provides Schwab with a complete view of its customers, which it uses to differentiate serious investors from nonserious investors. For example, automated deposits from paychecks are a sign of a serious investor, while stagnant balances signal a nonserious investor. Once Schwab is able to make this determination, the firm allocates its resources accordingly, saving money by not investing time or resources in subsidizing nonserious investors.[15]

Customer relationship management (CRM) involves managing all aspects of a customer's relationship with an organization to increase customer loyalty and retention and an organization's profitability. CRM allows an organization to gain insights into customers' shopping and buying behaviors. Kaiser Permanente undertook a CRM strategy to improve and prolong the lives of diabetics. After compiling CRM information on 84,000 diabetic patients, Kaiser found that only 20 percent were getting their eyes checked routinely. (Diabetes is the leading cause of blindness.) As a result, Kaiser is now enforcing rigorous eye-screening programs for diabetics, along with creating support groups for obesity and stress (two more factors that make diabetes even worse). This CRM-based "preventive medicine" approach is saving Kaiser money and, more importantly, improving the health of diabetic patients.[16]

Figure 2.13 provides an overview of a typical CRM system. Customers contact an organization through various means including call centers, Web access, e-mail, faxes, and direct sales. A single customer may access an organization multiple times through many different channels. The CRM system tracks every communication between the customer and the organization and provides access to CRM information across different systems from accounting to order fulfillment. Understanding all customer communications allows the organization to communicate effectively with each customer. It gives the organization a detailed understanding of each customer's products and services regardless of the customer's preferred communication channel. A customer service representative can easily view detailed account information and history through a CRM system when providing information to a customer such as expected delivery dates, complementary product information, and customer payment and billing information.

CRM Strategy

Eddie Bauer ships 110 million catalogs a year, maintains two Web sites, and has more than 600 retail stores. The company collects information through customer transactions and analyzes the information to determine the best way to market to each individual customer. Eddie Bauer discovered that customers who shop across all three of its distribution channels—catalogs, Web sites, and stores—spend up to five times more than customers who shop through only one channel.

Michael Boyd, director of CRM at Eddie Bauer, stated, "Our experience tells us that CRM is in no way, shape, or form a software application. Fundamentally, it is a business strategy to try to optimize profitability, revenue, and satisfaction at an individual customer level. Everything in an organization, every single process, every single application, is a tool that can be used to serve the CRM goal."[17]

FIGURE 2.13

Customer Relationship
Management Overview

Customer information flows
are represented by arrows.

It is important to realize that CRM is not just a technology, but also a strategy that an organization must embrace on an enterprise level. Although there are many technical components of CRM, it is actually a process and business goal simply enhanced by technology. Implementing a CRM system can help an organization identify customers and design specific marketing campaigns tailored to each customer, thereby increasing customer spending. A CRM system also allows an organization to treat customers as individuals, gaining important insights into their buying preferences and behaviors and leading to increased sales, greater profitability, and higher rates of customer loyalty.

BUSINESS PROCESS REENGINEERING

A *business process* is a standardized set of activities that accomplish a specific task, such as processing a customer's order. *Business process reengineering (BPR)* is the analysis and redesign of workflow within and between enterprises. The concept of BPR traces its origins to management theories developed as early as the 19th century. The purpose of BPR is to make all business processes best-in-class. Frederick Taylor suggested in the 1880s that managers could discover the best processes for performing work and reengineer the process to optimize productivity. BPR echoes the classical belief that there is one best way to conduct tasks. In Taylor's time, technology did not allow large companies to design processes in a cross-functional or

FIGURE 2.14

Seven Principles of Business
Process Reengineering

Seven Principles of Business Process Reengineering
1. Organize around outcomes, not tasks.
2. Identify all the organization's processes and prioritize them in order of redesign urgency.
3. Integrate information processing work into the real work that produces the information.
4. Treat geographically dispersed resources as though they were centralized.
5. Link parallel activities in the workflow instead of just integrating their results.
6. Put the decision point where the work is performed, and build control into the process.
7. Capture information once and at the source.

cross-departmental manner. Specialization was the state-of-the-art method to improve efficiency given the technology of the time.[18]

BPR reached its heyday in the early 1990s when Michael Hammer and James Champy published their best-selling book, *Reengineering the Corporation*. The authors promoted the idea that radical redesign and reorganization of an enterprise (wiping the slate clean) sometimes was necessary to lower costs and increase quality of service and that information technology was the key enabler for that radical change. Hammer and Champy believed that workflow design in most large corporations was based on invalid assumptions about technology, people, and organizational goals. They suggested seven principles of reengineering to streamline the work process and thereby achieve significant improvement in quality, time management, and cost (see Figure 2.14).[19]

Finding Opportunity Using BPR

Companies frequently strive to improve their business processes by performing tasks faster, cheaper, and better. Figure 2.15 displays different ways to travel the same road. A company could improve the way that it travels the road by moving from foot to horse and then from horse to car. However, true BPR would look at taking a different path. A company could forget about traveling on the same old road and use an airplane to get to its final destination. Companies often follow the same indirect path for doing business, not realizing there might be a different, faster, and more direct way of doing business.

Creating value for the customer is the leading factor for instituting BPR, and information technology often plays an important enabling role. Radical and

FIGURE 2.15

Better, Faster, Cheaper,
or BPR

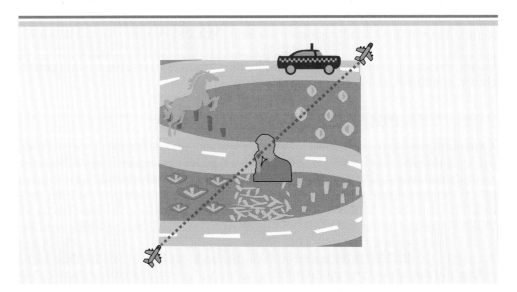

FIGURE 2.16

Auto Insurance Claims Processes

Company A: Claims Resolution Process

Progressive Insurance: Claims Resolution Process

Resolution Cycle Time: 3–8 weeks

Resolution Cycle Time 30 min–3 hours

fundamentally new business processes enabled Progressive Insurance to slash the claims settlement from 31 days to four hours. Typically, car insurance companies follow this standard claims resolution process: The customer gets into an accident, has the car towed, and finds a ride home. The customer then calls the insurance company to begin the claims process, which usually takes over a month (see Figure 2.16).[20]

Progressive Insurance improved service to its customers by offering a mobile claims process. When a customer has a car accident, he or she calls in the claim on the spot. The Progressive claims adjustor comes to the accident and performs a mobile claims process, surveying the scene and taking digital photographs. The adjustor then offers the customer on-site payment, towing services, and a ride home. (see Figure 2.16).[21]

A true BPR effort does more for a company than simply improve it by performing a process better, faster, and cheaper. Progressive Insurance's BPR effort redefined best practices for its entire industry. Figure 2.17 displays the different types of change an organization can achieve, along with the magnitude of change and the potential business benefit.

FIGURE 2.17

Process Change Spectrum

Process Change Spectrum

Redefine Industry

Define Best Practice

Match Best Practice

Improve Efficiency

No Benefit

Benefit

Strategic Reengineering

Business Process Reengineering

Streamline

Automate

Magnitude of Change

Pitfalls of BPR

One hazard of BPR is that the company becomes so wrapped up in fighting its own demons that it fails to keep up with its competitors in offering new products or services. While American Express tackled a comprehensive reengineering of its credit card business, MasterCard and Visa introduced a new product—the corporate procurement card. American Express lagged a full year behind before offering its customers the same service.[22]

ENTERPRISE RESOURCE PLANNING

Many organizations fail to maintain consistency across business operations. If a single department, such as sales, decides to implement a new system without considering the other departments, inconsistencies can occur throughout the company. Not all applications are built to talk to each other, and if the sales function suddenly implements a new system that marketing and production cannot use or is inconsistent in the way it handles information, the company's operations become isolated.

Enterprise resource planning systems provide organizations with consistency. **_Enterprise resource planning (ERP)_** integrates all departments and functions throughout an organization into a single IT system (or integrated set of IT systems) so that employees can make decisions by viewing enterprisewide information on all business operations. An ERP system provides a method for effective planning and controlling of all the resources required to take, make, ship, and account for customer orders in a manufacturing, distribution, or service organization. The key word in enterprise resource planning is _enterprise_.

Los Angeles is a city of 3.5 million people, with 44,000 city employees, and a budget of $4 billion. Yet a few years ago each of the departments conducted its own purchasing. That meant 2,000 people in 600 city buildings and 60 warehouses were ordering material. Some 120,000 purchase orders (POs) and 50,000 checks per year went to more than 7,000 vendors. Inefficiency was rampant.

"There was a lack of financial responsibility in the old system, and people could run up unauthorized expenditures," said Bob Jensen, the city's ERP project manager. Each department maintained its own inventories on different systems. Expense-item mismatches piled up. One department purchased one way, while others preferred a different approach. Mainframe-based systems were isolated. The city chose an ERP system as part of a $22 million project to integrate purchasing and financial reporting across the entire city. The project resulted in cutting the check processing staff in half, processing POs faster than ever, reducing the number of workers in warehousing by 40 positions, decreasing inventories from $50 million to $15 million, and providing a single point of contact for each vendor. In addition, $5 million a year has been saved in contract consolidation.[23]

ERP Software

The many ERP vendors on the market today each offer different ERP solutions, but the core functions are the same, focusing on financial, accounting, sales, marketing, human resources, operations, and logistics. Vendors differentiate themselves by offering distinct functionality such as CRM and SCM systems.

But many customers find that their chosen ERP solution does not meet expectations. Despite many improvements in the software, failed ERP implementations are still far too common. According to Gartner Inc., the average failure rate for an ERP project is 66 percent. With those results, it is no wonder that some organizations view ERP as a necessary, strategic evil. The key word here though is _necessary_.

Many companies strive to make good financial decisions by making smart investments. The best way to ensure a good investment in ERP is to understand why failure occurs and how to avoid it. The first challenge is that ERP comes in many flavors. Its main purpose is to provide support and automation to a business process.

The business world has many different business models with many ERP products available that serve them.

Finding the Right ERP Solution

A good ERP system will be highly reflective of the business process in place at the company. This means the software must perform many different tasks and that makes it complex. Most companies do not carry a high degree of ERP software expertise on their staff, making it easy to choose the wrong package. The key to making an effective purchase is to have solid business processes. Successful ERP projects share three basic attributes:

1. Overall fit
2. Proper business analysis
3. Solid implementation plans[24]

Overall Fit   This refers to the degree of gaps that exist between the system and the business process. A well-fitting ERP has no major process gaps and very few minor ones. Think of a new ERP system as a suit. Typically, a customer buys a suit three ways: off the rack, off the rack and tailored to fit, or custom-made.

The way the solution fits the business process will normally determine the client's satisfaction level. Buying ERP off the rack is the equivalent of buying a canned software package. It fits some well, but not all. The customer can tailor the software so that its processes better line up with company processes. This is a good strategy provided the chosen package supports this. The downside is that it can get very expensive. Choosing a custom system can provide a great fit, but the company must thoroughly understand what it is doing and be able to support the associated financial burden.

Proper Business Analysis   The best way to determine which fit strategy is right is to conduct a thorough business analysis. Successful companies normally spend up to 10 percent of the project budget on a business analysis. A proper analysis must result in a documented list of the business processes at work within the company. This will provide a basic tool that can measure vendor capability.

Solid Implementation Plans   As with the installation of any successful process or machinery, a plan is needed to monitor the quality objectives and timelines. The plan will also employ processes such as workflow analysis and job combination to harvest savings.

A thorough implementation will transfer knowledge to system users. When the project is complete, employees must be capable of using the tools the new system provides. The users must also know what to do in cases when the process fluctuates. Most failed systems result from low-quality implementation. ERP is simply a tool. Tools that people do not know how to use can be as useless as having no tools at all.

OPENING CASE QUESTIONS

Revving Up Sales at Harley-Davidson

4. Evaluate the HOG CRM strategy and recommend an additional benefit Harley-Davidson could provide to its HOG members to increase customer satisfaction.

5. Describe how Harley-Davidson's SCM system, Manugistics, could improve its business operations.

6. Provide a potential illustration of Harley-Davidson's SCM system including all upstream and downstream participants.

KEY TERMS

Analytical information   36
Artificial intelligence   43
Business intelligence   38
Business process   49
Business process reengineer-
   ing (BPR)   49
Consolidation   40
Customer relationship manage-
   ment (CRM)   48
Decision support system
   (DSS)   38
Digital dashboard   40
Drill-down   40

Enterprise resource planning
   (ERP)   52
Executive information system
   (EIS)   39
Expert system   44
Fuzzy logic   44
Genetic algorithm   44
Goal-seeking analysis   39
Intelligent agent   45
Intelligent system   43
Model   36
Neural network (artificial neural
   network)   44

Online analytical processing
   (OLAP)   38
Online transaction processing
   (OLTP)   37
Sensitivity analysis   38
Shopping bot   45
Slice-and-dice   40
Supply chain management
   (SCM)   46
Transaction processing system
   (TPS)   37
Transactional information   36
What-if analysis   38

Consolidating Touchpoints for Saab

Saab Cars USA imports more than 37,000 Saab sedans, convertibles, and wagons annually and distributes the cars to 220 U.S. dealerships. Saab competes in the premium automotive market, and its primary rivals attract customers through aggressive marketing campaigns, reduced prices, and inexpensive financing. Saab decided that the answer to beating its competition was not to spend capital on additional advertising, but to invest in Siebel Automotive, a customer relationship management system.

Until recently, the company communicated with its customers through three primary channels: (1) dealer network, (2) customer assistance center, (3) lead management center. Traditionally, each channel maintained its own customer database, and this splintered approach to managing customer information caused numerous problems for the company. For example, a prospective customer might receive a direct-mail piece from Saab one week, then an e-mail with an unrelated offer from a third-party marketing vendor the next week. The local dealer might not know of either activity, and therefore might deliver an ineffective pitch when the customer visited the showroom that weekend. Al Fontova, direct marketing manager with Saab Cars USA, stated he had over 3 million customer records and 55 files at three different vendors. Analyzing this information in aggregate was complicated, inefficient, and costly.

Saab required a solution that would provide a consolidated customer view from all three touchpoints. In 2003, Saab implemented the Siebel CRM solution, which provides Saab's call center employees with a 360-degree view of each customer, including prior service-related questions and all the marketing communications they have received. Known internally as "TouchPoint," the Siebel application provides Saab's dealers with a powerful Web-based solution for coordinating sales and marketing activities. These tracking capabilities enable Saab to measure the sales results of specific leads, recommend more efficient selling techniques, and target its leads more precisely in the future. Using Siebel Automotive, Saab received the following benefits:

- Direct marketing costs decreased by 5 percent.
- Lead follow-up increased from 38 percent to 50 percent.
- Customer satisfaction increased from 69 percent to 75 percent.
- Saab gained a single view of its customers across multiple channels.[25]

Questions

1. How has implementing a CRM system enabled Saab to gain a competitive advantage?
2. Estimate the potential impact to Saab's business if it had not implemented a CRM system.
3. What additional benefits could Saab receive from implementing a supply chain management system?
4. Model Saab's supply chain.
5. How is Saab's CRM implementation going to influence its SCM practices?

Made-to-Order Businesses

In the past, customers had two choices for purchasing products: (1) purchase a mass-produced product like a pair of jeans or a candy bar or (2) commission a custom-made item that was perfect but cost a small fortune. Mass customization is a new trend in the retail business. Mass customization hits that sweet spot between harnessing the cost efficiencies of mass production and offering so many options that customers feel the product has been designed just for them. Today, many companies are using strategic information systems to implement mass customization business strategies.

Lands' End

Lands' End built a decision support system that could pinpoint a person's body size by taking just a few measurements and running a series of algorithms. The process begins when the customer answers questions on Lands' End's Web site about everything from waist size to inseam. Lands' End saves the data in its customer relationship management system, which is used for reorders, promotions, and marketing campaigns. The order is then sent to San Francisco where supply chain management software determines which one of five contracted manufacturers should receive the order. The chosen manufacturer then cuts and sews the material and ships the finished garment directly to the customer.

Over 40 percent of Lands' End shoppers prefer a customized garment to the standard-sized equivalent, even though each customized garment costs at least $20 more and takes four weeks to deliver. Customized clothes account for a growing percentage of Lands' End's $511 million online business. Reorder rates for Lands' End custom-clothing buyers are 34 percent higher than for buyers of its standard-sized clothing.

Nike

The original business model for Nike iD concentrated on connecting with consumers and creating customer loyalty. Nike iD's Web site allows customers to build their own running shoes. The process begins when customers choose from one of seven different styles and orders from numerous color combinations. Dark-pink bottoms, red mesh, bright yellowing lining, purple laces, blue swoosh, and a eucalyptus green accent. Customers can even place eight-character personalized messages on the side. The cost averages about $30 more than buying the regular shoes in a store.

Once Nike receives the custom order, its supply chain management system sends it to one of 15 plants depending on production availability. Customers receive their shoes within four weeks. The program experienced triple-digit growth in just two years.

Stamps.com

Stamps.com made an agreement with the U.S. Postal Service to sell customized stamps. Customers could put pictures of their choice on an actual U.S. postage stamp. Pictures ranged from dogs to fiancées. The response was phenomenal: Within seven weeks Stamps.com processed and sold more than 2 million PhotoStamps at $1 for a first-class stamp.

Thinking about mass customization as a goal changes the way businesses think about their customers. Using supply chain management and customer relationship management to implement mass customization can have a direct impact on a business's bottom line.[26]

Questions

1. What role does supply chain management and customer relationship management play in a mass customization business strategy?

2. How can Lands' End use its CRM system to improve its business?

3. How can Nike use a CRM system to improve its customer relations?

4. Why is Nike's supply chain management system critical to its Nike iD order fulfillment process?

5. Choose one of the examples above and explain how an ERP system could help facilitate the mass customization effort.

6. Choose one of the examples above and explain how the company is attempting to gain a competitive advantage with mass customization.

7. Identify one other business that could benefit from the use of mass customization. Explain why this business would need customer relationship management and supply chain management systems to implement a mass customization business strategy.

Delta Air Lines Plays Catch-Up

The airline industry has a well-deserved reputation for creative use of IT. American Airlines is known as a leader in using IT to drive its business, and United Airlines is known as a fast follower. Delta Air Lines, while highly regarded as a well-run airline, has been a slow follower in IT. Recently, however, this has changed. In the past few years, Delta has invested more than $1.5 billion in technology, automating everything from gate and boarding tasks to baggage-handling, inventory control, and revenue accounting.

The airline reservation systems introduced by American Airlines and United Airlines, respectively, Sabre and Apollo, were the earliest examples of significant forays into business driven IT in the airline industry. The programs are inventory control systems that sell and manage available seats on upcoming flights. Travel agents received a special computer terminal from the airline when they signed up for the programs. Usually, a travel agent would sign up for one or the other system, but not both. Airline companies that did not have their own reservation systems (Frontier Airlines, for example) could become "co-hosts" on Sabre or Apollo. A fee was charged to co-hosts for the privilege of listing their flights on the reservation systems.

American and United obtained significant competitive advantages as owners of the reservation systems for several reasons. First, the systems were very profitable. Second, they gave American's and United's IT and operations personnel early and valuable experience with online transaction processing (OLTP) systems. Finally, they gave American and United access to information on the sales volumes of their competitors, such as Frontier, because the information was available in the reservation system's database. For example, if American wanted to consider adding a flight from Denver to Chicago, it could simply examine the historical information in the Sabre system to see if there was enough demand for the new route. It could also see what sort of traffic a competitor such as Frontier was generating on the same route in order to pick the best time to schedule a new flight along with the best price. American and United offered the same competitive intelligence information to their co-host airlines, but charged them for it, and often took weeks to provide it to them.

American and United soon realized they had a gold mine of customer-related information available in their reservation systems. They conceived and rolled out hugely successful frequent-flyer programs, which increased the likelihood that frequent business travelers, their most profitable customers, would fly with them instead of with a competitor. Frequent-flyer programs require sophisticated computer systems to properly account for and manage the flight activity of millions of customers, together with their eligibility for awards—another noteworthy example of business driven IT. Ultimately, frequent-flyer programs became an entry barrier for the industry because all airline companies felt they could not compete for the best customers without having their own frequent-flyer systems.

Follow-on IT Innovations

Yield management systems alter the price of available seats on a flight. The systems operate on a minute-by-minute basis as the date of the flight approaches, depending on the number of seats sold compared to the number expected. This is why an airfare quoted over the phone can be $100 higher if the airfare is quoted again an hour later. Most airlines use yield management systems to sell as many seats as possible at the best price. From the airlines' standpoint, it is better to sell a seat at a lower price than to have a plane take off with a vacant seat. At the same time, airlines want to avoid selling a seat for a price lower than what a passenger is willing to pay. Yield management systems are a great example of solving a business problem with IT because they help business managers maximize the revenue generated by each flight.

American Airlines went so far as to sell some of its systems, such as yield management, to other airlines. When asked why, American's then CIO, Max Hopper, said American might as well recover some of its development costs by selling systems to competitors because eventually competitors would develop their own systems. Besides, Hopper believed that by the time lagging competitors such as Delta figured out how to use the systems, American would have reached the next plateau of IT innovation.

Delta's IT Success

Delta always had a reputation in the industry as a slow follower, being reluctant to give up its paper-based systems for modern IT systems. The company did a turnaround when "CIO for Hire" Charlie Feld, a former Frito-Lay CIO, joined Delta in 1997. Feld quickly addressed some of Delta's most pressing IT issues including projects and people in disarray, departments hiring their own IT consultants to develop systems with no attention given to coordination with other Delta systems, as well as the pending Y2K problem. He established a separate wholly owned subsidiary called Delta Technology, and set out to replace Delta's antiquated IT systems with new applications to run the airline.

Feld began by building the gate and boarding application along with the supporting technical hardware, software, and network infrastructure. The gate and boarding application was chosen because it was most visible to Delta's 104 million passengers. The new system provided gate agents' information on which passengers had checked in, seat assignments, and standby status, and saved an average of 8 to 10 minutes of gate activity per flight. As Chief Technical Officer (CTO) Dean Compton recalled, "I remember when we put in the systems in Jacksonville. I saw an overbooked wide-body 767—where there is normally a lot of confusion around the gate—boarded by two agents on time and ahead of schedule. I'd seen a similar situation in Salt Lake City where we hadn't put in the technology yet, and they had to use nine agents to board the plane, and it still left late."

Delta Technology continued to roll out applications, but by early 2001, the airline industry began to feel the effects of the economic downturn. Delta's board of directors questioned the need to spend additional funds on IT when the airline was under great pressure to reduce its costs. After Delta Technology executives gave an overview of projects they were working on, Vickie Escarra, the chief marketing officer, spoke up in support of the IT initiatives like the gate and boarding application by saying, "Man, we couldn't have done what we're doing today if it wasn't for the technology." The overview from IT coupled with the endorsement from a satisfied business unit customer convinced the board that the IT projects should proceed. They insisted, however, that all projects be supported and justified by a solid business case analysis with emphasis placed on either lowered operating costs or increased revenues.

After September 11, 2001, when traffic fell off even more, Delta began to postpone projects showing a longer payoff (like new HR systems) and to speed up projects showing a faster payoff (like increasing the number of self-service check-in kiosks and replacing call center technology).

Currently, Delta processes almost 300 million transactions on its IT infrastructure each month. The company installed SAP software for inventory management, but altered the "flight plan" for Delta's new technology platform. "Today, we're working only on projects that pay off in 12 months and have ongoing impact for at least three years—either building revenue or lowering operating costs," said current CIO Curtis Robb. "I see this work going on for another five years. We'll be done when we run out of ideas."

Delta's Problems

Even after making great strides through IT, Delta could not shake financial woes caused by the 9/11 terrorist attacks and high oil prices. By staving off bankruptcy for a year, the carrier thought it was taking the high road. Unfortunately, it has not worked out that way. Delta CEO Gerald Grinstein stood before 1,700 retirees—men and women whose benefits and pensions will be slashed in Chapter 11 proceedings—and swore he shared their pain. "Bankruptcy is beyond strange," he told them in late 2005 at an Atlanta convention center. "I now know why we fought so hard to avoid it."

It is amazing that his remarks did not spark a riot. After all, Chapter 11 has become a last-resort management tool: a way for airlines to slash labor costs, offload pension obligations, dump unwanted jets, and reemerge as moneymakers. United Airlines, for instance, which exited bankruptcy in early 2006 after more than three years, projected more than $1 billion in profits by 2007. Yet Delta's retirees ended up giving the 73-year-old Grinstein, who outlined the airline's financial straits but made no promises about their benefits, a standing ovation. "That took a lot for [him] to be willing to come over and answer our questions," explains Cathy Cone, a retired flight attendant. While the Delta "family," as its workforce still calls itself, evinces plenty of hostility toward Grinstein's predecessor Leo Mullin, the current management team has avoided most of the blame.

Bankruptcies are notoriously unpredictable, and Delta's is still early in the process. CFO Edward Bastian insists the airline has a leg up on previous legacy carriers in Chapter 11, having entered it "with a transformation plan we've been working on for the past two years." The carrier also has an ace in the hole: GE, the world's biggest aircraft lessor and a major jet-engine maker. Sometimes called the "patron saint of failing airlines," GE knows that liquidations are bad for business. It helped keep US Airways aloft until that carrier finally merged with America West, and it is unlikely to let the third-biggest U.S. carrier disappear. (GE is already the lead provider of Delta's bankruptcy financing.) The real question is whether Delta's management will get its strategy together in time to ensure a post-Chapter 11 existence as a stand-alone carrier or whether Delta will survive only as part of another airline.[27]

Questions

1. What business risks would Delta be taking if it decided not to catch up with industry leaders in using IT to gain a competitive advantage?
2. What competitive advantages can an airline gain by using DSS and EIS?
3. What other industries could potentially benefit from the use of yield management systems?
4. How can American and United use customer information to gain a competitive advantage?
5. What types of metrics would Delta executives want to see in a digital dashboard?
6. How could Delta use supply chain management to improve its operations?

MAKING BUSINESS DECISIONS

1. **Making decisions**

   You are the vice president of human resources for a large consulting company. You are compiling a list of questions that you want each interviewee to answer. The first question on your list is, "How can information technology enhance your ability to make decisions at our organization?" Prepare a one-page report to answer this difficult question.

2. **DSS and EIS**

   Dr. Rosen runs a large dental conglomerate—Teeth Doctors—that staffs more than 700 dentists in six states. Dr. Rosen is interested in purchasing a competitor called Dentix that has 150 dentists in three additional states. Before deciding whether to purchase Dentix, Dr. Rosen must consider several issues:

   - The cost of purchasing Dentix.
   - The location of the Dentix offices.
   - The current number of customers per dentist, per office, and per state.

- The merger between the two companies.
- The professional reputation of Dentix.
- Other competitors.

Explain how Dr. Rosen and Teeth Doctors can benefit from the use of information systems to make an accurate business decision in regard to the potential purchase of Dentix.

3. SCM, CRM, and ERP

Jamie Ash is interested in applying for a job at a large software vendor. One of the criteria for the job is a detailed understanding of strategic initiatives such as SCM, CRM, and ERP. Jamie has no knowledge of any of these initiatives and cannot even explain what the acronyms mean. Jamie has come to you for help. She would like you to compile a summary of the three initiatives, including an analysis of how the three are similar and how they are different. Jamie would also like to perform some self-training via the Web so be sure to provide her with several additional links to key Web sites that offer detailed overviews on SCM, CRM, and ERP.

4. Finding information on decision support systems

You are working on the sales team for a small catering company that maintains 75 employees and generates $1 million in revenues per year. The owner, Pam Hetz, wants to understand how she can use decision support systems to help grow her business. Pam has an initial understanding of DSS systems and is interested in learning more about what types are available, how they can be used in a small business, and the cost associated with different DSS systems. In a group, research the Web site www.dssresources.com and compile a presentation that discusses DSS systems in detail. Be sure to answer all Pam's questions on DSS systems in the presentation.

5. Gaining business intelligence from strategic initiatives

You are a new employee in the customer service department at Premier One, a large pet food distributor. The company, founded by several veterinarians, has been in business for three years and focuses on providing nutritious pet food at a low cost. The company currently has 90 employees and operates in seven states. Sales over the past three years have tripled, and the manual systems currently in place are no longer sufficient to run the business. Your first task is to meet with your new team and create a presentation for the president and CEO describing supply chain management, customer relationship management, and enterprise resource planning systems. The presentation should highlight the main benefits Premier One can receive from these strategic initiatives along with any additional added business value that can be gained from the systems.

3

E-Business

CHAPTER OUTLINE

SECTION 3.1
Business and the Internet

- Disruptive Technology
- Evolution of the Internet
- Accessing Internet Information
- Providing Internet Information

SECTION 3.2
E-Business

- E-Business Basics
- E-Business Models
- Organizational Strategies for E-Business
- Measuring E-Business Success
- E-Business Benefits and Challenges
- New Trends in E-Business: E-Government and M-Commerce

Amazon.com—Not Your Average Bookstore

Jeffrey Bezos, CEO and founder of Amazon.com, is running what some people refer to as the "world's biggest bookstore." The story of Bezos's virtual bookstore teaches many lessons about online business. Out of nowhere, this digital bookstore turned an industry upside down. What happened here was more than just creating a Web site. Bezos conceived and implemented an intelligent, global digital business. Its business is its technology; its technology is its business. Shocking traditional value chains in the bookselling industry, Amazon opened thousands of virtual bookstores in its first few months of operation.

Bezos graduated from Princeton and was the youngest vice president at Banker's Trust in New York. He had to decide if he would stay and receive his 1994 Wall Street bonus or leave and start a business on the Internet. "I tried to imagine being 80 years old, looking back on my life. I knew that I would hardly regret having missed the 1994 Wall Street bonus. But having missed being part of the Internet boom—that would have really hurt," stated Bezos. One evening he compiled a list of 20 products he believed would sell on the Internet. Books, being small-ticket items that are easy and inexpensive to ship, were on the top of the list. It was also apparent that no book-store could conceivably stock more than a fraction of the 5 million books published annually. Bezos, who had never sold a book in his life, developed a strategic plan for selling books on the Internet. Amazon launched three years later. In the fall of 1994, Amazon filled its first book order—personally packaged by Bezos and his wife.

Amazon's E-Business Strategy

Amazon does not operate any physical stores. All of its sales occur through its Web site. It is consistently pushing the technological envelope in its search to provide a satisfying, personalized experience for its customers. What started as a human-edited list of product suggestions morphed into a sophisticated computer-generated recommendation engine. The company captures the comments and recommendations of buyers for site visitors to read—similar to the friendly salesperson in a store offering advice on which books to buy. The Web site tracks customer traffic, the number of visitors who access the site, how long they stay, what pages they click on, and so forth. The company uses the information to evaluate buying and selling patterns and the success of promotions. Amazon has quickly become a model success story for e-businesses around the globe.

Amazon retains customers with Web site features such as personalized recommendations, online customer reviews, and "1-click ordering"—the creation of a true one-stop shopping establishment where customers can find anything they want to buy online. Through the Amazon.com Auctions, zShops (independent third-party sellers), and more recently the Amazon.com Marketplace (where customers can sell used items), the company is able to offer its customers almost everything.

Shaping Amazon's Future

Amazon released a free Web service that enables its business partners (whom Amazon calls "associates") to interact with its Web site. More specifically, this Web service allows its partners to access catalog data, to create and populate an Amazon.com shopping cart, and even to initiate the checkout process. In 16 months, the company has inspired 30,000 associates to invent new ways to extend Amazon's visibility on the Internet. With over 30 million customers, Amazon has become a household brand.[1]

INTRODUCTION

One of the biggest forces changing business is the Internet. Technology companies such as Intel and Cisco were among the first to seize the Internet to overhaul their operations. Intel deployed Web-based automation to liberate its 200 salesclerks from tedious order-entry positions. Instead, salesclerks concentrate on customer relationship management functions such as analyzing sales trends and pampering customers. Cisco handles 75 percent of its sales online, and 45 percent of online orders never touch employees' hands. This type of Internet-based ordering has helped Cisco hike productivity by 20 percent over the past two years.[2]

E-business is the conducting of business on the Internet, not only buying and selling, but also serving customers and collaborating with business partners. Organizations realize that putting up simple Web sites for customers, employees, and partners does not create an e-business. E-business Web sites must create a buzz, much as Amazon has done in the bookselling industry. E-business Web sites must be innovative, add value, and provide useful information. In short, the site must build a sense of community and collaboration, eventually becoming the port of entry for business. Understanding e-business begins with understanding:

- Disruptive technology.
- Evolution of the Internet.
- Accessing Internet information.
- Providing Internet information.

section 3.1 BUSINESS AND THE INTERNET

LEARNING OUTCOMES

3.1. Compare disruptive and sustaining technologies.

3.2. Explain how the Internet caused disruption among businesses.

3.3. Define the relationship between the Internet and the World Wide Web.

3.4. Describe the different methods an organization can use to access information.

3.5. Compare the three different types of service providers.

DISRUPTIVE TECHNOLOGY

Polaroid, founded in 1937, produced the first instant camera in the late 1940s. The Polaroid camera was one of the most exciting technological advances the photography industry had ever seen. By using a Polaroid camera, customers no longer had to depend on others to develop their pictures. The technology was innovative and the product was high-end. The company eventually went public, becoming one of Wall Street's most prominent enterprises, with its stock trading above $60 in 1997. In 2002, the stock was down to 8 cents and the company declared bankruptcy.[3]

How could a company like Polaroid, which had innovative technology and a captive customer base, go bankrupt? Perhaps company executives failed to use Porter's Five Forces to analyze the threat of substitute products or services. If they had, would they have noticed the two threats, one-hour film processing and digital cameras, that eventually stole Polaroid's market share? Would they have understood that their customers, people who want instant access to their pictures without having a third party involved, would be the first to use one-hour film processing and the first to purchase digital cameras? Could the company have found a way to compete with one-hour film processing and the digital camera to save Polaroid?

Most organizations face the same dilemma as Polaroid—the criteria an organization uses to make business decisions for its present business could possibly create issues for its future business. Essentially, what is best for the current business could ruin it in the long term. Some observers of our business environment have an ominous vision of the future—digital Darwinism. **Digital Darwinism** implies that organizations which cannot adapt to the new demands placed on them for surviving in the information age are doomed to extinction.[4]

Disruptive versus Sustaining Technology

A **disruptive technology** is a new way of doing things that initially does not meet the needs of existing customers. Disruptive technologies tend to open new markets and destroy old ones. A **sustaining technology**, on the other hand, produces an improved product customers are eager to buy, such as a faster car or larger hard drive. Sustaining technologies tend to provide us with better, faster, and cheaper products in established markets. Incumbent companies most often lead sustaining technology to market, but virtually never lead in markets opened by disruptive technologies. Figure 3.1 displays companies that are expecting future growth to occur from new investments (disruptive technology) and companies that are expecting future growth to occur from existing investments (sustaining technology).

Disruptive technologies typically cut into the low end of the marketplace and eventually evolve to displace high-end competitors and their reigning technologies. Sony is a perfect example of a company that entered the low end of the marketplace and eventually evolved to displace its high-end competitors. Sony started as a tiny company that built portable, battery-powered transistor radios people could carry around with them. The sound quality of Sony's transistor radios was poor because

FIGURE 3.1

Disruptive versus Sustaining Technology

Fortune 500 Rank	Company	Expected Returns on New Investment	Expected Returns on Existing Investments
53	Dell Computer	78%	22%
47	Johnson & Johnson	66	34
35	Procter & Gamble	62	38
6	General Electric	60	40
77	Lockheed Martin	59	41
1	Wal-Mart	50	50
65	Intel	49	51
49	Pfizer	48	52
9	IBM	46	54
24	Merck	44	56
92	Cisco Systems	42	58
18	Home Depot	37	63
16	Boeing	30	70
11	Verizon	21	79
22	Kroger	13	87
32	Sears Roebuck	8	92
37	AOL Time Warner	8	92
3	General Motors	5	95
81	Phillips Petroleum	3	97

FIGURE 3.2

Companies That Capitalized
on Disruptive Technology

Company	Disruptive Technology
Charles Schwab	Online brokerage
Hewlett-Packard	Microprocessor-based computers; ink-jet printers
IBM	Minicomputers; personal computers
Intel	Low-end microprocessors
Intuit	QuickBooks software; TurboTax software; Quicken software
Microsoft	Internet-based computing; operating system software; SQL and Access database software
Oracle	Database software
Quantum	3.5-inch disks
Sony	Transistor-based consumer electronics

the transistor amplifiers were of lower quality than traditional vacuum tubes, which produce a better sound. But, customers were willing to overlook sound quality for the convenience of portability. With the experience and revenue stream from the portables, Sony improved its technology to produce cheap, low-end transistor amplifiers that were suitable for home use and invested those revenues to improve the technology further, which produced better radios.[5]

The *Innovator's Dilemma*, a book by Clayton M. Christensen, discusses how established companies can take advantage of disruptive technologies without hindering existing relationships with customers, partners, and stakeholders. Xerox, IBM, Sears, and DEC all listened to existing customers, invested aggressively in technology, had their competitive antennae up, and still lost their market-dominant positions. Christensen states that these companies may have placed too much emphasis on satisfying customers' current needs, while neglecting to adopt new disruptive technology that will meet customers' future needs, thus causing the companies to eventually lose market share. Figure 3.2 highlights several companies that launched new businesses by capitalizing on disruptive technologies.[6]

The Internet—Business Disruption

When the Internet was in its early days, no one had any idea how massive it would become. Computer companies did not think it would be a big deal; neither did the phone companies or cable companies. Difficult to access and operate, it seemed likely to remain an arcane tool of the Defense Department and academia. However, the Internet grew, and grew, and grew. It began with a handful of users in the mid-1960s and reached 1 billion by 2005 (see Figure 3.3). Estimates predict there will be more than 3 billion Internet users by 2010. Already, villages in Indonesia and India have Internet access before they have electricity.[7] Figure 3.4 displays several ways the Internet is changing business.

EVOLUTION OF THE INTERNET

During the Cold War in the mid-1960s, the U.S. military decided it needed a bombproof communications system, and thus the concept for the Internet was born. The system would link computers throughout the country, allowing messages to get though even if a large section of the country was destroyed. In the early days, the only linked computers were at government think tanks and a few universities. The Internet was essentially an emergency military communications system operated by the Department of Defense's Advanced Research Project Agency (ARPA) and called ARPANET. Formally defined, the **Internet** is a global public network of computer networks that pass information from one to another using common

FIGURE 3.3

Worldwide Internet Usage Statistics

Internet Usage Statistics–The Big Picture
World Internet Users and Population Statistics

Region	Population (2006)	% of World Population	Internet Users	Internet Penetration (% of Population)	% of World Usage	Usage Growth. 2000–2005
Africa	915,210,928	14.1%	22,737,500	2.5%	2.2%	403.7%
Asia	3,667,774,066	56.4	364,270,713	9.9	35.7	218.7
Europe	807,289,020	12.4	290,121,957	35.9	28.5	176.1
Middle East	190,084,161	2.9	18,203,500	9.6	1.8	454.2
North America	331,473,276	5.1	225,801,428	68.1	22.2	108.9
Latin America/ Caribbean	553,908,632	8.5	79,033,597	14.3	7.8	337.4
Oceania/ Australia	33,956,977	0.5	17,690,762	52.9	1.8	132.2
WORLD TOTAL	**6,499,697,060**	**100%**	**1,017,859,457**	**15.7%**	**100%**	**182%**

FIGURE 3.4

The Internet's Impact on Business

Industry	Business Changes Due to Technology
Travel	Travel site Expedia.com is now the biggest leisure-travel agency, with higher profit margins than even American Express. Thirteen percent of traditional travel agencies closed in 2002 because of their inability to compete with online travel.
Entertainment	The music industry has kept Napster and others from operating, but $35 billion annual online downloads are wrecking the traditional music business. U.S. music unit sales are down 20 percent since 2000. The next big entertainment industry to feel the effects of e-business will be the $67 billion movie business.
Electronics	Using the Internet to link suppliers and customers, Dell dictates industry profits. Its operating margins have risen from 7.3 percent in 2002 to 8 percent in 2003, even as it takes prices to levels where rivals cannot make money.
Financial services	Nearly every public e-finance company left makes money, with online mortgage service Lending Tree growing 70 percent a year. Processing online mortgage applications is now 40 percent cheaper for customers.
Retail	Less than 5 percent of retail sales occur online. eBay is on track this year to become one of the nation's top 15 retailers, and Amazon.com will join the top 40. Wal-Mart's e-business strategy is forcing rivals to make heavy investments in technology.
Automobiles	The cost of producing vehicles is down because of SCM and Web-based purchasing. eBay has become the leading U.S. used-car dealer, and most major car sites are profitable.
Education and training	Cisco saved $133 million last year by moving training sessions to the Internet, and the University of Phoenix online college classes please investors.

computer protocols. ***Protocols*** are standards that specify the format of data as well as the rules to be followed during transmission.

In time, every university in the United States that had defense-related funding installed ARPANET computers. Gradually, the Internet moved from a military pipeline to a communications tool for scientists. As more scholars came online, system administration transferred from ARPA to the National Science Foundation. Years later, businesses began using the Internet, and the administrative responsibilities were once again transferred. Today, no one party operates the Internet; however, several entities oversee the Internet and set standards including:

- Internet Engineering Task Force (IETF): The protocol engineering and development arm of the Internet.
- Internet Architecture Board (IAB): Responsible for defining the overall architecture of the Internet, providing guidance and broad direction to the IETF.
- Internet Engineering Steering Group (IESG): Responsible for technical management of IETF activities and the Internet standards process.

Evolution of the World Wide Web

People often interchange the terms *Internet* and the *World Wide Web*, but these terms are not synonymous. Throughout the 1960s, 1970s, and 1980s, the Internet was primarily used by the Department of Defense to support activities such as e-mail and transferring files. The Internet was restricted to noncommercial activities, and its users included government employees, researchers, university professors, and students. The World Wide Web changed the purpose and use of the Internet.

The ***World Wide Web (WWW)*** is a global hypertext system that uses the Internet as its transport mechanism. ***Hypertext transport protocol (HTTP)*** is the Internet standard that supports the exchange of information on the WWW. By defining universal resource locators (URLs) and how they can be used to retrieve resources anywhere on the Internet, HTTP enables Web authors to embed hyperlinks in Web documents. HTTP defines the process by which a Web client, called a browser, originates a request for information and sends it to a Web server, a program designed to respond to HTTP requests and provide the desired information. In a hypertext system, users navigate by clicking a hyperlink embedded in the current document. The action displays a second document in the same or a separate browser window. The Web has quickly become the ideal medium for publishing information on the Internet and serves as the platform for the electronic economy. Figure 3.5 displays the reasons for the popularity and growth in the WWW.

The WWW remained primarily text-based until 1991 when two events occurred that would forever change the Web and the amount and quality of information available (see Figure 3.6). First, Tim Berners-Lee built the first Web site on August 6, 1991 (http://info.cern.ch/—the site has been archived). The site provided details about the World Wide Web including how to build a browser and set up a Web server. It also housed the world's first Web directory, since Berners-Lee later maintained a list of other Web sites apart from his own.[8]

Reasons for Growth of the World Wide Web
■ The microcomputer revolution made it possible for an average person to own a computer.
■ Advancements in networking hardware, software, and media made it possible for business PCs to be inexpensively connected to larger networks.
■ Browser software such as Microsoft's Internet Explorer and Netscape Navigator gave computer users an easy-to-use graphical interface to find, download, and display Web pages.
■ The speed, convenience, and low cost of e-mail have made it an incredibly popular tool for business and personal communications.
■ Basic Web pages are easy to create and extremely flexible.

FIGURE 3.5

Reasons for World Wide Web Growth

FIGURE 3.6

The Internet's Impact on Information

Internet's Impact on Information	
Easy to compile	Searching for information on products, prices, customers, suppliers, and partners is faster and easier when using the Internet.
Increased richness	*Information richness* refers to the depth and breadth of information transferred between customers and businesses. Businesses and customers can collect and track more detailed information when using the Internet.
Increased reach	*Information reach* refers to the number of people a business can communicate with, on a global basis. Businesses can share information with numerous customers all over the world.
Improved content	A key element of the Internet is its ability to provide dynamic relevant content. Buyers need good content descriptions to make informed purchases, and sellers use content to properly market and differentiate themselves from the competition. Content and product description establish the common understanding between both parties to the transaction. As a result, the reach and richness of that content directly affects the transaction.

FIGURE 3.7

File Formats Offered over the WWW

Second, Marc Andreesen developed a new computer program called the NCSA Mosaic (National Center for Supercomputing Applications at the University of Illinois) and gave it away! The browser made it easier to access the Web sites that had started to appear. Soon Web sites contained more than just text; they also had sound and video files (see Figure 3.7). These pages, written in the hypertext markup language (HTML), have links that allow the user to quickly move from one document to another, even when the documents are stored in different computers. Web browsers read the HTML text and convert it into a Web page.[9]

By eliminating time and distance, the Internet makes it possible to perform business in ways not previously imaginable. The *digital divide* is when those with access to technology have great advantages over those without access to technology. People living in the village of Siroha, India, must bike five miles to find a telephone. For over 700 million rural people living in India, the digital divide was a way of life, until recently. Media Lab Asia sells telephony and e-mail services via a mobile Internet kiosk mounted on a bicycle, which is known as an "info-thelas." The kiosk has an onboard computer equipped with an antenna for Internet service and a specially designed all-day battery. Over 2,000 villages have purchased the kiosk for $1,200, and another 600,000 villages are interested.[10]

ACCESSING INTERNET INFORMATION

Many restaurant and franchise experts believe that Cold Stone Creamery's franchisee intranet is what keeps the company on the fast track. Franchisee owners communicate with other owners through Creamery Talk, the company's intranet-based chat room.

Since it launched, Creamery Talk has turned into a franchisee's black book, with tips on everything from storefront design to equipment repair. When one owner's freezer broke recently, a post to the chat room turned up an easy fix involving a $21 motor fan.

Four common tools for accessing Internet information include:

- Intranet
- Extranet
- Portal
- Kiosk

Intranet

An *intranet* is an internalized portion of the Internet, protected from outside access, that allows an organization to provide access to information and application software to only its employees. An intranet is an invaluable tool for presenting organizational information as it provides a central location where employees can find information. It can host all kinds of company-related information such as benefits, schedules, strategic directions, and employee directories. At many companies, each department has its own Web page on the intranet for departmental information sharing. An intranet is not necessarily open to the external Internet and enables organizations to make internal resources available using familiar Internet clients, such as Web browsers, newsreaders, and e-mail.

Intranet publishing is the ultimate in electronic publishing. Companies realize significant returns on investment (ROI) simply by publishing information, such as employee manuals or telephone directories, on intranets rather than printed media.

Citigroup's Global Corporate and Investment Banking division uses an intranet to provide its entire IT department with access to all IT projects including information on project owners, delivery dates, key resources, budget information, and project metrics. Providing this information via an intranet, or one convenient location, has enabled Citigroup to gain a 15 percent improvement in IT project delivery.[11]

Extranet

An *extranet* is an intranet that is available to strategic allies (such as customers, suppliers, and partners). Many companies are building extranets as they begin to realize the benefit of offering individuals outside the organization access to intranet-based information and application software such as order processing. Having a common area where employees, partners, vendors, and customers access information can be a major competitive advantage for an organization.

Wal-Mart created an extranet for its suppliers, which can view detailed product information at all Wal-Mart locations. Suppliers log on to Wal-Mart's extranet and view metrics on products such as current inventory, orders, forecasts, and marketing campaigns. This helps Wal-Mart's suppliers maintain their supply chains and ensure Wal-Mart never runs out of products.[12]

Portal

Portal is a very generic term for what is in essence a technology that provides access to information. A *portal* is a Web site that offers a broad array of resources and services, such as e-mail, online discussion groups, search engines, and online shopping malls. There are general portals and specialized or niche portals. Leading general portals include Yahoo!, Netscape, Microsoft, and America Online. Examples of niche portals include Garden.com (for gardeners), Fool.com (for investors), and SearchNetworking.com (for network administrators).

Pratt & Whitney, one of the largest aircraft-engine manufacturers in the world, has saved millions of dollars with its field service portal initiative. Pratt & Whitney's sales and service field offices are geographically scattered around the globe and were connected via expensive dedicated lines. The company saved $2.6 million annually by replacing the dedicated lines with high-speed Internet access to its field service portal. Field staff can find information they need in a fraction of the time it took before. The company estimates this change will save another $8 million per year in "process and opportunity" savings.[13]

Kiosk

A *kiosk* is a publicly accessible computer system that has been set up to allow interactive information browsing. In a kiosk, the computer's operating system has been hidden from view, and the program runs in a full-screen mode, which provides a few simple tools for navigation.

Jason Suker walked into the Mazda showroom in Bountiful, Utah, and quickly found what he was looking for in a car dealership—a Web kiosk, one of six stationed around the showroom. Using the Web kiosk, he could track down the latest pricing information from sites like Kelley Blue Book and Edmunds.com. Suker, eyeing a four-year-old limited-edition Miata in mint condition, quickly pulled up the average retail price on Kelley Blue Book. At $16,000, it was $500 more than the dealer's price. Then, on eBay, Suker checked bids for similar models and found they were going for far less. With a sales representative looking over his shoulder to confirm his findings, the skeptical Suker made a lowball offer and expected the worst: endless haggling over price. However, the sales representative, after commending Suker for his research talent, eventually compromised and offered up the Miata for $13,300.

It was an even better deal for Bountiful Mazda. By using a kiosk to help Suker find the bargain price he wanted, the dealership moved a used car (with a higher profit margin than a new model) and opened the door to the unexpected up-sell with a $1,300, 36,000-mile service warranty.[14]

PROVIDING INTERNET INFORMATION

British Airways, the $11.9 billion airline, outsourced the automation of its FAQ (frequently asked questions) Web pages. The airline needed to automatically develop, manage, and post different sets of FAQs for British Airway's loyalty program customers, allowing the company to offer special promotions based on the customer's loyalty program status (gold, silver, bronze). The company outsourced the project to application service provider RightNow Technologies. The new system is helping British Airways create the right marketing programs for the appropriate customer tier.[15]

There are three common forms of service providers including:

1. Internet service provider (ISP).
2. Online service provider (OSP).
3. Application service provider (ASP).

Internet Service Provider

An *Internet service provider (ISP)* is a company that provides individuals and other companies access to the Internet along with additional related services, such as Web site building. An ISP has the equipment and the telecommunication line access required to have a point of presence on the Internet for different geographic areas. Larger ISPs have their own high-speed leased lines so they are less dependent on telecommunication providers and can deliver better service to their customers. Among the largest national and regional ISPs are AT&T WorldNet, IBM Global Network, MCI, Netcom, UUNet, and PSINet.

Navigating the different options for an ISP can be daunting and confusing. There are more than 7,000 ISPs in the United States; some are large with household names, and others are literally one-person operations. Although Internet access is viewed as a commodity service, in reality features and performance can differ tremendously among ISPs. Figure 3.8 highlights common ISP features.

FIGURE 3.8

Common ISP Services

Common ISP Services

- **Web hosting.** Housing, serving, and maintaining files for one or more Web sites is a widespread offering.

- **Hard-disk storage space.** Smaller sites may need only 300 to 500 MB (megabytes) of Web site storage space, whereas other e-business sites may need at least 10 GB (gigabytes) of space or their own dedicated Web server.

- **Availability.** To run an e-business, a site must be accessible to customers 24x7. ISPs maximize the availability of the sites they host using techniques such as load balancing and clustering many servers to reach 100 percent availability.

- **Support.** A big part of turning to an ISP is that there is limited worry about keeping the Web server running. Most ISPs offer 24x7 customer service.

Another member of the ISP family is the ***wireless Internet service provider (WISP)***, an ISP that allows subscribers to connect to a server at designated hotspots or access points using a wireless connection. This type of ISP offers access to the Internet and the Web from anywhere within the zone of coverage provided by an antenna. This is usually a region with a radius of one mile. Figure 3.9 displays a brief overview of how this technology works.

One example of a WISP is T-Mobile International, a company that provides access to wireless laptop users in more than 2,000 locations including airports, airline clubs, Starbucks coffeehouses, and Borders Books. A wireless service called T-Mobile HotSpot allows customers to access the Internet and T-Mobile's corporate intranet via a wireless network from convenient locations away from their home or office. T-Mobile International is the first mobile communications company to extend service on both sides of the Atlantic, offering customers the advantage of using their wireless services when traveling worldwide.[16]

FIGURE 3.9

Wireless Access Diagram

Online Service Provider

An *online service provider (OSP)* offers an extensive array of unique services such as its own version of a Web browser. The term *online service provider* helps to distinguish ISPs that offer Internet access and their own online content, such as America Online (AOL), from ISPs that simply connect users directly with the Internet, such as EarthLink. Connecting to the Internet through an OSP is an alternative to connecting through one of the national ISPs, such as AT&T or MCI, or a regional or local ISP.

Application Service Provider

An *application service provider (ASP)* is a company that offers an organization access over the Internet to systems and related services that would otherwise have

FIGURE 3.10

Top ISPs, OSPs, and ASPs

Company	Description	Specialty
Appshop www.appshop.com	Application service provider	Oracle 11i e-business suite applications
BlueStar Solutions www.bluestarsolutions.com	Application service provider	Managing ERP solutions with a focus on SAP
Concur www.concur.com	Internet service provider	Integrates B2B procurement
Corio www.corio.com	Application service provider	Specializes in Oracle applications
Employease www.employease.com	Online service provider	Human resource applications services
Intacct www.intacct.com	Online service provider	Online general ledger service
LivePerson www.liveperson.com	Online service provider	Real-time chat provider
NetLedger www.netledger.com	Online service provider	Web based accounting platform
Outtask www.outtask.com	Application service provider	Integration of budgeting, customer service, sales management, and human resources applications
RightNow www.rightnow.com	Online service provider, Internet service provider	Suite of customer service applications
Salesforce.com www.salesforce.com	Online service provider	Suite of customer service applications
Salesnet www.salesnet.com	Online service provider	Suite of sales force automation products and services
Surebridge www.surebridge.com	Application service provider	High-tech manufacturing, distribution, health care applications
UpShot www.upshot.com	Online service provider	Sales force automation products and services
USi www.usinternetworking.com	Application service provider	Ariba, Siebel, Microsoft, and Oracle customer base

to be located in personal or organizational computers. Employing the services of an ASP is essentially outsourcing part of a company's business logic. Hiring an ASP to manage a company's software allows the company to hand over the operation, maintenance, and upgrade responsibilities for a system to the ASP.

custom company programs

One of the most important agreements between the customer and the ASP is the service level agreement. ***Service level agreements (SLAs)*** define the specific responsibilities of the service provider and set the customer expectations. SLAs include such items as availability, accessibility, performance, maintenance, backup/recovery, upgrades, equipment ownership, software ownership, security, and confidentiality. For example, an SLA might state that the ASP must have the software available and accessible from 7:00 a.m. to 7:00 p.m. Monday through Friday. It might also state that if the system is down for more than 60 minutes, there will be no charge for that day. Most industry analysts agree that the ASP market is growing rapidly. International Data Corporation (IDC) estimates the worldwide ASP market will grow from around $13 billion in 2005 to $23 billion by 2008.[17] Figure 3.10 displays the top ISPs, OSPs, and ASPs.

OPENING CASE QUESTIONS

Amazon.com—Not Your Average Bookstore

1. How has Amazon used technology to revamp the bookselling industry?

2. Is Amazon using disruptive or sustaining technology to run its business?

3. How is Amazon using intranets and extranets to run its business?

4. How could Amazon use kiosks to improve its business?

---

section 3.2 E-BUSINESS

LEARNING OUTCOMES

3.6. Compare the four types of e-business models.

3.7. Describe how an organization's marketing, sales, accounting, and customer service departments can use e-business to increase revenues or reduce costs.

3.8. Explain why an organization would use metrics to determine a Web site's success.

3.9. Describe e-business along with its benefits and challenges.

3.10. Define m-commerce and explain how an e-government could use it to increase its efficiency and effectiveness.

E-BUSINESS BASICS

In 2003, Tom Anderson and Chris DeWolf started MySpace, a social networking Web site that offers its members information about the independent music scene around the country representing both Internet culture and teenage culture. Musicians sign up for free MySpace home pages where they can post tour dates, songs, and lyrics. Fans sign up for their own Web pages to link to favorite bands and friends. As of February 2006, MySpace was the world's fifth most popular English-language Web site with over 60 million users.[18]

FIGURE 3.11

Overview of Several
Industries Using E-Business

One of the biggest benefits of the Internet is its ability to allow organizations to perform business with anyone, anywhere, anytime. *E-commerce* is the buying and selling of goods and services over the Internet. E-commerce refers only to online transactions. *E-business*, derived from the term e-commerce, is the conducting of business on the Internet, not only buying and selling, but also serving customers and collaborating with business partners. The primary difference between e-commerce and e-business is that e-business also refers to online exchanges of information. For example, a manufacturer allowing its suppliers to monitor production schedules or a financial institution allowing its customers to review their banking, credit card, and mortgage accounts.

In the past few years, e-business seems to have permeated every aspect of daily life. Both individuals and organizations have embraced Internet technologies to enhance productivity, maximize convenience, and improve communications globally. From banking to shopping to entertainment, the Internet has become integral to daily life. Figure 3.11 provides examples of a few of the industries using e-business.

E-BUSINESS MODELS

A *e-business model* is an approach to conducting electronic business on the Internet. E-business transactions take place between two major entities—businesses and consumers. All e-business activities happen within the framework of two types of business relationships: (1) the exchange of products and services between businesses (business-to-business, or B2B) and (2) the exchange of products and services with consumers (business-to-consumer, or B2C) (see Figure 3.12).

The primary difference between B2B and B2C are the customers; B2B customers are other businesses while B2C markets to consumers. Overall, B2B relations are more complex and have higher security needs; plus B2B is the dominant e-business force, representing 80 percent of all online business.[19] Figure 3.13 illustrates all the e-business models: Business-to-business, business-to-consumer, consumer-to-consumer, and consumer-to-business.

Business-to-Business (B2B)

Business-to-business (B2B) applies to businesses buying from and selling to each other over the Internet. Online access to data, including expected shipping date, delivery date, and shipping status, provided either by the seller or a third-party provider is widely supported by B2B models. Electronic marketplaces represent a new wave in B2B e-business models. *Electronic marketplaces*, or *e-marketplaces*, are interactive business communities providing a central market where multiple buyers and sellers can engage in e-business activities (see Figure 3.14). They present

FIGURE 3.12

Basic E-Business Models

E-Business Term	Definition
Business-to-business (B2B)	Applies to businesses buying from and selling to each other over the Internet.
Business-to-consumer (B2C)	Applies to any business that sells its products or services to consumers over the Internet.
Consumer-to-business (C2B)	Applies to any consumer that sells a product or service to a business over the Internet.
Consumer-to-consumer (C2C)	Applies to sites primarily offering goods and services to assist consumers interacting with each other over the Internet.

	Business	Consumer
Business	B2B	B2C
Consumer	C2B	C2C

FIGURE 3.13

E-Business Models

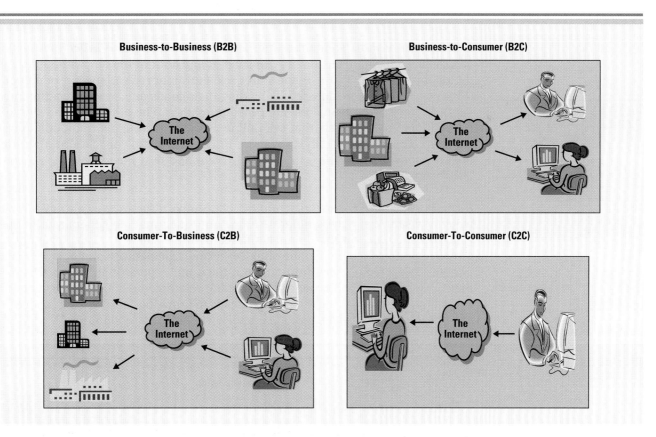

Business-to-Business (B2B)

Business-to-Consumer (B2C)

Consumer-To-Business (C2B)

Consumer-To-Consumer (C2C)

structures for conducting commercial exchange, consolidating supply chains, and creating new sales channels. Their primary goal is to increase market efficiency by tightening and automating the relationship between buyers and sellers. Existing e-marketplaces allow access to various mechanisms in which to buy and sell almost anything, from services to direct materials.

FIGURE 3.14

Business-to-Business
E-Marketplace Overview

Business-to-Consumer (B2C)

Business-to-consumer (B2C) applies to any business that sells its products or services to consumers over the Internet. Carfax has been in the vehicle history report business for 20 years with an original customer base of used-car dealers. "The Internet was just a new way for us to reach the consumer market," Carfax President Dick Raines said. Carfax spent $20 million on print and TV ads to attract customers to its Web site. Customers can purchase a Carfax report for $14.95 or six days of reports for $19.95. Carfax has now launched a partnership program for small auto dealers' Web sites and a cash-back program offering customers 20 percent of revenues received for their referrals. "We continue to look for more and more ways to add value," Raines said.[20] Common B2C e-business models include e-shops and e-malls.

E-Shop   An *e-shop*, sometimes referred to as an *e-store* or *e-tailer*, is a version of a retail store where customers can shop at any hour of the day without leaving their home or office. These online stores sell and support a variety of products and services. The online businesses channeling their goods and services via the Internet only, such as Amazon.com, are called pure plays. The others are an extension of traditional retail outlets that sell online as well as through a traditional physical store. They are generally known as "bricks and clicks" or "click and mortar" organizations, such as the Gap (www.gap.com) and Best Buy (www.bestbuy.com) (see Figure 3.15).

E-Mall   An *e-mall* consists of a number of e-shops; it serves as a gateway through which a visitor can access other e-shops. An e-mall may be generalized or specialized depending on the products offered by the e-shops it hosts. Revenues for e-mall operators include membership fees from participating e-shops, advertising, and possibly a fee on each transaction if the e-mall operator also processes payments. E-shops in e-malls benefit from brand reinforcement and increased traffic as visiting one shop on the e-mall often leads to browsing "neighboring" shops. An example of an e-mall is the Arizona e-mall www.1az1.com/shopping.

FIGURE 3.15

Types of Businesses

	Business Types
Brick-and-mortar business	A business that operates in a physical store without an Internet presence.
Pure-play (virtual) business	A business that operates on the Internet only without a physical store. Examples include Amazon.com and Expedia.com.
Click-and-mortar business	A business that operates in a physical store and on the Internet. Examples include REI and Barnes and Noble.

FIGURE 3.16

Online Auctions

Online Auctions	
Electronic Auction (e-auction)	Sellers and buyers solicit consecutive bids from each other and prices are determined dynamically.
Forward Auction	An auction that sellers use as a selling channel to many buyers and the highest bid wins.
Reverse Auction	An auction that buyers use to purchase a product or service, selecting the seller with the lowest bid.

FIGURE 3.17

C2C Communities

C2C Communities
■ **Communities of interest**—People interact with each other on specific topics, such as golfing and stamp collecting.
■ **Communities of relations**—People come together to share certain life experiences, such as cancer patients, senior citizens, and car enthusiasts.
■ **Communities of fantasy**—**People participate in** imaginary environments, such as fantasy football teams and playing one-on-one with Michael Jordan.

Consumer-to-Business (C2B)

Consumer-to-business (C2B) applies to any consumer that sells a product or service to a business over the Internet. One example of this e-business model is Priceline.com where bidders (or customers) set their prices for items such as airline tickets or hotel rooms, and a seller decides whether to supply them. The demand for C2B e-business will increase over the next few years due to customer's desire for greater convenience and lower prices.

Consumer-to-Consumer (C2C)

Consumer-to-consumer (C2C) applies to sites primarily offering goods and services to assist consumers interacting with each other over the Internet. eBay, the Internet's most successful C2C online auction Web site, links like-minded buyers and sellers for a small commission. Figure 3.16 displays the different types of online auctions.

C2C online communities, or virtual communities, interact via e-mail groups, Web-based discussion forums, or chat rooms. C2C business models are consumer-driven and opportunities are available to satisfy most consumers' needs, ranging from finding a mortgage to job hunting. They are global swap shops based on customer-centered communication. One C2C community, KazaA, allows users to download MP3 music files, enabling users to exchange files. Figure 3.17 highlights the different types of C2C communities that are thriving on the Internet.

ORGANIZATIONAL STRATEGIES FOR E-BUSINESS

To be successful in e-business, an organization must master the art of electronic relationships. Traditional means of customer acquisition such as advertising, promotions, and public relations are just as important with a Web site. Primary business areas taking advantage of e-business include:

■ Marketing/sales
■ Financial services

- Procurement
- Customer service
- Intermediaries

Marketing/Sales

Direct selling was the earliest type of e-business and has proven to be a stepping-stone to more complex commerce operations. Successes such as eBay, Barnes and Noble, Dell Inc., and Travelocity have sparked the growth of this segment, proving customer acceptance of e-business direct selling. Marketing and sales departments are initiating some of the most exciting e-business innovations (see Figure 3.18).

Cincinnati's WCPO-TV was a ratings blip in 2002 and is now the number three ABC affiliate in the nation. WCPO-TV credits its success largely to digital billboards that promote different programming depending on the time of day. The billboards are updated directly from a Web site. The station quickly noticed that when current events for the early-evening news were plugged during the afternoon, ratings spiked.

The digital billboards let several companies share one space and can change messages directly from the company's computer. In the morning, a department store can advertise a sale, and in the afternoon, a restaurant can advertise its specials. Eventually customers will be able to buy billboard sign time in hour or minute increments. Current costs to share a digital billboard are $40,000 a month, compared with $10,000 for one standard billboard.[21]

E-business provides an easy way to penetrate a new geographic territory and extend global reach. Large, small, or specialized businesses can use their online sales sites to sell on a worldwide basis with little extra cost. This ability to tap into expanded domestic or even international markets can be an immediate revenue boost to artists, jewelry makers, wineries, and the like, for initial orders and especially for reorders.

The Hotel Gatti (www.hotel-gatti.com) is a small hotel in northern Italy catering primarily to Italian travelers. By introducing its own Web site with English-language options, it significantly extended its geographic reach. Now, at very little cost, the hotel communicates with and takes reservations from potential customers in the United States and other English-speaking countries. The bottom line is that e-business now allows any company to market and sell products globally, regardless of its size.[22]

Financial Services

Financial services Web sites are enjoying rapid growth as they help consumers, businesses, and financial institutions distribute information with greater convenience and richness than is available in other channels. Consumers in e-business markets pay for products and services using a credit card or one of the methods outlined in Figure 3.19. Online business payments differ from online consumer payments because businesses tend to make large purchases (from thousands to millions of dollars) and typically do not pay with a credit card. Businesses make online payments using electronic data interchange (EDI) (see Figure 3.20). Transactions between businesses are complex and typically require a level of system integration between the businesses.

Many organizations are now turning to providers of electronic trading networks for enhanced Internet-based network and messaging services. Electronic trading networks are service providers that manage network services. They support business-to-business integration information exchanges, improved security, guaranteed

FIGURE 3.18

Generating Revenue on the Internet through Marketing and Sales Departments

Marketing and Sales E-Business Innovations

■ An *online ad* is a box running across a Web page that is often used to contain advertisements. The banner generally contains a link to the advertiser's Web site. Web-based advertising services can track the number of times users click the banner, generating statistics that enable advertisers to judge whether the advertising fees are worth paying. Banner ads are like living, breathing classified ads.

■ A *pop-up ad* is a small Web page containing an advertisement that appears on the Web page outside of the current Web site loaded in the Web browser. A *pop-under ad* is a form of a pop-up ad that users do not see until they close the current Web browser screen.

■ *Associate programs (affiliate programs)* allow businesses to generate commissions or royalties from an Internet site. For example, a business can sign up as an associate of a major commercial site such as Amazon. The business then sends potential buyers to the Amazon site using a code or banner ad. The business receives a commission when the referred customer makes a purchase on Amazon.

■ *Viral marketing* is a technique that induces Web sites or users to pass on a marketing message to other Web sites or users, creating exponential growth in the message's visibility and effect. One example of successful viral marketing is Hotmail, which promotes its service and its own advertisers' messages in every user's e-mail notes. Viral marketing encourages users of a product or service supplied by an e-business to encourage friends to join. Viral marketing is a word-of-mouth type advertising program.

■ *Mass customization* is the ability of an organization to give its customers the opportunity to tailor its products or services to the customers' specifications. For example, customers can order M&M's with customized sayings such as "Marry Me."

■ *Personalization* occurs when a Web site can know enough about a person's likes and dislikes that it can fashion offers that are more likely to appeal to that person. Personalization involves tailoring a presentation of an e-business Web site to individuals or groups of customers based on profile information, demographics, or prior transactions. Amazon uses personalization to create a unique portal for each of its customers.

■ A *blog* (the contraction of the phrase "Web log") is a Web site in which items are posted on a regular basis and displayed in reverse chronological order. Like other media, blogs often focus on a particular subject, such as food, politics, or local news. Some blogs function as online diaries. A typical blog combines text, images, and links to other blogs, Web pages, and other media related to its topic. Since its appearance in 1995, blogging has emerged as a popular means of communication, affecting public opinion and mass media around the world.

■ *Real simple syndications (RSS)* is a family of Web feed formats used for Web syndication of programs and content. RSS is used by (among other things) news Web sites, blogs, and podcasting, which allows consumers and journalists to have news constantly fed to them instead of searching for it. In addition to facilitating syndication, RSS allows a Web site's frequent readers to track updates on the site.

■ *Podcasting* is the distribution of audio or video files, such as radio programs or music videos, over the Internet to play on mobile devices and personal computers. Podcasting's essence is about creating content (audio or video) for an audience that wants to listen when they want, where they want, and how they want. Podcasters' Web sites also may offer direct download of their files, but the subscription feed of automatically delivered new content is what distinguishes a podcast from a simple download or real-time streaming. Usually, the podcast features one type of show with new episodes either sporadically or at planned intervals such as daily, weekly, etc.

■ *Search engine optimization (SEO)* is a set of methods aimed at improving the ranking of a Web site in search engine listings. Search engines display different kinds of listings in the search engine results pages (SERPs), including: pay-per-click advertisements, paid inclusion listings, and organic search results. SEO is primarily concerned with advancing the goals of Web sites by improving the number and position of organic search results for a wide variety of relevant keywords. SEO strategies can increase the number of visitors and the quality of visitors, where quality means visitors who complete the action the site intends (e.g., purchase, sign up, learn something).

SEO, or "white hat SEO," is distinguished from "black hat SEO," or spamdexing, by methods and objectives. *Spamdexing* uses a variety of deceptive techniques in an attempt to manipulate search engine rankings, whereas legitimate SEO focuses on building better sites and using honest methods of promotion. What constitutes an honest, or ethical, method is an issue that has been the subject of numerous debates.

FIGURE 3.19

Types of Online Consumer
Payments

Online Consumer Payments	
Financial cybermediary	A *financial cybermediary* is an Internet-based company that facilitates payments over the Internet. PayPal is the best-known example of a financial cybermediary.
Electronic check	An *electronic check* is a mechanism for sending a payment from a checking or savings account. There are many implementations of electronic checks, with the most prominent being online banking.
Electronic bill presentment and payment (EBPP)	An *electronic bill presentment and payment (EBPP)* is a system that sends bills over the Internet and provides an easy-to-use mechanism (such as clicking on a button) to pay the bill. EBPP systems are available through local banks or online services such as Checkfree and Quicken.
Digital wallet	A *digital wallet* is both software and information—the software provides security for the transaction and the information includes payment and delivery information (for example, the credit card number and expiration date).

service levels, and command center support (see Figure 3.21). As electronic trading networks expand their reach and the number of Internet businesses continues to grow, so will the need for managed trading services. Using these services allows organizations to reduce time to market and the overall development, deployment, and maintenance costs associated with their integration infrastructures.

Traders at Vanguard Petroleum Corporation spent most days on the phone, patrolling the market for pricing and volume information in order to strike the best possible deal. The process was slow and tied up traders on one negotiation at a time, making it inherently difficult to stay on top of quickly changing prices. One winter, for example, the weather got cold and stayed cold, causing propane prices to increase dramatically. The price was moving so fast that Vanguard was missing opportunities to buy, sell, and execute deals since it was able to complete only one deal at a time.

To bridge these shortcomings and speed the process, Vanguard became one of the first users of Chalkboard, a commodity markets electronic trading network that is now part of ChemConnect, a B2B e-marketplace. Vanguard uses Chalkboard to put bids and offers in front of hundreds of traders and complete various trades at multiple delivery points simultaneously. Vanguard now completes deals in real-time and is able to access a broader audience of buyers and sellers.[23]

Procurement

Web-based procurement of maintenance, repair, and operations (MRO) supplies is expected to reach more than $200 billion worldwide by the year 2009. *Maintenance, repair, and operations (MRO) materials* (also called *indirect materials*)

FIGURE 3.20

Types of Online Business
Payments

Online Business Payments
Electronic data interchange (EDI) is a standard format for exchanging business data. One way an organization can use EDI is through a value-added network. A *value-added network (VAN)* is a private network, provided by a third party, for exchanging information through a high-capacity connection. VANs support electronic catalogs (from which orders are placed), EDI-based transactions (the actual orders), security measures such as encryption, and EDI mailboxes.
Financial EDI (financial electronic data interchange) is a standard electronic process for B2B market purchase payments. National Cash Management System is an automated clearinghouse that supports the reconciliation of the payments.

FIGURE 3.21

Diagram of an Electronic Trading Network

are materials necessary for running an organization but do not relate to the company's primary business activities. Typical MRO goods include office supplies (such as pens and paper), equipment, furniture, computers, and replacement parts. In the traditional approach to MRO purchasing, a purchasing manager would receive a paper-based request for materials. The purchasing manager would need to search a variety of paper catalogs to find the right product at the right price. Not surprisingly, the administrative cost for purchasing indirect supplies often exceeded the unit value of the product itself. According to the Organization for Economic Cooperation and Development (OECD), companies with more than $500 million in revenue spend an estimated $75 to $150 to process a single purchase order for MRO supplies.[24]

E-Procurement *E-procurement* is the B2B purchase and sale of supplies and services over the Internet. The goal of many e-procurement applications is to link organizations directly to preapproved suppliers' catalogs and to process the entire purchasing transaction online. Linking to electronic catalogs significantly reduces the need to check the timeliness and accuracy of supplier information.

An *electronic catalog* presents customers with information about goods and services offered for sale, bid, or auction on the Internet. Some electronic catalogs manage large numbers of individual items, and search capabilities help buyers navigate quickly to the items they want to purchase. Other electronic catalogs emphasize merchandise presentation and special offers, much as a retail store is laid out to encourage impulse or add-on buying. As with other aspects of e-business, it is important to match electronic catalog design and functionality to a company's business goals.

Customer Service

E-business enables customers to help themselves by combining the communications capability of a traditional customer response system with the content richness only the Web can provide—all available and operating 24x7. As a result, conducting business via the Web offers customers the convenience they want while freeing key support staff to tackle more complex problems. The Web also allows an organization to provide better customer service through e-mail, special messages, and private password-Web access to special areas for top customers.

FIGURE 3.22

Consumer Protection

Issues for Consumer Protection
■ Unsolicited goods and communication
■ Illegal or harmful goods, services, and content
■ Insufficient information about goods or their suppliers
■ Invasion of privacy
■ Cyberfraud

Vanguard manages $690 billion in assets and charges the lowest fees in the industry: 0.26 percent of assets versus an industry average of 0.81 percent. Vanguard keeps fees down by teaching its investors how to better use its Web site. For good reason: A Web log-on costs Vanguard mere pennies, while each call to a service rep is a $9 expense.[25]

Customer service is the business process where the most human contact occurs between a buyer and a seller. Not surprisingly, e-business strategists are finding that customer service via the Web is one of the most challenging and potentially lucrative areas of e-business. The primary issue facing customer service departments using e-business is consumer protection.

Consumer Protection   An organization that wants to dominate by using superior customer service as a competitive advantage must not only consider how to service its customers, but also how to protect its customers. Organizations must recognize that many consumers are unfamiliar with their digital choices, and some e-businesses are well aware of these vulnerabilities. For example, 17-year-old Miami high school senior Francis Cornworth offered his "Young Man's Virginity" for sale on eBay. The offer attracted a $10 million phony bid. Diana Duyser of Hollywood, Florida, sold half of a grilled cheese sandwich that resembles the Virgin Mary to the owners of an online casino for $28,000 on eBay. Figure 3.22 highlights the different protection areas for consumers.[26]

Regardless of whether the customers are other businesses or end consumers, one of their greatest concerns is the security level of their financial transactions. This includes all aspects of electronic information, but focuses mainly on the information associated with payments (e.g., a credit card number) and the payments themselves, that is, the "electronic money." An organization must consider such issues as encryption, secure socket layers (SSL), and secure electronic transactions (SET), as explained in Figure 3.23.

FIGURE 3.23

E-Business Security

E-Business Security
Encryption scrambles information into an alternative form that requires a key or password to decrypt the information. Encryption is achieved by scrambling letters, replacing letters, replacing letters with numbers, and other ways.
A *secure socket layer (SSL)* (1) creates a secure and private connection between a client and server computer, (2) encrypts the information, and (3) sends the information over the Internet. SSL is identified by a Web site address that includes an "s" at the end—http**s**.
A *secure electronic transaction (SET)* is a transmission security method that ensures transactions are secure and legitimate. Similar to SSL, SET encrypts information before sending it over the Internet. However, SET also enables customer authentication for credit card transaction. SETs are endorsed by major e-commerce players including MasterCard, American Express, Visa, Netscape, and Microsoft.

FIGURE 3.24

Types of Intermediaries

Type of Intermediary	Description	Example
Internet service providers	Make money selling a service, not a product	Earthlink.com, Comcast.com, AOL.com
Portals	Central hubs for online content	Yahoo.com, MSN.com, Google.com
Content providers	Use the Internet to distribute copyrighted content	wsj.com, cnn.com, espn.com
Online brokers	Intermediaries between buyers and sellers of goods and services	charlesschwab.com, fidelity.com, datek.com
Market makers	Aggregate three services for market participants: a place, rules, and infrastructure	amazon.com, ebay.com, priceline.com
Online service providers	Extensive online array of services	xdrive.com, lawinfo.com
Intelligent agents	Software applications that follow instructions and learn independently	Sidestep.com, WebSeeker.com, iSpyNOW.com
Application service providers	Sell access to Internet-based software applications to other companies	ariba.com, commerceone.com, ibm.com
Infomedianies	Provide specialized information on behalf of producers of goods and services and their potential customers	autobytel.com, BizRate.com

Intermediaries

Intermediaries are agents, software, or businesses that bring buyers and sellers together that provide a trading infrastructure to enhance e-business. With the introduction of e-commerce there was much discussion about disintermediation of middle people/organizations; however, recent developments in e-business have seen more reintermediation. *Reintermediation* refers to using the Internet to reassemble buyers, sellers, and other partners in a traditional supply chain in new ways. Examples include New York-based e-Steel Corp. and Philadelphia-based PetroChemNet Inc. bringing together producers, traders, distributors, and buyers of steel and chemicals, respectively, in Web-based marketplaces. Figure 3.24 lists intermediaries and their functions.

MEASURING E-BUSINESS SUCCESS

Traffic on the Internet retail site for Wal-Mart has grown 66 percent in the last year. The site receives over 500,000 visitors daily (6.5 million per week), downloads 2 million Web pages daily, and averages 60,000 users logged on simultaneously. Wal-Mart's primary concern is maintaining optimal performance for online transactions. A disruption to the Web site directly affects the company's bottom line and customer loyalty. The company monitors and tracks the hardware, software, and network running the company's Web site to ensure high quality of service.[27]

The Yankee Group reports that 66 percent of companies determine Web site success solely by measuring the amount of traffic. Unfortunately, large amounts of Web site traffic does not necessarily indicate large sales. Many Web sites with lots of traffic have minimal sales. The best way to measure a Web site's success is to measure

FIGURE 3.25

Web Site Effectiveness
Metrics

Effectiveness Web Site Metrics

- *Cookie*—a small file deposited on a hard drive by a Web site containing information about customers and their Web activities. Cookies allow Web sites to record the comings and goings of customers, usually without their knowledge or consent.

- *Click-through*—a count of the number of people who visit one site and click on an advertisement that takes them to the site of the advertiser. Tracking effectiveness based on click-throughs guarantees exposure to target ads; however, it does not guarantee that the visitor liked the ad, spent any substantial time viewing the ad, or was satisfied with the information contained in the ad.

- A *banner ad*—advertises the products and services of another business, usually another dot-com business. Advertisers can track how often customers click on banner ads resulting in a click-through to their Web site. Often the cost of the banner ad depends on the number of customers who click on the banner ad. Tracking the number of banner ad clicks is one way to understand the effectiveness of the ad on its target audience.

such things as the revenue generated by Web traffic, the number of new customers acquired by Web traffic, any reductions in customer service calls resulting from Web traffic.[28]

Web Site Metrics

Figure 3.25 displays a few metrics an organization can use to measure Web site effectiveness.

To help understand advertising effectiveness, interactivity measures are tracked and monitored. *Interactivity* measures the visitor interactions with the target ad. Such interaction measures include the duration of time the visitor spends viewing the ad, the number of pages viewed, and even the number of repeat visits to the target ad. Interactivity measures are a giant step forward for advertisers, since traditional advertising methods—newspapers, magazines, radio, and television—provide few ways to track effectiveness metrics. Interactivity metrics measure actual consumer activities, something that was impossible to do in the past, and provide advertisers with tremendous amounts of business intelligence.

FIGURE 3.26

Clickstream Data Metrics

Clickstream Data Metrics

- The number of page views (i.e., the number of times a particular page has been presented to a visitor).

- The pattern of Web sites visited, including most frequent exit page and most frequent prior Web site.

- Length of stay on the Web site.

- Dates and times of visits.

- Number of registrations filled out per 100 visitors.

- Number of abandoned registrations.

- Demographics of registered visitors.

- Number of customers with shopping carts.

- Number of abandoned shopping carts.

The ultimate outcome of any advertisement is a purchase. Tying purchase amounts to Web site visits makes it easy to communicate the business value of the Web site. Organizations use metrics to tie revenue amounts and new customer creation numbers directly back to the Web sites or banner ads. Organization can observe through **clickstream data** the exact pattern of a consumer's navigation through a site. Clickstream data can reveal a number of basic data points on how consumers interact with Web sites. Figure 3.26 displays different types of clickstream metrics.

Marc Barach is the co-inventor and chief marketing officer of Ingenio, a start-up company that specializes in connecting people in real-time. When the Internet first emerged, banner ads were the prevalent marketing tools. Next came pay-per-click where the company pays the search engine each time its Web site is accessed from a search. Today 35 percent of online spending occurs through pay-per-clicks. Unfortunately, pay-per-clicks are not suitable for all businesses. Roofers, plumbers, auto repair people, and cosmetic surgeons rarely have Web sites and do not generate business via pay-per-clicks. Barach believes that the next line of Internet advertising will be pay-per-call, and Ingenio has invested five years and $50 million in building the platform to run the business. Here is how pay-per-call works:

- The user types a keyword into a search engine.
- The search engine passes the keyword to Ingenio.
- Ingenio determines the category and sends back the appropriate merchant's unique, traceable 800 telephone number.
- The 800 number routes through Ingenio's switches, and Ingenio charges the merchant when a customer calls.

A Jupiter Research study discovered that businesses were willing to pay between $2 and $35 for each call lead.[29]

Figure 3.27 provides definitions of common metrics based on clickstream data. To interpret such data properly, managers try to benchmark against other companies. For instance, consumers seem to visit their preferred Web sites regularly, even checking back to the Web site multiple times during a given session. Consumers tend to become loyal to a small number of Web sites, and they tend to revisit those Web sites a number of times during a particular session.

E-BUSINESS BENEFITS AND CHALLENGES

According to an NUA Internet Survey, the Internet links more than 1 billion people worldwide. Experts predict that global Internet usage will nearly triple between 2006 and 2010, making e-business a more significant factor in the global economy. As e-business improves, organizations will experience benefits and challenges alike. Figure 3.28 details e-business benefits for an organization.

The Internet is forcing organizations to refocus their information systems from the inside out. A growing number of companies are already using the Internet to streamline their business processes, procure materials, sell products, automate customer service, and create new revenue streams. Although the benefits of e-business systems are enticing, developing, deploying, and managing these systems is not always easy. Unfortunately, e-business is not something a business can just go out and buy. Figure 3.29 details the challenges facing e-business.

A key element of e-marketplaces is their ability to provide not only transaction capabilities but also dynamic, relevant content to trading partners. The original e-business Web sites provided shopping cart capabilities built around product catalogs. As a result of the complex e-marketplace that must support existing business processes and systems, content is becoming even more critical for e-marketplaces. Buyers need good content description to make informed purchases, and sellers use content to properly market and differentiate themselves from the competition. Content and product description establish the common understanding between both parties to the transaction. As a result, the accessibility, usability,

FIGURE 3.27

Definitions of Web Site Metrics

Visitor	Visitor Metrics
Unidentified visitor	A visitor is an individual who visits a Web site. An "unidentified visitor" means that no information about that visitor is available.
Unique visitor	A unique visitor is one who can be recognized and counted only once within a given period of time. An accurate count of unique visitors is not possible without some form of identification, registration, or authentication.
Session visitor	A session ID is available (e.g., cookie) or inferred by incoming address plus browser type, which allows a visitor's responses to be tracked within a given visit to a Web site.
Tracked visitor	An ID (e.g., cookie) is available which allows a user to be tracked across multiple visits to a Web site. No information, other than a unique identifier, is available for a tracked visitor.
Identified visitor	An ID is available (e.g., cookie or voluntary registration), which allows a user to be tracked across multiple visits to a Web site. Other information (name, demographics, possibly supplied voluntarily by the visitor) can be linked to this ID.
Exposure	**Exposure Metrics**
Page exposures (page-views)	The number of times a particular Web page has been viewed by visitors in a given time period, without regard to duplication.
Site exposures	The number of visitor sessions at a Web site in a given time period, without regard to visitor duplication.
Visit	**Visit Metrics**
Stickiness (visit duration time)	The length of time a visitor spends on a Web site. Can be reported as an average in a given time period, without regard to visitor duplication.
Raw visit depth (total Web pages exposure per session)	The total number of pages a visitor is exposed to during a single visit to a Web site. Can be reported as an average or distribution in a given time period, without regard to visitor duplication.
Visit depth (total unique Web pages exposure per session)	The total number of unique pages a visitor is exposed to during a single visit to a Web site. Can be reported as an average or distribution in a given time period, without regard to visitor duplication.
Hit	**Hit Metrics**
Hits	When visitors reach a Web site, their computer sends a request to the site's computer server to begin displaying pages. Each element of a requested page (including graphics, text, interactive items) is recorded by the Web site's server log file as a "hit."
Qualified hits	Exclude less important information recorded in a log file (such as error messages, etc.).

accuracy, and richness of that content directly affect the transaction. Figure 3.30 displays the different benefits and challenges of various e-marketplace revenue models.

NEW TRENDS IN E-BUSINESS: E-GOVERNMENT AND M-COMMERCE

Recent business models that have arisen to enable organizations to take advantage of the Internet and create value are within e-government. *E-government* involves the use of strategies and technologies to transform government(s) by improving the

FIGURE 3.28

E-Business Benefits

E-Business Benefits	
Highly Accessible	Businesses can operate 24 hours a day, 7 days a week, 365 days a year.
Increased Customer Loyalty	Additional channels to contact, respond to, and access customers helps contribute to customer loyalty.
Improved Information Content	In the past, customers had to order catalogs or travel to a physical facility before they could compare price and product attributes. Electronic catalogs and Web pages present customers with updated information in real-time about goods, services, and prices.
Increased Convenience	E-business automates and improves many of the activities that make up a buying experience.
Increased Global Reach	Business, both small and large, can reach new markets.
Decreased Cost	The cost of conducting business on the Internet is substantially smaller than traditional forms of business communication.

FIGURE 3.29

E-Business Challenges

E-Business Challenges	
Protecting Consumers	Consumers must be protected against unsolicited goods and communication, illegal or harmful goods, insufficient information about goods or their suppliers, invasion of privacy, and cyberfraud.
Leveraging Existing Systems	Most companies already use information technology to conduct business in non-Internet environments, such as marketing, order management, billing, inventory, distribution, and customer service. The Internet represents an alternative and complementary way to do business, but it is imperative that e-business systems integrate existing systems in a manner that avoids duplicating functionality and maintains usability, performance, and reliability.
Increasing Liability	E-business exposes suppliers to unknown liabilities because Internet commerce law is vaguely defined and differs from country to country. The Internet and its use in e-business have raised many ethical, social, and political issues, such as identity theft and information manipulation.
Providing Security	The Internet provides universal access, but companies must protect their assets against accidental or malicious misuse. System security, however, must not create prohibitive complexity or reduce flexibility. Customer information also needs to be protected from internal and external misuse. Privacy systems should safeguard the personal information critical to building sites that satisfy customer and business needs. A serious deficiency arises from the use of the Internet as a marketing means. Sixty percent of Internet users do not trust the Internet as a payment channel. Making purchases via the Internet is considered unsafe by many. This issue affects both the business and the consumer. However, with encryption and the development of secure Web sites, security is becoming less of a constraint for e-businesses.
Adhering to Taxation Rules	The Internet is not yet subject to the same level of taxation as traditional businesses. While taxation should not discourage consumers from using electronic purchasing channels, it should not favor Internet purchases over store purchases either. Instead, a tax policy should provide a level playing field for traditional retail businesses, mail-order companies, and Internet-based merchants. The Internet marketplace is rapidly expanding, yet it remains mostly free from traditional forms of taxation. In one recent study, uncollected state and local sales taxes from e-business are projected to exceed $60 billion in 2008.

FIGURE 3.30

The Benefits and Challenges
of Various E-Marketplace
Revenue Models

Revenue Models	Advantages	Limitation
Transaction fees	■ Can be directly tied to savings (both process and price savings) ■ Important revenue source when high level of liquidity (transaction volume) is reached	■ If process savings are not completely visible, use of the system is discouraged (incentive to move transactions offline) ■ Transaction fees likely to decrease with time
License fees	■ Creates incentives to do many transactions ■ Customization and back-end integration leads to lock-in of participants	■ Up front fee is a barrier to entry for participants ■ Price differentiation is complicated
Subscription fees	■ Creates incentives to do transactions ■ Price can be differentiated ■ Possibility to build additional revenue from new user groups	■ Fixed fee is a barrier to entry for participants
Fees for value-added services	■ Service offering can be differentiated ■ Price can be differentiated ■ Possibility to build additional revenue from established and new user groups (third parties)	■ Cumbersome process for customers to continually evaluate new services
Advertising fees	■ Well-targeted advertisements can be perceived as value-added content by trading participants ■ Easy to implement	■ Limited revenue potential ■ Overdone or poorly targeted advertisements can be disturbing elements on the Web site

delivery of services and enhancing the quality of interaction between the citizen-consumer within all branches of government (refer to Figure 3.31).

One example of an e-government portal, FirstGov.gov, the official U.S. gateway to all government information, is the catalyst for a growing electronic government. Its powerful search engine and ever-growing collection of topical and

FIGURE 3.31

Extended E-Business Models

	Business	Consumer	Government
Business	B2B conisint.com	B2C dell.com	B2G lockheedmartin.com
Consumer	C2B priceline.com	C2C ebay.com	C2G eGov.com
Government	G2B export.gov	G2C medicare.gov	G2G disasterhelp.gov

FIGURE 3.32

E-Government Models

E-Government Models	
Consumer-to-government (C2G)	C2G will mainly constitute the areas where a consumer (or citizen) interacts with the government. It will include areas like elections, when citizens vote for government officials; census, where the consumer provides demographic information to the government; taxation, where the consumer is paying taxes to the government.
Government-to-business (G2B)	This model includes all government interaction with business enterprises whether it is procurement of goods and services from suppliers or information regarding legal and business issues that is transmitted electronically.
Government-to-consumer (G2C)	Governments around the world are now dealing with consumers (or citizens) electronically, providing them with updated information. Governments are also processing applications for visas, renewal of passports and driver's licenses, advertising of tender notices, and other services online.
Government-to-government (G2G)	Governments around the world are now dealing with other governments electronically. Still at an inception stage, this e-business model will enhance international trade and information retrieval, for example, on criminal records of new migrants. At the state level, information exchange and processing of transactions online will enable enhanced efficiencies.

customer-focused links connect users to millions of Web pages, from the federal government, to local and tribal governments, to foreign nations around the world. Figure 3.32 highlights specific e-government models.

M-Commerce

In a few years, Internet-enabled mobile devices will outnumber PCs. *Mobile commerce*, or *m-commerce*, is the ability to purchase goods and services through a wireless Internet-enabled device. The emerging technology behind m-commerce is a mobile device equipped with a Web-ready micro-browser. To take advantage of the m-commerce market potential, handset manufacturers Nokia, Ericsson, Motorola, and Qualcomm are working with telecommunication carriers AT&T Wireless and Sprint to develop smartphones. Using new forms of technology, smartphones offer fax, e-mail, and phone capabilities all in one, paving the way for m-commerce to be accepted by an increasingly mobile workforce. Figure 3.33 gives a visual overview of m-commerce.

Amazon.com has collaborated with Nokia to pioneer a new territory. With the launch of its Amazon.com Anywhere service, it has become one of the first major online retailers to recognize and do something about the potential of Internet-enabled wireless devices. As content delivery over wireless devices becomes faster, more secure, and scalable, m-commerce will surpass landline e-business (traditional telephony) as the method of choice for digital commerce transactions. According to the research firm Strategy Analytics, the global m-commerce market was expected to be worth more than $200 billion by 2005, with some 350 million customers generating almost 14 billion transactions annually. Additionally, information activities like e-mail, news, and stock quotes will progress to personalized transactions, "one-click" travel reservations, online auctions, and videoconferencing.[30]

Organizations face changes more extensive and far reaching in their implications than anything since the modern industrial revolution occurred in the early

FIGURE 3.33

M-Commerce Technology Overview

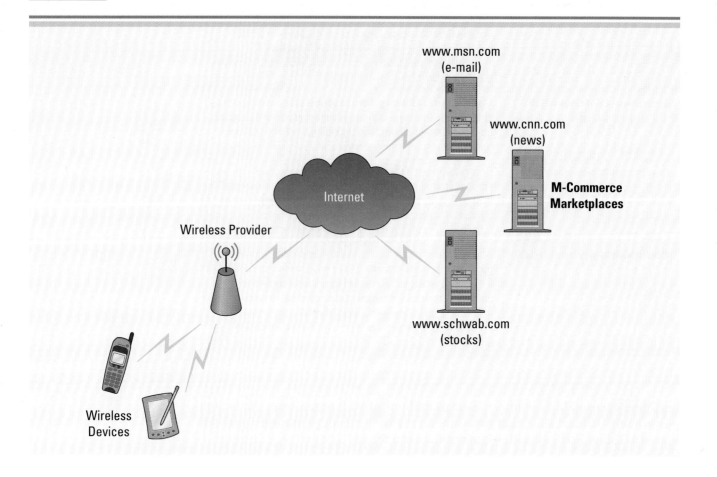

1900s. Technology is a primary force driving these changes. Organizations that want to survive must recognize the immense power of technology, carry out required organizational changes in the face of it, and learn to operate in an entirely different way.

OPENING CASE QUESTIONS

Amazon.com—Not Your Average Bookstore

5. What is Amazon's e-business model?

6. How can Amazon use m-commerce to influence its business?

7. Which metrics could Amazon use to assess the efficiency and effectiveness of Amazon's Web site?

8. What are some of the business challenges facing Amazon?

Application service provider
(ASP) 74
Associate program (affiliate
program) 81
Banner ad 86
Blog 81
Brick-and-mortar business 78
Business-to-business
(B2B) 76
Business-to-consumer
(B2C) 78
Clickstream data 87
Click-and-mortar business 78
Click-through 86
Consumer-to-business
(C2B) 79
Consumer-to-consumer
(C2C) 79
Cookie 86
Digital Darwinism 66
Digital divide 70
Digital wallet 82
Disruptive technology 66
E-business 65, 76
E-business model 76
E-commerce 76
E-government 88
E-mall 78
E-shop (e-store, e-tailer) 78
Electronic bill presentment and
payment (EBPP) 82

Electronic catalog 83
Electronic check 82
Electronic data interchange
(EDI) 82
Electronic marketplace
(e-marketplace) 76
Encryption 84
E-procurement 83
Extranet 71
Financial cybermediary 82
Financial EDI (financial
electronic data inter-
change) 82
Hypertext transport protocol
(HTTP) 69
Information reach 70
Information richness 70
Interactivity 86
Intermediary 85
Internet 67
Internet service provider
(ISP) 72
Intranet 71
Kiosk 72
Maintenance, repair, and op-
eration (MRO) material (indi-
rect material) 82
Mass customization 81
Mobile commerce, or
m-commerce 91
Online ad (banner ad) 86

Online service provider
(OSP) 74
Personalization 81
Podcasting 81
Pop-under ad 81
Pop-up ad 81
Portal 71
Protocol 69
Pure-play (virtual) business
78
Real simple syndication
(RSS) 81
Reintermediation 85
Search engine optimization
(SEO) 81
Secure electronic transaction
(SET) 84
Secure socket layer (SSL) 84
Service level agreement
(SLA) 75
Spamdexing 81
Sustaining technology 66
Value-added network
(VAN) 82
Viral marketing 81
Wireless Internet service pro-
vider (WISP) 73
World Wide Web (WWW) 69

eBay—The Ultimate E-Business

Pierre Omidyar was just 28 when he sat down over a long holiday weekend to write the original computer code for what eventually became an Internet super brand—the auction site eBay. Omidyar viewed auctions as a fair mechanism for Internet commerce where sellers could set their minimum prices, and buyers could then determine an item's market value by bidding up to what they were willingly to pay. A novel feedback system could allow buyers and sellers to rate each other, helping minimize fraud by enabling the community to police itself. "I really wanted to give the individual the power to be a producer as well. It was letting the users take responsibility for building the community," Omidyar would later explain.

The site launched on Labor Day, September 4, 1995, under the title of Auction Web, soon to be renamed after the site's domain name—ebay.com (a shortening of Echo Bay, Omidyar's consulting firm). The service was free at first, but started charging to cover Internet service provider costs.

A National Marketplace

Omidyar's auction Web site, eBay.com, took off. It provided something novel that its users craved: an efficient national marketplace with a strong community built on fairness and trust. A photography student looking for a used camera could choose from models across the nation and trust the timely delivery of the product. The owner of a vintage clothing store could sell to collectors nationwide. The community would expose a deceptive or fraudulent user and ban them from the marketplace.

Entrepreneurs in record numbers began setting up shop on eBay. According to a new survey conducted for eBay by ACNielsen International Research, in 2005 more than 724,000 people supported themselves by selling items on eBay, up from 75,000 in 2002. In addition to these professional eBay sellers, another 1.5 million individuals supplement their income by selling on eBay. In the first six months of 2005, Americans sold merchandise worth about $10.6 billion through eBay.

The stock market value of Omidyar's innovative company grew to $2 billion in just three years, and his site's staying power as an economic engine was evident. Jeffrey Skoll, a Stanford MBA, joined the company in 1996 after the site was already profitable. In March 1998, Meg Whitman took over as president and CEO. In September 1998, eBay launched a successful public offering, making both Omidyar and Skoll billionaires—three years after Omidyar created eBay. As of 2005, Omidyar's 214 million eBay shares were worth about $8 billion.

Collaborating with eBay

This e-business is collaborating with marketplace, payment, and communication companies that add value for its customers.

Marketplace—The U.S. Postal Service

People who sell items on eBay all have one thing in common: They need to ship their goods to their customers. To support this growing economic force, eBay and the U.S. Postal Service created an innovative economic and educational opportunity.

The Postal Service's bread and butter—first-class mail—is beset by rising costs and falling use. E-mail and faxes have reduced the amount of mail sent each day, but the Postal Service still bears the cost of delivering to every business and home, six days a week. Package shipping, however, remains a profitable and booming business, as evidenced by the number and earnings of private shippers in the market.

The Postal Service offers free boxes and heavy-duty envelopes for shippers using overnight or priority mail. To make it easier for those in the vanguard of the new, digital economy, the Postal Service will pick up shipments from the sender, and its Web site sells mailing labels with postage included that can be printed out from a home computer. Over 20 million shipping labels with postage were printed via the eBay/Postal Service link in 2005. Customers can also link to the United Parcel Service site, but eBay does not have a formal relationship with Federal Express.

Payment—PayPal

Founded in 1998, PayPal, an eBay company, enables any individual or business with an e-mail address to securely, easily, and quickly send and receive payments online. PayPal's service builds on the existing financial infrastructure of bank accounts and credit cards and utilizes the world's most advanced proprietary fraud prevention systems to create a safe, global, real-time payment solution.

PayPal has quickly become a global leader in online payment solutions with 96 million account members worldwide. Buyers and sellers on eBay, online retailers, online businesses, as well as traditional off-line businesses are transacting with PayPal, available in 55 countries.

Communication—Skype

Skype, a global Internet communications company, allows people everywhere to make free, unlimited, superior quality voice calls via its innovative peer-to-peer software. Since its launch in August 2003, Skype has been downloaded more than 163 million times in 225 countries and territories. Fifty-four million people are registered to use Skype's free services, with over 3 million simultaneous users on the network at any one time. Skype adds about 150,000 users a day.

In September 2005, eBay acquired Skype for approximately $2.6 billion, anticipating that Skype will streamline and improve communications between buyers and sellers as it is integrated into the eBay marketplace. Buyers will gain an easy way to talk to sellers quickly and get the information they need, and sellers can more easily build relationships. The auction company hopes the acquisition will strengthen its global marketplace and payments platform, while opening several new lines of business and creating significant new opportunities for the company.

Unforeseen Dangers of Collaboration

"Communications is at the heart of e-commerce and community," said Meg Whitman. "By combining the two leading e-commerce franchises, eBay and PayPal, with the leader in Internet voice communications, Skype, we will create an extraordinarily powerful environment for business on the Net."

In October 2005, one month after eBay's acquisition of Skype, a press release discussed two critical flaws in Skype's software, one of which could allow malicious hackers to take control of compromised systems and another that could allow attackers to crash the client software. While fixes for the issues were being addressed, businesses asked their users to refrain from using voice services based on proprietary protocols like Skype while on corporate networks because of network security issues. Perhaps Skype might not be the collaborative tool of choice for eBay. [31]

Questions

1. eBay is one of the only major Internet "pure plays" to consistently make a profit from its inception. What is eBay's e-business model and why has it been so successful?
2. Other major Web sites, like Amazon.com and Yahoo!, have entered the e-marketplace with far less success than eBay. How has eBay been able to maintain its dominant position?
3. eBay has long been an e-marketplace for used goods and collectibles. Today, it is increasingly a place where major businesses come to auction their wares. Why would a brand name vendor set up shop on eBay?

4. What are the three different types of online auctions and which one is eBay using?

5. What are the different forms of online payment methods for consumers and business? How might eBay's customer benefit from the different payment methods?

6. Which metrics would you use if you were hired to assess the efficiency and effectiveness of eBay's Web site?

Direct Groceries

In July 2002, FreshDirect made its first delivery. The online grocer, which began in the New York metropolitan area and has expanded slowly and cautiously from Brooklyn to Queens to Manhattan, now has annual revenues of $150 million. The company decided to revamp its IT infrastructure focusing on availability and scalability to support a new, more aggressive growth strategy. In early 2004, FreshDirect hired a new CTO, Myles Trachtenberg, to help expand its business. Trachtenberg led the company through its IT infrastructure revamp, which was completed in September 2004.

The company's growth strategy focuses on using a variety of industry best practices to succeed. "I like to think of us as three types of businesses pulled together," Trachtenberg said. FreshDirect has sought to emulate the e-business success of Amazon.com, the just-in-time manufacturing capabilities of Dell, and the distribution expertise of FedEx. FreshDirect generates 99 percent of its business through its Web site. To differentiate itself in the marketplace, the company concentrates on preparation and delivery of fresh foods, which account for about 70 percent of sales.

When Trachtenberg joined FreshDirect, its infrastructure was running on Sun Microsystems servers. Trachtenberg wanted to update the systems to create an infrastructure that would ensure high availability to meet customer demands for a quick and easy online experience, as well as the scalability to allow FreshDirect to continue to expand. Trachtenberg also wanted to move to an Intel-based system.

Keeping FreshDirect's Web site operational is essential to the company's growth strategy. The Web site must handle over 4,000 orders a day, each with an average of 30 items, which requires the movement of about 1 million items in the warehouse each week.

Before the new IT infrastructure revamp, the average response time on the FreshDirect Web site was about eight seconds. Today, the response time is two seconds during peak demand and one second during low demand periods.

Within its data center, FreshDirect runs SAP enterprise resource planning software and database. Inside the warehouse, each order is disassembled for sorting and packing. The order is first run through a logistics application by RouteSmart Technologies Inc., which uses algorithms to divide orders based on destination, delivery schedules, and capacity.

How rapidly FreshDirect will expand its territory has yet to be determined. "There's still a lot of growth left in the areas we serve now," Trachtenberg said. "In New York City alone, I'd say there's definitely potential for between $300 million and $500 million a year."[32]

Questions

1. What type of technology is FreshDirect using—disruptive or sustaining?
2. How could FreshDirect use a kiosk to improve its business?
3. How could FreshDirect use m-commerce to improve its business?
4. What are the three different types of service providers and which one would FreshDirect use to run its business?
5. What types of information would be contained in FreshDirect's intranet?
6. What types of information would be contained in FreshDirect's extranet?
7. Which metrics would you use if you were hired to assess the efficiency and effectiveness of FreshDirect's Web site?

How Do You Value Friendster?

Jonathan Abrams is keeping quiet about how he is going to generate revenue from his Web site, Friendster, which specializes in social networking. Abrams is a 33-year-old Canadian software developer whose experiences include being laid off by Netscape and then moving from one start-up to another. In 2002, Abrams was unemployed, not doing well financially, and certainly not looking to start another business when he developed the idea for Friendster. He quickly coded a working prototype and watched in amazement as his Web site took off.

The buzz around social networking start-ups has been on the rise. A number of high-end venture capital firms, including Sequoia and Mayfield, have invested more than $40 million into social networking start-ups such as LinkedIn, Spoke, and Tribe Networks. Friendster received over $13 million in venture capital from Kleiner, Perkins, Caufield, Byers, and Benchmark Capital, which reportedly valued the company at $53 million—a startling figure for a company that had yet to generate even a single dime in revenue.

A year after making its public debut, Friendster was one of the largest social networking Web sites, attracting over 5 million users and receiving more than 50,000 page views per day. The question is how do efficiency metrics, such as Web traffic and page views, turn into cash flow? Everyone is wondering how Friendster is going to begin generating revenue.

The majority of Abrams's competitors make their money by extracting fees from their subscribers. Friendster is going to continue to let its subscribers meet for free but plans to charge them for premium services such as the ability to customize their profile page. The company also has plans to extend beyond social networking to an array of value-added services such as friend-based job referrals and classmate searches. Abrams is also looking into using his high-traffic Web site to tap into the growing Internet advertising market.

Abrams does not appear concerned about generating revenue or about potential competition. "Match.com has been around eight years, has 12 million users, and has spent many millions of dollars on advertising to get them," he said. "We're a year old, we've spent zero dollars on advertising, and in a year or less, we'll be bigger than them—it's a given."

The future of Friendster is uncertain. Google offered to buy Friendster for $30 million even though there are signs, both statistical and anecdotal, that Friendster's popularity may have peaked. [33]

Questions

1. How could you use e-business metrics to place a value on Friendster?
2. Why would a venture capital company value Friendster at $53 million when the company has yet to generate any revenue?
3. Why would Google be interested in buying Friendster for $30 million when the company has yet to generate any revenue?
4. Identify Friendster's e-business model and explain how the company can generate revenue.
5. Explain the e-business benefits and challenges facing Friendster.

1. **Leveraging the competitive value of the Internet**

   Physical inventories have always been a major cost component of business. Linking to suppliers in real time dramatically enhances the classic goal of inventory "turn." The Internet provides a multitude of opportunities for radically reducing the costs of designing, manufacturing, and selling goods and services. E-mango.com, a fruit e-marketplace, must take advantage of these opportunities or find itself at a significant competitive disadvantage. Identify the disadvantages that confront E-mango.com if it does not leverage the competitive value of the Internet.

2. **Implementing an e-business model**

   The Genius is a revolutionary mountain bike with full-suspension and shock-adjustable forks that is being marketed via the Internet. The Genius needs an e-business solution that will easily enable internal staff to deliver fresh and relevant product information throughout its Web site. To support its large audience, the company also needs the ability to present information in multiple languages and serve over 1 million page views per month to visitors in North America and Europe. Explain what e-business model you would use to market The Genius on the Internet.

3. **Assessing Internet capabilities**

   Hoover's Rentals is a small privately owned business that rents sports equipment in Denver, Colorado. The company specializes in winter rentals including ski equipment, snowboarding equipment, and snowmobile equipment. Hoover's has been in business for 20 years and, for the first time, it is experiencing a decline in rentals. Brian Hoover, the company's owner, is puzzled by the recent decreases. The snowfall for the last two years has been outstanding, and the ski resorts have opened earlier and closed later than most previous years. Reports say tourism in the Colorado area is up, and the invention of loyalty programs has significantly increased the number of local skiers. Overall, business should be booming. The only reason for the decrease in sales might be the fact that big retailers such as Wal-Mart and Gart Sports are now renting winter sports equipment. Brian would like your team's help in determining how he can use the Internet to help his company increase sales and decrease costs to compete with these big retailers.

4. **Online auction sites**

   You are working for a new Internet start-up company, eMart.com, an online marketplace for the sale of goods and services. The company offers a wide variety of features and services that enable online members to buy and sell their goods and services quickly and conveniently. The company's mission is to provide a global trading platform where anyone can trade practically anything. Suggest some ways that eMart.com can extend its market reach beyond that of its competitor, eBay.com.

5. **Everybody needs an Internet strategy**

   An Internet strategy addresses the reasons businesses want to "go online." "Going online" because it seems like the right thing to do now or because everyone else is doing it is not a good enough reason. A business must decide how it will best utilize the Internet for its particular needs. It must plan for where it wants to go and how best the Internet can help shape that vision. Before developing a strategy a business should spend time on the Internet, see what similar businesses have grown, and what is most feasible, given a particular set of resources. Think of a new online business opportunity and answer the following questions:

1. Why do you want to put your business online?

2. What benefits will going online bring?

3. What effects will being connected to the Internet have on your staff, suppliers, and customers?

6. Analyzing Web Sites

Stars Inc. is a large clothing corporation that specializes in reselling clothes worn by celebrities. The company's four Web sites generate 75 percent of its sales. The remaining 25 percent of sales occur directly through the company's warehouse. You have recently been hired as the director of sales. The only information you can find on the success of the four Web sites follows:

Web Site	Classic	Contemporary	New Age	Traditional
Traffic analysis	5,000 hits/day	200 hits/day	10,000 hits/day	1,000 hits/day
Stickiness (average)	20 min.	1 hr.	20 min.	50 min.
Number of abandoned shopping carts	400/day	0/day	5,000/day	200/day
Number of unique visitors	2,000/day	100/day	8,000/day	200/day
Number of identified visitors	3,000/day	100/day	2,000/day	800/day
Average revenue per sale	$1,000	$1,000	$50	$1,300

You decide that maintaining four separate Web sites is expensive and adds little business value. You want to propose consolidating to one Web site. Create a report detailing the business value gained by consolidating to a single Web site, along with your recommendation for consolidation. Be sure to include your Web site profitability analysis.

Ethics and Information Security

4

CHAPTER

SECTION 4.1
Ethics

- Ethics
- Information Ethics
- Developing Information Management Policies
- Ethics in the Workplace

SECTION 4.2
Information Security

- Protecting Intellectual Assets
- The First Line of Defense—People
- The Second Line of Defense—Technology

CHAPTER OUTLINE

Sarbanes-Oxley: Where Information Technology, Finance, and Ethics Meet

Congress is cleaning up the way companies do business after accounting and governance scandals rocked investor confidence and damaged the reputation of companies large and small. The Sarbanes-Oxley Act (SOX) of 2002 was enacted in response to the high-profile Enron and WorldCom financial scandals to protect shareholders and the public from accounting errors and fraudulent practices by organizations.

Sarbanes-Oxley

One primary component of the SOX is the definition of which records are to be stored and for how long. For this reason, the legislation not only affects financial departments, but also IT departments whose job it is to store electronic records. SOX states that all business records, including electronic records and electronic messages, "must be saved for not less than five years." The consequences for noncompliance are fines, imprisonment, or both. Three rules of Sarbanes-Oxley affecting the management of electronic records address the following areas:

1. The destruction, alteration, or falsification of records. It states that persons who knowingly alter, destroy, mutilate, conceal, or falsify documents shall be fined or imprisoned for not more than 20 years, or both.
2. The retention period for records storage. Best practices indicate that corporations securely store all business records using the same guidelines set for public accountants. Organizations shall maintain all audit or review work papers for a period of five years from the end of the fiscal period in which the audit or review was concluded.
3. The business records and communications that need to be stored, including electronic communications. IT departments are facing the challenge of creating and maintaining a corporate records archive in a cost-effective fashion that satisfies the requirements put forth by the legislation.

Essentially, any public organization that uses IT as part of its financial business processes must implement IT controls to comply with SOX. The cost of implementing SOX is high at $35 million per year for large companies. William D. Zollars, CEO of Yellow Roadway Corp., the nation's largest trucking firm, said, "It requires an army of people to do the paperwork." Zollars dispatched 200 people to work on SOX compliance, paying more than $9 million for the work—roughly 3 percent of annual profits.

Benefits from Sarbanes-Oxley

Many businesses are promoting the benefits they received from implementing SOX. General Electric Co., which spent about $30 million on SOX compliance, has added controls that boost investors' confidence in the company. United Technologies used SOX to standardize bookkeeping audits in its disparate businesses around the world. The biggest advantage of all, though, may be the greater confidence investors have in financial results.

Some officials believe it will take another two years (around 2008) for companies, auditors, and regulators to apply the law efficiently. That might appear to be a long time, and it may seem to be expensive; however, it is a small price to pay to help organizations run smoothly and renew investor confidence.

Implementing Sarbanes-Oxley

Ultimately, Sarbanes-Oxley compliance will require a great deal of work among all departments. Compliance starts with running IT as a business and strengthening IT internal controls. The following are a few practices organizations can follow to ensure compliance with the Sarbanes-Oxley Act.

- Overhaul or upgrade financial systems to meet regulatory requirements for more accurate, detailed, and timely filings.
- Examine the control processes within the IT department and apply best practices to comply with the act's goals. For example, segregation of duties within the systems development staff is a widely recognized best practice that helps prevent errors and outright fraud. The people who code program changes should be different from the people who test them, and a separate team should be responsible for changes in production environments.
- Ensure that information system customizations are not overriding controls by working with internal and external auditors. Homegrown financial systems are fraught with potential information-integrity issues. Although leading enterprise resource planning (ERP) systems offer audit-trail functionality, customizations of these systems often bypass those controls.
- Work with the CIO, CEO, CFO, and corporate attorneys to create a document-retention-and-destruction policy that addresses what types of electronic documents should be saved, and for how long.[1]

INTRODUCTION

Ethics and security are two fundamental building blocks for all organizations. In recent years, such events as the Enron and Martha Stewart scandals along with 9/11 have shed new light on the meaning of ethics and security. When the behavior of a few individuals can destroy billion-dollar organizations, the value of ethics and security should be evident.

section 4.1 ETHICS

LEARNING OUTCOMES

4.1. Explain the ethical issues surrounding information.

4.2. Identify the differences between an ethical computer use policy and an acceptable use policy.

4.3. Describe the relationship between an e-mail privacy policy and an Internet use policy.

4.4. Explain the effects of spam on an organization.

4.5. Summarize the different monitoring technologies and explain the importance of an employee monitoring policy.

ETHICS

Ian Clarke, the inventor of a file-swapping service called Freenet, decided to leave the United States for the United Kingdom, where copyright laws are more lenient. Wayne Rosso, the inventor of a file-sharing service called Grokster, left the United States for Spain, again saying goodbye to tough U.S. copyright protections. The U.S. copyright laws, designed decades before the invention of the Internet, make file sharing and many other Internet technologies illegal. Although some individuals use file sharing in unethical manners, such as downloading music and movies illegally, file sharing has many positive benefits, such as improving drug research, software development, and the flow of information.[2]

The ethical issues surrounding copyright infringement and intellectual property rights are consuming the e-business world. Advances in technology make it easier for people to copy everything from music to pictures. Technology poses new challenges for our *ethics*—the principles and standards that guide our behavior toward other people. Review Figure 4.1 for an overview of concepts, terms, and ethical issues stemming from advances in technology.

The Securities Exchange Commission (SEC) began inquiries into Enron's accounting practices on October 22, 2001. David Duncan, the Arthur Andersen partner in charge of Enron, instructed his team to begin destroying paper and electronic Enron-related records on October 23, 2001. Kimberly Latham, a subordinate to

FIGURE 4.1

Technology-Related Ethical Issues

Intellectual property	Intangible creative work that is embodied in physical form.
Copyright	The legal protection afforded an expression of an idea, such as a song, video game, and some types of proprietary documents.
Fair use doctrine	In certain situations, it is legal to use copyrighted material.
Pirated software	The unauthorized use, duplication, distribution, or sale of copyrighted software.
Counterfeit software	Software that is manufactured to look like the real thing and sold as such.

FIGURE 4.2

Trust and E-Business

Primary Reasons Privacy Issues Reduce Trust for E-Business
1. Loss of personal privacy
2. 37 percent of Internet users are "a lot" more inclined to purchase a product on a Web site that has a privacy policy
3. Effective privacy and security would convert more Internet users to Internet buyers

Duncan, sent instructions on October 24, 2001, to her entire team to follow Duncan's orders and even compiled a list of computer files to delete. Arthur Andersen blames Duncan for destroying thousands of Enron-related documents. Duncan blames the Arthur Andersen attorney, Nancy Temple, for sending him a memo instructing him to destroy files. Temple blames Arthur Andersen's document deletion policies.[3]

Regardless of who is to blame, the bigger issue is that the destruction of files after a federal investigation has begun is both unethical and illegal. A direct corporate order to destroy information currently under federal investigation poses a dilemma for any professional. Comply, and you participate in potentially criminal activities; refuse, and you might find yourself looking for a new job.

Privacy is one of the largest ethical issues facing organizations. ***Privacy*** is the right to be left alone when you want to be, to have control over your own personal possessions, and not to be observed without your consent. Privacy is related to ***confidentiality***, which is the assurance that messages and information are available only to those who are authorized to view them. Some of the most problematic decisions facing organizations lie in the murky and turbulent waters of privacy. The burden comes from the knowledge that each time employees make a decision regarding issues of privacy, the outcome could potentially sink the company.

Trust between companies, customers, partners, and suppliers is the support structure of e-business. One of the main ingredients in trust is privacy. Privacy continues to be one of the primary barriers to the growth of e-business. People are concerned their privacy will be violated because of interactions on the Web. Unless an organization can effectively address this issue of privacy, its customers, partners, and suppliers might lose trust in the organization, which would hurt its business. Figure 4.2 displays the results from a *CIO* survey as to how privacy issues reduce trust for e-businesses.

INFORMATION ETHICS

Individuals determine how to use information and how information affects them. How individuals behave toward each other, how they handle information and technology, are largely influenced by their ethics. Ethical dilemmas usually arise not in simple, clear-cut situations but out of a clash between competing goals, responsibilities, and loyalties. Inevitably, the decision process has more than one socially acceptable "correct" decision. Figure 4.3 contains examples of ethically questionable or unacceptable uses of information technology.

People make arguments for or against—justify or condemn—the behaviors in Figure 4.3. Unfortunately, there are few hard and fast rules for always determining what is and is not ethical. Knowing the law will not always help because what is legal might not always be ethical, and what might be ethical is not always legal. For example, Joe Reidenberg received an offer for cell phone service from AT&T Wireless. The offer revealed that AT&T Wireless had used Equifax, a credit reporting agency, to identify Joe Reidenberg as a potential customer. Overall, this strategy seemed like good business. Equifax could generate additional revenue by selling information it already owned and AT&T Wireless could identify target markets, thereby increasing response rates to its marketing campaigns.

Unfortunately, the Fair Credit Reporting Act (FCRA) forbids repurposing credit information except when the information is used for "a firm offer of credit or insurance." In other words, the only product that can be sold based on credit information

Examples of Questionable Information Technology Use
Individuals copy, use, and distribute software.
Employees search organizational databases for sensitive corporate and personal information.
Organizations collect, buy, and use information without checking the validity or accuracy of the information.
Individuals create and spread viruses that cause trouble for those using and maintaining IT systems.
Individuals hack into computer systems to steal proprietary information.
Employees destroy or steal proprietary organization information such as schematics, sketches, customer lists, and reports.

is credit. A representative for Equifax stated, "As long as AT&T Wireless (or any company for that matter) is offering the cell phone service on a credit basis, such as allowing the use of the service before the consumer has to pay, it is in compliance with the FCRA." However, the question remains—is it ethical?[4]

This is a good example of the ethical dilemmas facing organizations. Because technology is so new and pervasive in unexpected ways, the ethics surrounding information are still being defined. Figure 4.4 displays the four quadrants of ethical and legal behavior. The ideal goal for organizations is to make decisions within quadrant I that are both legal and ethical.

Information Has No Ethics

Jerry Rode, CIO of Saab Cars USA, realized he had a public relations fiasco on his hands when he received an e-mail from an irate customer. Saab had hired four Internet marketing companies to distribute electronic information about Saab's new models to its customers. Saab specified that the marketing campaign be opt-in, implying that it would contact only the people who had agreed to receive promotions and marketing material via e-mail. Unfortunately, one of the marketing companies apparently had a different definition of opt-in and was e-mailing all customers regardless of their opt-in decision.

Rode fired the errant marketing company and immediately developed a formal policy for the use of customer information. "The customer doesn't see ad agencies and contracted marketing firms. They see Saab USA spamming them," Rode said. "Finger-pointing after the fact won't make your customers feel better."[5]

Information has no ethics. Information does not care how it is used. It will not stop itself from spamming customers, sharing itself if it is sensitive or personal, or revealing details to third parties. Information cannot delete or preserve itself. Therefore, it falls on the shoulders of those who own the information to develop ethical guidelines on how to manage the information. Figure 4.5 provides an overview of

FIGURE 4.4

Acting Ethically and Legally
Are Not Always the Same

FIGURE 4.5

Established Information-Related Laws

Established Information-Related Laws	
Privacy Act—1974	Restricts what information the federal government can collect; allows people to access and correct information on themselves; requires procedures to protect the security of personal information; and forbids the disclosure of name-linked information without permission.
Family Education Rights and Privacy Act—1974	Regulates access to personal education records by government agencies and other third parties and ensures the right of students to see their own records.
Cable Communications Act—1984	Requires written or electronic consent from viewers before cable TV providers can release viewing choices or other personally identifiable information.
Electronic Communications Privacy Act—1986	Allows the reading of communications by a firm and says that employees have no right to privacy when using their companies' computers.
Computer Fraud and Abuse Act—1986	Prohibits unauthorized access to computers used for financial institutions, the U.S. government, or interstate and international trade.
The Bork Bill (officially known as the Video Privacy Protection Act, 1988)	Prohibits the use of video rental information on customers for any purpose other than that of marketing goods and services directly to the customer.
Communications Assistance for Law Enforcement Act—1994	Requires that telecommunications equipment be designed so that authorized government agents are able to intercept all wired and wireless communications being sent or received by any subscriber. The Act also requires that subscriber call-identifying information be transmitted to a government when and if required.
Freedom of Information Act—1967, 1975, 1994, and 1998	Allows any person to examine government records unless it would cause an invasion of privacy. It was amended in 1974 to apply to the FBI, and again in 1994 to allow citizens to monitor government activities and information gathering, and once again in 1998 to access government information on the Internet.
Health Insurance Portability and Accountability Act (HIPPA)—1996	Requires that the health care industry formulate and implement regulations to keep patient information confidential.
Identity Theft and Assumption Deterrence Act—1998	Strengthened the criminal laws governing identity theft making it a federal crime to use or transfer identification belonging to another. It also established a central federal service for victims.
USA Patriot Act—2001 and 2003	Allows law enforcement to get access to almost any information, including library records, video rentals, bookstore purchases, and business records when investigating any act of terrorist or clandestine intelligence activities. In 2003, Patriot II broadened the original law.
Homeland Security Act—2002	Provided new authority to government agencies to mine data on individuals and groups including e-mails and Web site visits; put limits on the information available under the Freedom of Information Act; and gave new powers to government agencies to declare national heath emergencies.
Sarbanes-Oxley Act—2002	Sought to protect investors by improving the accuracy and reliability of corporate disclosures and requires companies to (1) implement extensive and detailed policies to prevent illegal activity within the company, and (2) to respond in a timely manner to investigate illegal activity.
Fair and Accurate Credit Transactions Act—2003	Included provisions for the prevention of identity theft including consumers' right to get a credit report free each year, requiring merchants to leave all but the last five digits of a credit card number off a receipt, and requiring lenders and credit agencies to take action even before a victim knows a crime has occurred when they notice any circumstances that might indicate identity theft.
CAN-Spam Act—2003	Sought to regulate interstate commerce by imposing limitations and penalties on businesses sending unsolicited e-mail to consumers. The law forbids deceptive subject lines, headers, return addresses, etc., as well as the harvesting of e-mail addresses from Web sites. It requires businesses that send spam to maintain a do-not-spam list and to include a postal mailing address in the message.

some of the important laws that individuals must follow when they are attempting to manage and protect information.

DEVELOPING INFORMATION MANAGEMENT POLICIES

Treating sensitive corporate information as a valuable resource is good management. Building a corporate culture based on ethical principles that employees can understand and implement is responsible management. In an effort to provide guidelines for ethical information management, *CIO* magazine (along with over 100 CIOs) developed six principles for ethical information management displayed in Figure 4.6.

Organizations should develop written policies establishing employee guidelines, personnel procedures, and organizational rules for information. These policies set employee expectations about the organization's practices and standards and protect the organization from misuse of computer systems and IT resources. If an organization's employees use computers at work, the organization should, at a minimum, implement ePolicies. *ePolicies* are policies and procedures that address the ethical use of computers and Internet usage in the business environment. These policies typically embody the following:

- Ethical computer use policy.
- Information privacy policy.
- Acceptable use policy.
- E-mail privacy policy.
- Internet use policy.
- Anti-spam policy.

Ethical Computer Use Policy

One of the essential steps in creating an ethical corporate culture is establishing an ethical computer use policy. An *ethical computer use policy* contains general principles to guide computer user behavior. For example, the ethical computer use policy might explicitly state that users should refrain from playing computer games during working hours. This policy ensures the users know how to behave at work and the organization has a published standard by which to deal with user infractions. For example, after appropriate warnings, the company may terminate an employee who spends significant amounts of time playing computer games at work.

FIGURE 4.6

CIO Magazine's Six Principles for Ethical Information Management

Six Principles for Ethical Information Management
1. Information is a valuable corporate asset and should be managed as such, like cash, facilities, or any other corporate asset.
2. The CIO is steward of corporate information and is responsible for managing it over its life cycle—from its generation to its appropriate destruction.
3. The CIO is responsible for controlling access to and use of information, as determined by governmental regulation and corporate policy.
4. The CIO is responsible for preventing the inappropriate destruction of information.
5. The CIO is responsible for bringing technological knowledge to the development of information management practices and policies.
6. The CIO should partner with executive peers to develop and execute the organization's information management policies.

There are variations in how organizations expect their employees to use computers, but in any approach, the overriding principle when seeking appropriate computer use should be informed consent. The users should be *informed* of the rules and, by agreeing to use the system on that basis, *consent* to abide by the rules.

An organization should make a conscientious effort to ensure all users are aware of the policy through formal training and other means. If an organization were to have only one ePolicy, it should be an ethical computer use policy since it is the starting point and the umbrella for any other policies the organization might establish.

Information Privacy Policy

Scott Thompson is the executive vice president of Inovant, the company Visa set up to handle its technology. Thompson errs on the side of caution in regard to Visa's information: He bans the use of Visa's customer information for anything outside its intended purpose—billing.

Visa's customer information details how people are spending their money, in which stores, on which days, and even at what time of day. Sales and marketing departments around the country no doubt are salivating at any prospect of gaining access to Visa's databases. "They would love to refine the information into loyalty programs, target markets, or even partnerships with Visa. There are lots of creative people coming up with these ideas. This whole area of information sharing is enormous and growing. For the marketers, the sky's the limit," Thompson said. Privacy specialists along with Thompson developed a strict credit card information policy, which the company follows.

The question now is can Thompson guarantee that unethical use of his information will not occur? Many experts do not believe that he can. In a large majority of cases, the unethical use of information happens not through the malicious scheming of a rogue marketer, but rather unintentionally. For instance, information is collected and stored for some purpose, such as record keeping or billing. Then, a sales or marketing professional figures out another way to use it internally, share it with partners, or sell it to a trusted third party. The information is "unintentionally" used for new purposes. The classic example of this type of unintentional information reuse is the Social Security number, which started simply as a way to identify government retirement benefits and is now used as a sort of universal personal ID, found on everything from drivers' licenses to savings accounts.

An organization that wants to protect its information should develop an information privacy policy. An ***information privacy policy*** contains general principles regarding information privacy. Figure 4.7 highlights a few guidelines an organization can follow when creating an information privacy policy.

Acceptable Use Policy

An ***acceptable use policy (AUP)*** is a policy that a user must agree to follow in order to be provided access to a network or to the Internet. ***Nonrepudiation*** is a contractual stipulation to ensure that e-business participants do not deny (repudiate) their online actions. A nonrepudiation clause is typically contained in an AUP.

Many businesses and educational facilities require employees or students to sign an acceptable use policy before gaining network access. When signing up with an Internet service provider (ISP), each customer is typically presented with an AUP, which states that they agree to adhere to certain stipulations (see Figure 4.8).

E-Mail Privacy Policy

E-mail is so pervasive in organizations that it requires its own specific policy. In a recent survey, 80 percent of professional workers identified e-mail as their preferred means of corporate communications. Trends also show a dramatic increase in the

Creating an Information Privacy Policy

1. **Adoption and implementation of a privacy policy.** An organization engaged in online activities or e-business has a responsibility to adopt and implement a policy for protecting the privacy of personal information. Organizations should also take steps that foster the adoption and implementation of effective online privacy policies by the organizations with which they interact, for instance, by sharing best practices with business partners.

2. **Notice and disclosure.** An organization's privacy policy must be easy to find, read, and understand. The policy must clearly state:
   - What information is being collected?
   - The use of information being collected.
   - Possible third-party distribution of that information.
   - The choices available to an individual regarding collection, use, and distribution of the collected information.
   - A statement of the organization's commitment to information security.
   - What steps the organization takes to ensure information quality and access.

3. **Choice and consent.** Individuals must be given the opportunity to exercise choice regarding how personal information collected from them online may be used when such use is unrelated to the purpose for which the information was collected. At a minimum, individuals should be given the opportunity to opt out of such use.

4. **Information security.** Organizations creating, maintaining, using, or disseminating personal information should take appropriate measures to assure its reliability and should take reasonable precautions to protect it from loss, misuse, or alteration.

5. **Information quality and access.** Organizations should establish appropriate processes or mechanisms so that inaccuracies in material personal information, such as account or contact information, may be corrected. Other procedures to assure information quality may include use of reliable sources, collection methods, appropriate consumer access, and protection against accidental or unauthorized alteration.

FIGURE 4.8

Acceptable Use Policy
Stipulations

Acceptable Use Policy Stipulations

1. Not using the service as part of violating any law.

2. Not attempting to break the security of any computer network or user.

3. Not posting commercial messages to groups without prior permission.

4. Not performing any nonrepudiation.

5. Not attempting to send junk e-mail or spam to anyone who does not want to receive it.

6. Not attempting to mail bomb a site. A *mail bomb* is sending a massive amount of e-mail to a specific person or system resulting in filling up the recipient's disk space, which, in some cases, may be too much for the server to handle and may cause the server to stop functioning.

adoption rate of instant messaging (IM) in the workplace. While e-mail and IM are common business communication tools, there are risks associated with using them. For instance, a sent e-mail is stored on at least three or four different computers (see Figure 4.9). Simply deleting an e-mail from one computer does not delete it off the other computers. Companies can mitigate many of the risks of using electronic messaging systems by implementing and adhering to an e-mail privacy policy.[6]

One of the major problems with e-mail is the user's expectations of privacy. To a large extent, this exception is based on the false assumption that e-mail privacy protection exists somehow analogous to that of U.S. first-class mail. This is simply not true.

FIGURE 4.9

E-Mail Is Stored on Multiple
Computers

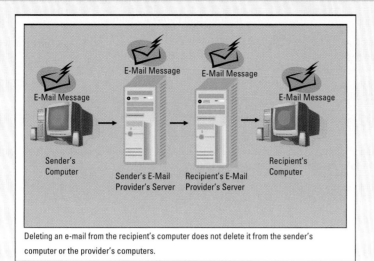

Deleting an e-mail from the recipient's computer does not delete it from the sender's computer or the provider's computers.

Generally, the organization that owns the e-mail system can operate the system as openly or as privately as it wishes. That means that if the organization wants to read everyone's e-mail, it can do so. If it chooses not to read any, that is allowable too. Hence, it is up to the organization to decide how much, if any, e-mail it is going to read. Then, when it decides, it must inform the users, so that they can consent to this level of intrusion. In other words, an ***e-mail privacy policy*** details the extent to which e-mail messages may be read by others.

Organizations must create an e-mail privacy policy. Figure 4.10 displays a few of the key stipulations generally contained in an e-mail privacy policy.

Internet Use Policy

Similar to e-mail, the Internet has some unique aspects that make it a good candidate for its own policy. These include the large amounts of computing resources that Internet users can expend, thus making it essential that such use be legitimate. In addition, the Internet contains numerous materials that some believe are offensive and, hence, some regulation is required. An ***Internet use policy*** contains general principles to guide the proper use of the Internet. Figure 4.11 lists a few important stipulations that might be included in an Internet use policy.

FIGURE 4.10

E-Mail Privacy Policy
Stipulations

E-Mail Privacy Policy Stipulations

1. The policy should be complementary to the ethical computer use policy.

2. It defines who legitimate e-mail users are.

3. It explains the backup procedure so users will know that at some point, even if a message is deleted from their computer, it will still be on the backup tapes.

4. It describes the legitimate grounds for reading someone's e-mail and the process required before such action can be taken.

5. It informs that the organization has no control of e-mail once it is transmitted outside the organization.

6. It explains what will happen if the user severs his or her connection with the organization.

7. It asks employees to be careful when making organizational files and documents available to others.

FIGURE 4.11

Internet Use Policy
Stipulations

Internet Use Policy Stipulations
1. The policy should describe available Internet services because not all Internet sites allow users to access all services.
2. The policy should define the organization's position on the purpose of Internet access and what restrictions, if any, are placed on that access.
3. The policy should complement the ethical computer use policy.
4. The policy should describe user responsibility for citing sources, properly handling offensive material, and protecting the organization's good name.
5. The policy should clearly state the ramifications if the policy is violated.

Anti-Spam Policy

Chief technology officer (CTO) of the law firm Fenwick and West, Matt Kesner reduced incoming spam by 99 percent and found himself a corporate hero. Before the spam reduction, the law firm's partners (whose time is worth $350 to $600 an hour) found themselves spending hours each day sifting through 300 to 500 spam messages. The spam blocking engineered by Kesner traps between 5,000 and 7,000 messages a day.[7]

Spam is unsolicited e-mail. An **anti-spam policy** simply states that e-mail users will not send unsolicited e-mails (or spam). Spam plagues all levels of employees within an organization from receptionists to CEOs. Estimates indicate that spam accounts for 40 percent to 60 percent of most organizations' e-mail traffic. Ferris Research says spam cost U.S. businesses over $10 billion in 2005, and Nucleus Research stated that companies forfeit $874 per employee annually in lost productivity from spam alone. Spam clogs e-mail systems and siphons IT resources away from legitimate business projects.[8]

It is difficult to write anti-spam policies, laws, or software because there is no such thing as a universal litmus test for spam. One person's spam is another person's newsletter. End users have to be involved in deciding what spam is because what is unwanted can vary widely not just from one company to the next, but from one person to the next. What looks like spam to the rest of the world could be essential business communications for certain employees.

John Zarb, CIO of Libbey, a manufacturer of glassware, china, and flatware, tested Guenivere (a virus and subject-line filter) and SpamAssassin (an open source spam filter). He had to shut them off after 10 days because they were rejecting important legitimate e-mails. As Zarb quickly discovered, once an organization starts filtering e-mail, it runs the risk of blocking legitimate e-mails that look like spam. Avoiding an unacceptable level of "false positives" requires a delicate balancing act. The IT team tweaked the spam filters and today, the filters block about 70 percent of Libbey's spam, and Zarb said the "false positive" rate is far lower, but still not zero. Figure 4.12 highlights a few methods an organization can follow to prevent spam.

FIGURE 4.12

Spam Prevention Tips

Spam Prevention Tips
■ **Disguise e-mail addresses posted in a public electronic place.** When posting an e-mail address in a public place, disguise the address through simple means such as replacing "jsmith@domain.com" with "jsmith at domain dot com." This prevents spam from recognizing the e-mail address.
■ **Opt out of member directories that may place an e-mail address online.** Choose not to participate in any activities that place e-mail addresses online. If an e-mail address is placed online be sure it is disguised in some way.
■ **Use a filter.** Many ISPs and free e-mail services now provide spam filtering. While filters are not perfect, they can cut down tremendously on the amount of spam a user receives.

ETHICS IN THE WORKPLACE

Concern is growing among employees that infractions of corporate policies—even accidental ones—will be a cause for disciplinary action. The Whitehouse.gov Internet site displays the U.S. president's official Web site and updates on bill signings and new policies. Whitehouse.com, however, leads to a trashy site that capitalizes on its famous name. A simple mistype from .gov to .com could potentially cost someone her or his job if the company has a termination policy for viewing illicit Web sites. Monitoring employees is one of the largest issues facing CIOs when they are developing information management policies.

Legal precedents that hold businesses financially responsible for their employees' actions drives the decision of whether to monitor what employees do on company time with corporate resources. Increasingly, employee monitoring is not a choice; it is a risk-management obligation. Michael Soden, CEO of the Bank of Ireland, issued a mandate stating that company employees could not surf illicit Web sites with company equipment. Next, he hired Hewlett-Packard to run the IT department. A Hewlett-Packard employee soon discovered illicit Web sites on Soden's computer. Soden resigned.[9]

A recent survey of workplace monitoring and surveillance practices by the American Management Association (AMA) and the ePolicy Institute showed the degree to which companies are turning to monitoring:

- 82 percent of the study's 1,627 respondents acknowledged conducting some form of electronic monitoring or physical surveillance.
- 63 percent of the companies stated that they monitor Internet connections.
- 47 percent acknowledged storing and reviewing employee e-mail messages.[10]

Monitoring Technologies

Many employees use their company's high-speed Internet access to shop, browse, and surf the Web. Fifty-nine percent of all 2004 Web purchases in the United States were made from the workplace, according to ComScore Networks. Vault.com determined that 47 percent of employees spend at least half an hour a day surfing the Web.[11]

This research indicates that managers should monitor what their employees are doing with their Web access. Most managers do not want their employees conducting personal business during working hours. For these reasons many organizations have increasingly taken the Big Brother approach to Web monitoring with software that tracks Internet usage and even allows the boss to read employees' e-mail. Figure 4.13 highlights a few reasons the effects of employee monitoring are worse than the lost productivity from employee Web surfing.

This is the thinking at SAS Institute, a private software company consistently ranked in the top 10 on many "Best Places to Work" surveys. SAS does not monitor its employees' Web usage. The company asks its employees to use company

---

FIGURE 4.13

Employee Monitoring Effects

Employee Monitoring Effects

1. Employee absenteeism is on the rise, almost doubling in 2004 to 21 percent. The lesson here might be that more employees are missing work to take care of personal business. Perhaps losing a few minutes here or there—or even a couple of hours—is cheaper than losing entire days.

2. Studies indicate that electronic monitoring results in lower job satisfaction, in part because people begin to believe the quantity of their work is more important than the quality.

3. Electronic monitoring also induces what psychologists call "psychological reactance": the tendency to rebel against constraints. If you tell your employees they cannot shop, they cannot use corporate networks for personal business, and they cannot make personal phone calls, then their desire to do all these things will likely increase.

resources responsibly, but does not mind if they occasionally check sports scores or use the Web for shopping.

Many management gurus advocate that organizations whose corporate cultures are based on trust are more successful than those whose corporate cultures are based on distrust. Before an organization implements monitoring technology it should ask itself, "What does this say about how the organization feels about its employees?" If the organization really does not trust its employees, then perhaps it should find new ones. If an organization does trust its employees, then it might want to treat them accordingly. An organization that follows its employees' every keystroke is unwittingly undermining the relationships with its employees.[12]

Information technology monitoring is tracking people's activities by such measures as number of keystrokes, error rate, and number of transactions processed. Figure 4.14 displays different types of monitoring technologies currently available.

Employee Monitoring Policies

The best path for an organization planning to engage in employee monitoring is open communication surrounding the issue. A recent survey discovered that communication about monitoring issues is weak for most organizations. One in five companies did not even have an acceptable use policy and one in four companies did not have an Internet use policy. Companies that did have policies usually tucked them into the rarely probed recesses of the employee handbook, and then the policies tended to be of the vague and legal jargon variety: "XYZ company reserves the right to monitor or review any information stored or transmitted on its equipment." Reserving the right to monitor is materially different from clearly stating that the company does monitor, listing what is tracked, describing what is looked for, and detailing the consequences for violations.

An organization must formulate the right monitoring policies and put them into practice. Employee monitoring policies explicitly state how, when, and where the company monitors its employees. CSOs that are explicit about what the company does in the way of monitoring and the reasons for it, along with actively

FIGURE 4.14

Monitoring Technologies

Common Monitoring Technologies	
Key logger, or key trapper, software	A program that, when installed on a computer, records every keystroke and mouse click.
Hardware key logger	A hardware device that captures keystrokes on their journey from the keyboard to the motherboard.
Cookie	A small file deposited on a hard drive by a Web site containing information about customers and their Web activities. Cookies allow Web sites to record the comings and goings of customers, usually without their knowledge or consent.
Adware	Software that generates ads that install themselves on a computer when a person downloads some other program from the Internet.
Spyware (sneakware or stealthware)	Software that comes hidden in free downloadable software and tracks online movements, mines the information stored on a computer, or uses a computer's CPU and storage for some task the user knows nothing about.
Web log	Consists of one line of information for every visitor to a Web site and is usually stored on a Web server.
Clickstream	Records information about a customer during a Web surfing session such as what Web sites were visited, how long the visit was, what ads were viewed, and what was purchased.

FIGURE 4.15

Employee Monitoring Policy
Stipulations

Employee Monitoring Policy Stipulations
1. Be as specific as possible.
2. Always enforce the policy.
3. Enforce the policy in the same way for everyone.
4. Expressly communicate that the company reserves the right to monitor all employees.
5. Specifically state when monitoring will be performed.
6. Specifically state what will be monitored (e-mail, IM, Internet, network activity, etc.).
7. Describe the types of information that will be collected.
8. State the consequences for violating the policy.
9. State all provisions that allow for updates to the policy.
10. Specify the scope and manner of monitoring for any information system.
11. When appropriate, obtain a written receipt acknowledging that each party has received, read, and understood the monitoring policies.

educating their employees about what unacceptable behavior looks like, will find that employees not only acclimate quickly to a policy, but also reduce the CSO's burden by policing themselves. Figure 4.15 displays several common stipulations an organization can follow when creating an employee monitoring policy.

OPENING CASE QUESTIONS

Sarbanes-Oxley: Where Information Technology, Finance, and Ethics Meet

1. Define the relationship between ethics and the Sarbanes-Oxley Act.
2. Why is records management an area of concern for the entire organization and not just the IT department?
3. Identify two policies an organization can implement to achieve Sarbanes-Oxley compliance.
4. What ethical dilemmas are being solved by implementing Sarbanes-Oxley?
5. What is the biggest ethical roadblock for organizations attempting to achieve Sarbanes-Oxley compliance?

section 4.2 INFORMATION SECURITY

LEARNING OUTCOMES

4.6. Describe the relationship between information security policies and an information security plan.

4.7. Summarize the five steps to creating an information security plan.

4.8. Provide an example of each of the three primary information security areas: (1) authentication and authorization, (2) prevention and resistance, and (3) detection and response.

4.9. Describe the relationships and differences between hackers and viruses.

PROTECTING INTELLECTUAL ASSETS

Organizational information is intellectual capital. Just as organizations protect their assets—keeping their money in an insured bank or providing a safe working environment for employees—they must also protect their intellectual capital. An organization's intellectual capital includes everything from its patents to its transactional and analytical information. With security breaches on the rise and computer hackers everywhere, an organization must put in place strong security measures to survive.

The Health Insurance Portability and Accountability Act (HIPAA) protects the privacy and security of personal health records and has the potential to impact every business in the United States. HIPAA affects all companies that use electronic data interchange (EDI) to communicate personal health records. HIPAA requires health care organizations to develop, implement, and maintain appropriate security measures when sending electronic health information. Most important, these organizations must document and keep current records detailing how they are performing security measures for all transmissions of health information. On April 21, 2005, security rules for HIPAA became enforceable by law.

According to recent Gartner polls, less than 10 percent of all health care organizations have begun to implement the security policies and procedures required by HIPAA. The Health Information Management Society estimates that 70 percent of all health care providers failed to meet the April 2005 deadline for privacy rule compliance. Health care organizations need to start taking HIPAA regulations seriously since noncompliance can result in substantial fines and even imprisonment.[13]

Beyond the health care industry, all businesses must understand the importance of information security, even if it is not enforceable by law. *Information security* is a broad term encompassing the protection of information from accidental or intentional misuse by persons inside or outside an organization. Figure 4.16 displays the typical size of an organization's information security budget relative to the organization's overall IT budget from the CSI/FBI 2004 Computer Crime and Security Survey. Forty-six percent of respondents indicated that their organization spent between 1 and 5 percent of the total IT budget on security. Only 16 percent indicated that their organization spent less than 1 percent of the IT budget on security.

Figure 4.17 displays the spending per employee on computer security broken down by both public and private industries. The highest average computer security investment per employee was found in the transportation industry.[14]

FIGURE 4.16

Organization's Security Budget

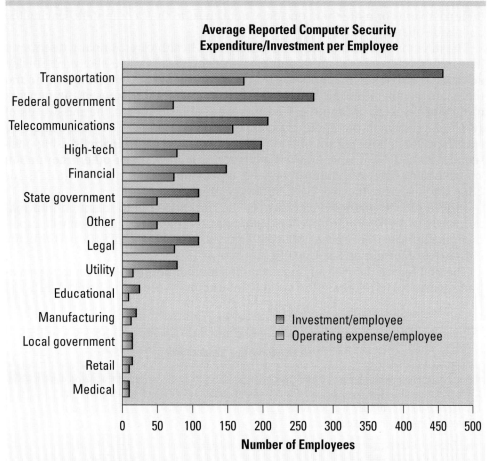

FIGURE 4.17

Security Spending per Employee

Average Reported Computer Security Expenditure/Investment per Employee

Legend:
- Investment/employee
- Operating expense/employee

X-axis: Number of Employees (0 to 500)

Transportation, Federal government, Telecommunications, High-tech, Financial, State government, Other, Legal, Utility, Educational, Manufacturing, Local government, Retail, Medical

Security is perhaps the most fundamental and critical of all the technologies/ disciplines an organization must have squarely in place to execute its business strategy. Without solid security processes and procedures, none of the other technologies can develop business advantages.

THE FIRST LINE OF DEFENSE—PEOPLE

With current advances in technologies and business strategies such as CRM, organizations are able to determine valuable information such as who are the top 20 percent of the customers that produce 80 percent of all revenues. Most organizations view this type of information as valuable intellectual capital, and they are implementing security measures to prevent the information from walking out the door or falling into the wrong hands. Enterprises can implement information security lines of defense through people first and through technology second.

Adding to the complexity of information security is the fact that organizations must enable employees, customers, and partners to access information electronically to be successful in this electronic world. Doing business electronically automatically creates tremendous information security risks for organizations. Surprisingly, the biggest issue surrounding information security is not a technical issue, but a people issue.

The CSI/FBI Computer Crime and Security Survey reported that 38 percent of respondents indicated security incidents originated within the enterprise. *Insiders* are legitimate users who purposely or accidentally misuse their access to the environment and cause some kind of business-affecting incident. Most information security breaches result from people misusing an organization's information either advertently or inadvertently. For example, many individuals freely give up their passwords or write them on sticky notes next to their computers, leaving the door wide open to intruders.[15]

The director of information security at a large health care company discovered how easy it was to create an information security breach when she hired outside auditors to test her company's security awareness. In one instance, auditors found that staff members testing a new system had accidentally exposed the network to outside hackers. In another, auditors were able to obtain the passwords of 16 employees when the auditors posed as support staff; hackers frequently use such "social engineering" to obtain passwords. **Social engineering** is using one's social skills to trick people into revealing access credentials or other information valuable to the attacker. Dumpster diving, or looking through people's trash, is another way social engineering hackers obtain information.[16]

Information security policies identify the rules required to maintain information security. An **information security plan** details how an organization will implement the information security policies. Figure 4.18 is an example of the University of Denver's Information Security Plan.

The first line of defense an organization should follow is to create an information security plan detailing the various information security policies. A detailed

FIGURE 4.18

Sample Information Security Plan

Interim Information Security Plan

This Information Security Plan ("Plan") describes the University of Denver's safeguards to protect information and data in compliance ("Protected Information") with the Financial Services Modernization Act of 1999, also known as the Gramm Leach Bliley Act, 15 U.S.C. Section 6801. These safeguards are provided to:

■ Ensure the security and confidentiality of Protected Information;

■ Protect against anticipated threats or hazards to the security or integrity of such information; and

■ Protect against unauthorized access to or use of Protected Information that could result in substantial harm or inconvenience to any customer.

This Information Security Plan also provides for mechanisms to:

■ Identify and assess the risks that may threaten Protected Information maintained by the University of Denver;

■ Develop written policies and procedures to manage and control these risks;

■ Implement and review the plan; and

■ Adjust the plan to reflect changes in technology, the sensitivity of covered data and information and internal or external threats to information security.

Identification and Assessment of Risks to Customer Information

The University of Denver recognizes that it has both internal and external risks. These risks include, but are not limited to:

■ Unauthorized access of Protected Information by someone other than the owner of the covered data and information

■ Compromised system security as a result of system access by an unauthorized person

■ Interception of data during transmission

■ Loss of data integrity

■ Physical loss of data in a disaster

■ Errors introduced into the system

FIGURE 4.18

(*continued*)

Interim Information Security Plan *(continued)*

- Corruption of data or systems

- Unauthorized access of covered data and information by employees

- Unauthorized requests for covered data and information

- Unauthorized access through hardcopy files or reports

- Unauthorized transfer of covered data and information through third parties

The University of Denver recognizes that this may not be a complete list of the risks associated with the protection of Protected Information. Since technology growth is not static, new risks are created regularly. Accordingly, the Information Technology Department and the Office of Student Affairs will actively participate with and seek advice from an advisory committee made up of university representatives for identification of new risks. The University of Denver believes current safeguards used by the Information Technology Department are reasonable and, in light of current risk assessments are sufficient to provide security and confidentiality to Protected Information maintained by the University.

Information Security Plan Coordinators

The University CIO and the Vice President for Student Affairs, in consultation with an advisory committee, have been appointed as the coordinators of this Plan. They are responsible for assessing the risks associated with unauthorized transfers of covered data and information and implementing procedures to minimize those risks to the University of Denver.

Design and Implementation of Safeguards Program

Employee Management and Training

During employee orientation, each new employee in departments that handle Protected Information will receive proper training on the importance of confidentiality of Protected Information.

Physical Security

The University of Denver has addressed the physical security of Protected Information by limiting access to only those employees who have a business reason to know such information.

Information Systems

The University of Denver has policies governing the use of electronic resources and firewall and wireless policies. The University of Denver will take reasonable and appropriate steps consistent with current technological developments to make sure that all Protected Information is secure and to safeguard the integrity of records in storage and transmission. The University of Denver will develop a plan to ensure that all electronic Protected Information is encrypted in transit.

Selection of Appropriate Service Providers

Due to the specialized expertise needed to design, implement, and service new technologies, vendors may be needed to provide resources that the University of Denver determines not to provide on its own. In the process of choosing a service provider that will maintain or regularly access Protected Information, the evaluation process shall include the ability of the service provider to safeguard Protected Information. Contracts with service providers may include the following provisions:

- A stipulation that the Protected Information will be held in strict confidence and accessed only for the explicit business purpose of the contract;

- An assurance from the contract partner that the partner will protect the Protected Information it receives.

Continuing Evaluation and Adjustment

This Information Security Plan will be subject to periodic review and adjustment, especially when due to the constantly changing technology and evolving risks. The Coordinators, in consultation with the Office of General Counsel, will review the standards set forth in this policy and recommend updates and revisions as necessary. It may be necessary to adjust the plan to reflect changes in technology, the sensitivity of student/customer data and internal or external threats to information security.

FIGURE 4.19

Creating an Information
Security Plan

Five Steps for Creating an Information Security Plan	
1. **Develop the information security policies**	Identify who is responsible and accountable for designing and implementing the organization's information security policies. Simple, yet highly effective types of information security policies include requiring users to log off of their systems before leaving for lunches or meetings, never sharing passwords with anyone, and changing personal passwords every 60 days. The chief security officer (CSO) will typically be responsible for designing these information security policies.
2. **Communicate the information security policies**	Train all employees on the policies and establish clear expectations for following the policies. For example, let all employees know that they will receive a formal reprimand for leaving a computer unsecured.
3. **Identify critical information assets and risks**	Require the use of user IDs, passwords, and antivirus software on all systems. Ensure any systems that contain links to external networks have the appropriate technical protections such as firewalls or intrusion detection software. A *firewall* is hardware and/or software that guards a private network by analyzing the information leaving and entering the network. *Intrusion detection software (IDS)* searches out patterns in information and network traffic to indicate attacks and quickly responds to prevent any harm.
4. **Test and reevaluate risks**	Continually perform security reviews, audits, background checks, and security assessments.
5. **Obtain stakeholder support**	Gain the approval and support of the information security polices from the board of directors and all stakeholders.

information security plan can alleviate people-based information security issues. Figure 4.19 displays the five steps for creating an information security plan.

Figure 4.20 provides the top 10 questions from Ernst & Young that managers should ask to ensure their information is secure.

Top 10 Questions Managers Should Ask Regarding Information Security
1. Does our Board of Directors recognize information security is a board level issue that cannot be left to the IT department alone?
2. Is there clear accountability for information security in our organization?
3. Do our Board members articulate an agreed-upon set of threats and critical assets? How often do we review and update these?
4. How much is spent on information security and what is it being spent on?
5. What is the impact on the organization of a serious security incident?
6. Does our organization view information security as an enabler? (For example, by implementing effective security, could we enable our organization to increase business over the Internet?)
7. What is the risk to our business of getting a reputation for low information security?
8. What steps have we taken to ensure that third parties will not compromise the security of our organization?
9. How do we obtain independent assurance that information security is managed effectively in our organization?
10. How do we measure the effectiveness of our information security activities?

THE SECOND LINE OF DEFENSE—TECHNOLOGY

Arkansas State University (ASU) recently completed a major network upgrade that brought gigabit-speed network capacity to every dorm room and office on its campus. The university was concerned that the new network would be a tempting playground for hackers. To reduce its fear, the university installed intrusion detection software (IDS) from Cisco Systems to stay on top of security and potential network abuses. Whenever the IDS spots a potential security threat, such as a virus or a hacker, it alerts the central management system. The system automatically pages the IT staff, who deal with the attack by shutting off access to the system, identifying the hacker's location, and calling campus security.[17]

Once an organization has protected its intellectual capital by arming its people with a detailed information security plan, it can begin to focus its efforts on deploying the right types of information security technologies such as the IDS installed at Arkansas State.

International Data Corp. estimated worldwide spending on IT security software, hardware, and services would top $35 billion in 2004. Organizations can deploy numerous technologies to prevent information security breaches. When determining which types of technologies to invest in, it helps to understand the three primary information security areas:

1. Authentication and authorization.
2. Prevention and resistance.
3. Detection and response.[18]

Authentication and Authorization

Authentication is a method for confirming users' identities. Once a system determines the authentication of a user, it can then determine the access privileges (or authorization) for that user. *Authorization* is the process of giving someone permission to do or have something. In multiple-user computer systems, user access or authorization determines such things as file access, hours of access, and amount of allocated storage space. Authentication and authorization techniques are broken down into three categories, and the most secure type involves a combination of all three:

1. Something the user knows such as a user ID and password.
2. Something the user has such as a smart card or token.
3. Something that is part of the user such as a fingerprint or voice signature.

Something the User Knows Such As a User ID and Password   The first type of authentication, using something the user knows, is the most common way to identify individual users and typically consists of a unique user ID and password. However, this is actually one of the most *ineffective* ways for determining authentication because passwords are not secure. All it typically takes to crack a password is enough time. More than 50 percent of help-desk calls are password related, which can cost an organization significant money, and passwords are vulnerable to being coaxed out of somebody by a social engineer.

Identity theft is the forging of someone's identity for the purpose of fraud. The fraud is often financial fraud, to apply for and use credit cards in the victim's name or to apply for a loan. Figure 4.21 displays several examples of identity theft.

Phishing is a common way to steal identities online. *Phishing* is a technique to gain personal information for the purpose of identity theft, usually by means of fraudulent e-mail. One way to accomplish phishing is to send out e-mail messages that look as though they came from legitimate businesses such as AOL, MSN, or Amazon. The messages appear to be genuine with official-looking formats and logos.

FIGURE 4.21

Examples of Identity Theft

Identity Theft Examples
An 82-year-old woman in Fort Worth, Texas, discovered that her identity had been stolen when the woman using her name was involved in a four-car collision. For 18 months, she kept getting notices of lawsuits and overdue medical bills that were really meant for someone else. It took seven years for her to get her financial good name restored after the identity thief charged over $100,000 on her 12 fraudulently acquired credit cards.
A 42-year-old retired Army captain in Rocky Hill, Connecticut, found that an identity thief had spent $260,000 buying goods and services that included two trucks, a Harley-Davidson motorcycle, and a time-share vacation home in South Carolina. The victim discovered his problem only when his retirement pay was garnished to pay the outstanding bills.
In New York, members of a pickpocket ring forged the driver's licenses of their victims within hours of snatching the women's purses. Stealing a purse typically results in around $200, if not less. But stealing the person's identity can net on average between $4,000 and $10,000.
A crime gang took out $8 million worth of second mortgages on victims' homes. It turned out the source of all the instances of identity theft came from a car dealership.
The largest identity-theft scam to date in U.S. history was broken up by police in 2002 when they discovered that three men had downloaded credit reports using stolen passwords and sold them to criminals on the street for $60 each. Many millions of dollars were stolen from people in all 50 states.

These e-mails typically ask for verification of important information like passwords and account numbers. The reason given is often that this personal information is required for accounting or auditing purposes. Since the e-mails look authentic, up to one in five recipients respond with the information, and subsequently becomes a victim of identity theft and other fraud. Figure 4.22 displays the amount of money lost to identity thefts based on stolen passwords, among other things.

Something the User Has Such As a Smart Card or Token   The second type of authentication, using something that the user has, offers a much more effective way to identify individuals than a user ID and password. Tokens and smart cards are two of the primary forms of this type of authentication. *Tokens* are small electronic devices that change user passwords automatically. The user enters his or her user ID and token-displayed password to gain access to the network. A *smart card* is a device that is around the same size as a credit card, containing embedded technologies that can store information and small amounts of software to perform some limited processing. Smart cards can act as identification instruments, a form of digital cash, or a data storage device with the ability to store an entire medical record.

Something That Is Part of the User Such As a Fingerprint or Voice Signature   The third kind of authentication, using something that is part of the user, is by far the best and most effective way to manage authentication. *Biometrics* (narrowly defined) is the identification of a user based on a physical characteristic, such as a fingerprint, iris, face, voice, or handwriting. Unfortunately, biometric authentication can be costly and intrusive. For example, iris scans are expensive and considered intrusive by most people. Fingerprint authentication is less intrusive and inexpensive but is also not 100 percent accurate.

Prevention and Resistance

Prevention and resistance technologies stop intruders from accessing intellectual capital. A division of Sony Inc., Sony Pictures Entertainment (SPE), defends itself from attacks by using an intrusion detection system to detect new attacks as they

Identity thefts are expected to increase anywhere from 900% to 2,250% over the next two years; dollar figures are billions.

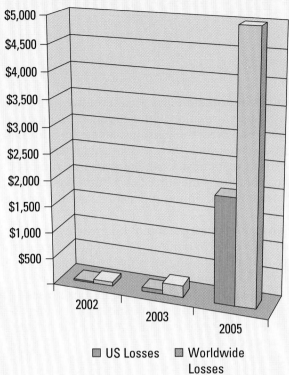

FIGURE 4.22

Identity Theft Losses by 2005 (billions of dollars)

occur. SPE develops and distributes a wide variety of products including movies, television, videos, and DVDs. A compromise to SPE security could result in costing the company valuable intellectual capital as well as millions of dollars and months of time. The company needed an advanced threat management solution that would take fewer resources to maintain and require limited resources to track and respond to suspicious network activity. The company installed an advanced intrusion detection system allowing it to monitor all of its network activity including any potential security breaches.[19]

The cost of downtime or network operation failures can be devastating to any business. For example, eBay experienced a 22-hour outage in June 2000 that caused the company's market cap to plunge an incredible $5.7 billion. Downtime costs for businesses can vary from $100 to $1 million per hour. An organization must prepare for and anticipate these types of outages resulting most commonly from hackers and viruses. Technologies available to help prevent and build resistance to attacks include content filtering, encryption, and firewalls. [20]

Content Filtering

Content filtering occurs when organizations use software that filters content to prevent the transmission of unauthorized information. Organizations can use content filtering technologies to filter e-mail and prevent e-mails containing sensitive information from transmitting, whether the transmission was malicious or accidental. It can also filter e-mails and prevent any suspicious files from transmitting such as potential virus-infected files. E-mail content filtering can also filter for spam, a form of unsolicited e-mail. Estimates predict organizational losses from spam will be about $198 billion by 2007 (see Figure 4.23).[21]

Encryption

Encryption scrambles information into an alternative form that requires a key or password to decrypt the information. If there is an information security breach and the information was encrypted, the person stealing the information will be unable to read it. Encryption can switch the order of characters, replace characters with other characters, insert or remove characters, or use a mathematical formula to convert the information into some sort of code. Companies that transmit sensitive customer information over the Internet, such as credit card numbers, frequently use encryption.

Some encryption technologies use multiple keys like public key encryption. ***Public key encryption (PKE)*** is an encryption system that uses two keys: a public key that everyone can have and a private key for only the recipient (see Figure 4.24). When implementing security using multiple keys, the organization provides the public key to all of its customers (end consumers and other businesses). The customers use the public key to encrypt their information and send it along the Internet. When it arrives at its destination, the organization would use the private key to unscramble the encrypted information.

Firewalls

One of the most common defenses for preventing a security breach is a firewall. A ***firewall*** is hardware and/or software that guards a private network by analyzing the information leaving and entering the network. Firewalls examine each message that wants entrance to the network. Unless the message has the correct markings, the firewall prevents it from entering the network. Firewalls can even detect computers communicating with the Internet without approval. As Figure 4.25 illustrates, organizations typically place a firewall between a server and the Internet.

FIGURE 4.24

Public Key Encryption (PKE)
System

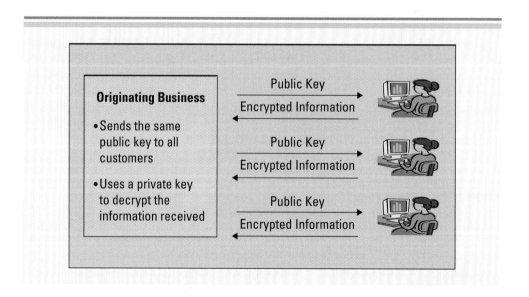

FIGURE 4.25

Sample Firewall Architecture Connecting Systems Located in Chicago, New York, and Boston

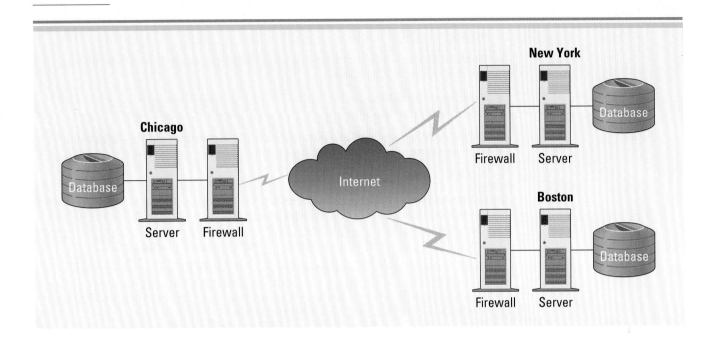

Detection and Response

The final area where organizations can allocate resources is in detection and response technologies. If prevention and resistance strategies fail and there is a security breach, an organization can use detection and response technologies to mitigate the damage. The most common type of defense within detection and response technologies is antivirus software.

A single worm can cause massive damage. In August 2003, the "Blaster worm" infected over 50,000 computers worldwide and was one of the worst outbreaks of the year. Jeffrey Lee Parson, 18, was arrested by U.S. cyber investigators for unleashing the damaging worm on the Internet. The worm replicated itself repeatedly, eating up computer capacity, but did not damage information or programs. The worm generated so much traffic that it brought entire networks down.

The FBI used the latest technologies and code analysis to find the source of the worm. Prosecutors said that Microsoft suffered financial losses that significantly exceeded $5,000, the statutory threshold in most hacker cases. Parson, charged with intentionally causing or attempting to cause damage to a computer, was sentenced to 18 months in prison, three years of supervised release, and 100 hours of community service. "What you've done is a terrible thing. Aside from injuring people and their computers, you shook the foundation of technology," U.S. District Judge Marsha Pechman told Parson.

"With this arrest, we want to deliver a message to cyber-hackers here and around the world," said U.S. Attorney John McKay in Seattle. "Let there be no mistake about it, cyber-hacking is a crime. We will investigate, arrest, and prosecute cyber-hackers."[22]

Typically, people equate viruses (the malicious software) with hackers (the people). While not all types of hackers create viruses, many do. Figure 4.26 provides an overview of the most common types of hackers and viruses.

Some of the most damaging forms of security threats to e-business sites include malicious code, hoaxes, spoofing, and sniffers (see Figure 4.27).

FIGURE 4.26

Hackers and Viruses

Hackers—people very knowledgeable about computers who use their knowledge to invade other people's computers.

- **White-hat hackers**—work at the request of the system owners to find system vulnerabilities and plug the holes.

- **Black-hat hackers**—break into other people's computer systems and may just look around or may steal and destroy information.

- **Hactivists**—have philosophical and political reasons for breaking into systems and will often deface the Web site as a protest.

- **Script kiddies** or **script bunnies**—find hacking code on the Internet and click-and-point their way into systems to cause damage or spread viruses.

- **Cracker**—a hacker with criminal intent.

- **Cyberterrorists**—seek to cause harm to people or to destroy critical systems or information and use the Internet as a weapon of mass destruction.

Viruses—software written with malicious intent to cause annoyance or damage.

- **Worm**—a type of virus that spreads itself, not only from file to file, but also from computer to computer. The primary difference between a virus and a worm is that a virus must attach to something, such as an executable file, in order to spread. Worms do not need to attach to anything to spread and can tunnel themselves into computers.

- **Denial-of-service attack (DoS)**—floods a Web site with so many requests for service that it slows down or crashes the site.

- **Distributed denial-of-service attack (DDoS)**—attacks from multiple computers that flood a Web site with so many requests for service that it slows down or crashes. A common type is the Ping of Death, in which thousands of computers try to access a Web site at the same time, overloading it and shutting it down.

- **Trojan-horse virus**—hides inside other software, usually as an attachment or a downloadable file.

- **Backdoor programs**—viruses that open a way into the network for future attacks.

- **Polymorphic viruses and worms**—change their form as they propagate.

Implementing information security lines of defense through people first and through technology second is the best way for an organization to protect its vital intellectual capital. The first line of defense is securing intellectual capital by creating an information security plan detailing the various information security policies. The second line of defense is investing in technology to help secure information through authentication and authorization, prevention and resistance, and detection and response.

FIGURE 4.27

Security Threats to
E-Business

Security Threats to E-Business

Elevation of privilege is a process by which a user misleads a system into granting unauthorized rights, usually for the purpose of compromising or destroying the system. For example, an attacker might log onto a network by using a guest account, and then exploit a weakness in the software that lets the attacker change the guest privileges to administrative privileges.

Hoaxes attack computer systems by transmitting a virus hoax, with a real virus attached. By masking the attack in a seemingly legitimate message, unsuspecting users more readily distribute the message and send the attack on to their co-workers and friends, infecting many users along the way.

Malicious code includes a variety of threats such as viruses, worms, and Trojan horses.

Spoofing is the forging of the return address on an e-mail so that the e-mail message appears to come from someone other than the actual sender. This is not a virus but rather a way by which virus authors conceal their identities as they send out viruses.

Spyware is software that comes hidden in free downloadable software and tracks online movements, mines the information stored on a computer, or uses a computer's CPU and storage for some task the user knows nothing about. According to the National Cyber Security Alliance, 91 percent of the study had spyware on their computers that can cause extremely slow performance, excessive pop-up ads, or hijacked home pages.

A *sniffer* is a program or device that can monitor data traveling over a network. Sniffers can show all the data being transmitted over a network, including passwords and sensitive information. Sniffers tend to be a favorite weapon in the hacker's arsenal.

Packet tampering consists of altering the contents of packets as they travel over the Internet or altering data on computer disks after penetrating a network. For example, an attacker might place a tap on a network line to intercept packets as they leave the computer. The attacker could eavesdrop or alter the information as it leaves the network.

OPENING CASE QUESTIONS

Sarbanes-Oxley: Where Information Technology, Finance, and Ethics Meet

6. What information security dilemmas are being solved by implementing Sarbanes-Oxley?

7. How can Sarbanes-Oxley help protect a company's information security?

8. What impact does implementing Sarbanes-Oxley have on information security in a small business?

9. What is the biggest information security roadblock for organizations attempting to achieve Sarbanes-Oxley compliance?

Acceptable use policy
(AUP) 109
Adware 114
Anti-spam policy 112
Authentication 121
Authorization 121
Backdoor program 126
Biometrics 122
Black-hat hacker 126
Clickstream 114
Confidentiality 105
Content filtering 123
Cookie 114
Copyright 104
Counterfeit software 104
Cracker 126
Cyberterrorist 126
Denial-of-service attack
(DoS) 126
Distributed denial-of-service
attack (DDoS) 126
Elevation of privilege 127
E-mail privacy policy 111
Encryption 124
ePolicies 108

Ethical computer use policy 108
Ethics 104
Fair use doctrine 104
Firewall 124
Hacker 126
Hactivist 126
Hardware key logger 114
Hoaxes 127
Identity theft 121
Information privacy policy 109
Information security 116
Information security plan 118
Information security
policies 118
Information technology
monitoring 114
Insider 117
Intellectual property 104
Internet use policy 111
Intrusion detection software
(IDS) 120
Key logger software (key
trapper) 114
Mail bomb 110
Malicious code 127

Nonrepudiation 109
Packet tampering 127
Phishing 121
Pirated software 104
Polymorphic virus
and worm 126
Privacy 105
Public key encryption (PKE) 124
Script kiddies or script
bunnies 126
Smart card 122
Sniffer 127
Social engineering 118
Spam 112
Spoofing 127
Spyware (sneakware
or stealthware) 114
Token 122
Trojan-horse virus 126
Virus 126
Web log 114
White-hat hacker 126
Worm 126

Banks Banking on Security

Bank of America, Commerce Bancorp, PNC Financial Services Group, and Wachovia were victims of a crime where a person tried to obtain customer data and sell it to law firms and debt-collection agencies. New Jersey police seized 13 computers from the alleged master-mind with 670,000 account numbers and balances. There is no indication the data were used for identity theft, but it highlights how increasingly difficult it is to protect information against such schemes as the market value of personal information grows. In the past, banks were wary of the cost or customer backlash from adopting network security technologies. Today, banks are beefing up network security as more customers begin to view security as a key fac-tor when choosing a bank.

Bank of America

Bank of America is moving toward a stronger authentication process for its 13 million online customers. Bank of America's new SiteKey service is designed to thwart scams in which cus-tomers think they are entering data on the bank's Web site, when they are actually on a thief's site built to steal data. This occurs when a worm tells a computer to reroute the bank's URL into a browser to another site that looks exactly like the banks.

SiteKey offers two-factor authentication. When enrolling in SiteKey, a customer picks an image from a library and writes a brief phrase. Each time the customer signs on, the image and phrase are displayed, indicating that the bank recognizes the computer the customer is using and letting the customer know that they are in fact at the bank's official Web site. The customer then enters a password and proceeds. When signing on from a different computer than usual the customer must answer one of three prearranged questions.

Wells Fargo & Company

"Out-of-wallet" questions contain information that is not found on a driver's license or ATM card. Wells Fargo is implementing a security strategy that operates based on "out-of-wallet" questions as a second factor for network password enrollment and maintenance. It is also of-fering network security hardware such as key fobs that change passwords every 60 seconds, and launching a two-factor authentication pilot in which small businesses making electronic funds transfers will need a key fob to complete transactions.

E-Trade Financial Corporation

E-Trade Financial Corporation provides customers with account balances exceeding $50,000 a free Digital Security ID for network authentication. The device displays a new six-digit code every 60 seconds, which the customer must use to log on. Accounts under $50,000 can pur-chase the Digital Security ID device for $25.

Barclay's Bank

Barclay's Bank instituted online-transfer delays of between several hours and one day. The delays, which apply the first time a transfer is attempted between two accounts, are intended to give the bank time to detect suspicious activity, such as a large number of transfers from multiple accounts into a single account. The online-transfer delay was adopted in response to a wave of phishing incidents in which thieves transferred funds from victims' bank accounts into accounts owned by "mules." Mules are people who open bank accounts based on an e-mail solicitations, usually under the guise of a business proposal. From the mule accounts, the thieves withdraw cash, open credit cards, or otherwise loot the account.

Barclay's also offers account monitoring of customer's actions to compare them with historical profile data to detect unusual behavior. For instance, the service would alert the bank to contact the customer if the customer normally logs on from England and suddenly logs on from New York and performs 20 transactions.[23]

Questions

1. What reason would a bank have for not wanting to adopt an online-transfer delay policy?
2. What are the two primary lines of security defense and why are they important to financial institutions?
3. Explain the differences between the types of security offered by the banks in the case. Which bank would you open an account with and why?
4. What additional types of security, not mentioned in the case above, would you recommend a bank implement?
5. Identify three policies a bank should implement to help it improve information security.
6. Describe monitoring policies along with the best way for a bank to implement monitoring technologies.

Hacker Hunters

Hacker hunters are the new breed of crime fighter. They employ the same methodology used to fight organized crime in the 1980s—informants and the cyberworld equivalent of wiretaps. Daniel Larking, a 20-year veteran who runs the FBI's Internet Crime Complaint Center, taps online service providers to help track down criminal hackers. Leads supplied by the FBI and eBay helped Romanian police round up 11 members of a gang that set up fake eBay accounts and auctioned off cell phones, laptops, and cameras they never intended to deliver.

On October 26, 2004, the FBI unleashed Operation Firewall, targeting the ShadowCrew, a gang whose members were schooled in identity theft, bank account pillage, and selling illegal goods on the Internet. ShadowCrew's 4,000 gang members lived in a dozen countries and across the United States. For months, agents had been watching their every move through a clandestine gateway into their Web site, shadowcrew.com. One member turned informant and called a group meeting, ensuring the members would be at home on their computers during a certain time, when the Secret Service issued orders to move in on the gang. The move was synchronized around the globe to prevent gang members from warning each other via instant messages. Twenty-eight gang members in eight states and six countries were arrested, most still at their computers. Authorities seized dozens of computers and found 1.7 million credit card numbers and more than 18 million e-mail accounts.

ShadowCrew's Operations

The alleged ringleaders of ShadowCrew included Andres Mantovani, 23, a part-time community college student in Arizona, and David Appleyard, 45, a former New Jersey mortgage broker. Mantovani and Appleyard allegedly were administrators in charge of running the Web site and recruiting members. The site created a marketplace for over 4,000 gang members who bought and sold hot information and merchandise. The Web site was open for business 24 hours a day, but since most of the members held jobs, the busiest time was from 10 p.m. to 2 a.m. on Sundays. Hundreds of gang members would meet online to trade credit card information, passports, and even equipment to make fake identity documents. Platinum credit cards cost more than gold ones and discounts were offered for package deals. One member known as "Scarface" sold 115,695 stolen credit card numbers in a single trade. Overall, the gang made more than $4 million in credit card purchases over two years. ShadowCrew was equivalent to an eBay for the underworld. The site even posted crime tips on how to use stolen credit cards and fake IDs at big retailers.

The gang stole credit card numbers and other valuable information through clever tricks. One of the favorites was sending millions of phishing e-mails—messages that appeared to be from legitimate companies such as Yahoo!— designed to steal passwords and credit card numbers. The gang also hacked into corporate databases to steal account data. According to sources familiar with the investigation, the gang cracked the networks of 12 unidentified companies that were not even aware their systems had been breached.

Police Operations

Brian Nagel, an assistant director at the Secret Service, coordinated the effort to track the ShadowCrew. Allies included Britain's national high-tech crimes unit, the Royal Canadian Mounted Police, and the Bulgarian Interior Ministry. Authorities turned one of the high-ranking members of the gang into a snitch and had the man help the Secret Service set up a new electronic doorway for ShadowCrew members to enter their Web site. The snitch spread the word that the new gateway was a more secure way to the Web site. It was the first-ever tap of a private computer network. "We became shadowcrew.com," Nagel said. Mantovani and Appleyard were slated for trail in late 2005. Authorities anticipated using case evidence to make additional arrests.[24]

Questions

1. What types of technology could big retailers use to prevent identity thieves from purchasing merchandise?

2. What can organizations do to protect themselves from hackers looking to steal account data?

3. Authorities frequently tap online service providers to track down hackers. Do you think it is ethical for authorities to tap an online service provider and read people's e-mail? Why or why not?

4. Do you think it was ethical for authorities to use one of the high-ranking officials to trap other gang members? Why or why not?

5. In a team, research the Internet and find the best ways to protect yourself from identity theft.

Thinking Like the Enemy

David and Barry Kaufman, the founders of the Intense School, recently added several security courses, including the five-day "Professional Hacking Boot Camp" and "Social Engineering in Two Days."

Information technology departments must know how to protect organizational information. Therefore, organizations must teach their IT personnel how to protect their systems, especially in light of the many new government regulations, such as the Health Insurance Portability and Accountability Act (HIPPA), that demand secure systems. The concept of sending IT professionals to a hacking school seems counterintuitive; it is somewhat similar to sending accountants to an Embezzling 101 course. The Intense School does not strive to breed the next generation of hackers, however, but to teach its students how to be "ethical" hackers: to use their skills to build better locks, and to understand the minds of those who would attempt to crack them.

The main philosophy of the security courses at the Intense School is simply "To know thy enemy." In fact, one of the teachers at the Intense School is none other than Kevin Mitnick, the famous hacker who was imprisoned from 1995 to 2000. Teaching security from the hacker's perspective, as Mitnick does, is more difficult than teaching hacking itself. A hacker just needs to know one way into a system, David Kaufman noted, but a security professional needs to know all of the system's vulnerabilities. The two courses analyze those vulnerabilities from different perspectives.

The hacking course, which costs $3,500, teaches ways to protect against the mischief typically associated with hackers: worming through computer systems through vulnerabilities that are susceptible to technical, or computer-based, attacks. Mitnick's $1,950 social engineering course, by contrast, teaches the more frightening art of worming through the vulnerabilities of the people using and maintaining systems—getting passwords and access through duplicity, not technology. People that take this class, or read Mitnick's book, *The Art of Deception*, never again think of passwords or the trash bin the same way.

So how does the Intense School teach hacking? With sessions on dumpster diving (the unsavory practice of looking for passwords and other bits of information on discarded papers), with field trips to case target systems, and with practice runs at the company's in-house "target range," a network of computers set up to thwart and educate students.

One feature of the Intense School that raises a few questions is that the school does not check on morals at the door: Anyone paying the tuition can attend the school. Given the potential danger that an unchecked graduate of a hacking school could represent, it is surprising that the FBI does not collect the names of the graduates. But perhaps it gets them anyhow—several governmental agencies have sent students to the school.[25]

Questions

1. How could an organization benefit from attending one of the courses offered at the Intense School?

2. What are the two primary lines of security defense and how can organizational employees use the information taught by the Intense School when drafting an information security plan?

3. Determine the differences between the two primary courses offered at the Intense School, "Professional Hacking Boot Camp" and "Social Engineering in Two Days." Which course is more important for organizational employees to attend?

4. If your employer sent you to take a course at the Intense School, which one would you choose and why?

5. What are the ethical dilemmas involved with having such a course offered by a private company?

1. Firewall decisions

You are the CEO of Inverness Investments, a medium-sized venture capital firm that specializes in investing in high-tech companies. The company receives over 30,000 e-mail messages per year. On average, there are two viruses and three successful hackings against the company each year, which result in losses to the company of about $250,000 per year. Currently, the company has antivirus software installed but does not have any firewalls.

Your CIO is suggesting implementing 10 firewalls for a total cost of $80,000. The estimated life of each firewall is about three years. The chances of hackers breaking into the system with the firewalls installed are about 3 percent. Annual maintenance costs on the firewalls is estimated around $15,000. Create an argument for or against supporting your CIO's recommendation to purchase the firewalls. Are there any considerations in addition to finances?

2. Preventing identity theft

The FBI states that identity theft is one of the fastest-growing crimes. If you are a victim of identity theft, your financial reputation can be ruined, making it impossible for you to cash a check or receive a bank loan. Learning how to avoid identity theft can be a valuable activity. Research the following Web sites and draft a document stating the best ways to prevent identity theft.

- The Federal Trade Commission Consumer Information on ID theft at www.consumer. gov/idtheft.
- The Office of the Comptroller of the Currency at www.occ.treas.gov/chcktfd.idassume.htm.
- The Office of the Inspector General at www.ssa.gov/oig/when.htm.
- U.S. Department of Justice at www.usdoj.gov/criminal/fraud/idtheft.html.

3. Discussing the three areas of information security

Great Granola Inc. is a small business operating out of northern California. The company specializes in selling homemade granola, and its primary sales vehicle is through its Web site. The company is growing exponentially and expects its revenues to triple this year to $12 million. The company also expects to hire 60 additional employees to support its growing number of customers. Joan Martin, the CEO, is aware that if her competitors discover the recipe for her granola, or who her primary customers are, it could easily ruin her business. Joan has hired you to draft a document discussing the different areas of information security, along with your recommendations for providing a secure e-business environment.

4. Information privacy

A study by the Annenberg Public Policy Center at the University of Pennsylvania shows that 95 percent of people who use the Internet at home think they should have a legal right to know everything about the information that Web sites collect from them. Research also shows that 57 percent of home Internet users incorrectly believe that when a Web site has an information privacy policy it will not share personal information with other Web sites or companies. In fact, the research found that after showing the users how companies track, extract, and share Web site information to make money, 85 percent found the methods unacceptable, even for a highly valued site. Write a short paper arguing for or against an organization's right to use and distribute personal information gathered from its Web site.

5. Spying on e-mail

Technology advances now allow individuals to monitor computers that they do not even have physical access. New types of software can capture an individual's incoming and outgoing e-mail and then immediately forward that e-mail to another person. For example, if you are at work and your child is home from school and she receives an e-mail from John at 3:00 pm, at 3:01 pm you will receive a copy of that e-mail sent to your e-mail address. A few minutes later, if she replies to John's e-mail, within seconds you will again receive a copy of what she sent to John. Describe two scenarios (other than the above) for the use of this type of software: (1) where the use would be ethical, (2) where the use would be unethical.

6. Stealing software

The software industry fights against pirated software on a daily basis. The major centers of software piracy are in places like Russia and China where salaries and disposable income are comparatively low. People in developing and economically depressed countries will fall behind the industrialized world technologically if they cannot afford access to new generations of software. Considering this, is it reasonable to blame someone for using pirated software when it could potentially cost him or her two months' salary to purchase a legal copy? Create an argument for or against the following statement: "Individuals who are economically less fortunate should be allowed access to software free of charge in order to ensure that they are provided with an equal technological advantage."

5

CHAPTER

IT Architectures

CHAPTER OUTLINE

SECTION 5.1
Hardware and Software Basics

- Hardware Basics
- Computer Categories
- Software Basics

SECTION 5.2
Managing Enterprise Architectures

- Enterprise Architectures
- Information Architecture
- Infrastructure Architecture
- Application Architecture

Electronic Breaking Points

What happens when someone accidentally spills a cup of hot coffee on a laptop, puts a USB memory key in a washing machine, or drops an iPod in the sand? How much abuse can electronic products take and keep on working? *PC World* tested several products to determine their breaking points.[1]

Laptop

A Gateway laptop was placed in a shoulder bag and smashed into several doors and walls. It was also dropped off a six-foot-high bookcase to simulate a drop from an airplane's overhead bin. Finally, it was knocked off a desk onto a carpeted floor without the bag. After all the abuse, the Gateway consistently rebooted and recognized the wireless network; however, the battery did become slightly dislodged and the optical drive opened.

Severe physical damage was caused when the laptop was dropped onto a hardwood floor. The laptop's screen cracked, and the black plastic molding above the keyboard cracked. Plastic splinters littered the floor, and the optical drive refused to open.

Spilling coffee in a travel-size mug onto the keyboard caused a slight sizzle, after which the Gateway's blue light winked out. The machine was quickly turned off, the battery removed, the liquid drained, the keys mopped, and the unit set aside. Unfortunately, the laptop never recovered.

Smart Phone

The PalmOne Treo 600 smart phone was stepped on, buried in the sand, bounced around in a car, and dropped off a desk onto carpeted and hardwood floors. Even though the Treo 600 was not protected by a shock-absorbent case or plastic screen cover, there were no signs of failure. Repeatedly knocking it off the desk onto a carpeted floor also left it undamaged, although the unit did turn off on several occasions.

The desk-to-hardwood-floor test produced scratches but nothing else. If dropped when in phone mode, the Treo automatically turned off. If an application was running—the calculator, for example—the device stayed on and the data remained on the screen, though a mysterious extra numeral nine appeared every time it was dropped.

MP3 Player

A 6 GB silver iPod Mini went for a bouncy car ride, was dropped on wet grass and dry pavement, was knocked off a desk onto carpeted and hardwood floors, and was finally dropped in dry sand. Bouncing inside the car caused a couple of skips. Drops on soft wet grass and carpet had no ill effect. Dropping it from the car seat to the curb and off a desk onto a hardwood floor produced a few nicks and caused songs to skip and the device to shut down repeatedly. Still, all the unit's features continued to work after the abuse, and songs played.

However, the Mini did not like the beach. Without the benefit of a protective case or plastic display covering on the unit, sand became wedged under the scroll wheel, affecting all controls. Feature settings could be seen and highlighted, but the crunching sand prevented the Mini from launching them. The unit turned on but could not turn off until the iPod's automatic shutdown feature took over.

Memory Stick

Lexar claims that its JumpDrive Sport 256 MB USB 2.0 Flash Drive is "built for the rugged life." A rubber cap protects the device, absorbing shock from any drops. For these experiments, the device was used without its cap. It was dropped, stepped on, buried in the sand, and knocked off a desk onto a hardwood floor. It also took a spin through the washing machine and dryer and was even run over by a car.

There is truth in advertising. Neither water, heat, sand, nor car could keep the memory stick from its appointed storage rounds. The car did squeeze the metal USB connector tip a tad tighter, but the device was still able to make contact with the USB port, and it worked perfectly.

Memory Card

The SanDisk SD 64 MB memory card is easy to misplace, but not easy to break. It was swatted off a desk onto a hardwood floor, dropped, stepped on, and buried in the sand. It also underwent a two-rinse cycle in the wash in a jeans pocket and then tumbled in the dryer for an hour on a high-heat setting. The SanDisk memory card aced every torture test.

For tips on how to protect electronic products, review Figure 5.1.

FIGURE 5.1

How to Protect Electronic Products

Protecting Electronic Products

Bag it. Place your products in a cushioned case or shock-absorbent travel bag. The secret is to make sure it has plenty of padding.

Get protection. Almost every technology manufacturer offers some type of warranty and equipment-replacement program. For example, Sprint provides the PCS Total Equipment Protection service, which costs $5 per month and covers loss, theft, and accidental damage to a cell phone.

Clean up spills. Try these tips to bring a laptop and data back from the dead after a spill.

1. **Disconnect the battery.** The faster the battery is disconnected the less likely components will burn out.

2. **Empty it.** Turn over the device and pour out as much liquid as possible.

3. **Open it up.** Remove the optical drive and keyboard. This can be tricky, so check the user manual for instructions. Once open, use a towel to soak up as much liquid as possible. According to Herman De Hoop, Hewlett-Packard's technical marketing manager, you can even use a hair dryer set on cool (not hot) to dry the liquid.

4. **Leave it alone.** Let the device sit for at least 12 to 24 hours. Robert Enochs, IBM's worldwide product manager for the ThinkPad Series, warns that you should not turn the device on until all the liquid is gone and it is completely dry.

5. **Plug and pray.** Reassemble the device, and if it powers up, copy off important data, and then call the manufacturer. Even if the unit works, a professional cleaning is recommended.

6. **Enter a recovery program.** For an average price of $900, enlist the help of data recovery services like DriveSavers to rescue data from drowned hard disks.

INTRODUCTION

Managers need to determine what types of hardware and software will satisfy their current and future business needs, the right time to buy the equipment, and how to protect their IT investments. This does not imply that managers need to be experts in all areas of technology; however, building a basic understanding of hardware and software can help them make the right IT investment choices.

Information technology (IT) is any computer-based tool that people use to work with information and support the information and information-processing needs of an organization. Information technology can be composed of the Internet, a personal computer, a cell phone that can access the Web, a personal digital assistant, or presentation software. All of these technologies help to perform specific information processing tasks. There are two basic categories of information technology: hardware and software. *Hardware* consists of the physical devices associated with a computer system. *Software* is the set of instructions that the hardware executes to carry out specific tasks. Software, such as Microsoft Excel, and various hardware devices, such as a keyboard and a monitor, interact to create a spreadsheet or a graph. This chapter covers the basics of computer hardware and software including terminology, characteristics, and the associated managerial responsibilities for building a solid enterprise architecture.

section 5.1 HARDWARE AND SOFTWARE BASICS

LEARNING OUTCOMES

5.1. Describe the six major categories of hardware and provide an example of each.

5.2. Identify the different computer categories and explain their potential business uses.

5.3. Explain the difference between primary and secondary storage.

5.4. List the common input, output, storage, and communication devices.

5.5. Describe the eight categories of computers by size.

5.6. Define the relationship between operating system software and utility software.

HARDWARE BASICS

In many industries, exploiting computer hardware is key to gaining a competitive advantage. Frito-Lay gained a competitive advantage by using handheld devices to track the strategic placement and sale of items in convenience stores. Sales representatives could track sale price, competitor information, the number of items sold, and item location in the store all from their handheld device.[2]

A *computer* is an electronic device operating under the control of instructions stored in its own memory that can accept, manipulate, and store data. A computer system consists of six hardware components (see Figure 5.2). Figure 5.3 displays how these components work together to form a computer system.

Central Processing Unit

The dominant manufacturers of CPUs today include Intel (with its Celeron and Pentium lines for personal computers) and Advanced Micro Devices (AMD) (with its Athlon series). AMD was initially dismissed as a company that simply cloned current chips, producing processors that mimic the features and capabilities of those from industry leader Intel. However, over the past few years, AMD has begun introducing innovative CPUs that are forcing Intel into the unfamiliar position of reacting to competition. AMD led the way in transforming the processor market by

FIGURE 5.2

Hardware Components of a
Computer System

Six Hardware Components	
Central processing unit (CPU)	The actual hardware that interprets and executes the program (software) instructions and coordinates how all the other hardware devices work together.
Primary storage	The computer's main memory, which consists of the random access memory (RAM), cache memory, and the read-only memory (ROM) that is directly accessible to the central processing unit (CPU).
Secondary storage	Equipment designed to store large volumes of data for long-term storage (e.g., diskette, hard drive, memory card, CD).
Input devices	Equipment used to capture information and commands (e.g., keyboard, scanner).
Output devices	Equipment used to see, hear, or otherwise accept the results of information processing requests (e.g., monitor, printer).
Communication devices	Equipment used to send information and receive it from one location to another (e.g., modem).

FIGURE 5.3

How the Hardware Components Work Together

creating chips that handle 64 bits of data at a time, up from 32 bits. It also broke new territory when it became the first provider of dual-core processors for the server market. Hector Ruiz, chairman and CEO of AMD, stated, "In our position there is only one thing we can do: Stay close to our customers and end users, understand what they need and want, and then simply out-innovate the competition. Innovation is at the center of our ability to succeed. We cannot win by just copying the competition."[3]

The ***central processing unit (CPU)*** (or ***microprocessor***) is the actual hardware that interprets and executes the program (software) instructions and coordinates how all the other hardware devices work together. The CPU is built on a small flake of silicon and can contain the equivalent of several million transistors. CPUs are unquestionably one of the 20th century's greatest technological advances.

A CPU contains two primary parts: control unit and arithmetic/logic unit. The ***control unit*** interprets software instructions and literally tells the other hardware devices what to do, based on the software instructions. The ***arithmetic-logic unit (ALU)*** performs all arithmetic operations (for example, addition and subtraction) and all logic operations (such as sorting and comparing numbers). The control unit and ALU perform different functions. The control unit obtains instructions from the software. It then interprets the instructions, decides which tasks other devices perform, and finally tells each device to perform the task. The ALU responds to the control unit and does whatever it dictates, performing either arithmetic or logic operations.

The number of CPU cycles per second determines how fast a CPU carries out the software instructions; more cycles per second means faster processing, and faster CPUs cost more than their slower counterparts. CPU speed is usually quoted in megahertz and gigahertz. ***Megahertz (MHz)*** is the number of millions of CPU cycles per second. ***Gigahertz (GHz)*** is the number of billions of CPU cycles per second. Figure 5.4 displays the factors that determine CPU speed.

Advances in CPU Design Chip makers are pressing more functionality into CPU technology. Most CPUs are ***complex instruction set computer (CISC) chips,*** which is a type of CPU that can recognize as many as 100 or more instructions,

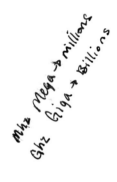

FIGURE 5.4

Factors That Determine CPU Speed

CPU Speed Factors
Clock speed—the speed of the internal clock of a CPU that sets the pace at which operations proceed within the computer's internal processing circuitry. Clock speed is measured in megahertz (MHz) and gigahertz (GHz). Faster clock speeds bring noticeable gains in microprocessor-intensive tasks, such as recalculating a spreadsheet.
Word length—number of bits (0s and 1s) that can be processed by the CPU at any one time. Computers work in terms of bits and bytes using electrical pulses that have two states: on and off. A ***binary digit (bit)*** is the smallest unit of information that a computer can process. A bit can be either a 1 (on) or a 0 (off). A group of eight bits represents one natural language character and is called a ***byte***.
Bus width—the size of the internal electrical pathway along which signals are sent from one part of the computer to another. A wider bus can move more data, hence faster processing.
Chip line width—the distance between transistors on a chip. The shorter the chip line width the faster the chip since more transistors can be placed on a chip and the data and instructions travel short distances during processing.

FIGURE 5.5

Chip Advancements by
Manufacturer

Chip Advancements
AMD: Security, virtualization, and advanced power-management technology.
IBM: Cryptography for additional security and floating point capability for faster graphics processing.
Intel: Cryptography for additional security, hardware-assisted virtualization, and Active Management Technology for asset tracking, patching, and software updates.
Sun Microsystems: Cryptography for additional security, increased speed for data transmission and receipt, and the ability to run 32 computations simultaneously.

enough to carry out most computations directly. ***Reduced instruction set computer (RISC) chips*** limit the number of instructions the CPU can execute to increase processing speed. The idea of RISC is to reduce the instruction set to the bare minimum, emphasizing the instructions used most of the time and optimizing them for the fastest possible execution. An RISC processor runs faster than a CISC processor.

In the next few years, better performance, systems management capabilities, virtualization, security, and features to help track computer assets will be built directly into the CPU (see Figure 5.5). ***Virtualization*** is a protected memory space created by the CPU allowing the computer to create virtual machines. Each virtual machine can run its own programs isolated from other machines.

Primary Storage

Primary storage is the computer's main memory, which consists of the random access memory (RAM), cache memory, and the read-only memory (ROM) that is directly accessible to the CPU.

Random Access Memory
Random access memory (RAM) is the computer's primary working memory, in which program instructions and data are stored so that they can be accessed directly by the CPU via the processor's high-speed external data bus.

RAM is often called read/write memory. In RAM, the CPU can write and read data. Most programs set aside a portion of RAM as a temporary workspace for data so that one can modify (rewrite) as needed until the data is ready for printing or storage on secondary storage media, such as a hard drive or memory key. RAM does not retain its contents when the power to the computer is switched off, hence individuals should save their work frequently. When the computer is turned off, everything in RAM is wiped clean. ***Volatility*** refers to RAM's complete loss of stored information if power is interrupted. RAM is volatile and its contents are lost when the computer's electric supply fails.

Cache Memory ***Cache memory*** is a small unit of ultra-fast memory that is used to store recently accessed or frequently accessed data so that the CPU does not have to retrieve this data from slower memory circuits such as RAM. Cache memory that is built directly into the CPU's circuits is called primary cache. Cache memory contained on an external circuit is called secondary cache.

*Flash mem → Compact Portable Rom
Memory card → Stores media files, removable
Cell phones
→ nonvolatile mem
memory sticks portable devices.

Read-Only Memory (ROM)

Read-only memory (ROM) is the portion of a computer's primary storage that does not lose its contents when one switches off the power. ROM contains essential system programs that neither the user nor the computer can erase. Since the computer's internal memory is blank during start-up, the computer cannot perform any functions unless given start-up instructions. These instructions are stored in ROM.

Flash memory is a special type of rewriteable read-only memory (ROM) that is compact and portable. **Memory cards** contain high-capacity storage that holds data such as captured images, music, or text files. Memory cards are removable; when one is full the user can insert an additional card. Subsequently, the data can be downloaded from the card to a computer. The card can then be erased and used again. Memory cards are typically used in digital devices such as cameras, cellular phones, and personal digital assistants (PDA). **Memory sticks** provide nonvolatile memory for a range of portable devices including computers, digital cameras, MP3 players, and PDAs.

Secondary Storage

Storage is a hot area in the business arena as organizations struggle to make sense of exploding volumes of data. Storage sales grew more than 16 percent to nearly $8 billion in 2004, according to IDC market research. **Secondary storage** consists of equipment designed to store large volumes of data for long-term storage. Secondary storage devices are nonvolatile and do not lose their contents when the computer is turned off. Some storage devices, such as a hard disk, offer easy update capabilities and a large storage capacity. Others, such as CD-ROMs, offer limited update capabilities but possess large storage capacities.

Storage capacity is expressed in bytes, with megabytes being the most common. A **megabyte (MB or M or Meg)** is roughly 1 million bytes. Therefore, a computer with 256 MB of RAM translates into the RAM being able to hold roughly 256 million characters of data and software instructions. A **gigabyte (GB)** is roughly 1 billion bytes. A **terabyte (TB)** is roughly 1 trillion bytes (refer to Figure 5.6).

Most standard desktops have a hard drive with storage capacity in excess of 80 GB. Hard drives for large organizational computer systems can hold in excess of 100 TB of information. For example, a typical double-spaced page of pure text is roughly 2,000 characters. Therefore, a 40 GB (40 gigabyte or 40 billion characters) hard drive can hold approximately 20 million pages of text.

FIGURE 5.6

Binary Terms

Term	Size
Kilobyte (KB)	1,024 Bytes
Megabyte (MB)	1,024 KB 1,048,576 Bytes
Gigabyte (GB)	1,024 MB (10^9 bytes)
Terabyte (TB)	1,024 GB (10^{12} bytes) 1 TB = Printing of 1 TB would require 50,000 trees to be made into paper and printed
Petabyte (PB)	1,024 TB (10^{15} bytes) 200 PB = All production of digital magnetic tape in 1995
Exabyte (EB)	1,024 PB (10^{18} bytes) 2 EB = total volume of information generated worldwide annually 5 EB = all words ever spoken by human beings

Common storage devices include:

- Magnetic medium
- Optical medium

Magnetic medium *Magnetic medium* is a secondary storage medium that uses magnetic techniques to store and retrieve data on disks or tapes coated with magnetically sensitive materials. Like iron filings on a sheet of waxed paper, these materials are reoriented when a magnetic field passes over them. During write operations, the read/write heads emit a magnetic field that orients the magnetic materials on the disk or tape to represent encoded data. During read operations, the read/write heads sense the encoded data on the medium.

One of the first forms of magnetic medium developed was magnetic tape. *Magnetic tape* is an older secondary storage medium that uses a strip of thin plastic coated with a magnetically sensitive recording medium. The most popular type of magnetic medium is a hard drive. A *hard drive* is a secondary storage medium that uses several rigid disks coated with a magnetically sensitive material and housed together with the recording heads in a hermetically sealed mechanism. Hard drive performance is measured in terms of access time, seek time, rotational speed, and data transfer rate.

Optical Medium Optical medium is a secondary storage medium for computers on which information is stored at extremely high density in the form of tiny pits. The presence or absence of pits is read by a tightly focused laser beam. Optical medium types include:

- **Compact disk-read-only memory (CD-ROM) drive**—an optical drive designed to read the data encoded on CD-ROMs and to transfer this data to a computer.
- **Compact disk-read-write (CD-RW) drive**—an optical drive that enables users to erase existing data and to write new data repeatedly to a CD-RW.
- **Digital video disk (DVD)**—a CD-ROM format capable of storing up to a maximum of 17 GB of data; enough for a full-length feature movie.
- **DVD-ROM drive**—a read-only drive designed to read the data encoded on a DVD and transfer the data to a computer.
- **Digital video disk-read/write (DVD-RW)**—a standard for DVD discs and player/recorder mechanisms that enables users to record in the DVD format.

CD-ROMs and DVDs offer an increasingly economical medium for storing data and programs. The overall trend in secondary storage is toward more direct-access methods, higher capacity with lower costs, and increased portability.

Input Devices

An *input device* is equipment used to capture information and commands. A keyboard is used to type in information, and a mouse is used to point and click on buttons and icons. Numerous input devices are available in many different environments, some of which have applications that are more suitable in a personal setting than a business setting. A keyboard, mouse, and scanner are the most common forms of input devices (see Figures 5.7 and 5.8).

FIGURE 5.7

Manual Input Devices

Manual Input Devices
Joystick—widely used as an alternative to the keyboard for computer games and some professional applications, such as computer-aided design.
Keyboard—provides a set of alphabetic, numeric, punctuation, symbol, and control keys.
Microphone—captures sounds such as a voice for voice-recognition software.
Mouse—one or more control buttons housed in a palm-sized case and designed so that one can move it about on the table next to the keyboard.
Pointing stick—causes the pointer to move on the screen by applying directional pressure (popular on notebooks and PDAs).
Touch screen—allows the use of a finger to point at and touch a particular function to perform.
Touchpad—a form of a stationary mouse on which the movement of a finger causes the pointer on the screen to move.

FIGURE 5.8

Automated Input Devices

Automated Input Devices
Bar code scanner—captures information that exists in the form of vertical bars whose width and distance apart determine a number.
Digital camera—captures still images or video as a series of 1s and 0s.
Magnetic ink character reader—reads magnetic ink numbers printed on checks that identify the bank, checking account, and check number.
Optical-character recognition—converts text into digital format for computer input.
Optical-mark recognition (OMR)—detects the presence or absence of a mark in a predetermined place (popular for multiple-choice exams).
Point-of-sale (POS)—captures information at the point of a transaction, typically in a retail environment.
Radio frequency identification (RFID)—uses active or passive tags in the form of chips or smart labels that can store unique identifiers and relay this information to electronic readers.

New forms of input devices allow people to exercise and play video games at the same time. The Kilowatt Sport from Powergrid Fitness lets people combine strength training with their favorite video games. Players can choose any PlayStation or Xbox game that uses a joystick to run the elliptical trainer. After loading the game, participants stand on a platform while pushing and pulling a resistance rod in all directions to control what happens in the game. The varied movement targets muscle groups on the chest, arms, shoulders, abdomen, and back. The machine's display shows information such as pounds lifted and current resistance level, and players can use one-touch adjustment to vary the degree of difficulty.[4]

Another new input device is a stationary bicycle. A computer design team of graduate and undergraduate students at MIT built the Cyclescore, an integrated video game and bicycle. The MIT students tested current games on the market but found users would stop pedaling to concentrate on the game. To engage users, the team is designing games that interact with the experience of exercise itself, for example, monitoring heart rate and adjusting the difficulty of the game according to the user's bicycling capabilities. In one game, the player must pedal to make a hot-air balloon float over mountains, while collecting coins and shooting at random targets.[5]

FIGURE 5.9

Output Devices

Output Devices
Cathode-ray tube (CRT)—a vacuum tube that uses an electron gun (cathode) to emit a beam of electrons that illuminates phosphors on a screen as the beam sweeps across the screen repeatedly. A monitor is often called a CRT.
Liquid crystal display (LCDs)—a low-powered display technology used in laptop computers where rod-shaped crystal molecules change their orientation when an electrical current flows through them.
Laser printer—a printer that forms images using an electrostatic process, the same way a photocopier works.
Ink-jet printer—a printer that makes images by forcing ink droplets through nozzles.
Plotter—a printer that uses computer-directed pens for creating high-quality images, blueprints, schematics, etc.

Output Devices

An *output device* is equipment used to see, hear, or otherwise accept the results of information processing requests. Among output devices, printers and monitors are the most common; however, speakers and plotters (special printers that draw output on a page) are widely used (see Figure 5.9). In addition, output devices are responsible for converting computer-stored information into a form that can be understood.

A new output device based on sensor technology aims to translate American Sign Language (ASL) into speech, enabling the millions of people who use ASL to better communicate with those who do not know the rapid gesturing system. The AcceleGlove is a glove lined on the inside with sensors embedded in rings. The sensors, called accelerometers, measure acceleration and can categorize and translate finger and hand movements. Additional, interconnected attachments for the elbow and shoulder capture ASL signs that are made with full arm motion. When users wear the glove while signing ASL, algorithms in the glove's software translate the hand gestures into words. The translations can be relayed through speech synthesizers or read on a PDA-size computer screen. Inventor Jose L. Hernandez-Rebollar started with a single glove that could translate only the ASL alphabet. Now, the device employs two gloves that contain a 1,000-word vocabulary.[6]

Other new output devices are being developed every day. Needapresent.com, a British company, has developed a vibrating USB massage ball, which plugs into a computer's USB port to generate a warm massage for sore body parts during those long evenings spent coding software or writing papers. Needapresent.com also makes a coffee cup warmer that plugs into the USB port.[7]

FIGURE 5.10

Comparing Modems

Carrier Technology	Description	Speed	Comments
Dial-up Access	On demand access using a modem and regular telephone line (POT).	2400 bps to 56 Kbps	■ Cheap but slow.
Cable	Special cable modem and cable line required.	512 Kbps to 20 Mbps	■ Must have existing cable access in area. ■ Bandwidth is shared.
DSL Digital Subscriber Line	This technology uses the unused digital portion of a regular copper telephone line to transmit and receive information. A special modem and adapter card are required.	128 Kbps to 8 Mbps	■ Doesn't interfere with normal telephone use. ■ Bandwidth is dedicated. ■ Must be within 5 km (3.1 miles) of telephone company switch.
Wireless (LMCS)	Access is gained by connection to a high speed cellular like local multipoint communications system (LMCS) network via wireless transmitter/receiver.	30 Mbps or more	■ Can be used for high speed data, broadcast TV and wireless telephone service.
Satellite	Newer versions have two-way satellite access, removing need for phone line.	6 Mbps or more	■ Bandwidth is not shared. ■ Some connections require an existing Internet service account. ■ Setup fees can range from $500–$1000.

Communication Devices

A *communication device* is equipment used to send information and receive it from one location to another. A telephone modem connects a computer to a phone line in order to access another computer. The computer works in terms of digital signals, while a standard telephone line works with analog signals. Each digital signal represents a bit (either 0 or 1). The modem must convert the digital signals of a computer into analog signals so they can be sent across the telephone line. At the other end, another modem translates the analog signals into digital signals, which can then be used by the other computer. Figure 5.10 displays the different types of modems.

COMPUTER CATEGORIES

Supercomputers today can hit processing capabilities of well over 200 teraflops—the equivalent of everyone on earth performing 35,000 calculations per second

FIGURE 5.11

Supercomputer

(see Figure 5.11). For the past 20 years, federally funded supercomputing research has given birth to some of the computer industry's most significant technology breakthroughs including:

- Clustering, which allows companies to chain together thousands of PCs to build mass-market systems.
- Parallel processing, which provides the ability to run two or more tasks simultaneously and is viewed as the chip industry's future.
- Mosaic browser, which morphed into Netscape and made the Web a household name.

Federally funded supercomputers have also advanced some of the country's most dynamic industries, including advanced manufacturing, gene research in the life sciences, and real-time financial-market modeling.[8]

Computers come in different shapes, sizes, and colors. Some are small enough to carry around, while others are the size of a telephone booth. Size does not always correlate to power, speed, and price (see Figure 5.12).

MIT's Media Lab is developing a laptop that it will sell for $100 each to government agencies around the world for distribution to millions of underprivileged schoolchildren. Using a simplified sales model and reengineering the device helped MIT reach the $100 price point. Almost half the price of a current laptop comprises marketing, sales, distribution, and profit. Of the remaining costs, the display panel and backlight account for roughly half while the rest covers the operating system. The low-cost laptop will use a display system that costs less than $25, a 500 MHz processor from AMD, a wireless LAN connection, 1 GB of storage, and the Linux operating system. The machine will automatically connect with others. China and Brazil have already ordered 3 million and 1 million laptops, respectively. MIT's goal is to produce around 150 million laptops per year.[9]

SOFTWARE BASICS

Hardware is only as good as the software that runs it. Over the years, the cost of hardware has decreased while the complexity and cost of software have increased. Some large software applications, such as customer relationship management systems, contain millions of lines of code, take years to develop, and cost millions of dollars. The two main types of software are system software and application software.

System Software

System software controls how the various technology tools work together along with the application software. System software includes both operating system software and utility software.

FIGURE 5.12

Computer Categories

Computer Category	Description	Size
Personal digital assistant (PDA)	A small handheld computer that performs simple tasks such as taking notes, scheduling appointments, and maintaining an address book and a calendar. The PDA screen is touch-sensitive, allowing a user to write directly on the screen, capturing what is written.	Fits in a person's hand
Laptop	A fully functional computer designed to be carried around and run on battery power. Laptops come equipped with all of the technology that a personal desktop computer has, yet weigh as little as two pounds.	Similar to a textbook
Tablet	A pen-based computer that provides the screen capabilities of a PDA with the functional capabilities of a laptop or desktop computer. Similar to PDAs, tablet PCs use a writing pen or stylus to write notes on the screen and touch the screen to perform functions such as clicking on a link while visiting a Web site.	Similar to a textbook
Desktop	Available with a horizontal system box (the box is where the CPU, RAM, and storage devices are held) with a monitor on top, or a vertical system box (called a tower) usually placed on the floor within a work area.	Fits on a desk
Workstation	Similar to a desktop but has more powerful mathematical and graphics processing capabilities and can perform more complicated tasks in less time. Typically used for software development, Web development, engineering, and e-business tools.	Fits on a desk
Minicomputer (midrange computer)	Designed to meet the computing needs of several people simultaneously in a small to medium-size business environment. A common type of minicomputer is a server and is used for managing internal company networks and Web sites. Minicomputers are more powerful than desktop computers but also cost more, ranging in price from $5,000 to several hundred thousand dollars.	Ranges from fitting on a desk to the size of a filing cabinet
Mainframe computer	Designed to meet the computing needs of hundreds of people in a large business environment. Mainframe computers are a step up in size, power, capability, and cost from minicomputers. Mainframes can cost in excess of $1 million. With processing speeds greater than 1 trillion instructions per second (compared to a typical desktop that can process about 2.5 billion instructions per second), mainframes can easily handle the processing requests of hundreds of people simultaneously.	Similar to a refrigerator
Supercomputer	The fastest, most powerful, and most expensive type of computer. Organizations such as NASA that are heavily involved in research and number crunching employ supercomputers because of the speed with which they can process information. Other large, customer-oriented businesses such as General Motors and AT&T employ supercomputers just to handle customer information and transaction processing.	Similar to a car

FIGURE 5.13

Operating System Software

Operating System Software	
Linux	An open source operating system that provides a rich environment for high-end workstations and network servers. Open source refers to any program whose source code is made available for use or modification as users or other developers see fit.
Mac OS X	The operating system of Macintosh computers.
Microsoft Windows	Generic name for the various operating systems in the Microsoft Windows family, including Microsoft Windows CE, Microsoft Windows 98, Microsoft Windows ME, Microsoft Windows 2000, Microsoft Windows XP, Microsoft Windows NT, and Microsoft Windows Server 2003.
MS-DOS	The standard, single-user operating system of IBM and IBM-compatible computers, introduced in 1981. MS-DOS is a command-line operating system that requires the user to enter commands, arguments, and syntax.
UNIX	A 32-bit multitasking and multiuser operating system that originated at AT&T's Bell Laboratories and is now used on a wide variety of computers, from mainframes to PDAs.

Operating System Software   Linus Torvalds, a shy Finnish programmer, may seem an unlikely choice to be one of the world's top managers. However, Linux, the software project he created while a university student, is now one of the most powerful influences on the computer world. Linux is an operating system built by volunteers and distributed for free and has become one of the primary competitors to Microsoft. Torvalds coordinates Linux development with a few dozen volunteer assistants and more than 1,000 programmers scattered around the globe. They contribute code for the kernel—or core piece—of Linux. He also sets the rules for dozens of technology companies that have lined up behind Linux, including IBM, Dell, Hewlett-Packard, and Intel.

While basic versions of Linux are available for free, Linux is having a considerable financial impact. According to market researcher IDC, the total market for Linux devices and software will increase from $11 billion in 2004 to $35.7 billion by 2008.[10]

Operating system software controls the application software and manages how the hardware devices work together. When using Excel to create and print a graph, the operating system software controls the process, ensures that a printer is attached and has paper, and sends the graph to the printer along with instructions on how to print it.

Operating system software also supports a variety of useful features, one of which is multitasking. *Multitasking* allows more than one piece of software to be used at a time. Multitasking is used when creating a graph in Excel and simultaneously printing a word processing document. With multitasking, both pieces of application software are operating at the same time. There are different types of operating system software for personal environments and for organizational environments (see Figure 5.13).

Utility Software   *Utility software* provides additional functionality to the operating system. Utility software includes antivirus software, screen savers, and antispam software. Figure 5.14 displays a few types of available utility software.

Application Software

Application software is used for specific information processing needs, including payroll, customer relationship management, project management, training, and many others. Application software is used to solve specific problems or perform specific tasks. From an organizational perspective, payroll software, collaborative software such as videoconferencing (within groupware), and inventory management software are all examples of application software (see Figure 5.15).

FIGURE 5.14

Utility Software

Types of Utility Software	
Crash-proof	Helps save information if a computer crashes.
Disk image for data recovery	Relieves the burden of reinstalling and tweaking scores of applications if a hard drive crashes or becomes irretrievably corrupted.
Disk optimization	Organizes information on a hard disk in the most efficient way.
Encrypt data	Protects confidential information from unauthorized eyes. Programs such as BestCrypt simply and effectively apply one of several powerful encryption schemes to hard drive information. Users unlock the information by entering a password in the BestCrypt control panel. The program can also secure information on rewritable optical disks or any other storage media assigned a drive letter.
File and data recovery	Retrieves accidental deletion of photos or documents in Windows XP by utilities such as Free Undelete, which searches designated hard drive deletion areas for recognizable data.
Text protect	In Microsoft Word, prevents users from typing over existing text after accidentally hitting the Insert key. Launch the Insert Toggle Key program, and the PC will beep whenever a user presses the Insert key.
Preventative security	Through programs such as Window Washer, erases file histories, browser cookies, cache contents, and other crumbs that applications and Windows leave on a hard drive.
Spyware	Removes any software that employs a user's Internet connection in the background without the user's knowledge or explicit permission.
Uninstaller	Can remove software that is no longer needed.

OPENING CASE QUESTIONS

Electronic Breaking Points

1. Identify the six hardware categories and place each product listed in the case in its appropriate category.

2. Describe the CPU and identify which products would use a CPU.

3. Describe the relationship between memory sticks and laptops. How can a user employ one to help protect information loss from the other?

4. What different types of software might each of the products listed in the case use?

section 5.2 MANAGING ENTERPRISE ARCHITECTURES

LEARNING OUTCOMES

5.7. Explain the three components of an enterprise architecture.

5.8. Describe how an organization can implement a solid information architecture.

5.9. List and describe the five *ilities* in an infrastructure architecture.

5.10. Compare Web services and open systems.

FIGURE 5.15

Application Software

Types of Application Software	
Browser	Enables the user to navigate the World Wide Web. The two leading browsers are Netscape Navigator and Microsoft Internet Explorer.
Communication	Turns a computer into a terminal for transmitting data to and receiving data from distant computers through the telephone system.
Data management	Provides the tools for data retrieval, modification, deletion, and insertion; for example, Access, MySQL, and Oracle.
Desktop publishing	Transforms a computer into a desktop publishing workstation. Leading packages include Adobe FrameMaker, Adobe PageMaker, and QuarkXpress.
E-mail	Provides e-mail services for computer users, including receiving mail, sending mail, and storing messages. Leading e-mail software includes Microsoft Outlook, Microsoft Outlook Express, and Eudora.
Groupware	Increases the cooperation and joint productivity of small groups of co-workers.
Presentation graphics	Creates and enhances charts and graphs so that they are visually appealing and easily understood by an audience. A full-features presentation graphics package such as Lotus Freelance Graphics or Microsoft PowerPoint includes facilities for making a wide variety of charts and graphs and for adding titles, legends, and explanatory text anywhere in the chart or graph.
Programming	Possesses an artificial language consisting of a fixed vocabulary and a set of rules (called syntax) that programmers use to write computer programs. Leading programming languages include Java, C ++, C#, and .NET.
Spreadsheet	Simulates an accountant's worksheet onscreen and lets users embed hidden formulas that perform calculations on the visible data. Many spreadsheet programs also include powerful graphics and presentation capabilities to create attractive products. The leading spreadsheet application is Microsoft Excel.
Word processing	Transforms a computer into a tool for creating, editing, proofreading, formatting, and printing documents. Leading word processing applications include Microsoft Word and WordPerfect.

ENTERPRISE ARCHITECTURES

A 66-hour failure of an FBI database that performed background checks on gun buyers was long enough to allow criminals to buy guns. The database failed at 1:00 p.m. on a Thursday and was not restored until 7:30 a.m. Sunday. The FBI must complete a gun check within three days; if it fails to do so, a merchant is free to make the sale. During this outage, any gun checks that were in progress were not finished, allowing merchants to complete those gun sales at their own discretion.[11]

To support the volume and complexity of today's user and application requirements, information technology needs to take a fresh approach to enterprise architectures by constructing smarter, more flexible environments that protect from system failures and crashes. *Enterprise architectures* include the plans for how an organization will build, deploy, use, and share its data, processes, and IT assets. A unified enterprise architecture will standardize enterprisewide hardware and software systems, with tighter links to the business strategy. A solid enterprise architecture can decrease costs, increase standardization, promote reuse of IT assets, and speed development of new systems. The end result being that the right enterprise architecture can make IT cheaper, strategic, and more responsive. The primary business goals of enterprise architectures are displayed in Figure 5.16.

Enterprise architectures are never static; they continually change. Organizations use enterprise architects to help manage change. An *enterprise architect (EA)* is a person grounded in technology, fluent in business, a patient diplomat, and provides

FIGURE 5.16

Primary Business Goals of
Enterprise Architectures

FIGURE 5.17

Three Components of
Enterprise Architecture

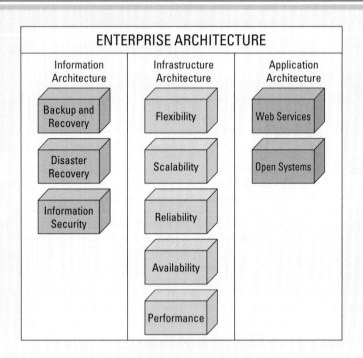

the important bridge between IT and the business. An EA is expensive and generally receives a salary upward of $150,000 per year. T-Mobile International's enterprise architects review projects to ensure they are soundly designed, meet the business objectives, and fit in with the overall enterprise architecture. One T-Mobile project was to create software that would let subscribers customize the ring sounds on their cell phones. The project group assumed it would have to create most of the software from scratch. However, T-Mobile's EAs found software already written elsewhere at T-Mobile that could be reused to create the new application. The reuse reduced the development cycle time by eight months, and the new application was available in less than six weeks.[12]

Companies that have created solid enterprise architectures, such as T-Mobile, are reaping huge rewards in savings, flexibility, and business alignment. Basic enterprise architectures contain three components (see Figure 5.17).

1. **Information architecture** identifies where and how important information, like customer records, is maintained and secured.

2. **Infrastructure architecture** includes the hardware, software, and telecommunications equipment that, when combined, provide the underlying foundation to support the organization's goals.

3. **Application architecture** determines how applications integrate and relate to each other.

INFORMATION ARCHITECTURE

Information architecture identifies where and how important information, like customer records, is maintained and secured. A single backup or restore failure can cost an organization more than time and money; some data cannot be recreated, and the business intelligence lost from that data can be tremendous. Chief information officers should have enough confidence that they could walk around and randomly pull out cables to prove that the systems are safe. The CIO should also be secure enough to perform this test during peak business hours. If the thought of this test makes the CIO cringe, then the organization's customers should be cringing also. Three primary areas an enterprise information architecture should focus on are:

1. Backup and recovery
2. Disaster recovery
3. Information security

Backup and Recovery

Each year businesses lose time and money because of system crashes and failures. One way to minimize the damage of a system crash is to have a backup and recovery strategy in place. A *backup* is an exact copy of a system's information. *Recovery* is the ability to get a system up and running in the event of a system crash or failure and includes restoring the information backup. Many different types of backup and recovery media are available, including redundant storage servers, tapes, disks, and even CDs and DVDs. All the different types of backup and recovery media are reliable; their primary differences are the speed and associated costs.

A chain of more than 4,000 franchise locations, 7-Eleven Taiwan uploads backup and recovery information from its central location to all its chain locations daily. The company implemented a new technology solution by Digital Fountain that could quickly and reliably download and upload backup and recovery information to all its stores. In addition, when a connection fails during the download or upload, the technology automatically resumes the download without having to start over, saving valuable time.[13]

Organizations should choose a backup and recovery strategy that is in line with its business goals. If the organization deals with large volumes of critical information, it will require daily backups, perhaps even hourly backups, to storage servers. If the organization deals with small amounts of noncritical information, then it might require only weekly backups to tapes, CDs, or DVDs. Deciding how often to back up information and what media to use is a critical business decision. If an organization decides to back up on a weekly basis, then it is taking the risk that, if a total system crash occurs, it could lose a week's worth of work. If this risk is acceptable, then a weekly backup strategy will work. If this risk is unacceptable, then the organization needs to move to a daily backup strategy. Some organizations find the risk of losing a day's worth of work too high and move to an hourly backup strategy.

Two techniques used to help in case of system failure are fault tolerance and failover. *Fault tolerance* is a computer system designed that in the event a component fails, a backup component or procedure can immediately take its place with no loss of service. Fault tolerance can be provided with software, or embedded in hardware, or provided by some combination. *Failover* is a backup operational mode in which the functions of a computer component (such as a processor, server, network, or database) are assumed by secondary system components when the primary component becomes unavailable through either failure or scheduled downtime. A failover procedure involves automatically offloading tasks to a standby system component so that the procedure is as seamless as possible to the end user. Used to make systems more fault tolerant, failover is typically an integral part of mission-critical systems that must be constantly available.

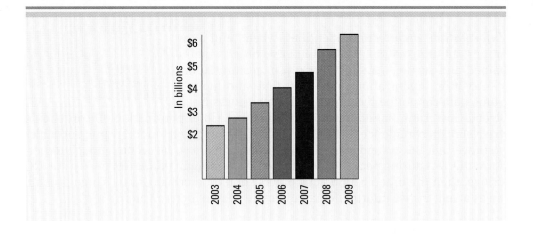

Disaster Recovery

A northern Ohio power company, FirstEnergy, missed signs that there were potential problems in its portion of North America's electrical grid. The events that followed left an estimated 50 million people in the Northeast and Canada in the dark. The failings are laid out in the widely reported findings of a joint U.S./Canada task force that investigated the causes of the blackout and recommended what to do to avoid big-scale outages in the future. The report detailed many procedures or best practices including:

- Mind the enterprise architectures.
- Monitor the quality of computer networks that provide data on power suppliers and demand.
- Make sure the networks can be restored quickly in the case of downtime.
- Set up disaster recovery plans.
- Provide adequate staff training, including verbal communication protocols "so that operators are aware of any IT-related problems that may be affecting their situational awareness of the power grid."[14]

Disasters such as power outages, floods, and even harmful hacking strike businesses every day. Organizations must develop a disaster recovery plan to prepare for such occurrences. A ***disaster recovery plan*** is a detailed process for recovering information or an IT system in the event of a catastrophic disaster such as a fire or flood. Spending on disaster recovery is rising worldwide among financial institutions (see Figure 5.18)

A comprehensive disaster recovery plan takes into consideration the location of the backup information. Many organizations store backup information in an off-site facility. StorageTek specializes in providing off-site information storage and disaster recovery solutions. A comprehensive disaster recovery plan also foresees the possibility that not only the computer equipment but also the building where employees work may be destroyed. A ***hot site*** is a separate and fully equipped facility where the company can move immediately after a disaster and resume business. A ***cold site*** is a separate facility that does not have any computer equipment, but is a place where employees can move after a disaster.

A ***disaster recovery cost curve*** charts (1) the cost to the organization of the unavailability of information and technology and (2) the cost to the organization of recovering from a disaster over time. Figure 5.19 displays a disaster recovery cost curve and shows that where the two lines intersect is the best recovery plan in terms of cost and time. Creating an organization's disaster recovery cost curve is no small task. It must consider the cost of losing information and technology within each department or functional area, and the cost of losing information and technology across the whole enterprise. During the first few hours of a disaster, those costs will be low but become increasingly higher over time. With those costs in hand, an organization must then determine the costs of recovery. Cost of recovery during the first few hours of a disaster is exceedingly high and diminishes over time.

FIGURE 5.19

The Disaster Recovery Cost
Curve

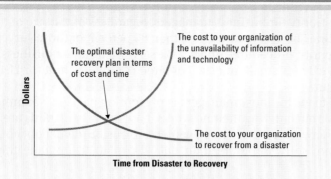

Marshall & Swift, which provides property valuation services, may be located in sunny Los Angeles, but the company barely averted a major disaster when Hurricane Charley ripped through southwest Florida in 2004. Many of the nation's largest insurance companies rely on Marshall & Swift's 200-plus servers to process claims and calculate the costs of rebuilding commercial and residential properties. Within one month of the Florida hurricane, the number of claims jumped from 20,000 to a whopping 180,000. This sudden surge in server utilization could have spelled disaster.

Fortunately, Marshall & Swift used an application performance management solution called ProactiveNet that identifies when an application or system is operating outside of its normal parameters and pinpoints the most likely source of the problem. ProactiveNet alerted the company's IT department to an improper balance of application, Web, and database servers. Some servers were being underutilized while others were being overburdened, thereby causing degradations in overall system performance. Marshall & Swift quickly began monitoring the usage patterns of each server and moved certain servers to ensure that all requests were processed in a timely matter.[15]

Information Security

Security professionals are under increasing pressure to do the job right and cost-effectively as networks extend beyond organizations to remote users, partners, and customers, and to cell phones, PDAs, and other mobile devices. Regulatory requirements to safeguard data have increased. Concerns about identity theft are at an all-time high. Hacking and other unauthorized access contribute to the approximately 10 million instances of identity theft each year, according to the Federal Trade Commission. A good information architecture includes a strong information security plan, along with managing user access and up-to-date antivirus software and patches.[16]

Managing User Access Managing user access to information is a critical piece of the information architecture. Passwords may still be the weakest link in the security chain. At Vitas Healthcare Corporation, with a workforce of 6,000 and operations across 15 states, authorized employees enter as many as a half-dozen passwords a day to access multiple systems. While it is important to maintain password discipline to secure customers' health care data, maintaining and managing the situation creates a drag on the IT department. "Our help desk spends 30 percent of their time on password management and provisioning," said John Sandbrook, senior IT director.

The company began using Fischer International Corporation's Identity Management Suite to manage passwords and comply with data-access regulations such as the Sarbanes-Oxley Act. The ID-management product includes automated audit, reporting, and compliance capabilities, plus a common platform for password management, provisioning, and self-service. With the software, Vitas can enforce stronger passwords with seven, eight, or nine characters, numbers, and capital letters that frequently change. The company anticipates curbing help-desk password time by 50 percent.[17]

Up-to-Date Antivirus Software and Patches There is little doubt that security is a top priority for business managers, regardless of the size of their company. Among Fortune 500 companies, more than 80 percent of those surveyed described updating security procedures, tools, and services as a key business priority. That desire holds true for small, midsize, or large companies and for IT managers and corporate managers.

The main focus for most managers is preventing hackers, spammers, and other malcontents from entering their networks, and nearly two-thirds are looking to enhance their network-security-management, intrusion-detection, content-filtering, and anti-spam software. More than half also plan to upgrade their encryption software.[18]

Microsoft issues patches for its software on the second Tuesday of every month. These patches must be downloaded and installed on all systems across the entire enterprise if the company wants to keep its systems protected. At OMD, a media buying and planning subsidiary of Omnicom Group Inc., the network administrator had to manually install critical patches on all 100 servers, taking more than a week to deploy the patch across the company. Now, OMD uses automated installation software for patches and upgrades. The company purchased Altiris Management Suite for Dell servers, which let it move ahead with applying patches without taking down entire systems and balancing patch-deployment timing among servers so that all departments were not down at once during a patch install. Given everything else that security professionals need to think about, automated installation software is a welcome relief.[19]

INFRASTRUCTURE ARCHITECTURE

Gartner Inc. estimates that the typical Web application goes down 170 hours per year. At Illinois-based online brokerage OptionsXpress, application performance problems can have a serious impact on livelihoods. Nearly 7,000 options traders

visit the OptionsXpress Web site at any given time, completing nearly 20,000 transactions a day. With all this online traffic, the brokerage's IT administrators were always up against the clock when recreating troublesome applications offline in the development environment. The company struggled to unlock the mystery behind a troublesome trading application that was forcing traders to resubmit orders. Sometimes the application would just die and then restart itself for no apparent reason.[20]

Infrastructure architecture includes the hardware, software, and telecommunications equipment that, when combined, provide the underlying foundation to support the organization's goals. As an organization changes, its systems must be able to change to support its operations. If an organization grows by 50 percent in a single year, its systems must be able to handle a 50 percent growth rate. Systems that cannot adapt to organizational changes can severely hinder the organization's ability to operate. The future of an organization depends on its ability to meet its partners and customers on their terms, at their pace, any time of the day, in any geographic location. The following are the five primary characteristics of a solid infrastructure architecture:

1. Flexibility
2. Scalability
3. Reliability
4. Availability
5. Performance

Flexibility

Organizations must watch today's business, as well as tomorrow's, when designing and building systems. Systems must be flexible enough to meet all types of business changes. For example, a system might be designed to include the ability to handle multiple currencies and languages, even though the company is not currently performing business in other countries. When the company starts growing and performing business in new countries, the system will already have the flexibility to handle multiple currencies and languages. If the company failed to recognize that its business would someday be global, it would need to redesign all its systems to handle multiple currencies and languages, not easy once systems are up and running.

Scalability

Estimating organizational growth is a challenging task. Growth can occur in a number of different forms including more customers and product lines and expansion into new markets. *Scalability* refers to how well a system can adapt to increased demands. A number of factors can create organizational growth including market, industry, and economy factors. If an organization grows faster than anticipated, it might experience all types of performance degradations, ranging from running out of disk space to a slowdown in transaction speeds. Anticipating expected—and unexpected—growth is key to building scalable systems that can support that growth.

MSNBC's Web site typically received moderate traffic. On September 11, 2001, the site was inundated with more than 91 million page views as its customers were trying to find out information about the terrorist attacks. Fortunately, MSNBC had anticipated this type of surging demand and built adaptable systems accordingly, allowing it to handle the increased page view requests.[21]

Capacity planning determines the future IT infrastructure requirements for new equipment and additional network capacity. Performing a capacity plan is one way to ensure the IT infrastructure is scalable. It is cheaper for an organization to implement an IT infrastructure that considers capacity growth at the beginning of a system launch than to try to upgrade equipment and networks after the system has been implemented. Not having enough capacity leads to performance issues and hinders the ability of knowledge workers to perform their jobs. If 100 workers are using the Internet to perform their jobs and the company purchases bandwidth that is too small and the network capacity is too small, the workers will spend a great deal of time just waiting to get information from the Internet. Waiting for an Internet site to return information is not very productive.

A computer glitch caused Delta Air Lines subsidiary Comair to cancel 1,100 flights Christmas Day 2004. The problem occurred when snowstorms caused the airline to ground flights, and the resulting quagmire overwhelmed its aging crew-scheduling system, causing further cancellations. Delta's crew-scheduling system is being replaced by one that can scale to handle more transaction.[22]

Reliability

Reliability ensures all systems are functioning correctly and providing accurate information. Reliability is another term for accuracy when discussing the correctness of systems within the context of efficiency IT metrics. Inaccurate information processing occurs for many reasons, from the incorrect entry of data to information corruption. Unreliable information puts the organization at risk when making decisions based on the information.

Availability

Availability (an efficiency IT metric) addresses when systems can be accessed by users. *High availability* refers to a system or component that is continuously operational for a desirably long length of time. Availability is typically measured relative to "100 percent operational" or "never failing." A widely held but difficult-to-achieve standard of availability for a system or product is known as "five 9s" (99.999 percent) availability.

Some companies have systems available 24x7 to support business operations and global customer and employee needs. With the emergence of the Web, companies expect systems to operate around the clock. A customer who finds that a Web site closes at 9:00 p.m. is not going to be a customer long.

Systems, however, must come down for maintenance, upgrades, and fixes. One challenge organizations face is determining when to schedule system downtime if the system is expected to operate continually. Exacerbating the negative impact of scheduled system downtime is the global nature of business. Scheduling maintenance during the evening might seem like a great idea, but the evening in one city is the morning somewhere else in the world, and global employees may not be able to perform their jobs if the system is down. Many organizations overcome this problem by having redundant systems, allowing the organization to take one system down by switching over to a redundant, or duplicate, system.

Performance

Performance measures how quickly a system performs a certain process or transaction (in terms of efficiency IT metrics of both speed and throughput). Not having enough performance capacity can have a devastating, negative impact on a business. A customer will wait only a few seconds for a Web site to return a request before giving up and moving on to another Web site. To ensure adaptable systems performance, capacity planning helps an organization determine future IT infrastructure requirements for new equipment and additional network capacity. It is cheaper for an organization to design and implement an IT infrastructure that envisions performance capacity growth than to update all the equipment after the system is already operational.

Abercrombie & Fitch (A&F) uses the Internet to market its distinctive image of being a fashion trendsetter to one of its largest customer segments, college students. The company designed its enterprise architecture with the help of IBM, which ensured www.abercrombie.com paralleled the same sleek but simple design of A&F Quarterly, the company's flagship magazine. Abercrombie & Fitch knew that its Web site had to be accessible, available, reliable, and scalable to meet the demands of its young customers. Young customers tend to be Internet savvy, and their purchasing habits vary from customers who only shop for sale items at midnight to customers who know exactly what they want immediately. The highly successful Web site gives customers not only an opportunity to shop online, but also a taste of the Abercrombie & Fitch lifestyle through downloadable MP3s, calendars, and desktop accessories.[23]

APPLICATION ARCHITECTURE

Gartner Inc. research indicates that application problems are the single largest source of downtime, causing 40 percent of annual downtime hours and 32 percent of average downtime costs. ***Application architecture*** determines how applications integrate and relate to each other. Advances in integration technology—primarily

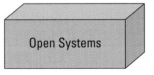

Web services and open systems—are providing new ways for designing more agile, more responsive enterprise architectures that provide the kind of value businesses need. With these new architectures, IT can build new business capabilities faster, cheaper, and in a vocabulary the business can understand.[24]

Web Services

Web services promise to be the next major frontier in computing. ***Web services*** contain a repertoire of Web-based data and procedural resources that use shared protocols and standards permitting different applications to share data and services. The major application of Web services is the integration among different applications. Before Web services, organizations had trouble with interoperability. ***Interoperability*** is the capability of two or more computer systems to share data and resources, even though they are made by different manufacturers. If a supply chain management (SCM) system can talk to (share information with) a customer relationship management (CRM) system, interoperability exists between the two systems. The traditional way that organizations achieved interoperability was to build integrations. Now, an organization can use Web services to perform the same task.

Verizon's massive enterprise architecture includes three different companies, GTE, Bell Atlantic, and Nynex, each with its own complex systems. To find a customer record in any of the three companies' systems, Verizon turns to its search engine, called Spider. Spider is Verizon's version of Google, and it's helping Verizon's business to thrive.

Spider contains a vital customer information Web service that encapsulates Verizon's business rules, which help it to access the correct data repository when looking for customer information. Whenever a new system is built that needs to link to customer information, all the developer has to do is reuse the Web service that will link to the customer records. Because Verizon has the Web service in place as part of its enterprise architecture, development teams can build new applications within a month, as opposed to six months.[25]

Web services encompass all the technologies that are used to transmit and process information on and across a network, most specifically the Internet. It is easiest to think of an individual Web service as software that performs a specific task, with that task being made available to any user who needs its service. For example, a "Deposit" Web service for a banking system might allow customers to perform the task of depositing money to their accounts. The Web service could be used by a bank teller, by the customer at an ATM, and/or by the customer performing an online transaction through a Web browser.

The "Deposit" Web service demonstrates one of the great advantages of using the Web service model to develop applications. Developers do not have to reinvent the wheel every time they need to incorporate new functionality. A Web service is really a piece of reusable software code. A software developer can quickly build a new application by using many of these pieces of reusable code. The two primary parts of Web services are events and services.

Events Events are the eyes and ears of the business expressed in technology—they detect threats and opportunities and alert those who can act on the information. Pioneered by telecommunication and financial services companies, this involves using IT systems to monitor a business process for events that matter—a stock-out in the warehouse or an especially large charge on a consumer's credit card—and automatically alert the people best equipped to handle the issue. For example, a credit monitoring system automatically alerts a credit supervisor and shuts down an account when the system processes a $7,000 charge on a credit card with a $6,000 limit.

Services Services are more like software products than they are coding projects. They must appeal to a broad audience, and they need to be reusable if they are going to have an impact on productivity. Early forms of services were defined at too low a level in the architecture to interest the business, such as simple "Print" and "Save" services. The new services are being defined at a higher level; they describe such things as "Credit Check," "Customer Information," and "Process Payment." These services describe a valuable business process. For example, "Credit Check" has value not just for programmers who want to use that code in another application, but also for businesspeople who want to use it across multiple products—say, auto loans and mortgages—or across multiple business.

The trick to building services is finding the right level of granularity. T-Mobile builds services starting at the highest level and then works its way down to lower levels, helping to ensure it does not build services that no one uses. The company first built a "Send Message" Web service and then built a "Send SMS Message" Web service that sends messages in special formats to different devices such as cell phones and pagers.

Lydian Trust's enterprise architects designed a Web service called "Get Credit" that is used by several different business units for loan applications. "Get Credit" seeks out credit ratings over the Internet from the major credit bureaus. One day, one of the credit bureaus' Web servers crashed, and Lydian Trust's "Get Credit" Web service could not make a connection. Since the connection to the server was loosely linked, the system did not know what to do. "Get Credit" was not built to make more than one call. So, while it waited for a response, hundreds of loan applications sat idle.

Lydian Trust's loan officers had to work overnight to ensure that all of the applications were completed within 24 hours as promised by the company. Fortunately, Lydian Trust's customers never felt the pain; however, its employees did. Systems must be designed to deal with the existence of certain events, or the lack of an event, in a way that does not interrupt the overall business. The "Get Credit" Web service has been modified to include an automatic e-mail alert to a supervisor whenever the Web service encounters a delay.[26]

Open Systems

Microsoft Internet Explorer's share of the Web browser market has dipped below 90 percent because of Mozilla's Firefox, an open source Web browser. According to WebSideStory, which has been tracking the Firefox versus Internet Explorer numbers, the Mozilla-made open source browser had captured 5 percent of the U.S. market in January 2005, an increase of almost a full percentage point in a month. Firefox claimed more than 25 million copies of the browser had been downloaded in its first 15 weeks of release.[27]

An **open system** is a broad, general term that describes nonproprietary IT hardware and software made available by the standards and procedures by which their products work, making it easier to integrate them. Amazon.com embraced open source technology converting from Sun's proprietary operating system to Linux. The switch to an open source operating system, such as Linux, is simplifying the process by which Amazon.com associates can build links to Amazon.com applications into their Web sites.[28]

The designs of open systems allow for information sharing. In the past, different systems were independent of each other and operated as individual islands of control. The sharing of information was accomplished through software drivers and devices that routed data allowing information to be translated and shared between systems. Although this method is still widely used, its limited capability and added cost are not an effective solution for most organizations. Another drawback to the stand-alone system is it can communicate only with components developed by a single manufacturer. The proprietary nature of these systems usually results in costly repair, maintenance, and expansion because of a lack of competitive forces. On the other hand, open system integration is designed to:

- Allow systems to seamlessly share information. The sharing of information reduces the total number of devices, resulting in an overall decrease in cost.

- Capitalize on enterprise architectures. This avoids installing several independent systems, which creates duplication of devices.

- Eliminate proprietary systems and promote competitive pricing. Often a sole-source vendor can demand its price and may even provide the customer with less than satisfactory service. Utilization of open systems allows users to purchase systems competitively.

OPENING CASE QUESTIONS
Electronic Breaking Points

5. How can an organization use an information architecture to protect its IT investment in electronic devices outlined in the case?

6. How can an organization use the devices mentioned in the case to protect information security?

7. Identify the five *ilities* and rank them in order of importance for a laptop (1 highest, 5 lowest).

8. Describe how a "Customer Phone Number" Web service could be used by one of the products outlined in the case.

Application architecture 140
Application software 151
Arithmetic-logic unit (ALU) 142
Availability 159
Backup 155
Binary digit (bit) 142
Byte 142
Cache memory 143
Capacity planning 159
Central processing unit (CPU)
   (or microprocessor) 142
Cold site 156
Communication device 148
Complex instruction set com-
   puter (CISC) chip 142
Computer 140
Control unit 142
Disaster recovery cost
   curve 156
Disaster recovery plan 156
Enterprise architect (EA) 153
Enterprise architecture 153

Failover 155
Fault tolerance 155
Flash memory 144
Gigabyte (GB) 144
Gigahertz (GHz) 142
Hard drive 145
Hardware 140
High availability 159
Hot site 156
Information architecture 154
Information technology (IT) 140
Infrastructure architecture 158
Input device 145
Interoperability 160
Magnetic medium 145
Magnetic tape 145
Megabyte (MB, M, or Meg) 144
Megahertz (MHz) 142
Memory card 144
Memory stick 144
Multitasking 151
Open system 162

Operating system
   software 151
Output device 147
Performance 160
Primary storage 141
Random access memory
   (RAM) 143
Read-only memory
   (ROM) 144
Recovery 155
Reduced instruction set
   computer (RISC) chip 143
Reliability 159
Scalability 159
Secondary storage 144
Software 140
System software 149
Terabyte (TB) 144
Utility software 151
Virtualization 143
Volatility 143
Web service 160

Chicago Tribune's Server Consolidation a Success

The *Chicago Tribune* is the seventh-largest newspaper in the country. Overhauling its data center and consolidating servers was a difficult task; however, the payoff was tremendous. The *Chicago Tribune* successfully moved its critical applications from a mishmash of mainframes and older Sun Microsystems servers to a new dual-site enterprise architecture, which has resulted in lower costs and increased reliability throughout the company.

The paper's new enterprise architecture clustered its servers over a two-mile distance, lighting up a 1 Gbps dark-fiber link—an optical fiber that is in place but not yet being used—between two data centers. This architecture lets the newspaper spread the processing load between the servers while improving redundancy and options for disaster recovery. The transfer to the new architecture was not smooth. A small piece of software written for the transition contained a coding error that caused the *Tribune*'s editorial applications to experience intermittent processing failures. As a result, the paper was forced to delay delivery to about 40 percent of its 680,000 readers and cut 24 pages from a Monday edition, costing the newspaper nearly $1 million in advertising revenue.

After editorial applications were stabilized, the *Tribune* proceeded to migrate applications for operations—the physical production and printing of the newspaper—and circulation to the new enterprise architecture. "As we gradually took applications off the mainframe, we realized that we were incurring very high costs in maintaining underutilized mainframes at two different locations," said Darko Dejanovic, vice president and CTO of the Tribune Co., which owns the *Chicago Tribune*, the *Los Angeles Times*, Long Island's *Newsday*, and about a dozen other metropolitan newspapers. "By moving from two locations to one, we've achieved several million dollars in cost savings. There's no question that server consolidation was the right move for us.

"The Tribune Co. is excited about its new enterprise architecture and is now looking to consolidate software across its newspapers. Currently, each newspaper maintains its own applications for classified advertising and billing, which means the parent company must support about 10 billing packages and the same number of classified-ad programs. The Tribune Co. has found that most of the business processes can be standardized. So far, it has standardized about 95 percent of classified-ad processes and about 90 percent of advertising-sales processes. Over the next three years, the Tribune Co. will replace the disparate billing and ad applications across the company with a single package that will be used by all business units. The different newspapers will not necessarily share the same data, but they will have the same processes and the same systems for accessing them. Over time, that will allow some of the call centers to handle calls for multiple newspapers; East Coast centers will handle the early-morning calls and West Coast centers the late-day and evening calls.

The Tribune Co. is looking at a few additional projects including the implementation of hardware that will allow its individual applications to run on partial CPUs, freeing up processor power and making more efficient use of disk space.[29]

Questions

1. Review the five characteristics of infrastructure architecture and rank them in order of their potential impact on the Tribune Co.'s business.
2. What is the disaster recovery cost curve? Where should the Tribune Co. operate on the curve?
3. Define backups and recovery. What are the risks to the Tribune Co.'s business if it fails to implement an adequate backup plan?

4. Why is a scalable and highly available enterprise architecture critical to the Tribune Co.'s current operations and future growth?

5. Identify the need for information security at the Tribune Co.

6. How could the Tribune Co. use a "Classified Ad" Web service across its different businesses?

UPS in the Computer Repair Business

When people think of UPS they usually think of brown delivery trucks and employees in shorts dropping off and picking up packages. This image is about to change. UPS has now entered the laptop repair business. Toshiba is handing over its entire laptop repair operation to UPS Supply Chain Solutions, the shipper's $2.4 billion logistics outsourcing division. Toshiba's decision to allow a shipping company to fix its laptops might appear odd to many individuals. However, when you understand that the primary challenge of computer repair is more logistical than technical—Toshiba's business decision seems brilliant. "Moving a unit around and getting replacement parts consumes most of the time," explains Mark Simons, general manager at Toshiba's digital products division. "The actual service only takes about an hour."

UPS will send broken Toshiba laptops to its facility in Louisville, Kentucky, where UPS engineers will diagnose and repair defects. Consumers will notice an immediate change: In the past, repairs could take weeks, depending on whether Toshiba needed components from Japan. Since the UPS repair site is adjacent to its air hub, customers should get their machines back, as good as new, in just a matter of days. UPS has been servicing Lexmark and Hewlett-Packard printers since 1996 and has been performing initial inspections on laptops being returned to Toshiba since 1999.

The expanded Toshiba relationship is another step in UPS's strategy to broaden its business beyond package delivery into commerce services. The company already works with clients to manage inventory, ordering, and custom processes. It recently introduced a service to dispose of unwanted electrical devices. To take on laptop repair, UPS put 50 technicians through a Toshiba-certified training course.[30]

Questions

1. Do you think UPS's entrance into the laptop repair business was a good business decision? Why or why not?
2. Identify the different types of hardware UPS technicians might be working on when fixing laptops.
3. Assume you are a technician working at UPS. Explain to a customer the different types of memory and why only certain types of data are lost during a computer failure. Also identify a potential backup strategy you can suggest to the customer.
4. Assume you are a technician working at UPS. Explain to a customer the different types of software found in a typical laptop.

Fear the Penguin

Linux has proved itself the most revolutionary software of the past decade. Spending on Linux was expected to reach $280 million by 2006. Linus Torvalds, who wrote the kernel (the core) of the Linux operating system at age 21, posted the operating system on the Internet and invited other programmers to improve his code and users to download his operating system for free. Since then, tens of thousands of people have, making Linux perhaps the single largest collaborative project in the planet's history.

Today, Linux, if not its penguin mascot, is everywhere. You can find Linux inside a boggling array of computers, machines, and devices. Linux is robust enough to run the world's most powerful supercomputers, yet sleek and versatile enough to run inside consumer items like TiVo, cell phones, and handheld portable devices. Even more impressive than Linux's increasing prevalence in living rooms and pockets is its growth in the market for corporate computers. According to a recent poll by CIO.com, 39 percent of IT managers agreed that Linux would dominate corporate systems by 2007.

Since its introduction in 1991, no other operating system in history has spread as quickly across such a broad range of systems as Linux, and it has finally achieved critical mass. According to studies by market research firm IDC, Linux is the fastest-growing server operating system, with shipments expected to grow by 34 percent per year over the next four years. With its innovative open source approach, strong security, reliability, and scalability, Linux can help companies achieve the agility they need to respond to changing consumer needs and stay ahead of the game.

Thanks to its unique open source development process, Linux is reliable and secure. A "meritocracy," a team specifically selected for their competence by the technical developer community, governs the entire development process. Each line of code that makes up the Linux kernel is extensively tested and maintained for a variety of different platforms and application scenarios.

This open collaborative approach means the Linux code base continually hardens and improves itself. If vulnerabilities appear, they get the immediate attention of experts from around the world, who quickly resolve the problems. According to Security Portal, which tracks vendor response times, it takes an average of 12 days to patch a Linux bug compared to an average of three months for some proprietary platforms. With the core resilience and reliability of Linux, businesses can minimize downtime, which directly increases their bottom line.

The Spread of Open Systems

Businesses and governments are opting for open source operating systems like Linux instead of Windows. One attendee at the Linux Desktop Consortium in 2004 was Dr. Martin Echt, a cardiologist from Albany, New York. Dr. Echt, chief operating officer of Capital Cardiology Associates, an eight-office practice, discussed his decision to shift his business from Microsoft's Windows to Linux. Dr. Echt is not your typical computer geek or Linux supporter, and he is not the only one switching to Linux.

The State Council in China has mandated that all ministries install the local flavor of Linux, dubbed Red Flag, on their PCs. In Spain, the government has installed a Linux operating system that incorporates the regional dialect. The city of Munich, despite a personal visit from Microsoft CEO Steve Ballmer, is converting its 14,000 PCs from Windows to Linux.

"It's open season for open source," declared Walter Raizner, general manager of IBM Germany. One of the biggest corporate backers of Linux, IBM has more than 75 government customers worldwide, including agencies in France, Spain, Britain, Australia, Mexico, the United States, and Japan.

The move toward Linux varies for each country or company. For Dr. Echt, it was a question of lower price and long-term flexibility. In China, the government claimed national security as a reason to move to open source code because it permitted engineers to make sure there were no security leaks and no spyware installed on its computers. In Munich, the move was largely political. Regardless of the reason, the market is shifting toward Linux.

Microsoft versus Linux

Bill Gates has openly stated that Linux is not a threat to Microsoft. According to IDC analysts, Microsoft's operating systems ship with 93.8 percent of all desktops worldwide. Ted Schadler, IDC research principal analyst, states that despite the push of lower cost Linux players into the market, Microsoft will maintain its desktop market share for the following three reasons:

1. Linux adds features to its applications that most computer users have already come to expect.
2. Linux applications might not be compatible with Microsoft applications such as Microsoft Word or Microsoft Excel.
3. Microsoft continues to innovate, and the latest version of Office is beginning to integrate word processing and spreadsheet software to corporate databases and other applications.

The Future of Linux

IDC analyst Al Gillen predicts that an open source operating system will not enjoy explosive growth on the desktop for at least six or eight years. Still, even Gillen cannot deny that Linux's penetration continues to rise, with an estimated 18 million users. Linux's market share has increased from 1.5 percent at the end of 2000 to 4.2 percent at the beginning of 2004. According to IDC, by the end of 2005 it was expected to have surpassed Apple's Mac OS, which has 2.9 percent of the market, as the second most popular operating system. Gartner Dataquest estimates Linux's server market share will grow seven times faster than Windows.[31]

Questions

1. How does Linux differ from traditional software?
2. Should Microsoft consider Linux a threat? Why or why not?
3. How is open source software a potential trend shaping organizations?
4. How can you use Linux as an emerging technology to gain a competitive advantage?
5. Research the Internet and discover potential ways that open source software might revolutionize business in the future.

1. Purchasing a computer

Dell is considered the fastest company on earth and specializes in computer customization. Connect to Dell's Web site at www.dell.com. Go to the portion of Dell's site that allows you to customize either a laptop or a desktop computer. First, choose an already prepared system and note its price and capability in terms of CPU speed, RAM size, monitor quality, and storage capacity. Now, customize that system to increase CPU speed, add more RAM, increase monitor size and quality, and add more storage capacity. What is the difference in price between the two? Which system is more in your price range? Which system has the speed and capacity you need?

2. Web-enabled cell phones

When categorizing computers by size for personal needs, we focused on PDAs, laptops, and desktop computers. Other variations include Web-enabled cell phones that include instant text messaging and Web computers. For this project, you will need a group of four people, which you will then split into two groups of two. Have the first group research Web-enabled cell phones, their capabilities and costs. Have that group make a purchase recommendation based on price and capability. Have the second group do the same for Web computers. What is your vision of the future? Will we ever get rid of clunky laptops and desktops in favor of more portable and cheaper devices such as Web-enabled cell phones and Web computers? Why or why not?

3. Small business computers

Many different types of computers are available for small businesses. Use the Internet to find three different vendors of laptops or notebooks that are good for small businesses. Find the most expensive and the least expensive that the vendor offers and create a table comparing the different computers based on the following:

- CPU
- Memory
- Hard drive
- Optical drive
- Operating system
- Utility software
- Application software
- Support plan

Determine which computer you would recommend for a small business looking for an inexpensive laptop. Determine which computer you would recommend for a small business looking for an expensive laptop.

4. Planning for disaster recovery

You are the new senior analyst in the IT department at Beltz, a large snack food manufacturing company. The company is located on the beautiful shoreline in Charleston, North Carolina. The company's location is one of its best and also worst features. The weather and surroundings are beautiful, but the threat of hurricanes and other natural disasters is high. Compile a disaster recovery plan that will minimize any risks involved with a natural disaster.

5. Comparing backup and recovery systems

Research the Internet to find three different vendors of backup and recovery systems. Compare and contrast the three systems and determine which one you would recommend if you were installing a backup and recovery system for a medium-sized business with 3,500 employees that maintains information on the stock market. Compile your findings in a presentation that you can give to your class that details the three systems' strengths and weaknesses, along with your recommendation.

6. Ranking the *-ilities*

In a group, review the list of IT infrastructure qualities and rank them in order of their impact on an organization's success. Use a rating system of 1 to 7, where 1 indicates the biggest impact and 7 indicates the least impact.

IT Infrastructure Qualities	Business Impact
Availability	
Accessibility	
Reliability	
Scalability	
Flexibility	
Performance	
Capacity Planning	

7. Designing an enterprise architecture

Components of a solid enterprise architecture include everything from documentation to business concepts to software and hardware. Deciding which components to implement and how to implement them can be a challenge. New IT components are released daily, and business needs continually change. An enterprise architecture that meets your organization's needs today may not meet those needs tomorrow. Building an enterprise architecture that is scalable, flexible, available, accessible, and reliable is key to your organization's success.

You are the enterprise architect (EA) for a large clothing company called Xedous. You are responsible for developing the initial enterprise architecture. Create a list of questions you will need answered to develop your architecture. Below is an example of a few of the questions you might ask.

- What are the company's growth expectations?
- Will systems be able to handle additional users?
- How long will information be stored in the systems?
- How much customer history must be stored?
- What are the organization's business hours?
- What are the organization's backup requirements?

Databases and Data Warehouses

6

CHAPTER

SECTION 6.1
Database Fundamentals

- Understanding Information
- Database Fundamentals
- Database Advantages
- Relational Database Fundamentals
- Database Management Systems
- Integrating Data Among Multiple Databases

SECTION 6.2
Data Warehouse Fundamentals

- Accessing Organizational Information
- History of Data Warehousing
- Data Warehouse Fundamentals
- Business Intelligence
- Data Mining

CHAPTER OUTLINE

Searching for Revenue—Google

Google founders Sergey Brin and Larry Page recently made *Forbes* magazine's list of world billionaires. Google, famous for its highly successful search engine, experienced a 850 percent revenue growth in 2005.

How Google Works

Figure 6.1 displays the life of an average Google query. The Web server sends the query to the index servers. The content inside the index server is similar to the index at the back of a book; it tells which pages contain the words that match any particular query term. Then the query travels to the document servers, which actually retrieve the stored documents and generate snippets to describe each search result. Finally, the search engine returns the results to the user. All these activities occur within a fraction of a second.

Google consists of three distinct parts:

1. The Web crawler, known as Googlebot, finds and retrieves Web pages and passes them to the Google indexer. Googlebot functions much like a Web browser. It

FIGURE 6.1

Sample Google Architecture

sends a request for a Web page to a Web server, downloads the entire page, and then hands it off to Google's indexer. Googlebot can request thousands of different Web pages simultaneously.

2. The indexer indexes every word on each page and stores the resulting index of words in a huge database. This index is sorted alphabetically by search term, with each index entry storing a list of documents in which the term appears and the location within the text where it occurs. Indexing the full text of Web pages allows Google to go beyond simply matching single search terms. Google gives more priority to pages that have search terms near each other and in the same order as the query. Google can also match multi-word phrases and sentences.

3. The query processor compares the search query to the index and recommends the documents that it considers most relevant. Google considers more than a hundred factors in determining which documents are most relevant to a query, including the popularity of the page, the position and size of the search terms within the page, and the proximity of the search terms to one another. The query processor has several parts, including the user interface (search box), the "engine" that evaluates queries and matches them to relevant documents, and the results formatter.

Selling Words

Google's primary line of business is its search engine; however, the company does not generate revenue from people using its site to search the Internet. It generates revenue from the marketers and advertisers that are paying to place their ads on the site.

Around 200 million times each day, people from all over the world access Google to perform searches. AdWords, a part of the Google site, allows advertisers to bid on common search terms. The advertisers simply enter in the keywords they want to bid on and the maximum amounts they want to pay per click, per day. Google then determines a price and a search ranking for those keywords based on how much other advertisers are willing to pay for the same terms. Pricing for keywords can range from 5 cents to $3 a click. A general search term like *tropical vacation* costs less than a more specific term like *Hawaiian vacation*. Whoever bids the most for a term appears in a sponsored advertisement link either at the top or along the side of the search-results page.

Paid search is the ultimate in targeted advertising because consumers type in exactly what they want. One of the primary advantages of paid search Web programs such as AdWords is that customers do not find it annoying, as is the problem with some forms of Web advertising such as banner ads and pop-up ads. According to the Interactive Advertising Bureau, overall industry revenues from paid search surpassed banner ads in the third quarter of 2003.

"A big percentage of queries we get are commercial in nature," said Salar Kamangar, Google's director of product management. "It is a marketplace where the advertisers tell us about themselves by telling us how much each lead is worth. They have an incentive to bid how much they really want to pay, because if they underbid, their competitors will get more traffic." Kamangar came up with the AdWords concept and oversees that part of the business. AdWords accounts for the vast majority of Google's annual revenue, and the company has over 150,000 advertisers in its paid-search program, up from zero in 2002.

Expanding Google

Google has a secret weapon working for its research and development department—hackers. Hackers actually develop many of the new and unique ways to expand Google. The company elicits hacker ideas through its application program interface (API), a large piece of the Google code. The API enables developers to build applications around the Google search engine. By making the API freely available, Google has inspired a community of programmers that are extending Google's capabilities. "It's working," said Nelson Minar, who runs the API effort. "We get clever hacks, educational uses, and wacky stuff. We love to see people do creative things with our product." A few of the successful developed applications include:

Banana Slug, www.bananaslug.com. For customers who hit a dead end with Google search, the site adds a random word to search text that generates surprising results.

Cookin' with Google, www.researchbuzz.org. Enter in the ingredients that are in the fridge and the site returns potential recipes for those ingredients.

Google Alert, www.googlealert.com. Google Alert automatically searches the Web for information on a topic and returns the results by e-mail.

RateMyProfessors.com, www.ratemyprofessors.com. The goal of this site was to create a place where students could rank their teachers. However, too many jokesters typing in false professor names such as "Professor Harry Leg" and "Professor Ima Dog" left the information on the site questionable. The developers turned to the Google API to create an automatic verification tool. If Google finds enough mentions in conjunction with a professor or university then it considers the information valid and posts it to the Web site.

Froogle, www.froogle.com. Google launched a beta version of a new shopping search tool called "Froogle" that the company claims is the most comprehensive product search engine available. Froogle has 15 product categories in its directory. Similar to the Google Directory, customers can view products either by using a keyword search or by drilling down through a particular category and its subcategories.

Stopping Google

As part of its Google Print Library Project, the company is working to scan all or parts of the book collections of the University of Michigan, Harvard University, Stanford University, the New York Public Library, and Oxford University. It intends to make those texts searchable on Google and to sell advertisements on the Web pages.

The Authors Guild filed a lawsuit against search engine Google, alleging that its scanning and digitizing of library books constitutes a "massive" copyright infringement. "This is a plain and brazen violation of copyright law," Nick Taylor, president of the New York-based Authors Guild, said in a statement about the lawsuit, which is seeking class action status. "It's not up to Google or anyone other than the authors, the rightful owners of these copyrights, to decide whether and how their works will be copied."

In response, Google defended the program in a company blog posting. "We regret that this group chose to sue us over a program that will make millions of books more discoverable to the world—especially since any copyright holder can exclude their books from the program," wrote Susan Wojcicki, vice president of product management. "Google respects copyright. The use we make of all the books we scan through the Library Project is fully consistent with both the fair use doctrine under U.S. copyright law and the principles underlying copyright law itself, which allow everything from parodies to excerpts in book reviews."[1]

INTRODUCTION

Information is powerful. Information is useful in telling an organization how its current operations are performing and estimating and strategizing how future operations might perform. New perspectives open up when people have the right information and know how to use it. The ability to understand, digest, analyze, and filter information is key to success for any professional in any industry. This chapter demonstrates the value an organization can uncover and create by learning how to manage, access, and analyze organizational information.

It is important to distinguish between data and information. ***Data*** are raw facts that describe the characteristics of an event. Characteristics for a sales event could include the date, item number, item description, quantity ordered, customer name, and shipping details. ***Information*** is data converted into a meaningful and useful context. Information from sales events could include best-selling item, worst-selling item, best customer, and worst customer.

section 6.1 DATABASE FUNDAMENTALS

LEARNING OUTCOMES

6.1. List, describe, and provide an example of each of the five characteristics of high quality information.

6.2. Define the relationship between a database and a database management system.

6.3. Describe the advantages an organization can gain by using a database.

6.4. Define the fundamental concepts of the relational database model.

6.5. Describe the role and purpose of a database management system and list the four components of a database management system.

6.6. Describe the two primary methods for integrating information across multiple databases.

UNDERSTANDING INFORMATION

Google recently reported a 200 percent increase in sales of its new Enterprise Search Appliance tool. Companies use the tool to search corporate information for answers to customer questions and to fulfill sales orders. Hundreds of Google's customers, including Xerox, Nextel Communications, Procter & Gamble, and Boeing, are using the tool. The ability to search, analyze, and comprehend information is vital for any organization's success. The incredible growth in sales of the Enterprise Search Appliance tool is a strong indicator that businesses desire technologies that help organize and provide access to information.[2]

When addressing a significant business issue, employees must be able to obtain and analyze all the relevant information so they can make the best decision possible. Organizational information comes at different levels, formats, and "granularities." ***Information granularity*** refers to the extent of detail within the information (fine and detailed or coarse and abstract information). On one end of the spectrum is coarse granularity, or highly summarized information. At the other end is fine granularity, or information that contains a great amount of detail. If employees are using a supply chain management (SCM) system to make decisions, they might find their suppliers send information in different formats and granularities, and at different levels. One supplier might send detailed information in a spreadsheet, another supplier might send summary information in a Word document, and still another might send aggregate information from a database. Employees must be able to correlate the different levels, formats, and granularities of information when making decisions.

Successfully collecting, compiling, sorting, and finally analyzing information from multiple levels, in varied formats, exhibiting different granularities can provide

Information Types	Range	Examples
Information Levels	Individual	Individual knowledge, goals, and strategies
	Department	Departmental goals, revenues, expenses, processes, and strategies
	Enterprise	Enterprisewide revenues, expenses, processes, and strategies
Information Formats	Document	Letters, memos, faxes, e-mails, reports, marketing materials, and training materials
	Presentation	Product, strategy, process, financial, customer, and competitor presentations
	Spreadsheet	Sales, marketing, industry, financial, competitor, customer, and order spreadsheets
	Database	Customer, employee, sales, order, supplier, and manufacturer databases
Information Granularities	Detail (Fine)	Reports for each salesperson, product, and part
	Summary	Reports for all sales personnel, all products, and all parts
	Aggregate (Coarse)	Reports across departments, organizations, and companies

tremendous insight into how an organization is performing. Taking a hard look at organizational information can yield exciting and unexpected results such as potential new markets, new ways of reaching customers, and even new ways of doing business. Figure 6.2 displays the different types of information found in organizations.

Samsung Electronics took a detailed look at over 10,000 reports from its resellers to identify "lost deals" or orders lost to competitors. The analysis yielded the enlightening result that 80 percent of lost sales occurred in a single business unit, the health care industry. Furthermore, Samsung was able to identify that 40 percent of its lost sales in the health care industry were going to one particular competitor. Before performing the analysis, Samsung was heading into its market blind. Armed with this valuable information, Samsung is changing its selling strategy in the health care industry by implementing a new strategy to work more closely with hardware vendors to win back lost sales.[3]

Not all companies are successful at managing information. Staples, the office-supplies superstore, opened its first store in 1986 with state-of-the-art technology. The company experienced rapid growth and soon found itself overwhelmed with the resulting volumes of information. The state-of-the-art technology quickly became obsolete and the company was unable to obtain any insight into its massive volumes of information. A simple query such as identifying the customers who purchased a computer, but not software or peripherals, took hours. Some of the queries required several days to complete and by the time the managers received answers to their queries it was too late.[4]

Information Quality

Westpac Financial Services (WFS), one of the four major banks in Australia, serves millions of customers from its many core systems, each with its own database.

FIGURE 6.3

Characteristics of
High-Quality Information

Characteristics of High-Quality Information	
Accuracy	Are all the values correct? For example, is the name spelled correctly? Is the dollar amount recorded properly?
Completeness	Are any of the values missing? For example, is the address complete including street, city, state, and zip code?
Consistency	Is aggregate or summary information in agreement with detailed information? For example, do all total fields equal the true total of the individual fields?
Uniqueness	Is each transaction, entity, and event represented only once in the information? For example, are there any duplicate customers?
Timeliness	Is the information current with respect to the business requirements? For example, is information updated weekly, daily, or hourly?

The databases maintain information and provide users with easy access to the stored information. Unfortunately, the company failed to develop information-capturing standards; one system had a field to capture e-mail addresses while another system did not, which led to inconsistent organizational information. Duplicate customer information among the different systems was another major issue, and the company continually found itself sending conflicting or competing messages to customers from different operations of the bank. A customer could also have multiple accounts within the company, one representing a life insurance policy and one representing a credit card. WFS had no way to identify that the two different customer accounts were for the same customer.

WFS had to solve its information quality problems immediately if it was to remain competitive. The company purchased NADIS (Name & Address Information Integrity Software), a software solution that filters customer information and highlights missing, inaccurate, and redundant information. Customer service ratings are on the rise for WFS now that the company can operate its business with a single and comprehensive view of each of its customers.[5]

Business decisions are only as good as the quality of the information used to make the decisions. Figure 6.3 reviews five characteristics common to high-quality information: accuracy, completeness, consistency, uniqueness, and timeliness. Figure 6.4 displays these issues in a sample information set.

FIGURE 6.4

Examples of Low-Quality Information

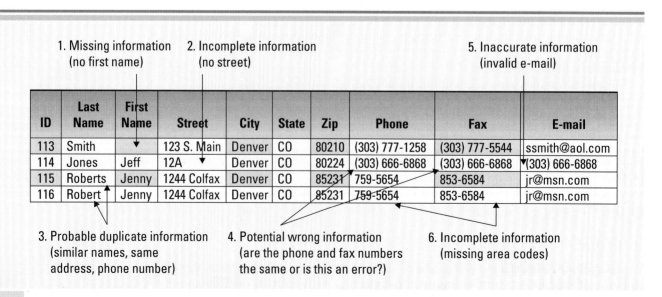

Figure 6.4 highlights several issues with low-quality information including:

1. The first issue is *missing* information. The customer's first name is missing. (See 1 in Figure 6.4.)

2. The second issue is *incomplete* information since the street address contains only a number and not a street name.

3. The third issue is a probable *duplication* of information since the only slight difference between the two customers is the spelling of the last name. Similar street addresses and phone numbers make this likely.

4. The fourth issue is potential *wrong* information because the customer's phone and fax numbers are the same. Some customers might have the same number for phone and fax line, but the fact that the customer also has this number in the e-mail address field is suspicious.

5. The fifth issue is definitely an example of *inaccurate* information since a phone number is located in the e-mail address field.

6. The sixth issue is *incomplete* information since there is not a valid area code for the phone and fax numbers.

Recognizing how quality issues occur will allow organizations to begin to correct them. The four primary sources of low-quality information are:

1. Online customers intentionally enter inaccurate information to protect their privacy.

2. Information from different systems have different information entry standards and formats.

3. Call center operators enter abbreviated or erroneous information by accident or to save time.

4. Third party and external information contain inconsistencies, inaccuracies, and errors.[6]

Addressing the above sources of information inaccuracies will significantly improve the quality of organizational information and the value extracted from the information.

Understanding the Costs of Poor Information   Using the wrong information can lead to making the wrong decision. Making the wrong decision can cost time, money, and even reputations. Every business decision is only as good as the information used to make the decision. Bad information can cause serious business ramifications such as:

- Inability to accurately track customers, which directly affects strategic initiatives such as customer relationship management and supply chain management.

- Difficulty identifying the organization's most valuable customers.

- Inability to identify selling opportunities and wasted revenue from marketing to nonexistent customers and nondeliverable mail.

- Difficulty tracking revenue because of inaccurate invoices.

- Inability to build strong relationships with customers, which increases their buyer power.

Understanding the Benefits of Good Information   High-quality information can significantly improve the chances of making a good decision and directly increase an organization's bottom line. Lillian Vernon Corp., a catalog company, used Web analytics to discover that men preferred to shop at Lillian Vernon's Web site instead of looking through its paper catalog. Based on this information, the company began placing male products more prominently on its Web site and soon realized a 15 percent growth in sales to men.[7]

Another company discovered that Phoenix, Arizona, is not a good place to sell golf clubs, even with its high number of golf courses. An analysis revealed that typical golfers in Phoenix are either tourists or conventioneers. These golfers usually bring their clubs with them while visiting Phoenix. The analysis further revealed that two of the best places to sell golf clubs in the United States are Rochester, New York, and Detroit, Michigan.[8]

There are numerous examples of companies that have used their high-quality information to make solid strategic business decisions. Quality information does not automatically guarantee that every decision made is going to be a good one, since people ultimately make decisions. But such information ensures that the basis of the decisions is accurate. The success of the organization depends on appreciating and leveraging the true value of timely and quality information.

DATABASE FUNDAMENTALS

Like any resource, an organization must manage information properly. That is, an organization must:

1. Determine what information it requires.
2. Acquire that information.
3. Organize the information in a meaningful fashion.
4. Assure the information's quality.
5. Provide software tools so that employees throughout the organization can access the information they require.

At the very heart of most—if not all—management information systems is a database and a database management system. A *database* maintains information about various types of objects (inventory), events (transactions), people (employees), and places (warehouses). A *database management system (DBMS)* is software through which users and application programs interact with a database. Think of it this way: A DBMS is to a database as word processing software is to a document or as spreadsheet software is to a spreadsheet. One is the information and the other is the software people use to manipulate the information.

The primary task of a database is to store and organize every piece of information related to transactions (for instance, the sale of a product) and business events (such as the hiring of a new employee). As such, databases store a tremendous amount of detailed information. The primary task of a DBMS then is to allow users to create, access, and use information stored in a database.

All kinds of information, from e-mails and contact information to financial information and sales records, are stored in databases. There are many different models for organizing information in a database, including the hierarchical database, network database, and the most prevalent—the relational database model. In a *hierarchical database model*, information is organized into a tree-like structure that allows repeating information using parent/child relationships, in such a way that it cannot have too many relationships. Hierarchical structures were widely used in the first mainframe database management systems. However, owing to their restrictions, hierarchical structures often cannot be used to relate to structures that exist in the real world. The *network database model* is a flexible way of representing objects and their relationships. Where the hierarchical model structures information as a tree of records, with each record having one parent record and many children, the network model allows each record to have multiple parent and child records, forming a lattice structure. The *relational database model* is a type of database that stores information in the form of logically related two-dimensional tables. This text focuses on the relational database model.

DATABASE ADVANTAGES

From a business perspective, databases offer many advantages, including:

- Increased flexibility.
- Increased scalability and performance.

- Reduced redundancy.
- Increased integrity (quality).
- Increased security.

Increased Flexibility

Databases tend to mirror business structures, and a good database can handle changes quickly and easily, just as any good business needs to be able to handle changes quickly and easily. Equally important, databases provide flexibility in allowing each user to access the information in whatever way best suits his or her needs.

The distinction between logical and physical views is important in understanding flexible database user views. The *physical view* of information deals with the physical storage of information on a storage device such as a hard disk. The *logical view* of information focuses on how users logically access information to meet their particular business needs. This separation of logical and physical views is what allows each user to access database information differently. That is, while a database has only one physical view, it can easily support multiple logical views. One user might want a customer report presented in alphabetical format, in which case last name should appear before first name. Another user might want customer names appearing as first name and then last name. Both are easily achievable, but different logical views of the same physical information.

Increased Scalability and Performance

The official Web site of The American Family Immigration History Center, www.ellisisland.org, generated over 2.5 billion hits in its first year of operation. The site offers easy access to immigration information about people who entered America through the Port of New York and Ellis Island between 1892 and 1924. The database contains over 25 million passenger names correlated to 3.5 million images of ships' manifests.[9]

Only a database could "scale" to handle the massive volumes of information and the large numbers of users required for the successful launch of the Ellis Island Web site. *Scalability* refers to how well a system can adapt to increased demands. *Performance* measures how quickly a system performs a certain process or transaction. Some organizations, such as eBay, must be able to support hundreds or thousands of online users including employees, partners, customers, and suppliers, who all want to access and share information. Databases today scale to exceptional levels, allowing all types of users and programs to perform information processing and information-searching tasks.

Reduced Redundancy

Redundancy is the duplication of information, or storing the same information in multiple places. Redundant information occurs because organizations frequently capture and store the same information in multiple locations. The primary problem with redundant information is it is often inconsistent, which makes it difficult to determine which values are the most current or most accurate. Not having correct information is confusing and frustrating for employees and disruptive to an organization. One primary goal of a database is to eliminate information redundancy by recording each piece of information in only one place in the database. Eliminating information redundancy saves space, makes performing updates easier, and improves quality.

Increased Integrity (Quality)

Information integrity is a measure of the quality of information. Within a database environment, *integrity constraints* are rules that help ensure the quality of information. Integrity constraints are defined and built into the database. The database (more appropriately, the database management system) ensures that users can never violate these constraints. There are two types of integrity constraints: (1) relational integrity constraints and (2) business-critical integrity constraints.

Relational integrity constraints are rules that enforce basic and fundamental information constraints. For example, a referential integrity constraint would not allow someone to create an order for a nonexistent customer, provide a markup percentage that was negative, or order zero pounds of raw materials from a supplier.

Business-critical integrity constraints enforce business rules vital to an organization's success and often require more insight and knowledge than relational integrity constraints. Consider a supplier of fresh produce to large grocery chains such as Safeway. The supplier might implement a business-critical integrity constraint stating that no produce returns are accepted after 15 days past delivery. That would make sense because of the chance of spoilage of the produce. These types of integrity constraints tend to mirror the very rules by which an organization achieves success.

The specification and enforcement of integrity constraints produce higher-quality information that will provide better support for business decisions. Organizations that establish specific procedures for developing integrity constraints typically see a decline in information error rates and an increase in the use of organizational information.

Increased Security

Information is an organizational asset. Like any asset, an organization must protect its information from unauthorized users or misuse. As systems become increasingly complex and more available over the Internet, security becomes an even bigger issue. Databases offer many security features including passwords, access levels, and access controls.

Passwords provide authentication of the user who is gaining access to the system. Access levels determine who has access to the different types of information, and access controls determine what type of access they have to the information. Customer service representatives might need read-only access to customer order information so they can answer customer order inquiries; they might not have or need the authority to change or delete order information. Managers might require access to employee files, but they should have access only to their own employees' files, not the employee files for the entire company. Various security features of databases ensure that individuals have only certain types of access to certain types of information.

Databases can increase personal security as well as information security. Since 1995, the Chicago Police Department (CPD) has relied on a crime-fighting system called Citizen and Law Enforcement Analysis and Reporting (CLEAR). CLEAR electronically streamlines the way detectives enter and access critical information to help them solve crimes, analyze crime patterns, and ultimately promote security in a proactive manner. The CPD enters 650,000 new criminal cases and 500,000 new arrests into CLEAR each year.[10]

RELATIONAL DATABASE FUNDAMENTALS

The relational database model is a type of database that stores information in the form of logically related two-dimensional tables. Consider how the Coca-Cola Bottling Company of Egypt (TCCBCE) implemented an inventory-tracking database to improve order accuracy by 27 percent, decrease order response time by 66 percent, and increase sales by 20 percent. With over 7,400 employees, TCCBCE owns and operates 11 bottling plants and 29 sales and distribution centers, making it one of the largest companies in Egypt.

Traditionally, the company sent distribution trucks to each customer's premises to take orders and deliver stock. Many problems were associated with this process including numerous information entry errors, which caused order-fulfillment time to take an average of three days. To remedy the situation, Coca-Cola decided to create presales teams equipped with handheld devices to visit customers and take orders electronically. On returning to the office, the teams synchronized orders with the company's inventory-tracking database to ensure automated processing and rapid dispatch of accurate orders to customers.[11]

Entities, Entity Classes, and Attributes

Figure 6.5 illustrates the primary concepts of the relational database model—entities, entity classes, attributes, keys, and relationships. An *entity* is a person, place, thing, transaction, or event about which information is stored. An *entity class* (often called a table) is a collection of similar entities. The entity classes of interest in Figure 6.5 are CUSTOMER, ORDER, ORDER LINE, PRODUCT, and DISTRIBUTOR. Notice that each entity class (the collection of similar entities) is stored in a different two-dimensional table. *Attributes*, also called fields or columns, are characteristics or properties of an entity class. In Figure 6.5, the attributes for CUSTOMER include *Customer ID, Customer Name, Contact Name,* and *Phone*. Attributes for PRODUCT include *Product ID, Product Description,* and Price. Each specific entity in an entity class (e.g., Dave's Sub Shop in the CUSTOMER table) occupies one row in its respective table. The columns in the table contain the attributes.

Keys and Relationships

To manage and organize various entity classes within the relational database model, developers must identify primary keys and foreign keys and use them to create logical relationships. A *primary key* is a field (or group of fields) that uniquely identifies a given entity in a table. In CUSTOMER, the *Customer ID* uniquely identifies each entity (customer) in the table and is the primary key. Primary keys are important because they provide a way of distinguishing each entity in a table.

A *foreign key* in the relational database model is a primary key of one table that appears as an attribute in another table and acts to provide a logical relationship between the two tables. Consider Hawkins Shipping, one of the distributors appearing in the DISTRIBUTOR table. Its primary key, *Distributor ID,* is DEN8001. Notice that *Distributor ID* also appears as an attribute in the ORDER table. This establishes the fact that Hawkins Shipping (*Distributor ID* DEN8001) was responsible for delivering orders 34561 and 34562 to the appropriate customer(s). Therefore, *Distributor ID* in the ORDER table creates a logical relationship (who shipped what order) between ORDER and DISTRIBUTOR.

DATABASE MANAGEMENT SYSTEMS

Ford's European plant manufactures more than 5,000 vehicles a day and sells them in over 100 countries. Every component of every model must conform to complex European standards, including passenger safety standards and pedestrian and environmental protection standards. These standards govern each stage of Ford's manufacturing process from design to final production. The company needs to obtain many thousands of different approvals each year to comply with the standards. Overlooking just one means the company cannot sell the finished vehicle, which brings the production line to a standstill and could potentially cost Ford up to 1 million euros per day. Ford built the Homologation Timing System (HTS), based on a relational database, to help it track and analyze these standards. The reliability and high performance of the HTS have helped Ford substantially reduce its compliance risk.[12]

As displayed in Figure 6.6, a user can directly interact with a database using different types of technology tools such as views and report generators. Users can also interact with a database by using application programs such as accounting, marketing, and manufacturing applications.

Austrian Federal Railways maintains its entire railway system—which includes over 5,849 kilometers of track, 5,993 bridges and viaducts, 240 tunnels, and 6,768 crossings—with an Oracle database. Multiple applications run on the database including accounting, order processing, and geographic applications that pinpoint railway equipment locations. The database contains over 80 billion characters and

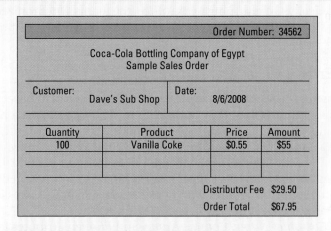

Order Number: 34562

Coca-Cola Bottling Company of Egypt
Sample Sales Order

Customer: Dave's Sub Shop	Date: 8/6/2008

Quantity	Product	Price	Amount
100	Vanilla Coke	$0.55	$55

	Distributor Fee	$29.50
	Order Total	$67.95

CUSTOMER

Customer ID	Customer Name	Contact Name	Phone
23	Dave's Sub Shop	David Logan	(555)333-4545
43	Pizza Palace	Debbie Fernandez	(555)345-5432
765	T's Fun Zone	Tom Repicci	(555)565-6655

ORDER

Order ID	Order Date	Customer ID	Distributor ID	Distributor Fee	Total Due
34561	7/4/2008	23	DEN8001	$22.00	$145.75
34562	8/6/2008	23	DEN8001	$12.95	$67.95
34563	6/5/2008	765	NY9001	$29.50	$249.50

ORDER LINE

Order ID	Line Item	Product ID	Quantity
34561	1	12345AA	75
34561	2	12346BB	50
34561	3	12347CC	100
34562	1	12349EE	300
34563	1	12345AA	100
34563	2	12346BB	100
34563	3	12347CC	50
34563	4	12348DD	50
34563	5	12349EE	100

DISTRIBUTOR

Distributor ID	Distributor Name
DEN8001	Hawkins Shipping
CHI3001	ABC Trucking
NY9001	Van Distributors

PRODUCT

Product ID	Product Description	Price
12345AA	Coca-Cola	$0.55
12346BB	Diet Coke	$0.55
12347CC	Sprite	$0.55
12348DD	Diet Sprite	$0.55
12349EE	Vanilla Coke	$0.55

FIGURE 6.6

User Interaction with a Database and DBMS

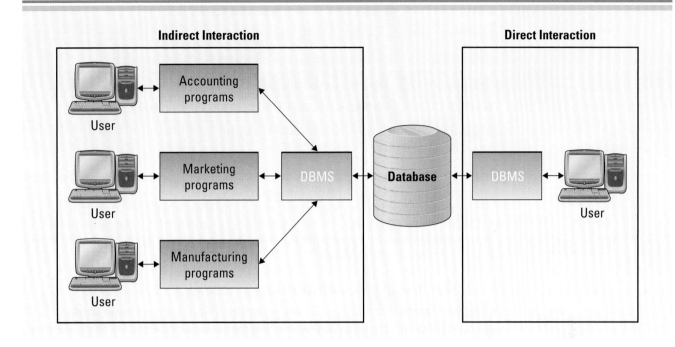

supports more than 1,200 users. Many organizations use databases similar to Austrian Federal Railways' to manage large amounts of information.[13]

A DBMS is composed of four primary components—data definition, data manipulation, application generation, and data administration (see Figure 6.7).

Data Definition Component

The ***data definition component*** of a DBMS helps create and maintain the data dictionary and the structure of the database. The ***data dictionary*** is a file that stores definitions of information types, identifies the primary and foreign keys, and maintains the relationships among the tables. The data dictionary essentially defines the logical properties of the information that the database contains. Figure 6.8 displays typical logical properties of information.

All the logical properties shown in Figure 6.8 are important, and they vary depending on the type of information. A typical address field might have a *Type* logical property of alphanumeric, meaning that the field can accept numbers, letters, and special characters. This would be an example of a relational integrity

FIGURE 6.7

Four Components of a Database Management System

FIGURE 6.8

Logical Field Properties
in a Database

Logical Property	Example
Field name	Name of field such as *Customer ID* or *Product ID*
Type	Alphanumeric, numeric, date, time, currency, etc.
Form	Each phone number must have the area code (XXX) XXX-XXXX
Default value	The default value for area code is (303)
Validation rule	A discount cannot exceed 100 percent
Entry rule	The field must have a valid entry—no blanks are allowed
Duplicate rule	Duplicate information is not allowed

constraint. The validation rule requiring that a discount cannot exceed 100 percent is an example of a business-critical integrity constraint.

The data dictionary is an important part of the DBMS because users can consult the dictionary to determine the different types of information. The data dictionary also supplies users with vital information when creating reports such as column names and information formats.

Data Manipulation Component

Of the four DBMS components, users probably spend the most time working with data manipulation. The ***data manipulation component*** allows users to create, read, update, and delete information in a database. A DBMS contains a variety of data

FIGURE 6.9

Sample Report Using
Microsoft Access

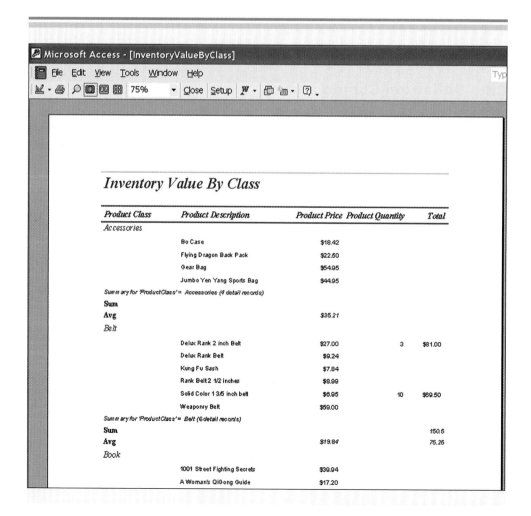

manipulation tools including views, report generators, query-by-example tools, and structured query language.

A *view* allows users to see the contents of a database, make any required changes, perform simple sorting, and query the database to find the location of specific information. *Report generators* allow users to define formats for reports along with what information they want to see in the report (see Figure 6.9).

Most often, users will create queries to access information in a database. A query is simply a question, such as "How many customers live in California?" *Query-by-example (QBE)* tools allow users to graphically design the answers to specific questions. Figure 6.10 displays Microsoft's Access QBE tool with a query asking which customers have ordered which products. Using a QBE, a user can design this query by asking the DBMS to pull all of the product descriptions for each order for every customer. Figure 6.11 displays the results to this query.

Structured query language (SQL) is a standardized fourth-generation query language found in most DBMSs. SQL performs the same function as QBE, except that the user must type statements instead of pointing, clicking, and dragging in a graphical environment. The basic form of an SQL statement is SELECT......FROM ......WHERE. Figure 6.12 displays the corresponding SQL statement required to perform the query from Figure 6.10. To write queries in SQL, users typically need some formal training and a solid technical background. Fortunately, QBE tools and their drag-and-drop design features allow nonprogrammers to quickly and easily design complex queries without knowing SQL.

FIGURE 6.10

Sample QBE Using Microsoft Access

FIGURE 6.11

Results to the QBE
in Figure 6.10

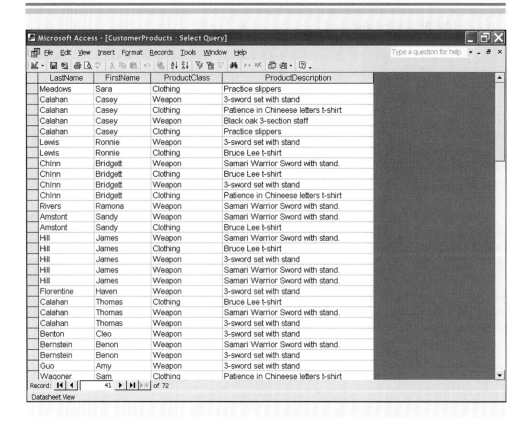

Application Generation and Data Administration Components

For the most part, users will be focusing on data manipulation tools to build views, reports, and queries. IT specialists primarily use the application generation and data administration components. Even though most users will probably not be using these components, it is still important they understand what they are and the functions they support.

The ***application generation component*** includes tools for creating visually appealing and easy-to-use applications. IT specialists use application generation components to build programs for users to enter and manipulate information with an interface specific to their application needs. Consider a manager involved in the

FIGURE 6.12

SQL Version of the QBE Query in Figure 6.10

```
SELECT  Customer.LastName, Customer.FirstName,
        Products.ProductClass, Products.ProductDescription
FROM    Products
        INNER JOIN ((Customer INNER JOIN Orders ON
        (Customer.CstmrID = Orders.CstmrID) AND (Customer.CstmrID
        = Orders.CstmrID))
        INNER JOIN OrderDetails ON Orders.OrderID =
        OrderDetails.OrderID) ON Products.Product ID =
        OrderDetails.ProductID;
```

management of an organization's supply chain. Using the application generation component, an IT specialist could build a supply chain management application software tool for the manager that would contain various menu options including add a supplier, order from a supplier, check the status of an order, and so on. This application would be easier and more intuitive for the manager to use on a consistent basis than requiring the manager to use views, report generators, and QBE tools.

The *data administration component* provides tools for managing the overall database environment by providing facilities for backup, recovery, security, and performance. Again, IT specialists directly interact with the data administration component.

Most organizations have several strategic-level IT positions—CIO (chief information officer), CTO (chief technology officer), CSO (chief security officer), CPO (chief privacy officer), and CKO (chief knowledge officer). People in these positions oversee the use of the data administration component. The CPO is responsible for ensuring the ethical and legal use of information. Therefore, he or she would direct the use of the security features of the data administration component, implement policies and procedures concerning who has access to different types of information, and control what functions they can perform on that information (read-only, update, delete). The CTO is responsible for ensuring the efficiency of IT systems and would direct the use of the backup, recovery, and performance features of the data administration component.

INTEGRATING DATA AMONG MULTIPLE DATABASES

Until the 1990s, each department in the United Kingdom's Ministry of Defense (MOD) and army headquarters had its own systems, each system had its own database, and sharing information among the departments was difficult. Manually inputting the same information multiple times into the different systems was also time-consuming and inefficient. In many cases, management could not even compile the information it required to answer questions and make decisions.

The army solved the problem by integrating its systems, or building connections between its many databases. These integrations allow the army's multiple systems to automatically communicate by passing information between the databases, eliminating the need for manual information entry into multiple systems because after entering the information once, the integrations sent the information immediately to all other databases. The integrations not only enable the different departments to share information, but have also dramatically increased the quality of the information. The army can now generate reports detailing its state of readiness and other vital issues, nearly impossible tasks before building the integrations among the separate systems.[14]

An *integration* allows separate systems to communicate directly with each other. Similar to the UK's army, an organization will maintain multiple systems, with each system having its own database. Without integrations, an organization will (1) spend considerable time entering the same information in multiple systems and (2) suffer from the low quality and inconsistency typically embedded in redundant information. While most integrations do not eliminate all redundant information, they can ensure the consistency of it across multiple systems.

An organization can choose from two integration methods. The first is to create forward and backward integrations that link processes (and their underlying databases) in the value chain. A *forward integration* takes information entered into a given system and sends it automatically to all downstream systems and processes. A *backward integration* takes information entered into a given system and sends it automatically to all upstream systems and processes.

Figure 6.13 demonstrates how this method works across the systems or processes of sales, order entry, order fulfillment, and billing. In the order entry system, for example, an employee can update the information for a customer. That information, via the integrations, would be sent upstream to the sales system and downstream to the order fulfillment and billing systems.

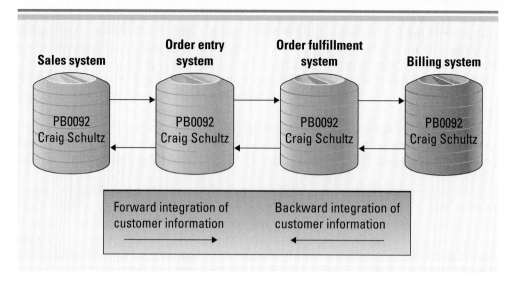

Ideally, an organization wants to build both forward and backward integrations, which provide the flexibility to create, update, and delete information in any of the systems. However, integrations are expensive and difficult to build and maintain and most organizations build only forward integrations (sales through billing in Figure 6.13). Building only forward integrations implies that a change in the initial system (sales) will result in changes occurring in all the other systems. Integration of information is not possible for any changes occurring outside the initial system, which again can result in inconsistent organizational information. To address this issue, organizations can enforce business rules that all systems, other than the initial system, have read-only access to the integrated information. This will require users to change information in the initial system only, which will always trigger the integration and ensure that organizational information does not get out of sync.

The second integration method builds a central repository for a particular type of information. Figure 6.14 provides an example of customer information integrated using this method across four different systems in an organization. Users can create, update, and delete customer information only in the central customer database. As users perform these tasks on the central customer database,

FIGURE 6.14

Integrating Customer
Information among
Databases

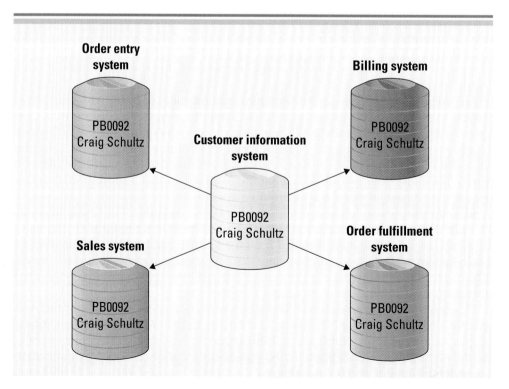

integrations automatically send the new and/or updated customer information to the other systems. The other systems limit users to read-only access of the customer information stored in them. Again, this method does not eliminate redundancy, but it does ensure consistency of the information among multiple systems.

OPENING CASE QUESTIONS

Searching for Revenue—Google

1. How did the Web site RateMyProfessors.com solve its problem of low-quality information?

2. Review the five common characteristics of high-quality information and rank them in order of importance to Google's business.

3. What would be the ramifications to Google's business if the search information it presented to its customers was of low quality?

4. Describe the different types of database. Why should Google use a relational database?

5. Identify the different types of entities, entity classes, attributes, keys, and relationships that might be stored in Google's AdWords relational database.

section 6.2 DATA WAREHOUSE FUNDAMENTALS

LEARNING OUTCOMES

6.7. Describe the roles and purposes of data warehouses and data marts in an organization.

6.8 Compare the multidimensional nature of data warehouses (and data marts) with two-dimensional nature of databases.

6.9. Identify the importance of ensuring cleanliness of information throughout an organization.

6.10. Explain the relationship between business intelligence and a data warehouse.

ACCESSING ORGANIZATIONAL INFORMATION

Applebee's Neighborhood Grill & Bar posts annual sales in excess of $3.2 billion and is actively using information from its data warehouse to increase sales and cut costs. The company gathers daily information for the previous day's sales into its data warehouse from 1,500 restaurants located in 49 states and seven countries.

Understanding regional preferences, such as patrons in Texas preferring steaks more than patrons in New England, allows the company to meet its corporate strategy of being a neighborhood grill appealing to local tastes. The company has found tremendous value in its data warehouse by being able to make business decisions about customers' regional needs. The company also uses data warehouse information to perform the following:

- Base its labor budgets on actual number of guests served per hour.
- Develop promotional sale item analysis to help avoid losses from overstocking or understocking inventory.
- Determine theoretical and actual costs of food and the use of ingredients.[15]

HISTORY OF DATA WAREHOUSING

In the 1990s as organizations began to need more timely information about their business, they found that traditional operational information systems were too cumbersome to provide relevant information efficiently and quickly. Operational systems typically include accounting, order entry, customer service, and sales and are not appropriate for business analysis for the following reasons:

- Information from other operational applications is not included.
- Operational systems are not integrated, or not available in one place.
- Operational information is mainly current—does not include the history that is required to make good decisions.
- Operational information frequently has quality issues (errors)— the information needs to be cleansed.
- Without information history, it is difficult to tell how and why things change over time.
- Operational systems are not designed for analysis and decision support.

During the latter half of the 20th century, the numbers and types of databases increased. Many large businesses found themselves with information scattered across multiple platforms and variations of technology, making it almost impossible for any one individual to use information from multiple sources. Completing reporting requests across operational systems could take days or weeks using antiquated reporting tools that were designed more or less to execute the business rather than run the business. From this idea, the data warehouse was born as a place where relevant information could be held for completing strategic reports for management. The key here is the word *strategic* as most executives were less concerned with the day-to-day operations than they were with a more overall look at the model and business functions.

A key idea within data warehousing is to take information from multiple platforms/technologies (as varied as spreadsheets, databases, and word files) and place them in a common location that uses a common querying tool. In this way operational databases could be held on whatever system was most efficient for the operational business, while the reporting/strategic information could be held in a common location using a common language. Data warehouses take this a step further by giving the information itself commonality by defining what each term means and keeping it standard. An example of this would be gender, which can be referred to in many ways (Male, Female, M/F, 1/0), but should be standardized on a data warehouse with one common way of referring to each sex (M/F).

This design makes decision support more readily available without affecting day-to-day operations. One aspect of a data warehouse that should be stressed is that it is *not* a location for *all* a business's information, but rather a location for information that is interesting, or information that will assist decision makers in making strategic decisions relative to the organization's overall mission.

Data warehousing is about extending the transformation of data into information. Data warehouses offer strategic level, external, integrated, and historical information so businesses can make projections, identify trends, and decide key business issues. The data warehouse collects and stores integrated sets of historical information from multiple operational systems and feeds them to one or more data marts. It may also provide end-user access to support enterprisewide views of information.

DATA WAREHOUSE FUNDAMENTALS

A ***data warehouse*** is a logical collection of information—gathered from many different operational databases—that supports business analysis activities and decision-making tasks. The primary purpose of a data warehouse is to aggregate information throughout an organization into a single repository in such a way that employees can make decisions and undertake business analysis activities. Therefore, while databases store the details of all transactions (for instance, the sale of a product) and events (hiring a new employee), data warehouses store that same information but in an aggregated form more suited to supporting decision-making tasks. Aggregation, in this instance, can include totals, counts, averages, and the like.

The data warehouse modeled in Figure 6.15 compiles information from internal databases or transactional/operational databases and external databases through ***extraction, transformation, and loading (ETL)***, which is a process that extracts information from internal and external databases, transforms the information using a common set of enterprise definitions, and loads the information into a data warehouse. The data warehouse then sends subsets of the information to data marts. A ***data mart*** contains a subset of data warehouse information. To distinguish between data warehouses and data marts, think of data warehouses as having a more organizational focus and data marts having focused information subsets particular to the needs of a given business unit such as finance or production and operations.

Lands' End created an organizationwide data warehouse so all its employees could access organizational information. Lands' End soon discovered that there could be "too much of a good thing." Many of its employees would not use the data warehouse because it was simply too big, too complicated, and had too much irrelevant information. Lands' End knew there was valuable information in its data warehouse, and it had to find a way for its employees to easily access the information. Data marts were the perfect solution to the company's information overload problem. Once the employees began using the data marts, they were ecstatic at the wealth of information. Data marts were a huge success for Lands' End.[16]

Multidimensional Analysis

A relational database contains information in a series of two-dimensional tables. In a data warehouse and data mart, information is multidimensional, meaning it contains layers of columns and rows. For this reason, most data warehouses and

FIGURE 6.15

Model of a Typical Data Warehouse

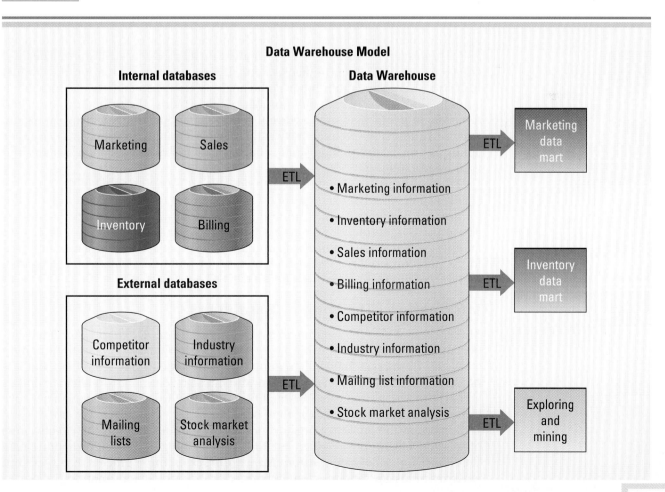

FIGURE 6.16

A Cube of Information for Performing a Multidimensional Analysis on Three Stores for Five Products and Four Promotions

data marts are *multidimensional databases*. A *dimension* is a particular attribute of information. Each layer in a data warehouse or data mart represents information according to an additional dimension. A **cube** is the common term for the representation of multidimensional information. Figure 6.16 displays a cube (cube a) that represents store information (the layers), product information (the rows), and promotion information (the columns).

Once a cube of information is created, users can begin to slice-and-dice the cube to drill down into the information. The second cube (cube b) in Figure 6.16 displays a slice representing promotion II information for all products at all stores. The third cube (cube c) in Figure 6.16 displays only information for promotion III, product B, at store 2. By using multidimensional analysis, users can analyze information in a number of ways and with any number of dimensions. Users might want to add dimensions of information to a current analysis including product category, region, and even forecasted versus actual weather. The true value of a data warehouse is its ability to provide multidimensional analysis that allows users to gain insights into their information.

Data warehouses and data marts are ideal for off-loading some of the querying against a database. For example, querying a database to obtain an average of sales for product B at store 2 while promotion III is under way might create a considerable processing burden for a database, essentially slowing down the time it takes another person to enter a new sale into the same database. If an organization performs numerous queries against a database (or multiple databases), aggregating that information into a data warehouse will be beneficial.

Information Cleansing or Scrubbing

Maintaining quality information in a data warehouse or data mart is extremely important. The Data Warehousing Institute estimates that low-quality information costs U.S. businesses $600 billion annually. That number may seem high, but it is not. If an organization is using a data warehouse or data mart to allocate dollars across advertising strategies, low-quality information will definitely have a negative impact on its ability to make the right decision.[17]

To increase the quality of organizational information and thus the effectiveness of decision making, businesses must formulate a strategy to keep information clean. This is the concept of **information cleansing or scrubbing,** a process that weeds out and fixes or discards inconsistent, incorrect, or incomplete information.

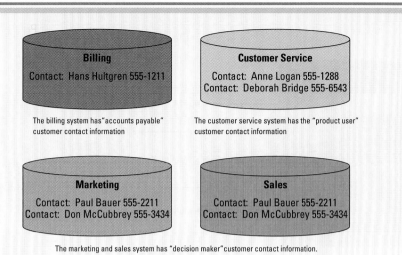

FIGURE 6.17

Contact Information in
Operational Systems

Specialized software tools exist that use sophisticated algorithms to parse, standardize, correct, match, and consolidate data warehouse information. This is vitally important because data warehouses often contain information from several different databases, some of which can be external to the organization. In a data warehouse, information cleansing occurs first during the ETL process and second on the information once it is in the data warehouse. Companies can choose information cleansing software from several different vendors including Oracle, SAS, Ascential Software, and Group 1 Software. Ideally, scrubbed information is error-free and consistent.

Dr Pepper/Seven Up, Inc., was able to integrate its myriad databases in a data warehouse (and subsequently data marts) in less than two months, giving the company access to consolidated, clean information. Approximately 600 people in the company regularly use the data marts to analyze and track beverage sales across multiple dimensions, including various distribution routes such as bottle/can sales, fountain food-service sales, premier distributor sales, and chain and national accounts. The company is now performing in-depth analysis of up-to-date sales information that is clean and error-free.[18]

Looking at customer information highlights why information cleansing is necessary. Customer information exists in several operational systems. In each system all details of this customer information could change from the customer ID to contact information (see Figure 6.17). Determining which contact information is accurate and correct for this customer depends on the business process that is being executed.

Figure 6.18 displays a customer name entered differently in multiple operational systems. Information cleansing allows an organization to fix these types of

FIGURE 6.18

Standardizing Customer
Name from Operational
Systems

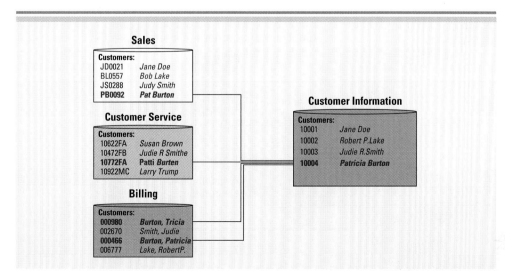

FIGURE 6.19

Information Cleansing
Activities

inconsistencies and cleans the information in the data warehouse. Figure 6.19 displays the typical events that occur during information cleansing.

Achieving perfect information is almost impossible. The more complete and accurate an organization wants its information to be, the more it costs (see Figure 6.20). The trade-off for perfect information lies in accuracy versus completeness. Accurate information means it is correct, while complete information means there are no blanks. A birth date of 2/31/10 is an example of complete but inaccurate information (February 31 does not exist). An address containing Denver, Colorado, without a ZIP code is an example of incomplete information that is accurate. For their information, most organizations determine a percentage high enough to make good decisions at a reasonable cost, such as 85 percent accurate and 65 percent complete.

BUSINESS INTELLIGENCE

Business intelligence (BI) is information that people use to support their decision-making efforts. An early reference to business intelligence occurs in Sun Tzu's book titled *The Art of War*. Sun Tzu claims that to succeed in war, one should have full knowledge of one's own strengths and weaknesses and full knowledge of the enemy's strengths and weaknesses. Lack of either one might result in defeat. A certain school of thought draws parallels between the challenges in business and those of war, specifically:

FIGURE 6.20

Accurate and Complete
Information

- Collecting information.
- Discerning patterns and meaning in the information.
- Responding to the resultant information.

Before the start of the information age in the late 20th century, businesses sometimes collected information from nonautomated sources. Businesses then lacked the computing resources to properly analyze the information and often made commercial decisions based primarily on intuition.

As businesses started automating more and more systems, more and more information became available. However, collection remained a challenge due to a lack of infrastructure for information exchange or to incompatibilities between systems. Reports sometimes took months to generate. Such reports allowed informed long-term strategic decision making. However, short-term tactical decision making continued to rely on intuition.

In modern businesses, increasing standards, automation, and technologies have led to vast amounts of available information. Data warehouse technologies have set up repositories to store this information. Improved ETL have increased the speedy collecting of information. Business intelligence has now become the art of sifting through large amounts of data, extracting information, and turning that information into actionable knowledge.

Enabling Business Intelligence

Competitive organizations accumulate business intelligence to gain sustainable competitive advantage, and they may regard such intelligence as a valuable core competence in some instances. The principal BI enablers are technology, people, and corporate culture.

Technology Even the smallest company with BI software can do sophisticated analyses today that were unavailable to the largest organizations a generation ago. The largest companies today can create enterprisewide BI systems that compute and monitor metrics on virtually every variable important for managing the company. How is this possible? The answer is technology—the most significant enabler of business intelligence.

People Understanding the role of people in BI allows organizations to systematically create insight and turn these insights into actions. Organizations can improve their decision making by having the right people making the decisions. This usually means a manager who is in the field and close to the customer rather than an analyst rich in information but poor in experience. In recent years "business intelligence for the masses" has been an important trend, and many organizations have made great strides in providing sophisticated yet simple analytical tools and information to a much larger user population than previously possible.

Culture A key responsibility of executives is to shape and manage corporate culture. The extent to which the BI attitude flourishes in an organization depends in large part on the organization's culture. Perhaps the most important step an organization can take to encourage BI is to measure the performance of the organization against a set of key indicators. The actions of publishing what the organization thinks are the most important indicators, measuring these indicators, and analyzing the results to guide improvement display a strong commitment to BI throughout the organization.

DATA MINING

Ruf Strategic Solutions helps organizations employ statistical approaches within a large data warehouse to identify customer segments that display common traits. Marketers can then target these segments with specially designed products and promotions. *Data mining* is the process of analyzing data to extract information

FIGURE 6.21

Data-Mining Tools Investment
Forecast

*In millions of dollars

Average Organizational Spending on Data-Mining Tools*

not offered by the raw data alone. Data mining can also begin at a summary information level (coarse granularity) and progress through increasing levels of detail (drilling down), or the reverse (drilling up).[19]

To perform data mining, users need data-mining tools. **Data-mining tools** use a variety of techniques to find patterns and relationships in large volumes of information and infer rules from them that predict future behavior and guide decision making. Data-mining tools for data warehouses and data marts include query tools, reporting tools, multidimensional analysis tools, statistical tools, and intelligent agents.

Sega of America, one of the largest publishers of video games, uses a data warehouse and statistical tools to distribute its advertising budget of more than $50 million a year. With its data warehouse, product line specialists and marketing strategists "drill" into trends of each retail store chain. Their goal is to find buying trends that help them determine which advertising strategies are working best and how to reallocate advertising resources by media, territory, and time. Figure 6.21 displays the average organizational spending on data-mining tools over the next few years.[20]

Data-mining tools apply algorithms to information sets to uncover inherent trends and patterns in the information, which analysts use to develop new business strategies. Analysts use the output from data-mining tools to build models that, when exposed to new information sets, perform a variety of information analysis functions. The analysts provide business solutions by putting together the analytical techniques and the business problem at hand, which often reveals important new correlations, patterns, and trends. The more common forms of data-mining analysis capabilities include cluster analysis, association detection, and statistical analysis.

Cluster Analysis

Cluster analysis is a technique used to divide an information set into mutually exclusive groups such that the members of each group are as close together as possible to one another and the different groups are as far apart as possible. Cluster analysis is frequently used to segment customer information for customer relationship management systems to help organizations identify customers with similar behavioral traits, such as clusters of best customers or one-time customers. Cluster analysis also has the ability to uncover naturally occurring patterns in information.

Such data-mining tools that "understand" human language are finding unexpected applications in medicine. IBM and the Mayo Clinic unearthed hidden patterns in medical records, discovering that infant leukemia has three distinct clusters, each of which probably benefits from tailored treatments. Caroline A. Kovac, general manager of IBM Life Sciences, expects that mining the records of cancer patients for clustering patterns will turn up clues pointing the way to "tremendous strides in curing cancer."[21]

Association Detection

Maytag Corporation, a $4.3 billion home and commercial appliance manufacturer, employs hundreds of R&D engineers, data analysts, quality assurance specialists, and customer service personnel who all work together to ensure that each generation of appliances is better than the previous generation. Maytag is an example of an organization that is gaining business intelligence with association detection data-mining tools.

Association detection reveals the degree to which variables are related and the nature and frequency of these relationships in the information. Maytag's warranty analysis tool, for instance, uses statistical analysis to automatically detect potential issues, provide quick and easy access to reports, and perform multidimensional analysis on all warranty information. This association detection data-mining tool enables Maytag's managers to take proactive measures to control product defects even before most of its customers are aware of the defect. The tool also allows Maytag personnel to devote more time to value-added tasks such as ensuring high quality on all products rather than waiting for or manually analyzing monthly reports.[22]

Many people refer to association detection algorithms as *association rule generators* because they create rules to determine the likelihood of events occurring together at a particular time or following each other in a logical progression. Percentages usually reflect the patterns of these events, for example, "55 percent of the time, events A and B occurred together," or "80 percent of the time that items A and B occurred together, they were followed by item C within three days."

One of the most common forms of association detection analysis is market basket analysis. *Market basket analysis* analyzes such items as Web sites and checkout scanner information to detect customers' buying behavior and predict future behavior by identifying affinities among customers' choices of products and services (see Figure 6.22). Market basket analysis is frequently used to develop marketing campaigns for cross-selling products and services (especially in banking, insurance, and finance) and for inventory control, shelf-product placement, and other retail and marketing applications.

Statistical Analysis

Statistical analysis performs such functions as information correlations, distributions, calculations, and variance analysis, just to name a few. Data-mining tools

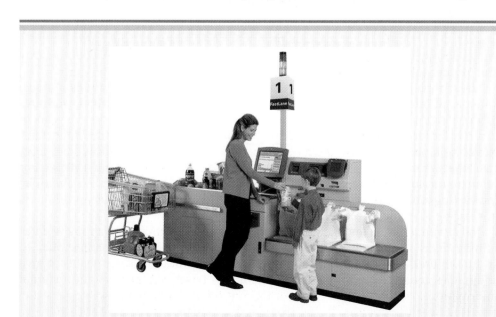

FIGURE 6.22

Market Basket Analysis

offer knowledge workers a wide range of powerful statistical capabilities so they can quickly build a variety of statistical models, examine the models' assumptions and validity, and compare and contrast the various models to determine the best one for a particular business issue.

Kraft is the producer of instantly recognizable food brands such as Oreo, Ritz, DiGiorno, and Kool-Aid. The company implemented two data-mining applications to assure consistent flavor, color, aroma, texture, and appearance for all of its food lines. One application analyzed product consistency and the other analyzed process variation reduction (PVR).

The product consistency tool SENECA (Sensory and Experimental Collection Application) gathers and analyzes information by assigning precise definitions and numerical scales to such qualities as chewy, sweet, crunchy, and creamy. SENECA then builds models, histories, forecasts, and trends based on consumer testing and evaluates potential product improvements and changes.

The PVR tool ensures consistent flavor, color, aroma, texture, and appearance for every Kraft product since even small changes in the baking process can result in huge disparities in taste. Evaluating every manufacturing procedure, from recipe instructions to cookie dough shapes and sizes, the PVR tool has the potential to generate significant cost savings for each product. Using these types of data-mining techniques for quality control and cluster analysis makes sure that the billions of Kraft products that reach consumers annually will continue to taste great with every bite.[23]

Forecasting is a common form of statistical analysis. Formally defined, **forecasts** are predictions made on the basis of time-series information. **Time-series information** is time-stamped information collected at a particular frequency. Examples of time-series information include Web visits per hour, sales per month, and calls per day. Forecasting data-mining tools allow users to manipulate the time series for forecasting activities. When discovering trends and seasonal variations in transactional information, use a time-series forecast to change the transactional information by units of time, such as transforming weekly information into monthly or seasonal information or hourly information into daily information. Companies base production, investment, and staffing decisions on a host of economic and market indicators in this manner. Forecasting models allow organizations to take into account all sorts of variables when making decisions.

Nestlé Italiana is part of the multinational giant Nestlé Group and currently dominates Italy's food industry. The company improved sales forecasting by 25 percent with its data-mining forecasting solution that enables the company's managers to make objective decisions based on facts instead of subjective decisions based on intuition. Determining sales forecasts for seasonal confectionery products is a crucial and challenging task. During Easter, Nestlé Italiana has only four weeks to market, deliver, and sell its seasonal products. The Christmas time frame is a little longer, lasting from six to eight weeks, while other holidays such as Valentine's Day and Mother's Day have shorter time frames of about one week.

The company's data-mining solution gathers, organizes, and analyzes massive volumes of information to produce powerful models that identify trends and predict confectionery sales. The business intelligence created is based on five years of historical information and identifies what is important and what is not important. Nestlé Italiana's sophisticated data-mining tool predicted Mother's Day sales forecasts that were 90 percent accurate. The company has benefited from a 40 percent reduction in inventory and a 50 percent reduction in order changes, all due to its forecasting tool. Determining sales forecasts for seasonal confectionery products is now an area in which Nestlé Italiana excels.[24]

Today, vendors such as Business Objects, Cognos, and SAS offer complete data-mining decision-making solutions. Moving forward, these companies plan to add more predictive analytical capabilities to their products. Their goal is to give companies more "what-if" scenario capabilities based on internal and external information.

Searching for Revenue—Google

6. How could Google use a data warehouse to improve its business operations?

7. Why would Google need to scrub and cleanse the information in its data warehouse?

8. Identify a data mart that Google's marketing and sales department might use to track and analyze its AdWords revenue.

Application generation
  component 188
Association detection 199
Attribute 183
Backward integration 189
Business intelligence 196
Business-critical integrity
  constraint 182
Cluster analysis 198
Cube 194
Data 176
Data administration component
  189
Database 180
Database management system
  (DBMS) 180
Data definition component 185
Data dictionary 185
Data manipulation component
  186

Data mart 193
Data mining 197
Data-mining tool 198
Data warehouse 192
Entity 183
Entity class 183
Extraction, transformation, and
  loading (ETL) 193
Forecast 200
Foreign key 183
Forward integration 189
Hierarchical database model
  180
Information 176
Information cleansing or
  scrubbing 194
Information granularity 176
Information integrity 181
Integration 189
Integrity constraint 181

Logical view 181
Market basket analysis 199
Network database model 180
Performance 181
Physical view 181
Primary key 183
Query-by-example (QBE) 187
Redundancy 181
Relational integrity constraint
  182
Relational database model 180
Report generator 187
Scalability 181
Structured query language
  (SQL) 187
Time-series information 200
View 187

Fishing for Quality

The Alaska Department of Fish and Game requires high-quality information to manage the state's natural resources, specifically to increase fishing yields, while ensuring the future of many species. Using fish counts, the department makes daily decisions as to which districts will be open or closed to commercial fishing. If the department receives low-quality information from fish counts, then either too many fish escape or too many are caught. Allowing too many salmon to swim upstream could deprive fishermen of their livelihoods. Allowing too many to be caught before they swim upstream to spawn could diminish fish populations—yielding devastating effects for years to come.

Because of the incredible size of Alaskan fisheries, the Commercial Fisheries Division's decisions have global impact. Its information is relied upon by individual fishermen who want to know the best places to fish, by corporations around the world that need information on which to base business strategies for seafood processing and marketing, by researchers, and by legislators. With so much at stake, the Division of Commercial Fisheries set out to improve the quality of its information by implementing a system that can gather the information from remote parts of the state and analyze it quickly to determine the daily outcomes.

Originally, the department captured information in spreadsheets that were e-mailed from station to station before being entered into the system. There was no central information set to work from, and more often than not, the information was low quality. Decisions were based on inaccurate and, because of delays in posting, untimely information.

With the implementation of an Oracle database, the department significantly improved the quality and timeliness of its information. Each time a commercial fishing boat within Alaska's jurisdiction unloads at a processing plant, the catch is weighed and details of the catch, such as species caught, weight, and quantity, are recorded on a fish ticket. This information is entered into the new system. To gather fish escapement information from remote areas, field workers positioned in towers scan rivers to visibly count fish. This information is radioed in the next morning.

Information from fish processed the previous day is keyed in by 10:00 a.m., and one hour later, the managers and fisheries across the state have all the information they require to make accurate decisions. They then announce on the radio and on their Web site, which receives more that 3,000 hits on an average day, whether or not fishermen can fish that day.

Fisheries are now managed with timely, centralized, and accurate information. Web pages summarize daily catches for certain areas, like Bristol Bay, whose annual sockeye salmon season, which lasts only a few weeks, is closely monitored by fish processors worldwide. With the enormous quantities of fish caught, salmon fisheries worldwide adjust their production levels based on the results of the annual Bristol Bay sockeye salmon season. This is just one reason why producing fast, quality information is critical to managing Alaska's natural resources.[25]

Questions

1. Explain the importance of high-quality information for the Alaska Department of Fish and Game.
2. Review the five common characteristics of quality information and rank them in order of importance for the Alaska Department of Fish and Game.
3. How could data warehouses and data marts be used to help the Alaska Department of Fish and Game improve the efficiency and effectiveness of its operations?
4. What two data marts might the Alaska Department of Fish and Game want to build to help it analyze its operational performance?

5. Do the managers at the Alaska Department of Fish and Game actually have all of the information they require to make an accurate decision? Explain the statement "it is never possible to have all of the information required to make the best decision possible."

Mining the Data Warehouse

According to a Merrill Lynch survey in 2006, business intelligence software and data-mining tools were at the top of CIOs' technology spending list. Following are a few examples of how companies are using data warehousing and data-mining tools to gain valuable business intelligence.

Ben & Jerry's

These days, when we all scream for ice cream, Ben & Jerry's cuts through the din by using integrated query, reporting, and online analytical processing technology from BI software vendor Business Objects. Through an Oracle database and with BI from Business Objects, Ben & Jerry's tracks the ingredients and life of each pint. If a consumer calls in with a complaint, the consumer affairs staff matches the pint with which supplier's milk, eggs, cherries, or whatever did not meet the organization's near-obsession with quality.

The BI tools let Ben & Jerry's officials access, analyze, and act on customer information collected by the sales, finance, purchasing, and quality-assurance departments. The company can determine what milk customers prefer in the making of the ice cream. The technology helped Ben & Jerry's track more than 12,500 consumer contacts in 2005. The information ranged from comments about the ingredients used in ice cream to queries about social causes supported by the company.

California Pizza Kitchen

California Pizza Kitchen (CPK) is a leading casual dining chain in the premium pizza segment with a recognized consumer brand and an established, loyal customer base. Founded in 1985, there are currently more than 130 full-service restaurants in over 26 states, the District of Columbia, and five foreign countries.

Before implementing its BI tool, Cognos, CPK used spreadsheets to plan and track its financial statements and line items. The finance team had difficulty managing the volumes of information, complex calculations, and constant changes to the spreadsheets. It took several weeks of two people working full time to obtain one version of the financial statements and future forecast. In addition, the team was limited by the software's inability to link cells and calculations across multiple spreadsheets, so updating other areas of corporate records became a time-consuming task. With Cognos, quarterly forecasting cycles have been reduced from eight days to two days. The finance team can now spend more time reviewing the results rather than collecting and entering the information.

Noodles & Company

Noodles & Company has more than 70 restaurants throughout Colorado, Illinois, Maryland, Michigan, Minnesota, Texas, Utah, Virginia, and Wisconsin. The company recently purchased Cognos BI tools to help implement reporting standards and communicate real-time operational information to field management throughout the United States.

Before implementing the first phase of the Cognos solution, IT and finance professionals spent days compiling report requests from numerous departments including sales and marketing, human resources, and real estate. Since completing phase one, operational Cognos reports are being accessed on a daily basis through the Noodles & Company Web site. This provides users with a single, 360-degree view of the business and consistent reporting throughout the enterprise.

Noodles & Company users benefit from the flexible query and reporting capabilities, allowing them to see patterns in the information to leverage new business opportunities. Cognos tools can pull information directly from a broad array of relational, operational, and other systems.[26]

Questions

1. How is Ben & Jerry's using BI tools to remain successful and competitive in a saturated market?

2. Why is information cleansing critical to California Pizza Kitchen's BI tools success?

3. Why is 100 percent accurate and complete information impossible for Noodles & Company to obtain?

4. Describe how each of the companies above is using BI from its data warehouse to gain a competitive advantage.

Harrah's—Gambling Big on Technology

The large investment made by Harrah's Entertainment Inc. in its information technology strategy has been tremendously successful. The results of Harrah's investment include:

- 10 percent annual increase in customer visits.
- 33 percent increase in gross market revenue.
- Yearly profits of over $208 million.
- Highest three-year ROI (return on investment) in the industry.
- A network that links over 42,000 gaming machines in 26 casinos across 12 states.
- Rated number six of the 100 best places to work in IT for 2003 by *ComputerWorld* magazine.
- Recipient of 2000 Leadership in Data Warehousing Award from the Data Warehousing Institute (TDWI), the premier association for data warehousing.

The casino industry is highly competitive (rivalry among existing competitors is fierce). Bill Harrah was a man ahead of his time when he opened his first bingo parlor in 1937 with the commitment of getting to know each one of his customers. In 1984, Phil Satre, president and CEO of Harrah's, continued that commitment to customers. In search of its competitive advantage, Harrah's invested in an enterprisewide technology infrastructure to maintain Bill Harrah's original conviction: "Serve your customers well and they will be loyal."

Harrah's Commitment to Customers

Harrah's recently implemented its patented Total Rewards™ program to help build strong relationships with its customers. The program rewards customers for their loyalty by tracking their gaming habits across its 26 properties and currently maintains information on over 19 million customers, information the company uses to analyze, predict, and maximize each customer's value.

One major reason for the company's success is Harrah's implementation of a service-oriented strategy. Total Rewards allows Harrah's to give every customer the appropriate amount of personal attention, whether it's leaving sweets in the hotel room or offering free meals. Total Rewards works by providing each customer with an account and a corresponding card that the player swipes each time he or she plays a casino game. The program collects information on the amount of time the customers gamble, their total winnings and losses, and their betting strategies. Customers earn points based on the amount of time they spend gambling, which they can then exchange for comps such as free dinners, hotel rooms, tickets to shows, and even cash.

Total Rewards helps employees determine which level of service to provide each customer. When a customer makes a reservation at Harrah's, the service representative taking the call can view the customer's detailed information including the customer's loyalty level, games typically played, past winnings and losses, and potential net worth. If the service representative notices that the customer has a Diamond loyalty level, the service representative knows that customer should never have to wait in line and always receive free upgrades to the most expensive rooms.

"Almost everything we do in marketing and decision making is influenced by technology," says Gary Loveman, Harrah's chief operating officer. "The prevailing wisdom in this business is that the attractiveness of property drives customers. Our approach is different. We stimulate demand by knowing our customers. For example, if one of our customers always vacations at Harrah's in April, they will receive a promotion in February redeemable for a free weekend in April."

Gaining Business Intelligence with a Data Warehouse

Over 90 million customers visit Harrah's each year, and tracking a customer base larger than the population of Australia is a challenge. To tackle this challenge Harrah's began developing a system called WINet (Winner's Data Network). WINet links all Harrah's properties, allowing the company to collect and share customer information on an enterprisewide basis. WINet collects customer information from all the company transactions, game machines, and hotel management and reservations systems and places the information in a central data warehouse. Information in the data warehouse includes both customer and gaming information recorded in hourly increments. The marketing department uses the data warehouse to analyze customer information for patterns and insights, which allows it to create individualized marketing programs for each customer based on spending habits. Most important, the data warehouse allows the company to make business decisions based on information, not intuition.

Casinos traditionally treat customers as though they belong to a single property, typically the place the customer most frequently visits. Harrah's was the first casino to realize the potential of rewarding customers for visiting more than one property. Today, Harrah's has found that customers who visit more than one of its properties represent the fastest growing revenue segment. In the first two years of the Total Rewards program, the company received a $100 million increase in revenue from customers who gambled at more than one casino.

Harrah's also uses business intelligence to determine gaming machine performance. Using the data warehouse, Harrah's examines the performance and cost structure of each individual gaming machine. The company can quickly identify games that do not deliver optimal operational performance and can make a decision to move or replace the games. The capability to assess the performance of each individual slot machine has provided Harrah's with savings in the tens of millions of dollars. CIO Tim Stanley stated, "As we leverage more data from our data warehouse and increase the use and sophistication of our decision science analytical tools, we expect to have many new ways to improve customer loyalty and satisfaction, drive greater revenues, and decrease our costs as part of our ongoing focus on achieving sustainable profitability and success."

Security and Privacy

Some customers have concerns about Harrah's information collection strategy since they want to keep their gambling information private. The good news for these customers is that casinos are actually required to be more mindful of privacy concerns than most companies. For example, casinos cannot send marketing material to any underage persons. To adhere to strict government regulations, casinos must ensure that the correct information security and restrictions are in place. Many other companies actually make a great deal of money by selling customer information. Harrah's will not be joining in this trend since its customer information is one of its primary competitive advantages.

The Future of Harrah's

Harrah's current systems support approximately $140,000 in revenue per hour (that's almost $25 million weekly). In the future, Harrah's hopes to become device-independent by allowing employees to access the company's data warehouse via PDAs, handheld computers, and even cell phones. "Managing relationships with customers is incredibly important to the health of our business," Stanley says. "We will apply whatever technology we can to do that."[27]

Questions

1. Identify the effects poor information might have on Harrah's service-oriented business strategy.
2. How does Harrah's use database technologies to implement its service-oriented strategy?
3. Harrah's was one of the first casino companies to find value in offering rewards to customers who visit multiple Harrah's locations. Describe the effects on the company if it did

not build any integrations among the databases located at each of its casinos. How could Harrah's use distributed databases or a data warehouse to synchronize customer information?

4. Estimate the potential impact to Harrah's business if there is a security breach in its customer information.

5. Identify three different types of data marts Harrah's might want to build to help it analyze its operational performance.

6. What might occur if Harrah's fails to clean or scrub its information before loading it into its data warehouse?

7. Describe cluster analysis, association detection, and statistical analysis and explain how Harrah's could use each one to gain insights into its business.

MAKING BUSINESS DECISIONS

1. Explaining relational databases

You have been hired by Vision, a start-up recreational equipment company. Your manager, Holly Henningson, is unfamiliar with databases and their associated business value. Holly has asked you to create a report detailing the basics of databases. Holly would also like you to provide a detailed explanation of relational databases along with their associated business advantages.

2. Entities and attributes

Martex Inc. is a manufacturer of athletic equipment, and its primary lines of business include running, tennis, golf, swimming, basketball, and aerobics equipment. Martex currently supplies four primary vendors including Sam's Sports, Total Effort, The Underline, and Maximum Workout. Martex wants to build a database to help it organize its products. In a group, identify the different types of entities, entity classes, attributes, keys and relationships Martex will want to consider when designing its database.

3. Integrating information

You are currently working for the Public Transportation Department of Chatfield. The department controls all forms of public transportation including buses, subways, and trains. Each department has about 300 employees and maintains its own accounting, inventory, purchasing, and human resource systems. Generating reports across departments is a difficult task and usually involves gathering and correlating the information from the many different systems. It typically takes about two weeks to generate the quarterly balance sheets and profit and loss statements. Your team has been asked to compile a report recommending what the Public Transportation Department of Chatfield can do to alleviate its information and system issues. Be sure that your report addresses the various reasons departmental reports are presently difficult to obtain as well as how you plan to solve this problem.

4. Information timeliness

Information timeliness is a major consideration for all organizations. Organizations need to decide the frequency of backups and the frequency of updates to a data warehouse. In a team, describe the timeliness requirements for backups and updates to a data warehouse for each of the following:

- Weather tracking systems.
- Car dealership inventories.

- Vehicle tire sales forecasts.
- Interest rates.
- Restaurant inventories.
- Grocery store inventories.

5. Improving information quality

HangUps Corporation designs and distributes closet organization structures. The company operates five systems—order entry, sales, inventory management, shipping, and billing. The company has severe information quality issues including missing, inaccurate, redundant, and incomplete information. The company wants to implement a data warehouse containing information from the five different systems to help maintain a single customer view, drive business decisions, and perform multidimensional analysis. Identify how the organization can improve its information quality when it begins designing and building its data warehouse.

6. Determining information quality issues

Real People is a magazine geared toward working individuals that provides articles and advice on everything from car maintenance to family planning. Real People is currently experiencing problems with its magazine distribution list. Over 30 percent of the magazines mailed are returned because of incorrect address information, and each month it receives numerous calls from angry customers complaining that they have not yet received their magazines. Below is a sample of Real People's customer information. Create a report detailing all of the issues with the information, potential causes of the information issues, and solutions the company can follow to correct the situation.

ID	First Name	Middle Initial	Last Name	Street	City	State	Zip Code
433	M	J	Jones	13 Denver	Denver	CO	87654
434	Margaret	J	Jones	13 First Ave.	Denver	CO	87654
434	Brian	F	Hoover	Lake Ave.	Columbus	OH	87654
435	Nick	H	Schweitzer	65 Apple Lane	San Francisco	OH	65664
436	Richard	A		567 55th St.	New York	CA	98763
437	Alana	B	Smith	121 Tenny Dr.	Buffalo	NY	142234
438	Trevor	D	Darrian	90 Fresrdestil	Dallas	TX	74532

7. Mining the data warehouse

Alana Smith is a senior buyer for a large wholesaler that sells different types of arts and crafts to greeting card stores such as Hallmark. Alana's latest marketing strategy is to send all of her customers a new line of handmade picture frames from Russia. All of Alana's information supports her decision for the new line. Her analysis predicts that the frames should sell an average of 10 to 15 per store, per day. Alana is excited about the new line and is positive it will be a success.

One month later Alana learns that the frames are selling 50 percent below expectations and averaging between five to eight frames sold daily in each store. Alana decides to access the company's data warehouse information to determine why sales are below expectations. Identify several different dimensions of information that Alana will want to analyze to help her decide what is causing the problems with the picture frame sales.

8. Cleansing information

You are working for BI, a start-up business intelligence consulting company. You have a new client that is interested in hiring BI to clean up its information. To determine how good your work is, the client would like your analysis of the following spreadsheet.

CUST ID	First Name	Last Name	Address	City	State	ZIP	Phone	Last Order Date
233620	Christopher	Lee	12421 W Olympic Blvd	Los Angeles	CA	75080-1100	(972)680-7848	4/18/2002
233621	Bruce	Brandwen	268 W 44th St	New York	PA	10036-3906	(212)471-6077	5/3/2002
233622	Glr	Johnson	4100 E Dry Creek Rd	Littleton	CO	80122-3729	(303)712-5461	5/6/2002
233623	Dave	Owens	466 Commerce Rd	Staunton	VA	24401-4432	(540)851-0362	3/19/2002
233624	John	Coulbourn	124 Action St	Maynard	MA	1754	(978)987-0100	4/24/2002
233629	Dan	Gagliardo	2875 Union Rd	Cheektowaga	NY	14227-1461	(716)558-8191	5/4/2002
23362	Damanceee	Allen	1633 Broadway	New York	NY	10019-6708	(212)708-1576	
233630	Michael	Peretz	235 E 45th St	New York	NY	10017-3305	(212)210-1340	4/30/2002
233631	Jody	Veeder	440 Science Dr	Madison	WI	53711-1064	(608)238-9690 X227	3/27/2002
233632	Michael	Kehrer	3015 SSE Loop 323	Tyler	TX	75701	(903)579-3229	4/28/
233633	Erin	Yoon	3500 Carillon Pt	Kirkland	WA	98033-7354	(425)897-7221	3/25/2002
233634	Madeline	Shefferly	4100 E Dry Creek Rd	Littleton	CO	80122-3729	(303)486-3949	3/33/2002
233635	Steven	Conduit	1332 Enterprise Dr	West Chester	PA	19380-5970	(610)692-5900	4/27/2002
233636	Joseph	Kovach	1332 Enterprise Dr	West Chester	PA	19380-5970	(610)692-5900	4/28/2002
233637	Richard	Jordan	1700 N	Philadelphia	PA	19131-4728	(215)581-6770	3/19/2002
233638	Scott	Mikolajczyk	1655 Crofton Blvd	Crofton	MD	21114-1387	(410)729-8155	4/28/2002
233639	Susan	Shragg	1875 Century Park E	Los Angeles	CA	90067-2501	(310)785-0511	4/29/2002
233640	Rob	Ponto	29777 Telegraph Rd	Southfield	MI	48034-1303	(810)204-4724	5/5/2002
233642	Lauren	Butler	1211 Avenue Of The Americas	New York	NY	10036-8701	(212)852-7494	4/22/2002
233643	Christopher	Lee	12421 W Olympic Blvd	Los Angeles	CA	90064-1022	(310)689-2577	3/25/2002
233644	Michelle	Decker	6922 Hollywood Blvd	Hollywood	CA	90028-6117	(323)817-4655	5/8/2002
233647	Natalia	Galeano	1211 Avenue Of The Americas	New York	NY	10036-8701	(646)728-6911	4/23/2002
233648	Bobbie	Orchard	4201 Congress St	Charlotte	NC	28209-4617	(704)557-2444	5/11/2002
233650	Ben	Konfino	1111 Stewart Ave	Bethpage	NY	11714-3533	(516)803-1406	3/19/2002
233651	Lenee	Santana	1050 Techwood Dr NW	Atlanta	GA	30318-KKRR	(404)885-2000	3/22/2002
233652	Lauren	Monks	7700 Wisconsin Ave	Bethesda	MD	20814-3578	(301)771-4772	3/19/2005
233653	Mark	Woolley	10950 Washington Blvd	Culver City	CA	90232-4026	(310)202-2900	4/20/2002

7

CHAPTER

Networks, Telecommunications, and Wireless Computing

SECTION 7.1
Networks and Telecommunications

- Network Basics
- Architecture
- Topology
- Protocols
- Media
- E-Business Networks

SECTION 7.2
Wireless Computing

- Wireless Fidelity
- Business Drivers for Wireless Technologies
- Advantages of Enterprise Mobility
- The Future of Wireless

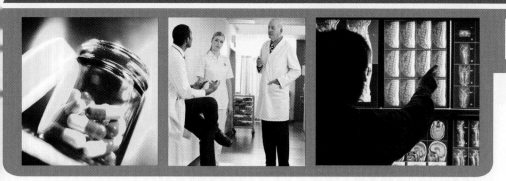

The Digital Hospital

For years, health care has missed the huge benefits that information technology has bestowed upon the rest of the economy. During the 1990s, productivity in health care services declined, according to estimates from Economy.com Inc. That is a huge underachievement in a decade of strong gains from the overall economy. This is beginning to change as hospitals, along with insurers and the government, are stepping up their IT investments. Hospitals are finally discarding their clumsy, sluggish first-generation networks and are beginning to install laptops, software, and Internet technologies.

Hackensack University Medical Center in Hackensack, New Jersey, is one of the nation's most aggressive technology adopters, investing $72 million in IT projects since 1998. The IT investments are paying off for the hospital with patient mortality rates decreasing—down 16 percent in four years—and quality of care and productivity increasing. The most important piece of Hackensack's digital initiatives is the networked software that acts as the hospital's central nervous system. Using wireless laptops, nurses log in to the system to record patient information and progress. Doctors tap into the network via wireless devices to order prescriptions and lab tests. Everything is linked, from the automated pharmacy to the X-ray lab, eliminating the need for faxes, phone calls, and other administrative hassles. Figure 7.1 displays the hospital's IT systems development projects.

Health care spending accounts for 15 percent of the U.S. economy, or $1.7 trillion. It is so gargantuan that any efficiency gains will affect the overall economy. Dr. David Brailer, President George W. Bush's point man on health IT initiatives, predicts that IT investments will lead to $140 billion a year in cost savings by 2014. More important than saving money is saving lives. Poor information kills some 7,000 Americans each year just by missing drug-interaction problems, according to the National Academy of Sciences Institute of Medicine. Hospital errors result in 100,000 deaths annually. Early evidence indicates that proper technology can reduce this amount. Hospitals using electronic prescription systems have seen 80 percent fewer prescription errors.[1]

FIGURE 7.1

Hospital IT Systems
Development Projects

Hackensack University Medical Center IT's Projects

- Patients can use 37-inch plasma TVs in their rooms to surf the Internet for information about their medical conditions. They can also take interactive classes about their condition and find out how to take care of themselves after discharge.

- From virtually anywhere in the world, physicians can make their hospital rounds with the help of a life-size robot, Mr. Rounder. Using laptops with joysticks and Web links, doctors drive the robot around the hospital to confer by remote video with patients and other doctors. When a blizzard prevented Dr. Garth Ballantynes from reaching the hospital, he used Mr. Rounder to make his rounds from his home 82 miles away.

- Pocket-sized PCs that hook wirelessly into the hospital's network allow doctors the freedom to place pharmacy orders and pull up medical records from anywhere in the hospital.

- Nurses use wireless laptops to record patients' vitals signs, symptoms and medications. Doctors can sign into the same central system from the laptops to order prescriptions and lab tests and read their patient's progress.

- The hospital's internal Web site stores all of its medical images. Doctors can view crystal-clear digital versions of their patients' X-rays, MRIs, and CT scans from any computer in or out of the hospital.

- A giant robot named Robbie, equipped with arms, reads prescriptions entered into the hospital's computer system and then grabs medications stored on pegs on the wall. The pills are then dropped into containers that are marked for each patient.

INTRODUCTION

elecommunication systems enable the transmission of data over public or private networks. A *network* is a communications, data exchange, and resource-sharing system created by linking two or more computers and establishing standards, or protocols, so that they can work together. Telecommunication systems and networks are traditionally complicated and historically inefficient. However, businesses can benefit from today's modern network infrastructures that provide reliable global reach to employees and customers. Businesses around the world are moving to network infrastructure solutions that allow greater choice in how they go to market—solutions with global reach. These alternatives include wireless, voice-over internet protocol (VoIP), and radio-frequency identification (RFID). This chapter takes a detailed look at key telecommunication, network, and wireless technologies being integrated into businesses around the world.

section 7.1 NETWORKS AND TELECOMMUNCIATIONS

LEARNING OUTCOMES

7.1. Compare LANs, WANs, and MANs.

7.2. List and describe the four components that differentiate networks.

7.3. Compare the two types of network architectures.

7.4. Explain topology and the different types found in networks.

7.5. Describe TCP/IP along with its primary purpose.

7.6. Identify the different media types found in networks.

NETWORK BASICS

Music is the hottest new product line at ubiquitous coffee retailer Starbucks. In Starbucks stores, customers can burn CDs while sipping coffee, thanks to the company's own online music library and increasingly sophisticated in-store network. Networks range from small two-computer networks to the biggest network of all, the Internet. A network provides two principle benefits: the ability to communicate and the ability to share. E-mail is the most popular form of network communication. Figure 7.2 highlights the three different types of networks, and Figure 7.3 graphically depicts each network type.

Networks are differentiated by the following:

- Architecture—peer-to-peer, client/server.
- Topology—bus, star, ring, hybrid, wireless.
- Protocols—Ethernet, Transmission Control Protocol/Internet Protocol (TCP/IP).
- Media—coaxial, twisted-pair, fiber-optic.

ARCHITECTURE

The two primary types of network architectures are: peer-to-peer networks and client/server networks.

Peer-to-Peer Networks

A *peer-to-peer (P2P) network* is any network without a central file server and in which all computers in the network have access to the public files located on all other workstations, as illustrated in Figure 7.4. Each networked computer can allow

FIGURE 7.2

Network Types

Network Types	
Local area network (LAN)	A computer network that uses cables or radio signals to link two or more computers within a geographically limited area, generally one building or a group of buildings. A networked office building, school, or home usually contains a single LAN. The linked computers are called workstations.
Wide area network (WAN)	A computer network that provides data communication services for business in geographically dispersed areas (such as across a country or around the world). The Internet is a WAN that spans the world.
Metropolitan area network (MAN)	A computer network that provides connectivity in a geographic area or region larger than that covered by a local area network, but smaller than the area covered by a wide area network. A college or business may have a MAN that joins the different LANs across its campus.

FIGURE 7.3

LAN, WAN, and MAN

FIGURE 7.4

Peer-to-Peer (P2P) Networks

other computers to access its files and use connected printers while it is in use as a workstation without the aid of a server.

While Napster may be the most widely known example of a P2P implementation, it may also be one of the most narrowly focused since the Napster model takes advantage of only one of the many capabilities of P2P computing: file sharing. The technology has far broader capabilities, including the sharing of processing, memory, and storage, and the supporting of collaboration among vast numbers of distributed computers. Peer-to-peer computing enables immediate interaction among people and computer systems.

Client/Server Networks

A *client* is a computer that is designed to request information from a server. A *server* is a computer that is dedicated to providing information in response to external requests. A *client/server network* is a model for applications in which the bulk of the back-end processing, such as performing a physical search of a database, takes place on a server, while the front-end processing, which involves communicating with the users, is handled by the clients (see Figure 7.5). A *network operating system (NOS)* is the operating system that runs a network, steering information between computers and managing security and users. The client/server model has become one of the central ideas of network computing. Most business applications written today use the client/server model.

A fundamental part of client/server architecture is packet-switching. *Packet-switching* occurs when the sending computer divides a message into a number of efficiently sized units called packets, each of which contains the address of the destination computer. Each packet is sent on the network and intercepted by routers. A *router* is an intelligent connecting device that examines each packet of data it receives and then decides which way to send it onward toward its destination. The packets arrive at their intended destination, although some may have actually traveled by different physical paths, and the receiving computer assembles the packets and delivers the message to the appropriate application. The number of network routers being installed by businesses worldwide is booming (see Figure 7.6).

Eva Chen, CIO at Trend Micro, built a router that helps prevent worms and viruses from entering networks. The problem with most existing antivirus software is that it starts working after a destructive sequence of code is identified, meaning it starts doing its job only after the virus or worm has been unleashed inside the network. Chen's router, the Network VirusWall, sits on the edge of a corporate network, scanning data packets and detaining those that might contain viruses or

FIGURE 7.5

Client/Server Network

FIGURE 7.6

Worldwide Router Growth

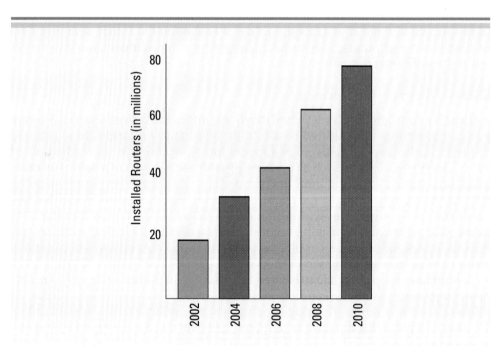

worms. Any suspicious packets are compared with up-to-the-second information from Trend Micro's virus-tracking command center. Viruses and worms are then deleted and refused entry to the network, allowing the company to perform a preemptive strike.[2]

TOPOLOGY

Networks are assembled according to certain rules. Cables, for example, have to be a certain length; each cable strand can support only a certain amount of network traffic. A ***network topology*** refers to the geometric arrangement of the

FIGURE 7.7

Five Network Topologies

Network Topologies	
Bus	All devices are connected to a central cable, called the bus or backbone. Bus networks are relatively inexpensive and easy to install for small networks.
Star	All devices are connected to a central device, called a hub. Star networks are relatively easy to install and manage, but bottlenecks can occur because all data must pass through the hub.
Ring	All devices are connected to one another in the shape of a closed loop, so that each device is connected directly to two other devices, one on either side of it. Ring topologies are relatively expensive and difficult to install, but they offer high bandwidth and can span large distances.
Hybrid	Groups of star-configured workstations are connected to a linear bus backbone cable, combining the characteristics of the bus and star topologies.
Wireless	Devices are connected by a receiver/transmitter to a special network interface card that transmits signals between a computer and a server, all within an acceptable transmission range.

FIGURE 7.8

Network Topologies

actual physical organization of the computers (and other network devices) in a network. Topologies vary depending on cost and functionality. Figure 7.7 highlights the five common topologies used in networks, and Figure 7.8 displays each topology.

PROTOCOLS

A **protocol** is a standard that specifies the format of data as well as the rules to be followed during transmission. Simply put, for one computer (or computer program) to talk to another computer (or computer program) they must both be talking the same language, and this language is called a protocol.

A protocol is based on an agreed-upon and established standard, and this way all manufacturers of hardware and software that are using the protocol do so in a similar fashion to allow for interoperability. **Interoperability** is the capability of two or more computer systems to share data and resources, even though they are made by different manufacturers. The most popular network protocols used are Ethernet and Transmission Control Protocol/Internet Protocol (TCP/IP).

Ethernet

Ethernet is a physical and data layer technology for LAN networking (see Figure 7.9). Ethernet is the most widely installed LAN access method, originally developed by Xerox and then developed further by Xerox, Digital Equipment Corporation, and Intel. When it first began to be widely deployed in the 1980s, Ethernet supported a maximum theoretical data transfer rate of 10 megabits per second (Mbps). More recently, Fast Ethernet has extended traditional Ethernet technology to 100 Mbps peak, and Gigabit Ethernet technology extends performance up to 1,000 Mbps.

Ethernet has survived as the major LAN technology—it is currently used for approximately 85 percent of the world's LAN-connected PCs and workstations—because its protocol has the following characteristics:

- Is easy to understand, implement, manage, and maintain.
- Allows low-cost network implementations.

FIGURE 7.9

Ethernet Protocol

FIGURE 7.10

TCP/IP Four-Layer Reference
Model

Applications	FTP, SMTP, Telnet, HTTP, SNTP
Transport	TCP
Internet	IP
Network Interface	Ethernet, Token Ring, FDDI

- Provides extensive flexibility for network installation.
- Guarantees successful interconnection and operation of standards-compliant products, regardless of manufacturer.

Transmission Control Protocol/Internet Protocol

The most common telecommunication protocol is Transmission Control Protocol/Internet Protocol (TCP/IP), which was originally developed by the Department of Defense to connect a system of computer networks that became known as the Internet. *Transmission Control Protocol/Internet Protocol (TCP/IP)* provides the technical foundation for the public Internet as well as for large numbers of private networks. The key achievement of TCP/IP is its flexibility with respect to lower-level protocols. TCP/IP uses a special transmission method that maximizes data transfer and automatically adjusts to slower devices and other delays encountered on a network. Although more than 100 protocols make up the entire TCP/IP protocol suite, the two most important of these are TCP and IP. **TCP** provides transport functions, ensuring, among other things, that the amount of data received is the same as the amount transmitted. **IP** provides the addressing and routing mechanism that acts as a postmaster. Figure 7.10 displays TCP/IP's four-layer reference model:

- Application layer—serves as the window for users and application processes to access network services.
- Transport layer—handles end-to-end packet transportation.
- Internet layer—formats the data into packets, adds a header containing the packet sequence and the address of the receiving device, and specifies the services required from the network.
- Network interface layer—places data packets on the network for transmission.

The TCP/IP suite of applications includes five protocols—file transfer, simple mail transfer, telnet, hypertext transfer, and simple network management (see Figure 7.11).

Another communication reference model is the seven-layer Open System Interconnection (OSI) reference model. Figure 7.12 show the OSI model's seven layers.

The lower layers (1 to 3) represent local communications, while the upper layers (4 to 7) represent end-to-end communications. Each layer contributes protocol functions that are necessary to establish and maintain the error-free exchange of information between network users.

For many years, users thought the OSI model would replace TCP/IP as the preferred technique for connecting multivendor networks. But the slow pace of OSI standards as well as the expense of implementing complex OSI software and having products certified for OSI interoperability will preclude this from happening.

FIGURE 7.11

TCP/IP Applications

TCP/IP Applications	
File Transfer Protocol (FTP)	Allows files containing text, programs, graphics, numerical data, and so on to be downloaded off or uploaded onto a network.
Simple Mail Transfer Protocol (SMTP)	TCP/IP's own messaging system for e-mail.
Telnet Protocol	Provides terminal emulation that allows a personal computer or workstation to act as a terminal, or access device, for a server.
Hypertext Transfer Protocol (HTTP)	Allows Web browsers and servers to send and receive Web pages.
Simple Network Management Protocol (SNMP)	Allows the management of networked nodes to be managed from a single point.

FIGURE 7.12

Open System Interconnection Model

OSI Model
7. Application
6. Presentation
5. Session
4. Transport
3. Network
2. Data Link
1. Physical

Voice over IP (VoIP)   Originally, phone calls made over the Internet had a reputation of offering poor call quality, lame user interfaces, and low call-completion rates. With new and improved technology and IT infrastructures, Internet phone calls now offer similar quality to traditional telephone calls. Today, many consumers are making phone calls over the Internet by using voice over Internet protocol (VoIP). *Voice over IP (VoIP)* uses TCP/IP technology to transmit voice calls over long-distance telephone lines. In fact, VoIP transmits over 10 percent of all phone calls in the United States and this number is growing exponentially.

VoIP and e-mail work in similar ways. The user sends a call over the Internet in packets of audio data tagged with the same destination. VoIP reassembles the packets once they arrive at their final destination.

Numerous vendors offer VoIP services; however, the service works differently depending on the vendor's IT infrastructure. The start-up Skype pairs P2P (peer-to-peer) technology with a PC's sound card to create a voice service, which the client can use to call other Skype users. Unfortunately, the user can talk only to other Skype users. Vonage lets the user place calls to any person who has a mobile or land-line (regular telephone) number. Vonage sends the call over a cable via a digital-to-analog converter. A few providers even offer an adapter for a traditional handset that plugs into a broadband modem. All of these vendors are providing VoIP, but the service and its features can vary significantly.

The telecom industry expects great benefits from combining VoIP with emerging standards that allow for easier development, interoperability among systems, and application integration. This is a big change for an industry that relies on proprietary systems to keep customers paying for upgrades and new features. The VoIP and open-standards combo should produce more choices, lower prices, and new applications.

FIGURE 7.13

Typical Telephone Start-up
Costs for a 1,000-Person
Office

Telephone System	Typical Telecom System	IP-Based System	Peerio
Requirements	■ Phones ■ Private branch exchange (PBX) ■ Voice switches ■ Dedicated voice network	■ Phones ■ IP PBX ■ Existing data network ■ Gateway	■ Phones ■ PC ■ Existing data network ■ Gateway
Total Cost	$1,000,000	$500,000	$100,000

Writing voice applications may never be as common as writing computer applications. But the spread of VoIP will make it easier to manage applications and add capabilities to the voice feature set. In a decade, the telecom network "will be like getting water out of the tap," predicts Stef van Aarle, vice president of marketing and strategy at Lucent Worldwide Services. "The only time you think of it will be when it doesn't work. And software is the glue that makes it all easy to use."

Upstarts like Vonage and Skype are bringing VoIP to the masses. But a bigger opportunity lurks in the $2 billion corporate phone market. New York-based start-up Popular Telephony is offering a new VoIP technology that dramatically cuts corporate phone costs while letting workers take their office phones anywhere. Its secret: peer-to-peer software called Peerio that is built right into handsets.

CEO Dmitry Goroshevsky founded the company three years ago to bring PC economics to the office telephone system. A traditional workplace setup requires a dedicated voice network and a private branch exchange, or PBX, to connect to the outside world and can cost up to $1 million (see Figure 7.13). Cisco has been selling an IP PBX, which uses a data network for voice calls. But Popular Telephony eliminates pricey hardware. Using an ordinary PC, network administrators assign an extension to each phone. Peerio-enabled handsets, which will be sold through discount retailers and office supply stores, plug directly into a company's data network, where calls are routed through a gateway and then out. Since Peerio is based on Internet protocol, office workers can use their phones wherever there is a broadband connection. And though companies pay the usual rates to call conventional landline and mobile phone numbers, ringing up other Peerio and VoIP users will not cost a dime. A handful of licensees are manufacturing the phones.[3]

MEDIA

Network transmission media refers to the various types of media used to carry the signal between computers. When information is sent across the network, it is converted into electrical signals. These signals are generated as electromagnetic waves (analog signaling) or as a sequence of voltage pulses (digital signaling). To be sent from one location to another, a signal must travel along a physical path. The physical path that is used to carry a signal between a signal transmitter and a signal receiver is called the transmission media. The two types of transmission media are wire (guided) and wireless (unguided).

Wire Media

Wire media are transmission material manufactured so that signals will be confined to a narrow path and will behave predictably. The three most commonly used types of guided media are (see Figure 7.14):

- Twisted-pair wiring
- Coaxial cable
- Fiber-optic cable

FIGURE 7.14

Twisted-Pair, Coaxial Cable,
and Fiber-Optic

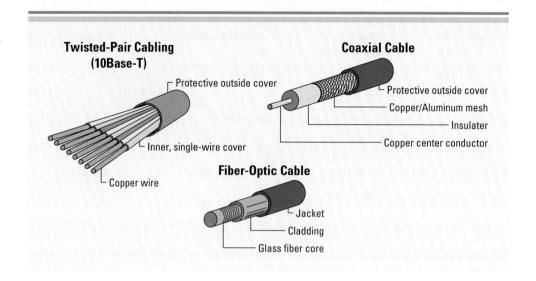

Twisted-Pair Wiring   *Twisted-pair wiring* refers to a type of cable composed of four (or more) copper wires twisted around each other within a plastic sheath. The wires are twisted to reduce outside electrical interference. Twisted-pair cables come in shielded and unshielded varieties. Shielded cables have a metal shield encasing the wires that acts as a ground for electromagnetic interference. Unshielded twisted-pair (UTP) is the most popular and is generally the best option for LAN networks. The quality of UTP may vary from telephone-grade wire to high-speed cable. The cable has four pairs of wires inside the jacket. Each pair is twisted with a different number of twists per inch to help eliminate interference from adjacent pairs and other electrical devices. The RJ-45 connectors on twisted-pair cables resemble large telephone connectors.

Coaxial Cable   *Coaxial cable* is cable that can carry a wide range of frequencies with low signal loss. It consists of a metallic shield with a single wire placed along the center of a shield and isolated from the shield by an insulator. This type of cable is referred to as coaxial because it contains one copper wire (or physical data channel) that carries the signal and is surrounded by another concentric physical channel consisting of a wire mesh. The outer channel serves as a ground for electrical interference. Because of this grounding feature, several coaxial cables can be placed within a single conduit or sheath without significant loss of data integrity.

Fiber-Optic Cable   *Fiber optic* (or *optical fiber*) refers to the technology associated with the transmission of information as light impulses along a glass wire or fiber. The 10Base-FL and 100Base-FX optical fiber cable are the same types of cable used by most telephone companies for long-distance service. Optical fiber cable can transmit data over long distances with little loss in data integrity. In addition, because data are transferred as a pulse of light, optical fiber is not subject to interference. The light pulses travel through a glass wire or fiber encased in an insulating sheath.

Optical fiber's increased maximum effective distance comes at a price. Optical fiber is more fragile than wire, difficult to split, and labor intensive to install. For these reasons, optical fiber is used primarily to transmit data over extended distances where the hardware required to relay the data signal on less expensive media would exceed the cost of optical fiber installation. It is also used where large amounts of data need to be transmitted on a regular basis.

Wireless Media

Wireless media are natural parts of the Earth's environment that can be used as physical paths to carry electrical signals. The atmosphere and outer space are examples of wireless media that are commonly used to carry signals. These media can carry such electromagnetic signals as microwave, infrared light waves, and radio waves.

Network signals are transmitted through all media as a type of waveform. When transmitted through wire and cable, the signal is an electrical waveform. When transmitted through fiber-optic cable, the signal is a light wave, either visible or infrared light. When transmitted through the Earth's atmosphere, the signal can take the form of waves in the radio spectrum, including microwaves, infrared, or visible light.

Recent advances in radio hardware technology have produced significant advancements in wireless networking devices: the cellular telephone, wireless modems, and wireless LANs. These devices use technology that in some cases has been around for decades but until recently was too impractical or expensive for widespread use.

E-BUSINESS NETWORKS

To set up an e-business even a decade ago would have required an individual organization to assume the burden of developing the entire network infrastructure. Today, industry-leading companies have developed Internet-based products and services to handle many aspects of customer and supplier interactions. "In today's retail market, you cannot be a credible national retailer without having a robust Web site," says Dennis Bowman, senior vice president and CIO of Circuit City, who adds that customers now expect seamless retailing just as they expect stores that are clean and well stocked. For this reason, retailers are working furiously to integrate their e-business sites with their inventory and point-of-sale (POS) systems so that they can accept in-store returns of merchandise bought online and allow customers to buy on the Web and pick up in the store.

Some companies, such as Best Buy, Circuit City, Office Depot, and Sears, already have their physical and online stores integrated. These companies have been the fast movers because they already had an area in their stores for merchandise pickup (usually for big, bulky items like TVs and appliances), and because long before the Web they had systems and processes in place that facilitated the transfer of a sale from one store to another. Other retailers are partially integrated. Ann Taylor, Bed Bath & Beyond, Eddie Bauer, Linens 'n' Things, Macy's, REI, Target, The Gap, and others let customers return but not pick up online-ordered merchandise in stores. To take on the challenge of e-business integration, an organization needs a secure and reliable IT infrastructure for mission-critical systems (see Figure 7.15)

A *virtual private network (VPN)* is a way to use the public telecommunication infrastructure (e.g., Internet) to provide secure access to an organization's network (see Figure 7.16). A *valued-added network (VAN)* is a private network, provided by a third party, for exchanging information through a high-capacity connection. To date, organizations engaging in e-business have relied largely on VPNs, VANs, and other dedicated links handling electronic data interchange transactions. These

FIGURE 7.15

E-Business Network Characteristics

E-Business Network Characteristics
■ Provide for the transparent exchange of information with suppliers, trading partners, and customers.
■ Reliably and securely exchange information internally and externally via the Internet or other networks.
■ Allow end-to-end integration and provide message delivery across multiple systems, in particular, databases, clients, and servers.
■ Respond to high demands with scalable processing power and networking capacity.
■ Serve as the integrator and transaction framework for both digital businesses and traditional brick-and-mortar businesses that want to leverage the Internet for any type of business.

FIGURE 7.16

Virtual Private Network
Example

traditional solutions are still deployed in the market and for many companies will likely hold a strategic role for years to come. However, conventional technologies present significant challenges:

- By handling only limited kinds of business information, these contribute little to a reporting structure intended to provide a comprehensive view of business operations.
- They offer little support for the real-time business process integration that will be essential in the digital marketplace.
- Relatively expensive and complex to implement, conventional technologies make it difficult to expand or change networks in response to market shifts.

OPENING CASE QUESTIONS

The Digital Hospital

1. Explain how hospitals are using telecommunication and network technologies to improve their operations.

2. Describe the two different types of network architectures and identify which one Hackensack University Medical Center is using.

3. Explain TCP/IP and the role it plays in Hackensack University Medical Center's IT projects.

4. Identify a new telecommunication or network product that Hackensack University Medical Center could use to improve its operations

section 7.2   WIRELESS COMPUTING

LEARNING OUTCOMES

7.7. Explain how a wireless device helps an organization conduct business anytime, anywhere, anyplace.

7.8. Describe RFID and how it can be used to help make a supply chain more effective.

7.9. List and discuss the key factors inspiring the growth of wireless technologies.

7.10. Describe the business benefits associated with enterprise mobility.

WIRELESS FIDELITY

An hour's drive west of Toronto sits a 120,000-square-foot building where Mike Lazaridis's 20-year dream is coming to life. Seven 125-foot-long assembly lines are stamping out wallet-size BlackBerrys—the wireless handhelds now in the hands of more than 1.3 million users worldwide—at a rate of about 230 an hour. Lazaridis, the co-CEO of Research in Motion (RIM), gave the go-ahead earlier this year to ratchet up plant production from five days a week to seven. Orders are surging, and so RIM's BlackBerry-making machine does not sleep.[4]

Wireless fidelity (wi-fi) is a means of linking computers using infrared or radio signals. Wi-fi is a type of Ethernet, which makes the wireless network a straightforward extension of the wired network. Wireless users can run the same network applications they use on an Ethernet LAN. Wireless communication can be installed using the existing network infrastructure with minimal retraining or system changes. Laptop users can roam throughout their locales while remaining in contact with the network via strategically placed access points that are plugged into the wired network. One of the biggest benefits of using wireless communications is its ability to deliver real-time information.

The Value of Timely Information

The need for timely information can change for each business decision. Some decisions require weekly or monthly information while other decisions require daily information. Timeliness is an aspect of information that depends on the situation. In some industries, information that is a few days or weeks old can be relevant, while in other industries information that is a few minutes old can be almost worthless. Some organizations, such as 911 centers, stock traders, and banks, require consolidated, up-to-the-second information, 24 hours a day, seven days a week. Other organizations, such as insurance and construction companies, require only daily or even weekly information.

Real-time information means immediate, up-to-date information. *Real-time systems* provide real-time information in response to query requests. Many organizations use real-time systems to exploit key corporate transactional information. In a survey of 700 IT executives by Evans Data Corp., 48 percent of respondents said they were already analyzing information in or near real-time, and another 25 percent reported plans to add real-time systems.[5]

Real-time systems provide valuable information for supporting corporate strategies such as customer relationship management. Bell Mobility Inc., Canada's largest wireless carrier, staffs over 550 customer service representatives and uses E.piphany Inc.'s Real-Time tool to make the right customer offers at the right time without having to rely on guesswork. The results from the first month after implementation of the Real-Time tool are displayed in Figure 7.17.[6]

The growing demand for real-time information stems from organizations' need to make faster and more effective decisions, keep smaller inventories, operate more efficiently, and track performance more carefully. Nevertheless, timeliness is

FIGURE 7.17

Results from Bell Mobility's Real-Time Tool

Bell Mobility's Real-Time Tool Results
■ 18 percent increase in sales per hour
■ 16 percent increase in total inbound marketing revenue
■ 75 percent decrease in total time to create and deploy a new marketing campaign

relative. Organizations need fresh, timely information to make good decisions. Information also needs to be timely in the sense that it meets employees' needs, but no more. If employees can absorb information only on an hourly or daily basis, there is no need to gather real-time information in smaller increments.

MBIA Insurance Corp. uses overnight updates to feed its real-time systems. Employees use this information to make daily risk decisions for mortgages, insurance policies, and other services. The company found that overnight updates were sufficient, as long as users could gain immediate access to the information they needed to make business decisions during the day.[7]

Most people request real-time information without understanding one of the biggest pitfalls associated with real-time information—continual change. Imagine the following scenario: Three managers meet at the end of the day to discuss a business problem. Each manager has gathered information at different times during the day to create a picture of the situation. Each manager's picture may be different because of this time discrepancy. Their views on the business problem may not match since the information they are basing their analysis on is continually changing. This approach may not speed up decision making, and may actually slow it down.

Organizations must evaluate the timeliness of the information required for each business decision. Organizations do not want to find themselves using real-time information to make a bad decision faster.

BUSINESS DRIVERS FOR WIRELESS TECHNOLOGIES

United Parcel Service and FedEx have been using wireless technologies for years, making it possible for information about dispatching and deliveries to travel between couriers and central stations. FedEx's famous tracking system, which can find a package's location from its tracking number, uses a wireless courier-management system.

The terms *mobile* and *wireless* are often used synonymously, but actually denote two different technologies. *Mobile technology* means the technology can travel with the user, but it is not necessarily in real-time; users can download software, e-mail messages, and Web pages onto their personal digital assistant (PDA), laptop, or other mobile device for portable reading or reference. Information collected while on the road can be synchronized with a PC or corporate server.

Wireless technology, on the other hand, gives users a live (Internet) connection via satellite or radio transmitters. International Data Corporation forecasts that by 2010 nearly two-thirds of handheld devices will include integrated wireless networking. For instance, newly announced PDAs integrate phones, text messaging, Web browsers, and organizers. Figure 7.18 displays the factors inspiring the growth of wireless technologies.[8]

State government agencies, such as transportation departments, use wireless devices to collect field information, tracking inventory, reporting times, monitoring logistics, and completing forms—all from a mobile environment. The

FIGURE 7.18

Wireless Drivers

Drivers of Wireless Technology Growth	
Universal access to information and applications	People are mobile and have more access to information than ever before, but they still need to get to the point where they can access all information anytime, anywhere, anyplace.
The automation of business processes	Wireless technologies have the ability to centralize critical information and eliminate redundant processes.
User convenience, timeliness, and ability to conduct business 24x7x365	People delayed in airports no longer have to feel cut off from the world or their office. Through wireless tools and wireless solutions such as a BlackBerry RIM device, they can access their information anytime, anywhere, anyplace.

FIGURE 7.19

U. S. Wireless Device Users

Number of U.S. Users	Wireless Device Technology
Less than 15,000	Smart phones
4,000,000	Web-enabled (WAP) phones
65,000,000	Digital cell phones

FIGURE 7.20

Wireless Technologies
Changing Business

Wireless Devices Changing Business

- **Wireless local area network (wLAN):** uses radio waves rather than wires to transmit information across a local area network.

- **Cellular phones and pagers:** provide connectivity for portable and mobile applications, both personal and business.

- **Cordless computer peripherals:** connect wirelessly to a computer, such as a cordless mouse, keyboard, and printer.

- **Satellite television:** allows viewers in almost any location to select from hundreds of channels.

- **WiMax wireless broadband:** enables wireless networks to extend as far as 30 miles and transfer information, voice, and video at faster speeds than cable. It is perfect for Internet service providers (ISPs) that want to expand into sparsely populated areas, where the cost of bringing in cable wiring or DSL is too high.

- **Security sensor:** alerts customers to break-ins and errant pop flies. Its dual sensors record vibration and acoustic disturbances—a shattered window—to help avoid false alarms.

transportation industry is using wireless devices to help determine current locations and alternate driving routes.

Wireless technology is rapidly evolving and is playing an increasing role in the lives of people throughout the world. The final key factor driving the increased use of wireless devices is the sheer number of U.S. wireless device users (see Figure 7.19). With such a large market, businesses simply must embrace wireless technologies or be left behind.

Wireless technologies are transforming how we live, work, and play. Handheld devices continue to offer additional functionality, and cellular networks are advancing rapidly in their increased speed and throughput abilities. These enabling technologies fuel widespread adoption and creation of new and innovative ways to perform business. The big changes that will re-create workplaces, industries, and organizations are coming from wireless technologies. Figure 7.20 displays a few common examples of wireless technologies that are changing our world.

ADVANTAGES OF ENTERPRISE MOBILITY

Organizations have realized that while the value of electronic corporate information can be nearly limitless, it is worth nothing if employees cannot access it. Work does not always get done at an office desk, and the ability to connect remote workers to the information they require to perform their job provides benefits to an organization.

Wireless laptops facilitate emergency room registration so doctors can start working on the patients as soon as the medics wheel them into the hospital. High-end tractors equipped with wireless sensors help farmers monitor everything from the weather to the amount of seed released. Tractors that break down automatically e-mail the service department with the information for the repair. Roaming ticket sellers armed with wi-fi-enabled devices and belt-mounted printers shorten the wait at the front gate at theme parks such as Universal Studios. Figure 7.21 lists the wireless technologies influencing business mobility, which are described in detail in the following section.

FIGURE 7.21

Wireless Technologies
Influencing Business Mobility

Wireless Technlogies Influencing Business Mobility
■ **Bluetooth:** creating a niche market for traditionally cabled devices.
■ **Radio frequency identification tags (RFID):** possessing the potential to reinvent the supply chain. Wal-Mart's suppliers must now use the tags for pallets and cases of merchandise.
■ **Satellite:** changing the way television and radio stations operate. Plus, global positioning systems (GPS) allow drivers of cars and trucks, captains of boats and ships, backpackers, hikers, skiers, and pilots of aircraft to ascertain their location anywhere on Earth.

FIGURE 7.22

Bluetooth Virtual Keyboard

Beams of light, which detect the user's movements, make up this virtual keyboard. It can be integrated into mobile phones, laptops, tablet PCs, or even sterile medical environments.

Bluetooth

One challenge to wireless devices is their size. Everyone wants their mobile devices to be small, but many people also curse the tiny, cryptic keyboards that manufacturers squeeze into smart phones and PDAs. The laws of physics have proved a significant barrier to solving this problem, but VKB Inc.'s Bluetooth Virtual Keyboard offers a possible solution (see Figure 7.22). VKB's technology uses a red laser to illuminate a virtual keyboard outline on any surface. Despite its futuristic look, the laser is really just a visual guide to where users put their fingers. A separate illumination and sensor module invisibly tracks when and where each finger touches the surface, translating that into keystrokes or other commands.[9]

Bluetooth is an omnidirectional wireless technology that provides limited-range voice and data transmission over the unlicensed 2.4-GHz frequency band, allowing connections with a wide variety of fixed and portable devices that normally would have to be cabled together. Bluetooth headsets allow users to cut the cord and make calls even while their cell phones are tucked away in a briefcase. Wireless Bluetooth printing allows users of a Bluetooth-enabled PDA or laptop to connect to any printer via a Bluetooth adapter connected to the printer's parallel port.

Since Bluetooth's development in 1994 by the Swedish telecommunications company Ericsson, more than 1,800 companies worldwide have signed on to build products to the wireless specification and promote the new technology in the marketplace. The engineers at Ericsson code-named the new wireless technology Bluetooth to honor a 10th-century Viking King, Harald Bluetooth, who is credited with uniting Denmark and bringing order to the country.

Bluetooth capability is enabled in a device by means of an embedded Bluetooth chip and supporting software. Although Bluetooth is slower than competing wireless LAN technologies, the Bluetooth chip enables Bluetooth networking to be built into a wide range of devices—even small devices such as cellular phones and PDAs. Bluetooth's maximum range is 30 feet, limiting it to gadget-to-gadget communication. There are more than 1,000 Bluetooth products on the market, with 10 more introduced each week.

Radio Frequency Identification (RFID)

Radio frequency identification (RFID) technologies use active or passive tags in the form of chips or smart labels that can store unique identifiers and relay this information to electronic readers. At Starbucks, good service is nearly as important as good coffee to customer loyalty. But when a delivery person comes knocking on the back door to drop off muffins, it means employees may need to leave their countertop posts, jeopardizing customer service. To help solve the problem, Starbucks is considering using radio frequency identification technology as part of a proposed plan to let its 40,000 suppliers drop off pastries, milk, coffee beans, and other supplies at night, after stores have closed. This solution solves one problem while causing another: How does Starbucks ensure that delivery people do not walk out with as much stuff as they dropped off?

To solve the problem, the company will distribute to its suppliers cards with RFID chips that give delivery people access to stores at night, while recording who is coming and going. *RFID tags* contain a microchip and an antenna, and typically work by transmitting a serial number via radio waves to an electronic reader, which confirms the identity of a person or object bearing the tag.

RFID technology is finally coming into its own. Wal-Mart, the nation's largest retailer, asked suppliers to attach RFID tags to product shipment pallets by the end of 2005 to automate tracking. However, drawbacks to RFID technology, including its high cost and concerns about consumer privacy, must be overcome before it finds widespread use. Figure 7.23 displays the three components of RFID, and Figure 7.24 shows how tracking with RFID tags is expected to work in the supply chain.

As many as 10,000 radio frequency identification tags are taking to the skies, affixed to everything from airline seats to brakes, as part of the Airbus A380, a 550-seat

FIGURE 7.23

Three RFID Components

The Three Components to an RFID System

Tag - A microchip holds data, in this case an EPC (electronic product code), a set of numbers unique to an item. The rest of the tag is an antenna that transmits data to a reader. EPC example: 01-0000A77-000136BR5

Reader - A reader uses radio waves to read the tag and sends the EPC to computers in the supply chain.

Computer Network - Each computer in the supply chain recognizes the EPC and pulls up information related to the item, such as dates made and shipped, price, and directions for use, from a server maintained by the manufacturer. The computers track the item's location throughout the supply chain.

FIGURE 7.24

RFID in the Supply Chain.

RFID in the Retail Supply Chain
RFID tags are added to every product and shipping box. At every step of an item's journey, a reader scans one of the tags and updates the information on the server.

The Manufacturer
A reader scans the tags as items leave the factory.

The Distribution Center
Readers in the unloading area scan the tags on arriving boxes and update inventory, avoiding the need to open packages.

The Store
Tags are scanned upon arrival to update inventory. At the racks, readers scan tags as shirts are stocked. At the checkout counter, a cashier can scan individual items with a handheld reader. As items leave the store, inventory is updated. Manufacturers and retailers can observe sales patterns in real time and make swift decisions about production, ordering, and pricing.

The Home
The consumer can have the tag disabled at the store for privacy or place readers in closets to keep track of clothes. With customers' approval, stores can follow purchasing patterns and notify them of sales.

jet scheduled to begin service in 2006. The tags will contain serial numbers, codes, and maintenance history that should make it easier to track, fix, and replace parts. Not to be outdone, Boeing is using tags on many of the parts in its upcoming 7E7 Dreamliner, a smaller commercial jet that is set to fly in 2007 and be in service by 2008.

These initiatives are not the first use of RFID in the airline industry, but they represent aggressive plans to further leverage the real-time and detail capabilities of RFID. In 2000, Boeing began equipping all its tools and toolboxes with RFID tags. Similarly, Airbus began tagging its ground equipment and tools soon after.[10]

Integrating RFID and Software Integrating RFID with enterprise software is expected to change the way companies manage maintenance, combat theft, and even augment Sarbanes-Oxley Act IT initiatives. Oracle and SAP have begun adding RFID capability to their enterprise application suites. Oracle's RFID and Sensor-Based Services analyze and respond to data from RFID so the information can be integrated with Oracle's applications.

RFID tags are evolving, too, and the advances will provide more granular information to enterprise software. Today's tags can store an electronic product code. In time, tags could hold more information, making them portable mini-databases.

The possibilities of RFID are endless. Delta Air Lines recently completed a pilot project that used baggage tags incorporating RFID chips instead of the standard bar codes. With RFID readers installed at counters and key sorting locations, not a single duffel was misplaced. The system worked so well that Delta intends to roll it out nationwide in 2007.[11]

Satellite

Microwave transmitters, especially satellite systems, are commonly used to transmit network signals over great distances. A microwave transmitter uses the atmosphere (or outer space) as the transmission medium to send the signal to a microwave receiver. The microwave receiver then either relays the signal to another microwave

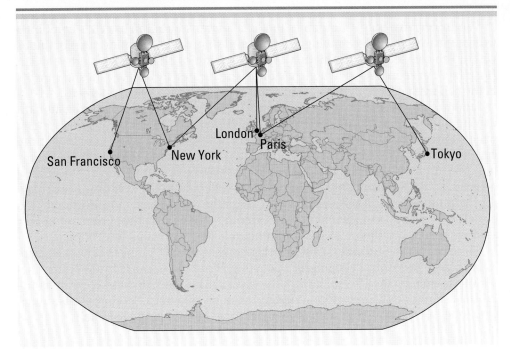

FIGURE 7.25

Satellite Microwave Link

transmitter or translates the signal to some other form, such as digital impulses, as illustrated in Figure 7.25. Originally, this technology was used almost exclusively for satellite and long-range communication. Recently, however, developments in cellular technology allow complete wireless access to networks, intranets, and the Internet via microwave transmission.

XM Satellite Radio made a tech-savvy decision when it decided to develop the chipsets for XM's radios in-house rather than outsourcing the job. The move allowed the XM service to launch faster and better, giving the company a lead over its archrival, Sirius Satellite Radio. Both companies are growing quickly. Satellite radio is big business, and Sirius recently signed a contract with Howard Stern for $500 million over five years.[12]

Global Positioning System (GPS)

The Department of Defense installed more than 30 satellites in space over the equator to help the military identify positions on Earth. In 1993, the Defense Department made this global positioning technology available for commercial use to anyone who has a GPS. A *global positioning system (GPS)* is a device that determines current latitude, longitude, speed, and direction of movement. GPS devices have special microprocessors that analyze satellite signals. Sirf Technology specializes in building GPS microprocessors and charges about $13 per device to put its GPS chipset in phones, electronics, and car navigation systems. Since going public in 2004, Sirf Technology has seen revenue climb 60 percent to $117 million with net profits of $30.7 million. With new federal regulation forcing wireless operators to include GPS in their phones and networking equipment, chip demand is sure to explode.[13]

The market for GPS services has grown to over $5 billion with expectations for demand to double over the next few years. Tracking, navigation, and hardware promise to be multibillion-dollar markets by 2010. UPS plans to outfit 75,000 drivers with GPS-enabled handhelds to help them reach destinations more efficiently. The handhelds will also trigger e-mail alerts if a company vehicle speeds or ventures into unauthorized areas. Steve Wozniak, Apple co-founder, started a company in 2002 named Wheels of Zeus that combines GPS data with local wireless networking. The technology helps parents keep tabs on their children or can alert IT managers when company-owned computers leave the premises. Zingo, in the United Kingdom, uses GPS-enabled cars and text messaging to help subscribers hail cabs.

A *geographic information system (GIS)* is designed to work with information that can be shown on a map. Companies that deal in transportation use GISs combined with database and GPS technology. Airlines and shipping companies can plot routes with up-to-the-second information on the location of all their transport vehicles. Hospitals can keep track of where personnel are located by using a GIS and sensors in the ceiling that pick up the transmission of badges worn by hospital staff.

Automobiles have GPSs linked to maps that display in a screen on the dashboard driving directions and exact location of the vehicle. GM offers the OnStar system, which sends a continuous stream of information to the OnStar center about the car's exact location. The new OnStar Vehicle Diagnostics automatically performs hundreds of diagnostic checks on four key operating systems—the engine/transmission, antilock brakes, air bags, and OnStar systems—in GM vehicles. The vehicle is programmed to send the results via e-mail to the owner each month. The unique e-mail report also provides maintenance reminders based on the current odometer reading, remaining engine oil life, and other relevant ownership information.[14]

Some cell phone providers equip their phones with GPS chips that enable users to be located to within a geographical location about the size of a tennis court. This allows emergency services such as 911 to find a cell phone user. Marketers are monitoring cell phone GPS development, hoping to be able to call potential customers when they are walking past their store to let them know of a special sale.[15]

THE FUTURE OF WIRELESS

One of the strangest Internet innovations in recent history was Microsoft's toilet project. It was a widely reported weird-news item in the spring of 2003, later revealed to be a hoax, and even later to be confirmed by Microsoft as an actual project, albeit a defunct one. The gist of the story was that Microsoft U.K. wanted to create a portable toilet, the iLoo, with a built-in high-speed Internet connection, wireless keyboard, and height-adjustable plasma monitor—a contraption, so they said, that would appeal to the British market.

Now it seems that the restroom and the Internet are converging yet again. A *hotspot* consists of one or more access points positioned on a ceiling, wall, or other strategic spot in a public place to provide maximum wireless coverage for a specific area. Users in range of the hotspot can then access the Internet from their wireless device. The latest front in the wireless hotspot movement is the interstate rest area. "I know it sounds strange at first, but when you think about it, rest areas are a great fit for wi-fi," said Mark Wheeler, CEO of I Spot Networks, a wireless Internet service provider. Wheeler noted that highway travelers often actively seek out an Internet connection because the Internet has become so integral to 21st century life.

Working in conjunction with state transportation departments, I Spot Networks is rolling out hotspots along interstates in Iowa, Missouri, and Nebraska. The company also targets more conventional hotspot locations, such as hotels and coffee shops, but it believes that heavily traveled interstate corridors are an overlooked hotspot opportunity.

Analysts predict that more than 120 million U.S. consumers will use wireless devices for Internet access by 2008. Overall, there will be more than 1.4 billion wireless subscribers by the end of 2010, with about 500 million of those using wireless Internet access. The growth of the wireless market will drive the development of new wireless technology, which in turn will create a larger market for Bluetooth connectivity, which allows wireless handheld devices, personal computers, and laptops to work together. Analysts expect Bluetooth shipments to rise from fewer than 1 million in 2001 to 3 billion in 2010.[16]

Gartner Inc. predicts that the future will belong to "The Real-Time Enterprise," the organization that thrives in uncertain times because it can detect sooner and respond faster. Wireless technologies clearly play a major role in increasing an organization's agility.

Wireless access to corporate e-mail systems, often the primary catalyst to an organization's first significant venture into wireless technology, has become the

FIGURE 7.26

Current Mobile Phone Users'
Applications Interest

Application	Western Europe	Eastern Europe	United States
On 6-point interest scale, 6 = high interest, and 1 = low interest:			
E-mail	4.5	4.7	4.3
Payment authorization/enablement	3.4	3.8	3.0
Banking/trading online	3.5	3.4	3.2
Shopping/reservations	3.0	3.1	2.9
Interactive games	2.0	2.2	2.4

focus of much attention. E-mail is the foremost communication system in most organizations, surpassing voice mail in importance and interest (see Figure 7.26).[17]

Organizations are fast approaching the point where they will have the technical wireless infrastructure to support an always-on connection that will let users roam seamlessly from Starbucks, to a customer site, to conference rooms, and even to a comfortable chair in front of the TV at home.

OPENING CASE QUESTIONS

The Digital Hospital

5. Why is real-time information important to hospitals?

6. How is Hackensack University Medical Center using wireless technology to improve its operations?

7. Identify three wireless technologies that are changing the way businesses operate and explain how hospitals can use these technologies to improve their operations.

Bluetooth 230
Client 217
Client/server network 217
Coaxial cable 224
Ethernet 220
Fiber optic (or optical fiber) 224
Geographic information system
    (GIS) 234
Global positioning system
    (GPS) 233
Interoperability 220
Local area network (LAN) 216
Metropolitan area network
    (MAN) 216
Microwave transmitter 232

Network 215
Network operating system
    (NOS) 217
Network topology 218
Network transmission media
    223
Packet-switching 217
Peer-to-peer (P2P) network 215
Protocol 220
Radio frequency identification
    (RFID) 231
Real-time information 227
Real-time system 227
RFID tag 231
Router 217

Server 217
Telecommunication system 215
Transmission Control Protocol/
    Internet Protocol
    (TCP/IP) 221
Twisted-pair wiring 224
Valued-added network
    (VAN) 225
Virtual private network
    (VPN) 225
Voice over IP (VoIP) 222
Wide area network (WAN) 216
Wire media 223
Wireless fidelity (wi-fi) 227
Wireless media 224

Tracking Students

The grade school that required students to wear radio frequency identification (RFID) tags that can track their every move has ended the program because the company that developed the technology pulled out. "I'm disappointed; that's about all I can say at this point," stated Earnie Graham, the superintendent and principal of Brittan Elementary School. "I think I let my staff down."

The tags, developed by Sutter-based technology company InCom Corp., were introduced in January 2005. Each student was required to wear identification cards around their necks with their picture, name, grade, and a wireless transmitter that beamed their ID number to a teacher's handheld computer when the child passed under an antenna posted above a classroom door. The system was imposed, without parental input, by the school as a way to simplify attendance-taking and potentially reduce vandalism and improve student safety. "I'm not convinced it's over," parent Dawn Cantrall, who filed a complaint with the American Civil Liberties Union, told the (Marysville) *Appeal-Democrat*. "I'm happy for now that kids are not being tagged, but I'm still fighting to keep it out of our school system. It has to stop here."

While many parents criticized the tags for violating privacy and possibly endangering children's health, some parents supported the plan. "Technology scares some people; it's a fear of the unknown," parent Mary Brower told the newspaper. "Any kind of new technology has the potential for misuse, but I feel confident the school is not going to misuse it."[18]

Questions

1. Explain the fundamentals of RFID and how it is being used to track students.
2. Describe the ethical dilemmas involved with tracking students with RFID.
3. Identify two types of wireless business opportunities schools could take advantage of to help improve operations.
4. How could RFID help schools deal with potential security issues?
5. Develop a Bluetooth, GPS, or satellite product that schools could use to improve operations.
6. Determine a way that schools could use RFID tags without violating privacy rights.

UPS versus FedEx: Head-to-Head on Wireless

Federal Express and United Parcel Service are always seeking a competitive edge over one another. And as the two companies are encroaching on each other's primary businesses (UPS on overnight delivery and FedEx on ground delivery), they are concurrently stepping up their wireless deployments as well. The reason: operational efficiency—a critical business requirement aimed at shaving costs, increasing reach, and doing more with the same resources.

Their approaches to deploying wireless technologies over the past 15 years have been markedly different; FedEx has led the way with cutting-edge applications, while UPS has been slower and more deliberate. FedEx deploys new technologies as soon as it can justify the cost and demonstrate improved efficiencies and customer benefit. UPS refreshes its technology base roughly every five to seven years, when it rolls out a unified system in stages that it synchronizes with the life span of the older system. But the goal is the same for both companies: to use next-generation wireless technologies to better manage the delivery of millions of packages that flow through dozens of sorting facilities every day.

The two companies are exploiting new wireless technologies in their differing attempts at aiding the two main components of their operations: pickup/delivery and packaging/sorting. Both are also looking ahead to potential applications of radio frequency identification and GPS wireless technologies.

	UPS	FedEx
Main hub:	Louisville, Kentucky	Memphis, Tennessee
Total packages handled each day:	13.6 million	5 million
Number of air deliveries daily:	2 million	3.1 million
Wireless devices in field:	90,000	80,000
Wireless devices in sorting facilities:	55,000	70,000
Wireless access points:	9,000	5,000

Seeking New Benefits from Wireless

In addition to their major package-scanning retooling efforts, FedEx and UPS continue to investigate what business benefits they might gain from other wireless technologies. Two have gained particular attention: RFID tags, which could replace bar code scanners, and GPS, which can precisely locate field units.

As UPS and FedEx are showing, wireless technology provides the medium through which dynamic exchange happens. Interconnectedness allows drivers to talk, computers to interact, and businesses to work together. Whether it is wireless routing or fueling of trucks, it is all happening dynamically. Although few companies have the scale of UPS and FedEx, they can adopt many of the wireless technologies scaled to their size, and use devices and network components that fit their operations.[19]

Questions

1. Explain the fundamentals of wireless fidelity.
2. Describe the differences between UPS and FedEx's use of wi-fi.
3. Identify two types of wireless business opportunities the companies could use to gain a competitive advantage.
4. How could RFID help the companies deal with potential security issues?
5. Develop a Bluetooth, GPS, or satellite product that the parcel delivery business could use to improve efficiencies.

Watching Where You Step—Prada

Prada estimates its sales per year at $22 million. The luxury retailer recently spent millions on IT for its futuristic "epicenter" store, but the flashy technology turned into a high-priced hassle. The company will need to generate annual sales of $75 million by 2007 to turn a profit on its new high-tech investment.

When Prada opened its $40 million Manhattan flagship, architect Rem Koolhaas promised a radically new shopping experience. He kept the promise—though not quite according to plan. Customers were soon enduring hordes of tourists, neglected technology, and the occasional thrill of being stuck in experimental dressing rooms. A few of the problems associated with the store:

- Fickle fitting rooms. Doors that turn from clear to opaque confuse shoppers and frequently fail to open on cue.
- Failed RFID. Touchscreens meant to spring to life when items are placed in the RFID "closets" are often just blank.
- Pointless personal digital assistants (PDA). Salesclerks let the handheld devices gather dust and instead check the stockroom for inventory.
- Neglected network. A lag between sales and inventory systems makes the wireless network nearly irrelevant.

This was not exactly the vision for the high-end boutique when it debuted its new high-tech store. Instead, the 22,000-square-foot SoHo shop was to be the first of four "epicenter" stores around the world that would combine cutting-edge architecture and 21st century technology to revolutionize the luxury shopping experience. Prada poured roughly 25 percent of the store's budget into IT, including a wireless network to link every item to an Oracle inventory database in real time using radio frequency identification (RFID) tags on the clothes. The staff would roam the floor armed with PDAs to check whether items were in stock, and customers could do the same through touchscreens in the dressing rooms.

However, most of the flashy technology today sits idle, abandoned by employees who never quite embraced the technology. On top of that, many gadgets, such as automated dressing-room doors and touchscreens, are either malfunctioning or ignored. Packed with experimental technology, the clear-glass dressing-room doors were designed to open and close automatically at the tap of a foot pedal, then turn opaque when a second pedal sent an electric current through the glass. Inside, an RFID-aware rack would recognize a customer's selections and display them on a touchscreen linked to the inventory system.

In practice, the process was hardly that smooth. Many shoppers never quite understood the pedals and disrobed in full view, thinking the door had turned opaque. That is no longer a problem, since the staff usually leaves the glass opaque, but often the doors are stuck. Some of the chambers are open only to VIP customers during peak traffic times.

With the smart closets and handhelds out of commission, the wireless network in the store is nearly irrelevant, despite its considerable expense. As Prada's debt reportedly climbed to around $1 billion in late 2001, the company shelved plans for the fourth epicenter store, in San Francisco. A second store opened in Tokyo in 2003 to great acclaim, albeit with different architects in a different market. Though that store incorporates similar cutting-edge concepts, architect Jacques Herzog emphasized that avant-garde retail plays well only in Japan. "This building is clearly a building for Tokyo," he told *The New York Times*. "It couldn't be somewhere else."

The multimillion-dollar technology is starting to look more like technology for technology's sake than an enhancement of the shopping experience, and the store's failings have prompted Prada to reevaluate its epicenter strategy.[20]

Questions

1. Would you consider Prada's use of technology cutting-edge? Why or why not?

2. Prada's attempt to use RFID to check inventory in real time failed because of the staff's refusal to use the system. What could Prada have done to make the implementation of RFID successful?

3. Identify an additional strategic use of RFID for Prada's high-tech store.

4. What should Prada do differently when designing its next store to ensure its success?

5. Identify a new use of wireless technology for Prada's next store.

MAKING BUSINESS DECISIONS

1. Wireless fitness

Sandifer's Fitness Club is located in beautiful South Carolina. Rosie Sandifer has owned and operated the club for 20 years. The club has three outdoor pools, two indoor pools, 10 racquetball courts, 10 tennis courts, an indoor and outdoor track, along with a four-story exercise equipment and massage therapy building. Rosie has hired you as a summer intern specializing in information technology. The extent of Rosie's current technology includes a few PCs in the accounting department and two PCs with Internet access for the rest of the staff. Your first assignment is to create a report detailing networks and wireless technologies. The report should explain how the club could gain a business advantage by implementing a wireless network. If Rosie likes your report, she will hire you as the full-time employee in charge of information technology. Be sure to include all of the different uses for wireless devices the club could implement to improve its operations.

2. Secure access

Organizations that have traditionally maintained private, closed systems have begun to look at the potential of the Internet as a ready-made network resource. The Internet is inexpensive and globally pervasive: Every phone jack is a potential connection. However, the Internet lacks security. What obstacles must organizations overcome to allow secure network connections?

3. Integrating wireless worlds

Tele-Messaging is a next-generation integrated Internet and wireless messaging service that offers services to ISPs, telecommunications carriers, and portal companies. According to Tele-Messaging's research, the primary reason that 90 percent of the people go online is for e-mail. However, the challenge for Tele-Messaging is how to successfully attract and retain these customers. Customers want more than free calls to sign up and are looking for a host of additional services with whiz-bang technology to give them the information they want, when they want it, anywhere, and in the method most convenient to them. List the infrastructures needed to deliver the technology with the necessary reliability, availability, and scalability demanded by Tele-Messaging's customers.

4. Communicating with instant messages

You are working for a new start-up magazine, *Jabber Inc.*, developed for information professionals that provides articles, product reviews, case studies, evaluation, and informed opinions. You need to collaborate on news items and projects, and exchange data with a variety of colleagues inside and outside the *Jabber Inc.* walls. You know that many companies are now embracing the instant messaging technology. Prepare a brief report for the CIO that will explain the reasons IM is not just a teenage fad, but also a valuable communications tool that is central to everyday business.

5. **Rolling out with networks**

   As organizations begin to realize the benefits of adding a wireless component to their network, they must understand how to leverage this emerging technology. Wireless solutions have come to the forefront for many organizations with the rollout of more standard, cost-effective, and secure wireless protocols. With wireless networks, increased business agility may be realized by continuous data access and synchronization. However, with the increased flexibility come many challenges. Develop a report detailing the benefits an organization could obtain by implementing wireless technology. Also, include the challenges that a wireless network presents along with recommendations for any solutions.

Supply Chain Management

8

SECTION 8.1
Supply Chain Fundamentals

SECTION 8.2
Applying a Supply Chain Design

- Basics of Supply Chain
- Information Technology's Role in the Supply Chain
- Supply Chain Management Success Factors
- SCM Success Stories

- Using Information Technology to Drive the Supply Chain
- Facilities Driver
- Inventory Driver
- Transportation Driver
- Information Driver
- Applying a Supply Chain Design
- Future Supply Chain Trends

Dell's Famous Supply Chain

Speed is at the core of everything Dell does. Dell assembles nearly 80,000 computers every 24 hours. The computer manufacturer has done more than any other company when it comes to tweaking its supply chain. About 10 years ago, Dell carried 20 to 25 days of inventory in a sprawling network of warehouses. Today, Dell does not have a single warehouse and carries only two hours of inventory in its factories and a maximum of just 72 hours across its entire operation. Dell's vast, global supply chain is in constant overdrive, making the company one of the fastest, most hyperefficient organizations on the planet.

Disaster Occurs

In 2002, a 10-day labor lockout shut down 29 West Coast ports extending from Los Angeles to Seattle, idled 10,000 union dockworkers, and blocked hundreds of cargo ships from unloading raw materials and finished goods. The port closings paralyzed global supply chains and ultimately cost U.S. consumers and businesses billions of dollars.

Analysts expected Dell, with its just-in-time manufacturing model, would be especially hard hit when parts failed to reach its two U.S.-based factories. Without warehouses filled with motherboards and hard drives the world's largest PC maker would simply find itself with nothing to sell within a matter of days. Dell knew all too well that its ultra-lean, high-speed business model left it vulnerable to just such a situation. "When a labor problem or an earthquake or a SARS epidemic breaks out, we've got to react quicker than anyone else," said Dick Hunter, the company's supply chain expert. "There's no other choice. We know these things are going to happen; we must move fast to fix them. We just can't tolerate any kind of delay."

Fortunately, the same culture of speed and flexibility that seems to put Dell at the mercy of disruptions also helps it deal with them. Dell was in constant, round-the-clock communication with its parts makers in Taiwan, China, and Malaysia and its U.S.-based shipping partners. Hunter dispatched a "tiger team" of 10 logistics specialists to Long Beach, California, and other ports; they worked with Dell's carrying and freight-forwarding networks to assemble a contingency plan.

When the tiger team confirmed that the closings were all but certain, Dell moved into high gear. It chartered 18 airplanes (747s) from UPS, Northwest Airlines, and China Airlines. A 747 holds the equivalent of 10 tractor-trailers—enough parts to manufacture 10,000 PCs. The bidding for the planes grew fierce, running as high as $1 million for a one-way flight from Asia to the West Coast. Dell got in the bidding early and kept costs around $500,000 per plane. Dell also worked with its Asia-based suppliers to ensure that its parts were always at the Shanghai and Taipei airports in time for its returning charters to land, reload, refuel, and take off. The company was consistently able to get its planes to the United States and back within 33 hours, which kept its costs down and its supply chain moving.

Meanwhile, Dell had people on the ground in every major harbor. In Asia, the freight specialists saw to it that Dell's parts were the last to be loaded onto each cargo ship so they would be unloaded first when the ship hit the West Coast. The biggest test came when the ports reopened and companies scrambled to sort through the backed-up mess of thousands of containers. Hunter's tiger team had anticipated this logistical nightmare. Even though Dell had PC components in hundreds of containers on 50 ships, it knew the exact moment when each component cycled through the harbor, and it was among the first to unload its parts and speed them to its factories in Austin, Texas, and Nashville, Tennessee. In the end, Dell did the impossible: It survived a 10-day supply chain blackout with roughly 72 hours of inventory without delaying a single customer order.

The aftershocks of the port closings reverberated for weeks. Many companies began to question the wisdom of running so lean in an uncertain world, and demand for warehouse space soared as they piled up buffer inventory to insure against labor unrest, natural disasters, and terrorist attacks.

Building a "Dell-like" Supply Chain

Dell's ultimate competitive weapon is speed, which gives the technical giant's bottom line a real boost. Figure 8.1 displays a five-point plan for building a fast supply chain—direct from Dell.[1]

FIGURE 8.1

How to Build a Dell-Like Supply Chain

Dell-Like Supply Chain Plan
1. **The supply chain starts with the customer.** By cutting out retailers and selling directly to its customers, Dell is in a far better position to forecast real customer demand.
2. **Replace inventory with information.** To operate with close to zero inventory, Dell communicates constantly with its suppliers. It sends out status updates three times a day from its assembly plants; every week it updates its quarterly demand forecasts. By making communication its highest priority, Dell ensures the lowest possible inventory.
3. **If you cannot measure it, you cannot manage it.** Dell knows what works because it measures everything from days in inventory to the time it takes to build a PC. As Dell slashed those numbers, it got more efficient.
4. **Complexity slows you down.** Dell cut the number of its core PC suppliers from several hundred to about 25. It standardized critical PC components, which streamlined its manufacturing. Dell got faster by making things simpler.
5. **Create a watershed mind-set.** Dell is not content with incremental improvement; it demands massive change. Each year, it wants its Austin-based PC-assembly plant—already very fast—to improve production by 30 percent. "You don't get a big result if you do not challenge people with big goals," Dell CEO Kevin Rollins said.

INTRODUCTION

Companies that excel in supply chain operations perform better in almost every financial measure of success, according to a report from Boston-based AMR Research Inc. When supply chain excellence improves operations, companies experience a 5 percent higher profit margin, 15 percent less inventory, 17 percent stronger "perfect order" ratings, and 35 percent shorter cycle times than their competitors. "The basis of competition for winning companies in today's economy is supply chain superiority," said Kevin O'Marah, vice president of research at AMR Research. "These companies understand that value chain performance translates to productivity and market-share leadership. They also understand that supply chain leadership means more than just low costs and efficiency: It requires a superior ability to shape and respond to shifts in demand with innovative products and services."[2]

Collecting, analyzing, and distributing transactional information to all relevant parties, supply chain management (SCM) systems help all the different entities in the supply chain work together more effectively. SCM systems provide dynamic holistic views of organizations. Users can "drill down" into detailed analyses of supply chain activities to find valuable information on the organizational operations. This chapter explores the details of supply chain management.

section 8.1 SUPPLY CHAIN FUNDAMENTALS

LEARNING OUTCOMES

8.1 List and describe the five components of a typical supply chain.

8.2 Define the relationship between information technology and the supply chain.

8.3 Identify the factors driving supply chain management.

8.4 Summarize the best practices for implementing a successful supply chain management system.

BASICS OF SUPPLY CHAIN

The average company spends nearly half of every dollar it earns on production needs—goods and services it needs from external suppliers to keep producing. A *supply chain* consists of all parties involved, directly or indirectly, in the procurement of a product or raw material. *Supply chain management (SCM)* involves the management of information flows between and among stages in a supply chain to maximize total supply chain effectiveness and profitability.

In the past, companies focused primarily on manufacturing and quality improvements within their four walls; now their efforts extend beyond those walls to influence the entire supply chain including customers, customers' customers, suppliers, and suppliers' suppliers. Today's supply chain is a complex web of suppliers, assemblers, logistic firms, sales/marketing channels, and other business partners linked primarily through information networks and contractual relationships. SCM systems enhance and manage the relationships. The supply chain has three main links (see Figure 8.2):

1. Materials flow from suppliers and their upstream suppliers at all levels.
2. Transformation of materials into semifinished and finished products—the organization's own production processes.
3. Distribution of products to customers and their downstream customers at all levels.

Organizations must embrace technologies that can effectively manage and oversee their supply chains. SCM is becoming increasingly important in creating organizational efficiencies and competitive advantages. Best Buy checks inventory levels at each of its 750 stores in North America as often as every half hour with its

FIGURE 8.2

A Typical Supply Chain

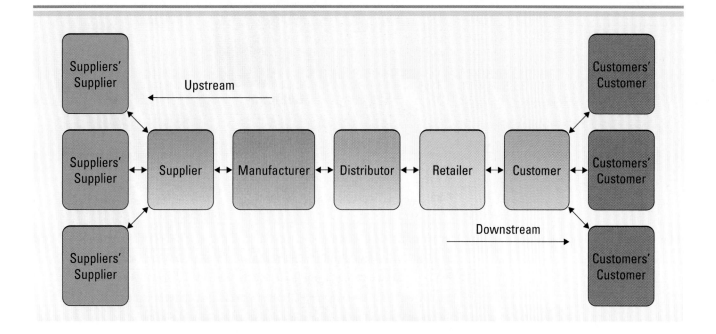

SCM system, taking much of the guesswork out of inventory replenishment. Supply chain management improves ways for companies to find the raw components they need to make a product or service, manufacture that product or service, and deliver it to customers. Figure 8.3 highlights the five basic components of supply chain management.[3]

Technology advances in the five SCM components have significantly improved companies' forecasting and business operations. Businesses today have access to modeling and simulation tools, algorithms, and applications that can combine information from multiple sources to build forecasts for days, weeks, and months in advance. Better forecasts for tomorrow result in better preparedness today.

Mattel Inc. spent the past several years investing heavily in software and processes that simplify its supply chain, cut costs, and shorten cycle times. Using supply chain management strategies, the company cut weeks out of the time it takes to design, produce, and ship everything from Barbies to Hot Wheels. Mattel installed optimization software that measures, tweaks, and validates the operations of its seven distribution centers, seven manufacturing plants, and other facilities that make up its vast worldwide supply chain. Mattel improved forecasting from monthly to weekly. The company no longer produces more inventory than stores require and delivers inventory upon request. Mattel's supply chain moves quickly to make precise forecasts that help the company meet demand.[4]

INFORMATION TECHNOLOGY'S ROLE IN THE SUPPLY CHAIN

As companies evolve into extended organizations, the roles of supply chain participants are changing. It is now common for suppliers to be involved in product development and for distributors to act as consultants in brand marketing. The notion of virtually seamless information links within and between organizations is an essential element of integrated supply chains.

Information technology's primary role in SCM is creating the integrations or tight process and information linkages between functions within a firm—such as marketing, sales, finance, manufacturing, and distribution—and between firms, which allow the smooth, synchronized flow of both information and product

FIGURE 8.3

The Five Basic Supply
Chain Management
Components

Company

| Plan | Source | Make | Deliver | Return |

THE FIVE BASIC SUPPLY CHAIN MANAGEMENT COMPONENTS
1. **Plan** – This is the strategic portion of supply chain management. A company must have a plan for managing all the resources that go toward meeting customer demand for products or services. A big piece of planning is developing a set of metrics to monitor the supply chain so that it is efficient, costs less, and delivers high quality and value to customers.
2. **Source** – Companies must carefully choose reliable suppliers that will deliver goods and services required for making products. Companies must also develop a set of pricing, delivery, and payment processes with suppliers and create metrics for monitoring and improving the relationships.
3. **Make** – This is the step where companies manufacture their products or services. This can include scheduling the activities necessary for production, testing, packaging, and preparing for delivery. This is by far the most metric-intensive portion of the supply chain, measuring quality levels, production output, and worker productivity.
4. **Deliver** – This step is commonly referred to as logistics. *Logistics* is the set of processes that plans for and controls the efficient and effective transportation and storage of supplies from suppliers to customers. During this step, companies must be able to receive orders from customers, fulfill the orders via a network of warehouses, pick transportation companies to deliver the products, and implement a billing and invoicing system to facilitate payments.
5. **Return** – This is typically the most problematic step in the supply chain. Companies must create a network for receiving defective and excess products and support customers who have problems with delivered products.

between customers, suppliers, and transportation providers across the supply chain. Information technology integrates planning, decision-making processes, business operating processes, and information sharing for business performance management (see Figure 8.4). Considerable evidence shows that this type of supply chain integration results in superior supply chain capabilities and profits.[5]

Adaptec, Inc., of California manufactures semiconductors and markets them to the world's leading PC, server, and end-user markets through more than 115

FIGURE 8.4

The Integrated Supply Chain

distributors and thousands of value-added resellers worldwide. Adaptec designs and manufactures products at various third-party locations around the world. The company uses supply chain integration software over the Internet to synchronize planning. Adaptec personnel at the company's geographically dispersed locations communicate in real time and exchange designs, test results, and production and shipment information. Internet-based supply chain collaboration software helped the company reduce inventory levels and lead times.[6]

Although people have been talking about the integrated supply chain for a long time, it has only been recently that advances in information technology have made it possible to bring the idea to life and truly integrate the supply chain. Visibility, consumer behavior, competition, and speed are a few of the changes resulting from advances in information technology that are driving supply chains (see Figure 8.5).

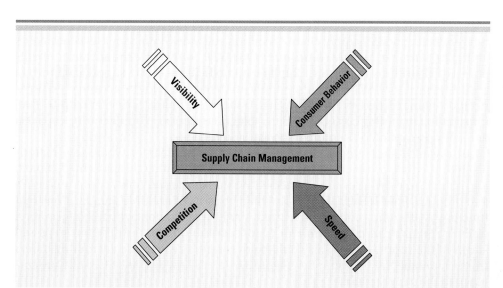

FIGURE 8.5

Factors Driving Supply Chain Management

Visibility

Supply chain visibility is the ability to view all areas up and down the supply chain. Making the change to supply chains requires a comprehensive strategy buoyed by information technology. Organizations can use technology tools that help them integrate upstream and downstream, with both customers and suppliers.

To make a supply chain work most effectively, organizations must create visibility in real time. Organizations must know about customer events triggered downstream, but so must their suppliers and their suppliers' suppliers. Without this information, partners throughout the supply chain can experience a bullwhip effect, in which disruptions intensify throughout the chain. The **bullwhip effect** occurs when distorted product demand information passes from one entity to the next throughout the supply chain. The misinformation regarding a slight rise in demand for a product could cause different members in the supply chain to stockpile inventory. These changes ripple throughout the supply chain, magnifying the issue and creating excess inventory and costs.

Today, information technology allows additional visibility in the supply chain. Electronic information flows allow managers to view their suppliers' and customers' supply chains. Some organizations have completely changed the dynamics of their industries because of the competitive advantage gained from high visibility in the supply chain. Dell is the obvious example. The company's ability to get product to the customer and the impact of the economics have clearly changed the nature of competition and caused others to emulate this model.

Consumer Behavior

The behavior of customers has changed the way businesses compete. Customers will leave if a company does not continually meet their expectations. They are more demanding because they have information readily available, they know exactly what they want, and they know when and how they want it. **Demand planning software** generates demand forecasts using statistical tools and forecasting techniques. Companies can respond faster and more effectively to consumer demands through supply chain enhancements such as demand planning software. Once an organization understands customer demand and its effect on the supply chain it can begin to estimate the impact that its supply chain will have on its customers and ultimately the organization's performance. The payoff for a successful demand planning strategy can be tremendous. A study by Peter J. Metz, executive directory of the MIT Center for e-business, found that companies have achieved impressive bottom-line results from managing demand in their supply chains, averaging a 50 percent reduction in inventory and a 40 percent increase in timely deliveries.[7]

Competition

Supply chain management software can be broken down into (1) supply chain planning software and (2) supply chain execution software. Both increase a company's ability to compete. **Supply chain planning (SCP) software** uses advanced mathematical algorithms to improve the flow and efficiency of the supply chain while reducing inventory. SCP depends entirely on information for its accuracy. An organization cannot expect the SCP output to be accurate unless correct and up-to-date information regarding customer orders, sales information, manufacturing capacity, and delivery capability is entered into the system.

An organization's supply chain encompasses the facilities where raw materials, intermediate products, and finished goods are acquired, transformed, stored, and sold. These facilities are connected by transportation links, where materials and products flow. Ideally, the supply chain consists of multiple organizations that function as efficiently and effectively as a single organization, with full information visibility. **Supply chain execution (SCE) software** automates the different steps and stages of the supply chain. This could be as simple as electronically routing orders from a manufacturer to a supplier. Figure 8.6 details how SCP and SCE software correlate to the supply chain.

FIGURE 8.6

Supply Chain Planning and Supply Chain Execution Software's Correlation to the Supply Chain

General Motors, Ford, and DaimlerChrysler made history when the three automotive giants began working together to create a unified supply chain planning/ execution system that all three companies and their suppliers could leverage. Gary Lapidus, Goldman Sachs Group's senior analyst, estimated that Newco, the name of the joint venture, will have a potential market capitalization of between $30 billion and $40 billion once it goes public, with annual revenues of around $3 billion.

The combined automotive giants' purchasing power is tremendous with GM spending $85 billion per year, Ford spending $80 billion, and DaimlerChrysler spending $73 billion. The ultimate goal of Newco is to process automotive production, from ordering materials and forecasting demand to making cars directly to consumer specifications through the Web. The automotive giants understand the impact strategic supply chain planning and execution can have on their competition.[8]

Speed

During the past decade, competition has focused on speed. New forms of servers, telecommunications, wireless applications, and software are enabling companies to perform activities that were once never thought possible. These systems raise the accuracy, frequency, and speed of communication between suppliers and customers, as well as between internal users. Another aspect of speed is the company's ability to satisfy continually changing customer requirements efficiently, accurately, and quickly. Timely and accurate information is more critical to businesses than ever before. Figure 8.7 displays the three factors fostering this change.

SUPPLY CHAIN MANAGEMENT SUCCESS FACTORS

To succeed in today's competitive markets, companies must align their supply chains with the demands of the markets they serve. Supply chain performance is now a distinct competitive advantage for companies proficient in the SCM area. Perdue Farms excels at decision making based on its supply chain management system. Perdue Farms moves roughly 1 million turkeys, each within 24 hours of

FIGURE 8.7

Factors Fostering Speed

Three Factors Fostering Speed
1. Pleasing customers has become something of a corporate obsession. Serving the customer in the best, most efficient, and most effective manner has become critical, and information about issues such as order status, product availability, delivery schedules, and invoices has become a necessary part of the total customer service experience.
2. Information is crucial to managers' abilities to reduce inventory and human resource requirements to a competitive level.
3. Information flows are essential to strategic planning for and deployment of resources.

FIGURE 8.8

Seven Principles
of Supply Chain
Management

Seven Principles of Supply Chain Management
1. Segment customers by service needs, regardless of industry, and then tailor services to those particular segments.
2. Customize the logistics network and focus intensively on the service requirements and on the profitability of the preidentified customer segments.
3. Listen to signals of market demand and plan accordingly. Planning must span the entire chain to detect signals of changing demand.
4. Differentiate products closer to the customer, since companies can no longer afford to hold inventory to compensate for poor demand forecasting.
5. Strategically manage sources of supply, by working with key suppliers to reduce overall costs of owning materials and services.
6. Develop a supply chain information technology strategy that supports different levels of decision making and provides a clear view (visibility) of the flow of products, services, and information.
7. Adopt performance evaluation measures that apply to every link in the supply chain and measure true profitability at every stage.

processing, to reach holiday tables across the nation yearly. The task is no longer as complicated as it was before Perdue Farms invested $20 million in SCM technology. SCM makes Perdue more adept at delivering the right number of turkeys, to the right customers, at the right time.[9]

To achieve success such as reducing operating costs, improving asset productivity, and compressing order cycle time, an organization should follow the seven principles of supply chain management outlined in Figure 8.8.

These seven principles run counter to previous built-in functional thinking of how companies organize, operate, and serve customers. Old concepts of supply chains are typified by discrete manufacturing, linear structure, and a focus on buy-sell transactions ("I buy from my suppliers, I sell to my customers"). Because the traditional supply chain is spread out linearly, some suppliers are removed from the end customer. Collaboration adds the value of visibility for these companies. They benefit by knowing immediately what is being transacted at the customer end of the supply chain (the end customer's activities are visible to them). Instead of waiting days or weeks (or months) for the information to flow upstream through the supply chain, with all the potential pitfalls of erroneous or missing information, suppliers can react in near real-time to fluctuations in end-customer demand.

Dell Inc. offers one of the best examples of an extremely successful SCM system. Dell's highly efficient build-to-order business model enables it to deliver customized computer systems quickly. As part of the company's continual effort to improve its supply chain processes, Dell deploys supply chain tools to provide global views of forecasted product demand and materials requirements, as well as improved factory scheduling and inventory management.

Organizations should study industry best practices to improve their chances of successful implementation of SCM systems. The following are keys to SCM success.

Make the Sale to Suppliers

The hardest part of any SCM system is its complexity because a large part of the system extends beyond the company's walls. Not only will the people in the organization need to change the way they work, but also the people from each supplier that is added to the network must change. Be sure suppliers are on board with the benefits that the SCM system will provide.

Wean Employees Off Traditional Business Practices

Operations people typically deal with phone calls, faxes, and orders scrawled on paper and will most likely want to keep it that way. Unfortunately, an organization cannot disconnect the telephones and fax machines just because it is implementing a supply chain management system. If the organization cannot convince people that using the software will be worth their time, they will easily find ways to work around it, which will quickly decrease the chances of success for the SCM system.

Ensure the SCM System Supports the Organizational Goals

It is important to select SCM software that gives organizations an advantage in the areas most crucial to their business success. If the organizational goals support highly efficient strategies, be sure the supply chain design has the same goals.

Deploy in Incremental Phases and Measure and Communicate Success

Design the deployment of the SCM system in incremental phases. For instance, instead of installing a complete supply chain management system across the company and all suppliers at once, start by getting it working with a few key suppliers, and then move on to the other suppliers. Along the way, make sure each step is adding value through improvements in the supply chain's performance. While a big-picture perspective is vital to SCM success, the incremental approach means the SCM system should be implemented in digestible bites, and also measured for success one step at a time.

Be Future Oriented

The supply chain design must anticipate the future state of the business. Because the SCM system likely will last for many more years than originally planned, managers need to explore how flexible the systems will be when (not if) changes are required in the future. The key is to be certain that the software will meet future needs, not only current needs.[10]

SCM SUCCESS STORIES

Figure 8.9 depicts the top reasons more and more executives are turning to SCM to manage their extended enterprises. Figure 8.10 lists several companies using supply chain management to drive operations.

Apple Computer initially distributed its business operations over 16 legacy applications. Apple quickly realized that it needed a new business model centered around an integrated supply chain to drive performance efficiencies. Apple devised an implementation strategy that focused on specific SCM functions—finance, sales, distribution, and manufacturing—that would most significantly help its business.

FIGURE 8.9

Top Reasons Executives
Use SCM to Manage
Extended Enterprises.

SCM Bottom-Line Benefits

Benefit	
Cost control/savings	~53%
Productivity improvements	~46%
Inventory reductions/improvements	~42%
Improved visibility into demand/supply	~37%
Process cycle time reductions	~37%
Quality improvements	~20%
Maintain/gain competitive advantage	~20%
Other	~6%

FIGURE 8.10

Companies Using Supply
Chain Management
Technologies to Drive
Operations

Companies Using Supply Chain To Drive Operations

Dell	Business grows 17 percent per year with a $40 billion revenue base.
Nokia	Supply chain best practices are turning ideas into profitable businesses.
Procter & Gamble	Consumer-driven supply chain is the defining architecture for large consumer companies. Best practices in product innovation and supply chain effectiveness are tops.
IBM	Hardware supply chain product-development processes overhauled to the tune of 70 percent better, faster, and cheaper.
Wal-Mart Stores	Everyday low prices define the customer demand driving Wal-Mart's partner integrated supply chain.
Toyota Motor	Lean is one of the top three best practices associated with benchmarked supply chain excellence.
The Home Depot	Cutting-edge supply chain management improved logistics and innovative services.
Best Buy	SCM has radically thinned inventories and delivered enviable business positions.
Marks & Spencer	A pioneer in the use of radio frequency identification (RFID) in stores, Marks & Spencer manages to grow and stay lean.

The company decided to deploy leading-edge functionality with a new business model that provided:

- Build-to-order and configure-to-order manufacturing capabilities.
- Web-enabled configure-to-order order entry and order status for customers buying directly from Apple at Apple.com.
- Real-time credit card authorization.
- Available-to-promise and rules-based allocations.
- Integration to advanced planning systems.

Since its SCM system went live, Apple Computer has experienced substantial benefits in many areas including measurable improvements in its manufacturing processes, a decrease by 60 percent in its build-to-order and configure-to-order cycle times, and the ability to process more than 6,000 orders daily.[11]

OPENING CASE QUESTIONS

Dell's Famous Supply Chain

1. How might Dell use each of the five basic SCM components?

2. How has Dell influenced visibility, consumer behavior, competition, and speed through the use of IT in its supply chain?

3. Explain the seven principles of SCM in reference to Dell's business model.

section 8.2 APPLYING A SUPPLY CHAIN DESIGN

LEARNING OUTCOMES

8.5 List and describe the four drivers of supply chain management.

8.6 Explain supply chain management strategies focused on efficiency.

8.7 Explain supply chain management strategies focused on effectiveness.

USING INFORMATION TECHNOLOGY TO DRIVE THE SUPPLY CHAIN

This section takes a detailed look at how an organization can create a supply chain strategy focusing on efficiency and effectiveness. **Efficiency IT metrics** measure the performance of the IT system including throughput, speed, and availability. **Effectiveness IT metrics** measure the impact IT has on business processes and activities including customer satisfaction, conversion rates, and sell-through increases. An organization's goals and strategic objectives should determine its overall supply chain management strategy. The SCM strategy in turn determines how the supply chain will perform with respect to efficiency and effectiveness. The four primary drivers of supply chain management are:

1. Facilities
2. Inventory
3. Transportation
4. Information

An organization can use information technology to influence these four drivers in varying measure to push it toward either a supply chain strategy focusing on efficiency or a supply chain strategy focusing on effectiveness. The organization must decide on the trade-off it desires between efficiency and effectiveness for each driver. The selected combined impact of the various drivers then determines the efficiency and effectiveness of the entire supply chain. Figure 8.11 provides an overview of the four supply chain drivers in terms of their effect on overall efficiency and effectiveness.

FACILITIES DRIVER

A facility processes or transforms inventory into another product or it stores the inventory before shipping it to the next facility. Toyota is an example of a company that stresses *effectiveness* in its facilities. Toyota's goal is to open a facility in every major market where it does business. These local facilities protect the company from currency fluctuations and trade barriers and thus are more effective for

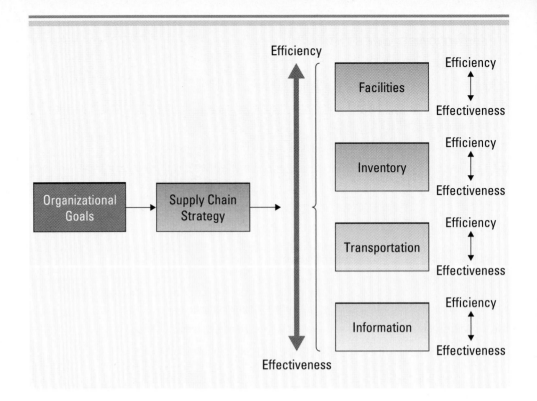

Toyota's customers. An organization should consider three primary components
when determining its facilities strategy:

1. Location
2. Capacity
3. Operational design

Location

An organization must determine where it will locate its facilities, an important decision that constitutes a large part of its supply chain strategy. Two primary options
when determining facilities location are: (1) centralize the location to gain economies of scale, which increases efficiency, or (2) decentralize the locations to be
closer to the customers, which increases effectiveness.

A company can gain economies of scale when it centralizes its facilities. However, this cost reduction decreases the company's effectiveness, since many of its
customers may be located far away from the facility. The opposite is also true; having a number of different facilities located closer to customers reduces efficiency
because of the increased costs associated with the additional facilities. Many other
factors will influence location decisions including facility costs, employee expense,
exchange rates, tax effects, and so on.

UPS uses package flow SCM systems at each of its locations. The custom-built
software combines operations research and mapping technology to optimize the
way boxes are loaded and delivered. The goal is to use the package flow software
to cut the distance that delivery trucks travel by more than 100 million miles each
year. The project will also help UPS streamline the profitability of each of its facility
locations.

Capacity

Demand planning SCM software can help an organization determine capacity.
An organization must determine the performance capacity level for each of its
facilities. If it decides a facility will have a large amount of excess capacity, which

provides the flexibility to respond to wide swings in demand, then it is choosing an effectiveness strategy. Excess capacity, however, costs money and can therefore decrease efficiency.

Operational Design

An organization must determine if it wants a product focus or a functional focus for its facilities operational design. If it chooses a product focus design, it is anticipating that the facility will produce only a certain type of product. All operations, including fabrication and assembly, will focus on developing a single type of product. This strategy allows the facility to become highly efficient in producing a single product.

If it chooses a functional design, the facility will perform a specific function (e.g., fabrication only or assembly only) on many different products. This strategy allows the facility to become more effective since it can use a single process on many different types of products (see Figure 8.12).

INVENTORY DRIVER

For most of business history, inventory has been a form of security. A warehouse bulging with components, or a distribution center packed with finished products, meant that even when a customer forecast went wildly awry, there would still be enough supply on hand to meet demand. Ever since the 1980s, when General Motors began adopting Toyota's pioneering methods in lean manufacturing, fast companies have delayered, reengineered, and scrubbed the waste from their assembly lines and supply chains by slashing lead time and stripping inventory and spare capacity from their operations.

Dillard's department store's competitive strategy is to appeal to higher-end customers who are willing to pay a premium to obtain products immediately. Dillard's carries large amounts of inventory to ensure products are always available for its customers. In return, its customers are willing to pay extra for their products.[12]

Companies require inventory to offset any discrepancies between supply and demand, but inventory is a major cost in any supply chain. Inventory's impact on a company's effectiveness versus efficiency can be enormous. Effectiveness results from more inventory, and efficiency results from less inventory. If a company's strategy requires a high level of customer effectiveness, then the company will locate large amounts of inventory in many facilities close to its customers, such as Dillard's strategy demands. If a company's strategy requires a high level of efficiency, the strategy of a low-cost producer, for instance, then the company will maintain low levels of inventory in a single strategic location.

Inventory management and control software provides control and visibility to the status of individual items maintained in inventory. The software maintains inventory record accuracy, generates material requirements for all purchased items, and analyzes inventory performance. Inventory management and control software provides the supply chain with information from a variety of sources including:

- Current inventory and order status.
- Cost accounting.
- Sales forecasts and customer orders.
- Manufacturing capacity.
- New-product introductions.

Inventory management and control software provides an organization with information when making decisions about two primary inventory strategies including:

1. Cycle inventory
2. Safety inventory

Cycle Inventory

Cycle inventory is the average amount of inventory held to satisfy customer demands between inventory deliveries. A company can follow either of two approaches regarding cycle inventory. The first approach is to hold a large amount of cycle inventory and receive inventory deliveries only once a month. The second approach is to hold a small amount of inventory and receive orders weekly or even daily. The trade-off is the cost comparison between holding larger lots of inventory for an effective supply chain and ordering products frequently for an efficient supply chain.

Safety Inventory

Safety inventory is extra inventory held in the event demand exceeds supply. For example, a toy store might hold safety inventory for the Christmas season. The risk a company faces when making a decision in favor of safety inventory is that in addition to the cost of holding it, if it holds too much, some of its products may go unsold and it may have to discount them—after the Christmas season, in the toy store example. However, if it holds too little inventory it may lose sales and risk losing customers. The company must decide if it wants to risk the expense of carrying too much inventory or to risk losing sales and customers (see Figure 8.13).

FIGURE 8.13

The Inventory Driver's Effect on Efficiency and Effectiveness

Inventory Driver

Efficiency

Increases Efficiency
- Maintains low levels of inventory
- Single inventory storage location

Increases Effectiveness
- Maintains large levels of inventory
- Multiple inventory storage locations close to customers

Effectiveness

TRANSPORTATION DRIVER

Organizations use IT-enabled supply chain management systems that use quantitative analysis, decision support systems, and intelligent systems for configuring shipping plans. FedEx's entire business strategy focuses on its customers' need for highly effective transportation methods. Any company that uses FedEx to transport a package is focusing primarily on a safe and timely delivery and not on the cost of delivery. Many businesses even locate their facilities near FedEx hubs so that they can quickly transport inventory overnight to their customers.

An organization can use many different methods of transportation to move its inventories between the different stages in the supply chain. Like the other supply chain drivers, transportation cost has a large impact either way on effectiveness and efficiency. If an organization focuses on a highly effective supply chain, then it can use transportation to increase the price of its products by using faster, more costly transportation methods. If the focus is a highly efficient supply chain, the organization can use transportation to decrease the price of its products by using slower, less costly transportation methods. Two primary facets of transportation an organization should consider when determining its strategy are:

1. Method of transportation
2. Transportation route

Method of Transportation

An organization must decide how it wants to move its inventory through the supply chain. There are six basic methods of transportation: truck, rail, ship, air, pipeline, and electronic. The primary differences between these methods are the speed of delivery and price of delivery. An organization might choose an expensive method of transportation to ensure speedy delivery if it is focusing on a highly effective supply chain. On the other hand, it might choose an inexpensive method of transportation if it is focusing on a highly efficient supply chain. Some organizations will use a *global inventory management system* that provides the ability to locate, track, and predict the movement of every component or material anywhere upstream or downstream in the supply chain. So regardless of the chosen method of transportation, the organization can find its inventory anywhere in the supply chain.

Transportation Route

An organization will also need to choose the transportation route for its products. Two supply chain software modules can aid in this decision. *Transportation planning software* tracks and analyzes the movement of materials and products to ensure the delivery of materials and finished goods at the right time, the right place, and the lowest cost. *Distribution management software* coordinates the process of transporting materials from a manufacturer to distribution centers to the final customer. Transportation route directly affects the speed and cost of delivery. An organization will use these software modules to help it decide if it wants to use an effectiveness route and ship its products directly to its customers, or use an efficiency route and ship its products to a distributor that ships the products to customers (see Figure 8.14).

INFORMATION DRIVER

Information is a driver whose importance has grown as companies use it to become both more efficient and more effective. An organization must decide what information is most valuable in efficiently reducing costs or in improving effectiveness. This decision will vary depending on a company's strategy and the design and organization of the supply chain. Two things to consider about information in the supply chain are:

1. Information sharing.
2. Push verses pull information strategy.

Information Sharing

An organization must determine what information it wants to share with its partners throughout the stages of the supply chain. Information sharing is a difficult decision since most organizations do not want their partners to gain insight into strategic or competitive information. However, they do need to share information so they can coordinate supply chain activities such as providing suppliers with inventory order levels to meet production forecasts. Building trusting relationships is one way to begin to understand how much information supply chain partners require.

If an organization chooses an efficiency focus for information sharing, then it will freely share lots of information to increase the speed and decrease the costs of supply chain processing. If an organization chooses an effectiveness focus for information sharing, then it will share only selected information with certain individuals, which will decrease the speed and increase the costs of supply chain processing.

Push versus Pull Information Strategy

In a *push technology* environment, organizations send information. In a *pull technology* environment, organizations receive or request information. An organization must decide how it is going to share information with its partners. It might decide that it wants to push information out to partners by taking on the responsibility of sending information to them. On the other hand, it might decide that it wants its partners to take on the responsibility of getting information by having them directly access the information from the systems and pull the information they require.

Again, an organization must determine how much it trusts its partners when deciding on a push versus pull information-sharing strategy. Using a push information-sharing strategy is more effective because the organization has control over exactly what information is shared and when the information is shared. However, a push strategy is less efficient because there are costs associated with sending information such as computer equipment, applications, time, resources, and so forth.

Using a pull information-sharing strategy is more efficient since the organization does not have to undertake the costs associated with sending information. However, the pull strategy is less effective since the organization has no control over when the information is pulled. For example, if the company needs inventory there is no guarantee that the suppliers will pick up the information. Hence, an organization could find itself in trouble if its partners forget to obtain the information and fail to deliver the required products (see Figure 8.15).

Information Driver

Efficiency

Increases Efficiency
- Openly shares information with all individuals
- Pull information strategy

Increases Effectiveness
- Selectively shares certain information with certain individuals
- Push information strategy

Effectiveness

APPLYING A SUPPLY CHAIN DESIGN

Figure 8.16 displays Wal-Mart's supply chain management design and how it correlates to its competitive strategy to be a reliable, low-cost retailer for a wide variety of mass consumption goods. Wal-Mart's supply chain emphasizes efficiency, but also maintains an adequate level of effectiveness.

- **Facilities focus**—efficiency: Wal-Mart maintains few warehouses and will build a new warehouse only when demand is high enough to justify one.
- **Inventory focus**—efficiency: Wal-Mart ships directly to its stores from the manufacturer. This significantly lowers inventory levels because stores maintain inventory, not stores and warehouses.
- **Transportation focus**—effectiveness: Wal-Mart maintains its own fleet of trucks. The benefits in terms of overall supply chain efficiency justify the expense of maintaining its own trucks because effective transportation allows Wal-Mart to keep low levels of inventory.
- **Information focus**—efficiency: Wal-Mart invests heavily in technology and the flow of information throughout its entire supply chain. Wal-Mart pushes inventory information all the way back up the supply chain to its suppliers who then manufacture only enough inventories to meet demand. The cost to build the information flows between its supply chain partners has been tremendous. However, the result of this investment is a highly successful and efficient supply chain.[13]

FUTURE SUPPLY CHAIN TRENDS

A television commercial shows a man in a uniform quietly moving through a family home. The man replaces the empty cereal box with a full one just before a hungry child opens the cabinet. He then opens a new sack of dog food as the hungry bulldog eyes him warily, and finally hands a full bottle of shampoo to the man in the shower who had just run out. The next wave in supply chain management will be home-based supply chain fulfillment.

Walgreens is differentiating itself from other national chains by marketing itself as the family's just-in-time supplier. Consumers today are becoming incredibly comfortable with the idea of going online to purchase products when they want, how they want, and at the price they want. Walgreens is developing custom Web sites for each household that allow families to order electronically and then at their convenience go to the store to pick up their goods at a special self-service counter or the drive-through window. Walgreens is making a promise that goes beyond low prices and customer service and extends right into the home.[14]

FIGURE 8.16

Wal-Mart's Supply Chain Management Drivers

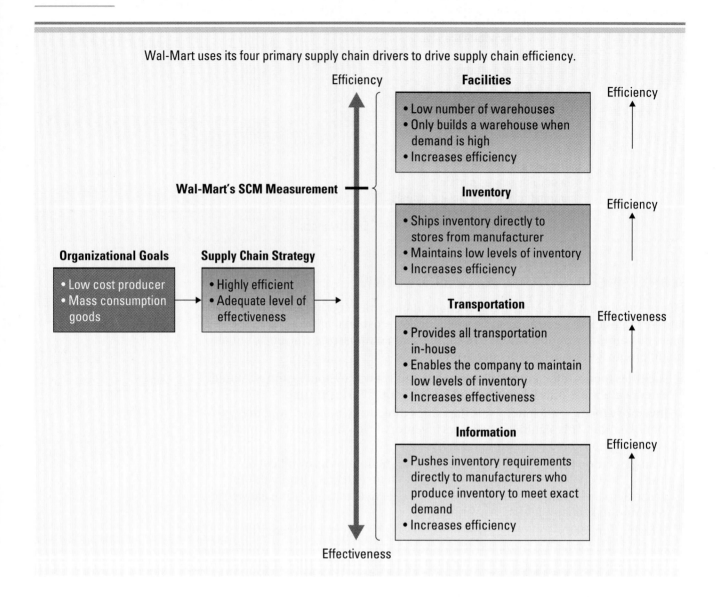

Wal-Mart uses its four primary supply chain drivers to drive supply chain efficiency.

The functionality in supply chain management systems is becoming more and more sophisticated as supply chain management matures. Now and in the future, the next stages of SCM will incorporate more functions such as marketing, customer service, and product development. This will be achieved through more advanced communication networks, adoption of more user-friendly decision support systems, and availability of shared information to all participants in the supply chain. SCM is an ongoing development as technology makes it possible to acquire information ever more accurately and frequently from all over the world, and introduces new tools to aid in the analytical processes that deal with the supply chain's growing complexity.

According to Forrester Research, Inc., U.S. firms will spend $35 billion over the next five years to improve business processes that monitor, manage, and optimize their extended supply chains. Figure 8.17 displays the fastest growing SCM components that can have the greatest potential impact on an organization's bottom line.[15]

New technologies are also going to improve the supply chain. Radio frequency identification (RFID) technologies use active or passive tags in the form of chips or smart labels that can store unique identifiers and relay this information to

Growing SCM Components	
Supply chain event management (SCEM)	Enables an organization to react more quickly to resolve supply chain issues. SCEM software increases real-time information sharing among supply chain partners and decreases their response time to unplanned events. SCEM demand will skyrocket as more and more organizations begin to discover the benefits of real-time supply chain monitoring.
Selling chain management	Applies technology to the activities in the order life cycle from inquiry to sale.
Collaborative engineering	Allows an organization to reduce the cost and time required during the design process of a product.
Collaborative demand planning	Helps organizations reduce their investment in inventory, while improving customer satisfaction through product availability.

FIGURE 8.17

Fast Growth SCM Components

electronic readers. RFID will become an effective tool for tracking and monitoring inventory movement in a real-time SCM environment. The real-time information will provide managers with an instant and accurate view of inventories within the supply chain.

Using current SCM systems, the RFID will check the inventory status and then trigger the replenishment process. Organizations using RFIDs will be able to quickly and accurately provide current inventory levels (in real-time) at any point in the supply chain. Reducing inventory levels to their reorder points allows electronic regeneration of replenishment orders. With quick and accurate information about inventories, the use of safety stock levels guarding against uncertainty can also be reduced. Hence, the potential benefits of RFIDs include a reduction of human intervention (or required labor) and holding fewer inventories, which nets a reduction in operating costs.

SCM applications have always been expensive, costing between $1 million and $10 million. As the industry matures and competition increases, vendors will continue adapting their pricing models to attract midsize and smaller companies.[16]

OPENING CASE QUESTIONS

Dell's Famous Supply Chain

4. Identify the four primary drivers of SCM and explain how Dell uses each one to gain efficiency or effectiveness in its supply chain.

5. Choose one of the fast growth SCM components and explain how Dell can use it to increase business operations.

6. What is RFID and how could Dell use the technology to improve its supply chain?

KEY TERMS

Bullwhip effect 250
Collaborative demand planning 263
Collaborative engineering 263
Cycle inventory 258
Demand planning software 250
Distribution management software 259
Effectiveness IT metrics 255
Efficiency IT metrics 255

Global inventory management system 259
Inventory management and control software 258
Logistics 248
Pull technology 260
Push technology 260
Safety inventory 250
Selling chain management 246
Supply chain 246

Supply chain event management (SCEM) 263
Supply chain execution (SCE) software 250
Supply chain management (SCM) 246
Supply chain planning (SCP) software 250
Supply chain visibility 250
Transportation planning software 259

BudNet

Every time a six-pack moves off the shelf, Anheuser-Busch's top-secret nationwide data network, BudNet, knows. BudNet is Anheuser-Busch's secret weapon and one of the reasons that Anheuser's share (by volume) of the $74.4 billion U.S. beer market inched up to 50.1 percent from 48.9 percent in a single year.

Dereck Gurden, a sales representative for Sierra Beverage, one of about 700 U.S. distributors that work for Anheuser-Busch, manages an 800-square-mile territory in California's Central Valley. His customers include 7-Eleven, Buy N Save, and dozens of liquor marts and restaurants. When Gurden enters one of his customers' stores he already knows what products are selling, which campaigns are successful, and what needs to be done to help the customer's business.

When entering a store, Gurden checks his handheld PC, which displays vital store information. "First I'll scroll through and check the accounts receivable, make sure everything's current," he says. "Then it'll show me an inventory screen with a four-week history. I can get past sales, package placements—facts and numbers on how much of the sales they did when they had a display in a certain location." Gurden also walks around the store and inputs competitor information into his PC relating to product displays, pricing strategies, and promotions.

How BudNet Works

Information is entered into BudNet nightly from several thousand beer distributors and sales representatives. The information allows Anheuser-Busch managers to constantly adjust production and fine-tune marketing campaigns. The system works as follows:

1. Sales representatives collect new orders and track competitors' marketing efforts on PDAs and laptops.
2. Distributors compile the information and transmit it daily to Anheuser corporate headquarters.
3. Anheuser brand managers analyze the information and make decisions for distributors.
4. Distributors log on to BudNet to get the latest intelligence.
5. Sales representatives rearrange displays and rotate stock based on the recommendations.

Anheuser-Busch uses BudNet's information to constantly change marketing strategies, to design promotions to suit the ethnic makeup of its markets, and as early warning radar that detects where rivals might have an edge. "If Anheuser-Busch loses shelf space in a store in Clarksville, Tennessee, they know it right away," says Joe Thompson, president of Independent Beverage Group, a research and consulting firm. "They're better at this game than anyone, even Coca-Cola."

According to dozens of analysts, beer-industry veterans, and distributor executives, Anheuser has made a deadly accurate science out of determining what beer lovers are buying, as well as when, where, and why. The last time you bought a six-pack of Bud Light at the corner store, Anheuser servers most likely recorded what you paid, when that beer was brewed, whether you purchased it warm or chilled, and whether you could have gotten a better deal down the street. BudNet has not just added efficiency into the beer supply chain; it is changing the dynamics of the industry.[17]

Questions

1. How can an SCM system help a distributor such as Anheuser-Busch make its supply chain more effective and efficient?

2. SCM is experiencing explosive growth. Explain why this statement is true using BudNet as an example.

3. Evaluate BudNet's effect on each of the five factors that are driving SCM success.

4. List and describe the components of a typical supply chain along with its ability to help Budweiser make effective decisions.

Listerine's Journey

When you use Listerine antiseptic mouthwash, you are experiencing the last step in a complex supply chain spanning several continents and requiring months of coordination by countless businesses and individuals. The resources involved in getting a single bottle of Listerine to a consumer are unbelievable. As raw material transforms into finished product, what will be Listerine travels around the globe and through multiple supply chains and information systems.

The Journey Begins

A farmer in Australia is harvesting a crop of eucalyptus for eucalyptol, the oil found in its leathery leaves. The farmer sells the crop to an Australian processing company, which spends about four weeks extracting the eucalyptol from the eucalyptus.

Meanwhile, in New Jersey, Warner-Lambert (WL) partners with a distributor to buy the oil from the Australian company and transport it to WL's Listerine manufacturing and distribution facility in Lititz, Pennsylvania. The load will arrive at Lititz about three months after the harvest.

At the same time, in Saudi Arabia, a government-owned operation is drilling deep under the desert for the natural gas that will yield the synthetic alcohol that gives Listerine its 43-proof punch. Union Carbide Corp. ships the gas via tanker to a refinery in Texas, which purifies it and converts it into ethanol. The ethanol is loaded onto another tanker, and then transported from Texas through the Gulf of Mexico to New Jersey, where it is transferred to storage tanks and transported via truck or rail to WL's plant. A single shipment of ethanol takes about six to eight weeks to get from Saudi Arabia to Lititz.

SPI Polyols Inc., a manufacturer of ingredients for the confectionery, pharmaceutical, and oral-care industries, buys corn syrup from farmers in the Midwest. SPI converts the corn syrup into sorbitol solution, which sweetens and adds bulk to the Cool Mint Listerine. The syrup is shipped to SPI's New Castle, Delaware, facility for processing and then delivered on a tank wagon to Lititz. The whole process, from the time the corn is harvested to when it is converted into sorbitol, takes about a month.

By now the ethanol, eucalyptol, and sorbitol have all arrived at WL's plant in Lititz, where employees test them, along with the menthol, citric acid, and other ingredients that make up Listerine, for quality assurance before authorizing storage in tanks. To mix the ingredients, flow meters turn on valves at each tank and measure out the right proportions, according to the Cool Mint formula developed by WL R&D in 1990. (The original amber mouthwash was developed in 1879.)

Next, the Listerine flows through a pipe to fillers along the packaging line. The fillers dispense the product into bottles delivered continuously from a nearby plastics company for just-in-time manufacturing. The bottles are capped, labeled, and fitted with tamper-resistant safety bands, then placed in shipping boxes that each hold one dozen 500-milliliter bottles. During this process, machines automatically check for skewed labels, missing safety bands, and other problems. The entire production cycle, from the delivery via pipe of the Listerine liquid to the point where bottles are boxed and ready to go, takes a matter of minutes. The line can produce about 300 bottles per minute—a far cry from the 80 to 100 bottles that the line produced per minute before 1994.

Each box travels on a conveyor belt to the palletizer, which organizes and shrink-wraps the boxes into 100-case pallets. Stickers with identifying bar codes are affixed to the pallets. Drivers forklift the pallets to the distribution center, located in the same Lititz facility, from which the boxes are shipped around the world.

Finally, the journey is completed when a customer purchases a bottle of Listerine at a local drugstore or grocery store. In a few days, the store will place an order for a replacement bottle of Listerine. And so begins the cycle again.[18]

Questions

1. Summarize SCM and describe Warner-Lambert's supply chain strategy. Diagram the SCM components.
2. Detail Warner-Lambert's facilities strategy.
3. Detail Warner-Lambert's inventory strategy.
4. What would happen to Warner-Lambert's business if a natural disaster in Saudi Arabia depletes its natural gas resources?
5. Assess the impact to Warner-Lambert's business if the majority of the eucalyptus crop was destroyed in a natural disaster.
6. Detail Warner-Lambert's information strategy.

How Levi's Got Its Jeans into Wal-Mart

People around the world recognize Levi's as an American icon, the cool jeans worn by movie stars James Dean and Marilyn Monroe. For one reason or another, however, the company failed to keep up with the fast-changing tastes of American teenagers. In particular, it missed the trend to baggy jeans that caught hold in the mid-1990s. Sales plummeted from $7.1 billion in 1996 to $4.1 billion in 2003, and Levi's U.S. market share dropped from 18.7 percent in 1997 to 12 percent in 2003, a huge decline of almost one-third in both dollars and market share.

Analyzing and Responding to What Happened

Competition hit Levi Strauss on both the high and low ends. Fashion-conscious buyers were drawn to high-priced brands like Blue Cult, Juicy, and Seven, which had more fashion cachet than Levi's. On the low end, parents were buying Wrangler and Lee jeans for their kids because on average they cost about $10 less than Levi's Red Tab brand. Wrangler and Lee were also the brands they found at discount retailers such as Wal-Mart, Target, and T. J. Maxx. David Bergen, Levi's chief information officer (CIO), described the company as "getting squeezed," and "caught in the jaws of death."

Levi Strauss's new CEO, Philip A. Marineau, came to the company from PepsiCo in 1999, a year after he helped PepsiCo surpass Coca-Cola in sales for the first time. Marineau recruited Bergen in 2000 from Carstation.com. Marineau quickly realized that turning Levi Strauss around would entail manufacturing, marketing, and distributing jeans that customers demanded, particularly customers at the low end where the mass market was located.

Bergen was eager to join Marineau's team because of his background in clothing, retailing, and manufacturing with companies such as The Gap and Esprit de Corps in the 1980s. He knew that Marineau's plan to anticipate customer wants would require up-to-date IT applications such as data warehousing, data mining, and customer relationship management (CRM) systems. He also knew that selling to mass market retailers would require upgrades to the supply chain management (SCM) systems, and he understood that globalization would necessitate standardized enterprise resource planning (ERP) systems. Overall, it was a challenge any ambitious CIO would covet. After all, designing and installing IT systems that drive and achieve key business initiatives is what it is all about.

Joining Wal-Mart

Wal-Mart was a pioneer in supply chain management systems, having learned early on that driving costs out of the supply chain would let it offer products to customers at the lowest possible prices, while at the same time assuring that products the customers demanded were always on the stores' shelves. Becoming one of Wal-Mart's 30,000 suppliers is not easy. Wal-Mart insists that its suppliers do business using up-to-date IT systems to manage the supply chain—not just the supply chain between Wal-Mart and its suppliers, but the supply chains between the suppliers and their suppliers as well. Wal-Mart has strict supply chain management system requirements that its business partners must meet.

Wal-Mart's requirements presented Levi Strauss with a serious hurdle to overcome because its supply chain management systems were in bad shape. Levi Strauss executives did not even have access to key information required to track where its products were moving in the supply chain. For example, they did not know how many pairs of jeans were in the factory awaiting shipment, how many were somewhere en route, or how many had just been unloaded at a customer's warehouse. According to Greg Hammann, Levi's U.S. chief customer officer, "Our supply chain could not deliver the services Wal-Mart expected."

Bergen created a cross-functional team of key managers from IT, finance, and sales to transform Levi Strauss's systems to meet Wal-Mart's requirements. Their recommendations included network upgrades, modifications to ordering and logistics applications, and data warehouse improvements, among others. Although Bergen realized that about half the changes required to current IT systems to accommodate the state-of-the-art demands of Wal-Mart would be a waste of resources since these systems were being replaced by a new SAP enterprise software system over the next five years, Levi Strauss could not wait for the SAP installation if it wanted Wal-Mart's business now, so it decided to move forward with the changes to the current systems.

The successful transformation of its supply chain management system allowed the company to collaborate with Wal-Mart. The company introduced its new signature line at Wal-Mart, which sells for around $23 and has fewer details in the finish than Levi's other lines, no trademark pocket stitching or red tab, for example. Wal-Mart wants big-name brands to lure more affluent customers into its stores, while still maintaining the low price points all Wal-Mart customers have come to expect. Wal-Mart Senior Vice President Lois Mikita noted that Wal-Mart "continues to tailor its selection to meet the needs of customers from a cross section of income levels and lifestyles." She also stated she is impressed with the level of detail Levi Strauss has put into its systems transformation efforts to "make the execution of this new launch 100 percent."

Achieving Business Success Through IT

Bergen's changes were a success and the percentage of products delivered on time quickly rose from 65 percent to 95 percent primarily because of the updated supply chain management system. Levi's total sales were also up in the third and fourth quarters of 2003, for the first time since 1996. NPD Group's Fashionworld is a research group that tracks apparel and footwear market trends. In 2003, Levi's appeared on NPD Fashionworld's top 10 list of brands preferred by young women, ending an absence of several years. Marshall Cohen, a senior industry analyst at NPD Fashionworld, noted that Levi's "hadn't been close to that for a while. Teens hadn't gravitated toward Levi's in years. That was incredible. A lot of that has to do with having the right style in the right place at the right time." The improved systems, Cohen noted, also helped the company get the right sizes to the right stores.

Another highly successful IT system implemented by Levi Strauss is a digital dashboard that executives can display on their PC screens. The dashboard lets an executive see the status of a product as it moves from the factory floor to distribution centers to retail stores. For example, the dashboard can display how Levi's 501 jeans are selling at an individual Kohl's store compared to forecasted sales. "When I first got here I didn't see anything," Hammann said. "Now I can drill down to the product level."

The digital dashboard alerts executives to trends that under the previous systems would have taken weeks to detect. For example, in 2003 Levi Strauss started to ship Dockers Stain Defender pants. Expected sales for the pants were around 2 million pairs. The digital dashboard quickly notified key executives that the trousers were selling around 2.5 million pairs. This information enabled them to adjust production upward in time to ship more pants, meet the increased demand, and avoid lost sales. Levi Strauss also uses the systems to control supply during key seasonal sales periods such as back-to-school and Christmas.

"If I look overconfident, I'm not," Bergen said. "I'm very nervous about this change. When we trip, we have to stand up real quick and get back on the horse, as they say." As if to reinforce Bergen's point, Gib Carey, a supply chain analyst at Bain, noted, "The place where companies do fail is when they aren't bringing anything new to Wal-Mart. Wal-Mart is constantly looking at 'How can I get the same product I am selling today at a lower price somewhere else?'"[19]

Questions

1. How did Levi Strauss achieve business success through the use of supply chain management?

2. What might have happened to Levi's if its top executives had not supported investments in SCM?

3. David Bergen, Levi's CIO, put together a cross-functional team of key managers from IT, finance, and sales to transform Levi's systems to meet Wal-Mart's requirements. Analyze the relationships between these three business areas and SCM systems. How can an SCM system help support these three critical business areas?

4. Describe the five basic SCM components in reference to Wal-Mart's business model.

5. Explain RFID and provide an example of how Levi's could use the technology to increase its business operations.

MAKING BUSINESS DECISIONS

1. **Analyzing Dell's supply chain management system**

   Dell's supply chain strategy is legendary. Essentially, if you want to build a successful SCM system your best bet is to model your SCM system after Dell's. In a team, research Dell's supply chain management strategy on the Web and create a report discussing any new SCM updates and strategies the company is currently using that were not discussed in this text. Be sure to include a graphical presentation of Dell's current supply chain model.

2. **Focusing on facilities**

   Focus is a large distributor of films and is owned and operated by Lauren O'Connell. The company has been in business for more than 50 years and distributes motion pictures to theaters all over the United States and Canada. Focus is in the middle of a supply chain overhaul and is currently deciding its supply chain strategy. Lauren has asked you to create a report discussing the company's options for its facilities including location, capacity, and operational design. The report should include two primary focuses: one on efficiency and one on effectiveness.

3. **Investing in inventory**

   Poppa's Toy Store Inc. has more then 150 stores in 38 states. The chain has been owned and operated for the last 30 years by CEO Taylor Coombe. Taylor has been reading reports on supply chain management and is particularly interested in updating the company's current supply chain. It is the beginning of April and Taylor wants a new SCM system up and running before the Christmas season starts in November. Taylor is particularly interested in demand planning and forecasting for the entire company's inventory during its busiest season—Christmas. Taylor has asked you to create a report discussing the company's options for its inventory management strategy including cycle and safety inventory. The report should include two primary focuses: one on efficiency and one on effectiveness.

4. **Increasing information**

   Galina's is a high-end auction house located in New York City. Galina's specializes in selling jewelry, art, and antique furniture primarily from estate sales. The owner, Galina Bucrya, would like to begin offering certain items for auction over the Internet. Galina is unfamiliar with the Internet and not quite sure how to pursue her new business strategy. You are working for Information Inc., a small business consulting company that specializes in e-business strategies. Galina has hired you to help her create her supply chain e-business strategy. Compile a report describing supply chain management, the potential benefits her company can receive from an SCM strategy, your recommendation for an efficient or effective SCM strategy, and your views on the future of SCM.

5. **Increasing revenues with SCM**

   Cold Cream is one of the premier beauty supply stores in the metro New York area. People come from all over to sample the store's unique creams, lotions, makeup, and perfumes. The company receives its products from manufacturers around the globe. The company would like to implement an SCM system to help it better understand its customers and their purchasing habits. Create a report summarizing SCM systems and explain how an SCM system can directly influence Cold Cream's revenues.

Customer Relationship Management

9

CHAPTER

SECTION 9.1
Customer Relationship Management

- Business Benefits of CRM

- CRM Basics

- Using Information Technology to Drive Operational CRM

- Using Information Technology to Drive Analytical CRM

SECTION 9.2
Customer Relationship Management Strategies

- Customer Relationship Management's Explosive Growth

- Customer Relationship Management Success Factors

- Current Trends: SRM, PRM, and ERM

- Future CRM Trends

CHAPTER OUTLINE

Customer First Awards

Profitable Player Award: Progressive

Fast Company granted Progressive the coveted Profitable Player Customer First Award. Imagine walking into a Circuit City prepared to buy an expensive digital camera and being told you could get it cheaper at Best Buy. Sound crazy? If a customer shopping for car insurance calls Progressive, that is what happens. For years, the company has handed out rivals' rates to potential customers. In 2002, it began scrolling competitors' rates—even when its own were higher—across its Web site.

It is a bold piece of Progressive's plan to foster long-term customer loyalty. Progressive may lose some customers who opt for lower rates, but CEO Glenn Renwick thinks transparency will keep the rest around. "We hope it establishes a feeling of trust for the company," he said.

Renwick seems to be getting his wish. The third-largest auto insurer in the United States, Progressive has averaged an awe-inducing 75 percent annual profit growth since 2001. Progressive continues to roll out still more customer-focused services, including a test program that lets drivers exchange a totaled vehicle for another of the same or better make, year, and mileage (Progressive does the shopping).

Progressive has long emphasized innovations that transform the customer experience and the efficiency of its operations. Its 2,900-plus immediate response vehicles (IRVs), which the company pioneered 10 years ago, are sent to accident sites or customers' homes to assess damage and in some cases pay claims immediately. Renwick says the IRVs—mobile offices for Progressive's claim representatives—were designed in part to help the customer's "emotional EKG." Reps arrive in the IRVs and quickly take care of the details so the accident victim can get back on the road as soon as possible. But the IRVs are more than just reassuring perks for stressed-out drivers. They save Progressive money by reducing costs of vehicle storage and rental cars on the 10,000 or so claims it handles in a typical day.

This results in happier customers like Dave Meisburger, whose wife was in a car accident a few years ago. Within four hours of her initial call to Progressive, an adjustor had been to their Mobile, Alabama, home, assessed the damage, and cut them a check, right in the driveway. Now Meisburger says he will never leave Progressive. "They could double their rate, and I wouldn't care. Their customer service means more to me than anything," he said.

More recently, Progressive has launched and expanded its Concierge Level claims-service facilities, now available in 18 metropolitan areas. Clients bring in their damaged cars, get a beeper and a rental car, and are notified when repairs are done. In addition to saving the customer time and energy, the centers help streamline communications among Progressive, the customer, and the body shop, increasing productivity of inspections and repairs.

"We're a company that has thought about claims continuously," Renwick said. "Rather than believing that there's one breakthrough that gets you to a new utopia of customer service, we're continuously trying to improve."

High-Tech Achiever Award: Mini USA

Fast Company granted Mini the coveted High-Tech Achiever Customer First Award. Before Angela DiFabio bought her Mini Cooper, she had been dreaming about it for a year. The Philadelphia-based Accenture consultant spent untold hours on Mini's Web site, playing with dozens of possibilities before coming up with the perfect combination: A chili-pepper-red exterior, white racing stripes on the hood, and a custom rally badge bar on the grill.

When DiFabio placed her order with her dealer, the same build-your-own tool—and all the price and product details it provided—left her feeling as if she were getting a fair deal. "He even used the site to order my car," she said. "That made me feel like I was getting the same information that he was, that I wasn't missing something."

While she waited for her Mini to arrive, DiFabio logged on to Mini's Web site every day, this time using its "Where's My Baby?" tracking tool to follow her car, like an expensive FedEx package, from the factory in Britain to its delivery. "I think most places you go to for a car, if you order one it's just a big black hole," DiFabio said. "To be able to check the process made the wait exciting. It definitely gave me a feeling of control in the process."

Being in control. Not missing anything. Making the wait, if there must be one, exciting. It's how every customer wants the service experience to be. And it is what Mini USA, whose customers must usually wait two to three months for their cars, is using technology to do. The Web site does more than just provide information or sell products or services. It keeps customers engaged, and when they are more engaged, they are usually happier, too. "Our ultimate goal was to make waiting fun," said Kerri Martin, Mini USA's marketing manager.

Mini's technology is not groundbreaking; however, it makes an impact on the customer experience because of how it is integrated with the brand: It is fun and makes users feel like part of the clan. Many car Web sites have build-your-own tools, but few are as customizable as Mini's, where the choices are endless and the on-screen car image changes to your specifications. The tracking service, which is unusual, acknowledges and soothes customers' anxiety and impatience—and perhaps stretches the nervous-parent metaphor a bit. In the "scheduled for production" phase, for example, the tracking tool assures them that their Mini "will begin to move through the 'birth canal' at our Oxford plant. Rest well knowing that your baby is in the best of hands."

The challenge for Mini is meeting the high expectations of such eager customers. Critics note that some dealerships are not as integrated with their Web site as they should be. And when expectant Mini owners, who it turns out are a fretful bunch, found a way to track their cars through independent shipping companies, some customers were upset that Mini's tool was not updated as quickly as the information they were finding on their own. To try to adjust these customers' expectations, Mini added an online video that explains everything that has to happen in the port and why its online tool might be slower than the independent data. It has not appeased everyone, but it has helped soothe some anxiety.

Some of Mini's technology is just for fun: Stay on the Mini site too long, and a pop-up window tells you to "save your retinas for the road." Owners are e-mailed birthday cards when their Mini is a year old and sent notices when new features are available on the site. DiFabio looks forward to these messages. "E-mails I get from other companies feel more like an ad. This feels more like a club," she said.[1]

INTRODUCTION

Customer relationship management (CRM) involves managing all aspects of a customer's relationship with an organization to increase customer loyalty and retention and an organization's profitability. As organizations begin to migrate from the traditional product-focused organization toward customer-driven organizations, they are recognizing their customers as experts, not just revenue generators. Organizations are quickly realizing that without customers, they simply would not exist and it is critical they do everything they can to ensure their customers' satisfaction. In an age when product differentiation is difficult, CRM is one of the most valuable assets a company can acquire. The sooner a company embraces CRM the better off it will be and the harder it will be for competitors to steal loyal and devoted customers.

section 9.1 CUSTOMER RELATIONSHIP MANAGEMENT

LEARNING OUTCOMES

9.1. Compare operational and analytical customer relationship management.

9.2. Explain the formula an organization can use to find its most valuable customers.

9.3. Describe and differentiate the CRM technologies used by sales departments and customer service departments.

9.4. Describe and differentiate the CRM technologies used by marketing departments and sales departments.

BUSINESS BENEFITS OF CRM

1-800-Flowers.com achieved operational excellence by building customer intimacy to continue to improve profits and business growth. The company turned brand loyalty into brand relationships by using the vast amounts of information it collected to understand customers' needs and expectations. The floral delivery company adopted SAS Enterprise Miner to analyze the information in its CRM systems. Enterprise Miner sifts through information to reveal trends, explain outcomes, and predict results so that businesses can increase response rates and quickly identify their profitable customers. With the help of Enterprise Miner, 1-800-Flowers.com is continuing to thrive with revenues averaging 17 percent annual increases in revenue.[2]

CRM is a business philosophy based on the premise that those organizations that understand the needs of individual customers are best positioned to achieve sustainable competitive advantage in the future. Many aspects of CRM are not new to organizations; CRM is simply performing current business better. Placing customers at the forefront of all thinking and decision making requires significant operational and technology changes.

A customer strategy starts with understanding who the company's customers are and how the company can meet strategic goals. *The New York Times* understands this and has spent the past decade researching core customers to find similarities among groups of readers in cities outside the New York metropolitan area. Its goal is to understand how to appeal to those groups and make *The New York Times* a national newspaper, expanding its circulation and the reach it offers to advertisers. *The New York Times* is growing in a relatively flat publishing market and has achieved a customer retention rate of 94 percent in an industry that averages roughly 60 percent.[3]

As the business world increasingly shifts from product focus to customer focus, most organizations recognize that treating existing customers well is the best source

FIGURE 9.1

CRM Benefits

CRM Benefits
Provide better customer service
Improve call center efficiency
Cross-sell products more effectively
Help sales staff close deals faster
Simplify marketing and sales processes
Discover new customers
Increase customer revenues

of profitable and sustainable revenue growth. In the age of e-business, however, an organization is challenged more than ever before to satisfy its customers. Figure 9.1 displays the benefits derived by an organization from a CRM strategy.

The National Basketball Association's New York Knicks are becoming better than ever at communicating with their fans. Thanks to a CRM solution, New York Knicks' management now knows which season-ticket holders like which players, what kind of merchandise they buy, and where they buy it. Management is finally able to send out fully integrated e-mail campaigns that do not overlap with other marketing efforts.[4]

CRM BASICS

An organization can find its most valuable customers by using a formula that industry insiders call RFM—**R**ecency, **F**requency, and **M**onetary value. In other words, an organization must track:

- How recently a customer purchased items (recency).
- How frequently a customer purchases items (frequency).
- How much a customer spends on each purchase (monetary value).

Once a company has gathered this initial CRM information, it can compile it to identify patterns and create marketing campaigns, sales promotions, and services to increase business. For example, if Ms. Smith buys only at the height of the season, then the company should send her a special offer during the off-season. If Mr. Jones always buys software but never computers, then the company should offer him free software with the purchase of a new computer.

The CRM technologies discussed in this chapter can help organizations find answers to RFM and other tough questions, such as who are their best customers and which of their products are the most profitable.

The Evolution of CRM

Knowing the customer, especially knowing the profitability of individual customers, is highly lucrative in the financial services industry. Its high transactional nature has always afforded the financial services industry more access to customer information than other industries have, but it has embraced CRM technologies only recently.

Barclays Bank is a leading financial services company operating in more than 70 countries. In the United Kingdom, Barclays has over 10 million personal customers and about 9.3 million credit cards in circulation, and it serves 500,000 small business customers. Barclays decided to invest in CRM technologies to help it gain valuable insights into its business and customers.

With the new CRM system, Barclays' managers are better able to predict the financial behavior of individual customers and assess whether a customer is likely to

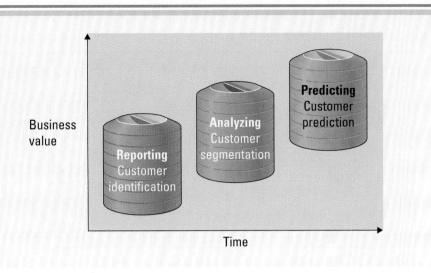

FIGURE 9.2

Evolution of CRM

pay back a loan in full and within the agreed-upon time period. This helps Barclays manage its profitability with greater precision because it can charge its customers a more appropriate rate of interest based on the results of the customer's risk assessment. Barclays also uses a sophisticated customer segmentation system to identify groups of profitable customers, both on a corporate and personal level, which it can then target for new financial products. One of the most valuable pieces of information Barclays discovered was that about 50 percent of its customers are nonprofitable and that less than 30 percent of its customers provide 90 percent of its profits.[5]

There are three phases in the evolution of CRM: (1) reporting, (2) analyzing, and (3) predicting. **CRM reporting technologies** help organizations identify their customers across other applications. **CRM analysis technologies** help organizations segment their customers into categories such as best and worst customers. **CRM predicting technologies** help organizations make predictions regarding customer behavior such as which customers are at risk of leaving (see Figure 9.2).

Both operational and analytical CRM technologies can assist in customer reporting (identification), customer analysis (segmentation), and customer prediction. Figure 9.3 highlights a few of the important questions an organization can answer using CRM technologies.

FIGURE 9.3

Reporting, Analyzing, and Predicting Examples

REPORTING "Asking What Happened"	ANALYZING "Asking Why It Happened"	PREDICTING "Asking What Will Happen"
What is the total revenue by customer?	Why did sales not meet forecasts?	What customers are at risk of leaving?
How many units did we manufacture?	Why was production so low?	What products will the customer buy?
Where did we sell the most products?	Why did we not sell as many units as last year?	Who are the best candidates for a mailing?
What were total sales by product?	Who are our customers?	What is the best way to reach the customer?
How many customers did we serve?	Why was customer revenue so high?	What is the lifetime profitability of a customer?
What are our inventory levels?	Why are inventory levels so low?	What transactions might be fradulent?

FIGURE 9.4

Operational CRM
and Analytical CRM

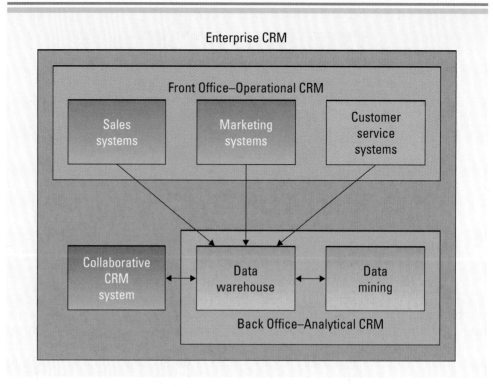

FIGURE 9.5

Operational CRM
Technologies for Sales,
Marketing, and Customer
Service Departments

Operational and Analytical CRM

Joe Guyaux knows the best way to win customers is to improve service. Under his leadership and with the help of Siebel CRM, the PNC retail banking team increased new consumer checking customers by 19 percent in one year. Over the past year, PNC retained 21 percent more of its consumer checking households as well as improved customer satisfaction by 9 percent.[6]

The two primary components of a CRM strategy are operational CRM and analytical CRM. **Operational CRM** supports traditional transactional processing for day-to-day front-office operations or systems that deal directly with the customers. **Analytical CRM** supports back-office operations and strategic analysis and includes all systems that do not deal directly with the customers. The primary difference between operational CRM and analytical CRM is the direct interaction between the organization and its customers. Figure 9.4 provides an overview of operational CRM and analytical CRM.

USING INFORMATION TECHNOLOGY TO DRIVE OPERATIONAL CRM

Figure 9.5 displays the different technologies marketing, sales, and customer service departments can use to perform operational CRM.

Operational CRM Technologies		
Marketing	**Sales**	**Customer Service**
1. List generator	1. Sales management	1. Contact center
2. Campaign management	2. Contact management	2. Web-based self-service
3. Cross-selling and up-selling	3. Opportunity management	3. Call scripting

Marketing and Operational CRM

Companies are no longer trying to sell one product to as many customers as possible; instead, they are trying to sell one customer as many products as possible. Marketing departments are able to transform to this new way of doing business by using CRM technologies that allow them to gather and analyze customer information to deploy successful marketing campaigns. In fact, a marketing campaign's success is directly proportional to the organization's ability to gather and analyze the right information. The three primary operational CRM technologies a marketing department can implement to increase customer satisfaction are:

1. List generator.
2. Campaign management.
3. Cross-selling and up-selling.

List Generator   *List generators* compile customer information from a variety of sources and segment the information for different marketing campaigns. Information sources include Web site visits, Web site questionnaires, online and off-line surveys, flyers, toll-free numbers, current customer lists, and so on. After compiling the customer list, an organization can use criteria to filter and sort the list for potential customers. Filter and sort criteria can include such things as household income, education level, and age. List generators provide the marketing department with a solid understanding of the type of customer it needs to target for marketing campaigns.

Campaign Management   *Campaign management systems* guide users through marketing campaigns performing such tasks as campaign definition, planning, scheduling, segmentation, and success analysis. These advanced systems can even calculate quantifiable results for return on investment (ROI) for each campaign and track the results in order to analyze and understand how the company can fine-tune future campaigns.

Cross-Selling and Up-Selling   Two key sales strategies a marketing campaign can deploy are cross-selling and up-selling. *Cross-selling* is selling additional products or services to a customer. *Up-selling* is increasing the value of the sale. For example, McDonald's performs cross-selling by asking customers if they would like an apple pie with their meal. McDonald's performs up-selling by asking customers if they would like to super-size their meals. CRM systems offer marketing departments all kinds of information about their customers and their products, which can help them identify cross-selling and up-selling marketing campaigns.

The California State Automobile Association (CSAA) had to take advantage of its ability to promote and cross-sell CSAA automotive, insurance, and travel services to beat its competition. Accomplishing this task was easy once the company implemented E.piphany's CRM system. The system integrated information from all of CSAA's separate databases, making it immediately available to all employees through a Web-based browser. Employees could quickly glance at a customer's profile and determine which services the customer currently had and which services the customer might want to purchase based on her or his needs as projected by the software.[7]

Sales and Operational CRM

Siebel, one of the largest providers of CRM software, had 33,000 subscribers in January 2005. Salesforce.com, provider of on-demand Web-based customer relationship management software, added 40,000 subscribers during the first three months of 2005, more than all of Siebel's subscribers. Salesforce.com's total number of subscribers is over 300,000. Merrill Lynch, one of the biggest customers in the sales force market, signed on for 5,000 subscriptions for its global private client division, making the brokerage firm Salesforce.com's largest customer. Salesforce.com's new product, Customforce, includes tools for adding data analysis capabilities, spreadsheet-style mathematical formulas, business processes, and forecasting models.[8]

Sales departments were the first to begin developing CRM systems. Sales departments had two primary reasons to track customer sales information electronically. First, sales representatives were struggling with the overwhelming amount of customer account information they were required to maintain and track. Second, companies were struggling with the issue that much of their vital customer and sales information remained in the heads of their sales representatives. One of the first CRM components built to help address these issues was the sales force automation component. *Sales force automation (SFA)* is a system that automatically tracks all of the steps in the sales process. SFA products focus on increasing customer satisfaction, building customer relationships, and improving product sales by tracking all sales information.

Serving several million guests each year, Vail Resorts Inc. maintains dozens of systems across all seven of its properties. These systems perform numerous tasks including recording lift ticket, lodging, restaurant, conference, retail, and ski rental sales. Since a significant percentage of the company's revenue results from repeat guests, building stronger, more profitable relationships with its loyal customers is Vail Resorts first priority.

To improve its customer service and marketing campaign success, Vail deployed the Ascential CRM system, which integrated the customer information from its many disparate systems. The CRM system is providing Vail Resorts with a detailed level of customer insight, which helps the company personalize its guest offerings and promotions. By using a CRM system that integrates information from across all of its resorts and business lines, the company can determine what, where, and how its guests behave across all of its properties. For example, the company can now offer discounts on lift ticket and ski rentals for customers staying in its resorts. The three primary operational CRM technologies a sales department can implement to increase customer satisfaction are:

1. Sales management CRM systems.
2. Contact management CRM systems.
3. Opportunity management CRM systems.[9]

Sales Management CRM Systems   Figure 9.6 depicts the typical sales process, which begins with an opportunity and ends with billing the customer for the sale. Leads and potential customers are the lifeblood of all sales organizations, whether the products they are peddling are computers, clothing, or cars. How the leads are handled can make the difference between revenue growth or decline. *Sales management CRM systems* automate each phase of the sales process, helping individual sales representatives coordinate and organize all of their accounts. Features include calendars to help plan customer meetings, alarm reminders signaling important tasks, customizable multimedia presentations, and document generation. These systems even have the ability to provide an analysis of the sales cycle and calculate how each individual sales representative is performing during the sales process.

Contact Management CRM Systems   A *contact management CRM system* maintains customer contact information and identifies prospective customers for future sales. Contact management systems include such features as maintaining organizational charts, detailed customer notes, and supplemental sales information. For example, a contact management system can take an incoming telephone number and display the caller's name along with notes detailing previous conversations. This allows the sales representative to answer the telephone and say, "Hi Sue, how is your new laptop working? How was your vacation to Florida?" without receiving any reminders of such details first from the customer. The customer feels valued since the sales associate knows her name and even remembers details of their last conversation!

FIGURE 9.6

Overview of the Sales Process

Sales Process

A $16 billion technology company, 3M is a leader in health care, safety, electronics, telecommunications, office, and consumer markets. The company began to focus on streamlining and unifying its sales processes with the primary goals of better customer segmentation and more reliable lead generation and qualification. To achieve these goals the company implemented a CRM system and soon found itself receiving the following benefits:

- Cutting the time it takes to familiarize sales professionals with new territories by 33 percent.

- Increasing management's visibility of the sales process.

- Decreasing the time it takes to qualify leads and assign sales opportunities by 40 percent.

One of the more successful campaigns driven by the CRM system allowed 3M to deliver direct mail to targeted government agencies and emergency services in response to the anthrax attacks in 2002. All inquiries to the mail campaign were automatically assigned to a sales representative who followed up with a quote. In little more than a week, the company had received orders for 35,000 respirator masks.[10]

Opportunity Management CRM Systems *Opportunity management CRM systems* target sales opportunities by finding new customers or companies for future sales. Opportunity management systems determine potential customers and competitors and define selling efforts including budgets and schedules. Advanced opportunity management systems can even calculate the probability of a sale, which can save sales representatives significant time and money when attempting to find new customers. The primary difference between contact management and opportunity management is that contact management deals with existing

FIGURE 9.7

CRM Pointers for Gaining
Prospective Customers

CRM Pointers for Gaining Prospective Customers	
1. Get their attention	If you have a good prospect, chances are that he or she receives dozens of offers from similar companies. Be sure your first contact is professional and gets your customer's attention.
2. Value their time	When you ask for a meeting, you are asking for the most valuable thing a busy person has—time. Many companies have had great success by offering high-value gifts in exchange for a meeting with a representative. Just be careful because some organizations frown on expensive gifts. Instead, offer these prospective customers a report that can help them perform their jobs more effectively.
3. Overdeliver	If your letter offered a free DVD in exchange for a meeting, bring a box of microwave popcorn along with the movie. Little gestures like these tell customers that you not only keep your word, but also can be counted on to overdeliver.
4. Contact frequently	Find new and creative ways to contact your prospective customers frequently. Starting a newsletter and sending out a series of industry updates are excellent ways to keep in contact and provide value.
5. Generate a trustworthy mailing list	If you are buying a mailing list from a third party be sure that the contacts are genuine prospects, especially if you are offering an expensive gift. Be sure that the people you are meeting have the power to authorize a sale.
6. Follow up	One of the most powerful prospecting tools is a simple thank-you note. Letting people know that their time was appreciated may even lead to additional referrals.

customers and opportunity management deals with new customers. Figure 9.7 displays six CRM pointers a sales representative can use to increase prospective customers.

Customer Service and Operational CRM

Andy Taylor became president of Enterprise, his father's $76 million rental-car company, in 1980. Today, it is the largest in North America, with $7 billion in revenue. How has he kept customer service a priority? By quantifying it. Enterprise surveys 1.7 million customers a year. If a branch's satisfaction scores are low, employees, even vice presidents, cannot be promoted. The result is self-propagating. Seeking better scores, managers make better hires. And because Enterprise promotes almost solely from within, nearly every executive—including Taylor, who started out washing cars—has a frontline understanding of what it takes to keep customers happy. "The company would never have gotten that 100-fold growth without Andy's knack for putting systems and processes in place so you can deliver consistent service," said Sandy Rogers, senior vice president of corporate strategy.

Sales and marketing are the primary departments that interact directly with customers before a sale. Most companies recognize the importance of building strong relationships during the marketing and sales efforts; however, many fail to realize the importance of continuing to build these relationships after the sale is complete. It is actually more important to build postsale relationships if the company wants to ensure customer loyalty and satisfaction. The best way to implement postsale CRM strategies is through the customer service department.

One of the primary reasons a company loses customers is bad customer service experiences. Providing outstanding customer service is a difficult task, and many CRM technologies are available to assist organizations with this important activity. For example, by rolling out Lotus Instant Messaging to its customers, Avnet Computer Marketing has established an efficient, direct route to push valuable information and updates out to its customers. The company uses Lotus Instant Messaging to provide real-time answers to customer questions by listing its support specialists' status by different colors on its Web site: green if they are available, red if they are not, or blue if they are out of the office. The customer simply clicks on a name to begin instant messaging or a chat session to get quick answers to questions.[11]

Before access to Lotus Instant Messaging, customers had to wait in "1-800" call queues or for e-mail responses for answers. The new system has increased customer satisfaction along with tremendous savings from fewer long-distance phone charges. Avnet also estimates that Lotus Instant Messaging saves each of its 650 employees 5 to 10 minutes a day. The three primary operational CRM technologies a customer service department can implement to increase customer satisfaction are:

1. Contact center.
2. Web-based self-service.
3. Call scripting.

Contact Center Knowledge-management software, which helps call centers put consistent answers at customer-service representative's fingertips, is often long on promise and short on delivery. The problem? Representatives have to take time out from answering calls to input things they have learned—putting the "knowledge" in knowledge management.

Brad Cleveland, who heads the Incoming Calls Management Institute, said, "Software is just a tool. It doesn't do any good unless people across the organization are using it to its potential." Sharp Electronics is making it happen. Sharp's frontline representatives built the system from scratch. And as Sharp rolled out its network over the past four years, representatives' compensation and promotions were tied directly to the system's use. As a result, the customer call experience at Sharp has improved dramatically: The proportion of problems resolved by a single call has soared from 76 percent to 94 percent since 2000.

A *contact center* (or *call center*) is where customer service representatives (CSRs) answer customer inquiries and respond to problems through a number of different customer touchpoints. A contact center is one of the best assets a customer-driven organization can have because maintaining a high level of customer support is critical to obtaining and retaining customers. Numerous systems are available to help an organization automate its contact centers. Figure 9.8 highlights a few of the features available in contact center systems.

Contact centers also track customer call history along with problem resolutions—information critical for providing a comprehensive customer view to the CSR. CSRs who can quickly comprehend and understand all of a customer's products and issues provide tremendous value to the customer and the organization. Nothing makes frustrated customers happier than not having to explain their problems to yet another CSR.

New emotion-detection software called Perform, created by Nice Systems, is designed to help companies improve customer service by identifying callers who are upset. When an elderly man distressed over high medical premiums hung up during his phone call to the Wisconsin Physician Services Insurance Corporation's call center, an IT system detected the customer's exasperation and automatically

FIGURE 9.8

Common Features Included in Contact Centers

Common Features Included in Contact Centers	
Automatic call distribution	A phone switch routes inbound calls to available agents.
Interactive voice response (IVR)	Directs customers to use touch-tone phones or keywords to navigate or provide information.
Predictive dialing	Automatically dials outbound calls and when someone answers, the call is forwarded to an available agent.

e-mailed a supervisor. The supervisor listened to a digital recording of the conversation, called the customer, and suggested ways to lower the premium. The system uses algorithms to determine a baseline of emotion during the first 5 to 10 seconds of a call, any deviation from the baseline triggers an alert.[12]

Web-Based Self-Service   *Web-based self-service systems* allow customers to use the Web to find answers to their questions or solutions to their problems. FedEx uses Web-based self-service systems to allow customers to track their own packages without having to talk to a CSR. FedEx customers can simply log on to FedEx's Web site and enter their tracking number. The Web site quickly displays the exact location of the package and the estimated delivery time.

Another great feature of Web-based self-service is click-to-talk buttons. Click-to-talk buttons allow customers to click on a button and talk with a CSR via the Internet. Powerful customer-driven features like these add tremendous value to any organization by providing customers with real-time information without having to contact company representatives. [13]

Call Scripting   Being a CSR is not an easy task, especially when the CSR is dealing with detailed technical products or services. *Call scripting systems* access organizational databases that track similar issues or questions and automatically generate the details for the CSR who can then relay them to the customer. The system can even provide a list of questions that the CSR can ask the customer to determine the potential problem and resolution. This feature helps CSRs answer difficult questions quickly while also presenting a uniform image so two different customers do not receive two different answers.

Documedics is a health care consulting company that provides reimbursement information about pharmaceutical products to patients and health care professionals. The company currently supports inquiries for 12 pharmaceutical companies and receives over 30,000 customer calls per month. Originally, the company had a data file for each patient and for each pharmaceutical company. This inefficient process resulted in the potential for a single patient to have up to 12 different information files if the patient was a client of all 12 pharmaceutical companies. To answer customer questions, a CSR had to download each customer file, causing tremendous inefficiencies and confusion. The company implemented a CRM system with a call scripting feature to alleviate the problem and provide its CSRs with a comprehensive view of every customer, regardless of the pharmaceutical company. The company anticipated 20 percent annual growth primarily because of the successful implementation of its new system.[14]

USING INFORMATION TECHNOLOGY TO DRIVE ANALYTICAL CRM

Maturing analytical CRM and behavioral modeling technologies are helping numerous organizations move beyond legacy benefits such as enhanced customer service and retention to systems that can truly improve business profitability. Unlike operational CRM that automates call centers and sales forces with the aim of enhancing customer transactions, analytical CRM solutions are designed to dig deep into a company's historical customer information and expose patterns of behavior on which a company can capitalize. Analytical CRM is primarily used to enhance and support decision making and works by identifying patterns in customer information collected from the various operational CRM systems.

For many organizations, the power of analytical CRM solutions provides tremendous managerial opportunities. Depending on the specific solution, analytical CRM tools can slice-and-dice customer information to create made-to-order views of customer value, spending, product affinities, percentile profiles, and segmentations. Modeling tools can identify opportunities for cross-selling, up-selling, and expanding customer relationships.

Personalization occurs when a Web site can know enough about a person's likes and dislikes that it can fashion offers that are more likely to appeal to that person.

Many organizations are now utilizing CRM to create customer rules and templates that marketers can use to personalize customer messages.

The information produced by analytical CRM solutions can help companies make decisions about how to handle customers based on the value of each and every one. Analytical CRM can help reveal information about which customers are worth investing in, which should be serviced at an average level, and which should not be invested in at all.

Data gained from customers can also reveal information about employees. Wachovia Bank surveys customers—25,000 every month—for feedback on their service experience. It asks about individual employees and uses those answers in one-on-one staff coaching. A recent 20-minute coaching session at a Manhattan branch made clear how this feedback—each customer surveyed rates 33 employee behaviors—can improve service. The branch manager urged an employee to focus on sincerity rather than on mere friendliness, to "sharpen her antenna" so she would listen to customers more intuitively, and to slow down rather than hurry up. That focus on careful, sincere, intuitive service has paid off: Wachovia has held the top score among banks in the American Customer Satisfaction Index since 2001.[15]

Analytical CRM relies heavily on data warehousing technologies and business intelligence to glean insights into customer behavior. These systems quickly aggregate, analyze, and disseminate customer information throughout an organization. Figure 9.9 displays a few examples of the kind of information insights analytical CRM can help an organization gain.

UPS's data-intensive environment is supported by the largest IBM DB2 database in the world, consisting of 236 terabytes of data related to its analytical CRM tool.

FIGURE 9.9

Analytical CRM Information
Examples

Analytical CRM Information Examples	
1. Give customers more of what they want	Analytical CRM can help an organization go beyond the typical "Dear Mr. Smith" salutation. An organization can use its analytical CRM information to make its communications more personable. For example, if it knows a customer's shoe size and preferred brand it can notify the customer that there is a pair of size 12 shoes set aside to try on the next time the customer visits the store.
2. Find new customers similar to the best customers	Analytical CRM might determine that an organization does a lot of business with women 35 to 45 years old who drive SUVs and live within 30 miles of a certain location. The company can then find a mailing list that highlights this type of customer for potential new sales.
3. Find out what the organization does best	Analytical CRM can determine what an organization does better than its competitors. For example, if a restaurant caters more breakfasts to midsized companies than its competition does, it can purchase a specialized mailing list of midsized companies in the area and send them a mailing that features the breakfast catering specials.
4. Beat competitors to the punch	Analytical CRM can determine sales trends allowing an organization to offer the best customers deals before the competition has a chance to. For example, a clothing store might determine its best customers for outdoor apparel and send them an offer to attend a private sale right before the competition runs its outdoor apparel sale.
5. Reactivate inactive customers	Analytical CRM can highlight customers who have not done any business with the organization in a while. The organization can then send them a personalized letter along with a discount coupon. It will remind them of the company and may help spark a renewed relationship.
6. Let customers know they matter	Analytical CRM can determine what customers want and need, so an organization can contact them with this information. Anything from a private sale to a reminder that the car is due for a tune-up is excellent customer service.

The shipping company's goal is to create one-to-one customer relationships, and it is using QuantumView tools that allow it to let customers tailor views of such things as shipment history and receive notices when a package arrives or is delayed. UPS has built more than 500 customer relationship management applications that run off of its data warehouse.[16]

Data warehouses are providing businesses with information about their customers and products that was previously impossible to locate, and the resulting payback can be tremendous. Organizations are now relying on business intelligence to provide them with hard facts that can determine everything from which type of marketing and sales campaign to launch, to which customers to target, at what time. Using CRM along with business intelligence allows organizations to make better, more informed decisions and to reap amazing unforeseen rewards.

Sears, Roebuck and Company is the third-largest U.S. retailer. Over the past two decades there has been a well-publicized encroachment by discount mass merchandisers. Even though Sears does not know exactly "who" its customers are (by name and address) since many customers use cash or non-Sears credit cards, it can still benefit from analytical CRM technologies. Sears uses these technologies to determine what its generic customers prefer to buy and when they buy it, which enables the company to predict what they will buy. Using analytical CRM, Sears can view each day's sales by region, district, store, product line, and individual item. Sears can now monitor the precise impact of advertising, weather, and other factors on sales of specific items. For the first time, Sears can even group together, or "cluster," widely divergent types of items. For example, merchandisers can track sales of a store display marked "Gifts under $25" that might include sweatshirts, screwdrivers, and other unrelated items. The advertising department can then follow the sales of "Gifts under $25" to determine which products to place in its newspaper advertisements.[17]

OPENING CASE QUESTIONS

Customer First Awards

1. Summarize the evolution of CRM and provide an example of a reporting, analyzing, and predicting question Progressive might ask its customers.
2. How could Progressive's marketing department use CRM technology to improve its operations?
3. How could Mini's sales department use CRM technology to improve its operations?
4. How could Progressive and Mini's customer service departments use CRM technology to improve their operations?
5. Define analytical CRM and its importance to companies like Progressive and Mini.

---

section 9.2   CUSTOMER RELATIONSHIP MANAGEMENT STRATEGIES

LEARNING OUTCOMES

9.5. Identify the primary forces driving the explosive growth of customer relationship management.

9.6. Summarize the best practices for implementing a successful customer relationship management system.

9.7. Compare customer relationship management, supplier relationship management, partner relationship management, and employee relationship management.

CUSTOMER RELATIONSHIP MANAGEMENT'S EXPLOSIVE GROWTH

Brother International Corporation experienced skyrocketing growth in its sales of multifunction centers, fax machines, printers, and labeling systems in the late 1990s. Along with skyrocketing sales growth came a tremendous increase in customer service calls. When Brother failed to answer the phone fast enough, product returns started to increase. The company responded by increasing call center capacity, and the rate of returns began to drop. However, Dennis Upton, CIO of Brother International, observed that all the company was doing was answering the phone. He quickly realized that the company was losing a world of valuable market intelligence (business intelligence) about existing customers from all those telephone calls. The company decided to deploy SAP's CRM solution. The 1.8 million calls Brother handled dropped to 1.57 million, which reduced call center staff from 180 agents to 160 agents. Since customer demographic information is now stored and displayed on the agent's screen based on the incoming telephone number, the company has reduced call duration by an average of one minute, saving the company $600,000 per year.[18]

In the context of increasing business competition and mature markets, it is easier than ever for informed and demanding customers to defect since they are just a click away from migrating to an alternative. When customers buy on the Internet, they see, and they steer, entire value chains. The Internet is a "looking glass," a two-way mirror, and its field of vision is the entire value chain. While the Internet cannot totally replace the phone and face-to-face communication with customers, it can strengthen these interactions at all customer touchpoints. Customer Web interactions become conversations, interactive dialogs with shared knowledge, not just business transactions. Web-based customer care can actually become the focal point of customer relationship management and provide breakthrough benefits for both the enterprise and its customers, substantially reducing costs while improving service.

According to an AMR Research survey of more than 500 businesses in 14 key vertical markets, half of all current CRM spending is by manufacturers. Current users are allocating 20 percent of their IT budgets to CRM solutions. Those who have not invested in CRM may soon come on board: Of the respondents in the study who are not currently using CRM, roughly one-third plan to implement these types of technology solutions within the next year. Figure 9.10 shows the top CRM business drivers, and Figure 9.11 displays the forecasts for CRM spending over the next few years.

When you are dealing with sick customers, flexibility is key. That is why Walgreens has made healthy investments in customer service over the past 30 years,

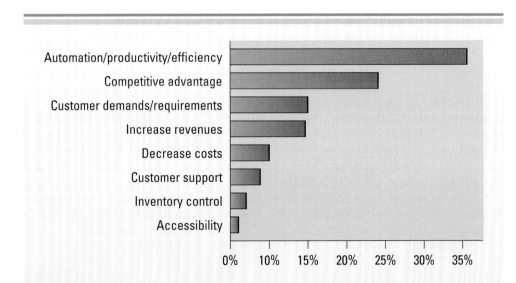

FIGURE 9.10

CRM Business Drivers

FIGURE 9.11

Forecasts for CRM
Spending ($ billions)

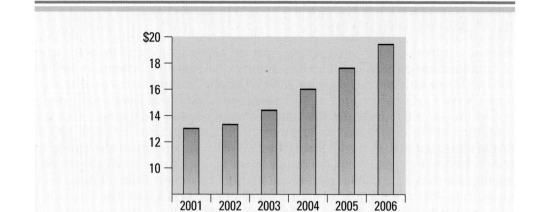

originating the drive-through pharmacy and pioneering a network for refilling prescriptions at any location. It should come as no surprise that Walgreens credited much of its growth to an increased investment in customer service. The company has developed new software that can print prescription labels in 14 languages and large-type labels for older patrons. Besides investing in customer-friendly technology, the 103-year-old chain is not forgetting the human touch. Walgreens spends more on payroll on stores where performance is below average, increasing the clerk-to-customer ratio; and it recently launched an online training program for all employees. With 19 straight quarters of double-digit earnings growth, the prescription appears to be working.[19]

CUSTOMER RELATIONSHIP MANAGEMENT SUCCESS FACTORS

When a "lucky ambassador" greets a Harrah's guest at a video-poker machine by name, wishes her a happy birthday, and offers free tickets to a show, luck has nothing to do with it. The moment customers insert their loyalty card into a slot machine, the casino giant's $30 million-plus CRM system reveals every move they have ever made at any of its 28 properties. "If you start to have a really unfortunate visit, you start to think, 'Man, that place is really just bad luck,'" said Gary Loveman, Harrah's president and CEO. "If we see that coming, we can intervene" with perks to soothe the pain of gambling losses. While many companies struggle to employ CRM successfully, gathering massive amounts of data without using it to benefit customers, Harrah's is building on its mastery. In the future, its slot machines will spout real-time monetary credits and dinner coupons using new customer-recognition software and hardware, leaving even its losing customers feeling a little luckier.

CRM solutions make organizational business processes more intelligent. Organizations achieve this by understanding customer behavior and preferences, then realigning product and service offerings and related communications to make sure they are synchronized with customer needs and preferences. If an organization is implementing a CRM system, it should study the industry best practices to help ensure a successful implementation (see Figure 9.12).

CRM is critical to business success. CRM is the key competitive strategy to stay focused on customer needs and to integrate a customer-centric approach throughout an organization. CRM can acquire enterprisewide knowledge about customers and improve the business processes that deliver value to an organization's customers, suppliers, and employees. Using the analytical capabilities of CRM can help a company anticipate customer needs and proactively serve customers in ways that build relationships, create loyalty, and enhance bottom lines.

FIGURE 9.12

CRM Industry Best
Practices

1. **Clearly Communicate the CRM Strategy**—Boise Office Solutions recently spent $25 million implementing a successful CRM system. One of the primary reasons for the system's success was that Boise started with a clear business objective for the system: to provide customers with greater economic value. Only after establishing the business objective did Boise Office Solutions invest in CRM technology to help meet the goal. Ensuring that all departments and employees understand exactly what CRM means and how it will add value to the organization is critical. Research by Gartner Dataquest indicates that enterprises that attain success with CRM have interested and committed senior executives who set goals for what CRM should achieve, match CRM strategies with corporate objectives, and tie the measurement process to both goals and strategies.

2. **Define Information Needs and Flows**—People who perform successful CRM implementations have a clear understanding of how information flows in and out of their organization. Chances are information comes into the organization in many different forms over many different touch points.

3. **Build an Integrated View of the Customer**—Essential to a CRM strategy is choosing the correct CRM system that can support organizational requirements. The system must have the corresponding functional breadth and depth to support strategic goals. Do not forget to take into account the system's infrastructure including ease of integration to current systems, discussed in greater detail later in this unit.

4. **Implement in Iterations**—Implement the CRM system in manageable pieces—in other words avoid the "big bang" implementation approach. It is easier to manage, measure, and track the design, building, and deployment of the CRM system when it is delivered in pieces. Most important, this allows the organization to find out early if the implementation is headed for failure and thus either kill the project and save wasted resources or change direction to a more successful path.

5. **Scalability for Organizational Growth**—Make certain that the CRM system meets the organization's future needs as well as its current needs. Estimating future needs is by far one of the hardest parts of any project. Understanding how the organization is going to grow, predicting how technology is going to change, and anticipating how customers are going to evolve are very difficult challenges. Taking the time to answer some tough questions up front will ensure the organization grows into, instead of out of, its CRM system.

CURRENT TRENDS: SRM, PRM, AND ERM

Organizations are discovering a wave of other key business areas where it is beneficial to take advantage of building strong relationships. These emerging areas include supplier relationship management (SRM), partner relationship management (PRM), and employee relationship management (ERM).

Supplier Relationship Management

Supplier relationship management (SRM) focuses on keeping suppliers satisfied by evaluating and categorizing suppliers for different projects, which optimizes supplier selection. SRM applications help companies analyze vendors based on a number of key variables including strategy, business goals, prices, and markets. The company can then determine the best supplier to collaborate with and can work on developing strong relationships with that supplier. The partners can then work together to streamline processes, outsource services, and provide products that they could not provide individually.

With the merger of the Bank of Halifax and Bank of Scotland, the new company, HBOS, implemented an SRM system to provide consistent information to its suppliers. The system integrates procurement information from the separate Bank of Halifax and Bank of Scotland operational systems, generating a single repository of management information for consistent reporting and analysis. Other benefits HBOS derived from the SRM solution include:

- A single consolidated view of all suppliers.
- Consistent, detailed management information allowing multiple views for every executive.
- Elimination of duplicate suppliers.[20]

Partner Relationship Management

Organizations have begun to realize the importance of building relationships with partners, dealers, and resellers. *Partner relationship management (PRM)* focuses on keeping vendors satisfied by managing alliance partner and reseller relationships that provide customers with the optimal sales channel. PRM's business strategy is to select and manage partners to optimize their long-term value to an organization. In effect, it means picking the right partners, working with them to help them be successful in dealing with mutual customers, and ensuring that partners and the ultimate end customers are satisfied and successful. Many of the features of a PRM application include real-time product information on availability, marketing materials, contracts, order details, and pricing, inventory, and shipping information.

PRM is one of the smaller segments of CRM that has superb potential. PRM grew from a $500 million business to a $1 billion business in under four years. This is a direct reflection of the growing interdependency of organizations in the new economy. The primary benefits of PRM include:

- Expanded market coverage.
- Offerings of specialized products and services.
- Broadened range of offerings and a more complete solution.

Employee Relationship Management

Jim Sinegal runs Costco, one of the largest wholesale club chains, but there are two things he does not discount: employee benefits and customer service. Average hourly wages trounce those of rival Sam's Club, and 86 percent of workers have health insurance (versus a reported 47 percent at Sam's). Sinegal is not just being nice. Happy employees, he believes, make for happier customers. Low prices (he caps per-item profits at 14 percent) and a generous return policy certainly help. Although Wall Street has long been arguing for smaller benefits, a stingier return policy, and bigger profits, Sinegal sides with customers and staff. "We're trying to run Costco in a fashion that is not just going to satisfy our shareholders this year or this month," he said, "but next year and on into the future."[21]

Employee relationship management (ERM) provides employees with a subset of CRM applications available through a Web browser. Many of the ERM applications assist the employee in dealing with customers by providing detailed information on company products, services, and customer orders.

At Rackspace, a San Antonio-based Web-hosting company, customer focus borders on the obsessive. Joey Parsons, 24, won the Straightjacket Award, the most coveted employee distinction at Rackspace. The award recognizes the employee who best lives up to the Rackspace motto of delivering "fanatical support," a dedication to customers that is so intense it borders on the loony. Rackspace motivates its staff by treating each team as a separate business, which is responsible for its own profits and losses and has its own ERM Web site. Each month, employees can earn bonuses of up to 20 percent of their monthly base salaries depending on the performance of their units by both financial and customer-centric measurements such as customer turnover, customer expansion, and customer referrals. Daily reports are available through the team's ERM Web site.[22]

FUTURE CRM TRENDS

CRM revenue forecast for 2008 is $11.5 billion. In the future, CRM applications will continue to change from employee-only tools to tools used by suppliers, partners, and even customers. Providing a consistent view of customers and delivering timely and accurate customer information to all departments across an organization will continue to be the major goal of CRM initiatives.

As technology advances (intranet, Internet, extranet, wireless), CRM will remain a major strategic focus for companies, particularly in industries whose product is difficult to differentiate. Some companies approach this problem by moving to a low-cost producer strategy. CRM will be an alternative way to pursue a differentiation strategy with a nondifferentiable product.

CRM applications will continue to adapt wireless capabilities supporting mobile sales and mobile customers. Sales professionals will be able to access e-mail, order details, corporate information, inventory status, and opportunity information all from a PDA in their car or on a plane. Real-time interaction with human CSRs over the Internet will continue to increase.

CRM suites will also incorporate PRM and SRM modules as enterprises seek to take advantage of these initiatives. Automating interactions with distributors, re-sellers, and suppliers will enhance the corporation's ability to deliver a quality experience to its customers.

OPENING CASE QUESTIONS

Customer First Awards

6. How might Progressive's business model change if it decreased its investments in CRM technologies?

7. How might Mini's business model change if it decreased its investments in CRM technologies?

8. Describe the CRM industry best practices and explain how Progressive is using each.

9. Explain SRM and how Mini could use it to improve its business.

10. Explain ERM and how Progressive could use it to improve its business.

Analytical CRM 280
Automatic call distribution 285
Call scripting system 286
Campaign management
system 281
Contact center (call center) 285
Contact management CRM
system 282
CRM analysis technology 279
CRM predicting technology 279
CRM reporting technology 279
Cross-selling 281

Customer relationship
management (CRM) 277
Employee relationship
management (ERM) 292
Interactive voice response
(IVR) 285
List generator 281
Operational CRM 280
Opportunity management CRM
system 283
Partner relationship
management (PRM) 292

Personalization 286
Predictive dialing 285
Sales management CRM
system 282
Sales force automation
(SFA) 282
Supplier relationship
management (SRM) 291
Up-selling 281
Web-based self service
system 286

Fighting Cancer with Information

"The mission of the American Cancer Society (ACS) is to cure cancer and relieve the pain and suffering caused by this insidious disease," said Zachary Patterson, chief information officer, ACS.

The ACS is a nationwide voluntary health organization dedicated to eliminating cancer as a major health problem by supporting research, education, advocacy, and volunteer service. Headquartered in Atlanta, Georgia, with 17 divisions and more than 3,400 local offices throughout the United States, the ACS represents the largest source of private nonprofit cancer research funds in the United States.

To support its mission, the ACS must perform exceptionally well in three key areas. First, it must be able to provide its constituents—more than 2 million volunteers, patients, and donors—with the best information available regarding the prevention, detection, and treatment of cancer. Second, ACS must be able to demonstrate that it acts responsibly with the funds entrusted to it by the public. "Among other things, that means being able to provide exceptional service when someone calls our call center with a question about mammography screening or our latest antismoking campaign," said Terry Music, national vice president for Information Delivery at the ACS. Third, ACS must be able to secure donations of time and money from its constituent base. Its success in this area is directly related to providing excellent information and service, as well as having an integrated view of its relationship with constituents. "To succeed, we need to understand the full extent of each constituent's relationship with us so we can determine where there might be opportunities to expand that relationship," Music said.

The ACS was experiencing many challenges with its current information. "Our call center agents did not know, for example, if a caller was both a donor and a volunteer, or if a caller was volunteering for the society in multiple ways," he said. "This splintered view made it challenging for American Cancer Society representatives to deliver personalized service and make informed recommendations regarding other opportunities within the society that might interest a caller."

The ACS chose to implement a customer relationship management solution to solve its information issues. Critical to the CRM system's success was consolidating information from various databases across the organization to provide a single view of constituents and all information required to serve them. After an evaluation process that included participation from individuals across the organization, the ACS chose Siebel Systems as its CRM solution provider. The society wanted to work with a company that could address both its immediate needs with a best-in-class e-business solution and its future requirements.

The Siebel Call Center is specifically designed for the next generation of contact centers, enabling organizations to provide world-class customer service, generate increased revenue, and create a closed-loop information flow seamlessly over multichannel sales, marketing, and customer service operations. Siebel Call Center empowers agents at every level by providing up-to-the-minute information and in-depth customer and product knowledge. This approach enables quick and accurate problem resolution and generates greater relationship opportunities. The ACS has received numerous benefits from the system including:

- Increased constituent satisfaction and loyalty by supporting personalized interactions between constituents and cancer information specialists.
- Improved productivity of cancer information specialists by consolidating all information required to serve constituents into a single view.
- Increased donations of time and money by helping call center agents identify callers who are likely to be interested in expanding their relationship with the ACS.[23]

Questions

1. How could the ACS's marketing department use operational CRM to strengthen its relationships with its customers?

2. How could the ACS's customer service department use operational CRM to strengthen its relationships with its customers?

3. Review all of the operational CRM technologies and determine which one would add the greatest value to ACS's business.

4. Describe the benefits ACS could gain from using analytical CRM.

5. Summarize SRM and describe how ACS could use it to increase efficiency in its business.

Calling All Canadians

With multiple communication channels available and so many CRM failures, many companies are concluding that the best method for providing customer service is good old-fashioned customer service provided by a real live person. At the same time that companies consider outsourcing their customer service departments to other countries in order to save money, many worry about foreign accents as well as time-zone issues related to offshore outsourcing.

Canada has become one of the primary targets for outsourcing customer service centers by U.S. companies. Not only are accent and time-zone issues nonexistent, but companies also receive a favorable exchange rate. The Bank of Canada estimates that over the past five years, the currency exchange rate between the United States and Canada favors Americans by 44 percent. For every dollar an American business spends in Canada, it receives over a dollar and a half in goods and services.

Additional factors that make Canada even more attractive include a high Canadian unemployment rate estimated at 7.5 percent in 2003, while the U.S. unemployment rate was 5.9 percent. Canadians also have high education rates with 63 percent of Canadians over the age of 15 being high school graduates. The country's predominantly rural population and strong work ethic along with a declining industrial base have made call center outsourcing an attractive solution for Canada, too.

Canada has been a leader in the call center industry for over a decade. Since the early 1990s, "the Canadian call center industry has grown at an annual rate of 20 percent," according to Steve Demmings, president of Site Selection Canada of Winnipeg, Manitoba. Site Selection Canada promotes and assists site selection for American and Canadian firms. Demmings estimated there are 14,000 call centers in Canada with six or more agents employing 500,000 people, contributing about $36 billion (Canadian) in annual salaries.

In 1994, two Canadian provinces—Manitoba and New Brunswick—made a concerted effort to develop a local call center industry, recognizing the area's high unemployment with little native industry, Demmings said. The other provinces soon followed. Then the call center industry "made a big move" to bring educational institutions on board. "Many colleges have set up call center training programs," Demmings reported. The result has been an established industry with an excellent skilled labor pool. "American companies come up here to go shopping and we need to have the tableware on the table," Demmings said.

What is important to outsourcing buyers is that many Canadian call center customer service representatives have made it their career. Consequently, there is a much lower turnover rate for call centers than in the United States. Demmings reported the CSR turnover rate in the Province of Ontario was 18.3 percent last year. Compare that to the United States, where call center staffing can be a problem. Christopher Fletcher, vice president and research director of CRM for the Aberdeen Group, stated, "It is tough to find people to staff a call center. Turnover ranges from 25 percent to 50 percent annually or above. The skill sets of the people you have available are often equivalent to McDonald's."[24]

Questions

1. What are the two different types of CRM and how can they be used to help an organization gain a competitive advantage?
2. Explain how a contact center (or call center) can help an organization achieve its CRM goals.
3. Describe three ways an organization can perform CRM functions over the Internet.
4. How will outsourcing contact centers (call centers) to Canada change as future CRM technologies replace current CRM technologies?

The Ritz-Carlton—Specializing in Customers

Bill Kapner, CEO of financial software provider Bigdough, checked into the Ritz-Carlton in Palm Beach, Florida. Before introducing himself, he was greeted—by name—at the front desk. Then a reception clerk asked, "Will you be having sushi tonight?" The interesting thing about these conversations is that Kapner never mentioned his fondness for Japanese cuisine. "I was wowed," he said.

Ritz-Carlton is the only service company to have won the prestigious Malcolm Baldrige National Quality Award twice—in 1992 and 1999. Companies worldwide strive to be "the Ritz-Carlton" of their industries. In 2000, the company launched the Ritz-Carlton Leadership Center, where anyone can study the brand's cult of customer service for $2,000. The center has addressed topics such as "talent benchmarking" and "empowerment using customer recognition to boost loyalty" for more than 800 companies, including Starbucks, Microsoft, and Coca-Cola. The following six steps can be followed and implemented by any company to become the Ritz-Carlton of its industry:

1. **Make customer service an elite club.** Ritz-Carlton has devised a rigorous interview process to identify the positive team players who, according to in-house statistics, become top performers. Executives believe that the company is effective not only in picking great talent, but also in conveying the message that working at Ritz-Carlton is a privilege.

2. **Once you have the right people, indoctrinate them.** Ritz-Carlton spends about $5,000 to train each new hire. It begins with a two-day introduction to company values (it is all about the service) along with a 21-day course focused on job responsibilities, such as a bellman's 28 steps to greeting a guest: "A warm and sincere greeting. Use the guest's name, if and when possible." Tracy Butler Hamilton, a retired bond trader who has stayed at a Ritz-Carlton in Atlanta several times, recalls that the hotel's bartenders remembered not only her name, but also the name and favorite drink of her brother, who would sometimes visit. "He wasn't even staying at the hotel," Hamilton said.

3. **Treat staffers the way they should treat customers.** The Ritz-Carlton motto—"We are ladies and gentlemen serving ladies and gentlemen"—might sound corny, but it is taken seriously. The company celebrates not just employee birthdays, but also employment anniversaries. Regardless of position, every staff member can spend as much as $2,000 without management approval to resolve a guest's problem. Employees say the exemption lets them make a personal impact on a guest's experience, resulting in higher job satisfaction. The median annual nonmanagement turnover rate at luxury hotels is 44 percent; at Ritz-Carlton, it is only 25 percent.

4. **Offer "memorable" service.** "What others call complaints," said John Timmerman, vice president for quality and productivity, "we call opportunities." A tired euphemism elsewhere, the idea is truly embraced at Ritz-Carlton. In one case, an administrative assistant at Ritz-Carlton Philadelphia overheard a guest lamenting that he had forgotten to pack formal shoes and would have to wear hiking boots to an important meeting; early the next morning, she delivered to the awestruck man a new pair in his size and favorite color. (In a more intimate example, a housekeeper recently traded shoes with a woman who needed a different pair.)

5. **Talk about values and stoke enthusiasm.** Every day at the chain's 57 hotels, all 25,000 Ritz-Carlton employees participate in a 15-minute "lineup" to talk about one of the basics. The ritual makes Ritz-Carlton one of the few large companies that set aside time for a daily discussion of core values.

6. **Eschew technology, except where it improves service.** Other hotels may be experimenting with automated check-in kiosks, but not Ritz-Carlton. "Not in a million years," said Vivian Deuschl, the company's vice president for public relations. "We will not replace human service with machines." But porters and doormen wear headsets, so when they spot your name on luggage tags, they can radio the information to the front desk. In addition, an in-house database called the Customer Loyalty Anticipation Satisfaction System stores guest preferences, such as whether an individual likes Seagram's ginger ale or Canada Dry. The software also alerts front-desk clerks when a guest who has stayed at other Ritz-Carltons has a habit of inquiring about the best sushi in town.[25]

Questions

1. What are the two different types of CRM and how has the Ritz-Carlton used them to become a world-class customer-service business?
2. Which of the Ritz-Carlton six steps of customer service is the most important for its business?
3. Rank the Ritz-Carlton's six steps of customer service in order of greatest to least importance in a CRM strategy for an online bookselling business such as Amazon.com.
4. Describe three ways the Ritz-Carlton can extend its customer reach by performing CRM functions over the Internet.
5. What benefits could the Ritz-Carlton gain from using analytical CRM?
6. Explain ERM and describe how the Ritz-Carlton could use it to increase efficiency in its business.

MAKING BUSINESS DECISIONS

1. Customer relationship management strategies

On average, it costs an organization six times more to sell to a new customer than to sell to an existing customer. As the co-owner of a medium-sized luggage distributor, you have recently been notified that sales for the past three months have decreased by an average of 17 percent. The reasons for the decline in sales are numerous, including a poor economy, people's aversion to travel because of the terrorist attacks, and some negative publicity your company received regarding a defective product line. In a group, explain how implementing a CRM system can help you understand and combat the decline in sales. Be sure to justify why a CRM system is important to your business and its future growth.

2. Comparing CRM vendors

As a team, search the Internet for at least one recent and authoritative article that compares or ranks customer relationship management systems. Select two packages from the list and compare their functions and features as described in the article(s) you found as well as on each company's Web site. Find references in the literature where companies that are using each package have reported their experiences, both good and bad. Draw on any other comparisons you can find. Prepare a presentation for delivery in class on the strengths and weaknesses of each package, which one you favor, and why.

3. Searching for employee loyalty

You are the CEO of Razz, a start-up Web-based search company, which is planning to compete directly with Google. The company had an exceptional first year and is currently receiving over 500,000 hits a day from customers all over the world. You have hired 250 people in the last four months, doubling the size of your organization. With so many new employees starting so quickly you are concerned about how your company's culture will evolve and whether your employees are receiving enough attention. You are already familiar with customer relationship management and how CRM systems can help an organization create strong customer relationships. However, you are unfamiliar with employee relationship management and you are wondering what ERM systems might be able to offer your employees and your company. Research the Web, create a report detailing features and functions of ERM systems, and determine what value will be added to your organization if you decide to implement an ERM solution.

4. **Employee relationship management**

   All new employees at the Shinaberry Inn & Spa wear bathing suits during orientation to experience the spa's exfoliating showers and hot mineral baths. At the Shinaberry San Francisco, new employees get the same penthouse champagne toast the hotel uses to woo meeting planners. And at many properties, employees arriving for their first day have their cars parked by the valet or get vouchers for a free night's stay. This innovative orientation program, which lets employees experience what guests experience began two years ago after focus groups pointed to empathy as a service differentiator. As a result, the company added empathy to the attributes for which it screens and a training program that involves listening to recorded guest phone calls. Even its discounted employee travel program gives employees yet another way to understand the guest experience. Design an ERM system that would help Shinaberry further its employee-centered culture. The ERM system must consider all employee needs.

5. **Increasing revenues with CRM**

   Cold Cream is one of the premier beauty supply stores in the metro New York area. People come from all over to sample the store's unique creams, lotions, makeup, and perfumes. The store is four stories high with each department located on a separate floor. The company would like to implement a CRM system to help it better understand its customers and their purchasing habits. Create a report summarizing CRM systems and detail how such a system can directly influence Cold Cream's revenues.

6. **Driving Up Profits with Successful Campaigns (or Driving Down?)**

   The Butterfly Café is a local hotspot located in downtown San Francisco and offers specialty coffee, teas, and organic fruits and vegetables. The café holds a number of events to attract customers such as live music venues, poetry readings, book clubs, charity events, and local artist's night. A listing of all participants attending each event is tracked in the café's database. The café uses the information for marketing campaigns and offers customers who attend multiple events additional discounts. A marketing database company, InTheKnow.com, has offered to pay The Butterfly Café a substantial amount of money for access to its customer database, which it will then sell to other local businesses. The owner of the Butterfly Café, Mary Conzachi, has come to you for advice. Mary is not sure if her customers would appreciate her selling their personal information and how it might affect her business. However, the amount of money InTheKnow.com is offering is enough to finance her much needed new patio for the back of the café. InTheKnow.com has promised Mary that the sale will be completely confidential. What should Mary do?

7. **Supporting Customers**

   Creative.com is an e-business that sells craft materials and supplies over the Internet. You have just started as the vice president of customer service, and you have a team of 45 customer service representatives. Currently, the only form of customer service is the 1-800 number and the company is receiving a tremendous number of calls regarding products, orders, and shipping information. The average wait time for a customer to speak to a customer service representative is 35 minutes. Orders are being cancelled and Creative.com is losing business due to its lack of customer service. Create a strategy to revamp the customer service center at Creative.com and get the company back on track.

Enterprise Resource Planning and Collaboration Systems

10
CHAPTER

SECTION 10.1
Enterprise Resource Planning

SECTION 10.2
Collaboration Systems

CHAPTER OUTLINE

- Enterprise Resource Planning
- Core and Extended ERP Components
- Core ERP Components
- Extended ERP Components
- ERP Vendor Overview
- ERP Benefits and Risks (Cost)
- The Connected Corporation— Integrating SCM, CRM, and ERP
- The Future of ERP

- Teams, Partnerships, and Alliances
- Collaboration Systems
- Knowledge Management
- Knowledge Management Systems
- Content Management Systems
- Workflow Management Systems
- Groupware Systems
- Collaboration Trends

Campus ERP

When Stefanie Fillers returned to college she needed to log in to the school's new online registration system to make certain that the courses she was taking would allow her to graduate. She also wanted to waive her participation in her college's health insurance plan. When the system crashed the day before classes began, Fillers, a senior, was annoyed. But at least she knew where her classes were—unlike most first-year students.

Several colleges around the country have experienced problems with nonfunctioning Web portals that prevented students from finding out where their classes were. At one college, financial aid was denied to 3,000 students by a buggy new ERP system, even though they had already received loan commitments. The college provided short-term loans for the cash-strapped students while the IT department and financial aid administrators scrambled to fix the complex system.

Disastrous ERP implementations have given more than a few colleges' black eyes. These recent campus meltdowns illustrate how the growing reliance on expensive ERP systems has created nightmare scenarios for some colleges. In every case, the new systems were designed to centralize business processes in what historically has been a hodgepodge of discrete legacy systems. College administrators are drawn to ERP systems offering integrated views of finance, HR, student records, financial aid, and more.

ERP implementations are difficult, even in very top-down corporate environments. Getting them to work in colleges, which are essentially a conglomeration of decentralized fiefdoms, has been nearly impossible. Staff members in the largely autonomous departments do not like the one-size-fits-all strategy of an ERP implementation. Plus, these nonprofit organizations generally lack the talent and financial resources to create and manage a robust enterprise system. Representatives from Oracle, which dominates the higher education market for ERP, say that much of the problem results from the inexperience of college IT departments and their tendency to rush implementations and inadequately test the new systems.

Standardizing at Stanford

Stanford University bought into the late 1990s enterprise software pitch and never slowed down its implementation engine. "In hindsight, we tried to do too much in too little time," said Randy Livingston, Stanford's vice president of business affairs and CFO.

Starting in 2001, Stanford implemented student administration systems, People-Soft HR, Oracle financials, and several other ancillary applications. Years later, users still complain that they have lower productivity with the new systems than with the previous ones, which were supported by a highly customized mainframe. Users also have had difficulty accessing critical information on a timely basis. Livingston said many transactions, such as initiating a purchase requisition or requesting a reimbursement, now take longer for users than with the prior legacy system.

Stanford has also not realized any of the projected savings the vendors promised. "We are finding that the new ERP applications cost considerably more to support than our legacy applications," Livingston said. He does not know how much it will cost to get the enterprise systems working at acceptable user levels.

Stanford's IT department is still trying to get campuswide buy-in for the enterprise applications, which have necessitated new ways of doing business, which leads to nonuse of the new systems and costly customizations to keep all users satisfied. For example, Stanford's law school operates on a semester schedule, while the other six schools operate on a trimester schedule. "This means that every aspect of the student administration system needs to be configured differently for the law school," Livingston said. Within the schools, some faculty members are paid a 12-month salary; other schools pay by 9 months, 10 months, or 11 months. "The standard HR payroll system is not designed to handle all these unusual pay schedules," Livingston said.

To resolve the issues, Livingston has reorganized the IT department, which he hopes will be better able to manage the enterprise projects going forward. He also created a separate administrative systems group that reports directly to him, with responsibility for development, integration, and support of the major ERP systems.

The hurdles Stanford and other colleges face with ERP systems are largely cultural ones. For instance, lean staffs and tight budgets at most university campuses usually lead to a lack of proper training and systems testing. At Stanford, plenty of training was offered, but many users did not take it, Livingston said. He has set up new training programs, including a group of trainers who sit side by side with users to help them learn how to do complex tasks; periodic user group meetings; Web site and e-mail lists that offer more help; and expert users embedded in the various departments who aid their colleagues.

Stanford's IT was still struggling with integrating the enterprise systems when the newly launched PeopleSoft Web portal (called Axess) crashed in 2004. Axess could not handle the load of all the returning students trying to log in to the untested Web-based system at the same time, Livingston said. Stanford was able to fix those problems relatively quickly, but Livingston and his staff continue to struggle with the enterprise projects. The university's departments remain "highly suspicious and resistant" of his efforts to standardize and centralize business processes, Livingston said.[1]

INTRODUCTION

*E*nterprise resource planning (ERP) integrates all departments and functions throughout an organization into a single IT system (or integrated set of IT systems) so that employees can make decisions by viewing enterprisewide information on all business operations.

SAP, the leading ERP vendor, boasts 20,000 installations and 10 million users worldwide. These figures represent only 30 percent of the overall ERP market. Figure 10.1 highlights a few reasons ERP solutions have proven to be such a powerful force.

ERP as a business concept resounds as a powerful internal information management nirvana: Everyone involved in sourcing, producing, and delivering the company's product works with the same information, which eliminates redundancies, reduces wasted time, and removes misinformation.

section 10.1 ENTERPRISE RESOURCE PLANNING

LEARNING OUTCOMES

10.1. Compare core enterprise resource planning components and extended enterprise resource planning components.

10.2. Describe the three primary components found in core enterprise resource planning systems.

10.3. Describe the four primary components found in extended enterprise resource planning systems.

10.4. Explain the business value of integrating supply chain management, customer relationship management, and enterprise resource planning systems.

ENTERPRISE RESOURCE PLANNING

Turner Industries grew from $300 million in sales to $800 million in sales in less than 10 years thanks to the implementation of an ERP system. Ranked number 369 on the Forbes 500 list of privately held companies, Turner Industries is a leading industrial services firm. Turner Industries develops and deploys advanced software applications designed to maximize the productivity of its 25,000 employees and construction equipment valued at more than $100 million.

The company considers the biggest challenges in the industrial services industry to be completing projects on time, within budget, while fulfilling customers' expectations. To meet these challenges the company invested in an ERP system and named the project Interplan. Interplan won Constructech's Vision award for software innovation in the heavy construction industry. Interplan runs all of Turner's construction, turnaround, shutdown, and maintenance projects and is so adept at estimating and planning jobs that Turner Industries typically achieves higher profit margins on projects that use Interplan. As the ERP solution makes the company more profitable, the company can pass on the cost savings to its customers, giving the company an incredible competitive advantage.[2]

FIGURE 10.1

Reasons ERP Systems Are Powerful Organizational Tools

Reasons ERP Systems Are Powerful Organizational Tools
ERP is a logical solution to the mess of incompatible applications that had sprung up in most businesses.
ERP addresses the need for global information sharing and reporting.
ERP is used to avoid the pain and expense of fixing legacy systems.

A common problem facing organizations is maintaining consistency across its business operations. If a single department, such as sales, decides to implement a new system without considering the other departments, it can cause inconsistencies throughout the company. A common problem occurs when one system saves (or fails to save) information that is not in other company systems. For example, a new sales system does not have a field to save e-mail addresses and the rest of the company's systems save e-mail addresses. Not all applications are built to talk to each other and if sales suddenly implements a new system that marketing and production cannot use or is inconsistent in the way it handles information, the company becomes siloed in its operations.

Enterprise resource planning systems provide organizations with consistency. An ERP system provides a method for the effective planning and controlling of all the resources required to take, make, ship, and account for customer orders in a manufacturing, distribution, or service organization. The key word in enterprise resource planning is *enterprise.*

Los Angeles is a city of 3.5 million, with 44,000 city employees, and a budget of $4 billion. Yet a few years ago each of the departments conducted its own purchasing. That meant 2,000 people in 600 city buildings and 60 warehouses ordering material. Some 120,000 purchase orders (POs) and 50,000 checks per year went to more than 7,000 vendors. Inefficiency was rampant.

"There was a lack of financial responsibility in the old system, and people could run up unauthorized expenditures," said Bob Jensen, the city's ERP project manager. Each department maintained its own inventories on different systems. Expense-item mismatches piled up. One department purchased one way, others preferred a different approach. Their mainframe-based systems were isolated. The city chose an ERP system as part of a $22 million project to integrate purchasing and financial reporting across the entire city. The project resulted in cutting the check-processing staff in half, processing POs faster than ever, reducing the number of workers in warehousing by 40 positions, decreasing inventories from $50 million to $15 million, and providing a single point of contact for each vendor. In addition, $5 million a year has been saved in contract consolidation.[3]

CORE AND EXTENDED ERP COMPONENTS

Figure 10.2 provides an example of an ERP system with its core and extended components. *Core ERP components* are the traditional components included in most ERP systems and they primarily focus on internal operations. *Extended ERP components* are the extra components that meet the organizational needs not covered by the core components and primarily focus on external operations.

CORE ERP COMPONENTS

The three most common core ERP components focusing on internal operations are:

1. Accounting and finance.
2. Production and materials management.
3. Human resources.

Accounting and Finance ERP Components

Deeley Harley-Davidson Canada, the exclusive Canadian distributor of Harley-Davidson motorcycles, has improved inventory, turnaround time, margins, and customer satisfaction—all with the implementation of a financial ERP system. The system has opened up the power of information to the company and is helping it make strategic decisions when it still has the time to change things. The ERP system provides the company with ways to manage inventory, turnaround time, and utilize warehouse space more effectively.[4]

FIGURE 10.2

Core ERP Components and Extended ERP Components

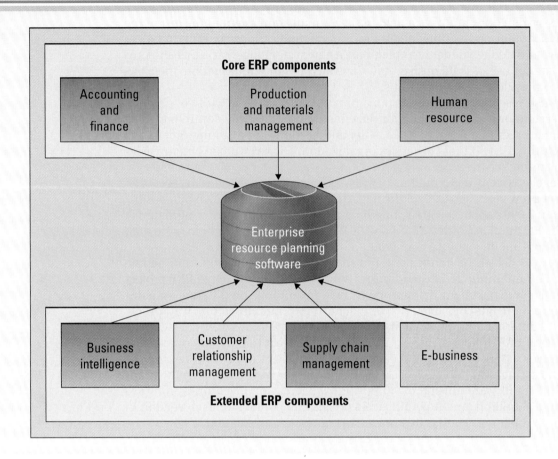

Accounting and finance ERP components manage accounting data and financial processes within the enterprise with functions such as general ledger, accounts payable, accounts receivable, budgeting, and asset management. One of the most useful features included in an ERP accounting/finance component is its credit-management feature. Most organizations manage their relationships with customers by setting credit limits, or a limit on how much a customer can owe at any one time. The company then monitors the credit limit whenever the customer places a new order or sends in a payment. ERP financial systems help to correlate customer orders with customer account balances determining credit availability. Another great feature is the ability to perform product profitability analysis. ERP financial components are the backbone behind product profitability analysis and allow companies to perform all types of advanced profitability modeling techniques.

Production and Materials Management ERP Components

One of the main functions of an ERP system is streamlining the production planning process. *Production and materials management ERP components* handle the various aspects of production planning and execution such as demand forecasting, production scheduling, job cost accounting, and quality control. Companies typically produce multiple products, each of which has many different parts. Production lines, consisting of machines and employees, build the different types of products. The company must then define sales forecasting for each product to determine production schedules and materials purchasing. Figure 10.3 displays the typical ERP production planning process. The process begins with forecasting sales in order to

FIGURE 10.3

The Production Planning Process

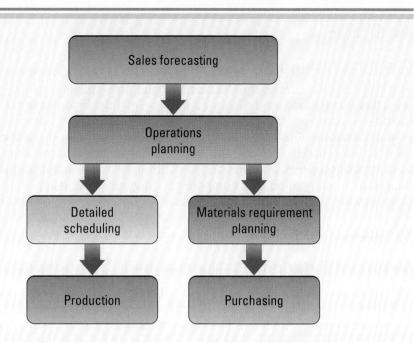

plan operations. A detailed production schedule is developed if the product is produced, and a materials requirement plan is completed if the product is purchased.

Grupo Farmanova Intermed, located in Costa Rica, is a pharmaceutical marketing and distribution company that markets nearly 2,500 products to about 500 customers in Central and South America. The company identified a need for software that could unify product logistics management in a single country. It decided to deploy PeopleSoft financial and distribution ERP components allowing the company to improve customer data management, increase confidence among internal and external users, and coordinate the logistics of inventory. With the new software the company enhanced its capabilities for handling, distributing, and marketing its pharmaceuticals.[5]

Human Resources ERP Components

Human resources ERP components track employee information including payroll, benefits, compensation, and performance assessment, and assure compliance with the legal requirements of multiple jurisdictions and tax authorities. Human resources components even offer features that allow the organization to perform detailed analysis on its employees to determine such things as the identification of individuals who are likely to leave the company unless additional compensation or benefits are provided. These components can also identify which employees are using which resources, such as online training and long-distance telephone services. They can also help determine whether the most talented people are working for those business units with the highest priority—or where they would have the greatest impact on profit.

EXTENDED ERP COMPONENTS

Extended ERP components are the extra components that meet the organizational needs not covered by the core components and primarily focus on external operations. Many of the numerous extended ERP components are Internet-enabled and require interaction with customers, suppliers, and business partners outside the organization. The four most common extended ERP components are:

1. Business intelligence.
2. Customer relationship management.

3. Supply chain management.

4. E-business.

Business Intelligence Components

ERP systems offer powerful tools that measure and control organizational operations. Many organizations have found that these valuable tools can be enhanced to provide even greater value through the addition of powerful business intelligence systems. *Business intelligence* describes information that people use to support their decision-making efforts. The business intelligence components of ERP systems typically collect information used throughout the organization (including data used in many other ERP components), organize it, and apply analytical tools to assist managers with decisions. Data warehouses are one of the most popular extensions to ERP systems, with over two-thirds of U.S. manufacturers adopting or planning such systems.[6]

Customer Relationship Management Components

ERP vendors are expanding their functionality to provide services formerly supplied by customer relationship management (CRM) vendors such as PeopleSoft and Siebel. *Customer relationship management (CRM)* involves managing all aspects of a customer's relationship with an organization to increase customer loyalty and retention and an organization's profitability. CRM components provide an integrated view of customer data and interactions allowing organizations to work more effectively with customers and be more responsive to their needs. CRM components typically include contact centers, sales force automation, and marketing functions. These improve the customer experience while identifying a company's most (and least) valuable customers for better allocation of resources.

Supply Chain Management Components

ERP vendors are expanding their functionality to provide services formerly supplied by supply chain management vendors such as i2 Technologies and Manugistics. *Supply chain management (SCM)* involves the management of information flows between and among stages in a supply chain to maximize total supply chain effectiveness and profitability. SCM components help an organization plan, schedule, control, and optimize the supply chain from its acquisition of raw materials to the receipt of finished goods by customers.

E-Business Components

The original focus of ERP systems was the internal organization. In other words, ERP systems are not fundamentally ready for the external world of e-business. The newest and most exciting extended ERP components are the e-business components. *E-business* means conducting business on the Internet, not only buying and selling, but also serving customers and collaborating with business partners. Two of the primary features of e-business components are e-logistics and e-procurement. *E-logistics* manages the transportation and storage of goods. *E-procurement* is the business-to-business (B2B) purchase and sale of supplies and services over the Internet.

E-business and ERP complement each other by allowing companies to establish a Web presence and fulfill orders expeditiously. A common mistake made by many businesses is deploying a Web presence before the integration of back-office systems or an ERP system. For example, one large toy manufacturer announced less than a week before Christmas that it would be unable to fulfill any of its Web orders. The company had all the toys in the warehouse, but it could not organize the basic order processing function to get the toys delivered to the consumers on time.

Customers and suppliers are now demanding access to ERP information including order status, inventory levels, and invoice reconciliation. Plus, the customers and partners want all this information in a simplified format available through a

Web site. This is a difficult task to accomplish because most ERP systems are full of technical jargon, which is why employee training is one of the hidden costs associated with ERP implementations. Removing the jargon to accommodate untrained customers and partners is one of the more difficult tasks when Web-enabling an ERP system. To accommodate the growing needs of the e-business world, ERP vendors need to build two new channels of access into the ERP system information—one channel for customers (B2C) and one channel for businesses, suppliers, and partners (B2B).[7]

ERP VENDOR OVERVIEW

Companies that are successful in the digital economy understand that current business designs and models are insufficient to meet the challenges of doing business in the e-business era. A close look at such leading companies as Amazon.com, Dell, and Cisco will provide insight into a new kind of business model that focuses on having a finely tuned integration of business, technology, and process. These companies frequently use technology to streamline supply chain operations, improve customer loyalty, gain visibility into enterprisewide information, and ultimately drive profit growth. To thrive in the e-business world, organizations must structurally transform their internal architectures. They must integrate their disparate systems into a potent e-business infrastructure.

Applications such as SCM, CRM, and ERP are the backbone of e-business. Integration of these applications is the key to success for many companies. Integration allows the unlocking of information to make it available to any user, anywhere, anytime. Figure 10.4 displays the top three ERP vendors until December 2004 when Oracle bought PeopleSoft for $10 billion, after a takeover battle that lasted for 18 months. Figure 10.5 displays the new vendor overview.

The vendors highlighted in Figure 10.5 offer CRM and SCM modules. However, these modules are not as functional or flexible as the modules offered by industry leaders of SCM and CRM such as Siebel and i2 technologies, as depicted in Figure 10.6 and Figure 10.7. As a result, organizations face the challenge of integrating their new e-business systems with their preexisting applications and other vendor products.

Component	Vendor		
	PeopleSoft	Oracle	SAP
Customer relationship management	X		X
Supply chain management	X	X	X
Financial management	X	X	X
Human resource management	X	X	X
Service automation	X		
Supplier relationship management	X		X
Enterprise performance management	X		
Business intelligence		X	
Learning management		X	
Order management		X	
Manufacturing		X	
Marketing		X	
Sales		X	

FIGURE 10.4

ERP Vendor Overview (before December 31, 2004)

FIGURE 10.5

ERP Vendor Overview
(after December 31, 2004)

	Vendor	
Component	**Oracle**	**SAP**
Customer relationship management	X	X
Supply chain management	X	X
Financial management	X	X
Human resource management	X	X
Service automation	X	
Supplier relationship management	X	X
Enterprise performance management	X	
Business intelligence	X	
Learning management	X	
Order management	X	
Manufacturing	X	
Marketing	X	
Sales	X	

FIGURE 10.6

SCM Market Overview

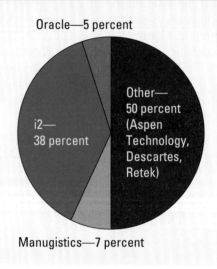

Oracle—5 percent

Other—
50 percent
(Aspen
Technology,
Descartes,
Retek)

i2—
38 percent

Manugistics—7 percent

FIGURE 10.7

CRM Market Overview

Oracle—8 percent

Siebel—25 percent

Other—67 percent
(Clarify, E.piphany,
Onyx, Kana, Pivitol)

ERP SOFTWARE

There are many different ERP vendors on the market today, each offering different ERP solutions. The core ERP functions for each vendor are the same and focus on financial, accounting, sales, marketing, human resource, operations, and logistics. ERP vendors differentiate themselves by offering unique functionality such as CRM and SCM systems.

Many customers find that their chosen ERP solution does not meet their expectations. Despite many improvements in the software, the industry itself is well aware that failed ERP implementations are still far too common. According to Gartner Research, the average failure rate for an ERP project is 66 percent. It is no wonder that some manufacturers view ERP as a necessary, strategic evil. The key word here though is *necessary*.

Many companies strive to make good financial decisions by making smart investments. The best way to ensure a good investment in ERP is to understand why failure occurs and how to avoid it. The first challenge is that ERP is a product that comes in many flavors. Its main purpose is to provide support and automation to a business process. The business world has many different business models, and there are just as many ERP products available that serve them.

Finding the Right ERP Solution

A good ERP system will be highly reflective of the business process in place at the company. This means that the software must perform many different tasks and that makes it complex. Most companies do not carry a high degree of ERP software expertise on their staff and do not understand ERP to the degree they should, and this makes it easy to choose the wrong package. The key to making an effective purchase is to have solid business processes. Successful ERP projects share three basic attributes:

1. Overall fit.
2. Proper business analysis.
3. Solid implementation plans.[8]

Overall Fit This refers to the degree of gaps that exist between the system and the business process. A well-fitting ERP has no major process gaps and very few minor ones. Think of a new ERP system as a suit. Typically, a customer buys a suit three ways:

1. Off the rack.
2. Off the rack and tailor it to fit.
3. Custom made.

The way the solution fits the business process will normally determine the satisfaction level of the client. Buying ERP off the rack is the equivalent of buying a canned software package. It fits some well, but some not at all. That is why a customer can tailor a suit so that it fits better. Modifications can be made to the software so that its processes line up better with the company processes. This is a good strategy, provided the chosen package supports this. The downside is that it can get very expensive. Finally, the custom system can provide a great fit, but the company must thoroughly understand what it is doing and be able to support the heavy financial burden associated with a custom-build.

Proper Business Analysis The best way to determine which fit strategy is right is to conduct a thorough business analysis. Successful companies normally spend up to 10 percent of the project budget on a business analysis. A proper analysis must result in a documented list of the business processes at work within the company. This will provide a basic tool that can measure vendor capability.

Solid Implementation Plans Like the installation of any successful process or piece of machinery, a plan is needed to monitor the quality objectives and timelines. It will also employ processes like workflow analysis and job combination to harvest savings.

A thorough implementation will transfer knowledge to the system users. When the project is complete the users of the new system must be capable of using the tools it provides. The users must also know what to do in cases when the process fluctuates. The majority of failed systems are the result of poor-quality implementation. It is important to remember that ERP is simply a tool. Tools that people do not know how to use can be as useless as having no tools at all.

ERP BENEFITS AND RISKS (COST)

There is no guarantee of success for an ERP system. ERPs focus on how a corporation operates internally, and optimizing these operations takes significant time and energy. According to Meta Group, it takes the average company 8 to 18 months to see any benefits from an ERP system. The good news is that the average savings from new ERP systems are $1.6 million per year. Figure 10.8 displays a list of the five most common benefits an organization can expect to achieve from a successful ERP implementation.[9]

Along with understanding the benefits an organization can gain from an ERP system, it is just as important to understand the primary risk associated with an ERP implementation—cost. ERP systems do not come cheap. Meta Group studied total cost of ownership (TCO) for an ERP system. The study included hardware, software, professional services, and internal staff costs. Sixty-three companies were surveyed ranging in size from small to large over a variety of industries. The average TCO was $15 million (highest $300 million and lowest $400,000). The price tag for an ERP system can easily start in the multiple millions of dollars and implementation can take an average of 23 months. Figure 10.9 displays a few of the costs associated with an ERP system.

THE CONNECTED CORPORATION—INTEGRATING SCM, CRM, AND ERP

Most organizations today have no choice but to piece their applications together since no one vendor can respond to every organizational need; hence, customers purchase applications from multiple vendors. As a result, large companies usually have multiple applications that are not designed to work together, and find themselves having to integrate business solutions. For example, a single organization might choose its CRM components from Siebel, SCM components from i2,

FIGURE 10.8

Common Benefits Received from ERP Systems

Common ERP Benefits
1. **Integrate financial information:** To understand an organization's overall performance, managers must have a single financial view.
2. **Integrate customer order information:** With all customer order information in a single system it is easier to coordinate manufacturing, inventory, and shipping to send a common message to customers regarding order status.
3. **Standardize and speed up manufacturing processes:** ERP systems provide standard methods for manufacturing companies to use when automating steps in the manufacturing process. Standardizing manufacturing processes across an organization saves time, increases production, and reduces head count.
4. **Reduce inventory:** With improved visibility in the order fulfillment process, an organization can reduce inventories and streamline deliveries to its customers.
5. **Standardize human resource information:** ERPs provide a unified method for tracking employees' time, as well as communicating HR benefits and services.

FIGURE 10.9

Associated ERP Risk (Cost)

Associated ERP Risk (Cost)
Software cost: Purchasing the software.
Consulting fees: Hiring external experts to help implement the system correctly.
Process rework: Redefining processes in order to ensure the company is using the most efficient and effective processes.
Customization: If the software package does not meet all of the company's needs, it may be required to customize the software.
Integration and testing: Ensuring all software products, including disparate systems not part of the ERP system, are working together or are integrated. Testing the ERP system includes testing all integrations.
Training: Training all new users.
Data warehouse integration and data conversion: Moving data from an old system into the new ERP system.

FIGURE 10.10

Primary Users and Business Benefits of Strategic Initiatives

financial components and human resources components from Oracle. Figure 10.10 displays the general audience and purpose for each of the applications that have to be integrated.

Effectively managing the transformation to an integrated enterprise will be critical to the success of the 21st century organization. The key to an integrated enterprise is the integration of the disparate IT applications. An integrated enterprise infuses support areas, such as finance and human resources, with a strong customer orientation. Integrations are achieved using *middleware*—several different types of software that sit in the middle of and provide connectivity between two or more software applications. Middleware translates information between disparate systems. *Enterprise application integration (EAI) middleware* represents a new approach to middleware by packaging together commonly used functionality, such as providing prebuilt links to popular enterprise applications, which reduces the time

FIGURE 10.11

Integration between SCM,
CRM, and ERP Applications

necessary to develop solutions that integrate applications from multiple vendors. A few leading vendors of EAI middleware include Active Software, Vitria Technology, and Extricity.

Figure 10.11 displays the data points where these applications integrate and illustrates the underlying premise of e-business architecture infrastructure design: Companies run on interdependent applications. If one application of the company does not function well, the entire customer value delivery system is affected. The world-class enterprises of tomorrow must be built on the foundation of world-class applications implemented today.

The heart of an ERP system is a central database that collects information from and feeds information into all the ERP system's individual application components (called modules), supporting diverse business functions such as accounting, manufacturing, marketing, and human resources. When a user enters or updates information in one module, it is immediately and automatically updated throughout the entire system, as illustrated in Figure 10.12.

FIGURE 10.12

ERP Integration Flow

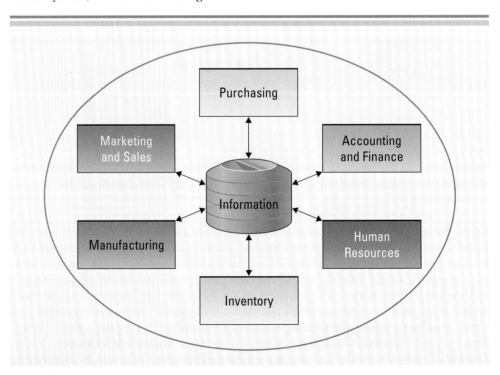

FIGURE 10.13

ERP Process Flow

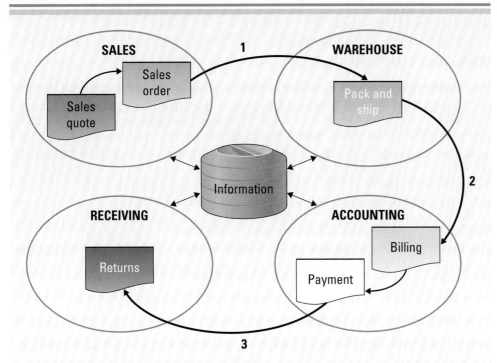

ERP automates business processes such as order fulfillment—taking an order from a customer, shipping the purchase, and then billing for it. With an ERP system, when a customer service representative takes an order from a customer, he or she has all the information necessary to complete the order (the customer's credit rating and order history, the company's inventory levels, and the delivery schedule). Everyone else in the company sees the same information and has access to the database that holds the customer's new order. When one department finishes with the order, it is automatically routed via the ERP system to the next department. To find out where the order is at any point, a user need only log in to the ERP system and track it down, as illustrated in Figure 10.13. The order process moves like a bolt of lightning through the organization, and customers get their orders faster and with fewer errors than ever before. ERP can apply that same magic to the other major business processes, such as employee benefits or financial reporting.

To qualify as a true ERP solution, the system not only must integrate various organization processes, but also must be:

- **Flexible**—An ERP system should be flexible in order to respond to the changing needs of an enterprise.
- **Modular and open**—An ERP system has to have an open system architecture, meaning that any module can be interfaced with or detached whenever required without affecting the other modules. The system should support multiple hardware platforms for organizations that have a heterogeneous collection of systems. It must also support third-party add-on components.
- **Comprehensive**—An ERP system should be able to support a variety of organizational functions and must be suitable for a wide range of business organizations.
- **Beyond the company**—An ERP system must not be confined to organizational boundaries but rather support online connectivity to business partners or customers.

Companies are expecting e-business to increase profitability, create competitive differentiation, and support innovative business practices. To achieve these goals, companies must evolve through distinct stages, from integrated processes to truly synchronized inter-enterprise communities. Getting e-business applications based on different technologies and with differing business models and data models to work together is a key issue for 21st century organizations.

THE FUTURE OF ERP

ERP places new demands not only on support and delivery information technology, but also on the way business processes have to be designed, implemented, monitored, and maintained. For example, several persons in different locations and with different hardware and software resources may simultaneously initiate a purchase process for the same product but with different selection criteria. Reliability, efficiency, and scalability are among the features that have to be embedded in e-business processes in ERP systems. Despite the rapid growth in the number of ERP installations, conducting ERP operations is still challenging.

Understanding the many different types of core and extended ERP components can help an organization determine which components will add the most value. The two biggest vendors in the ERP market are Oracle (which purchased PeopleSoft in 2004) and SAP. Figure 10.14 is an overview of a few of the components offered by each ERP vendor.

FIGURE 10.14

ERP Vendor Components

PeopleSoft (Purchased by Oracle)	
Component	**Description**
Application Integration	Integrate PeopleSoft and non-PeopleSoft applications at all levels with Portal Solutions, AppConnect, and Data Warehousing and Analytic Solutions.
Customer Relationship Management	Get immediate, seamless integration among customer, financial, supply chain, and employee management systems.
Enterprise Performance Management	Enable customers, suppliers, and employees to connect to set goals, develop plans, and measure progress with our integrated, scalable applications.
Financial Management	Get the power to compete in the business world with a comprehensive suite of pure Internet financial applications.
Human Capital Management (including Human Resources Management Solutions)	Manage and mobilize a unified, global workforce, and align workforce contribution with business objectives.
Service Automation	Optimize project investments, reduce project delivery costs, and maximize resources to increase utilization and value to your organization.
Supplier Relationship Management	Manage all aspects of supplier relationships including indirect and direct goods, as well as services procurement.
Supply Chain Management	Take advantage of solutions that promote business-to-business interaction throughout the supply chain, from customer to supplier.
Oracle	
Component	**Description**
Oracle Financials	Financial applications manage the flow of cash and assets into, out of, and within your enterprise: tracking thousands of transactions, setting fiscal goals for various departments, and allowing you to project future financial health as you record today's profits.
Oracle Human Resources Management	Oracle Human Resources Management System (HRMS) empowers businesses with the tools to find, extract, and analyze data related to human capital. This intelligence readies a company to rapidly deploy the best resources for maximum employee productivity, satisfaction, and retention.

FIGURE 10.14

(Continued)

Oracle Intelligence	Oracle Daily Business Intelligence accesses and shares unified information and analysis across the enterprise with a single definition of customers, suppliers, employees, and products.
Oracle Learning Management	Oracle Learning Management (Oracle iLearning, Oracle Training Management, and Oracle Human Resources Management System) provides a complete infrastructure that lets organizations manage, deliver, and track training, in both online and classroom environments.
Oracle Supply Chain Management	Oracle Supply Chain Management lets organizations gain global visibility, automate internal processes, and readily collaborate with suppliers, customers, and partners.
Oracle Manufacturing	Oracle Manufacturing optimizes production capacity beginning with raw materials through final products.
Oracle Order Management	Oracle's support of the complete fulfillment process from order to cash.
Oracle Marketing	Oracle Marketing drives profit by intelligently marketing to the most profitable customers. By leveraging a single repository of customer information, marketing professionals can better target and personalize their campaigns, and refine them in real time with powerful analytical tools.
Oracle Projects	To consistently deliver on time and on budget, an organization must fine-tune execution, align global organization with projects, and assign the right resources to the most important initiatives at the right time.
Oracle Sales	Oracle Sales allows an organization to learn more about its entire business to identify and target profitable opportunities.

SAP

Component	Description
mySAP™ Customer Relationship Management	The fully integrated CRM solution that facilitates world-class service across all customer touchpoints.
mySAP™ Financials	The leading solution for operational, analytical, and collaborative financial management.
mySAP™ Human Resources (mySAP HR)	The HR resource that helps more than 7,800 organizations worldwide maximize their return on capital.
mySAP™ Marketplace	An online marketplace solution that allows your company to buy, sell, and conduct business around the clock and around the world.
mySAP™ Product Lifecycle Management	The collaborative solution that helps designers, engineers, and suppliers achieve new levels of innovation.
mySAP™ Supplier Relationship Management	Covers the full supply cycle—from strategic sourcing for lower costs to faster process cycles.
mySAP™ Supply Chain Management	Gives an organization the power to dramatically improve its planning, responsiveness, and execution. suppliers, customers, and partners.

In the future, the line between ERP, SCM, and CRM will continue to blur as ERP vendors broaden the functionality of their product suites and redefine the packaging of their products. ERP vendors with comprehensive but modular components will dominate the next high-growth phase of the enterprise applications market. Since core functionality is virtually the same for all vendors, a vendor's success will primarily depend upon how quickly it incorporates other kinds of functionality such as the Internet, interface, and wireless technology.

Internet

The adoption of the Internet is one of the single most important forces reshaping the architecture and functionality of ERP systems and is responsible for the most important new developments in ERP. The Internet serves as a basis for extending ERP's traditional vision of integrating data and processes across an organization's functional departments to include sharing data and processes among multiple enterprises.

Interface

Most ERP suites offer a customizable browser that allows each employee to configure his or her own view of the system. A manager can also customize each employee's views of the system. This feature allows managers to control access to highly sensitive information such as payroll and performance appraisals. The same customizable browser will be used in the future to allow customers and partners to see only select ERP information via the Internet.

Wireless Technology

Wireless technologies provide a means for users with handheld devices, such as PDAs and Web-enabled telephones, to connect to and interact with ERP systems. Most large ERP vendors will acquire smaller companies that specialize in wireless access. If they fail to do so, they will need to develop their own expertise in this area to build wireless access packages.

Wireless technologies will enable users to carry out the same transactions from their mobile devices as they used to do from any fixed device. Being able to buy and sell goods and services over mobile devices is an important step toward achieving the anywhere-anytime paradigm. In the future, location and time will no longer constrain organizations from completing their operations.

OPENING CASE QUESTIONS

Campus ERP

1. How could core ERP components help improve business operations at your college?

2. How could extended ERP components help improve business operations at your college?

3. How can integrating SCM, CRM, and ERP help improve business operations at your college?

4. Review the different components in Figure 10.14. Which component would you recommend your college implement if it decided to purchase an ERP component?

---

section 10.2 COLLABORATION SYSTEMS

LEARNING OUTCOMES

10.5. Identify the different ways in which companies collaborate using technology.

10.6. Compare the different categories of collaboration technologies.

10.7. Define the fundamental concepts of a knowledge management system.

10.8. Provide an example of a content management system along with its business purpose.

10.9. Evaluate the advantages of using a workflow management system.

10.10. Explain how groupware can benefit a business.

TEAMS, PARTNERSHIPS, AND ALLIANCES

To be successful—and avoid being eliminated by the competition—an organization must constantly undertake new initiatives, address both minor and major problems, and capitalize on significant opportunities. To support these activities, an organization often will create and utilize teams, partnerships, and alliances because the expertise needed is beyond the scope of a single individual or organization. These teams, partnerships, and alliances can be formed internally among a company's employees or externally with other organizations (see Figure 10.15).

Businesses of all sizes and in all markets have witnessed the benefits of leveraging their IT assets to create competitive advantage. Whereas information technology efforts in the past were aimed at increasing operational efficiency, the advent and proliferation of network-based computing (the Internet being the most visible, but not only, example) has enabled organizations to build systems with which all sorts of communities can interact. The ultimate result will allow organizations to do business with customers, business partners, suppliers, governments and regulatory agencies, and any other community relevant to their particular operation or activity.

In the same way that organizations use internal teams, they are increasingly forming alliances and partnerships with other organizations. The *core competency* of an organization is its key strength, a business function that it does better than any of its competitors. Apple Computer is highly regarded for its strength in product design, while Accenture's core competency is the design and installation of information systems. A *core competency strategy* is one in which an organization chooses to focus specifically on what it does best (its core competency) and forms partnerships and alliances with other specialist organizations to handle nonstrategic business processes. Strategic alliances enable businesses to gain competitive advantages through access to a partner's resources, including markets, technologies, and people. Teaming up with another business adds complementary resources and capabilities, enabling participants to grow and expand more quickly and efficiently, especially fast-growing companies that rely heavily on outsourcing many areas of their business to extend their technical and operational resources. In the outsourcing process, they save time and boost productivity by not having to develop their own systems from scratch. They are then free to concentrate on innovation and their core business.

Information technology makes such business partnerships and alliances easier to establish and manage. An *information partnership* occurs when two or more organizations cooperate by integrating their IT systems, thereby providing customers with the best of what each can offer. The advent of the Internet has greatly increased the opportunity for IT-enabled business partnerships and alliances. Amazon developed a profitable business segment by providing e-business outsourcing services to other retailers that use Amazon's Web site software. Some well-known retailers partnering with Amazon include Marshall Fields, Office Depot, and Target.[10]

COLLABORATION SYSTEMS

Heineken USA has shortened its inventory cycle time for beer production and distribution from three months to four weeks. By using its collaborative system to forecast demand and expedite shipping, the company has dramatically cut inventory levels and shipping costs while increasing sales.

Over the past few years most business processes have changed on various dimensions (e.g., flexibility, interconnectivity, coordination style, autonomy) because of market conditions and organizational models. Frequently, information is located within physically separated systems as more and more organizations spread their reach globally. This creates a need for a software infrastructure that enables collaboration systems.

A *collaboration system* is an IT-based set of tools that supports the work of teams by facilitating the sharing and flow of information. Collaboration solves specific business tasks such as telecommuting, online meetings, deploying applications, and remote project and sales management (see Figure 10.16).

Collaboration systems allow people, teams, and organizations to leverage and build upon the ideas and talents of staff, suppliers, customers, and business partners. It involves a unique set of business challenges that:

- Include complex interactions between people who may be in different locations and desire to work across function and discipline areas.
- Require flexibility in work process and the ability to involve others quickly and easily.
- Call for creating and sharing information rapidly and effortlessly within a team.

Most organizations collaborate with other companies in some capacity. Consider the supplier-customer relationship, which can be thought of in terms of a continuous life cycle of engagement, transaction, fulfillment, and service activities. Rarely do companies excel in all four life cycle areas, either from a business process or from a technology-enabled aspect. Successful organizations identify and invest in their core competencies, and outsource or collaborate for those competencies that are not core to them. Collaboration systems fall into one of two categories:

1. **Unstructured collaboration** (sometimes referred to as *information collaboration*) includes document exchange, shared whiteboards, discussion forums, and

FIGURE 10.16

Collaborative Business Areas

e-mail. These functions can improve personal productivity, reducing the time spent searching for information or chasing answers.

2. **Structured collaboration** (or **process collaboration**) involves shared participation in business processes, such as workflow, in which knowledge is hard-coded as rules. This is beneficial in terms of improving automation and the routing of information.

Regardless of location or format—be it unstructured or structured—relevant accurate information must be readily and consistently available to those who need it anytime, anywhere, and on any device. The integration of IT systems enables an organization to provide employees, partners, customers, and suppliers with the ability to access, find, analyze, manage, and collaborate on content. The collaboration can be done across a wide variety of formats, languages, and platforms. Figure 10.17 illustrates many of the typical collaborative functions within most organizations.

Lockheed Martin Aeronautics Company's ability to share complex project information across an extended supply chain in real time was key in its successful bid of a $19 billion Department of Defense (DoD) contract to build 21 supersonic stealth fighters. New government procurement rules require defense contractors to communicate effectively to ensure that deadlines are met, costs are controlled, and projects are managed throughout the life cycle of the contract.[11]

In anticipation of the contract, the Fort Worth, Texas, unit of Lockheed Martin Corporation developed a real-time collaboration system that can tie together its partners, suppliers, and DoD customers via the Internet. The platform lets participants collectively work on product design and engineering tasks as well as supply chain and life cycle management issues. Lockheed will host all transactions and own the project information. The platform will let DoD and Lockheed project managers track the daily progress of the project in real time. This is the first major DoD project with such a requirement. The contract, awarded to the Lockheed unit and partners Northrop Grumman Corp. and BAE Systems, is the first installment in what could

Function	Collaborator(s)	Business Function(s)
Planning and forecasting	Supplier, Customer	Real-time information sharing (forecast information and sales information)
Product design	Supplier, Customer	Document exchange, computer-aided design (CAD)
Strategic sourcing	Supplier	Negotiation, supplier performance management
Component compatibility testing	Supplier	Component compatibility
Pricing	Supplier, Customer	Pricing in supply chain
Marketing	Supplier, Customer	Joint/coop marketing campaigns, branding
Sales	Customer	Shared leads, presentations, configuration and quotes
Make-to-order	Customer	Requirements, capabilities, contract terms
Order processing	Supplier, Customer	Order solution
Fulfillment: Logistics and service	Supplier, Customer	Coordination of distribution
International trade logistics	Customer	Document exchange, import/export documents
Payment	Customer	Order receipt, invoicing
Customer service/support	Supplier, Customer	Shared/split customer support

FIGURE 10.17

Typical Collaborative Business Functions

amount to a $200 billion program for 3,000 jet fighters over 40 years. The strengths of the collaboration process lie with the integration of many systems, namely:

- Knowledge management systems
- Content management systems
- Workflow management systems
- Groupware systems

KNOWLEDGE MANAGEMENT

Knowledge management (KM) involves capturing, classifying, evaluating, retrieving, and sharing information assets in a way that provides context for effective decisions and actions. It is best to think of KM in the broadest context. Succinctly put, KM is the process through which organizations generate value from their intellectual and knowledge-based assets. Most often, generating value from such assets involves codifying what employees, partners, and customers know, and sharing that information among employees, departments, and even with other companies to devise best practices. It is important to note that the definition says nothing about technology; while KM is often facilitated by IT, technology by itself is not KM.

Think of a golf caddie as a simplified example of a knowledge worker. Good caddies do more than carry clubs and track down wayward balls. When asked, a good caddie will give advice to golfers, such as, "The wind makes the ninth hole play 15 yards longer." Accurate advice may lead to a bigger tip at the end of the day. The golfer, having derived a benefit from the caddie's advice, may be more likely to play that course again. If a good caddie is willing to share what he knows with other caddies, then they all may eventually earn bigger tips. How would KM work to make this happen? The caddie master may decide to reward caddies for sharing their knowledge by offering them credits for pro shop merchandise. Once the best advice is collected, the course manager would publish the information in notebooks (or make it available on PDAs) and distribute them to all the caddies. The end result of a well-designed KM program is that everyone wins. In this case, caddies get bigger tips and deals on merchandise, golfers play better because they benefit from the collective experience of caddies, and the course owners win because better scores lead to repeat business.

KM in Business

KM has assumed greater urgency in American business over the past few years as millions of baby boomers prepare to retire. When they punch out for the last time, the knowledge they gleaned about their jobs, companies, and industries during their long careers will walk out with them—unless companies take measures to retain their insights. In addition, CIOs who have entered into outsourcing agreements must address the thorny issue of transferring the knowledge of their full-time staff members, who are losing their jobs because of an outsourcing deal, to the outsourcer's employees.

KNOWLEDGE MANAGEMENT SYSTEMS

Knowledge can be a real competitive advantage for an organization. Information technology can distribute an organization's knowledge base by interconnecting people and digitally gathering their expertise. The primary objective of knowledge management is to be sure that a company's knowledge of facts, sources of information, and solutions are readily available to all employees whenever it is needed.

Such knowledge management requires that organizations go well beyond providing information contained in spreadsheets, databases, and documents. It must include expert information that typically resides in people's heads. A ***knowledge management system (KMS)*** supports the capturing, organization, and dissemination of knowledge (i.e., know-how) throughout an organization. It is up to the organization to determine what information qualifies as knowledge.

Explicit and Tacit Knowledge

Not all information is valuable. Individual companies must determine what information qualifies as intellectual and knowledge-based assets. In general, intellectual and knowledge-based assets fall into one of two categories: explicit or tacit. As a rule, ***explicit knowledge*** consists of anything that can be documented, archived, and codified, often with the help of IT. Examples of explicit knowledge are assets such as patents, trademarks, business plans, marketing research, and customer lists.

Tacit knowledge is the knowledge contained in people's heads. The challenge inherent in tacit knowledge is figuring out how to recognize, generate, share, and manage knowledge that resides in people's heads. While information technology in the form of e-mail, instant messaging, and related technologies can help facilitate the dissemination of tacit knowledge, identifying it in the first place can be a major obstacle. Shadowing and joint problem solving are two best practices for transferring or re-creating tacit knowledge inside an organization.

Shadowing   With *shadowing*, less experienced staff observe more experienced staff to learn how their more experienced counterparts approach their work. Dorothy Leonard and Walter Swap, two knowledge management experts, stress the importance of having the protégé discuss his or her observations with the expert to deepen the dialog and crystallize the knowledge transfer.

Joint Problem Solving   Another sound approach is *joint problem solving* by expert and novice. Because people are often unaware of how they approach problems or do their work and therefore cannot automatically generate step-by-step instructions for doing whatever they do, having a novice and expert work together on a project will bring the expert's approach to light. The difference between shadowing and joint problem solving is that shadowing is more passive. With joint problem solving, the expert and the novice work hand in hand on a task.[12]

Information is of little use unless it is analyzed and made available to the right people, at the right place, and at the right time. To get the most value from intellectual assets, knowledge must be shared. An effective KMS system should help do one or more of the following:

- Foster innovation by encouraging the free flow of ideas.
- Improve customer service by streamlining response time.
- Boost revenues by getting products and services to market faster.
- Enhance employee retention rates by recognizing the value of employees' knowledge.
- Streamline operations and reduce costs by eliminating redundant or unnecessary processes.

A creative approach to knowledge management can result in improved efficiency, higher productivity, and increased revenues in practically any business function. Figure 10.18 indicates the reasons organizations launch KMS.

Software is helping ChevronTexaco Corporation improve how it manages the assets in oil fields by enabling employees in multiple disciplines to easily access and share the information they need to make decisions. ChevronTexaco teams of 10 to 30 people are responsible for managing the assets, such as the drilling equipment, pipelines, and facilities, for a particular oil field. Within each team, earth scientists and various engineers with expertise in production, reservoir, and facilities work together to keep the oil field up and running. Each member of the asset team needs to communicate with other members to make decisions based on the collection and analysis of huge amounts of information from various departments. Individual team members can look at information from the perspective of their own department.

This has helped ChevronTexaco achieve a 30 percent productivity gain, a 50 percent improvement in safety performance, and more than $2 billion in operating

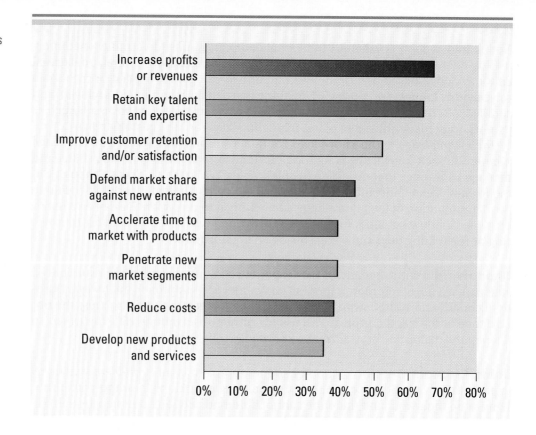

cost reductions. Through KMSs, ChevronTexaco has restructured its gasoline retailing business and now drills oil and gas wells faster and cheaper.[13]

Not every organization matches ChevronTexaco's success with KM. Numerous KM projects have failed over the past few years, generating an unwillingness to undertake—or even address—KM issues among many organizations. However, KM is an effective tool if it is tied directly to discrete business needs and opportunities. Beginning with targeted projects that deliver value quickly, companies can achieve the success that has proved elusive with many big-bang approaches. Successful KM projects typically focus on creating value in a specific process area, or even just for a certain type of transaction. Companies should start with one job at a time—preferably the most knowledge-oriented one—and build KM into a job function in a way that actually helps employees do their work better and faster, then expand to the next most knowledge-intensive job, and so on. Celebrating even small success with KM will help build a base of credibility and support for future KM projects.

KM Technologies

KM is not a purely technology-based concept. Organizations that implement a centralized database system, electronic message board, Web portal, or any other collaborative tool in the hope that they have established a KMS are wasting both their time and money.

Although tools don't make a KMS, such a system does need tools, from standard, off-the-shelf e-mail packages to sophisticated collaboration tools designed specifically to support community building and identity. Generally, KMS tools fall into one or more of the following categories:

- Knowledge repositories (databases).
- Expertise tools.
- E-learning applications.
- Discussion and chat technologies.
- Search and data mining tools.

KM and Social Networking

Companies that have been frustrated by traditional KM efforts are increasingly looking for ways to find out how knowledge flows through their organization, and social networking analysis can show them just that. *Social networking analysis (SNA)* is a process of mapping a group's contacts (whether personal or professional) to identify who knows whom and who works with whom. In enterprises, it provides a clear picture of how far-flung employees and divisions work together and can help identify key experts in the organization who possess the knowledge needed to, say, solve a complicated programming problem or launch a new product.

M&M maker Mars used SNA to identify how knowledge flows through its organizations, who holds influence, who gives the best advice, and how employees share information. The Canadian government's central IT unit used SNA to establish which skills it needed to retain and develop, and to determine who, among the 40 percent of the workforce that was due to retire within five years, had the most important knowledge and experience to begin transferring to others.[14]

SNA is not a replacement for traditional KM tools such as knowledge databases or portals, but it can provide companies with a starting point for how best to proceed with KM initiatives. As a component to a larger KM strategy, SNA can help companies identify key leaders and then set up a mechanism, such as communities of practice, so that those leaders can pass on their knowledge to colleagues. To identify experts in their organizations, companies can use software programs that track e-mail and other kinds of electronic communication.[15]

CONTENT MANAGEMENT SYSTEMS

A *content management system* provides tools to manage the creation, storage, editing, and publication of information in a collaborative environment. As a Web site grows in size and complexity, the business must establish procedures to ensure that things run smoothly. At a certain point, it makes sense to automate this process and use a content management system to manage this effectively. The content management system marketplace is complex, incorporating document management, digital asset management, and Web content management. Figure 10.19 highlights the three primary types of content management systems. Figure 10.20 lists the major content management system vendors.

Content management software is helping BMW Group Switzerland accelerate personalized, real-time information about products, services, prices, and events to

Common Types of Content Management Systems	
Document management system (DMS)	DMS—Supports the electronic capturing, storage, distribution, archiving, and accessing of documents. A DMS optimizes the use of documents within an organization independent of any publishing medium (for example, the Web). A DMS provides a document repository with information about other information. The system tracks the editorial history of each document and its relationships with other documents. A variety of search and navigation methods are available to make document retrieval easy. A DMS manages highly structured and regulated content, such as pharmaceutical documentation.
Digital asset management system (DAM)	DAM—Though similar to document management, DAM generally works with binary rather than text files, such as multimedia file types. DAM places emphasis on allowing file manipulation and conversion, for example, converting GIF files to JPEG.
Web content management system (WCM)	WCM—Adds an additional layer to document and digital asset management that enables publishing content both to intranets and to public Web sites. In addition to maintaining the content itself, WCM systems often integrate content with online processes like e-business systems.

FIGURE 10.19

Common Types of Content Management Systems

FIGURE 10.20

Major Content Management
Systems Vendors

Vendors	Strengths	Weaknesses	Costs
Documentum www.documentum.com	Document and digital asset management	Personalization features not as strong as competitors	Major components start at less than $100,000
FatWire www.fatwire.com	Web content management	May not scale to support thousands of users	SPARK, $25,000; Update Engine, $70,000 and up
InterWoven www.interwoven.com	Collaboration, enterprise content management	Requires significant customization	InterWoven 5 Platform, $50,000; average cost for a new customer, $250,000
Percussion www.percussion.com	Web content management	May not scale to support thousands of users	Rhythmyx Content Manager, about $150,000
Stellent www.stellent.com	Document conversion to Web-ready formats	Engineering for very large implementations with thousands of users	Content and Collaboration Servers, $50,000 to $250,000 each
Vignette www.vignette.com	Personalization	Document management and library services are not as robust as others	V6 Multisite Content Manager, $200,000 and up; V6 Content Suite, $450,000 and up

its dealers countrywide. BMW uses a process that allows dealers to specify what information is seen by which employee, as well as to deliver marketing materials solely to members of the sales department, and technical specifications and support documents only to mechanics. That enhanced personalization eliminates the chance that information is sent to the wrong dealership or to the wrong individual, which provides higher quality customer service. The content management software also enables nontechnical employees to create pages using predefined layout templates, simplifying the Web publishing process. More than 500 people use the solution daily, and all employees are able to publish information without calling on IT specialists, while maintaining the look and feel of the BMW brand.[16]

WORKFLOW MANAGEMENT SYSTEMS

A ***workflow*** defines all the steps or business rules, from beginning to end, required for a business process. Therefore, ***workflow management systems*** facilitate the automation and management of business processes and control the movement of work through the business process. Work activities can be performed in series or in parallel and involve people and automated computer systems. In addition, many workflow management systems allow the opportunity to measure and analyze the execution of the process because workflow systems allow the flow of work between individuals and/or departments to be defined and tracked. Workflow software helps automate a range of business tasks and electronically route the right information to the right people at the right time. Users are notified of pending work, and managers can observe status and route approvals through the system quickly.

There are two primary types of workflow systems: messaging-based and database-based. ***Messaging-based workflow systems*** send work assignments through an e-mail system. The workflow system automatically tracks the order for the work to be assigned and, each time a step is completed, the system automatically sends the work to the next individual in line. For example, each time a team member completes a piece of the project, the system would automatically send the document to the next team member.

Database-based workflow systems store documents in a central location and automatically ask the team members to access the document when it is their turn to edit the document. Project documentation is stored in a central location and team members are notified by the system when it is their turn to log in and work on their portion of the project.

Either type of workflow system helps to present information in a unified format, improves teamwork by providing automated process support, and allows team members to communicate and collaborate within a unified environment. Figure 10.21 lists some typical features associated with workflow management systems.

FIGURE 10.21

Workflow Management Systems Features

Workflow Feature	Description
Process definition tool	A graphical or textual tool for defining a business process. Each activity within the process is associated with a person or a computer application. Rules are created to determine how the activities progress across the workflow and which controls are in place to govern each activity.
Simulation, prototyping, and piloting	Some systems allow workflow simulation or create prototype and/or pilot versions of a particular workflow to test systems on a limited basis before going into production.
Task initiation and control	The business process defined above is initiated and the appropriate resources (either human and/or IT related) are scheduled and/or engaged to complete each activity as the process progresses.
Rules-based decision making	Rules are created for each step to determine how workflow-related information is to be processed, routed, tracked, and controlled. As an example, one rule might generate e-mail notifications when a condition has been met. Another rule might implement conditional routing of documents and tasks based on the content of fields.
Document routing	In simple systems, this is accomplished by passing a file or folder from one recipient to another (e.g., an e-mail attachment). In sophisticated systems, document routing is completed by checking the documents in and out of a central repository. Both systems might allow for "redlining" of the documents so that each person in the process can add their own comments without affecting the original document.
Applications to view and manipulate information	Word-processors, spreadsheets, and production systems are used to allow workers to create, update, and view information.
Work list	Current tasks are quickly identified along with such things as a due date, goal date, and priority by using work lists. In some systems, an anticipated workload is displayed as well. These systems analyze where jobs are in the workflow and how long each step should take, and then estimate when various tasks will reach a worker's desk.
Task automation	Computerized tasks are automatically invoked. These might include such things as letter writing, e-mail notices, or execution of production systems. Task automation often requires customization of the basic workflow product.
Event notification	Employees can be notified when certain milestones occur or when workload increases.
Process monitoring	The workflow system can provide an organization with valuable information on current workload, future workload, bottlenecks (current or potential), turn-around time, or missed deadlines.
Tracking and logging of activities	Information about each step can be logged. This might include such things as start and completion times, worker(s) assigned to the task, and key status fields. Later, this information can be used to analyze the process or to provide evidence that certain tasks were in fact completed.

New York City was experiencing a record number of claims, ranging from injuries resulting from slips on sidewalks to medical malpractice at city hospitals. The city processes over 30,000 claims and incurs $250 million in claim costs annually. Claims are generally filed with the Comptroller's Office, which investigates them and offers to settle meritorious claims. The New York City Comptroller's Office, with the assistance of its consultants Xerox and Universal Systems Inc., utilized a workflow management system to enhance revenues and decrease operating costs. With the implementation of the Omnibus Automated Image Storage Information System (OAISIS) for processing contracts and claims, New York City will save over $20 million.

Numerous city organizations were involved in the workflow management system, including Bureau of Law and Adjustment, Office of Contracts/Administration, Management and Accounting Systems, and Bureau of Information Systems.

In supporting all these New York City organizations, the system performs many functions that were previously labor-intensive and detracted from the quality and efficiency of investigations. The workflow management system screens claims to determine accordance with statutory requirements. Acknowledgment letters are generated automatically, with little or no resource allocation involved in assignment of claims or routing of claims to specific work locations. Status letters are automatically generated by the system for certain claim types, thus allowing the Comptroller's Office to keep claimants informed two months, five months, and one year from the date of their filing. All this is done automatically by the workflow management system.

Workflow management systems allow management to schedule individual systematic claim reviews without disrupting the investigation. Management can also see the entire claim process graphically and determine bottlenecks. Deployment of additional resources to needed areas occurs without a management analysis of a particular process problem.

GROUPWARE SYSTEMS

Groupware is software that supports team interaction and dynamics including calendaring, scheduling, and videoconferencing. Organizations can use this technology to communicate, cooperate, coordinate, solve problems, compete, or negotiate. While traditional technologies like the telephone qualify as groupware, the term refers to a specific class of technologies relying on modern computer networks, such as e-mail, newsgroups, videophones, and chat rooms. Groupware systems fall along two primary categories (see Figure 10.22):

1. Users of the groupware are working together at the same time (real-time or synchronous groupware) or different times (asynchronous groupware).

2. Users are working together in the same place (co-located or face-to-face) or in different places (non-co-located or distance).

The groupware concept integrates various systems and functionalities into a common set of services or a single (client) application. In addition, groupware can represent a wide range of systems and methods of integration. Figure 10.23 displays the advantages groupware systems offer an organization over single-user systems.

Lotus Notes is one of the world's leading software solutions for collaboration that combines messaging, groupware, and the Internet. The structure of Notes allows it to track, route, and manage documents. Systems that lend themselves to Notes involve tracking, routing, approval, document management, and organization.

Toyota developed an intranet system to promote information sharing within the company and to raise productivity. Unfortunately, the company's conventional e-mail system became overloaded, generating problems. Users did not receive incoming messages and were not able to send messages. Individual departments had introduced their own e-mail systems, which were not always compatible. Messages to other mail systems, including those outside the company, experienced delays. To deal with these difficulties, Toyota's information systems department reviewed the

FIGURE 10.22

Groupware Systems

	Same time "Synchronous"	Different time "Asynchronous"
Same place "Colocated"	Presentation support	Shared computers
Different place "Distance"	Videophones, Chat	E-mail, Workflow

FIGURE 10.23

Groupware Advantages

Groupware System Advantages
Facilitating communication (faster, easier, clearer, more persuasive)
Enabling telecommuting
Reducing travel costs
Sharing expertise
Forming groups with common interests where it would not be possible to gather a sufficient number of people face-to-face
Saving time and cost in coordinating group work
Facilitating group problem solving

e-mail system and restructured it so that e-mail, now recognized as an important communication tool, is utilized more effectively in business transactions.[17]

COLLABORATION TRENDS

E-mail is by far the dominant collaboration application, but real-time collaboration tools like instant messaging are creating a new communication dynamic within organizations. *Instant messaging* (sometimes called *IM* or *IMing*) is a type of communications service that enables someone to create a kind of private chat room with another individual in order to communicate in real-time over the Internet. In 1992, AOL deployed IM to the consumer market, allowing users to communicate with other IMers through a buddy list. Most of the popular instant messaging programs provide a variety of features, such as:

- Web links: Share links to favorite Web sites.
- Images: Look at an image stored on someone else's computer.
- Sounds: Play sounds.
- Files: Share files by sending them directly to another IMer.
- Talk: Use the Internet instead of a phone to talk.
- Streaming content: Receive real-time or near-real-time stock quotes and news.
- Instant messages: Receive immediate text messages.

Commercial vendors such as AOL and Microsoft offer free instant messaging tools. Real-time collaboration, such as instant messaging, live Web conferencing,

FIGURE 10.24

Instant Messaging
Application

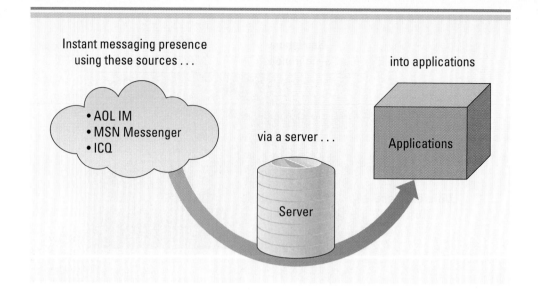

and screen or document sharing, creates an environment for decision making. AOL, Microsoft's MSN, and Yahoo! have begun to sell enterprise versions of their instant messaging services that match the capabilities of business-oriented products like IBM's Lotus Sametime. Figure 10.24 demonstrates the IM application presence within IT systems.

IBM Lotus software has released new versions of its real-time collaboration platform, IBM Lotus Instant Messaging and IBM Lotus Web Conferencing, plus its mobile counterpart, IBM Lotus Instant Messaging Everyplace. These built-for-business products let an organization offer presence awareness, secure instant messaging, and Web conferencing. The products give employees instant access to colleagues and company information regardless of time, place, or device.

The bigger issue in collaboration for organizations is cultural. Collaboration brings teams of people together from different regions, departments, and even companies—people who bring different skills, perceptions, and capabilities. A formal collaboration strategy helps create the right environment as well as the right systems for team members.

OPENING CASE QUESTIONS

Campus ERP

5. How can a college campus achieve business success through the use of collaboration tools?

6. How can your college use knowledge management systems to improve operations?

7. How can your college use content management systems to improve operations?

8. How can a team of college students use a workflow management system to complete a group project?

9. If your college wanted to implement a groupware system, what would be its primary purpose?

KEY TERMS

Accounting and finance ERP component 306
Business intelligence 308
Collaboration system 320
Content management system 325
Core competency 319
Core competency strategy 319
Core ERP component 305
Customer relationship management (CRM) 308
Database-based workflow system 327
Digital asset management system (DAM) 325
Document management system (DMS) 325
E-business 308
E-logistics 308

Enterprise application integration (EAI) 313
Enterprise resource planning (ERP) 304
E-procurement 308
Explicit knowledge 323
Extended ERP component 305
Groupware 328
Human resources ERP component 307
Information partnership 319
Instant messaging (IM, IMing) 329
Knowledge management (KM) 322
Knowledge management system (KMS) 322
Messaging-based workflow system 326

Middleware 313
Production and materials management ERP component 306
Social networking analysis (SNA) 325
Structured collaboration (process collaboration) 321
Supply chain management (SCM) 308
Tacit knowledge 323
Unstructured collaboration (information collaboration) 320
Web content management system (WCM) 325
Workflow 326
Workflow management system 326

DreamWorks Animation Collaboration

Hewlett-Packard (HP) and DreamWorks Animation SKG were the first to introduce a collaboration studio for simulating face-to-face business meetings across long distances. Vyomesh Joshi, executive vice president at HP, and Jeffrey Katzenberg, CEO of DreamWorks, officially unveiled the HP Halo Collaboration Studio in New York City in 2005. Halo enables people in different locations to communicate in a vivid, face-to-face environment in real time. Whether across a country or across the ocean, users can see and hear one another's physical and emotional reactions to conversation and information.

By giving participants the remarkable sense that they are in the same room, the Halo Collaboration Studio is already transforming the way businesses such as PepsiCo, Advanced Micro Devices, and DreamWorks communicate across the globe. Halo significantly increases team effectiveness, provides faster decision-making capabilities, and decreases the need for travel.

"The HP Halo Collaboration Studio enables remote teams to work together in a setting so lifelike that participants feel as though they are in the same room," Joshi said. "To create this experience, HP is harnessing its expertise in color science, imaging, and networking in this new category of innovation. It is something we believe will not only disrupt the traditional videoconferencing market, but will also change the way people work in a global market."

Early in the production of the animated film *Shrek 2,* DreamWorks realized a significant return on investment using the Halo technology. By connecting its California teams in Glendale and Redwood City, DreamWorks was able to speed up many aspects of the production.

"In 2002, while we were producing *Shrek 2,* we realized that DreamWorks needed face-to-face collaboration between key creative talent in different locations," Katzenberg said. "We weren't satisfied with the available videoconferencing systems, so we designed a collaboration solution that would fulfill our needs. HP took the system and turned it into Halo, which is now the only solution on the market that allows this kind of effective communication."

Halo Connection

To connect via Halo, organizations purchase at least two Halo rooms set up for six people each. Three plasma displays in each room enable participants to see those they are collaborating with in life-size images. The rooms come equipped with studio-quality audio and lighting, and participants use a simple on-screen user interface to begin collaborating with just a few mouse clicks.

An intricate software control system ensures Halo rooms work easily and seamlessly together. The control system also provides precise image and color calibration, so participants see each other as they appear in real life. A dedicated HP Halo Video Exchange Network provides a high-bandwidth experience with imperceptible delays between Halo studios worldwide.

To ensure a 24x7 connection and eliminate the need for enterprises to manage the operation and maintenance of a Halo room, services offered include network operations and management, remote diagnostics and calibration, concierge, equipment warranty, and ongoing service and repair.

Participants can easily share documents and data directly from their notebook PCs with individuals in other rooms using a collaboration screen mounted above the plasma displays. The rooms also contain a high-magnification camera that enables individuals to zoom in on objects on a table, revealing the finest of details and color shading, and a phone that opens a conference call line to those not in one of the Halo rooms.

"We believe there is a personal connection that comes with Halo that just clearly doesn't come from any other kind of technology we've used in the past," said Steve Reinemund, CEO of PepsiCo. "Halo is one of the best investments we've made to improve the effectiveness of our business and work/life balance for our people."[18]

Questions

1. How can companies use Halo to increase their business efficiency?
2. Explain how a company like PepsiCo can use Halo to gain a competitive advantage in its industry.
3. How can knowledge management be increased by using a product such as Halo?
4. Why would a company like DreamWorks, that is not IT focused, be interested in collaboration technology?
5. What are a few of the security issues surrounding this type of technology?

Improving Highway Safety Through Collaboration

Information on traffic-related deaths and accidents are two to three years out of date in some states, making it difficult to devise new safety regulations, rebuild unsafe roads, develop safer automobiles, and improve emergency services. Systems used by federal, state, and local agencies to collect and share information need to be overhauled, and the U.S. Department of Transportation's National Highway Traffic Safety Administration said it would ask Congress for $300 million over the next six years to upgrade them.

The goal is to eliminate antiquated paper-based reporting systems and implement a nationwide initiative to automate and synchronize the collection and sharing of information. The information will include vehicle-related injuries, associated health care costs, safety stops, driver licenses, vehicle registration, and adjudicated violations.

Safer Driving

Federal highway safety officials want $300 million to finance:

- Wireless communications equipment to facilitate electronic information collection and transmission during traffic safety stops.
- Real-time information transfer and editing processes to update driver's license or vehicle registration information from traffic stops or crash sites.
- Centralized access to query all traffic record databases.
- Standardized search capabilities on common queries and information transmission using XML formats.

Few states have the capability to capture and transmit traffic record and crash information electronically, and those that do are limited, according to Joseph Carra, director of the National Center for Statistics and Analysis at the highway safety agency. "Today, the information is written and stored in files. It's a paper process. The files are sent to the state office, whose clerks input the information into proprietary computer systems. And there it sits," he said.

Collaborating

Better information will save lives and money, says the federal highway safety administration. About 43,220 people were killed on the nation's highways in 2003, and another 2.9 million suffered serious injuries. Traffic accidents in 2000, the latest year for which information is available, cost the U.S. economy about $230 billion, the agency says.

The wide-ranging proposal calls for standardized formats to improve information sharing among various government agencies and private groups, more sophisticated sensors in cars and along highways to gather detailed information on crashes, and wireless handheld devices to let police officers check for outstanding warrants on drivers, among other ideas. Federal funding will encourage states to adopt federal standards. Many states, suffering from a slow economy and declining tax revenues, have not been able to fund upgrades themselves. Some, however, have projects under way.

Revamping Texas

Texas is about halfway done with an IT project to build a crash-records information system, a joint initiative between its Department of Public Safety and the Texas Department of Transportation. When completed, police officers will be able to file accident reports via the Web, and other state agencies will be able to electronically link their systems with it and share information.

Texas has been working on the crash-records system for several years. The state has a $9.9 million contract with IBM to build an information warehouse using a DB2 Universal Database, WebSphere Application Server, Tivoli Storage Manager, and MQ-Series, its message-queuing product. IBM says Florida, Arizona, and New Mexico are considering similar systems.

The Texas system is replacing a decades-old one that is "archaic and in need of many changes," said Carol Rawson, deputy division director for the traffic operations division with the state transportation department. The old system requires time-consuming manual entry of around 850,000 accident forms a year, as well as manual cross-checking and validation to ensure the information is correct. Because the process took so long, the state's accident information is backlogged some 30 months. "This is all about safety," Rawson said. "The way you tell if a road is safe is you look at accident information. So that information is critical."[19]

Questions

1. How are collaboration tools helping to save lives in Texas?

2. How could a police department use groupware to help with collaboration on accident reports?

3. Describe how a police department could use workflow systems to help with accident reports and health-care-related issues.

4. What would be the impact on lives if a state fails to implement collaboration tools to help track and analyze highway accidents?

5. How could police departments use wireless technologies to operate more efficiently and effectively?

6. What ethical issues surrounding wireless technologies should police departments understand?

Saving Costs at Costco

For Costco Wholesale to provide quality, brand-name merchandise at substantially lower prices, it must communicate quickly and effectively with thousands of vendors. The company cannot afford slow response times when accessing purchase orders, debit memos, or invoices; unsatisfactory image quality; or indirect access to transaction documents. Costco began the search for a technology that could handle its growing volume of paper, microfilm, and microfiche. The company processes 30,000 documents per day and has more than 75 million documents scanned in total.

Costco chose Stellent Imaging and Business Process Management because of its open architecture, competitive price, and multiple features, which provided a rapid return on investment. Costco worked with ImageSource, Inc., a Stellent solution provider, on design and implementation.

With Stellent, Costco processes about 6.7 million documents per year. Imaged documents can be accessed in seconds. Costco also gained easy storage and quick retrieval of information and integration of workflow processes with computer data. Faster payment processing and easier transaction storage and retrieval improved service to warehouse, depot, and vendor customers. Faster document retrieval times and quicker problem resolution led to increased vendor satisfaction. Costco recouped the cost of the Stellent solution in just 11 months of operation and saved $7 million in labor and payment term discounts. Today, 750 of Costco's 2,000 corporate office employees use the Stellent system including:

- The accounts payable group accesses invoices related to expense and merchandise functions.
- The accounting department scans and stores capital expenditure and fixed asset documents, which can be accessed by the facilities department.
- Costco's legal department uses Stellent to process and store vendor maintenance and setup agreements and other documents.
- The tax department improved its audit process now that it can randomly review a sampling of historical transaction documents.
- Regional offices can also quickly access vendor invoices and rebate documents via a Web browser.[20]

Questions

1. Identify content management and document management and explain how Costco is using them to improve business operations.
2. Provide an example of a few of the documents that Costco must maintain electronically.
3. How might other Costco departments benefit from a document management system?
4. The Stellent Imaging and Business Process Management solution allowed Costco to grow as a company without increasing expenses. Identify another business that could benefit from the Stellent Imaging and Business Process Management solution.

1. Implementing an ERP system

Blue Dog Inc. is a leading manufacturer in the high-end sunglasses industry, reaching record revenue levels of over $250 million last year. Blue Dog is currently deciding on the possibility of implementing an ERP system to help decrease production costs and increase inventory control. Many of the executives are nervous about making such a large investment in an ERP system due to its low success rates. As a senior manager at Blue Dog Inc. you have been asked to compile a list of the potential benefits and risks associated with implementing an ERP system along with your recommendations for the steps the company can take to ensure a successful implementation.

2. Most popular ERP component

Mackenzie Coombe is currently thinking about implementing an ERP solution in her online music company, The Burford Beat. The company is generating over $12 million in revenues and is growing by 150 percent a year. Create a one-page document explaining the advantages and disadvantages of ERP systems, why ERP systems include CRM and SCM components, and why the most popular ERP component in today's marketplace is the accounting and finance core component.

3. Value-added ERP

Pirate's Pizza is a large pizza chain that operates 700 franchises in 15 states. The company is currently contemplating implementing a new ERP system, which is expected to cost $7 million and take 18 months to implement. Once the system is completed, it is expected to generate $12 million a year in decreased costs and increased revenues. You are working in the finance department for the company and your boss has asked you to compile a report detailing the different financial metrics you can use to assess the business value of the new ERP system. Once your report is completed, the company will make a decision about purchasing the ERP system.

4. Collaboration on intranets

MyIntranet.com is a worldwide leader providing online intranet solutions. The MyIntranet. com online collaboration tool is a solution for small businesses and groups inside larger organizations that need to organize information, share files and documents, coordinate calendars, and enable efficient collaboration, all in a secure, browser-based environment. MyIntranet.com has just added conferencing and group scheduling features to its suite of hosted collaboration software. Explain why infrastructure integration is critical to the suite of applications to function within this environment.

5. Gaining efficiency with collaboration

During the past year, you have been working for a manufacturing firm to help improve its supply chain management by implementing enterprise resource planning and supply chain management systems. For efficiency gains, you are recommending that the manufacturing firm should be turning toward collaborative systems. The firm has a need to share intelligent plans and forecasts with supply chain partners, reduce inventory levels, improve working capital, and reduce manufacturing changeovers. Given the technologies presented to you in this unit, what type of system(s) would you recommend to facilitate your firm's future needs?

6. **Increasing revenues with ERP**

Cold Cream is one of the premier beauty supply stores in the metro New York area. People come from all over to sample the store's unique creams, lotions, makeup, and perfumes. The company receives its products from manufacturers around the globe. The company would like to implement an ERP system to help it better understand its customers and their purchasing habits. Create a report summarizing ERP systems and explain how an ERP system can directly influence Cold Cream's revenues.

Systems Development

11

SECTION 11.1
Developing Enterprise Applications

SECTION 11.2
The Systems Development Life Cycle (SDLC)

- Developing Software

- The Systems Development Life Cycle (SDLC)

- Software Development Methodologies

- Developing Successful Software

- Systems Development Life Cycle

- Phase 1: Planning

- Phase 2: Analysis

- Phase 3: Design

- Phase 4: Development

- Phase 5: Testing

- Phase 6: Implementation

- Phase 7: Maintenance

- Software Problems Are Business Problems

CHAPTER OUTLINE

HP's Software Problems

With IT projects, pessimism—otherwise known as contingency planning—is the only way to keep small technology problems from becoming full-blown business disasters. Christina Hanger had little reason to be pessimistic in May 2004, when she was moving one of Hewlett-Packard's biggest North American divisions onto a centralized ERP system from SAP. As the leader of an IT consolidation project rooted in HP's acquisition of Compaq two years earlier, Hanger, HP senior vice president of Americas operations and IT, had an unbroken record of success migrating five product groups within the two former companies onto one of two SAP systems.

Hanger had every reason to believe that the sixth would go well too. Even so, she knew to be prepared for problems. At approximately $7.5 billion in annual revenue, the division involved with this latest project, Industry Standard Servers (ISS), is much larger than any of the others that Hanger had migrated to SAP to that point. Hanger took the contingency plan that her team had developed for the other five migrations and adjusted it to accommodate the ISS division's larger sales volume. She planned for three weeks of IT snafus, mostly focused on what might happen as a result of tweaking a legacy order-entry system to work with the new SAP system. The contingency plan addressed business impacts too. HP banked three weeks' worth of extra servers and took over an empty portion of an HP factory in Omaha to stand by for any overflow of orders that needed special configurations (for example, an unusual component or software combination) and could not be stockpiled ahead of time.

"We had a series of small problems, none of which individually would have been too much to handle. But together they created the perfect storm," stated Gilles Bouchard, CIO and executive vice president of global operations. Starting when the system went live at the beginning of June and continuing throughout the rest of the month, as many as 20 percent of customer orders for servers stopped dead in their tracks between the legacy order-entry system and the SAP system. As IT problems go, this was not too big: Some data modeling issues between the legacy system and the SAP system prevented the SAP system from processing some orders for customized products. These programming errors were fixed within four or five weeks. However, Hanger and her business colleagues from the ISS division who were on the project steering committee never envisioned the degree to which these programming glitches would affect the business.

Orders began to backlog quickly, and HP did not have enough manual work-arounds to keep servers flowing fast enough to meet customer demand. Angry customers picked up the phone and called HP—or worse, competitors Dell and IBM. In a commodity market such as servers, customer loyalty is built upon a company's ability to configure products to order and get them delivered on time. HP could do neither for much of the summer. In a third-quarter conference call on August 12, HP Chairman and CEO Carly Fiorina pegged the financial impact at $160 million: a $120 million order backlog that resulted in $40 million in lost revenue. That is more than the cost of the project itself, which AMR Research estimates to be $30 million.

The headlines all claimed an IT disaster, but in fact, HP's disaster resulted from a few relatively small problems in IT that snowballed into a much bigger problem for the business: the inability to cope with the order backlog. This was a disaster that could have been prevented—not by trying to eliminate every possibility for error in a major IT system migration, which is virtually impossible, but by taking a much broader view of the impact that these projects can have on a company's supply chain.[1]

INTRODUCTION

Organizations must learn how to build and implement systems to remain competitive. Software that is built correctly can support agile organizations and can transform as the organization and its business transforms. Software that effectively meets employee needs will help an organization become more productive and enhance decision making. Software that does not meet employee needs may have a damaging effect on productivity and can even cause a business to fail. Employee involvement along with using the right implementation methodology when developing software is critical to the success of an organization.

section 11.1 DEVELOPING ENTERPRISE APPLICATIONS

LEARNING OUTCOMES

11.1. Identify the business benefits associated with successful software development.

11.2. Describe the seven phases of the systems development life cycle.

11.3. Summarize the different software development methodologies.

11.4. Define the relationship between the systems development life cycle and software development methodologies.

11.5. Compare the waterfall methodology and the agile methodology.

DEVELOPING SOFTWARE

Nike's SCM system failure, which spun out of control to the tune of $400 million, is legendary. Nike blamed the system failure on its SCM vendor, i2 Technologies. Nike states that i2 Technologies' demand and supply planning module created serious inventory problems. The i2 deployment, part of a multimillion-dollar e-business upgrade, caused Nike CEO Philip Knight to famously say, "This is what we get for our $400 million?" The SCM vendor saw its stock plummet with the Nike disaster, along with its reputation. Katrina Roche, i2's chief marketing officer, asserted that Nike failed to use the vendor's implementation methodology and templates, which contributed to the problem.[2]

Software development problems often lead to high-profile disasters. Hershey's glitch in its ERP implementation made the front page of *The Wall Street Journal* and cost the company millions. Hershey said computer problems with its SAP software system created a backlog of orders, causing slower deliveries, and resulting in lower earnings. Statistics released in 2006 by the National Research Council show that U.S. companies spent $250 billion in 2005 to repair damage caused by software defects.[3]

If software does not work, the organization will not work. Traditional business risk models typically ignored software development, largely because most organizations considered the impact from software and software development on the business to be minor. In the digital age, however, software success, or failure, can lead directly to business success, or failure. Almost every large organization in the world relies on software, either to drive its business operations or to make its products work. As organizations' reliance on software grows, so do the business-related consequences of software successes and failures as displayed in Figure 11.1.

The lucrative advantages of successful software implementations provide significant incentives to manage software development risks. However, according to the Chaos report from the Standish Group, a Massachusetts-based consultancy, more than half the software development projects undertaken in the United States come in late or over budget and the majority of successful projects maintain fewer features and functions than originally specified. Organizations also cancel around 33 percent of these projects during development. Understanding the basics of software

Business-Related Consequences of Software Success and Failure
Increase or decrease revenues—Organizations have the ability to directly increase profits by implementing successful IT systems. Organizations can also lose millions when software fails or key information is stolen or compromised. Nike's poorly designed supply chain management software delayed orders, increased excess inventories, and caused earnings to fall 24 percent below expectations.
Repair or damage to brand reputation—Technologies such as CRM can directly enhance a company's brand reputation. Software can also severely damage a company's reputation if it fails to work as advertised or has security vulnerabilities that affect its customers' trust. H&R Block customers were furious when the company accidentally placed its customers' passwords and Social Security numbers on its Web site.
Prevent or incur liabilities—Technology such as CAT scans, MRIs, and mammograms can save lives. Faulty technology used in airplanes, automobiles, pacemakers, or nuclear reactors can cause massive damage, injury, or death. The parent company of bankrupt pharmaceutical distributor FoxMeyer sued SAP for $500 million over ERP software failure that allegedly crippled its operations.
Increase or decrease productivity—CRM and SCM software can directly increase a company's productivity. Large losses in productivity can also occur when software malfunctions or crashes. The Standish Group estimates that defective software code accounted for 45 percent of computer-system downtime and cost U.S. companies $100 billion in lost productivity in 2003 alone.[4]

development, or the systems development life cycle, will help organizations avoid potential software development pitfalls and ensure that software development efforts are successful.[5]

THE SYSTEMS DEVELOPMENT LIFE CYCLE (SDLC)

Information systems are the support infrastructure that helps an organization change quickly when adapting to shifting business environments and markets. Many factors must come together to develop successful software. This chapter focuses on the *systems development life cycle (SDLC)*, also known as the "software life cycle" or the "application life cycle," which is the overall process for developing information systems from planning and analysis through implementation and maintenance (see Figure 11.2).

1. **Planning:** The *planning phase* involves establishing a high-level plan of the intended project and determining project goals. Planning is the first and most

FIGURE 11.2

The Systems
Development
Life Cycle

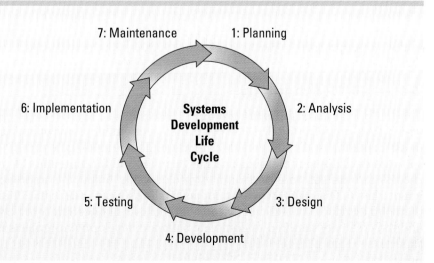

7: Maintenance — 1: Planning — 6: Implementation — 2: Analysis — Systems Development Life Cycle — 5: Testing — 3: Design — 4: Development

critical phase of any systems development effort an organization undertakes, regardless of whether the effort is to develop a system that allows customers to order products over the Internet, determine the best logistical structure for warehouses around the world, or develop a strategic information alliance with another organization. Organizations must carefully plan the activities (and determine why they are necessary) to be successful.

2. **Analysis:** The ***analysis phase*** involves analyzing end-user business requirements and refining project goals into defined functions and operations of the intended system. ***Business requirements*** are the detailed set of business requests that the system must meet in order to be successful. The analysis phase is obviously critical. A good start is essential and the organization must spend as much time, energy, and resources as necessary to perform a detailed, accurate analysis.

3. **Design:** The ***design phase*** involves describing the desired features and operations of the system including screen layouts, business rules, process diagrams, pseudo code, and other documentation.

4. **Development:** The ***development phase*** involves taking all of the detailed design documents from the design phase and transforming them into the actual system. In this phase the project transitions from preliminary designs to the actual physical implementation.

5. **Testing:** The ***testing phase*** involves bringing all the project pieces together into a special testing environment to test for errors, bugs, and interoperability and verify that the system meets all of the business requirements defined in the analysis phase.

6. **Implementation:** The ***implementation phase*** involves placing the system into production so users can begin to perform actual business operations with the system.

7. **Maintenance:** Maintaining the system is the final sequential phase of any systems development effort. The ***maintenance phase*** involves performing changes, corrections, additions, and upgrades to ensure the system continues to meet the business goals. This phase continues for the life of the system because the system must change as the business evolves and its needs change, demanding constant monitoring, supporting the new system with frequent minor changes (for example, new reports or information capturing), and reviewing the system to be sure it is moving the organization toward its strategic goals.

SOFTWARE DEVELOPMENT METHODOLOGIES

Today, systems are so large and complex that teams of architects, analysts, developers, testers, and users must work together to create the millions of lines of custom-written code that drive enterprises. For this reason, developers have created a number of different systems development life cycle methodologies including *waterfall, rapid application development (RAD), extreme programming,* and *agile.* The oldest of these, and the best known, is the waterfall methodology: a sequence of phases in which the output of each phase becomes the input for the next (see Figure 11.3).

Waterfall Methodology

The traditional ***waterfall methodology*** is a sequential, activity-based process in which each phase in the SDLC is performed sequentially from planning through implementation and maintenance. The waterfall methodology is one of the oldest software development methods and has been around for more than 30 years. The success rate for software development projects that follow this approach is only about 1 in 10. One primary reason for such a low success rate is that the waterfall methodology does not sufficiently consider the level of uncertainty in new projects and the creativity required to complete software development projects in several aspects (see Figure 11.4).

FIGURE 11.3

The Traditional
Waterfall Methodology

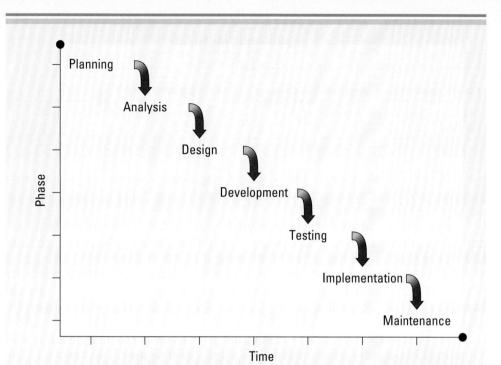

FIGURE 11.4

Issues Related to the
Waterfall Methodology

Issues Related to the Waterfall Methodology

The business problem	Any flaws in accurately defining and articulating the business problem in terms of what the business users actually require flow onward to the next phase.
The plan	Managing costs, resources, and time constraints is difficult in the waterfall sequence. What happens to the schedule if a programmer quits? How will a schedule delay in a specific phase impact the total cost of the project? Unexpected contingencies may sabotage the plan.
The solution	The waterfall methodology is problematic in that it assumes users can specify all business requirements in advance. Defining the appropriate IT infrastructure that is flexible, scalable, and reliable is a challenge. The final IT infrastructure solution must meet not only current but also future needs in terms of time, cost, feasibility, and flexibility. Vision is inevitably limited at the head of the waterfall.

Unfortunately, business requirements change as the business changes, which calls for considerable feedback and iterative consultation for all business requirements. Essentially, software is "soft" and it must be easily changed and manipulated to meet the changing dynamics of an organization. As people's understanding of the business problems evolve, so must the software. For this reason, it is counterproductive to define all requirements precisely upfront since, by the time the software goes into production, which can be several months or even years after completing the initial analysis phase, chances are the business problems have changed as well as the business.

Rapid Application Development Methodology (RAD)

In response to the faster pace of business, rapid application development has become a popular route for accelerating systems development. *Rapid application development (RAD)* (also called *rapid prototyping*) *methodology* emphasizes

FIGURE 11.5

Fundamentals of RAD

Fundamentals of RAD
Focus initially on creating a prototype that looks and acts like the desired system.
Actively involve system users in the analysis, design, and development phases.
Accelerate collecting the business requirements through an interactive and iterative construction approach.

extensive user involvement in the rapid and evolutionary construction of working prototypes of a system to accelerate the systems development process. Figure 11.5 displays the fundamentals of RAD.

A *prototype* is a smaller-scale representation or working model of the users' requirements or a proposed design for an information system. The prototype is an essential part of the analysis phase when using the RAD methodology.

PHH Vehicle Management Services, a Baltimore fleet-management company with over 750,000 vehicles, wanted to build an enterprise application that opened the entire vehicle information database to customers over the Internet. To build the application quickly, the company abandoned the traditional waterfall approach. Instead, a team of 30 developers began prototyping the Internet application, and the company's customers evaluated each prototype for immediate feedback. The development team released new prototypes that incorporated the customers' feedback every six weeks. The PHH Interactive Vehicle application went into production seven months after the initial work began. Over 20,000 customers, using a common browser, can now access the PHH Interactive site at any time from anywhere in the world to review their accounts, analyze billing information, and order vehicles.[6]

Extreme Programming Methodology

Extreme programming (XP) methodology breaks a project into tiny phases, and developers cannot continue on to the next phase until the first phase is complete. The primary difference between the waterfall and XP methodologies is that XP divides its phases into iterations with user feedback. The waterfall approach develops the entire system, whereas XP develops the system in iterations (see Figure 11.6). XP is a lot like a jigsaw puzzle; there are many small pieces. Individually the pieces make no sense, but when they are combined (again and again) an organization can gain visibility into the entire new system.

Microsoft Corporation developed Internet Explorer and Netscape Communications Corporation developed Communicator using extreme programming. Both companies did a nightly compilation (called a build) of the entire project, bringing together all the current components. They established release dates and expended considerable effort to involve customers in each release. The extreme programming approach allowed both Microsoft and Netscape to manage millions of lines of code as specifications changed and evolved over time. Most important, both companies frequently held user design reviews and strategy sessions to solicit and incorporate user feedback.[7]

XP is a significant departure from traditional software development methodologies, and many organizations in different industries have developed successful software using it. One reason for XP's success is its stress on customer satisfaction. XP empowers developers to respond to changing customer and business requirements, even late in the systems development life cycle, and XP emphasizes teamwork. Managers, customers, and developers are all part of a team dedicated to delivering quality software. XP implements a simple, yet effective way to enable groupware-style development. The XP methodology promotes quickly being able to respond to changing requirements and technology.

FIGURE 11.6

The Iterative Approach

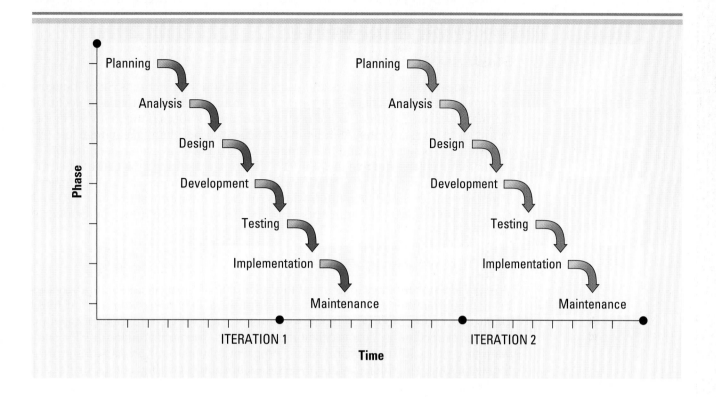

FIGURE 11.7

The Agile Alliance
Manifesto

The Agile Alliance Manifesto
Early and continuous delivery of valuable software will satisfy the customer.
Changing requirements, even late in development, are welcome.
Businesspeople and developers must work together daily throughout the project.
Projects should be built around motivated individuals. Give them the environment and support they need, and trust them to get the job done.
The best architectures, requirements, and designs emerge from self-organizing teams.
At regular intervals, the team should reflect on how to become more effective, then tune and adjust its behavior accordingly.

Agile Methodology

The *agile methodology*, a form of XP, aims for customer satisfaction through early and continuous delivery of useful software components. Agile is similar to XP but with less focus on team coding and more on limiting project scope. An agile project sets a minimum number of requirements and turns them into a deliverable product. Agile means what it sounds like: fast and efficient; small and nimble; lower cost; fewer features; shorter projects.

The Agile Alliance is a group of software developers whose mission is to improve software development processes and whose manifesto is displayed in Figure 11.7.

DEVELOPING SUCCESSFUL SOFTWARE

The Gartner Research estimates that 65 percent of agile projects are successful. This success rate is extraordinary compared to the 10 percent success rate of waterfall projects. The following are the primary principles an organization should follow for successful agile software development.[8]

Slash the Budget

Small budgets force developers and users to focus on the essentials. Small budgets also make it easier to kill a failing project. For example, imagine that a project that has already cost $20 million is going down the tubes. With that much invested, it is tempting to invest another $5 million to rescue it rather than take a huge loss. All too often, the system fails and the company ends up with an even bigger loss.

Jim Johnson, chairman of the Standish Group, says he forced the CIO of one Fortune 500 company to set a $100,000 ceiling on all software development projects. There were no exceptions to this business rule without approval from the CIO and CEO. Johnson claims the company's project success rate went from 0 percent to 50 percent.[9]

If It Doesn't Work, Kill It

Bring all key stakeholders together at the beginning of a project and as it progresses bring them together again to evaluate the software. Is it doing what the business wants and, more important, requires? Eliminate any software that is not meeting business expectations. This is called triage, and it's "the perfect place to kill a software project," said Pat Morgan, senior program manager at Compaq's Enterprise Storage Group. He holds monthly triage sessions and says they can be brutal. "At one [meeting], engineering talked about a cool process they were working on to transfer information between GUIs. No one in the room needed it. We killed it right there. In our environment, you can burn a couple of million dollars in a month only to realize what you're doing isn't useful."[10]

Keep Requirements to a Minimum

Start each project with what the software must absolutely do. Do not start with a list of everything the software should do. Every software project traditionally starts with a requirements document that will often have hundreds or thousands of business requirements. The Standish Group estimates that only 7 percent of the business requirements are needed for any given application. Keeping requirements to a minimum also means that scope creep and feature creep must be closely monitored. *Scope creep* occurs when the scope of the project increases. *Feature creep* occurs when developers add extra features that were not part of the initial requirements. Both scope creep and feature creep are major reasons software development fails.[11]

Test and Deliver Frequently

As often as once a week, and not less than once a month, complete a part of the project or a piece of software. The part must be working and it must be bug-free. Then have the customers test and approve it. This is the agile methodology's most radical departure from traditional development. In some traditional software projects, the customers did not see any working parts or pieces for years.

Assign Non-IT Executives to Software Projects

Non-IT executives should coordinate with the technical project manager, test iterations to make sure they are meeting user needs, and act as liaisons between executives and IT. Having the business side involved full-time will bring project ownership and a desire to succeed to all parties involved. SpreeRide, a Salt Lake City market research outfit, used the agile methodology to set up its company's Web site. The project required several business executives designated full-time. The company believes this is one of the primary reasons that the project was successfully deployed in less than three months.[12]

OPENING CASE QUESTIONS

HP's Software Problems

1. Identify the business benefits associated with successful software development for HP.

2. Which of the seven phases of the systems development life cycle is most important to HP?

3. Which of the seven phases of the systems development life cycle is least important to HP?

4. Which of the different software development methodologies should HP use to implement successful systems?

5. Explain what might happen if HP used the waterfall methodology to develop its ERP system.

section 11.2 THE SYSTEMS DEVELOPMENT LIFE CYCLE (SDLC)

LEARNING OUTCOMES

11.6. Summarize the activities associated with the planning phase in the SDLC.

11.7. Summarize the activities associated with the analysis phase in the SDLC.

11.8. Summarize the activities associated with the design phase in the SDLC.

11.9. Summarize the activities associated with the development phase in the SDLC.

11.10. Summarize the activities associated with the testing phase in the SDLC.

11.11. Summarize the activities associated with the implementation phase in the SDLC.

11.12. Summarize the activities associated with the maintenance phase in the SDLC.

SYSTEMS DEVELOPMENT LIFE CYCLE

The systems development life cycle is the foundation for all systems development methodologies, and there are literally hundreds of different activities associated with each phase in the SDLC. Typical activities include determining budgets, gathering system requirements, and writing detailed user documentation. The activities performed during each systems development project will vary. This section takes a detailed look at a few of the more common activities performed during the systems development life cycle, along with common issues facing software development projects (see Figures 11.8 and 11.9).

PHASE 1: PLANNING

The *planning phase* involves establishing a high-level plan of the intended project and determining project goals. The three primary activities involved in the planning phase are:

1. Identify and select the system for development.
2. Assess project feasibility.
3. Develop the project plan.

FIGURE 11.8

The Systems
Development
Life Cycle

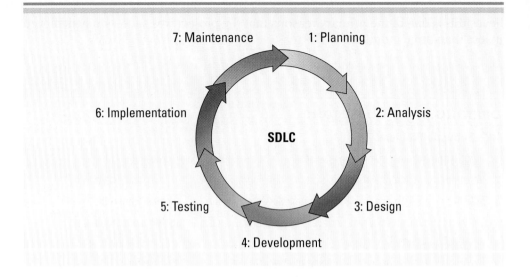

FIGURE 11.9

Common Activities
Performed During
Systems
Development

SDLC Phase	Activities
1. Planning	■ Identify and select the system for development ■ Assess project feasibility ■ Develop the project plan
2. Analysis	■ Gather business requirements ■ Create process diagrams ■ Perform a buy versus build analysis
3. Design	■ Design the IT infrastructure ■ Design system models
4. Development	■ Develop the IT infrastructure ■ Develop the database and programs
5. Testing	■ Write the test conditions ■ Perform the system testing
6. Implementation	■ Determine implementation method ■ Provide training for the system users ■ Write detailed user documentation
7. Maintenance	■ Build a help desk to support the system users ■ Perform system maintenance ■ Provide an environment to support system changes

Identify and Select the System for Development

Systems are successful only when they solve the right problem or take advantage of the right opportunity. Systems development focuses on either solving a problem or taking advantage of an opportunity. Determining which systems are required to support the strategic goals of an organization is one of the primary activities performed during the planning phase. Typically, employees generate proposals to build new information systems when they are having a difficult time performing their jobs. Unfortunately, most organizations have limited resources and cannot afford to develop all proposed information systems. Therefore, they look to critical success factors to help determine which systems to build.

A *critical success factor (CSF)* is a factor that is critical to an organization's success. To determine which system to develop, an organization tracks all the proposed

Evaluation Criteria	Description
Value chain analysis	The value chain determines the extent to which the new system will add value to the organization. Systems with greater value are given priority over systems with less value.
Strategic alignment	Projects that are in line with the organization's strategic goals and objectives are given priority over projects not in line with the organization's strategic goals and objectives.
Cost/benefit analysis	A cost/benefit analysis determines which projects offer the organization the greatest benefits with the least amount of cost.
Resource availability	Determine the amount and type of resources required to complete the project and determine if the organization has these resources available.
Project size, duration, and difficulty	Determine the number of individuals, amount of time, and technical difficulty of the project.

systems and prioritizes them by business impact or critical success factors. This allows the business to prioritize which problems require immediate attention and which problems can wait. Figure 11.10 displays possible evaluation criteria for determining which projects to develop.

Assess Project Feasibility

A *feasibility study* determines if the proposed solution is feasible and achievable from a financial, technical, and organizational standpoint. Typically, an organization will define several alternative solutions that it can pursue to solve a given problem. A feasibility study is used to determine if the proposed solution is achievable, given the organization's resources and constraints in regard to technology, economics, organizational factors, and legal and ethical considerations. Figure 11.11 displays the different types of feasibility studies an organization can perform.

Develop the Project Plan

Developing a project plan is one of the final activities performed during the planning phase and it is one of the hardest and most important activities. The project plan is the guiding force behind on-time delivery of a complete and successful system. It logs and tracks every single activity performed during the project. If an activity is missed, or takes longer than expected to complete, the project plan must be updated to reflect these changes. Updating the project plan must be performed in every subsequent phase during the systems development effort.

FIGURE 11.11

Different Types of
Feasibility Studies

Types of Feasibility Studies	
Economic feasibility study (often called a cost-benefit analysis)	Identifies the financial benefits and costs associated with the systems development project.
Legal and contractual feasibility study	Examines all potential legal and contractual ramifications of the proposed system.
Operational feasibility study	Examines the likelihood that the project will attain its desired objectives.
Schedule feasibility study	Assesses the likelihood that all potential time frames and completion dates will be met.
Technical feasibility study	Determines the organization's ability to build and integrate the proposed system.

PHASE 2: ANALYSIS

The *analysis phase* involves analyzing end-user business requirements and refining project goals into defined functions and operations of the intended system. The three primary activities involved in the analysis phase are:

1. Gather business requirements.
2. Create process diagrams.
3. Perform a buy versus build analysis.

Gather Business Requirements

Business requirements are the detailed set of business requests that the system must meet to be successful. At this point, there is little or no concern with any implementation or reference to technical details. For example, the types of technology used to build the system, such as an Oracle database or the Java programming language, are not yet defined. The only focus is on gathering the true business requirements for the system. A sample business requirement might state, "The system must track all customer sales by product, region, and sales representative." This requirement states what the system must do from the business perspective, giving no details or information on how the system is going to meet this requirement.

Gathering business requirements is basically conducting an investigation in which users identify all the organization's business needs and take measurements of these needs. Figure 11.12 displays different methods organizations use to gather business requirements.

The *requirements definition document* contains the final set of business requirements, prioritized in order of business importance. The system users review the requirements definition document and determine if they will sign off on the business requirements. *Sign-off* is the system users' actual signatures indicating they approve all of the business requirements. One of the first major milestones on the project plan is usually the users' sign-off on business requirements.

A large data storage company implemented a project called Python whose purpose was to control all the company's information systems. Seven years, tens of millions of dollars, and 35 programmers later, Python was canceled. At the end of the project, Python had over 1,800 business requirements of which 900 came from engineering and were written in order to make the other 900 customer requirements work. By the time the project was canceled, it was unclear what the primary goals, objectives, and needs of the project were. Management should have realized Python's issues when the project's requirements phase dragged on, bulged, and took years to complete. The sheer number of requirements should have raised a red flag.[13]

Create Process Diagrams

Once a business analyst takes a detailed look at how an organization performs its work and its processes, the analyst can recommend ways to improve these processes

FIGURE 11.12

Methods for Gathering Business Requirements

Methods for Gathering Business Requirements
Perform a *joint application development (JAD)* session where employees meet, sometimes for several days, to define or review the business requirements for the system.
Interview individuals to determine current operations and current issues.
Compile questionnaires to survey employees to discover issues.
Make observations to determine how current operations are performed.
Review business documents to discover reports, policies, and how information is used throughout the organization.

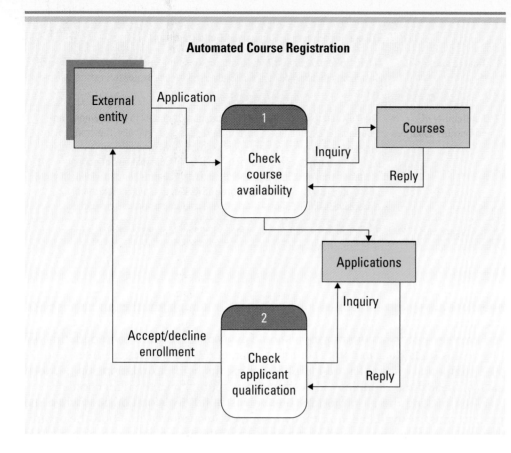

FIGURE 11.13

Sample Data Flow
Diagram

Automated Course Registration

to make them more efficient and effective. ***Process modeling*** involves graphically representing the processes that capture, manipulate, store, and distribute information between a system and its environment. One of the most common diagrams used in process modeling is the data flow diagram. A ***data flow diagram (DFD)*** illustrates the movement of information between external entities and the processes and data stores within the system (see Figure 11.13). Process models and data flow diagrams establish the specifications of the system. ***Computer-aided software engineering (CASE)*** tools are software suites that automate systems analysis, design, and development. Process models and data flow diagrams can provide the basis for the automatic generation of the system if they are developed using a CASE tool.

Perform a Buy versus Build Analysis

An organization faces two primary choices when deciding to develop an information system: (1) it can buy the information system from a vendor or (2) it can build the system itself. ***Commercial off-the-shelf (COTS)*** software is a software package or solution that is purchased to support one or more business functions and information systems. Most customer relationship management, supply chain management, and enterprise resource planning solutions are COTS. Typically, a cost-benefit analysis forms the basis of the buy versus build decision. Figure 11.14 displays a few

FIGURE 11.14

Buy versus Build
Decision Questions

Buy versus Build Decision Questions
Do any currently available products fit the organization's needs?
Are unavailable features important enough to warrant the expense of in-house development?
Can the organization customize or modify an existing COTS to fit its needs?
Is there a justification to purchase or develop based on the cost of acquisition?

FIGURE 11.15

Key Factors
in Buy versus
Build Decisions

Three Key Factors in Buy versus Build Decisions	
1. **Time to market**	If time to market is a priority, then purchasing a good base technology and potentially building on to it will likely yield results faster than starting from scratch.
2. **Availability of corporate resources**	The buy versus build decision is a bit more complex to make when considering the availability of corporate resources. Typically, the costs to an organization to buy systems such as SCM, CRM, and ERP are extremely high. These costs can be so high—in the multiple millions of dollars—that acquiring these technologies might make the entire concept economically unfeasible. Building these systems, however, can also be extremely expensive, take indefinite amounts of time, and constrain resources.
3. **Corporate core competencies**	The more an organization wants to build a technical core competency, the less likely it will want to buy.

questions an organization must consider when contemplating the buy versus build decision.

Three key factors an organization should also consider when contemplating the buy versus build decision are: (1) time to market, (2) corporate resources, and (3) core competencies (see Figure 11.15). Weighing the complex relationship between each of these three variables will help an organization make the right choice.

When making the all-important buy versus build decision consider when the product must be available, how many resources are available, and how the organization's core competencies affect the product. If these questions can be definitely answered either yes or no, then the answer is easy. However, most organizations cannot answer these questions with a solid yes or no. Most organizations need to make a trade-off between the lower cost of buying a system and the need for a system that meets all of their requirements. Finding a system to buy that meets all an organization's unique business requirements is next to impossible.

PHASE 3: DESIGN

The *design phase* involves describing the desired features and operations of the system including screen layouts, business rules, process diagrams, pseudo code, and other documentation. The two primary activities involved in the design phase are:

1. Design the IT infrastructure.
2. Design system models.

Design the IT Infrastructure

The system must be supported by a solid IT infrastructure or chances are the system will crash, malfunction, or not perform as expected. The IT infrastructure must meet the organization's needs in terms of time, cost, technical feasibility, and flexibility. Most systems run on a computer network with each employee having a client and the application running on a server. During this phase, the IT specialists recommend what types of clients and servers to buy including memory and storage requirements, along with software recommendations. An organization typically explores several different IT infrastructures that must meet current as well as future system needs. For example, databases must be large enough to hold the current volume of customers plus all new customers that the organization expects to gain over the next several years (see Figure 11.16).

Design System Models

Modeling is the activity of drawing a graphical representation of a design. An organization should model everything it builds including reports, programs, and

FIGURE 11.16

Sample IT Infrastructure

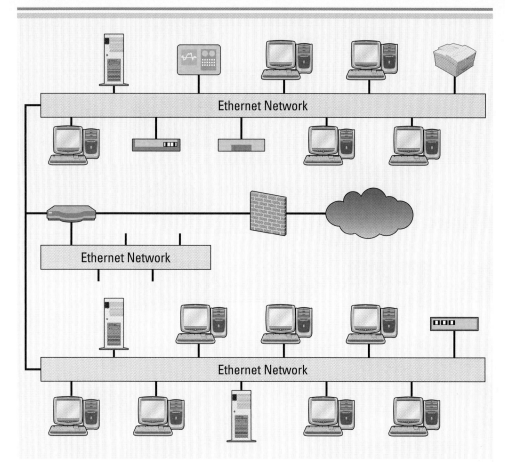

databases. Many different types of modeling activities are performed during the design phase including:

- The ***graphical user interface (GUI)*** is the interface to an information system. GUI screen design is the ability to model the information system screens for an entire system using icons, buttons, menus, and submenus.
- ***Data models*** represent a formal way to express data relationships to a database management system (DBMS).
- ***Entity relationship diagram (ERD)*** is a technique for documenting the relationships between entities in a database environment (see Figure 11.17).

PHASE 4: DEVELOPMENT

The ***development phase*** involves taking all of the detailed design documents from the design phase and transforming them into the actual system. The two primary activities involved in the development phase are:

1. Develop the IT infrastructure.
2. Develop the database and programs.

Develop the IT Infrastructure

The platform upon which the system will operate must be built before building the actual system. In the design phase, an organization creates a blueprint of the proposed IT infrastructure displaying the design of the software, hardware, and telecommunication equipment. In the development phase, the organization purchases and implements the required equipment to support the IT infrastructure.

Most new systems require new hardware and software. It may be as simple as adding memory to a client or as complex as setting up a wide area network across several states.

FIGURE 11.17

Sample Entity Relationship Diagram

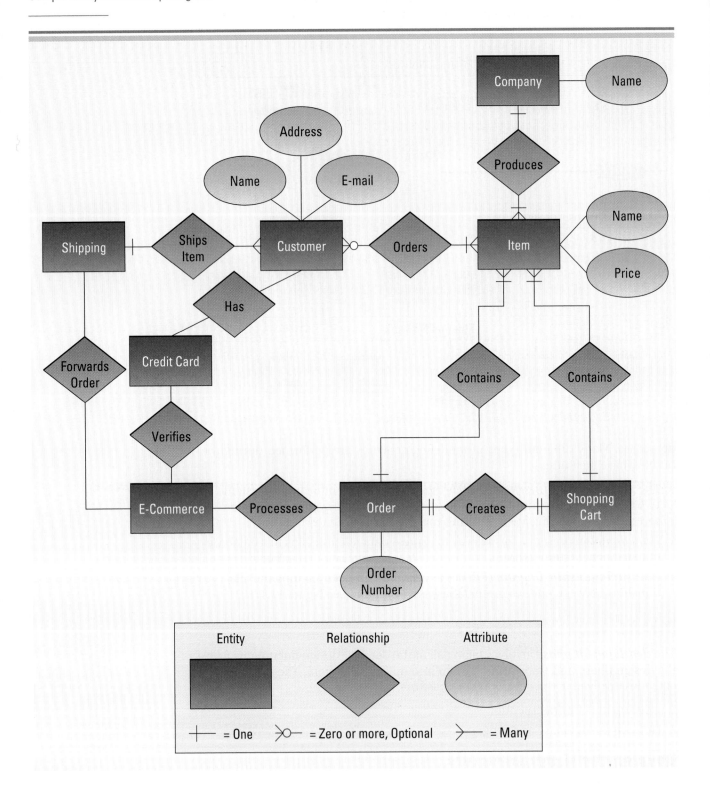

Develop the Database and Programs

Once the IT infrastructure is built, the organization can begin to create the database and write the programs required for the system. IT specialists perform these functions and it may take months or even years to design and create all the needed elements to complete the system.

PHASE 5: TESTING

According to a report issued in June 2003 by the National Institute of Standards and Technology (NIST), defective software costs the U.S. economy an estimated $59.5 billion each year. Of that total, software users incurred 64 percent of the costs and software developers 36 percent. NIST suggests that improvements in testing could reduce this cost by about a third, or $22.5 billion, but that unfortunately testing improvements would not eliminate all software errors.[14]

The **testing phase** involves bringing all the project pieces together into a special testing environment to test for errors, bugs, and interoperability, in order to verify that the system meets all the business requirements defined in the analysis phase. The two primary activities involved in the testing phase are:

1. Write the test conditions.
2. Perform the system testing.

Write the Test Conditions

Testing is critical. An organization must have excellent test conditions to perform an exhaustive test. **Test conditions** are the detailed steps the system must perform along with the expected results of each step. Figure 11.18 displays several test conditions for testing user log-on functionality in a system. The tester will execute each test condition and compare the expected results with the actual results in order to verify that the system functions correctly. Notice in Figure 11.18 how each test condition is extremely detailed and states the expected results that should occur when executing each test condition. Each time the actual result is different from the expected result, a "bug" is generated and the system goes back to development for a bug fix.

Test condition 6 in Figure 11.18 displays a different actual result than the expected result because the system failed to allow the user to log on. After this test

FIGURE 11.18

Sample Test Conditions

Test Condition Number	Date Tested	Tester	Test Condition	Expected Result	Actual Result	Pass/ Fail
1	1/1/05	Emily Hickman	Click on System Start Button	Main Menu appears	Same as expected result	Pass
2	1/1/05	Emily Hickman	Click on Logon Button in Main Menu	Logon Screen appears asking for Username and Password	Same as expected result	Pass
3	1/1/05	Emily Hickman	Type Emily Hickman in the User Name Field	Emily Hickman appears in the User Name Field	Same as expected result	Pass
4	1/1/05	Emily Hickman	Type Zahara 123 in the password field	XXXXXXXXX appears in the password field	Same as expected result	Pass
5	1/1/05	Emily Hickman	Click on O.K. button	User logon request is sent to database and user name and password are verified	Same as expected result	Pass
6	1/1/05	Emily Hickman	Click on Start	User name and password are accepted and the system main menu appears	Screen appeared stating logon failed and username and password were incorrect	Fail

FIGURE 11.19

Types of Tests
Performed During
the Testing Phase

Types of Tests Performed During the Testing Phase	
Application (or system) testing	Verifies that all units of code work together and the total system satisfies all of its functional and operational requirements.
Backup and recovery testing	Tests the ability of an application to be restarted after failure.
Documentation testing	Verifies that the instruction guides are helpful and accurate.
Integration testing	Exposes faults in the integration of software components or software units.
Regression testing	Determines if a functional improvement or repair to the system has affected the other functional aspects of the software.
Unit testing	Tests each unit of code as soon as the unit is complete to expose faults in the unit regardless of its interaction with other units.
User acceptance testing (UAT)	Determines whether a system satisfies its acceptance criteria, enabling the customer to decide whether or not to accept a system.

condition fails, it is obvious that the system is not functioning correctly and it must be sent back to development for a bug fix.

A typical system development effort has hundreds or thousands of test conditions. Every single test condition must be executed to verify that the system performs as expected. Writing all the test conditions and performing the actual testing of the software takes a tremendous amount of time and energy. Testing is critical to the successful development of any system.

Perform the System Testing

System developers must perform many different types of testing to ensure that the system works as expected. Figure 11.19 displays the more common types of tests performed during the testing phase.

PHASE 6: IMPLEMENTATION

The *implementation phase* involves placing the system into production so users can begin to perform actual business operations with the system. The three primary activities involved in the implementation phase are:

1. Write detailed user documentation.
2. Determine implementation method.
3. Provide training for the system users.

Write Detailed User Documentation

System users require *user documentation* that highlights how to use the system. This is the type of documentation that is typically provided along with the new system. System users find it extremely frustrating to have a new system without documentation.

Determine Implementation Method

An organization must choose the right implementation method to ensure a successful system implementation. There are four primary implementation methods an organization can use (see Figure 11.20).

FIGURE 11.20

Primary
Implementation
Methods

Primary Implementation Methods	
1. **Parallel implementation**	Using both the old and new systems until it is evident that the new system performs correctly.
2. **Phased implementation**	Implementing the new system in phases (e.g., accounts receivables then accounts payable) until it is evident that the new system performs correctly and then implementing the remaining phases of the new system.
3. **Pilot implementation**	Having only a small group of people use the new system until it is evident that the new system performs correctly and then adding the remaining people to the new system.
4. **Plunge implementation**	Discarding the old system completely and immediately using the new system.

Provide Training for the System Users

An organization must provide training for the system users. The two most popular types of training are online training and workshop training. *Online training* runs over the Internet or off a CD-ROM. System users perform the training at any time, on their own computers, at their own pace. This type of training is convenient for system users because they can set their own schedule for the training. *Workshop training* is set in a classroom-type environment and led by an instructor. Workshop training is recommended for difficult systems where the system users require one-on-one time with an individual instructor.

PHASE 7: MAINTENANCE

The *maintenance phase* involves performing changes, corrections, additions, and upgrades to ensure the system continues to meet the business goals. Once a system is in place, it must change as the organization changes. The three primary activities involved in the maintenance phase are:

1. Build a help desk to support the system users.
2. Perform system maintenance.
3. Provide an environment to support system changes.

Build a Help Desk to Support the System Users

A *help desk* is a group of people who respond to internal system user questions. Typically, internal system users have a phone number for the help desk they call whenever they have issues or questions about the system. Staffing a help desk that answers internal user questions is an excellent way to provide comprehensive support for new systems.

Perform System Maintenance

Maintenance is fixing or enhancing an information system. Many different types of maintenance must be performed on the system to ensure it continues to operate as expected. These include:

- **Adaptive maintenance**—making changes to increase system functionality to meet new business requirements.
- **Corrective maintenance**—making changes to repair system defects.

- **Perfective maintenance**—making changes to enhance the system and improve such things as processing performance and usability.
- **Preventive maintenance**—making changes to reduce the chance of future system failures.

Provide an Environment to Support System Changes

As changes arise in the business environment, an organization must react to those changes by assessing the impact on the system. It might well be that the system needs to adjust to meet the ever-changing needs of the business environment. If so, an organization must modify its systems to support the business environment.

A *change management system* includes a collection of procedures to document a change request and define the steps necessary to consider the change based on the expected impact of the change. Most change management systems require that a change request form be initiated by one or more project stakeholders (users, customers, analysts, developers). Ideally, these change requests are reviewed by a *change control board (CCB)* responsible for approving or rejecting all change requests. The CCB's composition typically includes a representative for each business area that has a stake in the project. The CCB's decision to accept or reject each change is based on an impact analysis of the change. For example, if one department wants to implement a change to the software that will increase both deployment time and cost, then the other business owners need to agree that the change is valid and that it warrants the extended time frame and increased budget.

SOFTWARE PROBLEMS ARE BUSINESS PROBLEMS

Only 28 percent of projects are developed within budget and delivered on time and as promised, says a Standish Group report. The primary reasons for project failure are:

- Unclear or missing business requirements.
- Skipping SDLC phases.
- Failure to manage project scope.
- Failure to manage project plan.
- Changing technology.[15]

Unclear or Missing Business Requirements

The most common reason systems fail is because the business requirements are either missing or incorrectly gathered during the analysis phase. The business requirements drive the entire system. If they are not accurate or complete, the system will not be successful.

It is important to discuss the relationship between the SDLC and the cost for the organization to fix errors. An error found during the analysis and design phase is relatively inexpensive to fix. All that is typically required is a change to a Word document. However, exactly the same error found during the testing or implementation phase is going to cost the organization an enormous amount to fix because it has to change the actual system. Figure 11.21 displays how the cost to fix an error grows exponentially the later the error is found in the SDLC.

Skipping SDLC Phases

The first thing individuals tend to do when a project falls behind schedule is to start skipping phases in the SDLC. For example, if a project is three weeks behind in the development phase, the project manager might decide to cut testing down from

FIGURE 11.21

The Cost of Finding Errors

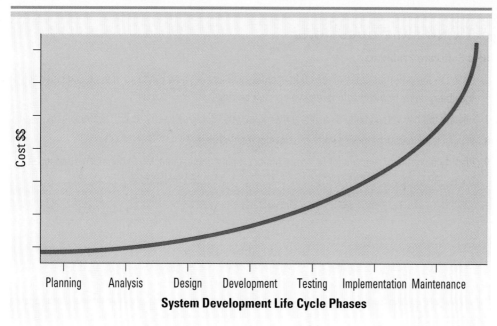

six weeks to three weeks. Obviously, it is impossible to perform all the testing in half the time. Failing to test the system will lead to unfound errors, and chances are high that the system will fail. It is critical that an organization perform all phases in the SDLC during every project. Skipping any of the phases is sure to lead to system failure.

Failure to Manage Project Scope

As the project progresses, the project manager must track the status of each activity and adjust the project plan if an activity is added or taking longer than expected. Scope creep occurs when the scope of the project increases. Feature creep occurs when developers add extra features that were not part of the initial requirements. Scope creep and feature creep are difficult to manage and can easily cause a project to fall behind schedule.

Failure to Manage Project Plan

Managing the project plan is one of the biggest challenges during systems development. The project plan is the road map the organization follows during the development of the system. Developing the initial project plan is the easiest part of the project manager's job. Managing and revising the project plan is the hard part. The project plan is a living document since it changes almost daily on any project. Failing to monitor, revise, and update the project plan can lead to project failure.

Changing Technology

Many real-world projects have hundreds of business requirements, take years to complete, and cost millions of dollars. Gordon Moore, co-founder of Intel Corporation, observed in 1965 that chip density doubles every 18 months. This observation, known as Moore's law, simply means that memory sizes, processor power, and so on, all follow the same pattern and roughly double in capacity every 18 months. As Moore's law states, technology changes at an incredibly fast pace; therefore, it is possible to have to revise an entire project plan in the middle of a project as a result of a change in technology. Technology changes so fast that it is almost impossible to deliver an information system without feeling the pain of changing technology.

HP's Software Problems

6. Describe the different types of feasibility studies and explain how HP could use a technical feasibility study to avoid software development failure.

7. Review the buy versus build decision and explain why HP chose to buy its ERP system.

8. Why is testing critical to HP's software development process?

9. Identify the primary reasons for software project failure and explain which ones HP experienced on its ERP build.

Agile methodology 347
Analysis phase 344
Business requirement 344
Change control board
(CCB) 360
Change management
system 360
Commercial off-the shelf
(COTS) 353
Computer-aided software
engineering (CASE) 353
Critical success factor
(CSF) 350
Data flow diagram (DFD) 353
Data model 355
Design phase 344
Development phase 344

Entity relationship diagram
(ERD) 355
Extreme programming (XP)
methodology 346
Feasibility study 351
Feature creep 348
Graphical user interface
(GUI) 355
Help desk 359
Implementation phase 344
Joint application development
(JAD) 352
Maintenance 359
Maintenance phase 344
Modeling 354
Online training 359
Planning phase 343

Process modeling 353
Prototype 346
Rapid application development
(RAD) (rapid prototyping)
methodology 345
Requirements definition
document 352
Scope creep 348
Sign-off 352
Systems development life cycle
(SDLC) 343
Test condition 357
Testing phase 344
User documentation 358
Waterfall methodology 344
Workshop training 359

Disaster at Denver International Airport

One good way to learn how to develop successful systems is to review past failures. One of the most infamous system failures is Denver International Airport's (DIA) baggage system. When the automated baggage system design for DIA was introduced, it was hailed as the savior of modern airport design. The design relied on a network of 300 computers to route bags and 4,000 telecars to carry luggage across 21 miles of track. Laser scanners were to read bar-coded luggage tags, while advanced scanners tracked the movement of toboggan-like baggage carts.

When DIA finally opened its doors for reporters to witness its revolutionary baggage handling system the scene was rather unpleasant. Bags were chewed up, lost, and misrouted in what has since became a legendary systems nightmare.

One of the biggest mistakes made in the baggage handling system fiasco was that not enough time was allowed to properly develop the system. In the beginning of the project, DIA assumed it was the responsibility of individual airlines to find their own way of moving the baggage from the plane to the baggage claim area. The automated baggage system was not involved in the initial planning of the DIA project. By the time the developers of DIA decided to create an integrated baggage system, the time frame for designing and implementing such a complex and huge system was not possible.

Another common mistake that occurred during the project was that the airlines kept changing their business requirements. This caused numerous issues including the implementation of power supplies that were not properly updated for the revised system design, which caused overloaded motors and mechanical failures. Besides the power supplies design problem, the optical sensors did not read the bar codes correctly, causing issues with baggage routing.

Finally, BAE, the company that designed and implemented the automated baggage system for DIA, had never created a baggage system of this size before. BAE had created a similar system in an airport in Munich, Germany, where the scope was much smaller. Essentially, the baggage system had an inadequate IT infrastructure since it was designed for a much smaller system.

DIA simply could not open without a functional baggage system so the city had no choice but to delay the opening date for over 16 months, costing taxpayers roughly $1 million per day, which totaled around $500 million.[16]

Questions

1. One of the problems with DIA's baggage system was inadequate testing. What types of tests could DIA have used to help ensure its baggage system's success?

2. Evaluate the different implementation approaches. Which one would have most significantly increased the chances of the project's success?

3. Explain the cost of finding errors. How could more time spent in the analysis and design phase have saved Colorado taxpayers hundreds of millions of dollars?

4. Why could BAE not take an existing IT infrastructure and simply increase its scale and expect it to work?

Reducing Ambiguity in Business Requirements

The number one reason projects fail is bad business requirements. Business requirements are considered "bad" because of ambiguity or insufficient involvement of end users during analysis and design.

A requirement is unambiguous if it has the same interpretation for all parties. Different interpretations by different participants will usually result in unmet expectations. Here is an example of an ambiguous requirement and an example of an unambiguous requirement:

- Ambiguous requirement: The financial report must show profits in local and U.S. currencies.
- Unambiguous requirement: The financial report must show profits in local and U.S. currencies using the exchange rate printed in *The Wall Street Journal* for the last business day of the period being reported.

Ambiguity is impossible to prevent completely because it is introduced into requirements in natural ways. For example:

- Requirements can contain technical implications that are obvious to the IT developers but not to the customers.
- Requirements can contain business implications that are obvious to the customer but not to the IT developers.
- Requirements may contain everyday words whose meanings are "obvious" to everyone, yet different for everyone.
- Requirements are reflections of detailed explanations that may have included multiple events, multiple perspectives, verbal rephrasing, emotion, iterative refinement, selective emphasis, and body language—none of which are captured in the written statements.

Tips for Reviewing Business Requirements

When reviewing business requirements always look for the following words to help dramatically reduce ambiguity:

- *And* and *or* have well-defined meanings and ought to be completely unambiguous, yet they are often understood only informally and interpreted inconsistently. For example, consider the statement "The alarm must ring if button T is pressed and if button F is pressed." This statement may be intended to mean that to ring the alarm, both buttons must be pressed or it may be intended to mean that either one can be pressed. A statement like this should never appear in a requirement because the potential for misinterpretation is too great. A preferable approach is to be very explicit, for example, "The alarm must ring if both buttons T and F are pressed simultaneously. The alarm should not ring in any other circumstance."
- *Always* might really mean "most of the time," in which case it should be made more explicit. For example, the statement "We always run reports A and B together" could be challenged with "In other words, there is never any circumstance where you would run A without B and B without A?" If you build a system with an "always" requirement, then you are actually building the system to never run report A without report B. If a user suddenly wants report B without report A, you will need to make significant system changes.
- *Never* might mean rarely, in which case it should be made more explicit. For example, the statement "We never run reports A and B in the same month" could be challenged

with, "So that means that if I see that A has been run, I can be absolutely certain that no one will want to run B." Again, if you build a system that supports a "never" requirement, then the system users can never perform that requirement. For example, the system would never allow a user to run reports A and B in the same month, no matter what the circumstances.

- Boundary conditions are statements about the line between true and false and do and do not. These statements may or may not be meant to include end points. For example, "We want to use method X when there are up to 10 pages, but method Y otherwise." If you were building this system, would you include page 10 in method X or in method Y? The answer to this question will vary causing an ambiguous business requirement.[17]

Questions

1. Why are ambiguous business requirements the leading cause of system development failures?

2. Why do the words *and* and *or* tend to lead to ambiguous requirements?

3. Research the Web and determine other reasons for "bad" business requirements.

4. What is wrong with the following business requirement: "The system must support employee birthdays since every employee always has a birthday every year."

Gearing Up at REI

Recreational Equipment Inc. (REI) boasts annual revenues between $500 million and $1 billion and more than 10,000 employees. According to Forrester Research, REI is an industry leader for its "best practice" multichannel CRM strategy, which allows customers to seamlessly purchase products at the company's 70 retail stores as well as by telephone, through mail order, and on the Internet.

REI's Internet Strategy

To boost in-store sales, REI developed a comprehensive Internet strategy. In June 2003, REI .com launched free in-store pickup for customers who ordered online. The belief was that people who visit stores to collect their online purchases might spend more money upon seeing the colorful displays of clothing, climbing gear, bikes, and camping equipment.

REI's strategy paid off. "One out of every three people who buy something online will spend an additional $90 in the store when they come to pick something up," said Joan Broughton, REI's vice president of multichannel programs. That tendency translated into a healthy 1 percent increase in store sales. Broughton's motto is "a sale is a sale is a sale—whether online, in stores, or through catalogs." The Internet is not an isolated channel with its own operational metrics or exclusive customer group.

As the Web has matured as a retail channel, consumers have turned to online shopping as an additional place to interact with a retailer rather than as a replacement for existing channels such as stores or catalogs. According to Jupiter Research, while its prediction of $117 billion in online sales for 2008 represents only 5 percent of total retail sales, the company estimates that 30 percent of off-line sales will be influenced by consumers' online research. Essentially, that means retailers will need to leverage their online properties in ways that are synergistic with and complementary to their offline operations.

REI's CRM Strategy

REI.com was one of the first companies to offer a broad selection of outdoor gear plus expert advice and in-depth information about outdoor products and recreation online. The highly successful Web site currently receives over 2.5 million visitors per day, and online sales represent 15 percent of REI's total sales revenue.

REI realized it could provide a consistent and seamless customer experience whether the customer is shopping via its Web site or at its in-store kiosks by consolidating its four disparate database systems into one customer relationship management system. The system integrates multiple sales channels to manage mail orders, in-store special orders, kiosk operations, and REI Adventures, the company's adventure travel service. This gives the company a complete view of all customers regardless of their shopping preference. In addition to finding items such as backpacks, bicycles, or tents through the system, customers can also research hiking trails, camping guides, and cycling techniques.

The system is providing REI with the confidence it needs to expand customer service, such as the new REI store pickup. REI has also expanded its multichannel philosophy to include services. In February 2004, the company launched an integrated gift registry that allows people to set up lists for gifts that can be purchased in any retail channel. The registry also allows consumers to post messages to other site visitors, seeking information or specific, hard-to-find products. Customers can create a gift registry in several ways: Visit a store and use a kiosk or scan products with a handheld device, call customer service, or visit REI.com. Once a registry is set up, REI sends an e-mail to a designated list of recipients, complete with a link to a personalized registry page. According to Brad Brown, REI's vice president of information services, the registry is a way to expand sales among consumers who do not traditionally shop at REI.

REI's SCM Strategy

REI offers free in-store pickup for online orders as a strategy specifically designed to get people into the stores. To make that strategy as cost-efficient as possible, the company uses the same trucks that restock its stores to fulfill online orders slated for in-store pickup. To do this, REI had to integrate order information from its Web site and replenishment orders from its stores.

Integrating the two types of order information was not complex, Brown said. What was difficult, however, was coordinating fulfillment of both online and replenishment orders because "orders placed on the Web [by customers] are nothing like replenishment orders that stores place," he said. Online orders are picked from the warehouse at the time of the order and then put in a queue until the appropriate truck is loaded, whereas store orders are picked by an automated replenishment system that typically picks orders at one time based on either a weekly or biweekly replenishment schedule.

To make in-store pickup a reality, Brown's group wrote a "promise algorithm" that informs customers of a delivery date when they place an online order. Timing can get tricky when orders are placed the day before a truck is scheduled to depart the warehouse with a store-replenishment delivery. For example, if an online order is placed on a Monday night and a truck is scheduled to depart Tuesday morning, the system promises the customer a pickup date of a week later, as if the order would be placed on the following week's truck. However, REI will shoot for fulfilling the order that night; if it can do it, REI (and, ultimately, the customer) is happy because the order arrives sooner than was promised.

Creating effective business-to-consumer retail Web sites entails more than simply calculating sales figures; it also involves multiple projects and delivering the functionality that users expect while mitigating risk and change.[18]

Questions

1. What business benefits did REI receive by developing its successful CRM system?
2. Identify the potential issues facing REI if it failed to implement a successful SCM system.
3. List and describe the seven phases of the SDLC and rank them in order of importance to REI's system development efforts.
4. Summarize the different software development methodologies and recommend one for REI to follow.
5. Describe the analysis phase of systems development along with its importance for successful system development efforts for REI.
6. Explain the importance of the testing phase along with three different tests REI should perform on each new system.

1. Selecting a systems development methodology

Exus Incorporated is an international billing outsourcing company. Exus currently has revenues of $5 billion, over 3,500 employees, and operations on every continent. You have recently been hired as the CIO. Your first task is to increase the software development project success rate, which is currently at 20 percent. To ensure that future software development projects are successful, you want to standardize the systems development methodology across the entire enterprise. Currently, each project determines which methodology it uses to develop software.

Create a report detailing three additional system development methodologies that were not covered in this text. Compare each of these methodologies to the traditional waterfall approach. Finally, recommend which methodology you want to implement as your organizational standard. Be sure to highlight any potential roadblocks you might encounter when implementing the new standard methodology.

2. Understanding project failure

You are the director of project management for Stello, a global manufacturer of high-end writing instruments. The company sells to primarily high-end customers, and the average price for one of its fine writing instruments is about $350. You are currently implementing a new customer relationship management system and you want to do everything you can to ensure a successful systems development effort. Create a document summarizing the five primary reasons why this project could fail, along with your strategy to eliminate the possibility of system development failure on your project.

3. Missing phases in the systems development life cycle

Hello Inc. is a large concierge service for executives operating in Chicago, San Francisco, and New York. The company performs all kinds of services from dog walking to airport transportation. Your manager, Dan Martello, wants to skip the testing phase during the company's financial ERP implementation. Dan feels that since the system came from a vendor it should work correctly. To meet the project's looming deadline he wants to skip the testing phase. Draft a memo explaining to Dan the importance of following the SDLC and the ramifications to the business if the financial system is not tested.

4. Refusing to sign off

You are the primary client on a large extranet development project. After carefully reviewing the requirements definition document, you are positive that there are missing, ambiguous, inaccurate, and unclear requirements. The project manager is pressuring you for your sign-off since he has already received sign-off from five of your co-workers. If you fail to sign off on the requirements, you are going to put the entire project at risk since the time frame is nonnegotiable. What would you do? Why?

5. Saving failing systems

Crik Candle Company manufactures low-end candles for restaurants. The company generates over $40 million in annual revenues and has more than 300 employees. You are in the middle of a large multimillion-dollar supply chain management implementation. Your project manager has just come to you with the information that the project might fail for the following reasons:

- Several business requirements were incorrect and the scope has to be doubled.
- Three developers recently quit.

■ The deadline has been moved up a month.

Develop a list of options that your company can follow to ensure the project remains on schedule and within budget.

6. **Feasibility studies**

John Lancert is the new managing operations director for a large construction company, LMC. John is currently looking for an associate who can help him prioritize the 60 proposed company projects. You are interested in working with John and have decided to apply for the job. John has asked you to compile a report detailing why project prioritization is critical for LMC, along with the different types of feasibility studies you would recommend that LMC use when determining which projects to pursue.

Project Management and Outsourcing

12

SECTION 12.1
Project Management

- Project Management
- Project Management Fundamentals
- Change Management Fundamentals
- Risk Management Fundamentals

SECTION 12.2
Outsourcing

- Outsourcing
- The Outsourcing Phenomenon
- Outsourcing Options
- Offshore Outsourcing
- The Challenges of Outsourcing
- Future Outsourcing Trends

Change at Toyota

At Toyota Motor Sales USA's headquarters in Torrance, California, a circular patch of manicured earth separates the IS building and corporate headquarters. A brook winds its way through lush flowers and pine trees, and a terraced path connects the two buildings. For many years, this was about the only thing the two groups shared with each other.

For the business executives at Toyota Motor Sales (TMS) peering across the courtyard at the Data building, the deep black windows were a symbol of IS's opacity. These executives felt that IS was unresponsive, and they had little clue where the money was going. "One of the complaints was that we spent a lot of money on IT projects, and the business was frequently disappointed with the results," recalled Bob Daly, group vice president of Toyota Customer Services. Daly says badly handled projects, such as a delayed PeopleSoft ERP implementation and a protracted parts inventory initiative, led to finger-pointing between the two factions.

Meanwhile, behind the darkened windows of the Data building, CIO Barbra Cooper's IS staff was buried under the weight of six enterprisewide projects. Called the Big Six, they included a new extranet for Toyota dealers and the PeopleSoft ERP rollout, as well as four new systems for order management, parts forecasting, advanced warranty, and financial document management. Feeling besieged, the IS group made the mistake of not explaining to the business side all the things it was doing and how much it all cost. It was a classic case of mismanaged expectations and fractured alignment.

By late 2002, Cooper realized that if she wanted to win back the respect of the business managers—and remain in her post—she would have to make some radical changes. A conversation with the Toyota Motor Sales CEO, in which he questioned the sharp incline of IS's spending curve, stopped her in her tracks. In her 30 years in IT, Cooper had developed something of a reputation for coming in to clean up other CIO's messes. Now, she had to take a long look in the mirror and fix herself.

Cooper's Path to Success

Cooper could no longer ignore the rumblings from across the courtyard that had worked their way into the rank-and-file business staff. To them, IS had become an unresponsive, bureaucratic machine.

Cooper started soliciting informal feedback from a wide range of businesspeople. What she discovered was an accumulation of "very painful projects for both IT and the business," she said. "Clearly there was not enough communication and education on our part."

In late 2002, Cooper hired an outside consultancy to interview TMS's top 20 executives. She wanted their honest opinions of how IS was doing. The results did not provide all the answers to the ailments, but she certainly saw the trouble spots. "Parts of the survey results were stinging," Cooper said. "But you can't be a CIO and not face that."

Cooper spent many introspective weeks in 2003 formulating her vision for a new IT department. What she developed was a strategy for a decentralized and transparent IS organization that focused all of its energy on the major business segments. In the summer of 2003, she presented her vision to her senior IS staffers. Some of the managers were excited by the prospect of change; others were less so.

The first thing Cooper did was set up the Toyota Value Action Program, a team of eight staffers responsible for translating her vision into actionable items for the department and her direct reports. Using the survey results and Cooper's direction, the team winnowed the list to 18 initiatives, including increasing employee training and development, gaining cost savings, making process improvements, ridding IS of inefficiencies, and implementing a metrics program. Each initiative got a project owner and a team. Cooper insisted that each initiative have a mechanism to check its success. The most significant initiative called for improved alignment with the business side. At the heart of this new effort would be a revamped Office of the CIO structure—with new roles, reporting lines, and responsibilities.

As part of the rehaul, Cooper took top-flight personnel out of the Data building and embedded them as divisional information officers, or DIOs, in all of the business units. These DIOs are accountable for IT strategy, development, and services, and they sit on the management committees headed by top business executives. The DIOs' goal is to forge relationships with tier-one executives and executives at the vice president level.

The DIOs were not alone. Business operation managers and relationship managers from IS sat alongside the business folks. "I still believe in managing IT centrally, but it was incumbent on us to physically distribute IT into the businesses," Cooper said. "They could provide more local attention while keeping the enterprise vision alive."

Cooper upended the structure of Toyota's IS department in six months in a bid to weave IT functions more closely into the daily business operations. The process was painful: She changed IS employees' jobs, exposed all of IS's shortcomings, and forced her staff into the business offices. Just over a year into the new plan, IS and the business were standing shoulder-to-shoulder when planning and implementing IT projects. And Cooper is still CIO of Toyota Motor Sales.

A Little Kicking and Screaming

Change can be scary for anyone, especially during an upheaval of an entire 400-person IS department. Cooper changed the jobs of 50 percent of her staffers within six months, yet no one left or was let go. Some took on new responsibilities; others took on expanded or new roles. Cooper said some mid- and upper-level staffers were initially uncomfortable with their new roles, but she spent a lot of time fostering a new attitude about the change. "I dragged them into the conversations kicking and screaming," Cooper said. "But I said to them, 'Unless you think of what it means to change on this level, you will never make it happen.'" The key, Cooper said, is that all IS staffers were brought into the development of the new organization early.[1]

INTRODUCTION

No one would think of building an office complex by turning loose 100 different construction teams to build 100 different rooms, with no single blueprint or agreed-upon vision of the completed structure. Yet this is precisely the situation in which many large organizations find themselves when managing information technology projects. Organizations routinely overschedule their resources (human and otherwise), develop redundant projects, and damage profitability by investing in nonstrategic efforts that do not contribute to the organization's bottom line. Project management offers a strategic framework for coordinating the numerous activities associated with organizational projects.

Business leaders face a rapidly moving and unforgiving global marketplace that will force them to use every possible tool to sustain competitiveness. A good project manager understands not only the fundamentals of project management, but also how to effectively deal with change management and risk management. This chapter explores project management, change management, risk management, and outsourcing in detail.[2]

---

section 12.1 PROJECT MANAGEMENT

LEARNING OUTCOMES

12.1. Describe the three primary activities performed by a project manager.

12.2. Describe the three common techniques an organization can use to select good projects.

12.3. List and describe the characteristics of a well-defined project plan.

12.4. Explain change management and how an organization can prepare for change.

12.5. Explain risk management and how an organization can mitigate risk.

12.6. Summarize the strategies a project manager can use to ensure a successful project.

PROJECT MANAGEMENT

A *project* is a temporary endeavor undertaken to create a unique product or service. According to the Project Management Institute, *project management* is the application of knowledge, skills, tools, and techniques to project activities in order to meet or exceed stakeholder needs and expectations from a project. *Project management software* specifically supports the long-term and day-to-day management and execution of the steps in a project (such as building a new warehouse or designing and implementing a new IT system).

Project management is essential to the success of almost every aspect of IT. Without it, projects tend to be delayed, over budget, and often never reach completion. Horizon Blue Cross Blue Shield of New Jersey, a $6 billion-plus health insurance provider, allocated several hundred million dollars to IT over a five-year period to tackle tasks such as consolidating five enterprise software platforms, managing compliance with regulatory offices, and simplifying new product development. These IT initiatives involve hundreds of skilled people working on hundreds of concurrently developing projects. Horizon's executives needed to gain visibility into all projects, subsets of projects, and existing and planned projects collectively. The company considered a rigorous and formalized project management strategy fundamental to the project's success.

Horizon decided to implement IT project management software from Business Engine Inc. to manage its projects. The software collects information through standardized templates created for Microsoft Project, which are stored in an enterprise database, and then fed into Business Engine's analytical tool, called Ben. Each user

FIGURE 12.1

Project Management
Interdependent
Variables

can then view and manipulate spreadsheets and graphs, share documents, track revisions, and run what-if scenarios in their personalized digital dashboard view. With the help from Business Engine, Horizon is managing IT projects and assets as if they were investments, tracking their performance against business goals, assessing their individual return and value to the company, and helping sort out which projects require greater attention and resources and which require reduced attention and resources. Horizon found itself ahead of schedule on over 70 percent of its IT projects.[3]

Figure 12.1 displays the relationships between the three primary variables in any project—(1) time, (2) cost, and (3) scope. These three variables are interdependent. For example, decreasing a project's time frame means either increasing the cost of the project or decreasing the scope of the project to meet the new deadline. Increasing a project's scope means either increasing the project's time frame or increasing the project's cost—or both—to meet the increased scope changes. Project management is the science of making intelligent trade-offs between time, cost, and scope. All three of the factors combined determine a project's quality.

Benjamin Franklin's timeless advice—by failing to prepare, you prepare to fail—especially applies to many of today's software development projects. A recent survey concluded that the failure rate of IT projects is much higher in organizations that do not exercise disciplined project management. Figure 12.2 displays the top

FIGURE 12.2

Why IT Projects Fall
Behind Schedule
or Fail

FIGURE 12.3

Expected Growth
for Project
Management
Software

Annual Sales of Project Management Tools

six reasons why IT projects fail according to *Information Week's* research survey of 150 IT managers.

A successful project is typically on time, within budget, meets the business's requirements, and fulfills the customer's needs. The Hackett Group, an Atlanta-based consultancy, analyzed its client database (which includes 2,000 companies, including 81 Fortune 100 companies) and discovered:

- Three in 10 major IT projects fail.
- 21 percent of the companies state that they cannot adjust rapidly to market changes.
- One in four validate a business case for IT projects after completion.[4]

Nicolas Dubuc, collaborative project manager at Rhodia Inc., a $6 billion worldwide manufacturer of specialty chemicals, uses Microsoft's software to develop project management templates and methodologies for its 18 divisions. "We're designing a platform for rapid application development that will enhance opportunities for innovation," Dubuc said.

Today, the leaders in the project management software market include Microsoft, Primavera, Oracle, and SAP. Microsoft Project is the core project management tool for many organizations and dominates with more than 8 million users and over 80 percent of the market share. Figure 12.3 displays the expected growth for project management software over the next few years. If an organization wants to deliver successful, high-quality software on time and under budget, it must take advantage of project management software.

PROJECT MANAGEMENT FUNDAMENTALS

Project deliverables are any measurable, tangible, verifiable outcome, result, or item that is produced to complete a project or part of a project. Examples of project deliverables include design documents, testing scripts, and requirements documents. *Project milestones* represent key dates when a certain group of activities must be performed. For example, completing the planning phase might be a project milestone. If a project milestone is missed, then chances are the project is experiencing problems. A *project manager* is an individual who is an expert in project planning and management, defines and develops the project plan, and tracks the plan to ensure all key project milestones are completed on time. The art and science of project

FIGURE 12.4

Project Management
Roles

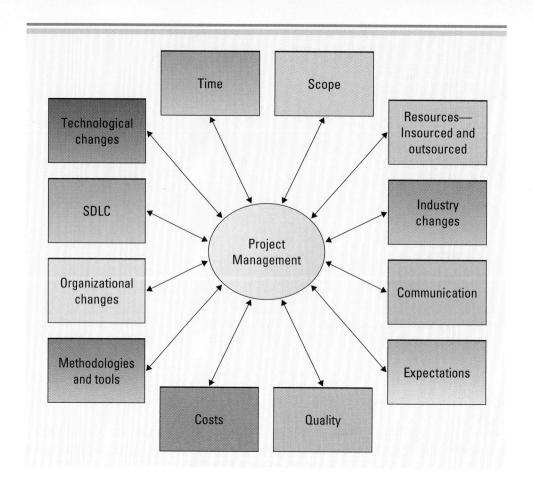

management must coordinate numerous activities as displayed in Figure 12.4. Project managers perform numerous activities, and three of these primary activities are:

1. Choosing strategic projects.
2. Setting the project scope.
3. Managing resources and maintaining the project plan.

Choosing Strategic Projects

Calpine Corp., a large energy producer, uses project management software to look at its IT investments from a business perspective. The company classifies projects in one of three ways: (1) run the business, (2) grow the business, and (3) transform the business. Calpine splits its $100 million in assets accordingly: 60 percent for running the business, 20 percent for growing the business, and 20 percent for transforming the business. Calpine evaluates each of its 30 to 35 active projects for perceived business value against project costs. For the company to pursue a project it must pass a return on investment (ROI) hurdle. A business project must minimally provide two times ROI, and a transformation project must provide five times ROI.[5]

One of the most difficult decisions organizations make is determining the projects in which to invest time, energy, and resources. An organization must identify what it wants to do and how it is going to do it. The "what" part of this question focuses on issues such as justification for the project, definition of the project, and expected results of the project. The "how" part of the question deals with issues such as project approach, project schedule, and analysis of project risks. Determining which projects to focus corporate efforts on is as necessary to projects as each project is to an organization. Figure 12.5 displays the three common techniques an organization can use to select projects.

Before its merger with Hewlett-Packard, Compaq decided to analyze and prioritize its system development projects. Knowing that the CIO wanted to be able to

FIGURE 12.5

Techniques for Choosing
Strategic Projects

Techniques for Choosing Strategic Projects

1. **Focus on organizational goals**—Managers are finding tremendous value in choosing projects that align with the organization's goals. Projects that address organizational goals tend to have a higher success rate since they are important to the entire organization.

2. **Categorize projects**—There are various categories that an organization can group projects into to determine a project's priority. One type of categorization includes problem, opportunity, and directives. Problems are undesirable situations that prevent an organization from achieving its goals. Opportunities are chances to improve the organization. Directives are new requirements imposed by management, government, or some other external influence. It is often easier to obtain approval for projects that address problems or directives because the organization must respond to these categories to avoid financial losses.

3. **Perform a financial analysis**—A number of different financial analysis techniques can be performed to help determine a project's priority. A few of these include net present value, return on investment, and payback analysis. These financial analysis techniques help determine the organization's financial expectations for the project.

view every project, project management leaders quickly identified and removed nonstrategic projects. At the end of the review process, the company canceled 39 projects, saving the organization $15 million. Most Fortune 100 companies are receiving bottom-line benefits similar to Compaq's from implementing a project management solution.[6]

Organizations also need to choose and prioritize projects in such a way that they can make responsible decisions as to which projects to eliminate. Jim Johnson, chairman of the Standish Group, a Massachusetts-based consultancy, has identified project management as the process that can make the difference in project success. According to Johnson, "Companies need a process for taking a regular look at their projects and deciding, again and again, if the investment is going to pay off. As it stands now, for most companies, projects can take on a life of their own."[7]

An organization must build in continuous self-assessment, which allows earlier termination decisions on failing projects, with the associated cost savings. This frees capital and personnel for dedication to projects that are worth pursuing. The elimination of a project should be viewed as successful resource management, not as an admission of failure.

Setting the Project Scope

Once an organization defines the projects it wants to pursue, it must set the project scope. **Project scope** defines the work that must be completed to deliver a product with the specified features and functions. The project scope statement is important because it specifies clear project boundaries. The project scope typically includes the following:

- **Project product**—a description of the characteristics the product or service has undertaken.
- **Project objectives**—quantifiable criteria that must be met for the project to be considered a success.
- **Project deliverables**—any measurable, tangible, verifiable outcome, result, or item that is produced to complete a project or part of a project.
- **Project exclusions**—products, services, or processes that are not specifically a part of the project.

The project objectives are one of the most important areas to define because they are essentially the major elements of the project. When an organization achieves the project objectives, it has accomplished the major goals of the project and the project scope is satisfied. Project objectives must include metrics so that the

FIGURE 12.6

SMART Criteria for
Successful Objective
Creation

- Specific
- Measurable
- Agreed upon
- Realistic
- Time framed

project's success can be measured. The metrics can include cost, schedule, and quality metrics along with a number of other metrics. Figure 12.6 displays the SMART criteria—useful reminders on how to ensure that the project has created understandable and measurable objectives.

Managing Resources and Maintaining the Project Plan

Managing people is one of the hardest and most critical efforts a project manager undertakes. How to resolve conflicts within the team and how to balance the needs of the project with the personal/professional needs of the team are a few of the challenges facing project managers. More and more project managers are the main (and sometimes sole) interface with the client during the project. As such, communication, negotiation, marketing, and salesmanship are just as important to the project manager as financial and analytical acumen. There are many times when the people management side of project management made the difference in pulling off a successful project. A ***project plan*** is a formal, approved document that manages and controls project execution. Figure 12.7 displays the characteristics of a well-defined project plan.

The most important part of the plan is communication. The project manager must communicate the plan to every member of the project team and to any key stakeholders and executives. The project plan must also include any project assumptions and be detailed enough to guide the execution of the project. A key to achieving project success is earning consensus and buy-in from all key stakeholders. By including key stakeholders in project plan development, the project manager allows them to have ownership of the plan. This often translates to greater commitment, which in turn results in enhanced motivation and productivity.

The two primary diagrams most frequently used in project planning are PERT and Gantt charts. A ***PERT (Program Evaluation and Review Technique) chart*** is a graphical network model that depicts a project's tasks and the relationships between those tasks. A ***dependency*** is a logical relationship that exists between the project tasks, or between a project task and a milestone. PERT charts define dependency between project tasks before those tasks are scheduled (see Figure 12.8). The boxes in Figure 12.8 represent project tasks, and the project manager can adjust the contents of the boxes to display various project attributes such as schedule and actual start and finish times. The arrows indicate that one task is dependent on the

FIGURE 12.7

Project Plan
Characteristics

Characteristics of a Well-Defined Project Plan
Easy to understand
Easy to read
Communicated to all key participants (key stakeholders)
Appropriate to the project's size, complexity, and criticality
Prepared by the team, rather than by the individual project manager

FIGURE 12.8

PERT Chart Expert,
a PERT Chart Example

start or completion of another task. The **critical path** is a path from the start to the finish that passes through all the tasks that are critical to completing the project in the shortest amount of time. PERT charts frequently display a project's critical path.

A **Gantt chart** is a simple bar chart that depicts project tasks against a calendar. In a Gantt chart, tasks are listed vertically and the project's time frame is listed horizontally. A Gantt chart works well for representing the project schedule. It also shows actual progress of tasks against the planned duration. Figure 12.9 displays a software development project using a Gantt chart.

CHANGE MANAGEMENT FUNDAMENTALS

Snap-on, a maker of tools and equipment for specialists such as car mechanics, is successful at managing change. The company recently increased profits by 12 percent while sales were down 6.7 percent. Dennis Leitner, vice president of IT, runs the IT group on a day-to-day basis and leads the implementation of all major software development initiatives. Each software development initiative is managed by both the business and IT. In fact, business resources are on the IT group's payroll, and they spend as much as 80 percent of their time learning what a business unit is doing and how IT can help make it happen. Leitner's role focuses primarily on strategic planning, change management, and setting up metrics to track performance.[8]

Dynamic organizational change is inevitable and an organization must effectively manage change as it evolves. With the numerous challenges and complexities that organizations face in today's rapidly changing environment, effective change management thus becomes a critical core competency. **Change management** is a set of techniques that aid in evolution, composition, and policy management of the design and implementation of a system. Figure 12.10 displays a few of the more common reasons change occurs.

A **change management system** includes a collection of procedures to document a change request and define the steps necessary to consider the change based on

FIGURE 12.9

Microsoft Project, a
Gantt Chart Example

FIGURE 12.10

Common Reasons
Why Change Occurs

Common Reasons Change Occurs

1. An omission in defining initial scope

2. A misunderstanding of the initial scope

3. An external event such as government regulations that create new requirements

4. Organizational changes, such as mergers, acquisitions, and partnerships, that create new business problems and opportunities

5. Availability of better technology

6. Shifts in planned technology that force unexpected and significant changes to the business organization, culture, and/or processes

7. The users or management simply wanting the system to do more than they originally requested or agreed to

8. Management reducing the funding for the project or imposing an earlier deadline

the expected impact of the change. Most change management systems require that a change request form be initiated by one or more project stakeholders (systems owners, users, customers, analysts, developers). Ideally, these change requests are considered by a ***change control board (CCB)*** that is responsible for approving or rejecting all change requests. The CCB's composition typically includes a representative from each business area that has a stake in the project. The CCB's decision to accept or reject each change is based on an impact analysis of the change. For example, if one department wants to implement a change to the software that will increase both deployment time and cost, then the other business owners need to agree that the change is valid and that it warrants the extended time frame and increased budget.

FIGURE 12.11

Three Important
Guidelines for
Effective Change
Management

Three Important Guidelines for Effectively Dealing with Change Management
1. **Institute change management polices**—Create clearly defined policies and procedures that must be followed each time a request for change is received.
2. **Anticipate change**—View change as an opportunity and embrace it.
3. **Seek change**—Every 6 to 12 months look for changes that may be windows of opportunity. Review successes and failures to determine if there are any opportunities for innovation.

Preparing for Change

Change is an opportunity, not a threat. Realizing that change is the norm rather than the exception will help an organization stay ahead. Becoming a change leader and accepting the inevitability of change can help ensure that an organization can survive and even thrive in times of change. Figure 12.11 displays the three important guidelines change leaders can follow to make change effective both inside and outside their organizations.

General Electric has successfully tackled change management through an innovative program trademarked "Work Out." Work Out is shorthand for the idea of taking excess work out of the system. The purpose is to eliminate bureaucracy and free people's time for more productive activities. The positive time-saving and productivity-enhancing results of the Work Out change management program include:

- **Reports**: Teams calculated the time it took to prepare routine reports and compared it with the value generated from the reports. It quickly became apparent that much more effort went into preparing the reports than their comparative value to the recipients warranted. Valuable time was freed when those reports were eliminated or scaled back.

- **Approvals**: The approval process was questioned and adjusted accordingly. One instance discovered that a simple purchase order request required 12 approval signatures.

- **Meetings**: Teams evaluated the need for meetings and changed the way they were conducted to take advantage of technologies such as teleconferencing.[9]

Change, whether it comes in the form of a crisis, a market shift, or a technological development, is challenging for all organizations. Successful organizations and successful people learn to anticipate and react appropriately to change.

RISK MANAGEMENT FUNDAMENTALS

Altria Group, Inc., the tobacco and food-products conglomerate, has a well-defined process for choosing projects based on project risk. The company gathers project information such as cash flow, return on investment, interfaces, and regulatory-compliance issues and creates a risk-based score of each project. The company then plots them on a grid with risk on the horizontal axis and value on the vertical axis. Managers then choose projects based on an optimal balance of risk and return.[10]

Project risk is an uncertain event or condition that, if it occurs, has a positive or negative effect on a project objective(s). ***Risk management*** is the process of proactive and ongoing identification, analysis, and response to risk factors. The best place to address project risk is during the project plan creation. Elements of risk management are outlined in Figure 12.12.

Risks vary throughout a project and in general are more significant at the later phases of a project. Figure 12.13 displays risk factors that may not be immediately obvious and are often the root causes of IT project success or failure.

FIGURE 12.12

Elements of Risk
Management

Elements of Risk Management
Risk identification—Determining which risks might affect the project and documenting their characteristics
Qualitative risk analysis—Performing a qualitative analysis of risks and conditions to prioritize their effects on project objectives
Quantitative risk analysis—Measuring the probability and consequences of risks as well as estimating their implications for the project objectives
Risk response planning—Developing procedures and techniques to enhance opportunities and reduce threats to the project's objectives

FIGURE 12.13

Common Project
Risk Factors

Common Project Risk Factors
Changing business circumstances that undermine expected benefits
Reluctance to report negative information or to "blow the whistle" on a project
Significant change management issues including resistance to change
The rush to get a project done quickly, often compromising the end result and desired outcome
Executives who are strongly wedded to a project and unwilling to admit that it may have been a mistake
A common tendency in IT projects to overengineer technology solutions, stemming from a belief in the superiority of technical solutions over simpler, people-based solutions
Building the project plan in conjunction with the budget or to validate some basic assumptions about the project's fiscal requirements and business base payback calculations

Mitigating Risk

An organization must devise strategies to reduce or mitigate risk. A wide range of strategies can be applied, with each risk category necessitating different mitigation strategies. When considering risk mitigation, the importance of choice, opportunities, and inexactitude should be kept clearly in mind. Organizations should take several actions at the enterprise level to improve risk management capabilities; these are displayed in Figure 12.14.

FIGURE 12.14

Actions to Improve Risk
Management Capabilities

Actions to Improve Risk Management Capabilities
Promote project leadership skills—Hire individuals with strong project management and project leadership skills as well as business management skills. These individuals can be extremely helpful in advisory and steering committee roles as well as coaching roles.
Learn from previous experience—Over many years of collective experiences, organizations have encountered hundreds of large IT projects. Document and revisit development methodologies, software tools, and software development best practices in order to share this vital information across the organization.
Share knowledge—Working in team or group environments tends to yield the most successful projects since individuals can share their unique learning experiences.
Create a project management culture—Orient people from day one on the importance of project management, change management, and risk management. Be sure to measure and reward project management skills and promote individuals based on successful projects.

Audit and tax firm KPMG LLP and software maker SeeCommerce unveiled a service, called SeeRisk, to help companies assess supply chain management risk. SeeRisk helps a company establish common metrics and measure performance against them by identifying operational problems and risks. The SeeRisk system is integrated with operational and transactional systems along with external vendor systems. The goal of the system is to improve revenue as well as reduce costs by increasing visibility of inventory, and by knowing what is on the shelf and what is downstream in production. SeeRisk can calculate the implications that defective components would have on revenue, operating costs, what it would cost to start production over, and ultimately the effect on corporate profitability.[11]

Successful Project Management Strategies

Recreational Equipment, Inc. (REI), needs to consistently develop quality products and decrease the time to deliver them to market. To do that, REI needs to efficiently manage product development processes, projects, and information. The REI Gear and Apparel division takes an integrated project management approach to designing, managing, and tracking its product development projects, while collaborating and managing its workflow. REI's strategy entails combining Microsoft .NET technology, the Microsoft Office Enterprise Project Management (EPM) Solution, and software based on Microsoft Office Visio 2003 to create an integrated business solution it can use to model as-is business processes, experiment with what-if scenarios, and then convert the optimized processes into detailed project plans.

Project managers can further develop these plans, assign resources divisionwide, manage projects online, and collaborate globally. REI predicts this integrated solution will help it improve its efficiency, consistency, and scalability so it can deliver its products to market more quickly. Figure 12.15 displays the top five successful project management strategies outlined in CIO magazine.

Large IT projects require significant investment of time and resources. Successful software development projects have proven challenging and often elusive, wasting many resources and jeopardizing the goodwill of stakeholders, including customers and employees. Bringing strong, effective project, change, and risk management disciplines to large IT projects is essential to successful organizations. The days when a project manager could just concentrate on bringing a project in on time, on budget, and with agreed-upon deliverables are fading.

Top Five Successful Project Management Strategies

1. **Define project success criteria.** At the beginning of the project, make sure the stakeholders share a common understanding of how they will determine whether the project is successful. Too often, meeting a predetermined schedule is the only apparent success factor, but there are certainly others. Some examples are increasing market share, reaching a specified sales volume or revenue, achieving specific customer satisfaction measures, retiring a high-maintenance legacy system, and achieving a particular transaction processing volume and correctness.

2. **Develop a solid project plan.** The hard part of developing a plan is the thinking, negotiating, balancing, and communication project managers will have to do to develop a solid and realistic plan. The time they spend analyzing what it will take to solve the business problem will reduce the number of changes later in the project.

3. **Divide and conquer.** Break all large tasks into multiple small tasks to provide more accurate estimates, reveal hidden work activities, and allow for more accurate, fine-grained status tracking.

4. **Plan for change.** Things never go precisely as planned on a project; therefore, the budget and schedule should include some contingency buffers at the end of major phases to accommodate change.

5. **Manage project risk.** Failure to identify and control risks will allow the risks to control the project. Be sure to spend significant time during project planning to brainstorm possible risk factors, evaluate their potential threat, and determine the best way to mitigate or prevent them.

FIGURE 12.15

Top Five Successful Project Management Strategies

OPENING CASE QUESTIONS

Change at Toyota

1. What would be the impact on Toyota's business if it failed to implement a project management solution and managed its projects using a myriad of spreadsheets and Word documents?

2. Why would Opportunity, Resource, and Time & Expense Manager applications be of value to a company like Toyota?

3. Why would Toyota find it important to focus on implementing good project management techniques?

4. Why are project management, change management, and risk management critical to a global company such as Toyota?

5. Why would Toyota find it important to focus on implementing solid risk management techniques?

6. Why would Toyota find it important to focus on implementing solid change management techniques?

7. Describe the ramifications to Toyota's business if it failed to anticipate change.

8. Explain the potential issues facing Toyota if it failed to analyze risk.

section 12.2 OUTSOURCING

LEARNING OBJECTIVES

12.7. Identify three primary outsourcing options and explain the advantages and disadvantages of each.

12.8. Explain the business benefits of outsourcing.

12.9. Identify the leading offshore outsourcing countries.

12.10. Identify the up-and-coming offshore outsourcing countries.

12.11. Identify the rookie offshore outsourcing countries.

12.12. Assess the reasons for developing strategic outsourcing partnerships.

OUTSOURCING

More than 400 people from Merrill Lynch, Thomson Financial (a large market data vendor), and a number of other vendors worked feverishly on Merrill Lynch's biggest outsourcing initiative ever. This highly complex $1 billion makeover of its wealth management system is designed to improve the efficiency of Merrill's financial advisers. With the new system, Merrill Lynch advisers can manage more of the assets of their high-net-worth customers.

The new system also represents a major shift in the way Merrill Lynch approaches IT initiatives. In the 1990s, Merrill Lynch developed its previous system, Trusted Global Advisor (TGA), as it did any other major system—it developed it in-house. The thought of outsourcing a critical business system to a vendor was viewed as highly unfavorable by most financial services organizations. Merrill Lynch signed a contract that outsourced much of the responsibility for its new platform to Thomson Financial.[12]

In the high-speed global business environment, an organization needs to maximize its profits, enlarge its market share, and restrain its ever-increasing costs. Businesses need to make every effort to rethink and adopt new processes, especially the prospective resources regarding insourcing and outsourcing.

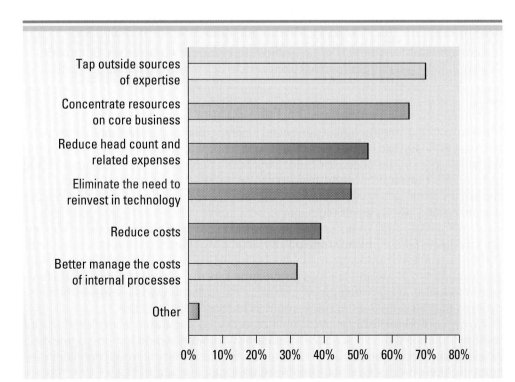

Percent of Functions Outsourced

- Information Technology
- Human Resources
- Facilities Management
- Finance and Accounting
- Marketing/Sales
- No Departments
- Other Departments

0% 10% 20% 30% 40% 50% 60%

FIGURE 12.16

Common Departments
Outsourced by
Organizations

Insourcing (*in-house development*) is a common approach using the professional expertise within an organization to develop and maintain the organization's information technology systems. Insourcing has been instrumental in creating a viable supply of IT professionals and in creating a better quality workforce combining both technical and business skills.

Outsourcing is an arrangement by which one organization provides a service or services for another organization that chooses not to perform them in-house. In some cases, the entire information technology department is outsourced, including planning and business analysis as well as the installation, management, and servicing of the network and workstations. Outsourcing can range from a large contract under which an organization such as IBM manages IT services for a company such as Xerox, to the practice of hiring contractors and temporary office workers on an individual basis. Figure 12.16 compares the functions companies have outsourced, and Figure 12.17 displays the primary reasons companies outsource.

FIGURE 12.17

Reasons Companies
Outsource

- Tap outside sources of expertise
- Concentrate resources on core business
- Reduce head count and related expenses
- Eliminate the need to reinvest in technology
- Reduce costs
- Better manage the costs of internal processes
- Other

0% 10% 20% 30% 40% 50% 60% 70% 80%

Ever since Eastman Kodak announced that it was outsourcing its information systems function in 1988 to IBM, DEC, and Businessland, large organizations have found it acceptable to transfer their IT assets, leases, and staff to outsourcers. In view of the changes in sourcing, the key question now is not "should we outsource IT?" but rather "where and how can we take advantage of the rapidly developing market of IT services providers?" Some of the influential drivers affecting the growth of the outsourcing market include:

- **Core competencies.** Many companies have recently begun to consider outsourcing as a means to fuel revenue growth rather than just a cost-cutting measure. Outsourcing enables an organization to maintain an up-to-date technology infrastructure while freeing it to focus on revenue growth goals by reinvesting cash and human capital in areas offering the greatest return on investment.

- **Financial savings.** It is typically cheaper to hire workers in China and India than similar workers in the United States. Technology is advancing at such an accelerated rate that companies often lack the resources, workforce, or expertise to keep up. It is close to impossible for an IT department to maintain a "best-of-breed" status, especially for small and medium-sized enterprises where cost is a critical factor.

- **Rapid growth.** A company's sustainability depends on both speed to market and ability to react quickly to changes in market conditions. By taking advantage of outsourcing, an organization is able to acquire best practices process expertise. This facilitates the design, building, training, and deployment of business processes or functions.

- **Industry changes.** High levels of reorganization across industries have increased demand for outsourcing to better focus on core competencies. The significant increase in merger and acquisition activity created a sudden need to integrate multiple core and noncore business functions into one business, while the deregulation of the utilities and telecom industries created a need to ensure compliance with government rules and regulations. Companies in either situation turned to outsourcing so they could better focus on industry changes at hand.

- **The Internet.** The pervasive nature of the Internet as an effective sales channel has allowed clients to become more comfortable with outsourcing. Barriers to entry, such as lack of capital, are dramatically reduced in the world of e-business due to the Internet. New competitors enter the market daily.

- **Globalization.** As markets open worldwide, competition heats up. Companies may engage outsourcing service providers to deliver international services.

THE OUTSOURCING PHENOMENON

The outsourcing market has experienced strong growth over the last several years because of businesses' need to focus on core competencies, Web implementation initiatives, consolidation across industries, and a tight labor pool. The outsourcing of noncore, transaction-based processes has gained significant momentum over the last few years as organizations have become more comfortable with the concept of outsourcing and its advantages.

Organizations elect to outsource for a variety of reasons. Some of these reasons are tactical, while others are strategic. In the past, outsourcing was often used tactically, as a quick-fix, short-term solution to a particular need or problem, that did not form part of an overall business strategy. In recent years, many companies have begun to use strategic outsourcing where an organization works with suppliers in order to make a significant improvement in business performance.

No one would seriously expect an oil company to outsource its exploration and refining functions; pharmaceutical companies probably would not outsource their research and development; and few, if any, major automakers would consider outsourcing their production planning or marketing campaigns. These activities are

FIGURE 12.18

Outsourcing
Opportunities

Industry	Outsourcing Opportunities
Banking and finance	Check and electronic payment processing, credit report issuance, delinquency management, securities, and trades processing
Insurance	Claims reporting and investigation, policy administration, check processing, risk assessment
Telecommunications	Invoice and bill production, transaction processing
Health care	Electronic data interchange, database management, accounting
Transportation	Ticket and order processing
Government	Loan processing, Medicaid processing
Retail	Electronic payment processing

core to their businesses and often the means for differentiation in the marketplace and a source of competitive advantage. Businesses outsource their noncore functions, such as payroll and IT. By outsourcing IT, most organizations can cut costs, improve service, and focus on their core business. According to research firm IDC, the worldwide IT outsourcing market will reach $230 billion by 2009.[13]

Best Buy Co. Inc. is the number one U.S. specialty retailer for consumer electronics, personal computers, entertainment software, and appliances. Best Buy needed to find a strategic IT partner that could help the company leverage its IT functions in order to meet its business objectives. Best Buy further wanted to integrate its disparate enterprise systems and minimize its operating expenses. Best Buy outsourced these functions to Accenture, a global management consulting, technology services, and outsourcing company. The comprehensive outsourcing relationship that drove Best Buy's transformation produced spectacular results that were measurable in every key area of its business, such as a 20 percent increase in key category revenue that translated into a $25 million profit improvement.[14]

According to PricewaterhouseCoopers' survey of CEOs from 452 of the fastest growing U.S. companies, "Businesses that outsource are growing faster, larger, and more profitably than those that do not. In addition, most of those involved in outsourcing say they are saving money and are highly satisfied with their outsourcing service providers." Figure 12.18 lists common areas for outsourcing opportunities across industries.

Outsourcing Benefits

The many benefits associated with outsourcing include:

- Increased quality and efficiency of a process, service, or function.
- Reduced operating expenses.
- Focusing resources on core profit-generating competencies.
- Reduced exposure to risks involved with large capital investments.
- Access to outsourcing service provider's economies of scale.
- Access to outsourcing services provider's expertise and best-in-class practices.
- Access to advanced technologies.
- Increased flexibility with the ability to respond quickly to changing market demands.
- Avoiding costly outlay of capital funds.
- Reduced head count and associated overhead expense.
- Reduced frustration and expense related to hiring and retaining employees in an exceptionally tight job market.
- Reduced time to market for products or services.

FIGURE 12.19

Outsourcing Models
and Cost Savings

OUTSOURCING OPTIONS

In the early 1990s, British Petroleum (BP) began looking at IT outsourcing as a way to radically reduce costs and gain more flexible and higher-quality IT resources that directly improve the overall business. Over the past decade, all companies within the global BP Group have incorporated outsourcing initiatives in their business plans. BP's information technology costs were reduced by 40 percent globally over the first three years of the outsourcing engagement and have continued at a 10 percent reduction year after year, leading to hundreds of millions of dollars in savings to BP.[15]

Information technology outsourcing enables organizations to keep up with market and technology advances—with less strain on human and financial resources and more assurance that the IT infrastructure will keep pace with evolving business priorities (see Figure 12.19). Planning, deploying, and managing IT environments is both a tactical and a strategic challenge that must take into account a company's organizational, industrial, and technological concerns. The three different forms of outsourcing options are:

1. **Onshore outsourcing** is the process of engaging another company within the same country for services.
2. **Nearshore outsourcing** refers to contracting an outsourcing arrangement with a company in a nearby country. Often this country will share a border with the native country.
3. **Offshore outsourcing** is using organizations from developing countries to write code and develop systems. In offshore outsourcing the country is geographically far away.

OFFSHORE OUTSOURCING

Since the mid-1990s, major U.S. companies have been sending significant portions of their software development work offshore—primarily to vendors in India, but also to vendors in China, Eastern Europe (including Russia), Ireland, Israel, and the Philippines. The big selling point for offshore outsourcing to these countries is "inexpensive good work." A programmer who earns as much as $63,000 per year in the United States is paid as little as $5,000 per year overseas (see Figure 12.20). Companies can easily realize cost savings of 30 percent to 50 percent through offshore outsourcing and still get the same, if not better, quality of service.[16]

Developed and developing countries throughout Europe and Asia offer some IT outsourcing services, but most are hampered to some degree by language, telecommunications infrastructure, or regulatory barriers. The first and largest offshore marketplace is India, whose English-speaking and technologically advanced population have built its IT services business into a $4 billion industry. Infosys, NIIT, Satyam, TCS, and Wipro are among the biggest Indian outsourcing service

Country	Salary Range Per Year
China	$5,000–$9,000
India	6,000–10,000
Philippines	6,500–11,000
Russia	7,000–13,000
Ireland	21,000–28,000
Canada	25,000–50,000
United States	60,000–90,000

FIGURE 12.20

Typical Salary Ranges for Computer Programmers

FIGURE 12.21

Categories of Outsourcing Countries

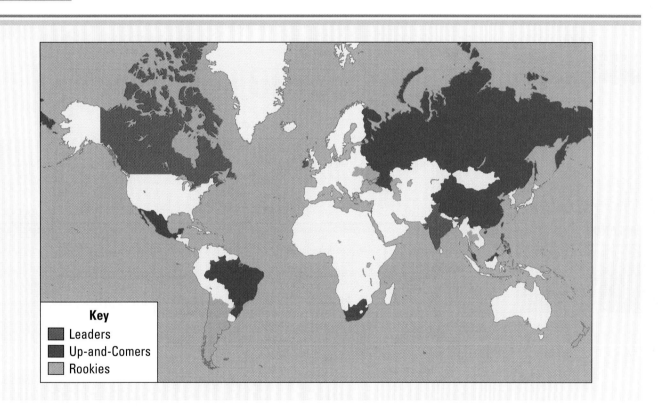

Key
- Leaders
- Up-and-Comers
- Rookies

providers, each with a significant presence in the United States. There are currently three categories of outsourcing countries (see Figure 12.21).

1. The leaders—countries that are leading the outsourcing industry.
2. The up-and-comers—countries that are beginning to emerge as solid outsourcing options.
3. The rookies—countries that are just entering the outsourcing industry.

The Leaders

The following countries are leaders in the outsourcing industry:

- Canada
- India

- Ireland
- Israel
- Philippines

CANADA

Expertise	■ Software development/maintenance, contact centers, technical support.
Major Customers	■ Allmerica, Agilent.
Advantages	■ Though labor costs are high, geographic proximity and cultural affinity with the United States make it highly desirable. ■ Contact center turnover is low.
Disadvantage	■ High cost of labor pool, but still less expensive than outsourcing in the United States.

INDIA

Expertise	■ Software development/maintenance, contact centers, financial processing.
Major Customers	■ Citigroup, GE Capital, American Express.
Advantages	■ India is the leader in business process and IT services outsourcing. ■ Two million English-proficient speakers graduate every year from more than 1,000 colleges that offer information technology education. ■ Strong history of software development. ■ Highly skilled labor pool. ■ Favorable cost structure.
Disadvantages	■ Political instability. ■ Labor costs are rising as demand for IT workers begins to exceed supply. ■ High turnover, particularly in contact centers, is becoming an issue.

IRELAND

Expertise	■ European shared-services centers, software development, contact centers.
Major Customers	■ Intel, Dell, Microsoft.
Advantages	■ Reputation for producing highly skilled IT professionals. ■ Strong cultural affinity with the United States. ■ Low political or financial risk. ■ Solid telecommunications infrastructure. ■ Strong educational system.
Disadvantage	■ High cost of salaries, however, labor costs are still lower than in the United States.

ISRAEL

Expertise	■ Software development/maintenance, packaged software implementation, application integration, security, e-business.
Major Customers	■ Merrill Lynch, Shaw Industries.
Advantages	■ Highly skilled workforce including scientists and engineers from Eastern Europe and Russia. ■ Excellent educational system. ■ Hotbed for IT innovation.
Disadvantages	■ Political instability. ■ Employee safety is a cause for concern. ■ High cost of IT salaries.

Expertise	■ Accounting, finance, contact centers, human resources.
Major Customers	■ Procter & Gamble, American International Group, Citigroup.
Advantages	■ The population boasts a high percentage of English speakers with American accents. ■ Culture dictates aim-to-please attitude. ■ Estimated 15,000 technology students graduate from universities annually.
Disadvantages	■ Filipinos are not nearly as strong in software development and maintenance as other outsourcing countries. ■ Political instability.

The Up-and-Comers

The following countries are up-and-coming in the outsourcing industry:

- Brazil
- China
- Malaysia
- Mexico
- Russia
- South Africa

Expertise	■ Software development/maintenance.
Major Customers	■ General Electric, Goodyear, Xerox.
Advantages	■ Big cost savings from a large supply of IT labor. ■ Brazil is Latin America's largest economy with a strong industrial base. ■ Brazil's national focus is on growing small and midsize businesses, including IT services. ■ Affinity with U.S. culture including minimal time zone differences.
Disadvantage	■ Remains on priority watch list of International Intellectual Property Alliance for copyright infractions.

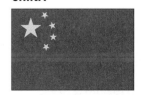

Expertise	■ Transaction processing, low-end software development/maintenance.
Major Customers	■ HSBC Bank, Microsoft.
Advantages	■ Large pool of educated IT workers with broad skill sets. ■ Government provides strong support for IT outsourcing industry. ■ Telecommunications infrastructure is improving. ■ Entry into World Trade Organization winning confidence of foreign investors. ■ Government has established 15 national software industrial parks.
Disadvantages	■ English proficiency low. ■ Workers lack knowledge of Western business culture. ■ Workers lack project management skills. ■ Intellectual property protections weak. ■ Piracy. ■ Red tape and corruption from a highly bureaucratic government.

MALAYSIA

Expertise	■ Wireless applications.
Major Customers	■ IBM, Shell, DHL, Motorola, Electronic Data Systems Corporation.
Advantages	■ Good business environment with strong government support for IT and communications industries. ■ Workforce has strong global exposure. ■ World-class telecommunications infrastructure. ■ Over half of the 250,000 students in higher education major in scientific or technical disciplines.
Disadvantages	■ Labor costs higher than India. ■ Few suppliers, which limits business choices. ■ Shortage of skilled IT talent.

MEXICO

Expertise	■ Software development, contact centers.
Major Customers	■ AOL Time Warner, General Motors, IBM.
Advantages	■ Solid telecommunications infrastructure. ■ Shares cultural affinity and time zones with the United States. ■ Second-largest U.S. trading partner. ■ Programmers highly proficient on latest technologies, including Sun's J2EE and Microsoft's .NET.
Disadvantages	■ English proficiency low. ■ Government corruption.

RUSSIA

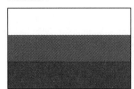

Expertise	■ Web design, complex software development, aerospace engineering.
Major Customer	■ Boeing.
Advantages	■ Large number of highly skilled workers with degrees in science, engineering, and math. ■ Strong venue for research and development. ■ Programmers have skills for both cutting-edge projects and working with legacy applications. ■ European-based companies benefit from historic cultural affinity and geographic proximity.
Disadvantages	■ English proficiency not as widespread as in India or the Philippines, making contact centers impractical. ■ Government corruption and red tape. ■ Copyright piracy. ■ Outsourcing industry is fragmented and many firms have 20 programmers or less, making them unattractive to companies with large IT projects. ■ Telecommunications infrastructure needs work.

SOUTH AFRICA

Expertise	■ Contact centers, e-business, software development, IT security.
Major Customers	■ AIG, Old Mutual, Sage Life, Swissair.
Advantages	■ Time zone compatibility with Europe. ■ English is a native language. ■ Solid telecommunications infrastructure.
Disadvantages	■ Small pool of IT skilled workers. ■ IT talent tends to emigrate. ■ Crime.

The Rookies

The following countries are just beginning to offer outsourcing and are considered rookies in the industry:

- Argentina
- Chile
- Costa Rica

ARGENTINA

Expertise	■ Software development/maintenance, contact centers.
Major Customers	■ BankOne, Citibank, Principal Financial Group.
Advantages	■ Low costs resulting from an economic collapse in 2001. ■ Economy began to rebound in 2003, growing more than 8 percent, but unemployment remains high. ■ Large labor pool, including solid base of engineering talent.
Disadvantages	■ Country has yet to reach agreement with creditors on restructuring debt. ■ Foreign investors are cautious.

CHILE

Expertise	■ Software development/maintenance.
Major Customer	■ Compaq.
Advantages	■ Large highly skilled pool of IT talent. ■ State-of-the-art telecommunications infrastructure. ■ Good satellite connectivity and digital network. ■ Government actively supports business process and software development sectors. ■ Government plans to begin offering English classes to technical workers.
Disadvantages	■ English proficiency lacking. ■ Slightly higher costs than neighboring countries.

COSTA RICA

Expertise	■ Contact centers, e-business.
Major Customer	■ Unisys.
Advantages	■ Business-friendly environment. ■ Highly skilled pool of engineering talent. ■ Well-educated workforce. ■ Favorable cost structure. ■ English and Spanish widely spoken.
Disadvantage	■ Relatively small labor supply.

NEW ZEALAND

Expertise	■ Contact centers, e-business, Web hosting, Web design.
Major Customers	■ IBM, Microsoft, Cisco.
Advantages	■ Stable political and economic environment. ■ Well-established telecommunications infrastructure. ■ Thriving contact center industry. ■ Limited supply of domestic labor. To meet demand, the government has eased visa restrictions allowing entry of workers from countries such as Bangladesh.
Disadvantage	■ New Zealand cannot compete on costs with India and the Philippines.

THAILAND

Expertise	■ Software development/maintenance.
Major Customers	■ Dell, Glovia, Sungard.
Advantages	■ Reasonable telecommunications infrastructure. ■ Cost structure is slightly lower than Malaysia.
Disadvantages	■ Demand for skilled IT labor exceeds supply. ■ Population is not as educated as in neighboring countries. ■ English is not widely spoken.

UKRAINE

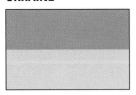

Expertise	■ Software development, Web site development.
Major Customers	■ Sears, Roebuck and Company; Target Corporation.
Advantages	■ History of training highly educated scientists and engineers. (The Soviet Union based the majority of its space and aviation technology work here.) ■ Information technology outsourcing growth predicted to double over the next couple of years.
Disadvantages	■ Unstable political climate. ■ Fears that the country is drifting away from democracy and pro-Western stance.

■ New Zealand

■ Thailand

■ Ukraine

In summary, many countries are racing to participate in the outsourcing phenomenon. When an organization outsources, it needs to analyze all of its options and weigh all of the advantages and disadvantages. When faced with an outsourcing decision, be sure to evaluate the countries on such things as geopolitical risk, English proficiency, and salary cost (see Figure 12.22).

THE CHALLENGES OF OUTSOURCING

Outsourcing comes with several challenges. These arguments are valid and should be considered when a company is thinking about outsourcing. Many challenges can be avoided with proper research on the outsourcing service provider. The challenges include:

■ **Contract length.** Most of the outsourced IT contracts are for a relatively long time period (several years). This is because of the high cost of transferring assets and employees as well as maintaining technological investment. The long time period of the contract causes three particular problems:

1. Difficulties in getting out of a contract if the outsourcing service provider turns out to be unsuitable.

2. Problems in foreseeing what the business will need over the next 5 or 10 years (typical contract lengths), hence creating difficulties in establishing an appropriate contract.

3. Problems in reforming an internal IT department after the contract period is finished.

■ **Competitive edge.** Effective and innovative use of IT can give an organization a competitive edge over its rivals. A competitive business advantage provided by an internal IT department that understands the organization and is committed to its goals can be lost in an outsourced arrangement. In an outsourced arrangement, IT staff are striving to achieve the goals and objectives of the outsourcing service provider, which may conflict with those of the organization.

THE LEADERS

Country	Geopolitical Risk	English Proficiency	Average Programmer Salary
Canada	Low	Good	>$12K
India	Moderate	Good	$4K–$12K
Ireland	Low	Good	>$12K
Israel	Moderate	Good	>$12K
Philippines	Moderate	Good	$4K–$12K

THE UP-AND-COMERS

Country	Geopolitical Risk	English Proficiency	Average Programmer Salary
Brazil	Moderate	Poor	$4K–$12K
China	Low	Poor	$4K–$12K
Malaysia	Low	Fair	$4K–$12K
Mexico	Moderate	Poor	>$12K
Russia	Moderate	Poor	$4K–$12K
South Africa	Moderate	Good	>$12K

THE ROOKIES

Country	Geopolitical Risk	English Proficiency	Average Programmer Salary
Argentina	Moderate	Fair	$4K–$12K
Chile	Low	Poor	<$4K
Costa Rica	Moderate	Good	$4K–$12K
New Zealand	Low	Good	>$12K
Thailand	Low	Poor	$4K–$12K
Ukraine	Moderate	Poor	$4K-$12K

FIGURE 12.22

Outsourcing Options

- **Confidentiality.** In some organizations, the information stored in the computer systems is central to the enterprise's success or survival, such as information about pricing policies, product mixing formulas, or sales analysis. Some companies decide against outsourcing for fear of placing confidential information in the hands of the provider, particularly if the outsourcing service provider offers services to companies competing in the same marketplace. Although the organization usually dismisses this threat, claiming it is covered by confidentiality clauses in a contract, the organization must assess the potential risk and costs of a confidentiality breach in determining the net benefits of an outsourcing agreement.

- **Scope definition.** Most IT projects suffer from problems associated with defining the scope of the system. The same problem afflicts outsourcing arrangements. Many difficulties result from contractual misunderstandings between the organization and the outsourcing service provider. In such circumstances, the organization believes that the service required is within the contract scope while the service provider is sure it is outside the scope and so is subject to extra fees.

FUTURE OUTSOURCING TRENDS

Companies are getting smarter about outsourcing and about aligning efficiency with core business priorities. As businesses become increasingly networked—global, commoditized, 24x7, and collaborative—outsourcing is becoming less of a cost-saving strategy and more an overall context for business.

Outsourcing is rapidly approaching commodity status, and this will transform the outsourcing value equation from high margins and vendor control into a classic buyers' market with competition driving down margins, adding features and services, and increasing buyer choices. U.S. companies should consider Mexico and Canada for nearshore outsourcing since those countries often provide very competitive pricing. Vendors in these countries can be viable alternatives, such as IBM Global Services (Mexico and Canada), Softtek (Mexico), CGI (Canada), and Keane (Canada).[17]

Companies should look for value-based pricing rather than the lowest possible price. The emerging trend of companies using reverse auction bidding to select offshore vendors is a dangerous one; it could result in low prices, but also low value and low customer satisfaction.

Outsourcing IT services and business functions is becoming an increasingly common global practice among organizations looking for competitive advantage. The guiding principle is that noncore and critical activities of an enterprise can be handed over to companies with expertise in those activities, thereby freeing internal resources to focus on enhancing the added-value of the organization's core business. Outsourcing is no longer a simple matter of cutting costs and improving service levels. As more companies consider the benefits of outsourcing their IT functions and their business processes, they will find new ways to create business value. Companies that succeed will find innovative solutions to help drive costs down, select only the problem areas to outsource, and more important, learn to use outsourcing as a strategic weapon.

OPENING CASE QUESTIONS

Change at Toyota

9. How could Toyota benefit from outsourcing?

10. If you had to choose a country to recommend for outsourcing, which country would it be and why?

11. Explain the issues facing Toyota from its internal IT department if it decided to outsource the project management of the development of a new system.

12. What types of ethical issues might Toyota encounter when considering outsourcing?

13. What types of security issues might Toyota encounter when considering outsourcing?

Change control board
    (CCB) 382
Change management 381
Change management
    system 381
Critical path 381
Dependency 380
Gantt chart 381
Insourcing (in-house
    development) 387
Nearshore outsourcing 390

Offshore outsourcing 390
Onshore outsourcing 390
Outsourcing 387
PERT (Program Evaluation and
    Review Technique)
    chart 380
Project 375
Project deliverable 377
Project exclusion 379
Project management 375

Project management
    software 375
Project manager 377
Project milestone 377
Project objective 379
Project plan 380
Project product 379
Project risk 383
Project scope 379
Risk management 383

Staying on Track—Toronto Transit

Schedules are at the heart of Toronto Transit Commission's (TTC) celebrated transit system, which services over 1 million customers daily. More than 50 large engineering and construction projects are under way to expand, upgrade, and maintain Toronto's transit systems and structures. One such project is the Sheppard project, which consists of constructing the new six-kilometer line north of the city. Sheppard is estimated to take more than five years to complete, with a total cost of $875 million.

TTC's challenge is to keep its 50 individual projects, most of which fall within the $2 million to $100 million price range and span an average of five years, on schedule and under budget. Staying on top of so many multifaceted, multiyear, and often interdependent projects adds additional complexity for the company. TTC uses Primavera Project Planner (P3) to create a single master schedule for all of its engineering and construction projects.

TTC's 50 individual projects average 100 to 150 activities each, with some projects encompassing as many as 500 to 600 activities. "Seeing the big picture is important, not only for the 300 people who work in the Engineering and Construction branch of the TTC, but for the entire 9,000-person organization," said Vince Carroll, head scheduler for the Engineering and Construction branch. "Engineering managers need to see how other projects may impact their own. Materials and procurement managers need to track project progress. Senior managers need to be able to communicate with city government to secure funding. Marketing and public relations people need the latest information to set public expectations. And most important of all," Carroll said, "the operations group needs to stay informed of what is happening so that they can adjust the schedules that run the trains."

Carroll and his team of 25 people create, update, and publish a master schedule that summarizes the individual status of each project, shows the logical links between projects, and provides an integrated overview of all projects. The master schedule helps the team effectively and regularly communicate the status of all projects currently under way throughout the Toronto Transit system.

The master schedule organizes projects according to their location in the capital budget. For example, projects can be organized according to those that have been allotted funding for expansion, state of good repair, legislative reasons, or environmental reasons. Each project is organized by its logical flow—from planning, analysis, design, through the maintenance phase. The final report shows positive and negative balances for each project and a single overview of the status of all the engineering and construction projects. Carroll and his team use PERT charts to create time-scaled logic diagrams and then convert this information to bar charts for presentation purposes in the master schedule. TTC is currently linking its master schedule directly to its payroll system, enabling it to track the number of hours actually worked versus hours planned. [18]

Questions

1. Describe Gantt charts and explain how TTC could use one to communicate project status.
2. Describe PERT charts and explain how TTC could use one to communicate project status.
3. How could TTC use its master schedule to identify change management issues along with potential resolutions?
4. How could TTC use its master schedule to identify risk management issues along with potential resolutions?

Changing Circuits at Circuit City

When Circuit City expanded the big-box warehouse format to consumer electronics retailing in the 1980s, the company was on its way to becoming the place to go for TVs and stereos. By the late 1980s, it had sidestepped its then top competitor, Silo, and it soon put the squeeze on the likes of Tweeter and RadioShack. Circuit City was doing so well in the 1990s that business consultant Jim Collins, in his best seller *Good to Great*, wrote: "From 1982 to 1999, Circuit City generated cumulative stock returns 22 times better than the market, handily beating Intel, Wal-Mart, GE, Hewlett-Packard and Coca-Cola."

Today, Circuit City is in a markedly different position. By 2001, Best Buy had raced past the Richmond, Virginia-based chain, usurping its position as the number one consumer electronics retailer. Best Buy now has 608 stores compared with Circuit City's 599 and nearly $25 billion in revenue to Circuit City's $9.7 billion. Circuit City is ranked by consultancy Retail Forward as the number three seller of consumer electronics, behind Best Buy and Wal-Mart. "Circuit City was the 800-pound gorilla," said Joseph Feldman, a research analyst with the investment bank SG Cowen & Co. However, "they woke up one morning and Best Buy had doubled its size with the same number of stores."

Catching Best Buy

Circuit City has been trying to catch up to Best Buy, or at least cement its position as a serious contender in consumer electronics retailing. Recently, its top executives announced plans to turn the company into a customer-focused business that delivers a personalized experience to all customers across all its channels (stores, Web, and call centers). Michael Jones, who took over as Circuit City's CIO in January 2004, speaks passionately about the high-profile role technology will play in delivering personalized customer experiences. However, before he can achieve his vision of store associates recognizing customers through their loyalty cards as soon as they enter the store, he has a lot of unglamorous groundwork to lay. Circuit City's strategy hinges on a robust IT infrastructure that makes information readily accessible to decision makers. Everything the company is doing to improve its business—from developing more effective promotions to deciding which products should be displayed at the ends of aisles in stores—hinges on data. "This is heavy analytical work. It's fact-based, data-driven," said Philip Schoonover, Circuit City's new president who was hired in October 2004 from Best Buy.

Circuit City is just starting to invest heavily in the technology needed to act on this strategy. It is upgrading its mostly proprietary point-of-sale (POS) system and building an enterprise data warehouse to replace siloed databases. However, some analysts say Circuit City's turnaround effort has been hampered by a stodgy, overly complacent leadership that lacks vision. Top executives saw the Best Buy locomotive coming but failed to react as it steamed past them. Indeed, some analysts say they doubt Circuit City will ever catch up.

Bottom-Up Changes

As part of its turnaround effort over the past few years, Circuit City has sold all of its noncore businesses to focus on its core: consumer electronics. It also has changed the pay structure for in-store employees, begun relocating stores (it recently closed 19), and hired new management. In addition, the company is finally starting to hone its customer-centric strategy. Circuit City is already improving the customer experience in its stores by, among other things, locating accessories and services close to big-ticket items so that customers can see more quickly what they might need to furnish their home office or outfit a home theater. For example, when a customer is looking at a high-definition television, nearby is a selection of furniture to hold the TV, the cables needed to hook it up, and DirectTV or digital cable service products. Circuit

City is also making merchandising decisions based on what is important to the customer. For example, its stores are beginning to feature products deemed most important to customers on the displays at the ends of aisles. The company is trying to nail the basics of customer service by making sure that items are not out of stock.[19]

Questions

1. Explain why anticipating change would have helped Circuit City remain as an industry leader.
2. Why are project management, change management, and risk management critical to a global company such as Circuit City?
3. Assess the impact on Circuit City's business if it failed to implement change management strategies as it revamped its global organization.
4. What are some of the potential risks facing Circuit City's new business model?
5. Why would Opportunity, Resource, and Time & Expense applications be of value to a company like Circuit City?
6. Why would Circuit City benefit from implementing good risk management and change management techniques?

Outsourcing Brew

Coors Brewing Company, the third-largest brewer in the United States, manufactures and markets more than a dozen varieties of beer and malt beverages in 30 markets around the world. In a rapidly consolidating industry, Coors had a choice: keep growing or be acquired. To create the optimal conditions for growth, the company needed to improve access to information, consolidate systems, and reduce costs.

In less than a decade, Coors Brewing Company had more than doubled in size. Managing that growth became increasingly difficult for the company's internal IT staff. The company wanted to maintain responsibility for the technologies directly related to making and selling beer. Therefore, Coors was looking for a partner with deep industry expertise, mature application experience, and global reach to help revitalize its technology to support its business goals, including bringing new acquisitions online quickly.

The company decided to outsource the day-to-day management of its technical operations, conversion of legacy applications, and systems. Coors outsourced these functions to EDS to create a globally integrated enterprise solution, helping to optimize the supply chain from beginning to end. EDS is an experienced outsourcing services company with more than 130,000 employees and 2003 revenues of $21.5 billion, ranked 80th on the Fortune 500.

EDS offered Coors an infrastructure "on demand." Coors avoids a huge up-front investment in infrastructure, but is able to access increased capacity when business volumes increase. Now IT costs are predictable, and additional infrastructure is instantly available when the company needs it. Coors also controls costs by using EDS's Best ShoreSM Services, which enables Coors to reduce the cost of applications management by as much as 40 percent through a combination of offshore, nearshore, and local service centers and personnel.

EDS's solutions at Coors deliver much more than lower costs and increased reliability. As EDS assumed control of Coors's help desk, staff increased service levels while identifying patterns that let Coors focus training where it was most needed and kept the company aware of where potential problems lay. Standardizing the company's desktop environment has allowed Coors to get rid of many obsolete applications.

EDS is much more than an information technology outsourcing service provider, it is Coors's business partner. "They work with us on project management and root-cause analysis, which have helped us to add a lot of discipline in our organization," CIO Virginia Guthrie said. With a modernized and efficient information environment taking shape, EDS and Coors have ambitious plans for the future, from improving manufacturing processes to enhancing Coors's global presence. Guthrie said, "What we really want here is for this partnership to be a poster child for how outsourcing partnerships should work." With the help of EDS, Coors was able to:

- Within just 60 days, reduce cost of application maintenance by 70 percent.
- Save more than $1.2 million on project resources related to SAP implementation.
- Reduce applications in use by 48 percent.
- Work to retire 70 percent of legacy systems.[20]

Questions

1. Describe an alternative approach that Coors could have used instead of outsourcing to EDS.
2. What would be the advantages of offshore outsourcing the Coors IT department?
3. What are some other reasons Coors outsourced its information technology functions that were not mentioned in the case?

4. Describe some of the factors causing Coors to be "forced" to outsource its information technology functions.

1. **Saving failing systems**

Signatures Inc. specializes in producing for companies personalized products such as coffee mugs and pens with company logos. The company generates over $40 million in annual revenues and has more than 300 employees. The company is in the middle of a large multimillion-dollar SCM implementation, and it has just hired your Project Management Outsourcing firm to take over the project management efforts. On your first day, your team is told that the project is failing for the following reasons:

- The project is using the traditional waterfall methodology.
- The SDLC was not followed and the developers decided to skip the testing phase.
- A project plan was developed during the analysis phase, but the old project manager never updated or followed the plan.
- In a group determine what your first steps would be to get this project back on track.

2. **Explaining project management**

Prime Time Inc. is a large consulting company that specializes in outsourcing people with project management capabilities and skills. You are in the middle of an interview for a job with Prime Time. The manager performing the interview asks you to explain why managing a project plan is critical to a project's success. The manager also wants you to explain scope creep and feature creep and your tactics for managing them on a project. Finally, the manager wants you to elaborate on your strategies for delivering successful projects and reducing risks.

3. **Applying project management techniques**

You have been hired by a medium-sized airline company, Sun Best. Sun Best currently flies over 300 routes in the East. The company is experiencing tremendous issues coordinating its 3,500 pilots, 7,000 flight attendants, and 2,000 daily flights. Determine how Sun Best could use a Gantt chart to help it coordinate pilots, flight attendants, and daily flights. Using Excel, create a sample Gantt chart highlighting the different types of activities and resources Sun Best could track with the tool.

4. **Mitigating risk**

Alicia Fernandez owns and operates a chain of nine seafood restaurants in the Boston area. Alicia is currently considering purchasing one of her competitors, which would give her an additional six restaurants. Alicia's primary concerns with the purchase are the constantly changing seafood prices and high staff turnover rate in the restaurant industry. Explain to Alicia what risk management is and how she can use it to mitigate the risks for the potential purchase of her competitor.

5. **The Travel Store**

In 2006, The Travel Store faced a dilemma. The retailer had tripled in size over a three-year period to $1 billion in sales, but it had done so despite operational deficiencies. The company's inability to evolve its business processes as it grew was causing problems. Within a year, sales and profits fell below expectations, and its stock price plummeted from approximately $10 a share to less than $2 a share. The Travel Store is determined to take quick and decisive action to restore profitability and improve its credibility in the marketplace. One of its top priorities is to overhaul its inventory management system in an effort to create optimal levels of inventory to support sales demand. This would prevent higher volume stores from running out of key sale items while also ensuring that lower sales stores would not be burdened with excess inventory that could only be moved at closeout prices. The company would like to outsource this function but is worried about the challenges of transferring the responsibility of this important business function, as well as the issues surrounding confidentiality, and scope definition. Make a list of the competitive advantages outsourcing could give to The Travel Store, along with recommendations for addressing the company's outsourcing concerns.

6. Software solutions

Founded in 2003, Gus Software provides innovative search software, Web site demographics, and testing software. All serve as part of its desktop and enterprise resource planning solutions for government, corporate, educational, and consumer markets. Web site publishers, digital media publishers, content managers, document managers, business users, consumers, software companies, and consulting services companies use the Gus solutions. The company is currently thinking about offshore outsourcing its call center functions, e-business strategies, and application development. Describe how Gus could use outsourcing along with the potential advantages it might receive.

THE PLUG-INS

The overall goal of the plug-ins is to provide additional information not covered in the text such as personal productivity using information technology, business basics, and business process. The plug-ins also offer faculty who find themselves in the situation of having to purchase an extra book to support Microsoft Office an all-in-one text. The plug-ins presented here offer integration with the core chapters and provide critical knowledge using essential business applications, such as Microsoft Excel, Microsoft Access, and Microsoft FrontPage using hands-on tutorials for comprehension and mastery. Plug-Ins T1 – T12 are located on the CD that accompanies this text.

Plug-In	Description
T1. Personal Productivity Using IT	Plug-In T1 covers a number of things to do to keep a personal computer running effectively and efficiently. There are 12 topic areas covered in this plug-in. ■ Creating strong passwords ■ Performing good file management ■ Implementing effective backup and recovery strategies ■ Using Zip files ■ Writing professional e-mails ■ Stopping spam ■ Preventing phishing ■ Detecting spyware ■ Restricting instant messaging ■ Increasing PC performance ■ Using anti-virus software ■ Installing a personal firewall
T2. Basic Skills Using Excel	Plug-In T2 provides an introduction to the basics of using Microsoft Excel, a spreadsheet program for data management. It is designed to show the basics, along with a few fancy features. There are six topic areas covered in this plug-in. ■ Workbooks and worksheets ■ Working with cells and cell data ■ Printing worksheets ■ Formatting worksheets ■ Formulas ■ Working with charts and graphics
T3. Problem Solving Using Excel	Plug-In T3 provides a comprehensive tutorial on how to use a variety of Microsoft Excel functions and features for problem solving. There are five areas covered in this plug-in. ■ Lists ■ Conditional Formatting ■ AutoFilter ■ Subtotals ■ PivotTables
T4. Decision Making Using Excel	Plug-In T4 examines a few of the advanced business analysis tools used in Microsoft Excel that have the capability to identify patterns, trends, rules, and create "what-if" models. There are four topic areas covered in this plug-in. ■ IF ■ Goal Seek ■ Solver ■ Scenario Manager

(continued)

T5. Designing Database Applications	Plug-In T5 provides specific details on how to design relational database applications. One of the most efficient and powerful information management computer-based applications is the relational database. There are four topic areas covered in this plug-in. ■ Entities and data relationships ■ Documenting logical data relationships ■ The relational data model ■ Normalization
T6. Basic Skills and Tools Using Access	Plug-In T6 focuses on creating a Microsoft Access database file. One of the most efficient information management, computer-based applications, is Microsoft Access. Access provides a powerful set of tools for creating and maintaining a relational database. There are two topic areas covered in this plug-in. ■ Create a new database file ■ Create and modify tables
T7. Problem Solving Using Access	Plug-In T7 provides a comprehensive tutorial on how to query a database in Microsoft Access. Queries are essential for problem solving; allowing a user to sort information, summarize data (display totals, averages, counts, and so on), display the results of calculations on data, and choose exactly which fields are shown. There are three topic areas covered in this plug-in. ■ Create simple queries using the Simple Query Wizard ■ Advanced queries using calculated fields ■ Format results displayed in calculated fields
T8. Creating Forms and Reports Using Access	Plug-In T8 provides a comprehensive tutorial on entering data in a well-designed form and creating functional reports using Microsoft Access. A form is essential to use for data entry and a report is an effective way to present data in a printed format. There are two topic areas covered in this plug-in. ■ Creating, modifying, and running forms ■ Creating, modifying, and running reports
T9. Designing Web Pages	Plug-In T9 provides a comprehensive assessment into the functional aspects of Web design. Web sites are beginning to look more alike and to employ the same metaphors and conventions. The Web has now become an everyday tool whose design should not make users think. There are six topic areas in this plug-in. ■ The World Wide Web ■ The unknown(s) ■ The process of Web Design ■ HTML basics ■ Web Fonts ■ Web Graphics
T10. Basic Skills Using FrontPage	Plug-In T10 provides a tour of using FrontPage to create Web pages. FrontPage allows anyone with limited Web page design experience to create, modify, and maintain full-featured, professional-looking pages without having to learn how to code all the functions and features from scratch. There are seven topic areas covered in this plug-in. ■ Web sites, Web pages, and HTML ■ Navigation in FrontPage ■ Building a Web site ■ Working with graphics ■ Including hyperlinks ■ Presenting information in lists and tables ■ Formatting pages
T11. Business Basics	Plug-In T11 offers an introduction to the basics of business. There are nine topic areas covered in this plug-in. ■ Types of businesses ■ Internal operations of a corporation ■ Accounting ■ Marketing ■ Finance

(continued)

	■ Human resources ■ Management information systems ■ Production/operations ■ Sales
T12. Business Process	Plug-In T12 shows how investment in continuous process improvement, business process reengineering, or business process management is the same as any other technology-related investment. There are five topic areas covered in this plug-in. ■ Examining business processes ■ Business process design ■ Business process improvement ■ Business process management ■ Business process modeling examples

Apply Your Knowledge Project Overview

Project Number	Project Name	Project Type	Focus Area	Skill Set	Page Number
1	Capitalizing on Your Career	Business	IT/MIS	Careers in IT	412
2	Achieving Alignment	Business	General Business	Business-IT Alignment	413
3	Market Dissection	Business	General Business	Porter's Three Generic Strategies	413
4	Grading Security	Business	Security	Information Security Plan/Policies	414
5	Eyes Everywhere	Business	Security	Biometrics	415
6	Setting Boundaries	Business	Ethics	Ethical Dilemmas	416
7	Contemplating Sharing	Business	Ethics	Peer-to-Peer	416
8	Dashboard Design	Business	EIS	Digital Dashboard	417
9	Great Stories	Business	CRM	Disgruntled Customers	417
10	Classic Car Problems	Business	CRM	Business Efficiency	418
11	Building Visibility	Business	SCM	Business Effectiveness	418
12	Bean Integration	Business	ERP/CRM	Information Integration	419
13	Working Together	Business	Collaboration	Workflow	420
14	Different Dimensions	Business	Business Intelligence	Data Warehouse	421
15	Connecting Components	Business	Enterprise Architecture	Developing Systems	422
16	Internet Groceries	Business	E-Business	Business Analysis	422
17	Getting Personal	Business	E-Business	Mass Customization	423
18	Express Yourself	Business	E-Business	Web Site Development	423
19	Creating a Presence	Business	E-Business	Web Site Development	424
20	GoGo Gadgets	Business	Wireless	Competitive Advantage	424
21	Back on Your Feet	Business	Enterprise Architecture	Backup and Disaster Recovery	425
22	GEM Athletic Center	Business	SDLC	Business Requirements	425

(Continued)

Project Number	Project Name	Project Type	Focus Area	Skill Set	Page Number
23	Confusing Coffee	Business	SDLC	Business Requirements	426
24	Picking Projects	Business	Project Management	Prioritizing Projects	426
25	Keeping Time	Business	Project Management	Project Plan	426
26	Controlling Your Spending	Excel	Personal Budget	Introductory Development: Formulas	427
27	Gearing for Cash	Excel	Cash Flow	Introductory Development: Formulas	428
28	Book Boxes	Excel	Strategic Analysis	Intermediate Development: Formulas	428
29	SplashEm	Excel	Strategic Analysis	Intermediate Development: Formulas	429
30	Tally's Purchases	Excel	Hardware and Software	Introductory Development: Formulas	430
31	Tracking Donations	Excel	Employee Relationships	Introductory Development: Formulas	430
32	All Aboard	Excel	Global Commerce	Introductory Development: Formulas	430
33	In with the Out	Excel	Outsourcing	Advanced Development: Formulas	430
34	Woods You	Excel	SCM	Advanced Development: Formulas	432
35	Bill's Boots	Excel	Profit Maximization	Intermediate Development: Formulas	432
36	Adequate Acquisitions	Excel	Break-Even Analysis	Intermediate Development: Formulas	433
37	Formatting Grades	Excel	Streamlining Data	Advanced Development: If, LookUp	433
38	Moving Espressos	Excel	SCM	Advanced Development: Absolute vs. Relative Values	434
39	Reducing Transports	Excel	SCM	Advanced Development: Pivot Table	434
40	Better Business	Excel	CRM	Intermediate Development: Pivot Table	435
41	Too Much Information	Excel	CRM	Advanced Development: Pivot Table	435
42	Gizmo Turnover	Excel	Data Mining	Advanced Development: Pivot Table	436
43	Managing Martin	Excel	Data Mining	Advanced Development: Pivot Table	436

(Continued)

Project Number	Project Name	Project Type	Focus Area	Skill Set	Page Number
44	Mountain Cycle	Excel	Break Even Analysis	Advanced Development: Goal Seek	437
45	Lutz Motors	Excel	Sales Analysis	Advanced Development: Scenario Manager	437
46	Animal Relations	Access	Business Analysis	Introductory Development	438
47	On-The-Level	Access	Business Intelligence	Introductory Development	439
48	iToys Inventory	Access	SCM	Intermediate Development	440
49	Call Around	Access	CRM	Intermediate Development	441
50	MoveIt	Access	Business Intelligence	Advanced Development	443

Project 1:

Capitalizing on Your Career

Business leaders need to be involved in information technology—any computer-based tool that people use to work with information and support the information and information-processing needs of an organization—for the following (primary) reasons:

- The sheer magnitude of the dollars spent on IT must be managed to ensure business value.
- Research has consistently shown that when business leaders are involved in information technology, it enables a number of business initiatives, such as gaining a competitive advantage, streamlining business processes, and even transforming entire organizations.
- Research has consistently shown that when business leaders are not involved in IT, systems fail, revenue is lost, and even entire companies can fail as a result of poorly managed IT.

One of the biggest challenges facing organizations is, "How do we get general business leaders involved in IT?" Research has shown that involvement is highly correlated with personal experience with IT and IT education, including university classes and IT executive seminars. Once general business leaders understand IT through experience and education, they are more likely to be involved in IT, and more likely to lead their organizations in achieving business success through IT.

Project Focus

1. Search the Internet to find examples of the types of technologies that are currently used in the field or industry that you plan to pursue. For example, if you are planning on a career in accounting or finance, you should become familiar with financial systems such as Oracle Financials. If you are planning a career in logistics or distribution, you should research supply chain management systems. If you are planning a career in marketing, you should research customer relationship management systems, blogs, and eMarketing.

2. IT is described as an enabler/facilitator of competitive advantage, organizational effectiveness, and organizational efficiency. As a competitive tool, IT can differentiate an organization's products, services, and prices from its competitors by improving product quality, shortening product development or delivery time, creating new IT-based products and services, and improving customer service before, during, and after a transaction. Search the Internet and find several examples of companies in the industry where you plan to work that have achieved a competitive advantage through IT.

3. Create a simple report of your findings; include a brief overview of the type of technologies you found and how organizations are using them to achieve a competitive advantage.

Project 2:

Achieving Alignment

Most companies would like to be in the market-leading position of JetBlue, Dell, or Wal-Mart, all of which have used information technology to secure their respective spots in the marketplace. These companies have a relentless goal of keeping the cost of technology down by combining the best of IT and business leadership.

It takes more than a simple handshake between groups to start on the journey toward financial gains; it requires operational discipline and a linkage between business and technology units. Only recently have companies not on the "path for profits" followed the lead of their successful counterparts, requiring more operational discipline from their IT groups as well as more IT participation from their business units. Bridging this gap is one of the greatest breakthroughs a company can make.

Companies that master the art of finely tuned, cost-effective IT management will have a major advantage. Their success will force their competitors to also master the art or fail miserably. This phenomenon has already occurred in the retail and wholesale distribution markets, which have had to react to Wal-Mart's IT mastery, as one example. Other industries will follow. This trend will change not only the face of IT, but also the future of corporate America.

As world markets continue to grow, the potential gains are greater than ever. However, so are the potential losses. The future belongs to those who are perceptive enough to grasp the significance of IT and resourceful enough to synchronize business management and information technology.

Project Focus

1. Use any resource to answer the question, "Why is business-IT alignment so difficult?" Use the following questions to begin your analysis:

   a. How do companies prioritize the demands of various business units as they relate to IT?

   b. What are some of the greatest IT challenges for the coming year?

   c. What drives IT decisions?

   d. Who or what is the moving force behind IT decisions?

   e. What types of efficiency metrics and effectiveness metrics might these companies use to measure the impact of IT?

   f. How can a company use financial metrics to monitor and measure IT investments?

   g. What are some of the issues with using financial metrics to evaluate IT?

Project 3:

Market Dissection

To illustrate the use of the three generic strategies, consider Figure AYK.1. The matrix shown demonstrates the relationships among strategies (cost leadership versus differentiation) and market segmentation (broad versus focused).

■ Hyundai is following a broad cost leadership strategy. Hyundai offers low-cost vehicles, in each particular model stratification, that appeal to a large audience.

■ Audi is pursuing a broad differentiation strategy with its Quattro models available at several price points. Audi's differentiation is safety and it prices its various Quattro models (higher than Hyundai) to reach a large, stratified audience.

■ Kia has a more focused cost leadership strategy. Kia mainly offers low-cost vehicles in the lower levels of model stratification.

■ Hummer offers the most focused differentiation strategy of any in the industry (including Mercedes-Benz).

	Cost Leadership strategy	Differentiation strategy
Broad market		
Focused market		

FIGURE AYK.1

Porter's Three Generic
Strategies

Project Focus

Create a similar graph displaying each strategy for a product of your choice. The strategy must include an example of the product in each of the following markets: (1) cost leadership, broad market, (2) differentiation, broad market, (3) cost leadership, focused market, and (4) differentiation, focused market. Potential products include:

- Cereal
- Dog food
- Soft drinks
- Computers
- Shampoo
- Snack foods
- Jeans
- Sneakers
- Sandals
- Mountain bikes
- TV shows
- Movies

Project 4:
Grading Security

Making The Grade is a nonprofit organization that helps students learn how to achieve better grades in school. The organization has 40 offices in 25 states and more than 2,000 employees. The company wants to build a Web site to offer its services online. Making The Grade's online services will provide parents seven key pieces of advice for communicating with their children to help them achieve academic success. The Web site will offer information on how to maintain open lines of communication, set goals, organize academics, regularly track progress, identify trouble spots, get to know their child's teacher, and celebrate their children's successes.

Project Focus

You and your team work for the director of information security. Your team's assignment is to develop a document discussing the importance of creating information security polices and an information security plan. Be sure to include the following:

- The importance of educating employees on information security.
- A few samples of employee information security policies specifically for Making The Grade.
- Other major areas the information security plan should address.
- Signs the company should look for to determine if the Web site is being hacked.
- The major types of attacks the company should expect to experience.

Project 5:

Eyes Everywhere

The movie *Minority Report* chronicled a futuristic world where people are uniquely identifiable by their eyes. A scan of each person's eyes gives or denies them access to rooms, computers, and anything else with restrictions. The movie portrayed a black market in new eyeballs to help people hide from the authorities. (Why did they not just change the database entry instead? That would have been much easier, but a lot less dramatic.)

The idea of using a biological signature is entirely plausible since biometrics is currently being widely used and is expected to gain wider acceptance in the near future because forging documents has become much easier with the advances in computer graphics programs and color printers. The next time you get a new passport, it may incorporate a chip that has your biometric information encoded on it. Office of Special Investigations (OSI) agents with fake documents found that it was relatively easy to enter the United States from Canada, Mexico, and Jamaica, by land, sea, and air.

The task of policing the borders is daunting. Some 500 million foreigners enter the country every year and go through identity checkpoints. More than 13 million permanent-resident and border-crossing cards have been issued by the U.S. government. Also, citizens of 27 countries do not need visas to enter this country. They are expected to have passports that comply with U.S. specifications that will also be readable at the border.

In the post-9/11 atmosphere of tightened security, unrestricted border crossing is not acceptable. The Department of Homeland Security (DHS) is charged with securing the nation's borders, and as part of this plan, new entry/exit procedures were instituted at the beginning of 2003. An integrated system, using biometrics, will be used to identify foreign visitors to the United States and reduce the likelihood of terrorists entering the country.

Early in 2003, after 6 million biometric border-crossing cards had been issued, a pilot test conducted at the Canadian border detected more than 250 imposters. The testing started with two biometric identifiers: photographs for facial recognition and fingerprint scans. As people enter and leave the country, their actual fingerprints and facial features are compared to the data on the biometric chip in the passport.

Project Focus

In a team, discuss the following:

1. How do you feel about having your fingerprints, facial features, and perhaps more of your biometric features encoded in documents like your passport? Explain your answer.
2. Would you feel the same way about having biometric information on your driver's license as on your passport? Why or why not?
3. Is it reasonable to have different biometric identification requirements for visitors from different nations? Explain your answer. What would you recommend as criteria for deciding which countries fall into what categories?
4. The checkpoints U.S. citizens pass through upon returning to the country vary greatly in the depth of the checks and the time spent. The simplest involves simply walking past the

border guards who may or may not ask you your citizenship. The other end of the spectrum requires that you put up with long waits in airports where you have to line up with hundreds of other passengers while each person is questioned and must produce a passport to be scanned. Would you welcome biometric information on passports if it would speed the process, or do you think that the disadvantages of the reduction in privacy, caused by biometric information, outweighs the advantages of better security and faster border processing? Explain your answer.

Project 6:

Setting Boundaries

Even the most ethical people sometimes face difficult choices. Acting ethically means behaving in a principled fashion and treating other people with respect and dignity. It is simple to say, but not so simple to do since some situations are complex or ambiguous. The important role of ethics in our lives has long been recognized. As far back as 44 B.C., Cicero said that ethics are indispensable to anyone who wants to have a good career. Having said that, Cicero, along with some of the greatest minds over the centuries, struggled with what the rules of ethics should be.

Our ethics are rooted in our history, culture, and religion, and our sense of ethics may shift over time. The electronic age brings with it a new dimension in the ethics debate—the amount of personal information that we can collect and store, and the speed with which we can access and process that information.

Project Focus

In a team, discuss how you would react to the following situations:

1. A senior marketing manager informs you that one of her employees is looking for another job and she wants you to give her access to look through her e-mail.
2. A vice president of sales informs you that he has made a deal to provide customer information to a strategic partner, and he wants you to burn all of the customer information onto a DVD.
3. You are asked to monitor your employee's e-mail to discover if he is sexually harassing another employee.
4. You are asked to install a video surveillance system in your office to watch if employees are taking office supplies home with them.
5. You are looking on the shared network drive and discover that your boss's entire hard drive has been copied to the network for everyone to view. What do you do?
6. You have been accidentally copied on an e-mail from the CEO, which details who will be the targets of the next round of layoffs. What would you do?

Project 7:

Contemplating Sharing

Bram Cohen is the creator of one of the most successful peer-to-peer (P2P) programs ever developed, BitTorrent. BitTorrent allows users to quickly upload and download enormous amounts of data, including files that are hundreds or thousands of times bigger than a single MP3. BitTorrent's program is faster and more efficient than traditional P2P networking.

Cohen showed his code to the world at a hacker conference, as a free, open source project aimed at computer users who need a cheap way to swap software online. But the real audience turns out to be TV and movie fanatics. It takes hours to download a ripped episode of *Alias* or *Monk* off Kazaa, but BitTorrent can do it in minutes. As a result, more than 20 million people have downloaded the BitTorrent application. If any one of them misses a favorite TV show, no worries. Surely, someone has posted it as a "torrent." As for movies, if you can find it at Blockbuster, you can probably find it online somewhere—and use BitTorrent to download it. "Give and ye shall receive" became Cohen's motto, which he printed on T-shirts and sold to supporters.

Project Focus

There is much debate surrounding the ethics of peer-to-peer networking. Do you believe Bit-Torrent is ethical or unethical? Justify your answer.

Project 8:
Dashboard Design

Digital dashboards offer an effective and efficient way to view enterprisewide information at near real time. According to Nucleus Research, there is a direct correlation between use of digital dashboards and a company's return on investment (ROI), hence all executives should be using or pushing the development of digital dashboards to monitor and analyze organizational operations.

Project Focus

Design a digital dashboard for a CRM and ERP system. Be sure to address all of the following:

CRM System	ERP System
■ Customers	■ Accounting
■ Marketing	■ Finance
■ Order entry	■ Logistics
■ Collections	■ Production
■ Sales	■ Distribution
■ Customer service	■ Manufacturing
■ Billing	■ Human resources
■ Credit limits	■ SCM
■ Transportation	■ CRM

Project 9:
Great Stories

With the advent of the Internet, when customers have an unpleasant customer experience, the company no longer has to worry about them telling a few friends and family; the company has to worry about them telling everyone. Internet service providers are giving consumers frustrated with how they were treated by a company another means of fighting back. Free or low-cost computer space for Internet Web sites is empowering consumers to tell not only their friends, but also the world about the way they have been treated. A few examples of disgruntled customer stories from the Internet include:

■ **Bad Experience with Blue Marble Biking**—Tourist on biking tour is bitten by dog, requires stitches. Company is barred from hotel because of incident, and in turn it bars the tourist from any further tours.

■ **Best Buy Receipt Check**—Shopper declines to show register receipt for purchase to door guard at Lakewood Best Buy, which is voluntary. Employees attempt to seize cart, stand in shopper's path, and park a truck behind shopper's car to prevent departure.

■ **Enterprise Rent-A-Car Is a Failing Enterprise**—Enterprise Rent-A-Car did not honor reservations, did not have cars ready as stated, rented cars with nearly empty tanks, and charged higher prices to corporate account holders.

Project Focus

The Internet is raising the stakes for customer service. With the ability to create a Web site dedicated to a particular issue, a disgruntled customer can have nearly the same reach as a manufacturer. The Internet is making it more difficult for companies to ignore their customers' complaints. In a group, search the Web for the most outrageous story of a disgruntled customer. A few places to start include:

- **Complain Complain (complaincomplain.net)**— Provides professionally written, custom complaint letters to businesses.
- **The Complaint Department (www.thecomplaintdepartment.ca)**— A for-fee consumer complaint resolution and letter writing service.
- **The Complaint Station (www.thecomplaintstation.com)**— Provides a central location to complain about issues related to companies' products, services, employment, and get rich quick scams.
- **Complaints.com Consumer Complaints (www.complaints.com)**— Database of consumer complaints and consumer advocacy.
- **Baddealings.com (www.baddealings.com)**— Forum and database on consumer complaints and scams on products and services.

Project 10:

Classic Car Problems

Classic Cars Inc. operates high-end automotive dealerships that offer luxury cars along with luxury service. The company is proud of its extensive inventory, top-of-the-line mechanics, and especially its exceptional service, which even includes a cappuccino bar at each dealership.

The company currently has 40 sales representatives at four locations. Each location maintains its own computer systems, and all sales representatives have their own contact management systems. This splintered approach to operations causes numerous problems including customer communication issues, pricing strategy issues, and inventory control issues. A few examples include:

- A customer shopping at one dealership can go to another dealership and receive a quote for a different price for the same car.
- Sales representatives are frequently stealing each other's customers and commissions.
- Sales representatives frequently send their customers to other dealerships to see specific cars and when the customer arrives, the car is not on the lot.
- Marketing campaigns are not designed to target specific customers; they are typically generic, such as 10 percent off a new car.
- If a sales representative quits, all of his or her customer information is lost.

Project Focus

You are working for Customer One, a small consulting company that specializes in CRM strategies. The owner of Classic Cars Inc., Tom Repicci, has hired you to help him formulate a strategy to put his company back on track. Develop a proposal for Tom detailing how a CRM system can alleviate the company's issues and create new opportunities.

Project 11:

Building Visibility

Visionary companies are building extended enterprises to best compete in the new Internet economy. An extended enterprise combines the Internet's power with new business structures and processes to eliminate old corporate boundaries and geographic restrictions. Networked supply chains create seamless paths of communication among partners, suppliers, manufacturers, retailers, and customers. Because of advances in manufacturing and distribution, the cost of developing new products and services is dropping, and time to market is speeding up. This has resulted in increasing customer demands, local and global competition, and increased pressure on the supply chain.

To stay competitive, companies must reinvent themselves so that the supply chain—sourcing and procurement, production scheduling, order fulfillment, inventory management, and customer care—is no longer a cost-based back-office exercise, but rather a flexible operation designed to effectively address today's challenges.

The Internet is proving an effective tool in transforming supply chains across all industries. Suppliers, distributors, manufacturers, and resellers now work together more closely and effectively than ever. Today's technology-driven supply chain enables customers to manage their own buying experiences, increases coordination and connectivity among supply partners, and helps reduce operating costs for every company in the chain.

Project Focus

In the past, assets were a crucial component of success in supply chain management. In today's market, however, a customer-centric orientation is key to retaining competitive advantage. Using the Internet and any other resources available, develop a strategic plan for implementing a networked, flexible supply chain management system for a start-up company of your choice. Research Netflix if you are unfamiliar with how start-up companies are changing the supply chain. Be sure that your supply chain integrates all partners—manufacturers, retailers, suppliers, carriers, and vendors—into a seamless unit and views customer relationship management as a key competitive advantage. There are several points to consider when creating your customer-centric supply chain strategy:

- Taking orders is only one part of serving customer needs.
- Businesses must fulfill the promise they make to customers by delivering products and information upon request—not when it is convenient for the company.
- Time to market is a key competitive advantage. Companies must ensure uninterrupted supply, and information about customer demands and activities is essential to this requirement.
- Cost is an important factor. Companies need to squeeze the costs from internal processes to make the final products less expensive.
- Reducing design-cycle times is critical, as this allows companies to get their products out more quickly to meet customer demand.

Project 12:

Bean Integration

At Flavors, a premium coffee shop, customers receive more than just a great cup of coffee—they receive exposure to music, art, literature, and town events. Flavor's calendar for programs gives their customers a quick view into their corner of the world—from live music and art displays, to volunteering or a coffee tasting. Flavors offers the following:

- Music Center—Information to all live music events occurring in the area. The store also hosts an open microphone two nights a week for local musicians.
- Art Gallery—A space in the store filled with great pieces from local artists.
- Book Clubs—Customers can meet to discuss current and classic literature.
- Coffee Sampler—Customers can sample coffees from around the world with the experts.
- Community Events—Weekly meetings are held where customers can find ways to become more involved in their community.
- Brewing Courses—Offer the finer details of the brewing, grinding, and blending equipment for sale in Flavor stores—from the traditional press to a digital espresso machine. Also includes a trouble-shooting guide developed by brewing specialists.

Project Focus

Flavors sales are great and profits are soaring however, current operations need a complete overhaul. The owners of Flavors, J.P. Field and Marla Lily, built the business piece-by-piece over the last 12 years. The following offers a quick look at current operations.

- Flavors does not receive any information on how many of its customers attend live music events. Musicians typically maintain a fan e-mail listing and CD sales records for the event, however this information is not always provided to the store.
- Book club events are booked and run through the local book store—Pages Up. Pages Up runs a tab during the book club and provides Flavor with a check at the end of each month for all book club events. Flavors has no access to book club customer information or sales information.
- Artist gallery is run by several local artists who pay Flavors a small commission on each sale. Flavors has no input into the art contained in the store or information on customers who purchase art.
- Coffee sampler events are run through Flavors primary operations.
- Community event information is open to all members of the community. Each event is run by a separate organization, which provides monthly event feedback to Flavors in a variety of formats from Word to Access files.
- Brewing and machine resource courses are run by the equipment manufacturer and all customer and sales information is provided to Flavors in a Word document at the end of each year.

You have been hired as a consultant to Flavors. The owners want to revamp the way the company operates so it can take advantage of marketing and sales opportunities across its many different lines of business. For example, offering customers who attend book club events discounts on art and brewing and machine resource courses. They also want to gain a better understanding of how the different events impact sales. For example, should they have more open microphone nights or more book clubs? Currently, they have no way to tell which events result in higher sales. Flavors would like you to create a CRM marketing strategy to help them gain visibility across their company.

Project 13:

Working Together

Upon execution of a business process, a workflow system dictates the presentation of the information, tracks the information, and maintains the information's status. For example, the following highlights the common steps performed during a team project:

1. Find out what information and deliverables are required for the project and the due date.
2. Divide the work among the team members.
3. Determine due dates for the different pieces of work.
4. Compile all the completed work together into a single project.

One of the hardest parts of a team project is getting team members to complete their work on time. Often one team member cannot perform his or her work until another team member has finished. This situation causes work to sit idle waiting for a team member to pick it up to either approve it, continue working on it, or reformat it. Workflow systems help to automate the process of presenting and passing information around a team.

Project Focus

You have just received an assignment to work on a group project with 10 other students. The project requires you to develop a detailed business plan for a business of your choice. The types of activities you will need to perform include market analysis, industry analysis, growth opportunities, Porter's Five Forces analysis, financial forecasts, competitive advantage analysis, and so on.

For your project, determine the following:

1. How could you use collaboration tools to facilitate the sharing of information and the completion of the project?
2. What advantages can your group gain from using Groupware?
3. What advantages can your group gain from using IM?
4. How could you use a workflow system to manage the tasks for the group members?
5. Describe a few of the biggest issues you anticipate experiencing during the group project. Identify ways that you can resolve these issues using collaboration tools.

Project 14:

Different Dimensions

The focus of data warehousing is to extend the transformation of data into information. Data warehouses offer strategic level, external, integrated, and historical information so businesses can make projections, identify trends, and make key business decisions. The data warehouse collects and stores integrated sets of historical information from multiple operational systems and feeds them to one or more data marts. It may also provide end-user access to support enterprisewide views of information.

Project Focus

You are currently working on a marketing team for a large corporation that sells jewelry around the world. Your boss has asked you to look at the following dimensions of data to determine which ones you want in your data mart for performing sales and market analysis (see Figure AYK.2). As a team, categorize the different dimensions ranking them from 1 to 5, with 1 indicating that the dimension offers the highest value and must be in your data mart and 5 indicating that the dimension offers the lowest value and does not need to be in your data mart.

FIGURE AYK.2

Data Warehouse Data

Dimension	Value (1–5)	Dimension	Value (1–5)
Product number		Season	
Store location		Promotion	
Customer net worth		Payment method	
Number of sales personnel		Commission policy	
Customer eating habits		Manufacturer	
Store hours		Traffic report	
Sales person ID		Customer language	
Product style		Weather	
Order date		Customer gender	
Product quantity		Local tax information	
Ship date		Local cultural demographics	
Current interest rate		Stock market closing	
Product cost		Customer religious affiliation	
Customer's political affiliation		Reason for purchase	
Local market analysis		Employee dress code policy	
Order time		Customer age	
Customer spending habits		Employee vacation policy	
Product price		Employee benefits	
Exchange rates		Current tariff information	
Product gross margin			

Project 15:

Connecting Components

Components of a solid enterprise architecture include everything from documentation to business concepts to software and hardware. Deciding which components to implement and how to implement them can be a challenge. New IT components are released daily, and business needs continually change. An enterprise architecture that meets your organization's needs today may not meet those needs tomorrow. Building an enterprise architecture that is scalable, flexible, available, accessible, and reliable is key to your organization's success.

Project Focus

You are the enterprise architect for a large clothing company called Xedous. You are responsible for developing the initial enterprise architecture. Create a list of questions you will need answered to develop your architecture. Below is an example of a few questions you might ask.

- What are the company's growth expectations?
- Will systems be able to handle additional users?
- How long will information be stored in the systems?
- How much customer history must be stored?
- What are the organization's business hours?
- What are the organization's backup requirements?

Project 16:

Internet Groceries

E-Grocery, founded in 2005, is an online grocery shopping and delivery service. The company caters to thousands of customers in the Phoenix, Seattle, and Denver areas. Established on the idea that people will buy groceries over the Internet, e-Grocery offers over 25,000 items.

Ninety percent of e-Grocery's orders come in via computer; the rest are received by fax. Orders are received at the central office in Lakewood, Colorado, and then distributed by e-mail to a local affiliate store. The store receives the order, the delivery address, and a map to the order location. A store employee designated to online orders will fill, deliver, and collect for the order. E-Grocery members are charged actual shelf prices, plus a per-order charge of $5.00 or 5 percent of the order amount, whichever is greater. Members also receive additional benefits such as electronic coupons, customer discounts, recipes, and tips.

Project Focus

The company is using interactive technology to change the shopping experience. The success of e-Grocery lies within many areas. Analyze the e-Grocery business model using the questions below. Feel free to think outside the box to develop your own analysis of online grocery shopping and e-business models.

1. What is e-Grocery's e-business model?
2. How does e-Grocery compete with traditional retailers?
3. What value can e-Grocery offer as a true competitive advantage in this marketplace?
4. What is the threat of new entrants in this market segment?
5. How is e-Grocery using technology to change the shopping experience?
6. What are the logistics for making e-Grocery profitable?
7. How does e-Grocery profit from online customer interaction?
8. What kinds of e-business strategies can e-Grocery's marketing department use to help grow its business?
9. What are some of the benefits and challenges facing e-Grocery?

Project 17:

Getting Personal

Consider Sally Albright the reigning queen of customization in the movie *When Harry Met Sally*. Take, for example, the scene where she orders pie a la mode: "I'd like the pie heated. And I don't want the ice cream on top; I want it on the side. And I'd like strawberry instead of vanilla if you have it. If not, then no ice cream, just whipped cream, but only if it's real." Particular, yes, but Sally knew what she liked—and was not afraid to ask for it.

Project Focus

A growing number of online retailers are letting you have it your way, too. Choose a company highlighted in Figure AYK.3 and create your own product. Was the Web site easy to use? Would this service entice you as a customer to make a purchase over a generic product? If you could personalize a product what would it be and how would the Web site work?

Company	Product
Tommy Hilfiger, custom.tomm.com	Premium-cotton chinos and jeans ($98)
Lands' End, www.landsend.com	Utilitarian jeans and chinos made of luxurious twill in traditional silhouettes ($59)
JCPenney, www.custom.jcpenney.com	Substantial twill pants in classic cuts ($44)
Ralph Lauren Polo, www.polo.com	Everything from basic polos to oxford shirts ($80)
TIMBUK2; www.timbuk2.com	Hip nylon messenger bags ($105)
L.L. Bean, www.llbean.com	Sturdy and colorful books, totes, and messenger bags ($70)
Nike, www.nikeid.com	Full range of athletic shoes and accessories ($90)
VANS, www.vans.com	Classic "Old Skool" lace-up or slip-on sneakers ($50)
Converse, www.converseone.com	Custom Chuck Taylors, the company's most classic style ($60)

FIGURE AYK.3

Customization Companies

Project 18:

Express Yourself

One of the most popular Web sites among students is MySpace, a site that allows students to express themselves by personalizing their home page. What is your favorite band? Who is your favorite author? What is your favorite movie? You can find out a lot about a person by finding out the answers to these questions.

Project Focus

Build a Web site dedicated to your favorite band, book, or movie. Your Web site must contain all of the following:

- An image.
- Two different size headings.
- Different sizes and colors of text.
- Two horizontal rules.

- Text that is bolded, underlined, and/or italicized.
- A textured background.
- A link to a Web site.
- A link to your e-mail.
- One numbered and one unnumbered list.

Project 19:

Creating a Presence

More than 1 billion people are on the Internet. Having an Internet presence is critical for any business that wants to remain competitive. Businesses need their Web sites to create a "buzz" to attract customers. E-business Web sites must be innovative, stimulating, add value, and provide useful information. In short, the site must build a sense of community and collaboration, eventually becoming the "port of entry" for business.

Project Focus

You are applying for a job at BagEm, a start-up e-business devoted to selling custom book bags that does not have any physical stores and only sells bags over the Internet. You are up against several other candidates for the job. BagEm has asked you to use your business expertise and Web site development skills to design and build a potential Web site. The candidate with the best Web site will be awarded the job. Good luck!

Project 20:

GoGo Gadgets

Now that wi-fi and other types of high-speed wireless networks are becoming common, devices using that technology are multiplying rapidly. Wireless gadgets run the gamut from cell phones to kitchen appliances and digital cameras. Here are some of the hottest new wireless broadband gadgets.

- Samsung's $3,499 POPCON refrigerator will feature a wi-fi enabled, detachable screen that can function as a TV. The fridge also can be programmed to remember products' expiration dates and generate alerts when the milk is getting old.
- The Nokia 770 Internet Tablet is small enough to fit in a pocket. It comes with a 4.13-inch-wide touch screen that can be used to access the Web over a wi-fi network. The $350 device can also access the Web via a cell phone with a Bluetooth connection.
- Motorola's latest E815 mobile phone operates over Verizon Wireless's new EVDO (Evolution Data Optimized) wireless network, offering speeds comparable to digital subscriber line (DSL). The phone can even record and play back video clips. It also features a built-in MP3 digital music player.
- Hop-On's just-announced HOP 1515 may look like a typical cell phone, but it actually makes calls over wi-fi networks. Typically sold with a $20 to $30 monthly service plan, the phone allows for unlimited over-the-Web international and long-distance calling. The $39 HOP 1515 is sold through wi-fi hotspot operators, wireless carriers, and retailers.
- Eastman Kodak's EasyShare-One is a digital camera with wi-fi capabilities, allowing users to share their snapshots wirelessly. You will be able to snap a photo and immediately show it to a friend on a wi-fi-enabled PC or TV.

Project Focus

A dizzying array of new wireless technologies now promises to make today's wi-fi networks seem like poky dial-up connections by comparison. These new technologies will extend the reach of wireless networks, not just geographically but also into new uses in the home and office.

1. Research the Internet and discover new wireless devices that entrepreneurs and established companies can use to improve their business.

2. Explain how businesses can use these devices to create competitive advantages, streamline production, and improve productivity.

Project 21:

Back on Your Feet

You are working for GetSmart, a document creation company for legal professionals. Due to the highly sensitive nature in the industry, employees must store all work on the network drive and are not allowed to backup the data to a CD, flash drive, or any other type of external storage including home computers. The company has been following this policy for the last three years without any issues. You return to work Monday morning after a long weekend to find that the building was struck by lightning destroying several servers. Unfortunately, the backup strategy failed and all of the data from your department has been lost.

When the head of the company demanded an explanation as to why they did not have any individual backups, he was shown the company policy he had signed not once but three times. The end result was the head of IT along with four of his cronies that had developed this ridiculous policy were fired.

Project Focus

You have been placed on a committee with several of your peers to revamp the backup and recovery policies and create a new disaster recovery plan. You must create policies and procedures that will preserve the sensitive nature of the documents, while ensuring the company is safe from disasters. Be sure to address a worst case scenario where the entire building is lost.

Project 22:

GEM Athletic Center

First Information Corporation is a large consulting company that specializes in systems analysis and design. The company has over 2,000 employees and first-quarter revenues reached $15 million. The company prides itself on maintaining an 85 percent success rate for all project implementations. The primary reason attributed to the unusually high project success rate is the company's ability to define accurate, complete, and high quality business requirements.

The GEM Athletic Center located in Cleveland, Ohio, is interested in implementing a new payroll system. The current payroll process is manual and takes three employees two days each month to complete. The GEM Athletic Center does not have an IT department and is outsourcing the entire procurement, customization, and installation of the new payroll system to First Information Corporation.

Project Focus

You have been working for First Information for a little over one month. Your team has just been assigned the GEM Athletic Center project and your first task is to define the initial business requirements for the development of the new payroll system.

1. Review the testimony of three current GEM Athletic Center accounting employees who detail the current payroll process along with their wish list for the new system. Use the files MaggieCleaver.doc, AnneLogan.doc, JimPoulos.doc.
2. Review the Characteristics of Good Business Requirements document (BusinessRequirements.doc) that highlights several techniques you can use to develop solid business requirements.
3. After careful analysis, create a report detailing the business requirements for the new system. Be sure to list any assumptions, issues, or questions in your document.

   Data Folder: AYK 22_Data

Project 23:

Confusing Coffee

Business requirements are the detailed set of business requests that any new system must meet in order to be successful. A sample business requirement might state "The system must track all customer sales by product, region, and sales representative." This requirement states what the system must do from the business perspective, giving no details or information on how the system is going to meet this requirement.

Project Focus

You have been hired to build an employee payroll system for a new coffee shop. Review the following business requirements and highlight any potential issues.

- All employees must have a unique employee ID.
- The system must track employee hours worked based on employee's last name.
- Employees must be scheduled to work a minimum of eight hours per day.
- Employee payroll is calculated by multiplying the employee's hours worked by $7.25.
- Managers must be scheduled to work morning shifts.
- Employees cannot be scheduled to work more than eight hours per day.
- Servers cannot be scheduled to work morning, afternoon, or evening shifts.
- The system must allow managers to change and delete employees from the system.

Project 24:

Picking Projects

You are a project management contractor attempting to contract work at a large telecommunications company, Hex Incorporated. Your interview with Debbie Fernandez, the senior vice president of IT, went smoothly. The last thing Debbie wants to see from you before she makes her final hiring decision is a prioritized list of the projects below. You are sure to land the job if Debbie is satisfied with your prioritization.

Project Focus

Create a report for Debbie prioritizing the following projects and be sure to include the business justifications for your prioritization.

- Upgrade accounting system.
- Develop employee vacation tracking system.
- Enhance employee intranet.
- Cleanse and scrub data warehouse information.
- Performance test all hardware to ensure 20 percent growth scalability.
- Implement changes to employee benefits system.
- Develop backup and recovery strategy.
- Implement supply chain management system.
- Upgrade customer relationship management system.
- Build executive information system for CEO.

Project 25:

Keeping Time

Time Keepers Inc. is a small firm that specializes in project management consulting. You are a senior project manager, and you have recently been assigned to the Tahiti Tanning Lotion account. The Tahiti Tanning Lotion company is currently experiencing a 10 percent success rate (90 percent failure rate) on all internal IT projects. Your first assignment is to analyze one of the current project plans being used to develop a new CRM system (see Figure AYK.4).

Project Focus

1. Review the project plan and create a document listing the numerous errors in the plan. Be sure to also provide suggestions on how to fix the errors.
2. If you have access to Microsoft Project, open the file BadProject.mpp. Fix the errors you found in question 1 directly to BadProject.mpp. (If you are new to using Microsoft Project, review the document MSProjectGuidelines.doc for an overview of several tips for using Microsoft Project.)

Data Folder: AYK 25_Data

Project 26:

Controlling Your Spend

You have been introduced to Microsoft Excel and are ready to begin using it to help track your monthly expenses and take charge of your financial destiny. The first step is to create a personal budget so you can see where you are spending money and if you need to decrease your monthly expenses or increase your monthly income.

Project Focus

Create a template for a monthly budget of your income and expenditures, with some money set aside for savings. Create variations of this budget to show how much you could save if you cut back on certain expenses, found another roommate, or got a part-time job. Compare costs of meal plan to costs of groceries. Consider how much interest would be earned on savings if $100 saved monthly. Or how much debt paid on student loans or credit card bills. To expand your data set, make a fantasy budget for 10 years from now, when you might own a home, owe student loan payments, and have a good salary.

Project 27:

Gearing for Cash

Gears is a five year old company that specializes in bike components. The company is having trouble paying for its monthly supplies and would like to perform a cash flow analysis so it can understand its financial position. Cash flow represents the money an investment produces after subtracting cash expenses from income. The statement of cash flows summarizes sources and uses of cash, indicates whether enough cash is available to carry on routine operations, and offers an analysis of all business transactions, reporting where the firm obtained its cash and how it chose to allocate the cash. The cash flow statement shows where money comes from, how the company is going to spend it, and when the company will require additional cash. Gears would like to project a cash flow statement for the next month.

Project Focus

Please create the following cash flow statement for Gears in Excel. Be sure to create formulas so the company can simply input numbers in the future to determine cash flow.

Gears Cash Flow Statement January 2009	
Cash on Hand (beginning of month)	$18,456
CASH RECEIVED	
Cash Sales	$23,894
Credit Sales Accounts	$36,421
TOTAL CASH RECEIVED	$60,315
CASH PAID OUT	
Inventory	$15,340
Payroll expenses	$17,560
Supplies (office & oper.)	$ 4,500
Repairs & maintenance	$ 3,500
Advertising	$ 2,890
Car, delivery & travel	$ 1,500
Accounting & legal	$ 750
Rent	$ 4,000
Telephone	$ 120
Utilities	$ 430
Insurance	$ 1,020
Taxes (real estate, etc.)	$ 600
Miscellaneous	$ 350
TOTAL CASH PAID OUT	$52,560
CASH POSITION (END OF MONTH)	$ 7,755

Project 28:

Book Boxes

Books, Books, Books is a wholesale distributor of popular books. The business buys overstocked books and sells them for a discount of over 50 percent to local area bookstores. The owner of the company, BK Kane, would like to determine the best approach to boxing books so he can make the most profit possible. The local bookstores accept all shipments from Books, Books, Books because of BK's incredibly low prices. BK can order as many over-stocked books as he requires, and this week's options include:

Title	Weight	Cost	Sale Price
Harry Potter, JK Rowling	5 lb	$9	$17
The Lord of the Rings, JRR Tolkien	4 lb	$8	$13
Chronicles of Narnia, CS Lewis	3.5 lb	$7	$11
A Series of Unfortunate Events, Lemony Snicket	3 lb	$6	$9
Charlie and the Chocolate Factory, Roald Dahl	2.5 lb	$5	$7
A Wrinkle in Time, Madeleine L'Engle	1 lb	$4	$5

Project Focus

When packing a single box BK must adhere to the following:

- 20 books or less.
- Books by three different authors.
- Between four and eight books from each author.
- Weight equal to or less than 50 pounds.

BK has come to you to help him determine which books he should order to maximize his profit based on the above information. Using Excel, determine the optimal book order for a single box of books.

Project 29:

SplashEm

SplashEm is a popular amusement park filled with roller coasters, games, and a water park. Boasting 24 roller coasters, 10 of which exceed 200 feet and 70 miles per hour, and five water parks, the park's attendance remains steady throughout the season. Due to the park's popularity, it is not uncommon for entrance lines to exceed one hour on busy days. SplashEm would like your help to find a solution to decrease park entrance lines.

Project Focus

SplashEm would like to implement a scanner system that can allow employees to walk around the front gates and accept credit card purchases and print tickets on the spot. The park anticipates an overall increase in sales of 4 percent per year with online ticketing, with an expense of 6 percent of total sales for the scanning equipment. SplashEm would like you to create a workbook that compares scanning sales and traditional sales. Be sure to include formulas for all assumptions including:

- Tickets sold at the booth.
- Tickets sold by the scanner.
- Revenues generated by booth sales.
- Revenues generated by scanner sales.
- Scanner ticket expense.
- Revenue with and without scanner sales.
- Three year row totals.

    Data Folder: AYK 29_Data

Project 30:

Tally's Purchases

Tally is a start-up Web site development company located in Seattle, Washington. The company currently has seven employees and is looking to hire six new employees in the next month.

Project Focus

You are in charge of purchasing for the Tally company. Your first task is to purchase the computers for the new employees. Your budget is $250,000 to buy the best computer systems with a scanner, three color printers, and business software. Use the Web to research various products and calculate the costs of different systems using Excel. Use plenty of formulas as you analyze costs and compare prices.

Project 31:

Tracking Donations

Lazarus Consulting is a large computer consulting company in New York. Pete Lazarus, the CEO and founder, is well known for his philanthropic efforts. Pete knows that most of his employees contribute to nonprofit organizations and wants to reward them for their efforts while encouraging others to contribute to charities. Pete began a program that matches 50 percent of each employee donation. The only stipulations are that the charity must be a nonprofit organization and the company will only match up to $2,000 per year per employee.

Project Focus

Open the file Lazarus_data.xls and determine the following:

- What was the total donation amount per organization?
- What were the average donations per organization?

  Data Folder: AYK 31_Data

Project 32:

All Aboard

You have decided to spend the summer traveling abroad with your friends. Your trip is going to take you to France, England, Italy, Switzerland, Germany, Norway, and Ireland. You want to use Excel to convert currencies as you travel around the world.

Project Focus

Locate one of the exchange rate calculators on the Internet (www.xe.com or www.x-rates.com). Find the exchange rates for each of the countries listed above and create formulas in Excel to convert $100, $500, and $1,000.

Project 33:

In With the Out

Founded in 2005, Innovative Software provides advanced search software, Web site accessibility testing/repair software, and usability testing/repair software. All serve as part of its desktop and enterprise content management solutions for government, corporate, educational, and consumer markets. The company's solutions are used by Web site publishers, digital media publishers, content managers, document managers, business users, consumers, software companies, and consulting services companies. Innovative Software solutions help organizations develop long-term strategies to achieve Web content accessibility, enhance usability, and comply with U.S. and search standards.

In the past, Innovative Software has continually focused on providing outstanding customer service. With the informal motto of "Grow big, but stay small," the company takes pride in achieving 100 percent customer care callback. Its personal service has been an integral part of its outstanding customer service. However, the success of its "grow big" philosophy has presented new challenges.

Innovative Software has experienced rapid growth to six times its original customer-base size and is forced to deal with difficult questions for the first time, such as, "Can we serve this many customers?" "How do we ensure our commitment to personal service is not compromised as we grow?" In addition, the number of phone calls from customers having problems with one of the newer applications is on the rise.

As customer service manager for Innovative Software, your goal is to maintain the company's reputation for excellent customer service. You have been considering the option of outsourcing as a means of keeping up with the expanding call volume and are currently reviewing e-Bank, a company that has had great success with outsourcing. E-Bank outsourced its customer service to handle its large number of customers who interact with the company through several customer interaction channels. The company felt that its competencies were primarily in finance, rather than in customer service, and that it could greatly benefit from the expertise of a customer service-focused provider. E-Bank discovered that it was cost-effective to outsource its customer service center. Additionally, the outsourcing approach was relatively hassle-free, since e-Bank did not have to set up its own customer contact center (i.e., call center).

Project Focus

1. Create an analysis from the data provided in Forecast_Data.xls, which includes:

   - DATE—the actual date of the phone calls made to customer service about the search software.
   - SALES VOLUME—the number of search software units sold that day.
   - NUMBER OF CALLS—the number of calls received in customer service for the search software.

   Business assumptions include:

   - Innovative Software's customer service department is already near its call volume capacity. Any significant increase in calls would result in a decline in the company's 100 percent callback record.
   - You need to consider what approach would be more cost effective—adding customer service representatives or outsourcing—if your forecast predicts sudden growth in call volume. All else being equal, it would cost 30 percent less to increase call volume capacity by 50 percent if you outsourced.
   - The price of the products, the actual product type, and any warrantee information is irrelevant.
   - Develop a growth, trend, and forecast analysis. You should use a three-day moving average; a shorter moving average might not display the trend well and a much longer moving average would shorten the trend too much. Hint: A three-day moving average is done by taking the Actual Calls and dividing that by the Forecast Calls over a three-day period. As an example, on the fourth day you would calculate the average for the Actual Calls for days 1, 2, and 3.
   - You can create an effective forecast as long as you have a reasonable baseline to create a forecast. A baseline is a set of numeric observations made over time that is ordered from the earliest observation to the most recent. All the time periods in the baseline are of equal length.
   - You will want to use the TREND worksheet function in Excel to create a regression forecast. The regression approach to forecasting will help you to make projections into the future. The TREND function creates forecasts based on a linear relationship between the times that the observation was made. However, you will have to create a GROWTH pattern to determine the nonlinear forecasts if the line has a dramatic upward or downward curve to it.
   - Upon completing your analysis, provide detailed and thorough documentation (in narrative, numeric, and graphic forms) that justifies your outsourcing recommendations.

Data Folder: AYK 33_Data

Project 34:

Woods You

One of the main products of the Fairway Woods Company is custom-made golf clubs. The clubs are manufactured at three plants (Denver, Colorado; Phoenix, Arizona; and Dallas, Texas) and are then shipped by truck to five distribution warehouses in Sacramento, California; Salt Lake City, Utah; Chicago, Illinois; Albuquerque, New Mexico; and New York City, New York. Since shipping costs are a major expense, management has begun an analysis to determine ways to reduce them. For the upcoming golf season, an estimate has been made of what the output will be from each manufacturing plant and how much each warehouse will require to satisfy its customers.

The CIO from Fairway Woods Company has created a workbook for you, Fairways_Data.xls, of the shipping costs from each manufacturing plant to each warehouse as a baseline analysis. Some business rules and requirements you should be aware of include:

- The problem presented involves the shipment of goods from three plants to five regional warehouses.
- Goods can be shipped from any plant to any warehouse, but it costs more to ship goods over long distances than over short distances.

Project Focus

1. Your goal is to minimize the costs of shipping goods from production plants to warehouses, thereby meeting the demand from each metropolitan area while not exceeding the supply available from each plant. To complete this project it is recommended that you use the Solver function in Excel to assist with the analysis.

2. Specifically you want to focus on:

   - Minimize the total shipping costs.
   - Total shipped must be less than or equal to supply at a plant.
   - Total shipped to warehouses must be greater than or equal to the warehouse demand.
   - Number to ship must be greater than or equal to 0.

   Data Folder: AYK 34_Data

Project 35:

Bill's Boots

Bill Schultz is thinking of starting a store that specializes in handmade cowboy boots. Bill is a longtime rancher in the town of Taos, New Mexico. Bill's reputation for honesty and integrity is well-known around town, and he is positive that his new store will be highly successful.

Project Focus

Before opening his store, Bill is curious about how his profit, revenue, and variable costs will change depending on the amount he charges for his boots. Bill would like you to perform the work required for this analysis and has put together a workbook called BillsBoots_Data.xls. Here are a few things to consider while you perform your analysis:

- Current competitive prices for custom cowboy boots are between $225 and $275 a pair.
- Variable costs will be either $100 or $150 a pair depending on the types of materials Bill chooses to use.
- Fixed costs are $10,000 a month.

   Data Folder: AYK 35_Data

Project 36:

Adequate Acquisitions

XMark.com is a major Internet company specializing in organic food. XMark.com is thinking of purchasing GoodGrow, another organic food Internet company. GoodGrow has current revenues of $100 million, with expenses of $150 million. Current projections indicate that Good-Grow's revenues are increasing at 35 percent per year and its expenses are increasing by 10 percent per year. XMark.com understands that projections can be erroneous, however; the company must determine the number of years before GoodGrow will return a profit.

Project Focus

You need to help XMark.com determine the number of years required to break even, using annual growth rates in revenue between 20 percent and 60 percent and annual expense growth rates between 10 and 30 percent.

Data Folder: AYK 36_Data

Project 37:

Formatting Grades

Professor Streterstein is a bit absentminded. His instructor's grade book is a mess, and he would like your help cleaning it up and making it easier to use. In Professor Sterterstein's course, the maximum possible points a student can earn is 750. The following table displays the grade equivalent to total points for the course.

Total Points	Calculated Grade
675	A
635	A-
600	B
560	B-
535	C
490	C-
450	D
0	F

Project Focus

Help Professor Streterstein rework his grade book. Open the file Streterstein_data.xls and perform the following:

1. Reformat the workbook so it is readable, understandable, and consistent. Replace column labels, format and align the headings, add borders and shading.
2. Add a column in the grade book for final grade next to the total points earned column.
3. Use the VLookup Function to automatically assess final grades based on the total points column.
4. Using the If Function, format the workbook so each student's grade shows a high level pass or fail—P for pass, F for Fail—based on the total points.

Data Folder: AYK 37_Data

Project 38:

Moving Espressos

Pony Espresso is a small business that sells specialty coffee drinks at office buildings. Each morning and afternoon, trucks arrive at offices' front entrances, and the office employees purchase various beverages such as Java du Jour and Café de Colombia. The business is profitable. Pony Espresso offices, however, are located to the north of town, where lease rates are less expensive, and the principal sales area is south of town. This means that the trucks must drive cross-town four times each day.

The cost of transportation to and from the sales area, plus the power demands of the truck's coffee brewing equipment, is a significant portion of variable costs. Pony Espresso could reduce the amount of driving and, therefore, the variable costs, if it moved the offices closer to the sales area.

Pony Espresso presently has fixed costs of $10,000 per month. The lease of a new office, closer to the sales area, would cost an additional $2,200 per month. This would increase the fixed costs to $12,200 per month.

Although the lease of new offices would increase the fixed costs, a careful estimate of the potential savings in gasoline and vehicle maintenance indicates that Pony Espresso could reduce the variable costs from $0.60 per unit to $0.35 per unit. Total sales are unlikely to increase as a result of the move, but the savings in variable costs should increase the annual profit.

Project Focus

Consider the information provided to you from the owner (PonyEspresso.xls). Especially look at the change in the variability of the profit from month to month. From November through January, when it is much more difficult to lure office workers out into the cold to purchase coffee, Pony Espresso barely breaks even. In fact, in December 2004, the business lost money.

1. Develop the cost analysis on the existing lease information using the monthly sales figures provided to you in the file PonyEspresso.xls.
2. Develop the cost analysis from the new lease information provided above.
3. Calculate the variability that is reflected in the month-to-month standard deviation of earnings for the current cost structure and the projected cost structure.
4. Do not consider any association with downsizing such as overhead—simply focus on the information provided to you.
5. You will need to calculate the EBIT (earnings before interest and taxes).

Data Folder: AYK 38_Data

Project 39:

Reducing Transports

Hoover Transportation, Inc., is a large distribution company located in Denver, Colorado. The company is currently looking to gain operational efficiencies in its supply chain by reducing the number of transportation carriers that it is using to outsource. Operational efficiencies for Hoover Transportation, Inc., suggest that reducing the number of carriers from the Denver distribution center to warehouses in the selected states will lead to reduced costs. Brian Hoover, the CEO of Hoover Transportation, requests that the number of carriers transporting products from its Denver distribution center to wholesalers in Arizona, Arkansas, Iowa, Missouri, Montana, Oklahoma, Oregon, and Washington be reduced from the current five carriers to one or two carriers.

Project Focus

Carrier selection should be based on the assumptions that all environmental factors are equal and historical cost trends will continue. Review the historical raw data from the past several years to determine your recommendation for the top two carriers that Hoover Transportation should continue to use.

1. Analyze the last 24 months of Hoover's Transportation carrier transactions found in HooverTransportation.xls.

2. Create a report detailing your recommendation for the top two carriers with which Hoover Transportation should continue to do business. Be sure to use PivotTables and PivotCharts in your report. A few questions to get you started include:

- Calculate the average cost per carrier.
- Calculate the total shipping costs per state.
- Calculate the total shipping weights per state.
- Calculate the average shipping costs per pound.
- Calculate the average cost per carrier.

Data Folder: AYK 39_Data

Project 40:

Better Business

Schweizer Distribution specializes in distributing fresh produce to local restaurants in the Chicago area. The company currently sells 12 different products through the efforts of three sales representatives to 10 restaurants. The company, like all small businesses, is always interested in finding ways to increase revenues and decrease expenses.

The company's founder, Bob Schweizer, has recently hired you as a new business analyst. You have just graduated from college with a degree in marketing and a specialization in customer relationship management. Bob is eager to hear your thoughts and ideas on how to improve the business and help the company build strong lasting relationships with its customers.

Project Focus

Bob has provided you with last year's sales information in the file RestaurantSales_Data.xls. Help Bob analyze his distribution company by using a Pivot Table to determine the following:

1. Who is Bob's best customer by total sales?
2. Who is Bob's worst customer by total sales
3. Who is Bob's best customer by total profit?
4. Who is Bob's worst customer by total profit?
5. What is Bob's best selling product by total sales?
6. What is Bob's worst selling product by total sales?
7. What is Bob's best selling product by total profit?
8. What is Bob's worst selling product by total profit?
9. Who is Bob's best sales representative by total profit?
10. Who is Bob's worst sales representative by total profit?
11. What is the best sales representative's best selling product (by total profit)?
12. Who is the best sales representative's best customer (by total profit)?
13. What is the best sales representative's worst selling product (by total profit)?
14. Who is the best sales representative's worst customer (by total profit)?

Data Folder: AYK 40_Data

Project 41:

Too Much Information

You have just landed the job of vice president of operations for The Pitt Stop Restaurants, a national chain of full-service, casual-themed restaurants. During your first week on the job, Suzanne Graham, your boss and CEO of the company, has asked you to provide an analysis of how well the company's restaurants are performing. Specifically, she would like to know which units and regions are performing extremely well, which ones are performing moderately well, and which ones are underperforming. Her goal is to identify where you should be spending time and focusing efforts to improve the overall health of the company.

Project Focus

Review the workbook entitled PittStop_Data.xls and determine how best to analyze and interpret the data. Create a formal presentation of your findings. A few things to consider include:

- Should underperforming restaurants be closed or sold?
- Should high performing restaurants be expanded to accommodate more seats?
- Should the company spend more or less on advertising?
- Which markets should adjustments be made to the advertising budget?
- How are The Pitt Stop Restaurants performing compared to its competition?
- How are units of like size performing relative to each other?

Data Folder: AYK 41_Data

Project 42:

Gizmos Turnover

Employee turnover rates are at an all-time high at Gizmo's Manufacturing plants. The company is experiencing severe worker retention issues, which are leading to productivity and quality control problems. The majority of the company's workers perform a variety of tasks and are paid by the hour. The company currently tests each potential applicant to ensure they have the skills necessary for the intense mental concentration and dexterity required to fill the positions. Since there are significant costs associated with employee turnover, Gizmo Manufacturing wants to find a way to predict which applicants have the characteristics of being a short-term versus a long-term employee.

Project Focus

1. Review the information that Gizmo Manufacturing has collected from two of its different data sources. The first file, Gizmo_Data.xls, contains information regarding employee wages. The second file, Gizmo2_Data.xls, contains information regarding employee retention.
2. Using Excel analysis functions, determine the employee characteristics that you would recommend Gizmo Manufacturing look for when hiring new personnel. It is highly recommended that you use PivotTables as part of your analysis.
3. Prepare a report based on your findings (which should include several forms of graphical representation) for your recommendations.

Data Folder: AYK 42_Data

Project 43:

Managing Martin

Martin Resorts, Inc., owns and operates four Spa and Golf resorts in Colorado. The company has five traditional lines of business: (1) golf sales; (2) golf lessons; (3) restaurants; (4) retail and rentals; and (5) hotels. David Logan, director of marketing technology at Martin Resorts, Inc., and Donald Mayer, the lead strategic analyst for Martin Resorts, are soliciting your input for their CRM strategic initiative.

Martin Resorts' IT infrastructure is pieced together with various systems and applications. Currently, the company has a difficult time with CRM because its systems are not integrated. The company cannot determine vital information such as which customers are golfing and staying at the hotel or which customers are staying at the hotel and not golfing.

For example, the three details that the customer Diego Titus (1) stayed four nights at a Martin Resorts' managed hotel, (2) golfed three days, and (3) took an all-day spa treatment the first day, are discrete facts housed in separate systems. Martin Resorts hopes that by using data warehousing technology to integrate its data, the next time Diego reserves lodging for another trip, sales associates may ask him if he would like to book a spa treatment as well, and even if he would like the same masseuse that he had on his prior trip.

Martin Resorts is excited about the possibility of taking advantage of customer segmentation and CRM strategies to help increase its business.

Project Focus

The company wants to use CRM and data warehouse technologies to improve service and personalization at each customer touch point. Using a data warehousing tool, important customer information can be accessed from all of its systems either daily, weekly, monthly, or once or twice per year. Analyze the sample data in Martin_Data.xls for the following:

1. Currently, the quality of the data within the above disparate systems is low. Develop a report for David and Donald discussing the importance of high quality information and how low quality information can affect Martin Resorts' business.

2. Review the data that David and Donald are working with from the data warehouse in the file Martin_Data.xls and Key_Data.doc.

    A. Give examples from the data showing the kind of information Martin Resorts might be able to use to gain a better understanding of its customers. Include the types of data quality issues the company can anticipate and the strategies it can use to help avoid such issues.

    B. Determine who are Martin Resorts' best customers, and provide examples of the types of marketing campaigns the company should offer these valuable customers.

    C. Prepare a report that summarizes the benefits Martin Resorts can receive from using business intelligence to mine the data warehouse. Include a financial analysis of the costs and benefits.

    Data Folder: AYK 43_Data

Project 44:

Mountain Cycle

Mountain Cycle is a company that specializes in making custom mountain bikes. The company founder, PJ Steffan, is having a hard time making the store profitable. Knowing that you have great business knowledge and solid financial sense, PJ has come to you for your advice.

Project Focus

PJ would like you to determine how many bikes Mountain Cycle needs to sell per year to break even. Using Goal Seek in Excel solve the following:

- Fixed cost equals $65,000.
- Variable cost equals $1,575.
- Bike price equals $2,500.

Project 45:

Lutz Motors

Murry Lutz owns a small shop that sells and services vintage motorcycles, Lutz Motors. Murry is curious how his profit will be affected by his sales over the next year.

Project Focus

Murry would like your help creating best, worst, and most-likely scenarios for his motorcycle sales over the next year. Using Scenario Manager help Murry analyze the worksheet Lutz_Data.xls.

Data Folder: AYK 45_Data

Project 46:

Animal Relations

Foothills Animal Hospital is a full-service small animal veterinary hospital located in Morrison, Colorado, specializing in routine medical care, vaccinations, laboratory testing, and surgery. The hospital has experienced tremendous growth over the past six months due to customer referrals. While Foothills Animal Hospital has typically kept its daily service records in a workbook format, it feels the need to expand its reporting capabilities to develop a relational database as a more functional structure.

Foothills Animal Hospital needs help developing a database, specifically:

- Create a customer table—name, address, phone, and date of entrance.
- Create a pet table—pet name, type of animal, breed, gender, color, neutered/spayed, weight, and comments.
- Create a medications table—medication code, name of medication, and cost of medication.
- Create a visit table—details of treatments performed, medications dispensed, and the date of the visit.
- Produce a daily invoice report.

Figure AYK.5 displays a sample daily invoice report that the Foothills Animal Hospital accountants have requested. Foothills Animal Hospital organizes its treatments using the codes displayed in Figure AYK.6. The entity classes and primary keys for the database have been identified in Figure AYK.7.

The following business rules have been identified:

1. A customer can have many pets but must have at least one.
2. A pet must be assigned to one and only one customer.

FIGURE AYK.5

Foothills Animal Hospital Daily Invoice Report Sample

Foothills Daily Hospital Report   6/15/2006

Customer Name	Pet Name	Type of Anim	Treatment	Amount
Amanda Smith				
	Indigo	Cat	Eye/Ear Examination	$20.00
Summary for Amanda Smith				**$20.00**
Anita Zimmerman				
	Midnight	Cat	Lab Work - Blood	$50.00
Summary for Anita Zimmerman				**$50.00**
Betsy Walsh				
	Stimpy	CAT	General Exam	$50.00
	Ren	DOG	General Exam	$50.00
Summary for Betsy Walsh				**$100.00**
John Williamson				
	Barney	DOG	Flea Spray	$50.00
Summary for John Williamson				**$50.00**
Mike Phillips				
	Thunder	DOG	General Exam	$50.00
	Micro	CAT	General Exam	$50.00
Summary for Mike Phillips				**$100.00**
Sam Jackson				
	Cuddles	CAT	Reset dislocation	$165.00
	Cuddles	CAT	Rabonius Shot	$75.00
Summary for Sam Jackson				**$240.00**
Sandra Williams				
	Flower	CAT	Tetrinious Shot	$10.00
	Shadow	CAT	General Exam	$50.00
	Flower	CAT	General Exam	$50.00
Summary for Sandra Williams				**$110.00**

Treatment Code	Treatment	Price
0100	Tetrinious Shot	$10.00
0201	Rabonius Shot	$20.00
0300	General Exam	$50.00
0303	Eye/Ear Examination	$20.00
0400	Spay/Neuter	$225.00
0405	Reset Dislocation	$165.00
0406	Amputation of Limb	$450.00
0407	Wrap Affected Area	$15.00
0408	Cast Affected Area	$120.00
1000	Lab Work—Blood	$50.00
1003	Lab Work—Misc	$35.00
2003	Flea Spray	$25.00
9999	Other Not Listed	$10.00

FIGURE AYK.6

Treatment Codes, Treatments, and Price Descriptions

Entity	Primary Key
CUSTOMER	Customer Number
PET	Pet Number
VISIT	Visit Number
VISIT DETAIL	Visit Number and Line Number (a composite key)
TREATMENT	Treatment Code
MEDICATION	Medication Code

FIGURE AYK.7

Entity Names and Primary Keys for Foothills Animal Hospital

3. A pet can have one or more treatments per visit but must have at least one.

4. A pet can have one or more medications but need not have any.

Project Focus

Your job is to complete the following tasks as they relate to this project:

1. Develop and describe the entity-relationship diagram.

2. Use normalization to assure the correctness of the tables (relations).

3. Create the database using a personal DBMS package (preferably Microsoft Access).

4. Use the data in Figure AYK.5 to populate your tables. Feel free to enter your own personal information.

5. Use the DBMS package to create the basic report in Figure AYK.5.

Project 47:

On-The-Level

On-The-Level Construction Company is a Denver-based construction company that specializes in subcontracting the development of single-family homes. In business since 1998, On-The-Level Construction has maintained a talented pool of certified staff and independent consultants providing the flexibility and combined experience required to meet the needs of its nearly 300 completed projects in the Denver metropolitan area. The field of operation methods that On-The-Level Construction is responsible for includes structural development, heating and cooling, plumbing, and electricity.

The company charges its clients by billing the hours spent on each contract. The hourly billing rate is dependent on the employee's position according to the field of operations (as noted above).

Figure AYK.8 shows a basic report that On-The-Level Construction foremen would like to see every week concerning what projects are being assigned, the overall assignment hours, and the charges for the assignment. On-The-Level Construction organizes its internal structure in four different operations—Structure (500), Plumbing (501), Electrical (502), and Heating and Ventilation (503). Each of these operational departments can and should have many subcontractors who specialize in that area.

Due to the boom in home sales over the last several years, On-The-Level Construction has decided to implement a relational database model to track project details according to project

ON-THE-LEVEL CONSTRUCTION PROJECT DETAIL

PROJECT NAME	ASSIGN DATE	EMPLOYEE LAST NAME	FIRST NAME	JOB DESCRIPTION	ASSIGN HOUR	CHARGE/HOUR
Chatfield						
	6/10/2004	Olenkoski	Glenn	Structure	2.1	$35.75
	6/10/2004	Ramora	Anne	Plumbing	2.6	$96.75
	6/10/2004	Sullivan	David	Electrical	1.2	$105.00
	6/11/2004	Frommer	Matt	Plumbing	1.4	$96.75
Summary of Assignment Hours and Charges					7.30	$588.08
Evergreen						
	6/10/2004	Sullivan	David	Electrical	1.8	$105.00
	6/10/2004	Jones	Anne	Heating and Ventalation	3.4	$84.50
	6/11/2004	Frommer	Matt	Plumbing	4.1	$96.75
	6/16/2004	Bavangi	Terry	Plumbing	4.1	$96.75
	6/16/2004	Newman	John	Electrical	1.7	$105.00
Summary of Assignment Hours and Charges					15.10	$1,448.15
Roxborough						
	6/10/2004	Ramora	Anne	Plumbing	2.6	$96.75
	6/10/2004	Washberg	Jeff	Plumbing	3.9	$96.75
	6/11/2004	Smithfield	William	Structure	2.4	$35.75
	6/11/2004	Bavangi	Terry	Plumbing	2.7	$96.75
	6/16/2004	Joen	Denise	Plumbing	2.5	$96.75
	6/16/2004	Johnson	Peter	Electrical	5.2	$105.00
Summary of Assignment Hours and Charges					19.30	$1,763.78

name, hours assigned, and charges per hour for each job description. Originally, On-The-Level Construction decided to let one of its employees handle the construction of the database. However, that employee has not had the time to completely implement the project. On-The-Level Construction has asked you to take over and complete the development of the database.

The entity classes and primary keys for the database have been identified in Figure AYK.9. The following business rules have been identified:

1. A job can have many employees assigned but must have at least one.
2. An employee must be assigned to one and only one job number.
3. An employee can be assigned to work on one or more projects.
4. A project can be assigned to only one employee but need not be assigned to any employee.

Entity	Primary Key
PROJECT	Project Number
EMPLOYEE	Employee Number
JOB	Job Number
ASSIGNMENT	Assignment Number

Project Focus

Your job is to complete the following tasks:

1. Develop and describe the entity-relationship diagram.
2. Use normalization to assure the correctness of the tables (relations).
3. Create the database using a personal DBMS package (preferably Microsoft Access).
4. Use the DBMS package to create the basic report in Figure AYK.8.
5. You may not be able to develop a report that looks exactly like the one in Figure AYK.8. However, your report should include the same information.
6. Complete personnel information is tracked by another database. For this application, include only the minimum: employee number, last name, and first name.
7. Information concerning all projects, employees, and jobs is not readily available. You should, however, create information for several fictitious projects, employees, and jobs to include in your database.

Project 48:

iToys Inventory

An independent retailer of mobile entertainment and wireless phones, iToys.com has built its business on offering the widest selection, expert advice, and outstanding customer service. However, iToys.com does not use a formal, consistent inventory tracking system. Periodically, an iToys.com employee visually checks to see what items are in stock. Although iToys.com does try to keep a certain level of each "top seller" in stock, the lack of a formal inventory tracking system has led to the overstocking of some items and understocking of other items. In fact, on occasion, a customer will request a hot item, and it is only then that iToys.com realizes that the item is out of stock. If an item is not available, iToys.com risks losing a customer to a competitor.

Lately, iToys.com has become concerned with its inventory management methods. The owner of iToys.com, Dan Connolly, wants to better manage his inventory.

The company receives orders by mail, telephone or through its Web site. Regardless of how the orders are received, what Dan needs is for a database to automate the inventory checking and ordering process.

Project Focus

Dan has provided you with a simplified version of the company's current system (an Excel workbook) for recording inventory and orders (iToys_Data.xls).

1. Develop an ERD diagram before you begin to create the database. You will need to use the information provided here as well as the data given in the Excel workbook.
2. Create an Access database that will track items (i.e., products), orders, order details, categories, suppliers, and shipping methods.
3. In addition to what is mentioned above, the database needs to track the inventory levels for each product, according to a reorder level and lead time.
4. At this time, Dan does not need information stored about the customer; he simply needs you to focus on the inventory structure.
5. Develop a query that will display the products that need to be ordered from their supplier. To complete this, you will want to compare a reorder level with how many units are in stock.
6. Develop several reports that displays:

   a. Each product ordered by its supplier. The report should include the product name, quantity on hand, and reorder level.
   b. Each supplier ordered by shipping method.
   c. Each product that requires more than five days lead time. (Hint: You will want to create a query for this first).
   d. Each product ordered by category.

7. Here are some additional business rules to assist you in completing this task:

   a. An order must have at least one product, but can contain more than one product.
   b. A product can have one or more orders, but need not have any orders.
   c. A product must belong to one and only one category, but a category many contain many different products.
   d. A product can only be stocked by one supplier, but a supplier can provide more than one product.
   e. A supplier will use one type of shipping method, but shipping methods can be used by more than one supplier.

   Data Folder: AYK 48_Data

Project 49:

Call Around

A manufacturing company, Teleworks, has been a market leader in the wireless telephone business for the last 10 years. Other firms have imitated its product with some degree of success, but they occupy a dominant position in the marketplace because Teleworks was there first with a quality product.

Just recently Teleworks began selling a new, enhanced wireless phone. This new phone does not replace its current product, but offers additional features, greater durability, and better performance for a somewhat higher price. Offering this enhanced phone has established a new revenue stream for the company.

Many sales executives at Teleworks seem to subscribe to the-more-you-have, the-more-you-want theory of managing customer data. That is, they believe they can never accumulate too much information about their customers, and that they can do their jobs more effectively by collecting infinite amounts of customer details. Having a firm grasp on a wide range of customer-focused details—specifically reports summarizing call center information—can be critical in enabling your company to successfully manage a customer relationship management (CRM) solution that creates a positive impact.

To continue to provide excellent customer support, and in anticipation of increased calls due to the release of its new product, Teleworks needs a database that it can use to record, track, and query call center information. Teleworks CIO, KED Davisson, has hired you to develop this database.

Project Focus

1. Teleworks has provided you with a workbook data file; its current approach for recording cell center information (Telworks_Data.xls).

2. Develop an ERD diagram before you begin to create the database.

3. Create an Access database that will allow data analysts to enter call center data according to the type of issue, the customer, assign each call to a consultant, and prioritize the call.

4. Develop a query that will display all issues that are "open."

5. Develop a screen form to browse all issues.

6. Develop several reports that display:

   a. All closed issues.

   b. Each issue in detail ordered by issue ID.

   c. Each issue in detail ordered by consultant.

   d. Each issue in detail ordered by category.

   e. Each issue in detail ordered by status.

7. Here are some additional business rules to assist you in completing this task:

   a. An issue must have at least one customer.

   b. A customer can have more than one issue.

   c. Each issue must be assigned to one consultant.

   d. Each consultant can be assigned to more than one issue.

   e. An issue can only belong to one category.

   f. An issue must be assigned only one status code.

   g. An issue must be assigned a priority code.

8. Priorities are assigned accordingly:

Priority Level
Critical
High
Moderate
Standard
Low

9. Status is recorded as either open or closed.

10. The categories of each issue needs to be recorded as:

Data Folder: AYK 49_Data

Project 50:
MoveIT

MoveIT is a moving company that provides moving and storage services in Colorado, New Mexico, and Wyoming. MoveIT provides a truck, driver, and one or more moving assistants to move residential and commercial items from one location to another within the defined coverage area. In addition to moving services, the company provides temporary and long-term storage in its warehouses. MoveIT's customers are commercial and residential. Some of the storage warehouses are climatically controlled for customers who need to store items that are sensitive to extreme temperatures.

The business started in 1990 with a single truck and a single warehouse in Colorado. Due to a very satisfied clientele, the company has grown over the years into a much larger business. Currently, MoveIT has one warehouse in each state it services and is working on a merger with another company that offers similar services in different service areas. When the merger is complete, MoveIT will acquire additional storage warehouses, trucks, and employees and will expand its operations into different states.

Colin Baker is the general manager of MoveIT. In the past, Colin managed the business using a combination of workbooks and paper forms. However, with a merger in the company's future, Colin needs to expand his system to manage data better. Colin recently hired Zachary Wilson, an information systems specialist, to recommend and implement a new plan for managing the company's data.

Zach's first task is to understand the current system and its limitations by talking extensively with Colin about data management and user needs. Colin explains that the office in each state accepts reservations for moving and storage services by completing a form that includes the customer's name, address, phone number, and the job's details. Jobs that involve trucking items from one location to another or from an outside location to a storage unit in a warehouse are maintained in a filing cabinet that is organized by customer name. Leases for storage space are stored alphabetically in a separate filing cabinet for each warehouse. All of the forms are stored in the on-site offices at the warehouse from which they were purchased.

Each warehouse has its own manager, office staff, and moving assistants. Drivers are contract employees and can work for any warehouse. Colin wants the new system to manage employee data, including personal information, salary information, and work performance. In addition to managing personnel data, Colin also wants to use the new system to manage information about drivers, including their personal information and driving records. The system also needs to store information about the trucks and vans that MoveIT owns and operates.

Finally, the system must maintain data about customers who utilize moving and storage services. Some customers might require storage in more than one location. When there is a request for services, the request is recorded on a form.

Zach gathered a collection of documents that will help you design the database. You need to be certain that every data item in the existing documents is also represented in the tables in your design.

Employee Information Form

Name: _Donald McCubbrey_

Address: _101 South Pine Street_

City: _Denver_   State: **CO**   Zip: _80210_

Phone: _307-444-1212_   Cell Phone: _307-441-3331_

SSN: _145-30-0001_   DOB: _9/12/1949_

The following Information will be completed by the MoveIT human resources manager.

Hire Date: _1/22/1999_   Termination Date: _____

Position: _General Manager_

Annual Salary: _$72,000_   or Hourly Rate: _____

Date of Personnel Review: _____

Notes: _____
_____
_____
_____
_____

FIGURE AYK.10

MoveIT Employee Data

Project Focus

Phase 1: Design the database

1. Zach gave you the form shown in Figure AYK.10, which collects data about employees. In addition to storing the data shown in Figure AYK.10, Zach also needs to identify the warehouse in which the employee works. On paper, design an employee table based on this form. The table design for all tables that you create should include field names, data types, field properties (as necessary), and field descriptions. Remember that each table must have a primary key field.

2. The database must manage data about drivers, who are hired on a contract basis. Design a table that stores information about drivers. The table should include the same information stored for employees, except for an indication about the warehouse in which the driver works, in addition to storing the following additional information:

   ▪ Drivers are not paid an hourly rate or salary; they are paid based on the number of miles driven for any job. The payment for a job is determined by multiplying the rate per mile by the number of miles for the job.

   ▪ MoveIT rates drivers based on their safety records, successful on-time deliveries, and other factors. The company's rating system uses the values A, B, C, D, and F to rate drivers, with A being the highest rating and F being the lowest rating. (You do not need to worry about how MoveIT assigns ratings to drivers; you only need to store the driver's rating.)

3. Design a table that stores data about the trucks and vans owned by MoveIT. Each vehicle has a unique identification number appearing on the vehicle in the format TRK-001 for trucks or VAN-009 for vans. Colin wants to store the vehicle's license plate number, number of axles, and color.

4. Design a table that stores data about warehouses using the data shown below. The warehouse identification number is the two-letter state abbreviation in which the warehouse is located followed by a dash and then a number. For example, the warehouse in Wyoming is WY-1.

Warehouse ID	Address	City	State	ZIP	Phone	Climate	Security Gate
CO-1	101 Park Way	Denver	CO	80210	(503) 551-2432	No	Yes
NM-1	1A Warehouse	Santa Fe	NM	87501	(206) 324-2312	Yes	Yes
WY-1	510 Hixson Pike	Jackson Hole	WY	83001	(307) 541-3571	Yes	No

5. Currently, information about storage units is stored in an Excel workbook; a portion of this data is shown in Figure AYK.11. Use this information to help you design a table that manages data about the storage units.

6. You also need to manage data to indicate which customer rents each unit. Colin wants to store the date the lease started and ended on each unit in each warehouse. For current customers, the ending lease date will be null. Design a table that manages data about the unit rentals.

7. When the customer requests a job, the administrative assistant from the warehouse that will perform the services fills out the form shown in Figure AYK.12. This form is considered a job order.

8. Colin needs to store the following data about customers: company name (for commercial customers only), the job contact's name, and the address, city, state, ZIP code, and phone number. Design a customer table using this information.

9. The administrative assistant uses a scheduling program to manage and assign vehicles and drivers for moving jobs, and then this information is entered into the database. Upon completion of a job, the database must store the details about the job, including the customer, truck or van used, driver, actual mileage, and actual weight. This step is considered to be the job detail. Colin wants to store job detail data separately from job order data. Design a table that manages the job detail information.

10. For each table you designed, use a piece of paper to sketch the table design so that you can enter five sample records into it. After creating five records, determine whether you need to adjust your table designs so that each table is in third normal form. If you need to make any changes to your table designs, do so on your paper and add the necessary documentation to the existing table designs.

11. Review each table design to ensure you have created all of the necessary fields. Be certain that you have designated a primary key field in each table and that your primary key field will contain unique values for each record.

12. Draw arrows to indicate the fields that will form the relationships in the database.

Phase 2: Build the database

1. Use the table designs you created in Phase 1 to build the tables in Access.

2. Check your database carefully to ensure that you have created all the tables, all the fields and set their properties, and all the necessary relationships.

FIGURE AYK.11

MoveIT Workbook

	A	B	C	D
1	UnitID	WarehouseID	UnitSize	Rent
2	1	CO-1	8 x 8	25
3	1	NM-1	12 x 12	35
4	1	WY-1	12 x 12	45
5	2	CO-1	8 x 12	30
6	2	NM-1	12 x 12	35
7	2	WY-1	12 x 12	45
8	3	CO-1	8 x 8	25
9	3	NM-1	9 x 12	30
10	3	WY-1	12 x 12	45
11	4	CO-1	8 x 12	30
12	4	NM-1	9 x 12	30
13	4	WY-1	12 x 18	70
14	5	CO-1	8 x 8	25
15	5	NM-1	12 x 12	85
16	5	WY-1	12 x 18	70
17	6	CO-1	8 x 12	30
18	6	NM-1	12 x 12	85
19	6	WY-1	12 x 12	45
20	7	CO-1	8 x 10	25
21	7	NM-1	12 x 10	80
22	7	WY-1	12 x 12	85
23	8	CO-1	15 x 15	95
24	8	NM-1	12 x 10	80
25	8	WY-1	12 x 8	35

FIGURE AYK.12

Customer Request Form

MoveIT

Job Order Information Form

Customer: _Donald McCubbrey_

Move Date: _9/1/2005_

Moving From: _1610 Pine Street, Apt #3A_
Denver, CO

Moving To: _101 Parkview Lane_
Highlands Ranch, CO

Estimated Mileage: _30_ Estimated Weight: _1250 lbs_

Packing Service Needed: Yes _x_ No ____

Heavy Items to Move? Yes _x_ No ____

Do You Need to Store Any Items? Yes ___ No _x_

3. Use the data shown below to populate the Position table.

PositionID	Title
1	General Manager
2	Warehouse Manager
3	Administrative Assistant
4	Accountant
5	Maintenance
6	Moving Assistant
7	Information Systems

4. Use the data shown below to populate the Warehouse table.

Warehouse ID	Address	City	State	ZIP	Phone	Climate	Security Gate
CO-1	101 Park Way	Denver	CO	80210	(503) 551-2432	No	Yes
NM-1	1A Warehouse	Santa Fe	NM	87501	(206) 324-2312	Yes	Yes
WY-1	510 Hixson Pike	Jackson Hole	WY	83001	(307) 541-3571	Yes	No

5. Populate the tables in your database using the data stored in the MoveIT.xls file.

Phase 3: Queries

Now that you have worked with Zach to develop the design for the MoveIT database, he explains that the most pressing task is to serve the needs of the human resources department. Haley Adams is an administrative assistant responsible for many human resources tasks, and she asks for your help extracting information from the MoveIT database. Although an outside company processes payroll for MoveIT, Haley and others maintain complete employment information and strive to meet management's goal of recruiting and retaining skilled, qualified employees who are well-trained in customer service. Having employees working in three warehouses in three states has made it difficult to track employee information, and the potential merger and expansion means that human resources must take advantage of the MoveIT database to maintain and retrieve employee information. Haley asks for your help in filtering data and creating queries that provide the information that she needs.

1. The truck drivers for MoveIT are a special type of employee, and their data are stored in a table separate from the rest of the employees because of driving certification requirements. Drivers are certified to drive trucks with a specified number of axles, and MoveIT must be certain that a driver is certified to drive a particular truck.

   a. When Haley meets with Colin, she learns that only drivers who have a driving record of A or B are allowed to drive the large trucks (those with four axles or more). She asks you to identify the drivers qualified to drive the four-axle trucks. Because she will use the list you create to call drivers when she needs a substitute, include the phone numbers and driving record for each driver. Save the query as 4AxleDrivers.

b. Haley also learns that she must immediately review drivers who have a driving record lower than A or B. Those drivers who have a record of C will be put on notice, and those with a record D or F can be terminated immediately. List the drivers with these low driving records, and sort the list so that Haley can easily determine the driving record of each driver. Because she can enroll long-term drivers in a training program, she also needs to know when each driver started working for MoveIT and whether the driver is still employed. Save the query as DriversWithLowRecords.

c. If drivers have been terminated because of their driving record, Haley wants to include them in an additional list. Create this list for Haley, and include all relevant employment information. Save this query as DriversForTermination.

2. Colin is considering providing bonuses to long-term employees. Haley asks you to list the 10 employees who have worked for MoveIT the longest. Name the query LongestEmployment.

3. To prepare for a payroll, Haley must provide a list of employees that includes their salary or hourly pay rate. The list must also include Social Security numbers and employee IDs so that an outside firm can properly process the payroll. Produce an employee list that provides this information, and sort it so that it's easy to find an employee by name. For those employees who are on a salary, the list should show their monthly wage. Save the query as Payroll.

Phase 4: Forms

Zach asks you to begin building forms that let users view and enter data. He suggests that you start by building some simple forms that will be used for entering data into the customers, drivers, employees, trucks, and warehouses tables.

1. Zach states that he wants to have simple data-entry forms for each of the following tables: customers (CustomerData), drivers (DriverData), employees (EmployeeData), vehicles (VehicleData), and warehouses (WarehouseData). Create those forms and save them in the database. As you create the forms, consider the design and layout of the form. Make selections that you feel are most appropriate for this application.

2. Open each form and view it from the perspective of the user. As you observe the form, make decisions as to what fields need to be rearranged, sized, aligned, and so on. You might even decide that a particular field doesn't need to be on the data-entry form. For example, when you are entering a customer's records, would you need the balance field for that customer? Be sure each form is attractively presented.

3. Zach has given you the logo for MoveIT (MoveIT-logo.jpg). He asks you to include the logo as well as a title on each of your forms.

Phase 5: Reports

In this project, you work with Olivia Benson, an accountant in the New Mexico warehouse of MoveIT Inc. Olivia needs to prepare a series of financial reports to present to Colin, the warehouse managers, and the accountants at MoveIT at their annual meeting. They are naturally interested in how much revenue recent jobs have generated, as well as the labor costs that offset this revenue.

1. Because Olivia will discuss all the reports at the same time, she wants them to look similar and present a consistent, unified package. She suggests that you use the following guidelines as you design the reports:

- Include the MoveIT logo at the top of every report.
- Provide an appropriate title that clearly states the purpose of each report.
- Show all dollar amounts with a dollar sign and two decimal places.

- At the bottom of every page, include the page number, total number of pages, date, and name of the person who prepared the report in the format "Prepared By: Your Name."

2. Olivia also needs a report that shows the income from the storage units. Group the information by warehouse and show the name of the renter so that it's easy to identify the renter by last name. The report should also include the rent per unit, the total rent for each warehouse, and a grand total of rent for all warehouses. Name the report StorageRevenue.

3. Olivia suspects that MoveIT could increase its income from storage units by encouraging more long-term rentals. Add a calculation to StorageRevenue that shows how long each renter has rented a storage unit. Show the figure in years with one decimal place. Name the report Longevity.

Chapter 1

1. "Apple Profit Surges 95 Percent on iPod Sales," Yahoo! News, http://news.yahoo.com/s/afp/20060118/bs_afp/uscompanyearningsit_060118225009, accessed January 18, 2005; "Apple's IPod Success Isn't Sweet Music for Record Company Sales," Bloomberg.com, http://quote.bloomberg.com/apps/news?pid=nifea&&sid=aHP5Ko1pozM0, accessed November 2, 2005; Peter Burrows, "How Apple Could Mess Up Again," BusinessWeek online, http://yahoo.businessweek.com/technology/content/jan2006/tc20060109_432937.htm, accessed January 9, 2006.

2. en.wikipedia.org/wiki/Organizational_culture, accessed July 2005.

3. "IT Master of the Senate," *CIO Magazine*, www.cio.com, accessed May 1, 2004.

4. "Integrating Information at Children's Hospital," *KMWorld*, www.kmworld.com/Articles/ReadArticle.aspx?ArticleID=10253, June 1, 2005.

5. Dave Lindorff, "General Electric and Real Time," www.cioinsight.com/article2/0,3959,686147,00.asp, accessed March 1, 2004.

6. Cisco Press, www.ciscopress.com/index.asp?rl=1, accessed March 15, 2004 .

7. Ken Blanchard, "Effectiveness vs. Efficiency," Wachovia Small Business, www.wachovia.com, accessed October 14, 2003.

8. United Nations Division for Public Economics and Public Administration, www.un.com, accessed November 10, 2003.

9. Ibid.

10. eBay Financial News, Earnings and Dividend Release, January 15, 2002.

11. "Sun and eBay Celebrate Record Uptime," www.sun.com/service/about/features/ebay.html, accessed January 14, 2004.

12. Gabriel Kahn and Cris Prystay, "'Charge It' Your Cellphone Tells Your Bank," *The Wall Street Journal*, August 13, 2003.

13. "Innovative Managers," *BusinessWeek,* April 24, 2005.

14. www.thomaslfriedman.com, accessed September 2005.

Chapter 2

1. www.investor.harley-davidson.com, accessed October 10, 2003; Bruce Caldwell, "Harley-Davidson Revs up IT Horsepower," Internetweek.com, December 7, 2000; "Computerworld 100 Best Places to Work in IT 2003," *Computerworld,* June 9, 2003, pp. 36–48; Leroy Zimdars, "Supply Chain Innovation at Harley-Davidson: An Interview with Leroy Zimdars," *Ascet 2,* April 15, 2000; "Customer Trust: Reviving Loyalty in a Challenging Economy," Pivotal Webcast, September 19, 2002; "Harley-Davidson Announces Go-Live: Continues to Expand Use of Manugistics Supplier Relationship Management Solutions," www.manugistics.com, May 7, 2002; and Roger Villareal, "Docent Enterprise Increases Technician and Dealer Knowledge and Skills to Maximize Sales Results and Customer Service," www.docent.com, August 13, 2002.

2. "1,000 Executives Best Skillset," *The Wall Street Journal*, July 15, 2003.

3. "The Visionary Elite," *Business 2.0*, December 2003, pp. S1–S5.

4. "Boston Coach Aligns Service with Customer Demand in Real Time," www-1.ibm.com/services/us/index.wss, November 4, 2003.

5. "Industry Facts and Statistics," Insurance Information Institute, www.iii.org, accessed December 2005.

6. Neil Raden, "Data, Data Everywhere," *DSSResources.com*, February 16, 2003.

7. Christopher Koch, "How Verizon Flies by Wire," *CIO Magazine*, November 1, 2004.

8. Beth Bacheldor, "Steady Supply," *InformationWeek*, November 24, 2003, www.informationweek.com, accessed June 6, 2003.

9. Neil McManus, "Robots at Your Service," *Wired*, January 2003, p. O59.

10. "Put Better, Faster Decision-Making in Your Sights," www.teradata.com, accessed July 7, 2003.

11. S. Begley, "Software au Natural," *Newsweek*, May 8, 2005.

12. McManus, "Robots at Your Service."

13. "Trek Standardizes Worldwide Operations on J. D. Edwards," www.jdedwards.com, accessed November 15, 2003.

14. Christopher Koch, "The ABC's of Supply Chain Management," www.cio.com, accessed October 12, 2003.

15. "Customer Success Stories," www.siebel.com, accessed November 12, 2003.

16. "Kaiser's Diabetic Initiative," www.businessweek.com, accessed November 15, 2003.

17. "Integrated Solutions—The ABCs of CRM," www.integratedsolutionsmag.com, accessed November 12, 2003.

18. Maureen Weicher, "Business Process Reengineering: Analysis and Recommendation," www.netlib.com, accessed February 12, 2005.

19. Michael Hammer and James Champy, *Reengineering the Corporation* (New York: HarperCollins Publishers, 2001).

20. Ibid.

21. Bruce Caldwell, "Missteps, Miscues—Business Reengineering Failures," *InformationWeek*, June 20, 1994, p. 50.

22. Barbara Ettorre, "Reengineering Tales from the Front," *Management Review*, January 1995; p. 13.

23. Thomas H. Davenport, "Will Participative Makeovers of Business Processes Succeed Where Reengineering Failed?" *Planning Review*, January 1995, p. 24.

24. Saul Berman, "Strategic Direction: Don't Reengineer Without It; Scanning the Horizon for Turbulence," *Planning Review*, November 1994, p. 18.

25. "Customer Success Stories," www.siebel.com, accessed November 12, 2005.

26. Rachel Metz, "Changing at the Push of a Button," *Wired,* September 27, 2004.

27. "The Incredible Lateness of Delta," *CIO Magazine*, www.cio.com, accessed February 15, 2003; "Can American Keep Flying?" *CIO Magazine*, www.cio.com, accessed February 15, 2003; Max Hopper, "Rattling SABRE," *Harvard Business Review,* October 2002; and John Helyar, "Delta's Chapter 11 Dogfight," *Fortune*, December 12, 2005, pp. 61–62.

Chapter 3

1. Beth Bacheldor, "From Scratch: Amazon Keeps Moving," *Information Week,* March 5, 2004; Gary Wolf, "The Great Library of Amazonia," *Wired*, October 23, 2003; "Amazon Company Information," *Forbes*, www.forbes.com, September 2005; and Rob Hof, "Amazon's Newest Product: Storage," *BusinessWeek*, March 13, 2006.

2. Cisco Press, www.ciscopress.com/index.asp?rl=1, accessed March 1, 2005

3. Adam Lashinsky, "Kodak's Developing Situation," *Fortune*, January 20, 2003, p. 176.

4. www.wired.com, accessed November 15, 2003.

5. Adam Lashinsky, "Kodak's Developing Situation," *Fortune*, January 20, 2003, p.176.

6. Clayton Christensen, *The Innovator's Dilemma* (Boston: Harvard Business School, 1997).

7. Internet World Statistics, www.internetworldstats.com, January 2005.

8. info.cern.ch, accessed March 1, 2005.

9. "Internet Pioneers," www.ibiblio.org/pioneers/andreesen.html, accessed March 1, 2005.

10. Gunjan Bagla, "Bringing IT to Rural India One Village at a Time," *CIO Magazine*, March 1, 2005.

11. "Info on 3.9M Citigroup," *Money*, June 6, 2005.

12. Amy Johnson, "A New Supply Chain Forged," *Computerworld*, September 30, 2002.

13. "Pratt & Whitney," *BusinessWeek*, June 2004.

14. "Let's Remake a Deal," *Business 2.0*, March 2004.

15. Laura Rohde, "British Airways Takes Off with Cisco," *Network World*, May 11, 2005.

16. www.t-mobile.com, accessed June 2005.

17. www.idc.com, accessed June 2005.

18. "A Site Stickier Than a Barroom Floor," *Business 2.0*, June 2005, p. 74.

19. www.emarketer.com, accessed January 2006.

20. Heather Harreld, "Lemon Aid," *CIO Magazine*, July 1, 2000.

21. Rachel Metz, "Changing at the Push of a Button," *Wired*, September 27, 2004.

22. www.hotel-gatti.com, accessed June 2003.

23. Frank Quinn, "The Payoff Potential in Supply Chain Management," www.ascet.com, accessed June 15, 2003.

24. www.oecd.org, accessed June 2005.

25. www.vanguard.com, accessed June 2005.

26. "Watch Your Spending," *BusinessWeek*, May 23, 2004.

27. Jack Welch, "What's Right About Wal-Mart," *CIO Magazine*, www.cio.com, accessed May 2005.

28. www.yankeegroup.com, accessed May 2005.

29. www.ingenio.com, accessed July 2005.

30. "E-Commerce Taxation," www.icsc.org/srch/government/ECommerceFebruary2003.pdf, accessed June 8, 2004.

31. Robert Hof, "Pierre M. Omidyar: The Web for the People," *BusinessWeek*, December 6, 2004; Margaret Kane, "eBay picks up PayPal for 1.5 Billion," Cnet News, news.com.com, accessed July 8, 2002; John Blau, "Are eBay and Skype a Good Fit?" Infoworld, www.inforworld.com, accessed September 8, 2005; and "Better Ask: IRS May Consider eBay Sales as Income," *USA Today,* March 27, 2005.

32. Success Stories, www.oracle.com, accessed June 2004.

33. John Heilmann, "What's Friendster Selling?" *Business 2.0*, March 2004, p. 34.

Chapter 4

1. "Sarbanes-Oxley Act," www.workingvalues.com, accessed March 3, 2004.

2. Michael Schrage, "Build the Business Case," *CIO Magazine,* www.cio.com, accessed November 17, 2003.

3. Scott Berianato, "Take the Pledge," *CIO Magazine,* www.cio.com, accessed November 17, 2003.

4. Ibid.

5. Ibid.

6. AMA Research, "Workplace Monitoring and Surveillance," www.amanet.org, accessed March 1, 2004.

7. Ibid.

8. Ibid.

9. Andy McCue, "Bank Boss Quits after Porn Found on PC," www.businessweek.com, accessed June 2004.

10. AMA Research, "Workplace Monitoring and Surveillance," www.amanet.org, accessed March 1, 2004.

11. www.vault.com, accessed January 2006.

12. AMA Research, "Workplace Monitoring and Surveillance."
13. "Health Information Management," www.gartner.com, accessed November 16, 2003.
14. "2005 CSI/FBI Computer Crime and Security Survey,". www.gocsi.com, accessed February 20, 2006.
15. "2005 CSI/FBI Computer Crime and Security Survey," www.gocsi.com, accessed February 20, 2006.
16. www.ey.com, accessed November 25, 2003.
17. "The Security Revolution," *CIO Magazine*, www.cio.com, accessed June 6, 2003.
18. Alice Dragoon, "Eight (Not So) Simple Steps to the HIPAA Finish Line," *CIO Magazine*, www.cio.com, accessed July 7, 2003.
19. "Losses from Identity Theft to Total $221 Billion Worldwide," www.cio.com, accessed May 23, 2003.
20. "Sony Fights Intrusion with 'Crystal Ball,'" *CIO Magazine*, www.cio.com, accessed August 9, 2003.
21. Mark Leon, "Keys to the Kingdom," www.computerworld.com, accessed August 8, 2003.
22. Spam Losses to Grow to $198 Billion," *CIO Magazine*, www.cio.com, accessed August 9, 2003.
23. "Teen Arrested in Internet 'Blaster' Attack," www.cnn.com, August 29, 2003.
24. "Hacker Hunters," *BusinessWeek*, May 30, 2005.
25. Berinato and Scalet, "The ABCs of Information Security." *CIO Magazine*, www.cio.com, accessed July 7, 2003.

Chapter 5

1. "Electronic Breaking Points," *PC World*, August 2005.
2. Tom Davenport, "Playing Catch-Up," *CIO Magazine*, May 1, 2001.
3. "Hector Ruiz, Advanced Micro Devices," *BusinessWeek*, January 10, 2005.
4. www.powergridfitness.com, accessed October 2005.
5. Denise Brehm, "Sloan Students Pedal Exercise," www.mit.edu, accessed May 5, 2003.
6. Margaret Locher, "Hands That Speak," *CIO Magazine*, June 1, 2005.
7. www.needapresent.com, accessed October 2005.
8. Aaron Ricadela, "Seismic Shift," *Information Week*, March 14, 2005.
9. www.mit.com, accessed October 2005.
10. "The Linux Counter," counter.li.org, accessed October 2005.
11. Christine McGeever, "FBI Database Problem Halts Gun Checks," www.computerworld.com, accessed May 22, 2000.
12. www.cio.com, accessed November 2005.
13. "Distribution of Software Updates of Thousands of Franchise Locations Was Slow and Unpredictable," www.fountain.com, accessed October 10, 2003.
14. Christopher Koch, "A New Blueprint for the Enterprise," *CIO Magazine*, March 1, 2005.

15. www.marshall&swift.com, accessed November 2005.
16. "What Every Executive Needs to Know," www.akamai.com, accessed September 10, 2003.
17. Martin Garvey, "Manage Passwords," *Information Week*, May 20, 2005.
18. Ibid.
19. Ibid.
20. Martin Garvey, "Security Action Plans," *Information Week*, May 30, 2005.
21. Ibid.
22. "Can American Keep Flying?" *CIO Magazine*, www.cio.com, accessed February 15, 2003.
23. www.abercrombie&fitch.com, accessed November 2005.
24. Erick Schonfeld, "Linux Takes Flight," *Business 2.0*, January 2003, pp. 103–5.
25. "Looking at the New," *Information Week*, May 2005.
26. John Fontana, "Lydian Revs up with Web Services," *Network World*, March 10, 2004.
27. www.websidestory.com, accessed November 2005.
28. Ibid.
29. Tim Wilson, "Server Consolidation Delivers," *Information Week*, May 30, 2005.
30. Geoffrey James, "The Next Delivery? Computer Repair," CNNMoney.com, accessed July 1, 2004.
31. Erick Schonfeld, "Linux Takes Flight," *Business 2.0*, January 2003, pp. 103–5. Otis Port, "Will the Feud Choke the Life Out of Linux?" *BusinessWeek*, July 7, 2003, p. 81.

Chapter 6

1. Michael S. Malone, "IPO Fever," *Wired*, March 2004; and Google Knows Where You Are," *BusinessWeek*, February 2, 2004.
2. "Google Reveals High-Profile Users of Data Search Machine," Reuters News Service, August 13, 2003, www.chron.com, accessed September 3, 2003.
3. Mitch Betts, "Unexpected Insights," *Computerworld*, April 14, 2003, www.computerworld.com, accessed September 4, 2003.
4. Ibid.
5. "Data Mining: What General Managers Need to Know," *Harvard Management Update*, October 1999.
6. Barbara DePompa Reimers, "Too Much of a Good Thing," *Computerworld*, April 14, 2003.
7. Ibid.
8. Ibid.
9. www.ellisisland.org, accessed April 15, 2004.
10. "Why Data Quality," www.trilliumsoft.com, accessed October 3, 2003.
11. Julia Kiling, "OLAP Gains Fans among Data-Hungry Firms," *Computerworld*, January 8, 2001, p. 54.
12. Ibid.
13. Customer Success Stories, www.oracle.com, accessed September 20, 2003.

14. Ibid., accessed September 22, 2003.
15. Kathleen Melymuka, "Premier 100: Turning the Tables at Applebee's," *Computerworld,* www.computerworld.com, accessed February 24, 2003.
16. Alice LaPante, "Big Things Come in Smaller Packages," *Computerworld,* June 24, 1996, pp. DW/6–7.
17. Tommy Peterson, "Data Cleansing," *Computerworld,* February 10, 2003.
18. "Dr Pepper/Seven Up, Inc.," www.cognos.com, accessed September 10, 2003.
19. "What Every Executive Needs to Know," www.akamai. com, accessed September 10, 2003.
20. Nikhil Hutheesing, "Surfing with Sega," *Forbes,* November 4, 2002, p. 58.
21. "Privacy, Security, Personal Health Records and the Enterprise," *CIO Magazine,* www.cio.com, accessed November 10, 2003.
22. LaPante, "Big Things Come in Smaller Packages," *Computerworld.*
23. "What Every Executive Needs to Know," www.akamai. com.
24. Ibid.
25. "Alaska Fish and Game Yields a Bounty of High-Quality Information to Manage Natural Resources," www.oracle. com, accessed September 20, 2003.
26. Julie Schlosser, "Looking for Intelligence in Ice Cream," *Fortune,* March 17, 2003; Leslie Goff, "Summertime Heats Up IT at Ben & Jerry's," *Computerworld,* July 2001; and Customer Success Stories, www.cognos.com, accessed January 2005.
27. Meridith Levinson, "Harrah's Knows What You Did Last Night," *Darwin Magazine,* May 2001; "Harrah's Entertainment Wins TDWI's 2000 DW Award," www. hpcwire.com, accessed October 10, 2003; Gary Loveman, "Diamonds in the Data Mine," *Harvard Business Review*, May 2003, p. 109; "NCR—Harrah's Entertainment, Inc.," www.ncr.com, accessed October 12, 2003; "Cognos and Harrah's Entertainment Win Prestigous Data Warehousing Award," 2002 News Release, www.cognos. com, accessed October 14, 2003; Kim Nash, "Casinos Hit Jackpot with Customer Data," www.cnn.com, accessed October 14, 2003.

Chapter 7

1. Timothy Mullaney and Arlene Weintraub, "The Digital Hospital," *BusinessWeek,* March 28, 2005, and Michelle Delio, "How Secure Is Digital Hospital," *Wired,* March 28, 2001.
2. Eva Chen, "Shop Talk," *CIO Magazine,* October 15, 2004.
3. www.perrio.com, accessed November 2005.
4. Chris Murphy, "RIM Settles BlackBerry Suit," *InformationWeek,* March 6, 2006.
5. "Data Mining: What General Managers Need to Know," *Harvard Management Update,* October 1999.
6. Barbara DePompa Reimers, "Too Much of a Good Thing," *Computerworld,* www.computerworld.com, April 14, 2003.
7. Ibid.
8. "Handheld 2006–2010 Forecast and Analysis," *IDC,* www. idc.com, March 2006.
9. "The I-Tech Virtual Keyboard," www.laser-keyboard.com, accessed September 2005.
10. "Airbus Working with LogicaCMG on Tracking," www. usingrfid.com, accessed August 16, 2004.
11. Ibid.
12. "Howard Stern Making Jump to Satellite Radio," www. msnbc.msn.com, October 6, 2004.
13. "SiRF Technology and NEC Electronics Partner," www. sirf.com, accessed February 2002.
14. "GM Owners Are Finding an Easy and Convenient Way to Manage Car Care Through E-Mail," www.cnnmoney.com, accessed April 10, 2006.
15. Joe Wilcox, "Sit and Surf," Cnet news, news.com.com, accessed May 2, 2003.
16. Tiffany Kary, "Palm Plugs and Premiers," Cnet news, news.com.com, accessed March 19, 2005.
17. Ibid.
18. www.businessweek.com, accessed October 14, 2005.
19. Galen Gruman, "UPS vs. FedEx: Head-to-Head on Wireless," *BusinessWeek,* June 1, 2004.
20. "Overcoming Software Development Problems," www.samspublishing.com, October 7, 2002, accessed November 16, 2003.

Chapter 8

1. Bill Breen, "Living in Dell Time," *Fast Company,* November 2004, p. 86.
2. John Hagerty, "How Best to Measure Our Supply Chain," www.amrresearch.com, accessed March 3, 2005.
3. Andrew Binstock, "Virtual Enterprise Comes of Age," *InformationWeek,* November 6, 2004.
4. Mitch Betts, "Kinks in the Chain," *Computerworld,* December 17, 2005.
5. Walid Mougayar, "Old Dogs Learn New Tricks," *Business 2.0,* October 2000, www.Business2.com, accessed June 14, 2003.
6. "Creating a Value Network," *Wired,* September 2003, p. S13.
7. Fred Hapgood, "Smart Decisions," *CIO Magazine,* www. cio.com, accessed August 15, 2001.
8. "Creating a Value Network," *Wired.*
9. "Success Story," www.perdue.com, accessed September 2003.
10. "Creating a Value Network," *Wired.*
11. "The e-Biz Surprise," *BusinessWeek,* May 12, 2003, pp. 60–65.
12. Hagerty, "How Best to Measure Our Supply Chain."
13. Frank Quinn, "The Payoff Potential in Supply Chain Management," www.ascet.com, accessed June 15, 2003.

14. Mougayar, "Old Dogs Learn New Tricks."
15. Quinn, "The Payoff Potential," and William Copacino, "How to Become a Supply Chain Master," *Supply Chain Management Review,* September 1, 2001, www.manufacturing.net, accessed June 12, 2003.
16. Bob Evans, "Business Technology: Sweet Home," *InformationWeek,* February 7, 2005.
17. Kevin Kelleher, "BudNet: 66,207,896 Bottles of Beer on the Wall," *Business 2.0,* February 2004.
18. Jennifer Bresnahan, "The Incredible Journey," *CIO Enterprise Magazine,* August 15, 1998, www.cio.com, accessed March 12, 2004.
19. Kim Girard, "How Levi's Got Its Jeans into Wal-Mart," *CIO Magazine*, July 15, 2003.

Chapter 9

1. "Customer First Awards," *Fast Company,* May 2005.
2. "1800 flowers.com," *Business 2.0,* February 2004.
3. "The 'New' New York Times," *Business 2.0,* January 2004.
4. "New York Knicks—Success," www.jdedwards.com, accessed January 15, 2004.
5. "Barclays, Giving Voice to Customer-Centricity," crm.insightexec.com, accessed July 15, 2003.
6. "Customer Success—PNC Retail Bank," www.siebel.com, accessed May 5, 2003.
7. California State Automobile Association Case Study, www.epiphany.com/customers/detail_csaa.html, accessed July 4, 2003.
8. www.salesforce.com, accessed June 2005.
9. "Vail Resorts Implements FrontRange HEAT," *CRM Today,* October 16, 2003, ww.crm2day.com/news/crm/EpyykllFyAqEUbqOhW.php, accessed December 2, 2003.
10. "3M Accelerates Revenue Growth Using Siebel eBusiness Applications," www.siebel.com, July 30, 2002, accessed July 10, 2003.
11. "Avnet Brings IM to Corporate America with Lotus Instant Messaging," www.websphereadvisor.com/doc/12196, accessed July 11, 2003.
12. www.nicesystems.com, accessed June 2005.
13. www.FedEx.com, accessed July 13, 2003.
14. "Documedics," www.siebel.com, accessed July 10, 2003.
15. Bob Evans, "Business Technology: Sweet Home," *InformationWeek,* February 7, 2005.
16. "Customer Success—UPS," www.sap.com, accessed April 5, 2003.
17. Supply Chain Planet, June 2003, http://newsweaver.co.uk/supplychainplanet/e_article000153342.cfm, accessed July 12, 2003.
18. "Customer Success—Brother," www.sap.com, accessed January 12, 2004.
19. "Customer Success," www.siebel.com, accessed May 5, 2003.
20. "Customer Success—Cisco," www.sap.com, accessed April 5, 2003.
21. "Customer Success," www.costco.com, accessed June 2005.
22. "Customer Success," www.rackspace.com, accessed June 2005.
23. "Partnering in the Fight against Cancer," www.siebel.com, accessed July 16, 2003.
24. "The Expanding Territory of Outsourcing," www.outsourcing.com, accessed August 15, 2003.
25. "Customer First Awards," *Fast Company,* May 2005.

Chapter 10

1. Thomas Wailgum, "Big Mess on Campus," *CIO Magazine,* May 1, 2005.
2. "Customer Success Story—Turner Industries," www.jdedwards.com, accessed October 15, 2003.
3. "Success Stories," www.sap.com, accessed April 2005.
4. "Harley-Davidson on the Path to Success," www.peoplesoft.com/media/success, accessed October 12, 2003.
5. "Customer Success Story—Grupo Farmanova Intermed," www.jdedwards.com, accessed October 15, 2003.
6. "Customer Success Stories," www.jdedwards.com, accessed October 15, 2003.
7. Michael Doane, "A Blueprint for ERP Implementation Readiness," www.metagroup.com, accessed October 17, 2003.
8. Ibid.
9. Ibid.
10. "Amazon Finds Profits in Outsourcing," *CIO Magazine,* October 15, 2002, www.cio.com/archive/101502/tl_ec.html, accessed November 14, 2003.
11. "D-FW Defense Contractors Show Mixed Fortunes since September 11," www.bizjournals.com/dallas/stories/2002/09/09/focus2.htm, accessed June 8, 2004.
12. Steve Konicki, "Collaboration Is Cornerstone of $19B Defense Contract," www.business2.com/content/magazine/indepth/2000/07/11/17966, accessed June 8, 2004.
13. "Knowledge Management Research Center," *CIO Magazine,* www.cio.com/research/knowledge, accessed December 2005.
14. Megan Santosus, "In The Know," *CIO Magazine,* January 2006.
15. Ibid.
16. "Speeding Information to BMW Dealers," www.kmworld.com/resources/featurearticles/index.cfm?action=readfeature&Feature_ID=337, accessed June 8, 2004.
17. "Toyota's One-Stop Information Shop," www.istart.co.nz/index/HM20/PC0/PV21873/EX236/CS25653, accessed June 8, 2004.
18. "HP Unveils Halo Collaboration Studio," www.hp.com, December 12, 2005.
19. Laurie Sullivan, "Collaboration Can Better Highway Safety," *InformationWeek,* August 9, 2004.
20. "Customer Success," www.costco.com, accessed June 2005.

Chapter 11

1. "Overcoming Software Development Problems," www.samspublishing.com, accessed October 2005.
2. www.businessweek.com, accessed November 1, 2005.
3. "Software Costs," *CIO Magazine,* www.cio.com, accessed December 5, 2003.
4. "Defective Software Costs," *National Institute of Standards and Technology (NIST),* June 2002.
5. Ibid.
6. "Customer Success Story—PHH," www.informatica.com, accessed December 12, 2003.
7. "Building Events," www.microsoft.com, accessed November 15, 2003.
8. Agile Alliance Manifesto, www.agile.com, accessed November 1, 2003.
9. "Software Metrics," *CIO Magazine,* www.cio.com, accessed December 2, 2003.
10. "Building Software That Works," www.compaq.com, accessed November 14, 2003.
11. "Software Metrics," *CIO Magazine.*
12. www.agile.com, accessed November 10, 2003.
13. "Python Project Failure," www.systemsdev.com, accessed November 14, 2003.
14. Gary McGraw, "Making Essential Software Work," *Software Quality Management,* April 2003, www.sqmmagazine.com, accessed November 14, 2003.
15. www.standishgroup.com, accessed November 14, 2003.
16. "Baggage Handling System Errors," www.flavors.com, accessed November 16, 2003.
17. www.microsoft.com, accessed November 16, 2003.
18. "REI Pegs Growth on Effective Multi-channel Strategy," *Internet Retailer,* www.internetretailer.com, accessed February 17, 2005, and Alison Overholt, "Smart Strategies: Putting Ideas to Work," *Fast Company,* April 2004, p. 63.

Chapter 12

1. "Toyota's One-Stop Information Shop," www.istart.co.nz/index/HM20/PC0/PV21873/EX236/CS25653, accessed June 8, 2004.
2. "Top Reasons Why IT Projects Fail," *InformationWeek,* www.infoweek.com, accessed November 5, 2003.
3. "Customer Success—Horizon," www.businessengine.com, accessed October 15, 2003.
4. "Top Reasons Why IT Projects Fail," *InformationWeek,* www.infoweek.com, accessed November 5, 2003.
5. www.calpine.com, accessed December 14, 2003.
6. "The Project Manager in the IT Industry," www.si2.com, accessed December 15, 2003.
7. www.standishgroup.com, accessed December 12, 2003.
8. www.snapon.com, accessed December 13, 2003.
9. www.change-management.org, accessed December 12, 2003.
10. www.altria.com, accessed December 15, 2003.
11. "Supply and Demand Chain," www.isourceonline.com, accessed December 14, 2003.
12. "Merrill Lynch and Thomson Financial to Develop Wealth Management Workstation," www.advisorpage.com/modules.php?name=News&file=print&sid=666, accessed June 8, 2004.
13. "IBM/Lotus Domino Server Hosting Service," www.macro.com.hk/solution_Outsourcing.htm, accessed June 8, 2004.
14. www.forrester.com/find?SortType=Date&No=350&N=32, accessed June 8, 2004.
15. "BP: WebLearn," www.accenture.com/xd/xd.asp?it=enweb&xd=industries%5Cresources%5Cenergy%5Ccase%5Cener_bpweblearn.xml, accessed June 8, 2004.
16. Todd Datz, "Outsourcing World Tour," *CIO Magazine,* July 15, 2004, pp. 42–48.
17. "Call Center and CRM Statistics," www.cconvergence.com/shared/printableArticle.jhtml?articleID=7617915, accessed June 8, 2004.
18. "Staying on Track at the Toronto Transit Commission," www.primavera.com, accessed December 16, 2003.
19. Meridith Levinson, "Circuit City Rewires," *CIO Magazine,* July 1, 2005.
20. "Coors Brewing Company," www.eds.com/case-studies, accessed June 8, 2004.

A

acceptable use policy (AUP)   A policy that a user must agree to follow in order to be provided access to a network or to the Internet.

accounting   Analyzes the transactional information of the business so the owners and investors can make sound economic decisions.

accounting and finance ERP component   Manages accounting data and financial processes within the enterprise with functions such as general ledger, accounts payable, accounts receivable, budgeting, and asset management.

accounting department   Provides quantitative information about the finances of the business including recording, measuring, and describing financial information.

adware   Software that generates ads that install themselves on a computer when a person downloads some other program from the Internet.

agile methodology   A form of XP, aims for customer satisfaction through early and continuous delivery of useful software components.

analysis phase   Analyzing end-user business requirements and refining project goals into defined functions and operations of the intended system.

analytical CRM   Supports back-office operations and strategic analysis and includes all systems that do not deal directly with the customers.

analytical information   Encompasses all organizational information, and its primary purpose is to support the performing of managerial analysis tasks.

anti-spam policy   States that e-mail users will not send unsolicited e-mails (or spam).

application architecture   Determines how applications integrate and relate to each other.

application generation component   Includes tools for creating visually appealing and easy-to-use applications.

application service provider (ASP)   A company that offers an organization access over the Internet to systems and related services that would otherwise have to be located in personal or organizational computers.

application software   Used for specific information processing needs, including payroll, customer relationship management, project management, training, and many others.

arithmetic/logic unit (ALU)   Performs all arithmetic operations (for example, addition and subtraction) and all logic operations (such as sorting and comparing numbers).

artificial intelligence (AI)   Simulates human intelligence such as the ability to reason and learn.

As-Is process model   Represent the current state of the operation that has been mapped, without any specific improvements or changes to existing processes.

asset   Anything owned that has value or earning power.

associates program (affiliate program)   Businesses can generate commissions or royalties from an Internet site.

association detection   Reveals the degree to which variables are related and the nature and frequency of these relationships in the information.

attribute   Characteristics or properties of an entity class.

authentication   A method for confirming users' identities.

authorization   The process of giving someone permission to do or have something.

automatic call distribution   A phone switch routes inbound calls to available agents.

availability   Addresses when systems can be accessed by users.

B

backdoor program   Viruses that open a way into the network for future attacks.

backup   An exact copy of a system's information.

backward integration   Takes information entered into a given system and sends it automatically to all upstream systems and processes.

balance sheet   Gives an accounting picture of property owned by a company and of claims against the property on a specific date.

banner ad   Small ad on one Web site that advertises the products and services of another business, usually another dot-com business.

benchmark   Baseline values the system seeks to attain.

benchmarking   The process of continuously measuring system results, comparing those results to optimal system performance (benchmark values), and identifying steps and procedures to improve system performance.

binary digit (bit)   The smallest unit of information that a computer can process.

biometric   The identification of a user based on a physical characteristic, such as a fingerprint, iris, face, voice, or handwriting.

black-hat hacker   Breaks into other people's computer systems and may just look around or steal and destroy information.

blog   Web site in which items are posted on a regular basis and displayed in reverse chronological order.

Bluetooth   An omnidirectional wireless technology that provides limited-range voice and data transmission over the unlicensed 2.4-GHz frequency band, allowing connections with a wide variety of fixed and portable devices that normally would have to be cabled together.

bookkeeping   The actual recording of the business's transactions, without any analysis of the information.

break-even point   The point at which revenues equal costs.

brick-and-mortar business   A business that operates in a physical store without an Internet presence.

bullwhip effect   Occurs when distorted product demand information passes from one entity to the next throughout the supply chain.

business-critical integrity constraint   Enforces business rules vital to an organization's success and often requires more insight and knowledge than relational integrity constraints.

business facing process   Invisible to the external customer but essential to the effective management of the business and includes goal setting, day-to-day planning, performance feedback, rewards, and resource allocation.

business intelligence   Information that people use to support their decision-making efforts.

business process   A standardized set of activities that accomplish a specific task, such as processing a customer's order.

business process management (BPM)   Integrates all of an organization's business processes to make individual processes more efficient.

business process management tool   Used to create an application that is helpful in designing business process models and also helpful in simulating, optimizing, monitoring, and maintaining various processes that occur within an organization.

business process model   A graphic description of a process, showing the sequence of process tasks, which is developed for a specific purpose and from a selected viewpoint.

business process modeling (or **mapping**)   The activity of creating a detailed flow chart or process map of a work process showing its inputs, tasks, and activities, in a structured sequence.

business process outsourcing   The contracting of a specific business task, such as payroll, to a third-party service provider.

business process reengineering (BPR)   The analysis and redesign of workflow within and between enterprises.

business requirement   The detailed set of business requests that the system must meet in order to be successful.

business-to-business (B2B)   Applies to businesses buying from and selling to each other over the Internet.

business-to-business (B2B) marketplace   An Internet-based service that brings together many buyers and sellers.

business-to-consumer (B2C)   Applies to any business that sells its products or services to consumers over the Internet.

buyer power   High when buyers have many choices of whom to buy from and low when their choices are few.

byte   Group of eight bits represents one natural language character.

C

cache memory   A small unit of ultra-fast memory that is used to store recently accessed or frequently accessed data so that the CPU does not have to retrieve this data from slower memory circuits such as RAM.

call scripting system   Accesses organizational databases that track similar issues or questions and automatically generate the details for the CSR who can then relay them to the customer.

campaign management system   Guides users through marketing campaigns performing such tasks as campaign definition, planning, scheduling, segmentation, and success analysis.

capacity planning   Determines the future IT infrastructure requirements for new equipment and additional network capacity.

capital   Represents money whose purpose is to make more money, for example, the money used to buy a rental property or a business.

central processing unit (CPU) (or microprocessor)   The actual hardware that interprets and executes the program (software) instructions and coordinates how all the other hardware devices work together.

change control board (CCB)   Responsible for approving or rejecting all change requests.

change management   A set of techniques that aid in evolution, composition, and policy management of the design and implementation of a system.

change management system   Includes a collection of procedures to document a change request and define the steps necessary to consider the change based on the expected impact of the change.

chief information officer (CIO)   Responsible for (1) overseeing all uses of information technology and (2) ensuring the strategic alignment of IT with business goals and objectives.

chief knowledge officer (CKO)   Responsible for collecting, maintaining, and distributing the organization's knowledge.

chief privacy officer (CPO)   Responsible for ensuring the ethical and legal use of information within an organization.

chief security officer (CSO)   Responsible for ensuring the security of IT systems and developing strategies and IT safeguards against attacks from hackers and viruses.

chief technology officer (CTO)   Responsible for ensuring the throughput, speed, accuracy, availability, and reliability of an organization's information technology.

clickstream   Records information about a customer during a Web surfing session such as what Web sites were visited, how long the visit was, what ads were viewed, and what was purchased.

clickstream data Exact pattern of a consumer's navigation through a site.

click-and-mortar business A business that operates in a physical store and on the Internet.

click-through A count of the number of people who visit one site and click on an advertisement that takes them to the site of the advertiser.

click-to-talk Buttons allow customers to click on a button and talk with a CSR via the Internet.

client Computer that is designed to request information from a server.

client/server network A model for applications in which the bulk of the back-end processing, such as performing a physical search of a database, takes place on a server, while the front-end processing, which involves communicating with the users, is handled by the clients.

cluster analysis A technique used to divide an information set into mutually exclusive groups such that the members of each group are as close together as possible to one another and the different groups are as far apart as possible.

coaxial cable Cable that can carry a wide range of frequencies with low signal loss.

cold site A separate facility that does not have any computer equipment, but is a place where employees can move after a disaster.

collaboration system An IT-based set of tools that supports the work of teams by facilitating the sharing and flow of information.

collaborative demand planning Helps organizations reduce their investment in inventory, while improving customer satisfaction through product availability.

collaborative engineering Allows an organization to reduce the cost and time required during the design process of a product.

commercial off-the-shelf (COTS) A software package or solution that is purchased to support one or more business functions and information systems.

communication device Equipment used to send information and receive it from one location to another.

competitive advantage A product or service that an organization's customers place a greater value on than similar offerings from a competitor.

complex instruction set computer (CISC) chip Type of CPU that can recognize as many as 100 or more instructions, enough to carry out most computations directly.

computer Electronic device operating under the control of instructions stored in its own memory that can accept, manipulate, and store data.

computer-aided software engineering (CASE) Software suites that automate systems analysis, design, and development.

confidentiality The assurance that messages and information are available only to those who are authorized to view them.

consolidation Involves the aggregation of information and features simple roll-ups to complex groupings of interrelated information.

consumer-to-business (C2B) Applies to any consumer that sells a product or service to a business over the Internet.

consumer-to-consumer (C2C) Applies to sites primarily offering goods and services to assist consumers interacting with each other over the Internet.

contact center (call center) Customer service representatives (CSRs) answer customer inquiries and respond to problems through a number of different customer touchpoints.

contact management CRM system Maintains customer contact information and identifies prospective customers for future sales.

content filtering Occurs when organizations use software that filters content to prevent the transmission of unauthorized information.

content management system Provides tools to manage the creation, storage, editing, and publication of information in a collaborative environment.

content provider Companies that use the Internet to distribute copyrighted content, including news, music, games, books, movies, and many other types of information.

continuous process improvement model Attempts to understand and measure the current process, and make performance improvements accordingly.

control unit Interprets software instructions and literally tells the other hardware devices what to do, based on the software instructions.

cookie A small file deposited on a hard drive by a Web site containing information about customers and their Web activities.

copyright The legal protection afforded an expression of an idea, such as a song, video game, and some types of proprietary documents.

core competency An organization's key strength or business function that it does better than any of its competitors.

core competency strategy When an organization chooses to focus specifically on what it does best (its core competency) and forms partnerships and alliances with other specialist organizations to handle nonstrategic business processes.

core ERP component Traditional components included in most ERP systems and they primarily focus on internal operations.

corporation (also called, **organization, enterprise,** or **business**) An artificially created legal entity that exists separate and apart from those individuals who created it and carry on its operations.

counterfeit software Software that is manufactured to look like the real thing and sold as such.

cracker A hacker with criminal intent.

critical path A path from the start to the finish that passes through all the tasks that are critical to completing the project in the shortest amount of time.

critical success factor (CSF) A factor that is critical to an organization's success.

CRM analysis technologies Help organizations segment their customers into categories such as best and worst customers.

CRM predicting technologies Help organizations make predictions regarding customer behavior such as which customers are at risk of leaving.

CRM reporting technologies Help organizations identify their customers across other applications.

cross-selling Selling additional products or services to a customer.

cube The common term for the representation of multidimensional information.

customer facing process Results in a product or service that is received by an organization's external customer.

customer metric Assesses the management of customer relationships by the organization.

customer relationship management (CRM) Involves managing all aspects of a customer's relationship with an organization to increase customer loyalty and retention and an organization's profitability.

cyberterrorist Seeks to cause harm to people or to destroy critical systems or information and use the Internet as a weapon of mass destruction.

cycle inventory The average amount of inventory held to satisfy customer demands between inventory deliveries.

D

data Raw facts that describe the characteristics of an event.

data administration component Provides tools for managing the overall database environment by providing facilities for backup, recovery, security, and performance.

database Maintains information about various types of objects (inventory), events (transactions), people (employees), and places (warehouses).

database management system (DBMS) Software through which users and application programs interact with a database.

database-based workflow system Stores documents in a central location and automatically asks the team members to access the document when it is their turn to edit the document.

data definition component Helps create and maintain the data dictionary and the structure of the database.

data dictionary A file that stores definitions of information types, identifies the primary and foreign keys, and maintains the relationships among the tables.

data flow diagram (DFD) Illustrates the movement of information between external entities and the processes and data stores within the system.

data manipulation component Allows users to create, read, update, and delete information in a database.

data mart Contains a subset of data warehouse information.

data mining The process of analyzing data to extract information not offered by the raw data alone.

data-mining tool Uses a variety of techniques to find patterns and relationships in large volumes of information and infer rules from them that predict future behavior and guide decision making.

data model A formal way to express data relationships to a database management system (DBMS).

data warehouse A logical collection of information—gathered from many different operational databases—that supports business analysis activities and decision-making tasks.

decision support system (DSS) Models information to support managers and business professionals during the decision-making process.

demand planning software Generates demand forecasts using statistical tools and forecasting techniques.

denial-of-service attack (DoS) Floods a Web site with so many requests for service that it slows down or crashes the site.

dependency A logical relationship that exists between the project tasks, or between a project task and a milestone.

design phase Involves describing the desired features and operations of the system including screen layouts, business rules, process diagrams, pseudo code, and other documentation.

development phase Involves taking all of the detailed design documents from the design phase and transforming them into the actual system.

digital asset management system (DAM) Though similar to document management, DAM generally works with binary rather than text files, such as multimedia file types.

digital Darwinism Organizations that cannot adapt to the new demands placed on them for surviving in the information age are doomed to extinction.

digital dashboard Integrates information from multiple components and tailors the information to individual preferences.

digital divide When those with access to technology have great advantages over those without access to technology.

digital wallet Both software and information—the software provides security for the transaction and the information includes payment and delivery information (for example, the credit card number and expiration date).

disaster recovery cost curve Charts (1) the cost to the organization of the unavailability of information and technology and (2) the cost to the organization of recovering from a disaster over time.

disaster recovery plan A detailed process for recovering information or an IT system in the event of a catastrophic disaster such as a fire or flood.

disruptive technology   A new way of doing things that initially does not meet the needs of existing customers.

distributed denial-of-service attack (DDoS)   Attacks from multiple computers that flood a Web site with so many requests for service that it slows down or crashes.

distribution management software   Coordinates the process of transporting materials from a manufacturer to distribution centers to the final customer.

dividend   A distribution of earnings to shareholders.

document management system (DMS)   Supports the electronic capturing, storage, distribution, archival, and accessing of documents.

drill-down   Enables users to get details, and details of details, of information.

E

e-business   The conducting of business on the Internet, not only buying and selling, but also serving customers and collaborating with business partners.

e-business model   An approach to conducting electronic business on the Internet.

e-commerce   The buying and selling of goods and services over the Internet.

effectiveness IT metric   Measures the impact IT has on business processes and activities including customer satisfaction, conversion rates, and sell-through increases.

efficiency IT metric   Measures the performance of the IT system itself including throughput, speed, and availability.

e-government   Involves the use of strategies and technologies to transform government(s) by improving the delivery of services and enhancing the quality of interaction between the citizen-consumer within all branches of government.

e-logistics   Manages the transportation and storage of goods.

electronic bill presentment and payment (EBPP)   System that sends bills over the Internet and provides an easy-to-use mechanism (such as clicking on a button) to pay the bill.

electronic catalog   Presents customers with information about goods and services offered for sale, bid, or auction on the Internet.

electronic check   Mechanism for sending a payment from a checking or savings account.

electronic data interchange (EDI)   A standard format for exchanging business data.

electronic marketplace, or e-marketplace   Interactive business communities providing a central market space where multiple buyers and suppliers can engage in e-business activities.

electronic tagging   A technique for identifying and tracking assets and individuals via technologies such as radio frequency identification and smart cards.

elevation of privilege   Process by which a user misleads a system into granting unauthorized rights, usually for the purpose of compromising or destroying the system.

e-mail privacy policy   Details the extent to which e-mail messages may be read by others.

e-mall   Consists of a number of e-shops; it serves as a gateway through which a visitor can access other e-shops.

employee monitoring policy   States how, when, and where the company monitors its employees.

employee relationship management (ERM)   Provides employees with a subset of CRM applications available through a Web browser.

encryption   Scrambles information into an alternative form that requires a key or password to decrypt the information.

enterprise application integration (EAI) middleware   Represents a new approach to middleware by packaging together commonly used functionality, such as providing prebuilt links to popular enterprise applications, which reduces the time necessary to develop solutions that integrate applications from multiple vendors.

enterprise architect (EA)   Person grounded in technology, fluent in business, a patient diplomat, and provides the important bridge between IT and the business.

enterprise architecture   Includes the plans for how an organization will build, deploy, use, and share its data, processes, and IT assets.

enterprise resource planning (ERP)   Integrates all departments and functions throughout an organization into a single IT system (or integrated set of IT systems) so that employees can make decisions by viewing enterprisewide information on all business operations.

entity   In the relational database model is a person, place, thing, transaction, or event about which information is stored.

entity class   In the relational database model is a collection of similar entities.

entity-relationship diagram (ERD)   A technique for documenting the relationships between entities in a database environment.

entry barrier   A product or service feature that customers have come to expect from organizations in a particular industry and must be offered by an entering organization to compete and survive.

environmental scanning   The acquisition and analysis of events and trends in the environment external to an organization.

ePolicies   Policies and procedures that address the ethical use of computers and Internet usage in the business environment.

e-procurement   The B2B purchase and sale of supplies and services over the Internet.

e-shop (e-store or e-tailer)   A version of a retail store where customers can shop at any hour of the day without leaving their home or office.

ethernet   A physical and data layer technology for LAN networking.

ethical computer use policy   Contains general principles to guide computer user behavior.

ethics   Principles and standards that guide our behavior toward other people.

executive information system (EIS)   A specialized DSS that supports senior level executives within the organization.

expense   Refers to the costs incurred in operating and maintaining a business.

expert system   Computerized advisory programs that imitate the reasoning processes of experts in solving difficult problems.

explicit knowledge   Consists of anything that can be documented, archived, and codified, often with the help of IT.

extended ERP component   The extra components that meet the organizational needs not covered by the core components and primarily focus on external operations.

extraction, transformation, and loading (ETL)   A process that extracts information from internal and external databases, transforms the information using a common set of enterprise definitions, and loads the information into a data warehouse.

extranet   An intranet that is available to strategic allies (such as customers, suppliers, and partners).

extreme programming (XP) methodology   Breaks a project into tiny phases, and developers cannot continue on to the next phase until the first phase is complete.

F

failover   Backup operational mode in which the functions of a computer component (such as a processor, server, network, or database) are assumed by secondary system components when the primary component becomes unavailable through either failure or scheduled down time.

fair use doctrine   In certain situations, it is legal to use copyrighted material.

fault tolerance   A computer system designed that in the event a component fails, a backup component or procedure can immediately take its place with no loss of service.

feasibility study   Determines if the proposed solution is feasible and achievable from a financial, technical, and organizational standpoint.

feature creep   Occurs when developers add extra features that were not part of the initial requirements.

fiber optic (optical fiber)   The technology associated with the transmission of information as light impulses along a glass wire or fiber.

finance   Deals with the strategic financial issues associated with increasing the value of the business while observing applicable laws and social responsibilities.

financial accounting   Involves preparing financial reports that provide information about the business's performance to external parties such as investors, creditors, and tax authorities.

financial cybermediary   Internet-based company that facilitates payments over the Internet.

financial EDI (financial electronic data interchange)   Standard electronic process for B2B market purchase payments.

financial quarter   A three-month period (four quarters per year).

financial statement   Written records of the financial status of the business that allow interested parties to evaluate the profitability and solvency of the business.

firewall   Hardware and/or software that guards a private network by analyzing the information leaving and entering the network.

first-mover advantage   An organization can significantly impact its market share by being first to market with a competitive advantage.

Five Forces model   Helps determine the relative attractiveness of an industry.

flash memory   A special type of rewriteable read-only memory (ROM) that is compact and portable.

for profit corporations   Primarily focus on making money and all profits and losses are shared by the business owners.

forecast   Predictions made on the basis of time-series information.

foreign key   A primary key of one table that appears as an attribute in another table and acts to provide a logical relationship between the two tables.

forward integration   Takes information entered into a given system and sends it automatically to all downstream systems and processes.

fuzzy logic   A mathematical method of handling imprecise or subjective information.

G

Gantt chart   A simple bar chart that depicts project tasks against a calendar.

genetic algorithm   An artificial intelligence system that mimics the evolutionary, survival-of-the-fittest process to generate increasingly better solutions to a problem.

geographic information system (GIS)   Designed to work with information that can be shown on a map.

gigabyte (GB)   Roughly 1 billion bytes.

gigahertz (GHz)   The number of billions of CPU cycles per second.

global inventory management system   Provides the ability to locate, track, and predict the movement of every component or material anywhere upstream or downstream in the supply chain.

global positioning system (GPS)   A device that determines current latitude, longitude, speed, and direction of movement.

goal-seeking analysis   Finds the inputs necessary to achieve a goal such as a desired level of output.

graphical user interface (GUI)   The interface to an information system.

groupware Software that supports team interaction and dynamics including calendaring, scheduling, and video-conferencing.

H

hacker People very knowledgeable about computers who use their knowledge to invade other people's computers.

hactivist Person with philosophical and political reasons for breaking into systems and will often deface the Web site as a protest.

hard drive Secondary storage medium that uses several rigid disks coated with a magnetically sensitive material and housed together with the recording heads in a hermetically sealed mechanism.

hardware Consists of the physical devices associated with a computer system.

hardware key logger A hardware device that captures keystrokes on their journey from the keyboard to the motherboard.

help desk A group of people who respond to internal system user questions.

hierarchical database model Information is organized into a tree-like structure that allows repeating information using parent/child relationships, in such a way that it cannot have too many relationships.

high availability Refers to a system or component that is continuously operational for a desirably long length of time.

hoaxes Attack computer systems by transmitting a virus hoax, with a real virus attached.

hot site A separate and fully equipped facility where the company can move immediately after a disaster and resume business.

human resource ERP component Tracks employee information including payroll, benefits, compensation, and performance assessment, and assures compliance with the legal requirements of multiple jurisdictions and tax authorities.

human resources management (HRM) Includes the policies, plans, and procedures for the effective management of employees (human resources).

hypertext transfer protocol (HTTP) The Internet standard that supports the exchange of information on the WWW.

I

identity theft The forging of someone's identity for the purpose of fraud.

implementation phase Involves placing the system into production so users can begin to perform actual business operations with the system.

income statement (also referred to as earnings report, operating statement, and **profit-and-loss (P&L) statement)** Reports operating results (revenues minus expenses) for a given time period ending at a specified date.

information Data converted into a meaningful and useful context.

information accuracy Extent to which a system generates the correct results when executing the same transaction numerous times.

information architecture Identifies where and how important information, like customer records, is maintained and secured.

information cleansing or scrubbing A process that weeds out and fixes or discards inconsistent, incorrect, or incomplete information.

information granularity Refers to the extent of detail within the information (fine and detailed or "coarse" and abstract information).

information integrity A measure of the quality of information.

information partnership Occurs when two or more organizations cooperate by integrating their IT systems, thereby providing customers with the best of what each can offer.

information privacy policy Contains general principles regarding information privacy.

information reach Refers to the number of people a business can communicate with, on a global basis.

information richness Refers to the depth and breadth of information transferred between customers and businesses.

information security A broad term encompassing the protection of information from accidental or intentional misuse by persons inside or outside an organization.

information security plan Details how an organization will implement the information security policies.

information security policy Identifies the rules required to maintain information security.

information technology (IT) Any computer-based tool that people use to work with information and support the information and information-processing needs of an organization.

information technology monitoring Tracking people's activities by such measures as number of keystrokes, error rate, and number of transactions processed.

infrastructure architecture Includes the hardware, software, and telecommunications equipment that, when combined, provide the underlying foundation to support the organization's goals.

input device Equipment used to capture information and commands.

insider Legitimate users who purposely or accidentally misuse their access to the environment and cause some kind of business-affecting incident.

insourcing (in-house development) A common approach using the professional expertise within an organization to develop and maintain the organization's information technology systems.

instant messaging (IM or **IMing)** A type of communications service that enables someone to create a kind of private chat room with another individual in order to communicate in real-time over the Internet.

integration Allows separate systems to communicate directly with each other.

integrity constraint The rules that help ensure the quality of information.

intellectual property Intangible creative work that is embodied in physical form.

intelligent agent A special-purpose knowledge-based information system that accomplishes specific tasks on behalf of its users.

intelligent system Various commercial applications of artificial intelligence.

interactive voice response (IVR) Directs customers to use touch-tone phones or keywords to navigate or provide information.

interactivity Measures the visitor interactions with the target ad.

intermediary Agents, software, or businesses that bring buyers and sellers together that provide a trading infrastructure to enhance e-business.

Internet A global public network of computer networks that pass information from one to another using common computer protocols.

Internet service provider (ISP) A company that provides individuals and other companies access to the Internet along with additional related services, such as Web site building.

Internet use policy Contains general principles to guide the proper use of the Internet.

interoperability Capability of two or more computer systems to share data and resources, even though they are made by different manufacturers.

intranet An internalized portion of the Internet, protected from outside access, that allows an organization to provide access to information and application software to only its employees.

intrusion detection software (IDS) Searches out patterns in information and network traffic to indicate attacks and quickly responds to prevent any harm.

inventory management and control software Provides control and visibility to the status of individual items maintained in inventory.

IT infrastructure Includes the hardware, software, and telecommunications equipment that, when combined, provide the underlying foundation to support the organization's goals.

J

joint application development (JAD) A session where employees meet, sometimes for several days, to define or review the business requirements for the system.

K

key logger, or key trapper, software A program that, when installed on a computer, records every keystroke and mouse click.

key performance indicator (KPI) Measures that are tied to business drivers.

kiosk Publicly accessible computer system that has been set up to allow interactive information browsing.

knowledge management (KM) Involves capturing, classifying, evaluating, retrieving, and sharing information assets in a way that provides context for effective decisions and actions.

knowledge management system (KMS) Supports the capturing, organization, and dissemination of knowledge (i.e., know-how) throughout an organization.

L

liability An obligation to make financial payments.

limited liability Means that the shareholders are not personally liable for the losses incurred by the corporation.

limited liability corporation (LLC) A hybrid entity that has the legal protections of a corporation and the ability to be taxed (one time) as a partnership.

limited partnership Much like a general partnership except for one important fundamental difference; the law protects the limited partner from being responsible for all of the partnership's losses.

list generator Compiles customer information from a variety of sources and segments the information for different marketing campaigns.

local area network (LAN) Computer network that uses cables or radio signals to link two or more computers within a geographically limited area, generally one building or a group of buildings.

logical view Focuses on how users logically access information to meet their particular business needs.

logistics The set of processes that plans for and controls the efficient and effective transportation and storage of supplies from suppliers to customers.

loss Occurs when businesses sell products or services for less than they cost to produce.

loyalty program Rewards customers based on the amount of business they do with a particular organization.

M

magnetic medium Secondary storage medium that uses magnetic techniques to store and retrieve data on disks or tapes coated with magnetically sensitive materials.

magnetic tape   Older secondary storage medium that uses a strip of thin plastic coated with a magnetically sensitive recording medium.

mail bomb   Sends a massive amount of e-mail to a specific person or system resulting in filling up the recipient's disk space, which, in some cases, may be too much for the server to handle and may cause the server to stop functioning.

maintenance   The fixing or enhancing of an information system.

maintenance phase   Involves performing changes, corrections, additions, and upgrades to ensure the system continues to meet the business goals.

maintenance, repair, and operations (MRO) materials (also called **indirect materials)**   Materials necessary for running an organization but do not relate to the company's primary business activities.

malicious code   Includes a variety of threats such as viruses, worms, and Trojan horses.

management information system (MIS)   The function that plans for, develops, implements, and maintains IT hardware, software, and applications that people use to support the goals of an organization.

managerial accounting   Involves analyzing business operations for internal decision making and does not have to follow any rules issued by standard-setting bodies such as GAAP.

market basket analysis   Analyzes such items as Web sites and checkout scanner information to detect customers' buying behavior and predict future behavior by identifying affinities among customers' choices of products and services.

marketing   The process associated with promoting the sale of goods or services.

marketing communication   Seeks to build product or service awareness and to educate potential consumers on the product or service.

marketing mix   Includes the variables that marketing managers can control in order to best satisfy customers in the target market.

market maker   Intermediaries that aggregate three services for market participants: (1) a place to trade, (2) rules to govern trading, and (3) an infrastructure to support trading.

market segmentation   The division of a market into similar groups of customers.

market share   Calculated by dividing the firm's sales by the total market sales for the entire industry.

mass customization   Ability of an organization to give its customers the opportunity to tailor its products or services to the customers' specifications.

megabyte (MB or M or Meg)   Roughly 1 million bytes.

megahertz (MHz)   The number of millions of CPU cycles per second.

memory card   Contains high-capacity storage that holds data such as captured images, music, or text files.

memory stick   Provides nonvolatile memory for a range of portable devices including computers, digital cameras, MP3 players, and PDAs.

messaging-based workflow system   Sends work assignments through an e-mail system.

metropolitan area network (MAN)   A computer network that provides connectivity in a geographic area or region larger than that covered by a local area network, but smaller than the area covered by a wide area network.

microwave transmitter   Commonly used to transmit network signals over great distances.

middleware   Different types of software that sit in the middle of and provide connectivity between two or more software applications.

mobile commerce, or m-commerce   The ability to purchase goods and services through a wireless Internet-enabled device.

model   A simplified representation or abstraction of reality.

modeling   The activity of drawing a graphical representation of a design.

multisourcing   A combination of professional services, mission-critical support, remote management, and hosting services that are offered to customers in any combination needed.

multitasking   Allows more than one piece of software to be used at a time.

N

nearshore outsourcing   Contracting an outsourcing agreement with a company in a nearby country.

net income   The amount of money remaining after paying taxes.

network   A communications, data exchange, and resource-sharing system created by linking two or more computers and establishing standards, or protocols, so that they can work together.

network database model   A flexible way of representing objects and their relationships.

network operating system (NOS)   The operating system that runs a network, steering information between computers and managing security and users.

network topology   Refers to the geometric arrangement of the actual physical organization of the computers (and other network devices) in a network.

network transmission media   Various types of media used to carry the signal between computers.

neural network (an artificial neural network)   A category of AI that attempts to emulate the way the human brain works.

nonrepudiation   A contractual stipulation to ensure that e-business participants do not deny (repudiate) their online actions.

not for profit (or **nonprofit**) **corporation** Usually exists to accomplish some charitable, humanitarian, or educational purpose, and the profits and losses are not shared by the business owners.

O

offshore outsourcing Using organizations from developing countries to write code and develop systems.

online ad Box running across a Web page that is often used to contain advertisements.

online analytical processing (OLAP) The manipulation of information to create business intelligence in support of strategic decision making.

online broker Intermediaries between buyers and sellers of goods and services.

online service provider (OSP) Offers an extensive array of unique services such as its own version of a Web browser.

online training Runs over the Internet or off a CD-ROM.

online transaction processing (OLTP) The capturing of transaction and event information using technology to (1) process the information according to defined business rules, (2) store the information, and (3) update existing information to reflect the new information.

onshore outsourcing The process of engaging another company within the same country for services.

open system A broad, general term that describes non-proprietary IT hardware and software made available by the standards and procedures by which their products work, making it easier to integrate them.

operating system software Controls the application software and manages how the hardware devices work together.

operational CRM Supports traditional transactional processing for day-to-day front-office operations or systems that deal directly with the customers.

operations management (also called **production management**) Includes the methods, tasks, and techniques organizations use to produce goods and services.

opportunity management CRM system Targets sales opportunities by finding new customers or companies for future sales.

opt-in Implying that a company will contact only the people who have agreed to receive promotions and marketing material via e-mail.

output device Equipment used to see, hear, or otherwise accept the results of information processing requests.

outsourcing An arrangement by which one organization provides a service or services for another organization that chooses not to perform them in-house.

owner's equity The portion of a company belonging to the owners.

P

packet tampering Altering the contents of packets as they travel over the Internet or altering data on computer disks after penetrating a network.

packet-switching Occurs when the sending computer divides a message into a number of efficiently sized units called packets, each of which contains the address of the destination computer.

partner relationship management (PRM) Focuses on keeping vendors satisfied by managing alliance partner and reseller relationships that provide customers with the optimal sales channel.

partnership Similar to sole proprietorships, except that this legal structure allows for more than one owner.

partnership agreement A legal agreement between two or more business partners that outlines core business issues.

peer-to-peer (P2P) network Any network without a central file server and in which all computers in the network have access to the public files located on all other workstations.

performance Measures how quickly a system performs a certain process or transaction (in terms of efficiency IT metrics of both speed and throughput).

personalization Occurs when a Web site can know enough about a person's likes and dislikes that it can fashion offers that are more likely to appeal to that person.

PERT (Program Evaluation and Review Technique) chart A graphical network model that depicts a project's tasks and the relationships between those tasks.

phishing Technique to gain personal information for the purpose of identity theft, usually by means of fraudulent e-mail.

physical view The physical storage of information on a storage device such as a hard disk.

pirated software The unauthorized use, duplication, distribution, or sale of copyrighted software.

planning phase Involves establishing a high-level plan of the intended project and determining project goals.

podcasting Distribution of audio or video files, such as radio programs or music videos, over the Internet to play on mobile devices and personal computers.

polymorphic virus and worm Change their form as they propagate.

pop-under ad Form of a pop-up ad that users do not see until they close the current Web browser screen.

pop-up ad Small Web page containing an advertisement that appears on the Web page outside of the current Web site loaded in the Web browser.

portal A Web site that offers a broad array of resources and services, such as e-mail, online discussion groups, search engines, and online shopping malls.

predictive dialing Automatically dials outbound calls and when someone answers, the call is forwarded to an available agent.

primary key   A field (or group of fields) that uniquely identifies a given entity in a table.

primary storage   Computer's main memory, which consists of the random access memory (RAM), cache memory, and the read-only memory (ROM) that is directly accessible to the CPU.

privacy   The right to be left alone when you want to be, to have control over your own personal possessions, and not to be observed without your consent.

private exchange   A B2B marketplace in which a single buyer posts its need and then opens the bidding to any supplier who would care to bid.

process modeling   Involves graphically representing the processes that capture, manipulate, store, and distribute information between a system and its environment.

product life cycle   Includes the four phases a product progresses through during its life cycle including introduction, growth, maturity, and decline.

production and materials management ERP component   Handles the various aspects of production planning and execution such as demand forecasting, production scheduling, job cost accounting, and quality control.

profit   Occurs when businesses sell products or services for more than they cost to produce.

project   A temporary endeavor undertaken to create a unique product or service.

project deliverable   Any measurable, tangible, verifiable outcome, result, or item that is produced to complete a project or part of a project.

project exclusion   Products, services, or processes that are not specifically a part of the project.

project management   The application of knowledge, skills, tools, and techniques to project activities in order to meet or exceed stakeholder needs and expectations from a project.

project management software   Supports the long-term and day-to-day management and execution of the steps in a project.

project manager   An individual who is an expert in project planning and management, defines and develops the project plan, and tracks the plan to ensure all key project milestones are completed on time.

project milestone   Represents key dates when a certain group of activities must be performed.

project objective   Quantifiable criteria that must be met for the project to be considered a success.

project plan   A formal, approved document that manages and controls project execution.

project product   A description of the characteristics the product or service has undertaken.

project risk   An uncertain event or condition that, if it occurs, has a positive or negative effect on a project objective(s).

project scope   Defines the work that must be completed to deliver a product with the specified features and functions.

protocol   A standard that specifies the format of data as well as the rules to be followed during transmission.

prototype   A smaller-scale representation or working model of the user's requirements or a proposed design for an information system.

public key encryption (PKE)   Encryption system that uses two keys: a public key that everyone can have and a private key for only the recipient.

pull technology   Organizations receive or request information.

pure-play (virtual) business   A business that operates on the Internet only without a physical store.

push technology   Organizations send information.

Q

query-by-example (QBE) tool   Allows users to graphically design the answers to specific questions.

R

radio frequency identification (RFID)   Technologies using active or passive tags in the form of chips or smart labels that can store unique identifiers and relay this information to electronic readers.

random access memory (RAM)   The computer's primary working memory, in which program instructions and data are stored so that they can be accessed directly by the CPU via the processor's high-speed external data bus.

rapid application development (RAD) (also called rapid prototyping) methodology   Emphasizes extensive user involvement in the rapid and evolutionary construction of working prototypes of a system to accelerate the systems development process.

read-only memory (ROM)   The portion of a computer's primary storage that does not lose its contents when one switches off the power.

real simple syndication (RSS)   Family of Web feed formats used for Web syndication of programs and content.

real-time information   Immediate, up-to-date information.

real-time system   Provides real-time information in response to query requests.

recovery   The ability to get a system up and running in the event of a system crash or failure and includes restoring the information backup.

reduced instruction set computer (RISC) chip   Limits the number of instructions the CPU can execute to increase processing speed.

redundancy   The duplication of information, or storing the same information in multiple places.

reintermediation   Using the Internet to reassemble buyers, sellers, and other partners in a traditional supply chain in new ways.

relational database model A type of database that stores information in the form of logically related two-dimensional tables.

relational integrity constraint The rules that enforce basic and fundamental information-based constraints.

reliability Ensures all systems are functioning correctly and providing accurate information.

report generator Allows users to define formats for reports along with what information they want to see in the report.

requirements definition document Contains the final set of business requirements, prioritized in order of business importance.

response time The time it takes to respond to user interactions such as a mouse click.

revenue Refers to the amount earned resulting from the delivery or manufacture of a product or from the rendering of a service.

reverse auction An auction format in which increasingly lower bids are solicited from organizations willing to supply the desired product or service at an increasingly lower price.

RFID tag Contains a microchip and an antenna, and typically works by transmitting a serial number via radio waves to an electronic reader, which confirms the identity of a person or object bearing the tag.

risk management The process of proactive and ongoing identification, analysis, and response to risk factors.

rivalry among existing competitors High when competition is fierce in a market and low when competition is more complacent.

router An intelligent connecting device that examines each packet of data it receives and then decides which way to send it onward toward its destination.

S

safety inventory Includes extra inventory held in the event demand exceeds supply.

sales The function of selling a good or service and focuses on increasing customer sales, which increases company revenues.

sales force automation (SFA) A system that automatically tracks all of the steps in the sales process.

sales management CRM system Automates each phase of the sales process, helping individual sales representatives coordinate and organize all of their accounts.

scalability Refers to how well a system can adapt to increased demands.

scope creep Occurs when the scope of the project increases.

script kiddies or **script bunnies** Find hacking code on the Internet and click-and-point their way into systems to cause damage or spread viruses.

search engine optimization (SEO) Set of methods aimed at improving the ranking of a Web site in search engine listings.

secondary storage Consists of equipment designed to store large volumes of data for long-term storage.

secure electronic transaction (SET) Transmission security method that ensures transactions are secure and legitimate.

secure socket layer (SSL) (1) Creates a secure and private connection between a client and server computer, (2) encrypts the information, and (3) sends the information over the Internet.

selling chain management Applies technology to the activities in the order life cycle from inquiry to sale.

sensitivity analysis The study of the impact that changes in one (or more) parts of the model have on other parts of the model.

server Computer that is dedicated to providing information in response to external requests.

service level agreement (SLA) Defines the specific responsibilities of the service provider and sets the customer expectations.

shareholder Another term for business owners.

shopping bot Software that will search several retailer Web sites and provide a comparison of each retailer's offerings including price and availability.

sign-off The system users' actual signatures indicating they
approve all of the business requirements.

slice-and-dice The ability to look at information from different perspectives.

smart card A device that is around the same size as a credit card, containing embedded technologies that can store information and small amounts of software to perform some limited processing.

sniffer A program or device that can monitor data traveling over a network.

social engineering Using one's social skills to trick people into revealing access credentials or other information valuable to the attacker.

social networking analysis (SNA) A process of mapping a group's contacts (whether personal or professional) to identify who knows whom and who works with whom.

software The set of instructions that the hardware executes to carry out specific tasks.

sole proprietorship A business form in which a single person is the sole owner and is personally responsible for all the profits and losses of the business.

solvency Represents the ability of the business to pay its bills and service its debt.

source document Describes the basic transaction data such as its date, purpose, and amount and includes cash receipts, canceled checks, invoices, customer refunds, employee time sheets, etc.

spam Unsolicited e-mail.

spamdexing Uses a variety of deceptive techniques in an attempt to manipulate search engine rankings, whereas legitimate search engine optimization focuses on building better sites and using honest methods of promotion.

spoofing   The forging of the return address on an e-mail so that the e-mail message appears to come from someone other than the actual sender.

spyware   Software that comes hidden in free download-able software and tracks online movements, mines the information stored on a computer, or uses a computer's CPU and storage for some task the user knows nothing about.

statement of cash flow   Summarizes sources and uses of cash, indicates whether enough cash is available to carry on routine operations, and offers an analysis of all business transactions, reporting where the firm obtained its cash and how it chose to allocate the cash.

statement of owner's equity (also called the **statement of retained earnings** or **equity statement**)   Tracks and communicates changes in the shareholder's earnings.

structured collaboration (or **process collaboration**)   Involves shared participation in business processes, such as workflow, in which knowledge is hard coded as rules.

structured query language (SQL)   A standardized fourth-generation query language found in most DBMSs.

supplier power   High when buyers have few choices of whom to buy from and low when their choices are many.

supplier relationship management (SRM)   Focuses on keeping suppliers satisfied by evaluating and categorizing suppliers for different projects, which optimizes supplier selection.

supply chain   Consists of all parties involved, directly or indirectly, in the procurement of a product or raw material.

supply chain event management (SCEM)   Enables an organization to react more quickly to resolve supply chain issues.

supply chain execution (SCE) software   Automates the different steps and stages of the supply chain.

supply chain management (SCM)   Involves the management of information flows between and among stages in a supply chain to maximize total supply chain effectiveness and profitability.

supply chain planning (SCP) software   Uses advanced mathematical algorithms to improve the flow and efficiency of the supply chain while reducing inventory.

supply chain visibility   The ability to view all areas up and down the supply chain.

sustaining technology   Produces an improved product customers are eager to buy, such as a faster car or larger hard drive.

switching cost   The costs that can make customers reluctant to switch to another product or service.

system availability   Number of hours a system is available for users.

systems development life cycle (SDLC)   The overall process for developing information systems from planning and analysis through implementation and maintenance.

system software   Controls how the various technology tools work together along with the application software.

T

tacit knowledge   The knowledge contained in people's heads.

telecommunication system   Enables the transmission of data over public or private networks.

terabyte (TB)   Roughly 1 trillion bytes.

test condition   The detailed steps the system must perform along with the expected results of each step.

testing phase   Involves bringing all the project pieces together into a special testing environment to test for errors, bugs, and interoperability and verify that the system meets all of the business requirements defined in the analysis phase.

threat of new entrants   High when it is easy for new competitors to enter a market and low when there are significant entry barriers to entering a market.

threat of substitute products or services   High when there are many alternatives to a product or service and low when there are few alternatives from which to choose.

throughput   The amount of information that can travel through a system at any point in time.

time-series information   Time-stamped information collected at a particular frequency.

To-Be process model   Shows the results of applying change improvement opportunities to the current (As-Is) process model.

token   Small electronic devices that change user passwords automatically.

transaction   Exchange or transfer of goods, services, or funds involving two or more people.

transaction processing system   The basic business system that serves the operational level (analysts) in an organization.

transaction speed   Amount of time a system takes to perform a transaction.

transactional information   Encompasses all of the information contained within a single business process or unit of work, and its primary purpose is to support the performing of daily operational tasks.

Transmission Control Protocol/Internet Protocol (TCP/IP)   Provides the technical foundation for the public Internet as well as for large numbers of private networks.

transportation planning software   Tracks and analyzes the movement of materials and products to ensure the delivery of materials and finished goods at the right time, the right place, and the lowest cost.

Trojan-horse virus   Hides inside other software, usually as an attachment or a downloadable file.

twisted-pair wiring　A type of cable composed of four (or more) copper wires twisted around each other within a plastic sheath.

U

unstructured collaboration (or **information collaboration**) Includes document exchange, shared whiteboards, discussion forums, and e-mail.

up-selling　Increasing the value of a sale.

user documentation　Highlights how to use the system.

utility software　Provides additional functionality to the operating system.

V

value-added network (VAN)　A private network, provided by a third party, for exchanging information through a high-capacity connection.

value chain　Views an organization as a series of processes, each of which adds value to the product or service for each customer.

view　Allows users to see the contents of a database, make any required changes, perform simple sorting, and query the database to find the location of specific information.

viral marketing　Technique that induces Web sites or users to pass on a marketing message to other Web sites or users, creating exponential growth in the message's visibility and effect.

virtualization　Protected memory space created by the CPU allowing the computer to create virtual machines.

virtual private network (VPN)　A way to use the public telecommunication infrastructure (e.g., Internet) to provide secure access to an organization's network.

virus　Software written with malicious intent to cause annoyance or damage.

voice over IP (VoIP)　Uses TCP/IP technology to transmit voice calls over long-distance telephone lines.

volatility　Refers to RAM's complete loss of stored information if power is interrupted.

W

waterfall methodology　A sequential, activity-based process in which each phase in the SDLC is performed sequentially from planning through implementation and maintenance.

Web-based self-service system　Allows customers to use the Web to find answers to their questions or solutions to their problems.

Web content management system (WCM)　Adds an additional layer to document and digital asset management that enables publishing content both to intranets and to public Web sites.

Web log　Consists of one line of information for every visitor to a Web site and is usually stored on a Web server.

Web service　Contains a repertoire of Web-based data and procedural resources that use shared protocols and standards permitting different applications to share data and services.

Web traffic　Includes a host of benchmarks such as the number of page views, the number of unique visitors, and the average time spent viewing a Web page.

what-if analysis　Checks the impact of a change in an assumption on the proposed solution.

white-hat hacker　Works at the request of the system owners to find system vulnerabilities and plug the holes.

wide area network (WAN)　Computer network that provides data communication services for business in geographically dispersed areas (such as across a country or around the world).

wireless fidelity (wi-fi)　A means of linking computers using infrared or radio signals.

wireless Internet service provider (WISP)　An ISP that allows subscribers to connect to a server at designated hotspots or access points using a wireless connection.

wireless media　Natural parts of the Earth's environment that can be used as physical paths to carry electrical signals.

wire media　Transmission material manufactured so that signals will be confined to a narrow path and will behave predictably.

workflow　Defines all the steps or business rules, from beginning to end, required for a business process.

workflow management system　Facilitates the automation and management of business processes and controls the movement of work through the business process.

workshop training　Set in a classroom-type environment and led by an instructor.

World Wide Web (WWW)　A global hypertext system that uses the Internet as its transport mechanism.

worm　A type of virus that spreads itself, not only from file to file, but also from computer to computer.

PHOTO CREDITS

Chapter 1

Cut 1.1A, page 2, © McGraw-Hill Companies/Jill Braaten, photographer.

Cut 1.1B, page 2, The McGraw-Hill Companies, Inc./Lars A. Niki, photographer.

Cut 1.1C, page 2, The McGraw-Hill Companies, Inc./Christopher Kerrigan, photographer.

Figure 1.1, page 6, Paige Baltzan.

Figure 1.6 top left, page 21, Photo courtesy Hyundai Motor America.

Figure 1.6 top right, page 21, Photo courtesy Audi of America.

Figure 1.6 bottom left, page 21, Courtesy Kia Motors American, Inc.

Figure 1.6 bottom right, page 21, Courtesy General Motors.

Figure 1.8. page 11, "What Concerns CIOs the Most?" www.cio.com. Accessed November 17, 2003.

Figure 1.9, page 12, www.cio.com, accessed August 2005.

Figure 1.10, page 14, United National Division for Public Economics and Public Administration, www.un.com, accessed November 10, 2003.

Chapter 2

Cut 2.1A, page 32, AP/Wide World.

Cut 2.1B, page 32, Scott Olsen/Getty Images.

Cut 2.1C, page 32, AP/Wide World.

Page 43 (left), Alexander Heimann/AFP/Getty Images.

Page 43 (center), AP/Wide World.

Page 43 (right), Jeff Greenberg/Photoedit.

Figure 2.9, page 42, www.visualmining.com, accessed June 24, 2005.

Figure 2.10, page 42, www.visualmining.com, accessed June 24, 2005.

Figure 2.14, page 50, Michael Hammar and James Champy, *Beyond Reengineering, How the Process-Centered Organization Is Changing Our Work and Our Lives, New York:* HarperCollins, Publisher, 1996.

Chapter 3

Cut 3.1A, page 63, Macduff Everton/Corbis.

Cut 3.1B, page 63, Jack Kurtz/The Image Works.

Cut 3.1C, page 63, AP/Wide World.

Figure 3.1, page 66, Adam Lashinsky, "The Disrupters," *Fortune*, August 11, 2003, pp. 62–65.

Figure 3.3, page 68, www.internetworldstats.com/stats.htm, accessed January 2005.

Figure 3.4, page 68, www.expedia.com, accessed October 13, 2003; www.apple.com, accessed October 13, 2003: www.dell.com, accessed October 13, 2003; www.lendingtree.com, accessed October 13, 2003: www.amazon.com, accessed October 13, 2003: www.ebay.com, accessed October 13, 2003; www.cisco.com, accessed October 13, 2003.

Figure 3.28, page 89, Internet World Statistics, www.internetworldstats.com, accessed January 2006.

Figure 3.29, page "E-Commerce Taxation," www.icsc.org/srch/government/ECommerceFebruary2003.pdf, accessed June 8, 2004.

Chapter 4

Cut 4.1A, page 102, PhotoLink/Getty Images.

Cut 4.1B, page 102, PhotoLink/Getty Images.

Cut 4.1C, page 102, Janis Christie/Getty Images.

Figure 4.2, page 105, Scott Berianato, "Take the Pledge," www.cio.com, accessed November 17, 2003.

Figure 4.12, page 112, Paul Roberts, "Report: Spam Costs $874 per Employee per Year," www.computerworld.com, July 2, 2003, accessed March 9, 2004.

Figure 4.13, page 113, AMA Research, "Workplace Monitoring and Surveillance," www.amanet.org, April 2003, accessed March 1, 2004.

Figure 4.16, page 116, "2004 CSI/FBI Computer Crime and Security Survey."

Figure 4.17, page 117, "2005 CSI/FBI Computer Crime and Security Survey," www.usdoj.gov/criminal/cybercrime/FBI2005.pdf.

Figure 4.21, page 122, "The Security Revolution," www.cio.com, accessed June 6, 2003.

Figure 4.22, page 123, "Losses from Identity Theft to Total $221 Billion Worldwide," www.cio.com, May 23, 2003.

Figure 4.23, page 1224, "Spam Losses to Grow to $198 Billion," www.cio.com, accessed August 9, 2003.

Chapter 5

Cut 5.1A, page 137, Stockbyte/Punchstock Images.

Cut 5.1B, page 137, John A. Rizzo/Getty Images.

Cut 5.1C, page 137, Steve Mason/Getty Images.

Figure 5.1, page 139, "Electronic Breaking Points," *PC World*, August 2005.

Figure 5.3, page 141 (left top), (c) Stockbyte/PunchStock.

Figure 5.3, page 141 (left bottom), (c) Stockbyte/PunchStock.

Figure 5.3, page 141(top left), Royalty-Free/CORBIS.

Figure 5.3, page 141(top center), Stockbyte/Punchstock Images.

Figure 5.3, page 141 (top right), SimpleTech Inc.

Figure 5.3, page 141(right top), Courtesy of Panasonic.

Figure 5.3 page 141 (right bottom), Courtesy of Dell Inc.

Figure 5.3, page 141 (bottom left), Daisuke Morita/Getty Images.

Figure 5.3, page 141(bottom right), Royalty-Free/CORBIS.

Page 142 (left), Daisuke Morita/Getty Images.

Page 142 (right), Stockbyte/Punchstock Images.

Figure 5.4, page 142, "Chip Wars," *PC World*, August 2005.

Page 143, SimpleTech Inc.

Page 143, Getty Images.

Page 145 (top), Daisuke Morita/Getty Images.

Page 145 (bottom left), (c) Stockbyte/PunchStock.

Page 145 (bottom right), (c) Stockbyte/PunchStock.

Page 147 (left), Courtesy of Panasonic.

Page 147 (right), Courtesy of Dell Inc.

Page 148 (right), Getty Images.

Page 148 (left), Royalty-Free/CORBIS.

Figure 5.12, page 150, Aaron Ricadela, "Seismic Shift," *Information Week*, March 14, 2005.

Figure 5.11, page 149, Photo courtesy of Cray, Inc.

Figure 5.16, page 154, *BusinessWeek*, January 10, 2005.

Figure 5.18, page 156, *InformationWeek*, August 9, 2004.

Chapter 6

Page 172 (left) no credit necessary.

Page 172 (center), Photo courtesy of Cray, Inc.

Page 172 (right), no credit necessary.

Figure 6.22, page 199, Courtesy NCR Corporation.

Chapter 7

Cut 7.1A, page 213, Dynamic Graphics/JupiterImages.

Cut 7.1B, page 213, (c) image100/PunchStock.

Cut 7.1C, page 213, Dynamic Graphics/JupiterImages.

Figure 7.6, page 218, www.pcmagazine.com, accessed October 10, 2005.

Figure 7.13, page 223, www.businessweek.com, accessed October 20, 2005.

Figure 7.22, page 230, AP/Wide World.

Chapter 8

Cut 8.1A, page 244, C. Sherburne/PhotoLink/Getty Images.

Cut 8.1B, page 244, Digital Vision/Getty Images.

Cut 8.1C, page 244, Ryan McVay/Getty Images.

Figure 8.8, page 252, William Copacino, "How to Become a Supply Chain Master," Supply Chain Management Review, September 1, 2001, www.manufacutirng.net, accessed June 12, 2003.

Chapter 9

Cut 9.1A, page 274, Stockbyte/Punchstock Images.

Cut 9.1B, page 274, Steve Cole/Getty Images.

Cut 9.1C, page 274, The McGraw-Hill Companies, Inc./Lars A. Niki, photographer.

Figure 9.10, page 289, "Finding Value in the Real-Time Enterprise," *Business 2.0,* November 2003, pp. S1–S5.

Figure 9.11, page 290, "Finding Value in the Real-Time Enterprise," Business 2.0, November 2003, pp. S1–S5.

Figure 9.12, page 291, "Finding Value in the Real-Time Enterprise,"Business 2.0, November 2003, pp. S1–S5 "Customer Success," www.siebel.com, accessed May 5, 2003.

Chapter 10

Cut 10.1A, page 302, Doug Menuez/Getty Images.

Cut 10.1B, page 302, Patrick Clark/Getty Images.

Cut 10.1C, page 302, Jules Frazier/Getty Images.

Figure 10.1, page 304, "ERP Knowledge Base," www.cio.com, accessed July 2005.

Figure 10.9, page 313, Michael Doane, "A Blueprint for ERP Implementation Readiness," www.metagroup.com, accessed October 17, 2003.

Figure 10.14, page 316, www.sap.com.

Chapter 11

Cut 11.1A, page 340, The McGraw-Hill Companies, Inc./Christopher Kerrigan, photographer.

Cut 11.1B, page 340, Getty Images.

Cut 11.1C, page 340, The McGraw-Hill Companies, Inc./Christopher Kerrigan, photographer.

Figure 11.1, page 343, "Software Costs," CIO Magazine, www.cio .com, accessed December 5, 2003.

Figure 11.7, page 347, Agile Alliance Manifesto, www.agile.com, accessed November 1, 2003.

Chapter 12

Cut 12.1A, page 372, (c) Comstock/PunchStock.

Cut 12.1B, page 372, © 2000 Image 100 Ltd.

Cut 12.1C, page 372, Royalty-Free/CORBIS.

Figure 12.2, page 376, "Top Reasons Why IT Projects Fail," InformationWeek, www.infoweek.com, accessed November 5, 2003.

Figure 12.15, page 385, www.microsoft.com, accessed December 13, 2003.

Figure 12.18, page 389, Deni Connor, "IT Outlook Declines Due to Outsourcing, Offshoring," www.nwfusion.com/careers/2004/0531manside.html, accessed June 8, 2004.

Figure 12.21, page 391, Todd Datz, "Outsourcing World Tour," *CIO Magazine*, July 15, 2004, pp. 42–48.

A

Abercrombie & Fitch (A&F), 160
Aberdeen Group, 297
Abrams, Jonathan, 98
Accenture, 14, 389
Acceptable-use policy, 109, 110
Accounting, in organizational structure, 7
Accounting and finance ERP components, 305–306
Accuracy, 178
ACLU (American Civil Liberties Union), 237
ACNielsen International Research, 94
ACS (American Cancer Society), 295
Adaptec, Inc., 248–249
Adaptive maintenance, 359
Advanced Micro Devices (AMD), 140, 142, 143, 149
Advanced Research Project Agency (ARPA), 67, 69
Adware, 114
A&F (Abercrombie & Fitch), 160
Affiliate (associate) programs, 81
Agile Alliance, 347
Agile methodology, 347
Airbus, 231–232
Alaska Department of Fish and Game, 203
Albertsons, 20
Altec Lansing Technologies, 3
Altria Group, Inc., 383
ALU (arithmetic-logic unit), 142
AMA (American Management Association), 113
Amazon.com, 19, 63–64, 78, 91, 97, 162, 309, 319
AMD (see Advanced Micro Devices)
America Online (AOL), 74
American Airlines, 58, 59
American Cancer Society (ACS), 295–296
American Civil Liberties Union (ACLU), 237
American Express, 52
American Family Immigration History Center, 181
American Management Association (AMA), 113
American Sign Language (ASL), 147
AMR Research, 246, 289, 341
Analysis phase (systems development life cycle), 352–354
Analytical CRM, 280, 286–288
Analytical information, 37
Andersen, Bjorn, 456
Anderson, Tom, 75
Andreesen, Marc, 70
Anheuser-Busch, 265–266
Ann Taylor, 225
Annenberg Public Policy Center, 134
Anti-spam policy, 111, 112
Antivirus software, 157
AOL (America Online), 74
AOL Time Warner, 66, 329–330
Apple Computer Inc., 2–5, 23, 168, 233, 253, 254, 319
Applebee's, 191
Appleyard, David, 131, 132
Application architecture, 154, 160–162
    defined, 160
    and open systems, 162
    Web services in, 160–162

Application generation component (of DBMS), 188, 189
Application service provider (ASP), 74, 85
Application software, 151, 153
Applications (system) testing, 358
Approvals, and change management, 383
Appshop, 74
Architecture (see Network architecture)
Argentina, 395
Arithmetic-logic unit (ALU), 142
Arkansas State University (ASU), 121
ARPA (see Advanced Research Project Agency)
The Art of War (Sun Tzu), 196
Arthur Andersen, 104–105
Artificial intelligence, 43–45
Artificial neural network, 44
ASL (American Sign Language), 147
ASP (see Application service provider)
Associate (affiliate) programs, 81
Association detection, 199
ASU (Arkansas State University), 121
AT&T Bell Laboratories, 151
AT&T Wireless, 105, 108, 150
Attributes, 183
Auctions, online, 79
Audi, 20–21
Austrian Federal Railways, 183
Authentication, 121
Authorization, 121
Authors Guild, 175
Automated input devices, 146
Automatic call distribution, 285
Automation, as CRM business driver, 289
Availability, 73, 159–160
Avnet Computer Marketing, 284–285

B

B2B (see Business-to-business model)
B2C (business-to-consumer) model, 78
Bacheldor, Beth, 450, 451
Backdoor programs, 126
Backup and recovery, 155, 358
Backward integration, 189
BAE, 364
Bagla, Gunjan, 451
Bain, 270
Ballantynes, Garth, 214
Ballmer, Steve, 167
Banana Slug, 174
Bank of America, 129
Bank of Canada, 297
Bank of Halifax, 291
Bank of Ireland, 113
Bank of Scotland, 291
Banner ads, 81, 86
Bar code scanner, 146
Barach, Marc, 87
Barclay's Bank, 129–130, 278–279
Bastian, Edward, 60

Bed Bath & Beyond, 225
Begley, S., 450
Belkin, 3
Bell Atlantic, 161
Ben & Jerry's, 205
Benchmarks and benchmarking, 4, 14
Bergen, David, 269, 270
Berianato, Scott, 451, 452
Berman, Saul, 451
Berners-Lee, Tim, 69
Best Buy, 78, 225, 254, 389, 401
Betts, Mitch, 452, 453
Bezos, Jeffrey, 63
BI (*see* Business intelligence)
Binary digit (bit), 142
Binary terms, 144
Binstock, Andrew, 453
Biometrics, 122
Bit (binary digit), 142
Black-hat hackers, 126
Blanchard, Ken, 450
Blau, John, 451
Blog, 81
BlueStar Solutions, 74
Bluetooth, 230–231
BMW Group Switzerland, 325–326
Boeing, 66, 232
Bork Bill, 107
Boston Red Sox, 26–27
Bowman, Dennis, 225
Boyd, Michael, 48
BP (British Petroleum), 390
BPR (*see* Business process reengineering)
Brailer, David, 213
Brand reputation, and software success, 343
Brazil, 393
Breen, Bill, 453
Brehm, Denise, 452
Bresnahan, Jennifer, 454
Brin, Sergey, 172
British Airways, 72
British Petroleum (BP), 390
Brittan Elementary School, 237
Brother International Corporation, 289
Broughton, Joan, 367
Brower, Mary, 237
Brown, Brad, 368
Browsers, 153
Bulgaria, 131
Bullwhip effect, 250
Burlington Northern and Santa Fe Railroad (BNSF), 39
Burrows, Peter, 450
Bus topology, 219
Bus width, 142
Bush, George W., 213
Business analysis, 311
Business decisions, making, 209–211
Business drivers, 228–229, 255
Business intelligence (BI), 38, 196, 197, 308
Business Objects (company), 200, 205
Business process, 21, 49
Business process reengineering (BPR), 49–52
    opportunity in, 50–51
    pitfalls of, 52

Business process reengineering (BPR)—*Cont.*
    principles of, 50
Business requirements, 352
    in analysis phase, 344
    case study, 365–366
    unclear/missing, 360
Business strategy, 17–23
    Apple case study, 2–4
    business decision projects for, 29
    cell phone credit card case study, 25
    creating globalization case study, 28–29
    Five Forces Model of, 17–20
    generic, 20–21
    innovative business managers case study, 26–27
    value chain approach to, 20–23
Business-critical integrity constraints, 182
Business-to-business (B2B) model, 18, 19, 76
Business-to-consumer (B2C) model, 78
Buy versus build decision, 353–354
Buyer power, 18
Byte, 142

C

C2B (consumer-to-business) model, 79
C2C (consumer-to-consumer) model, 79
C2G (consumer-to-government) model, 91
Cable, 148
Cable Communications Act of 1984, 107
Cache memory, 143
Caldwell, Bruce, 450, 451
California Pizza Kitchen, 205
California State Automobile Association (CSAA), 281
Caliper Associates, 35
Call center case study, 285, 297
Call scripting systems, 286
Calpine Corp., 378
Campaign management systems, 281
Canada, 297, 392, 398
CAN-Span Act of 2003, 107
Cantrall, Dawn, 237
Capacity (supply chain management), 256
Capacity planning, 159
Capital Cardiology Associates, 167
Carey, Gib, 270
Carfax, 78
Carra, Joseph, 334
Carroll, Vince, 400
CASE (computer-aided software engineering), 353
Cathode-ray tube (CRT), 147
CCB (change control board), 360
CD-ROM (compact disk-read-only memory), 145
CD-RW (compact disk-read-write), 145
Cell phones, 25, 229
Central processing unit (CPU), 140–143
CGI (company), 398
Champy, James, 50, 450
Change
    preparing for, 383
    reasons for, 382
Change control board (CCB), 360
Change management, 381–383
Change management system, 360, 381–383
Changing technology, 361

Charles Schwab, 47–48, 67
Chen, Eva, 217–218, 453
ChevronTexaco Corporation, 323–324
Chicago Police Department, 182
Chicago Tribune, 164–165
Chief information officer (CIO), 10
Chief knowledge officer (CKO), 11–12
Chief privacy officer (CPO), 11
Chief security officer (CSO), 11
Chief technology officer (CTO), 11
Children's Hospital (Boston), 12
Chile, 395
China, 393
China Airlines, 244
Chip line width, 142
Christensen, Clayton M., 67, 451
CIO (chief information officer), 10
Circuit City, 225, 401–402
CISC chips (*see* Complex instruction set computer chips)
Cisco Systems, 13, 65, 66, 121, 309
Citigroup, 71
Citizen and Law Enforcement Analysis and Reporting (CLEAR), 182
CKO (*see* Chief knowledge officer)
Clarke, Ian, 104
Cleansing, information, 194–196
CLEAR (Citizen and Law Enforcement Analysis and Reporting), 182
Cleveland, Brad, 285
Clickstream, 114
Clickstream data, 86, 87
Click-through, 86
Client/server network, 217–218
Clock speed, 142
Cluster analysis, 198
Coaxial cable wiring, 224
Coca-Cola Bottling Company, 269
Coca-Cola Bottling Company of Egypt, 182–183
Cognos, 200, 205
Cohen, Marshall, 270
Cold site, 156
Cold Stone Creamery, 70–71
Collaboration, trends in, 329–330
Collaboration systems, 318–330
    business decision projects for, 337
    and content management, 325–326
    Costco case study, 336
    defined, 320
    DreamWorks/Halo case study, 332–333
    functions of, 321
    and groupware, 328–329
    highway safety case study, 334–335
    internal/external, 319
    and knowledge management, 322–325
    Stanford University case study, 302–303
    trends in, 329–330
    types of, 320–321
    and workflow management, 326–328
Collaborative business functions, 321
Collaborative demand planning, 263
Collaborative engineering, 263
Collins, Jim, 401
Comair, 159
Commerce Bancorp, 129
Commercial off-the-shelf (COTS), 353
Communication devices, 141, 148

Communication software, 153
Communications Assistance for Law Enforcement Act of 1994, 107
Communities of fantasy, 79
Communities of interest, 79
Communities of relations, 79
Compact disk-read-only memory (CD-ROM), 145
Compact disk-read-write (CD-RW), 145
Compaq, 378–379
Compaq Enterprise Storage Group, 348
Competitive advantage, 17, 289
Competitive edge, 396
Completeness, 178
Complex instruction set computer (CISC) chips, 142, 143
Compton, Dean, 59
Computer Fraud and Abuse Act of 1986, 107
Computer-aided software engineering (CASE), 353
Computers, 140, 148, 150
Computer-use policy, 108–109
ComScore Networks, 113
Concur (company), 74
Confidentiality, 105, 397
Consistency, 178
Consolidation, 40
Consulting fees, 313
Consumer protection, 84
Consumer-to-business (C2B) model, 79
Consumer-to-consumer (C2C) model, 79
Consumer-to-government (C2G) model, 91
Contact center, 285
Contact management CRM systems, 282
Content filtering, 123
Content management systems, 325–326
Content provider, 85
Contracts, IT, 396
Control unit, 142
Conversion rates, 15
Cookies, 86, 114
Cookin' with Google, 174
Cooper, Barbara, 372–374
Coors, 403
Copacino, William, 454
Copyright, 104
Cordless computer peripherals, 229
Core competencies, 388
Core competency strategy, 319
Corio, 74
Cornworth, Francis, 84
Corrective maintenance, 359
Cost drivers, 42, 289
Cost leadership strategy, 20
Costa Rica, 395
Cost/benefit analysis, 351
Costco, 292, 336
Costco Wholesale, 336
Counterfeit software, 104
CPO (chief privacy officer), 11
CPU (*see* Central processing unit)
Crackers, 126
Crash-proof utility software, 152
Credit Union National Association, 44
Critical path, 381
Critical success factor (CSF), 350
CRM (*see* Customer relationship management)
Cross-selling, 281

CRT (cathode-ray tube), 147
CSAA (California State Automobile Association), 281
CSF (critical success factor), 350
CSI/FBI 2004 Computer Crime and Security Survey, 116–117
CSO (chief security officer), 11
CTO (chief technology officer), 11
Cultures
    in business intelligence, 197
    information, 10
    IT, 9, 10
Customer relationship management (CRM), 48, 274–288, 308
    American Cancer Society case study, 295–296
    analysis technologies of, 279
    analytical, 286–288
    benefits of, 277–278
    best practices, 291
    business decision projects for, 299–300
    business drivers in, 289
    Canadian call center case study, 297
    as component of ERP, 308
    defined, 277, 308
    in enterprise systems, 47, 49
    evolution of, 278–279
    growth of, 289–290
    integrating ERP with, 312–316
    market overview, 310
    Mini USA, 275–276
    operational, 280–286
    predicting technologies of, 279
    Progressive Insurance case study, 274–275
    reporting technologies of, 279
    RFM in, 278
    Ritz-Carlton case study, 298
    strategies for, 288–294
    success factors, 290–291
    trends in, 291–293
Customer relationship strategy, 48–49
Customer satisfaction, 15
Customer service, 41, 83–84, 284–285
Customer support, 289
Customization, 313
Cyberterrorists, 126
Cycle inventory, 258

D

DaimlerChrysler, 251
Daly, Bob, 372
DAM (digital asset management), 325
Danescu, Adrian, 455
Data, information vs., 9
Data administration component (of DBMS), 176, 188, 189
Data definition component (of DBMS), 185, 186
Data dictionary, 185
Data encryption (see Encryption)
Data flow diagram (DFD), 353
Data management software, 153
Data manipulation component (of DBMS), 186–188
Data mining, 45, 197–200, 205–206
Data models, 355
Data warehouses (data warehousing), 191–200, 192
    Applebee's use of, 191
    business decision projects for, 209–211
    and business intelligence, 196, 197

Data warehouses (data warehousing)—Cont.
    and data mining, 197–200
    data mining case studies of, 205–206
    defined, 192
    and ERP integration, 313
    fisheries case study, 203–204
    and information cleansing/scrubbing, 194–196
    and information maintenance, 193
    model of, 193, 194
    multidimensional analysis, 193, 194
The Data Warehousing Institute (TDWI), 194, 207
Database(s), 176–191
    advantages of, 180
    business decision projects for, 209–211
    characteristics of, 176
    fisheries case study, 203–204
    flexibility of, 181
    fundamentals of, 182–184
    Google case study, 172–175
    Harrah's case study, 207–209
    and information quality, 177–180
    integrating data among multiple, 189–191
    integrity of, 181–182
    levels/formats/granulations of, 176–177
    management of, 180 (See also Database management systems)
    redundancy of, 181
    scalability/performance of, 181
    security of, 182
Database management systems (DBMS), 180, 183–189
    application generation component of, 188, 189
    components of, 185
    data administration component of, 188, 189
    data definition component of, 185, 186
    data manipulation component of, 186–188
    user interaction with, 185
Database-based workflow systems, 327
Datbase program development, 356
Datz, Todd, 455
Davenport, Thomas H., 451, 452
DDoS (distributed denial-of-service attack), 126
De Hoop, Herman, 139
DEC (see Digital Equipment Corporation)
Decision making, 36, 37
Decision support systems (DSS), 38, 39, 40
Decision-making systems, 32–45
    business decision projects for, 60–61
    decision support systems in, 38–40
    Delta Air Lines case study, 58–60
    examples of, 35
    executive information systems in, 39–45
    Harley-Davidson case study, 32–34
    importance of information in, 35, 37
    mass customization case study, 56–57
    Saab case study, 55
    transaction processing systems in, 36–38
    types of, 35, 37
Deeley Harley-Davidson Canada, 305
Default value (database field property), 186
Dejanovic, Darko, 164
Delio, Michelle, 453
Dell Computer, 66, 97, 169, 244–245, 250, 252–254, 271, 309
Delta Air Lines, 58–60, 159, 232
Delta Technology, 59
Demand planning software, 250

Demmings, Steve, 297
Denial-of-service (DoS) attack, 126
Denver International Airport (DIA), 364
Dependency, 380
DePompa Reimers, Barbara, 452, 453
Design phase (systems development life cycle), 354–355
Desktop, 150
Desktop publishing software, 153
Detection and response, 125
Deuschl, Vivian, 299
Development phase (systems development life cycle), 355–356
DeWolf, Chris, 75
DFD (data flow diagram), 353
DIA (Denver International Airport), 364
Dial-up access, 148
Differentiation strategy, 20
Digital asset management (DAM), 325
Digital cameras, 146
Digital cell phones, 229
Digital Darwinism, 66
Digital dashboards, 40, 41–43
Digital divide, 70
Digital Equipment Corporation (DEC), 67, 220
Digital Fountain, 155
Digital hospital case study, 213–214
Digital subscriber line (DSL), 148
Digital video disk (DVD), 145
Digital video disk-read/write (DVD-RW), 145
Digital wallet, 82
Dillard's (department store), 257
Disaster recovery, 155–157
Disk image for data recovery, 152
Disk optimization utility software, 152
Disruptive technology, 65–68
Distributed denial-of-service attack (DDoS), 126
Distribution management software, 259
Doane, Michael, 454
Document management system (DMS), 325
Documentum, 326
DoD (see U.S. Department of Defense)
DoS (denial-of-service) attack, 126
Dr Pepper/Seven Up, Inc., 195
Dragoon, Alice, 452
DreamWorks, 26–27, 332–333
Drill-down, 40
Drucker, Peter, 13
DSL (digital subscriber line), 148
Dubuc, Nicholas, 377
Duncan, David, 104–105
Duplicate information, 179
Duplicate rule (database field property), 186
Duyser, Diana, 84
DVD (digital video disk), 145
DVD-ROM drive, 145
DVD-RW (digital video disk-read/write), 145

E

EA (enterprise architect), 153
EAI (enterprise application integration), 313
Eastman Kodak, 388
E-auctions, 79
EB (exabyte), 144
eBay, 15–16, 84, 94–96, 123, 181

EBPP (electronic bill presentment and payment), 82
E-business, 65, 75–92
    Amazon.com case study, 63–64
    benefits/challenges of, 87–90, 89
    business decision project for, 99–100
    as component of ERP, 308–309
    and customer service capability, 83–84
    defined, 76, 308
    eBay case study, 94–96
    extended models of, 90
    financial services, 80, 82, 83
    FreshDirect case study, 97
    innovations, 81
    intermediaries' roles in, 85
    and Internet, 65
    marketing/sales, 80, 81
    measuring success of, 85–88
    models of, 76–79
    procurement, 82, 83
    security issues, 84, 127
    trends in, 88, 90–92
E-business model, 76
E-business networks, 225–226
Echo Bay, 94
Echt, Martin, 167, 168
E-commerce, 76
Economic feasibility study (cost-benefit analysis), 351
Eddie Bauer, 48, 225
EDI (electronic data interchange), 82
Edwards, J. D., 450
Effectiveness IT metrics, 13–16, 86, 255
Efficiency, as CRM business driver, 289
Efficiency IT metrics, 13–16, 255
E-government models, 91
EIS (see Executive information systems)
Electronic auction (e-auction), 79
Electronic bill presentment and payment (EBPP), 82
Electronic catalog, 83
Electronic Communications Privacy Act of 1986, 107
Electronic data interchange (EDI), 82
Electronic marketplaces, 76
Elevation of privilege, 127
Ellis Island, 181
E-logistics, 308
E-mail, 109–111, 153
E-malls, 78
E-marketplaces, 76, 90
Employease, 74
Employee management and training, 119
Employee relationship management (ERM), 292
Employee-monitoring policy, 114, 115
Encryption, 84, 124, 152
Enochs, Robert, 139
Enron, 102, 104–105
Enterprise (car rental), 284
Enterprise application integration (EAI), 313
Enterprise applications, 342–349
    business decision projects for, 369–370
    business requirements case study, 365–366
    consequences of, 343
    Denver International Airport case study, 364
    developing, 342–343
    HP case study, 340–341
    methodologies for development of, 344–347

Enterprise applications—*Cont.*
  principles of successful, 348–349
  REI case study, 367–368
  systems development life cycle for, 343–344
Enterprise architect (EA), 153
Enterprise architecture, 152–162
  application architecture component of, 160–162
  business decision projects for, 170
  business goals of, 154
  Chicago Tribune case study, 164–165
  components of, 154
  defined, 153
  information architecture component of, 154–158
  infrastructure architecture component of, 158–160
  Linux case study, 167–168
  UPS case study, 166
Enterprise Miner, 277
Enterprise resource planning (ERP), 52–53, 302–318
  associated costs of, 313
  benefits of, 304, 312, 313
  and business analysis, 53
  business decision projects for, 337, 338
  business intelligence components of, 308
  core components of, 305–307
  costs of, 313
  customer relationship management components of, 308
  defined, 304
  e-business components of, 308–309
  examples of, 304, 305
  extended components of, 307–309
  future of, 316–318
  human components of, 307
  and implementation plans, 53
  integrating SCM/CRM with, 312–316
  overall fit of, 53
  production/materials management components of, 306–307
  risks of, 312, 313
  selection of, 53
  software for, 52–53, 311–312
  Stanford University case study, 302–303
  supply chain management components of, 308
  system needs, 315
  vendor components of, 316–317
  vendors offering, 309–310
Enterprise systems, 46–53
  business decision projects for, 60–61
  business process reengineering in, 49–52
  customer relationship management in, 47, 49
  Delta Air Lines case study, 58–60
  Harley-Davidson case study, 32–34
  mass customization case study, 56–57
  resource planning in, 52–53
  Saab case study, 55
  supply chain management in, 46–47
Entity, 183
Entity class, 183
Entity relationship diagram (ERD), 355
Entry rule (database field property), 186
Environmental scanning, 17
ePolicies, 108
ePolicy Institute, 113
E-procurement, 83, 308
Equifax, 105, 108
ERD (entity relationship diagram), 355

Ericsson, 91
ERM (employee relationship management), 292
Ernst & Young, 120
Escarra, Vickie, 59
E-shops, 78
E-stores, 78
E-tailers, 78
Ethernet, 220, 221
Ethical computer use policy, 108
Ethics, 49–52, 102–115
  hacker case studies, 131–133
  information, 105–108
  and information management policies, 108–112
  issues of, 104–105
  and making business decisions, 134–135
  monitoring technologies to enforce, 113–114
  privacy, 105
  Sarbanes-Oxley case study, 102–103
  in workplace, 113–115
ETL (extraction, transformation, and loading), 193
E-Trade Financial Corporation, 129
Ettorre, Barbara, 451
Etymotic Research, 3
Evans, Bob, 454
Evans Data Corp., 227
Events, 161
Exabyte (EB), 144
Executive information systems (EIS), 39–45
  artificial intelligence in, 43–45
  data mining in, 45
  digital dashboards, 40–43
Expert systems, 44
Explicit knowledge, 323–324
Exposure metrics, 88
Extended enterprise resource planning, 305, 306
Extended ERP components, 305, 307–309
External collaboration systems, 319
Extraction, transformation, and loading (ETL), 193
Extranet, 71
Extreme programming (XP) methodology, 346–347

F

Facilities, as supply chain driver, 255–257, 259–261
Facilities focus (supply chain management), 261
Failover, 155
Failure, project, 361
Fair and Accurate Credit Transactions Act of 2003, 107
Fair Credit Reporting Act (FCRA), 105
Fair use doctrine, 104
Family Education Rights and Privacy Act of 1974, 107
Fashionworld, 270
FatWire, 326
Fault tolerance, 155
FBI, 125, 131, 134, 152–153
FCRA (Fair Credit Reporting Act), 105
Feasibility study, 350, 351
Federal Trade Commission, 134, 157
FedEx, 17, 95, 97, 228, 238–239, 259, 286
Feld, Charlie, 59
Feldman, Joseph, 401
Fenwick and West (law firm), 112
Fiber optic wiring, 224
Field name (database field property), 186

File and data recovery utility software, 152
File transfer protocol (FTP), 222
Finance, in organizational structure, 7
Financial cybermediary, 82
Financial EDI, 82
Financial metrics, 15
Financial services, 80, 82, 83
Financial Services Modernization Act of 1999, 118
Fingerprint, 122
Fiorina, Carly, 341
Firewall, 120, 124, 125
FirstEnergy (Ohio), 155–156
First-mover advantage, 17
Fischer International Corporation, 157
Fisheries case study, 203–204
Five Forces Model, 17–20, 22–23, 65
Flash memory, 143
Fletcher, Christopher, 297
Flexibility, 158–159, 181
Focused strategy, 20
Fontana, John, 452
Fontova, Al, 57
Ford Motor Company, 183, 251
Ford-Woens, Betsy, 25
Forecasts, 200
Foreign key, 183
Form (database field property), 186
Forrester Research, Inc., 262, 367
Forward auction, 79
Forward integration, 189
Freedom of Information Acts, 107
Freenet, 104
FreshDirect (case study), 97
Friedman, Thomas, 28–29
Friendster, 98
Frito-Lay, 17, 59, 140
Froogle, 174
FTP (file transfer protocol), 222
Fuzzy logic, 44

G

G2B (government-to-business) model, 91
G2C (government-to-consumer) model, 91
G2G (government-to-government) model, 91
Galina (auction house), 271
Gantt chart, 381
The Gap, 78, 225
Gartner, Inc., 52, 116, 158, 160, 234, 348
Garvey, Martin, 452
Gates, Bill, 29, 168
Gateway, 137
GB (gigabyte), 144
Geffen, David, 26–27
General Electric Co., 13, 26, 60, 66, 103, 383
General Motors, 66, 150, 234, 251, 257
Genetic algorithm, 44–45
Geographic information system (GIS), 234
GHz (gigahertz), 142
Gigabyte (GB), 144
Gigahertz (GHz), 142
Gillen, Al, 168
Girard, Kim, 454
GIS (geographic information system), 234

Global inventory management system, 259
Global positioning system (GPS), 233–234
Globalization, 28–29, 388
Goal-seeking analysis, 39
Goldman Sachs Group, 251
Google, 98, 172–175
Goroshevsky, Dmitry, 223
Gouchard, Gilles, 340
Government-to-business (G2B) model, 91
Government-to-consumer (G2C) model, 91
Government-to-government (G2G) model, 91
GPS (see Global positioning system)
Graham, Earnie, 237
Gramm Leach Bliley Act, 118
Granularity, information, 176–177
Graphical user interface (GUI), 355
Green, Tonja, 46
Griffin Technology, 3
Grinstein, Gerald, 59–60
Grokster, 104
Groupware, 153, 328, 329
Gruman, Galen, 453
Grupo Farmanova Intermed, 307
GTE, 161
GUI (graphical user interface), 355
Gurden, Dereck, 265
Gus Software, 405
Guthrie, Virginia, 403
Guyaux, Joe, 280

H

Hackensack University Medical Center, 213–214
Hackers, 126, 131–133
Hackett Group, 377
Hactivists, 126
Hagerty, John, 453, 454
Halo (case study), 332–333
Hammann, Greg, 269
Hammer, Michael, 50, 450, 455, 456
Hanger, Christina, 340
Hanson, J. Greg, 10
Hapgood, Fred, 453
Hard drive, 145
Hard-disk storage space, 73
Hardware, 140–148
    business decision projects for, 169
    case studies of, 137–139
    central processing unit, 140–143
    components of, 141
    computer categories, 148–150
    input devices, 145–146
    output devices, 147
    primary storage, 143–144
    secondary storage, 144–145
Hardware key logger, 114
Harley-Davidson (case study), 32–34
Harrah, Bill, 207
Harrah's (case study), 207–209
Harreld, Heather, 451
Harrington, H. James, 456
Harvard Universtiy, 175
Health Information Management Society, 116

Health Insurance Portability and Accountability Act of 1996 (HIPAA), 107, 116
Heilmann, John, 451
Heineken USA, 320
Help desk, 359
Helyar, John, 451
Henry, John, 26–27
Hernandez-Rebollar, Jose L., 147
Hershey, 342
Herzog, Jacques, 240
Hewlett-Packard (HP), 67, 113, 139, 166, 332, 340–341, 378
Hierarchical database model, 180
High availability, 159
Highway safety case study, 334–335
HIPAA (see Health Insurance Portability and Accountability Act of 1996)
Hit metrics, 88
Hoaxes, 127
Hof, Robert, 451
The Home Depot, 26–27, 66, 254
Homeland Security Act of 2002, 107
Hopper, Max, 59, 451
Horizon Blue Cross Blue Shield of New Jersey, 375–376
Hot sites, 156
Hotel Gatti, 80
HP (see Hewlett-Packard)
HR (see Human resources)
H&R Block, 343
HTTP (see Hypertext transport protocol)
Human resources (HR), 7, 307
Hummer, 20–21
Hunter, Dick, 244
Hutheesing, Nikhil, 453
Hybrid topology, 219
Hypertext transport protocol (HTTP), 69, 222
Hyundai, 20–21

I Spot Networks, 234
I2 Technologies, 342
IAB (Internet Architecture Board), 69
IBM, 38, 66, 67, 139, 143, 198, 254, 329–330, 387
IBM Germany, 167
IBM Global Services, 398
IBM Life Sciences, 198–199
IDC (see International Data Corporation)
Identity theft, 121, 122
Identity Theft and Assumption Deterrence Act of 1998, 107
IDS (intrusion detection software), 120
IESG (Internet Engineering Steering Group), 69
ImageSource, Inc., 336
Immelt, Jeffrey, 26
Implementation phase (systems development life cycle), 358–359
InCom Corp., 237
Incoming Calls Management Institute, 285
India, 392
Indirect materials, 82
Infomediaries, 85
Information, 9
    data vs., 9
    and ethics, 105–108
    levels/formats/granularities of, 176–177
    quality of, 177–180

Information—Cont.
    as supply chain management driver, 259–261
    types of, 177
Information architecture, 154–158
    backup/recovery in, 155
    defined, 154
    disaster recovery in, 155–157
    information security in, 157–158
Information cleansing/scrubbing, 194–196
Information collaboration, 320, 321
Information ethics, 105–108
Information focus (supply chain management), 261
Information granularity, 176–177
Information integrity, 181–182
Information management policy(-ies), 108–112
    acceptable use, 109, 110
    anti-spam, 111, 112
    computer use, 108–109
    e-mail privacy, 109–111
    employee monitoring, 114, 115
    guidelines for, 110
    Internet use, 111, 112
    and privacy, 109, 110
Information partnership, 319
Information privacy policy, 109
Information quality, 177–180
    characteristics of, 178–179
    costs/benefits of, 179–180
Information reach, 70
Information richness, 70
Information security, 115–127, 157–158
    and authentication/authorization, 121–123
    banking case studies of, 129–130
    business decision projects in, 134–135
    and content filtering, 123–124
    courses in, 133
    and detection/response, 125–127
    and encryption, 124
    and firewalls, 124, 125
    five step plan for, 120
    hacker case studies of, 131–133
    and intellectual assets, 116–117
    and people risks, 117–121
    plan for, 118–119
    and prevention/resistance, 122, 123
    and privacy policy, 110
    questions for managers regarding, 120
    Sarbanes-Oxley Act case study, 103
    technology for, 121–127
Information security policies, 118
Information sharing, 260
Information systems, 119, 353
Information technology (IT), 5–16, 8, 140, 247–251
    Apple case study, 2–4
    business decision projects for, 29–30
    and business operations, 5–6
    business role of, 5–6
    cell phone credit card case study, 25
    components of, 248
    creating globalization case study, 28–29
    information-sharing cultures of, 9, 10
    information vs. data in, 9
    innovative business managers case study, 26–27
    managing, 9

Information technology (IT)—*Cont.*
    measuring, 13
    questionable use of, 105
    roles and responsibilities in, 10–13
    in supply chain management, 247–251
Information technology architecture, 167–168
Information technology monitoring, 114
Information-discovery cultures, 10
Information-functional cultures, 10
Information-inquiring cultures, 10
Information-sharing cultures, 10
Infosys, 390
Infrastructure, IT
    design of, 354
    development of, 355
    simple, 355
Infrastructure architecture, 154, 158–160
    availability of, 159–160
    defined, 158
    flexibility of, 158–159
    performance of, 160
    reliability of, 159
    scalability of, 159
Ingenio, 87
Ink-jet printer, 147
Innovative business managers case study, 26–27
Innovator's Dilemma (Christensen), 67
Inovant, 109
Input devices, 141, 145–146
Insiders, 117
Insourcing (in-house development), 387
Instant messaging, 329
Intacct, 74
Integrated supply chain, 249
Integrating enterprise resource planning, 312–316
Integration, 189
    of RFID and software, 232
    of SCM/CRM/ERP, 312–316
    and testing, 313
Integration flow, 314
Integration testing, 358
Integrity constraints, 181
Intel, 65–67, 143, 220, 361
Intellectual assets, 116
Intellectual property, 104
Intelligent agents, 45, 85
Intelligent systems, 43
Intense School, 133
Interactive Advertising Bureau, 173
Interactive voice response (IVR), 285
Interactivity, 86
Interface, 318
Intermediaries, 85
Internal collaboration systems, 319
International Data Corporation (IDC), 75, 121, 151, 167, 168, 228
International Federation of Robotics, 45
International Federation of the Phonographic Industry, 4
Internet, 67, 68
    business decision project for, 99–100
    as driver of outsourcing, 388
    eBay case study, 94–96
    evolution of the, 63–70, 67
    FreshDirect case study, 97
    Friendster case study, 98

Internet—*Cont.*
    and future of ERP, 317–318
    service providers on, 72–75
Internet Architecture Board (IAB), 69
Internet Crime Complaint Center, 131
Internet Engineering Steering Group (IESG), 69
Internet Engineering Task Force (IETF), 69
Internet Explorer, 346
Internet service providers (ISPs), 72–75, 85
Internet-use policy, 111, 112
Interoperability, 160, 220
InterWoven, 326
Intranet, 71
Intrusion detection software (IDS), 120
Intuit, 67
Inventory, as supply chain driver, 257–258
Inventory focus, 261
Inventory management and control software, 258
Inverness Investments, 134
Ireland, 392
Iriondo-Coysh, Eneka, 4
ISPs (*see* Internet service providers)
Israel, 392
IT (*see* Information technology)
IT cultures, 9, 10
Iterative approach, 347
IVR (interactive voice response), 285

J

James, Geoffrey, 452
Jensen, Bob, 52, 305
Jobs, Steve, 2
Johnson, Amy, 451
Johnson, Jim, 348, 379
Johnson & Johnson, 66
Joint problem solving, 323–324
Joshi, Vyomesh, 332
Joystick, 146
Jupiter Research, 87, 367

K

Kahn, Gabriel, 450
Kaiser Permanente, 48
Kamangar, Salar, 173–174
Kane, Margaret, 451
Kapner, Bill, 298
Kary, Tiffany, 453
Kate Spade (company), 3
Katzenberg, Jeffrey, 26–27, 332
Kaufman, Barry, 133
Kaufman, David, 133
KB (kilobyte), 144
Keane, 398
Keighley, Geoff, 455
Kelleher, Kevin, 454
Kesner, Matt, 112
Key logger software, 114
Key performance indicators (KPIs), 13
Key trapper software, 114
Keyboard, 146
Kheradpir, Shaygan, 41–42
Kia, 20–21

Kiling, Julia, 453
Kilobyte (KB), 144
Kiosk, 72
Kleiner, Perkins, Caufield, Byers, and Benchmark Capital, 98
KM (see Knowledge management)
KMS (see Knowledge management systems)
Knight, Phil, 26–27, 342
Knowledge management (KM), 322, 324
Knowledge management systems (KMS), 322–325
    defined, 322
    and explicit/tacit knowledge, 323–324
    reasons for launching, 324
    and social networking, 325
    technologies, 324
Koch, Christopher, 450, 452
Konicki, Steve, 454
Koolhaas, Rem, 240
Kovac, Caroline A., 198
KPIs (key performance indicators), 13
KPMG LL5, 385
Kraft, 200
Kroger, 20, 66

L

LAN (local area network), 216
Lands' End Inc., 56, 193
LaPante, Alice, 453
Lapidus, Gary, 251
Laptops, 150
Larking, Daniel, 131
Laser printers, 147
Lashinsky, Adam, 451
Latham, Kimberly, 104
Laws, information-related, 107
Lazaridis, Mike, 227
LCDs (liquid crystal displays), 147
Legal and contractual feasibility study, 351
Leitner, Dennis, 381
Leon, Mark, 452
Leonard, Dorothy, 323
Levi Strauss, 269–271
Levinson, Meridith, 453, 455
Lexar, 138
Lexmark, 166
Liabilities, 343
Libbey, 112
Lillian Vernon Corp., 179
Lin, John, 3
Lindorff, Dave, 450
Linens 'n' Things, 225
LinkedIn, 98
Linux, 151, 167–168
Liquid crystal displays (LCDs), 147
List generators, 281
Listerine (case study), 267–268
LivePerson, 74
Livingston, Randy, 302–303
LMCS (local multipoint communications network), 148
Local area network (LAN), 216
Local multipoint communications network (LMCS), 148
Locher, Margaret, 452
Lockheed Martin, 66, 321
Logical field properties, 186

Logical view, 181
Los Angeles, California, 52, 305
Loveman, Gary, 207, 290, 453
Loyalty programs, 18
Lucent Worldwide Services, 223
Lumish, Phil, 43
Lydian Trust, 161–162

M

M (megabyte), 144
Mac OS X, 151
Macy's, 225
Magnetic ink character reader, 146
Magnetic medium, 145
Magnetic tape, 145
Mail bombs, 110
Mainframe computer, 150
Maintenance, 82
    of system, 359
    types of, 359–360
Maintenance, repair, and operations (MRO) materials, 82
Maintenance phase, 359
Maintenance phase (systems development life cycle), 359–360
Malaysia, 394
Malicious code, 127
Malone, Michael S., 452
MAN (metropolitan area network), 216
Management information systems (MIS), 7, 8
Managing user access, 157
Manchester Airport (England), 43
Manitoba, 297
Mantovani, Andres, 131, 132
Manual input devices, 146
Marineau, Philip A., 269
Market basket analysis, 199
Market maker, 85
Market pulse, 41
Marketing, 80, 81
    in e-business, 80
    and operational CRM, 281
    in organizational structure, 7
Marks & Spencer, 254
Mars (company), 325
Marshall & Swift, 156–157
Marshall Fields, 319
Martin, Kerri, 275
Mass customization, 53, 56–57, 81
Massachusetts Institute of Technology (MIT), 146, 250
MasterCard International, 25, 52
Matsushita, 43
Mattel, Inc., 247
Mayfield, 98
Mayo Clinic, 198
Maytag Corporation, 199
Mazda, 72
MB (megabyte), 144
MBIA Insurance Corp., 228
McCue, Andy, 451
McDonald's, 281
McGeever, Christine, 452
McGraw, Gary, 455
McKay, John, 125
McManus, Neil, 450

M-commerce, 91
Media Lab Asia, 70
Meetings, 383
Megabyte (MB, M, Meg), 144
Megahertz (MHz), 142
Meisburger, Dave, 274
Melymuka, Kathleen, 453
Memory card, 144
Merck, 66
Merrill Lynch, 205, 281, 386
Messaging-based workflow systems, 326
Meta Group, 312
Metrics, e-business, 85–88
Metropolitan area network (MAN), 216
Metz, Peter J., 250
Metz, Rachel, 451
Mexico, 394, 398
MHz (megahertz), 142
Microphone, 146
Microprocessors, 142, 143
Microsoft, 67, 125, 151, 167, 168, 329–330, 346, 377
Microsoft Windows, 151
Microwave transmitters, 232
Middleware, 313
Mikita, Lois, 270
Minar, Nelson, 174
Mini USA, 275–276
Minicomputers, 150
Missing information, 179
MIT (*see* Massachusetts Institute of Technology)
MIT Center for e-business, 250
MIT Media Lab, 149
Mitnick, Kevin, 133
Mobile commerce, 91
Mobile technology, 228
Modeling, 354–355
Models, 36
Modems, 148
Monitoring technologies, 113–114
Moore, Gordon, 361
Morgan, Pat, 348
Motorola, 91
Mougayar, Walid, 453, 454
Mouse, 146
Mr. Rounder (robot), 214
MS-DOS, 151
Mullaney, Timothy, 453
Multidimensional analysis, 193, 194
Multitasking, 151
Murphy, Chris, 453
Music, Terry, 295

N

Nagel, Brian, 131, 132
Nardelli, Robert, 26–27
NASA, 150
Nash, Kim, 453
National Academy of Sciences Institute of Medicine, 213
National Basketball Association, 278
National Center for Statistics and Analysis, 334
National Center for Supercomputing Applications, 70
National Highway Traffic Safety Administration, 334
National Institute of Standards and Technology (NIST), 357

National Research Council, 342
National Science Foundation, 69
Nearshore outsourcing, 390
Nestlé Group, 200
Nestlé Italiana, 200
NetLedger, 74
Netscape Communications Corporation, 346
Network(s), 213–226
    business decision projects for, 241–242
    characteristics of, 215
    defined, 215
    digital hospital case study, 213–214
    e-business, 225–226
    media used in, 223–225
    protocols of, 220–223
    and telecommunication systems, 215
    topology of, 218–219
    types of, 216
Network architecture, 215–218
    client/server, 217–218
    peer-to-peer, 215, 217
Network database model, 180
Network media
    wire, 223–224
    wireless, 224–225
Network operating system (NOS), 217
Network topologies, 218–219
Network transmission media, 223–225
Neural network, 44
New Brunswick, 297
New York City, 181, 328
New York Knicks, 278
New York Public Library, 175
New Zealand, 395
Newco, 251
Nice Systems, 285
NIIT, 390
Nike, 26–27, 56, 342, 343
NIST (*see* National Institute of Standards and Technology)
Nokia, 25, 91, 254
Noodles & Company, 205–206
Northrop Grumman Corp., 321–322
Northwest Airlines, 244
NOS (network operating system), 217
NPD Group, 270
Nucleus Research, 41
Nynex, 161

O

OECD (Organization for Economic Cooperation and Development), 83
Office Depot, 225, 319
Office of the Comptroller of the Currency, 134
Office of the Inspector General, 134
Offshore outsourcing, 390
OLAP (online analytical processing), 38
OLTP (online transaction processing), 37
O'Marah, Kevin, 246
OMD, 158
Omidyar, Pierre, 94, 451
Omnicom Group Inc., 158
Online ads, 81, 86
Online analytical processing (OLAP), 38
Online auctions, 79

Online broker, 85
Online business payments, 82
Online consumer payments, 82
Online service provider (OSP), 74, 85
Online training, 359
Online transaction processing (OLTP), 37
Onshore outsourcing, 390
Open System Interconnection (OSI) model, 222
Open systems, 162
Operating system software, 149, 151–152
Operation Firewall, 131
Operational CRM, 280–286
    customer service technologies for, 284–286
    marketing technologies for, 281
    sales technologies for, 281–284
    technologies for, 280
Operational design (of SCM), 257
Operational feasibility study, 351
Operations management, 7
Opportunity management CRM systems, 283
Optical fiber, 224
Optical medium, 145
Optical-character recognition, 146
OptionsXpress, 158
Oracle, 67, 232, 309, 316, 377
Organization for Economic Cooperation and Development (OECD), 83
Organizational information cultures, 10
OSI (Open System Interconnection) model, 222
OSP (see Online service provider)
Ostermann, Ken, 33
Output devices, 146, 147
Outsourcing, 386–398
    benefits of, 389
    business decision projects for, 404–405
    challenges of, 396
    Coors case study, 403
    countries for, 391–396
    drivers of, 388
    by function, 387
    future trends in, 398
    Merrill Lynch example of, 386–387
    offshore, 390–397
    opportunities in, 389
    options for, 390, 397
    reasons for, 387
Outtask, 74
Overall fit, 45, 311
Overholt, Alison, 455
Oxford University, 175

P

P2P network (see Peer-to-peer network)
Packet tampering, 127
Packet-switching, 217
Page, Larry, 172
Parallel implementation, 359
Parson, Jeffrey Lee, 125
Partner relationship management (PRM), 292
Password, 121
Patterson, Zachary, 295
PayPal, 95
PB (petabyte), 144
PDA (personal digital assistant), 150

Pechman, Marsha, 125
Peer-to-peer (P2P) network, 215, 217
People, 197
PeopleSoft, 309
PepsiCo, 26, 269, 332–333
Percussion, 326
Perdue Farms, 251–252
Perfective maintenance, 360
Performance, 160, 181
Personal digital assistant (PDA), 150
Personalization, 81, 286–288
PERT chart (see Program Evaluation and Review Technique chart)
Petabyte (PB), 144
Peterson, Tommy, 453
Pfizer, 66
P&G (see Procter & Gamble)
Phased implementation, 359
PHH Vehicle Management Services, 346
Philippines, 393
Phillips Petroleum, 66
Phishing, 121
Physical security, 119
Physical view, 181
Physician Services Insurance Corporation, 285–286
Pilot implementation, 359
PING, Inc., 36
Pirated software, 104
PKE (public key encryption), 124
Planning phase (systems development life cycle), 343, 349–351
Plotter, 147
Plunge implementation, 359
PNC Financial Services Group, 129, 280
Podcasting, 81
Pointing stick, 146
Point-of-sale (POS), 146
Polaroid, 65
Polymorphic viruses and worms, 126
Popular Telephony, 223
Pop-under ad, 81
Pop-up ad, 81
Port, Otis, 452
Portal, 71, 85
Porter, Michael, 17, 20, 21, 23
POS (point-of-sale), 146
Powergrid Fitness, 146
Prada (case study), 240–241
Pratt & Whitney, 71
Predictive dialing, 285
Premier One, 60
Presentation graphics, 153
Prevention technology, 122
Preventive maintenance, 360
Preventive security utility software, 152
PricewaterhouseCoopers, 389
Primary key, 183
Primary storage, 141, 143–144
Primavera, 377
Privacy Act of 1974, 107
Privacy and privacy policies, 105, 109, 110
Private exchange, 18, 19
PRM (partner relationship management), 292
Problem solving, 323–324
Process diagrams, 352
Process flow, 315

Process modeling, 353
Process rework, 313
Procter & Gamble (P&G), 47, 66, 254
Procurement, 80, 82, 83
Production and materials management ERP components, 306–307
Productivity, 289, 343
Program Evaluation and Review Technique (PERT) chart, 380–381
Programming software, 153
Progressive Insurance, 51, 274–275
Project
    defined, 375
    evaluation criteria for, 351
    product undertaken in, 379
    selection of, 379
Project deliverables, 377, 379
Project exclusions, 379
Project failure, 360
Project management, 372–385
    activities of, 377–381
    business decision projects for, 404–405
    change management in, 381–383
    Circuit City case study, 401–402
    Coors case study, 403
    defined, 375
    growth of software for, 377
    PERT chart example, 381
    and project plan, 380–381
    resource management in, 380
    risk management in, 383–385
    roles in, 378
    scope of, 379–380
    selecting projects for, 378
    SMART criteria for, 380
    strategies for success in, 385
    successful strategies for, 385
    Toronto Transit Commission case study, 400
    Toyota case study, 372–374
    variables of, 376
Project Management Institute, 375
Project management software, 375
Project managers, 377
Project milestones, 377
Project objectives, 379
Project plan, 380–381
Project risk, 383–385
Project scope, 379–380
Protocols, 67, 220–223
    ethernet, 220, 221
    TCP/IP, 221–223
Prototype, 346
Prystay, Cris, 450
Public key encryption (PKE), 124
Pull technology, 260
Push technology, 260

Q

QBE (query-by-example), 187
Qualcomm, 91
Qualitative risk analysis, 384
Quality, information, 177–180
Quantum, 67
Query-by-example (QBE), 187
Quinn, Frank, 451, 454

R

Rackspace, 292
RAD (rapid application development), 345
Raden, Neil, 450
Radio frequency identification (RFID), 146, 230–232
RadioShack, 401
Raines, Dick, 78
Raizner, Walter, 167
RAM (random access memory), 143
Random access memory (RAM), 143
Rapid application development (RAD), 345
Rapid prototyping methodology (*see* Rapid application development)
RateMyProfessors.com, 174
Rawson, Carol, 335
Read-only memory (ROM), 144
Real simple syndications (RSS), 81
Real-time information, 227
Real-time systems, 227
Recency, frequency, and monetary value (RFM), 278
Recovery, 155, 358
Reduced instruction set computer (RISC) chips, 143
Redundancy, 181
Referential integrity constraints, 182
Regression testing, 358
REI, 367–368, 385
Reidenberg, Joe, 105
Reinemund, Steven, 26, 333
Reintermediation, 85
Relational database model, 180, 183
Relational databases, 182–184
Reliability, 159
Renwick, Glen, 274, 275
Repair, 82
Report generators, 187
Reports, and change management, 383
Requirements definition document, 352
Research in Motion (RIM), 227
Resistance technology, 122
Resource availability, 351
Resource planning, 52–53
Resources, IT, 9
Response time, 15
Revenues, 343
Reverse auction, 19, 79
RFID (*see* Radio frequency identification)
RFID tags, 230, 231
RFM (recency, frequency, and monetary value), 278
Rhodia Inc., 377
Ricadela, Aaron, 452
RightNow Technologies, 72, 74
RIM (Research in Motion), 227
Ring topology, 219
RISC (reduced instruction set computer) chips, 143
Risk, 118–119, 384
Risk management, 383, 384
Risk mitigation, 384
Risk response planning, 384
Ritz-Carlton (case study), 298
Rivalry, among existing competitors, 20
RivalWatch, 43
Robb, Curtis, 59
Robbie (robot), 214
Robbin, Jeff, 2
Roche, Katrina, 342

Rode, Jerry, 108
Rogers, Sandy, 284
Rohde, Laura, 451
ROM (read-only memory), 144
Rookies, outsourcing, 395–396
Rosso, Wayne, 104
Router, 217
RouteSmart Technologies, Inc., 97
Royal Canadian Mounted Police, 131
RSS (real simple syndications), 81
Ruf Strategic Solutions, 197
Ruiz, Hector, 142, 452
Russia, 394

S

Saab, 55, 57, 108
Safety inventory, 258
Safeway, 20, 182
Sales
    e-business, 80, 81
    and operational CRM, 281–284
    in organizational structure, 7
Sales force automation (SFA), 282
Sales management CRM systems, 282
Salesforce.com, 74
Salesnet, 74
Sam's Club, 292
Samsung Electronics, 177
Santosus, Megan, 454
SAP, 232, 377
Sarbanes-Oxley Act (SOX), 102–103, 107
SAS Institute, 113, 200, 277
Satellite, 148, 230
Satellite television, 229
Satellite wireless computing, 232–233
Satre, Phil, 207
Satyam, 390
Scalability, 159, 181
Scalet, Sarah, 452
SCE (supply chain execution), 250
SCEM (supply chain event management), 263
Schedule feasibility study, 351
Schlosser, Julie, 453, 455
Schonfeld, Erick, 452
Schoonover, Philip, 401
Schrage, Michael, 451
SCM (see Supply chain management)
Scope definition, 397
SCP (supply chain planning), 250
Script bunnies, 126
Script kiddies, 126
SDLC (see Systems development life cycle)
Search engine optimization (SEO), 81
Sears Roebuck, 66, 67, 225, 288
SEC (Securities and Exchange Commission), 104
Secondary storage, 141, 144–145
Secure electronic transaction (SET), 84
Secure socket layer (SSL), 84
Securities and Exchange Commission (SEC), 104
Security
    database, 182
    physical, 119
    preventive, 152

Security—Cont.
    training for, 119
    (See also Information security)
Security plan, 118–119
Security Portal (company), 167
Security sensor, 229
SeeCommerce (company), 385
Sega of America, 198
Selling chain management, 263
Sensitivity analysis, 38
SEO (search engine optimization), 81
Sequoia, 98
Server, 217
Service level agreements (SLAs), 75
Service providers, 119
Services, 161
SET (secure electronic transaction), 84
7–Eleven Taiwan, 155
SFA (sales force automation), 282
ShadowCrew, 131
Shadowing, 323
Sharp Electronics, 285
Shaw, Danny, 12
Shell Oil, 43
Shopping bot, 45
Siebel Automotive, 57
Siebel Systems, 47–48, 281, 295, 309
Sierra Beverage, 265
Sign-off, 352
Simons, Mark, 166
Simple mail transfer protocol (SMTP), 222
Simple network management protocol (SNMP), 222
Sinegal, Jim, 292
Sirf Technology, 233
Sirius Satellite Radio, 233
Site Selection Canada, 297
Skoll, Jeffrey, 94
Skype, 95, 222, 223
SLAs (service level agreements), 75
Slice-and-dice, 40
Smart card, 122
SMART criteria, 380
Smart phones, 229
SMTP (simple mail transfer protocol), 222
SNA (social networking analysis), 325
Snap-on, 381
Sniffer, 127
SNMP (simple network management protocol), 222
Social engineering, 118
Social networking analysis (SNA), 325
Soden, Michael, 113
Softtek, 398
Software, 140, 149, 151–153
    application, 151, 153
    business decision projects for, 169
    cost of, 313
    enterprise applications, 342–343
    ERP, 52–53, 311–312
    key logger, 114
    key trapper, 114
    success/failure of, 343
    successful development of, 348
    system, 149, 151–152
Software development projects, 351

Solheim, Karsten, 36
Sony, 66, 67, 122
Sony Pictures Entertainment (SPE), 122–123
SoundStep, 2
South Africa, 394
SOX (*see* Sarbanes-Oxley Act)
Spam, 112
Spamdexing, 81
SPE (Sony Pictures Entertainment), 122–123
Speed, 251
SPI Polyols Inc., 267
Spielberg, Steven, 26–27
Spoke, 98
Spreadsheet software, 153
SpreeRide, 348
Sprint, 139
Spyware (sneakware, stealthware), 114, 127, 152
SRM (*see* Supplier relationship management)
SSL (secure socket layer), 84
Stamps.com, 56
Standish Group, 342, 343, 348, 379
Stanford University, 175, 302–303
Stanley, Tim, 208
Staples, 177
Star topology, 219
Starbucks, 215, 231
Statistical analysis, 199
Stellent Imaging and Business Process Management, 326, 336
Stern, Howard, 453
StorageTek, 156
Strategic alignment, 351
Strategy (*see* Business strategy)
Strategy Analytics, 91
Structured collaboration (process collaboration), 321
Structured query language, 188
Student tracking case study, 237
Suker, Jason, 72
Sullivan, Laurie, 455
Sun Microsystems, 97, 143, 162, 164
Sun Tzu, 196
Supercomputers, 150
Supplier power, 18, 19
Supplier relationship management (SRM), 291–292
Supply chain, 18, 19, 246
    growing components of, 263
    integrated supply chain, 249
    operation of, 46
    superiority of, 246
    visibility of, 250
Supply chain event management (SCEM), 263
Supply chain execution (SCE), 250
Supply chain logistics, 46
Supply chain management (SCM), 24, 46–47, 244–263
    Anheuser-Busch case study, 265–266
    Apple example of, 253, 254
    business decision projects for, 271–272
    case study, 267–268
    companies using, 254
    and competition, 250–251
    as component of ERP, 308
    components of, 247, 248
    and consumer behavior, 250
    defined, 251, 308
    Dell case study, 244–245, 252–253

Supply chain management (SCM)—*Cont.*
    design of, 261, 262
    drivers of, 255
    in enterprise systems, 46–47
    example of, 252–253
    facilities driver of, 255–257
    factors driving, 249
    future trends in, 261–263
    information driver of, 259–261
    information technology in, 247–251
    integrated supply chain, 249
    integrating ERP with, 312–316
    inventory driver of, 257–258
    and IT, 247–251
    Levi's case study, 269–271
    Listerine case study, 267–268
    market overview, 310
    principles of, 252
    and speed, 251, 252
    success factors in, 251–254
    transportation driver of, 259, 260
    visibility of, 250
Supply chain partners, 46
Supply chain planning (SCP), 250
Supply chain strategy, 46
Support, 73
Surebridge, 74
Sustaining technology, 66
Swap, Walter, 323
Switching costs, 19
Synergistics, Inc., 30
System availability, 15
System model design, 354–355
System software, 149
System (applications) testing, 358
Systems, IT, 37
Systems development life cycle (SDLC), 343–344, 349–362
    activities of, 350
    analysis phase of, 352–354
    business decision projects for, 369–370
    business requirements case study, 365–366
    defined, 343
    Denver International Airport case study, 364
    design phase of, 354–355
    development phase of, 355–356
    HP case study, 340–341
    implementation phase of, 358–359
    maintenance phase of, 359–360
    phases of, 343–344
    planning phase of, 349–351
    and reasons for project failure, 360–361
    REI case study, 367–368
    testing phase of, 357–358

T

T. J. Maxx, 269
Tablet, 150
Tacit knowledge, 323
Target (company), 225, 269, 319
Taylor, Andy, 284
Taylor, Frederick, 49
Taylor, Nick, 175
TB (terabyte), 144

TCP/IP, 221–223
TCS, 390
TDWI (*see* The Data Warehousing Institute)
Technical feasibility study, 351
Technology
   in business intelligence, 197
   disruptive, 65–68
   pull/push, 260
   wireless, 228, 229, 318
   (*See also* Information technology [IT])
Telecommunication systems, 215
Telnet protocol, 222
Temple, Nancy, 105
Terabyte (TB), 144
Test conditions, 357
Testing phase (systems development life cycle), 357–358
Texas Department of Transportation, 334–335
Text protect utility software, 152
Thailand, 396
Thomas Financial, 386
Thomas J. Watson Research Center, 38
Thompson, Joe, 265
Thompson, Scott, 109
Threat of new entrants, 19–20
Threat of substitute products or services, 19
3M, 282
Throughput, 15
Timeliness, 178
Time-series information, 200
T-Mobile International, 73, 153–154
Token, 122
Tong, Eric, 3
Topology, 218–219
Toronto Transit Commission (TTC), 400
Torvalds, Linus, 151, 167
Toshiba, 166
Touch screen, 146
Touchpad, 146
Toyota, 255–257, 328–329, 372–374
TPS (*see* Transaction processing systems)
Trachtenberg, Myles, 97
Training
   and ERP, 313
   security, 119
   user, 359
Transaction processing systems (TPS), 36–38, 37
Transaction speed, 15
Transactional information, 36, 38
Transmission Control Protocol/Internet Protocol (TCP/IP), 221
Transportation, 259–261
Transportation planning software, 259
Trek, 46
Trend Micro, 217–218
Tribe Networks, 98
Tribune Co., 164
Trojan-horse virus, 126
TTC (Toronto Transit Commission), 400
Turner Industries, 304
Tweeter, 401
Twisted-pair wiring, 224
Type (database field property), 186

U

UAT (user acceptance testing), 358
Ukraine, 396
Uninstaller utility software, 152
Union Carbide Corp., 267
Uniqueness, 178
Unit testing, 358
United Airlines, 58, 60
United Nations, 45
United Nations Division for Public Economics and Public
   Administration, 14
U.S. Department of Defense (DoD), 67, 69, 233, 321
U.S. Department of Justice, 134
U.S. Department of Transportation, 334
U.S. Postal Service, 56, 94–95
U.S. Secret Service, 131
U.S. Senate, 10
Universal Studios, 229
Universal Systems Inc., 328
University of Denver Security Plan, 118–119
University of Illinois, 70
University of Michigan, 175
University of Pennsylvania, 134
Unix, 151
Unstructured collaboration, 320, 321
Up-and-comers, outsourcing, 393–395
UPS, 95, 166, 228, 238–239, 244, 256, 287–288
UPS Supply Chain Solutions, 166
Up-selling, 281
UpShot, 74
Upton, Dennis, 289
U.S. Bankcorp, 43
US Airways, 60
USA Patriot Acts, 107
Usability, 15
User acceptance testing (UAT), 358
User documentation, 358
User ID, 121
User interaction, 185
USi, 74
Utility software, 151, 152

V

Vail Resorts Inc., 282
Validation rule (database field property), 186
Value chain, 21
Value chain analysis, 22–23, 351
Value chain approach, 20–23
Value creation, 21
Van Aarle, Stef, 223
Vanguard Petroleum Corporation, 82, 84
Vendor components (of ERP), 309–310, 316–317
Verizon Communications, 41–42, 66, 161
Video Privacy Protection Act of 1988, 107
View, 187
Vignette, 326
Villareal, Roger, 450
Viral marketing, 81
Virtual private network, 226
Virtualization, 143

Viruses, 126
Visa, 52, 109
Visibility, 250
Visit metrics, 88
Visitor metrics, 88
Visual mining, 42
Vitas Healthcare Corporation, 157
Voice over IP (VoIP), 222
Voice signature, 122
VoIP (voice over IP), 222
Volatility, 143
Vonage, 223

W

Wachovia Bank, 129, 287
Wailgum, Thomas, 454
Walgreens, 261–262, 269
Wal-Mart, 20, 45, 47, 66, 71, 85, 230, 231, 254, 261, 262, 269–271, 401
WAN (wide area network), 216
WAP phones, 229
Warner-Lambert (WL), 267–268
Waterfall methodology, 344–345
WCM (Web content management), 325
WCPO-TV, 80
Web content management system (WCM), 325
Web hosting, 73
Web log, 81, 114
Web services, 160–162
Web site metrics, 86
Web traffic, 15
Web-based self-service systems, 286
Web-enabled (WAP) phones, 229
Weicher, Maureen, 450
Weintraub, Arlene, 453
Welch, Jack, 26, 451
Wells Fargo & Company, 129
Westpac Financial Services (WFS), 177–178
What-if analysis, 38–39
Wheeler, Mark, 234
White-hat hackers, 126
Whitman, Meg, 94, 95
Wide area network (WAN), 216
Wi-fi wireless computing, 227
Wilcox, Joe, 453
Wilson, Tim, 452
WiMax wireless broadband, 229
Wipro, 390
Wire media, 223–224
Wireless carrier technology, 148
Wireless computing, 226–235
    advantages of, 229–230
    bluetooth, 230–231
    business decision projects for, 241–242

Wireless computing—Cont.
    business drivers for, 228–229
    digital hospital case study, 213–214
    future of, 234–235
    GPS, 233–234
    Prada case study, 240–241
    RFID, 231–232
    satellite, 232–233
    student tracking case study, 237
    UPS vs. FedEx case study, 238–239
Wireless fidelity (wi-fi), 227
Wireless Internet service provider (WISP), 73
Wireless local area network (wLAN), 229
Wireless media, 224–225, 235
Wireless technology, 228
    and future of ERP, 318
    U.S. users of, 229
Wireless topology, 219
WISP (wireless Internet service provider), 73
WL (see Warner-Lambert)
wLAN (wireless local area network), 229
Wojcicki, Susan, 175
Wolf, Gary, 451
Word length, 142
Word processing software, 153
Workflow, 326
Workflow management systems, 326–328
Workplace ethics, 113–115
Workshop training, 359
Workstation, 150
The World is Flat (Friedman), 28–29
World Wide Web (WWW), 69–70
WorldCom, 102
Worm, 126
Wozniak, Steve, 233
Wrong information, 179
WWW (see World Wide Web)

X

Xerox, 67, 220, 328, 387
XM Satellite Radio, 233
XP methodology (see Extreme programming methodology)

Y

Yankee Group, 85
Yellow Roadway Corp., 103

Z

Zarb, John, 112
Zimdars, Leroy, 450
Zollars, William D., 102–103